THE BEST OF
JAMES HERRIOT

Published by Reader's Digest (Australia)
Pty Limited (Inc. in NSW),
in association with
Michael Joseph Limited.

Reprinted 1989

First published 1982 in Great Britain by
The Reader's Digest Association Limited,
25 Berkeley Square,
London WIX 6AB,
in association with
Michael Joseph Limited,
27 Wrights Lane,
London W8 5TZ.

THE BEST OF JAMES HERRIOT was edited and designed by
The Reader's Digest Association Limited, London.

The typeface used for text in this book
is 11 pt and 10 pt Baskerville Roman.

THE BEST OF
JAMES HERRIOT
Favourite memories of a country vet

JAMES HERRIOT'S OWN SELECTION FROM HIS ORIGINAL BOOKS,
WITH ADDITIONAL MATERIAL BY READER'S DIGEST EDITORS

PUBLISHED BY READER'S DIGEST
SYDNEY   LONDON   MONTREAL
IN ASSOCIATION WITH MICHAEL JOSEPH LIMITED

Contents

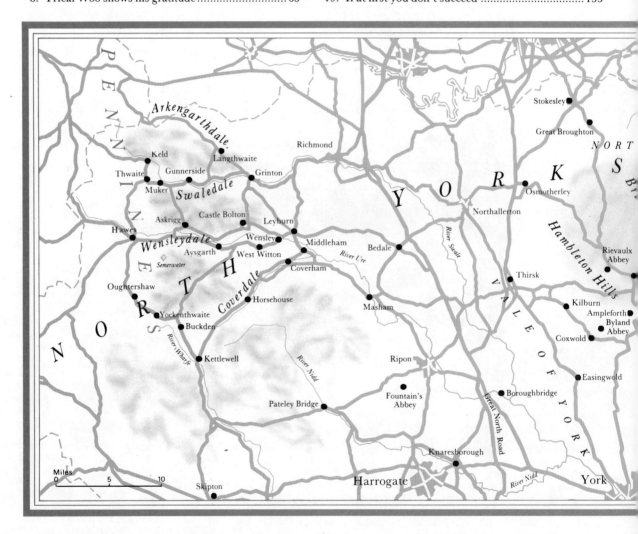

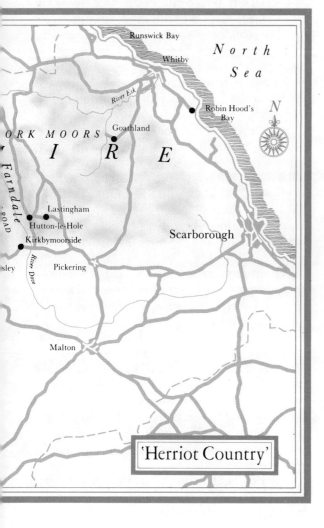

'Herriot Country'

SPECIAL FEATURES

The books I almost never wrote

BY JAMES HERRIOT

I wrote my books because of a compulsion to make some record of a fascinating era in veterinary practice. I wanted to tell people what it was like to be an animal doctor in the days before penicillin and about the things which made me laugh on my daily rounds, working in conditions which now seem primitive.

This compulsion, however, took a long time to assume any practical form. I seemed to sublimate it by recounting the daily happenings to my wife, finishing invariably with the remark, 'I'll put that in my book.'

There is no doubt this situation would have gone on for ever if my wife, at the end of one of my recitals, had not remarked, 'Jim, you are never going to write a book.' She said it kindly but, nevertheless, I was aghast.

'Whatever do you mean?' I said.

'Well,' she replied, 'You have been talking about this book for twenty-five years. Remember we celebrated our silver wedding last week?'

I tried to point out that I was not an impulsive type and always liked to take a little time to think things over, but women can be very unreasonable.

She smiled at me. 'Don't take it to heart, Jim. You are only one of thousands of people who think they are going to write a book, but they never do it.'

'But I will, I will,' I protested indignantly.

She smiled again with a touch of sadness. 'You must realise that it is impossible. Old vets of fifty don't suddenly start writing books.'

That did it. I went straight out, bought a lot of paper and got down to the job.

I suppose I started out with the intention of just writing a funny book, because veterinary life was funny in those days, but as I progressed I found that there were so many other things I wanted to say. I wanted to tell about the sad things, too, because they are inseparable from a vet's experiences; about the splendid old characters among the animal owners of that time and about the magnificent Yorkshire countryside which at all times was the backdrop to my work.

I was a city boy, brought up in Glasgow, and I was thrown into this rural community quite by accident because there was no other job available when I qualified. I was totally unprepared for the beauty of the Yorkshire Dales but their wildness and peace captivated me instantly. I fell under an enchantment which has remained until this day.

As I wrote, I found that I instinctively put down my memories in chronological order so that as one book was finished another one followed on naturally, taking up the advances in veterinary science and the events of my own life as they came along.

And now the richest threads of those years have been gathered together in one handsome volume. The publication of this book gives me the chance to pick out my favourite chapters – the ones my family and I have laughed at over the years and the ones my readers have said they most enjoyed.

The story of my early professional life is all here and as I turn the pages and study the pictures of the places where I have worked and played I am grateful that I found the time to put it all on paper; because it is a time that will not come again. The marginal drawings are particularly nostalgic, pulling my memory gently back again and again to the ambience of things past.

The rich old farming characters who formed such fertile soil for my writing have vanished, leaving behind them another generation of scientific agriculturists. These modern men are the most efficient farmers in the world. They are likeable and they work harder than any people I have ever known, but they are not as much fun as their fathers.

And talking of fun, a lot of it has gone from my own profession as the new drugs and procedures have flooded in. There is always a laugh to be found in veterinary practice because animals are unpredictable things and often embarrass their doctors, but oh, those old black magic days with their exotic, largely useless medicines reeking of witchcraft. They have gone for good and though as a veterinary surgeon I rejoice, as a writer I mourn their passing.

It has been a source of wonder to me that people all over the world have become interested in my personal life. In the beginning I used it mainly as a framework on which to hang the episodes which I encountered as an animal doctor, but over the years it has become an integral part of the books. It is here to be read in this big volume; my courtship and marriage, war service, the births of my children and the joys they brought with them.

They say we should not live in the past and I have no reason to do so because I am still a practising veterinary surgeon, still enjoying life. But to me, my past is a sweet, safe place to be, and through the medium of this book I shall spend a little time there now and then.

James Herriot

PART ONE
Early days in Darrowby

The narrow street opened on to a square where we stopped. Above the window of an unpretentious grocer shop I read 'Darrowby Co-operative Society'. We had arrived.

1

Arrival at Darrowby

It was hot in the rickety little bus and I was on the wrong side where the July sun beat on the windows. I shifted uncomfortably inside my best suit and eased a finger inside the constricting white collar. It was a foolish outfit for this weather but a few miles ahead, my prospective employer was waiting for me and I had to make a good impression.

There was a lot hanging on this interview; being a newly qualified veterinary surgeon in this year of 1937 was like taking out a ticket for the dole queue. Agriculture was depressed by a decade of government neglect, the draught horse which had been the mainstay of the profession was fast disappearing. It was easy to be a prophet of doom when the young men emerging from the colleges after a hard five years' slog were faced by a world indifferent to their enthusiasm and bursting knowledge. There were usually two or three situations vacant in the *'Record'* each week and an average of eighty applicants for each one.

It hadn't seemed true when the letter came from Darrowby in the Yorkshire Dales. Mr Siegfried Farnon M.R.C.V.S. would like to see me on the Friday afternoon; I was to come to tea and if we were mutually suited I could stay on as assistant. I had grabbed at the lifeline unbelievingly; so many friends who had qualified with me were unemployed or working in shops or as labourers in the shipyards that I had given up hope of any other future for myself.

The driver crashed his gears again as he went into another steep bend. We had been climbing steadily now for the last fifteen miles or so, moving closer to the distant blue swell of the Pennines. I had never been in Yorkshire before but the name had always raised a picture of a county as stodgy and unromantic as its pudding; I was prepared for solid worth, dullness and a total lack of charm. But as the bus groaned its way higher I began to wonder. The formless heights were resolving into high, grassy hills and wide valleys. In the valley bottoms, rivers twisted among the trees and solid grey-stone farmhouses lay among islands of cultivated land which pushed bright green promontories up the hillsides into the dark tide of heather which lapped from the summits.

I had seen the fences and hedges give way to dry stone walls which bordered the roads, enclosed the fields and climbed endlessly over the surrounding fells. The walls were everywhere, countless miles of them, tracing their patterns high on the green uplands.

But as I neared my destination the horror stories kept forcing their way into my mind; the tales brought back to college by veterans hardened and embittered by a few months of practice. Assistants were just little bits of dirt to be starved and worked into the ground by the

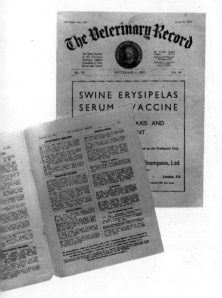

THE VET'S MAGAZINE William Hunting, twice president of the National Veterinary Medical Association of Great Britain and Ireland, founded *The Veterinary Record* in 1888. For many years his portrait appeared on the front page. Members of the association, who numbered 2,050 in 1937, paid an annual subscription of 2 guineas (£2.10) for the journal. It kept its readers informed about what was going on in the profession, and for newly qualified vets hunting for jobs, its classified advertisements were material to be pored over anxiously each week. It still flourishes.

principals who were heartless and vicious to a man. Dave Stevens, lighting a cigarette with trembling hand: 'Never a night off or a half day. He made me wash the car, dig the garden, mow the lawn, do the family shopping. But when he told me to sweep the chimney I left.' Or Willie Johnstone: 'First job I had to do was pass the stomach tube on a horse. Got it into the trachea instead of the oesophagus. Couple of quick pumps and down went the horse with a hell of a crash – dead as a hammer. That's when I started these grey hairs.' Or that dreadful one they passed around about Fred Pringle. Fred had trocarised a bloated cow and the farmer had been so impressed by the pent up gas hissing from the abdomen that Fred had got carried away and applied his cigarette lighter to the canula. A roaring sheet of flame had swept onto some straw bales and burned the byre to the ground. Fred had taken up a colonial appointment immediately afterwards – Leeward Islands wasn't it?

Oh hell, that one couldn't be true. I cursed my fevered imagination and tried to shut out the crackling of the inferno, the terrified bellow of the cattle as they were led to safety. No, it couldn't be as bad as all that; I rubbed my sweating palms on my knees and tried to concentrate on the man I was going to meet.

Siegfried Farnon. Strange name for a vet in the Yorkshire Dales. Probably a German who had done his training in this country and decided to set up in practice. And it wouldn't have been Farnon in the beginning; probably Farrenen. Yes, Siegfried Farrenen. He was beginning to take shape; short, fat, roly poly type with merry eyes and a bubbling laugh. But at the same time I had trouble with the obtruding image of a hulking, cold-eyed, bristle-skulled Teuton more in keeping with the popular idea of the practice boss.

I realised the bus was clattering along a narrow street which opened on to a square where we stopped. Above the window of an unpretentious grocer shop I read 'Darrowby Co-operative Society'. We had arrived.

I got out and stood beside my battered suitcase, looking about me. There was something unusual and I couldn't put my finger on it at first. Then I realised what it was – the silence. The other passengers had dispersed, the driver had switched off his engine and there was not a sound or a movement anywhere. The only visible sign of life was a group of old men sitting round the clock tower in the centre of the square but they might have been carved from stone.

Darrowby didn't get much space in the guide books but when it was mentioned it was described as a grey little town on the river Darrow with a cobbled market place and little of interest except its two ancient bridges. But when you looked at it, its setting was beautiful on the pebbly river where the houses clustered thickly and straggled unevenly along the lower slopes of Herne Fell. Everywhere in Darrowby, in the streets, through the windows of the houses you could see the Fell rearing its calm, green bulk more than two thousand feet above the huddled roofs.

There was a clarity in the air, a sense of space and airiness that made

TROCAR AND CANULA If a cow eats too much easily fermented food, its first stomach, the rumen, can become bloated with gas. This condition is fatal unless emergency treatment is rapidly given by a vet. One remedy is to drive a trocar and canula through the body wall into the rumen. The 5 in. spike of the trocar fits into the sleeve of the canula and the two are driven in together. Then the trocar is withdrawn and gas escapes through the canula, which is left in place as long as necessary.

me feel I had shed something on the plain, twenty miles behind. The confinement of the city, the grime, the smoke – already they seemed to be falling away from me.

Trengate was a quiet street leading off the square and I had my first sight of Skeldale House. I knew it was the right place before I was near enough to read 'S. Farnon M.R.C.V.S.' on the old fashioned brass plate hanging slightly askew on the iron railings. I knew by the ivy which climbed untidily over the mellow brick to the topmost windows. It was what the letter had said – the only house with ivy; and this could be where I would work for the first time as a veterinary surgeon.

Now that I was here, right on the doorstep, I felt breathless, as though I had been running. If I got the job, this was where I would find out about myself. There were many things to prove.

But I liked the look of the old house. It was Georgian with a fine, white-painted doorway. The windows, too, were white – wide and graceful on the ground floor and first storey but small and square where they peeped out from under the overhanging tiles far above. The paint was flaking and the mortar looked crumbly between the bricks, but there was a changeless elegance about the place. There was no front garden and only the railings separated the house from the street a few feet away.

The only visible sign of life was a group of old men sitting round the clock tower in the centre of the square.

I rang the doorbell and instantly the afternoon peace was shattered by a distant baying like a wolf pack in full cry. The upper half of the door was of glass and, as I peered through, a river of dogs poured round the corner of a long passage and dashed itself with frenzied yells against the door. If I hadn't been used to animals I would have turned and run for my life. As it was I stepped back warily and watched the dogs as they appeared, sometimes two at a time, at the top of their leap, eyes glaring, jaws slavering. After a minute or two of this I was able to sort them out and I realised that my first rough count of about fourteen was exaggerated. There were, in fact, five; a huge fawn greyhound who appeared most often as he hadn't so far to jump as the others, a cocker spaniel, a Scottie, a whippet and a tiny, short-legged hunt terrier. This terrier was seldom seen since the glass was rather high for him, but when he did make it he managed to get an even more frantic note into his bark before he disappeared.

I was thinking of ringing the bell again when I saw a large woman in the passage. She rapped out a single word and the noise stopped as if by magic. When she opened the door the ravening pack was slinking round her feet ingratiatingly, showing the whites of their eyes and wagging their tucked-in tails. I had never seen such a servile crew.

'Good afternoon,' I said with my best smile. 'My name is Herriot.'

The woman looked bigger than ever with the door open. She was about sixty but her hair, tightly pulled back from her forehead, was jet black and hardly streaked with grey. She nodded and looked at me with grim benevolence, but she seemed to be waiting for further information. Evidently, the name struck no answering spark.

'Mr Farnon is expecting me. He wrote asking me to come today.'

'Mr Herriot?' she said thoughtfully. 'Surgery is from six to seven o'clock. If you wanted to bring a dog in, that would be your best time.'

'No, no.' I said, hanging on to my smile. 'I'm applying for the position of assistant. Mr Farnon said to come in time for tea.'

'Assistant? Well, now, that's nice.' The lines in her face softened a little. 'I'm Mrs Hall. I keep house for Mr Farnon. He's a bachelor, you know. He never said anything to me about you, but never mind, come in and have a cup of tea. He shouldn't be long before he's back.'

I followed her between whitewashed walls, my feet clattering on the tiles. We turned right at the end into another passage and I was beginning to wonder just how far back the house extended when I was shown into a sunlit room.

It had been built in the grand manner, high-ceilinged and airy with a massive fireplace flanked by arched alcoves. One end was taken up by a french window which gave on a long, high-walled garden. I could see unkempt lawns, a rockery and many fruit trees. A great bank of paeonies blazed in the hot sunshine and at the far end, rooks cawed in the branches of a group of tall elms. Above and beyond were the green hills with their climbing walls.

Ordinary looking furniture stood around on a very worn carpet.

13

SCOTTISH TERRIER The Scottie dog, formerly called the Aberdeen terrier, has an air of elderly wisdom. The long, narrow face is bearded, with intelligent eyes set under beetling brows. The ears are always pricked on the alert. The wiry coat is usually black and the broad, short-legged body is tough and active. The terrier instinct to pursue small game and vermin to and even into their holes is still strong – one glimpse of a mouse and the Scottie sets out to chase it to the kill.

Hunting prints hung on the walls and books were scattered everywhere, some on shelves in the alcoves but others piled on the floor in the corners. A pewter pint pot occupied a prominent place at one end of the mantelpiece. It was an interesting pot. Cheques and bank notes had been stuffed into it till they bulged out of the top and overflowed on to the hearth beneath. I was studying this with astonishment when Mrs Hall came in with a tea tray.

'I suppose Mr Farnon is out on a case.' I said.

'No, he's gone through to Brawton to visit his mother. I can't really say when he'll be back.' She left me with my tea.

The dogs arranged themselves peacefully around the room and, except for a brief dispute between the Scottie and the cocker spaniel about the occupancy of a deep chair, there was no sign of their previous violent behaviour. They lay regarding me with friendly boredom and, at the same time, fighting a losing battle against sleep. Soon the last nodding head had fallen back and a chorus of heavy breathing filled the room.

But I was unable to relax with them. A feeling of let-down gripped me; I had screwed myself up for an interview and I was left dangling. This was all very odd. Why should anyone write for an assistant, arrange a time to meet him and then go to visit his mother? Another thing – if I was engaged, I would be living in this house, yet the housekeeper had no instructions to prepare a room for me. In fact, she had never even heard of me.

My musings were interrupted by the door bell ringing and the dogs, as if touched by a live wire, leaped screaming into the air and launched themselves in a solid mass through the door. I wished they didn't take their duties so seriously. There was no sign of Mrs Hall so I went out to the front door where the dogs were putting everything into their fierce act.

'Shut up!' I shouted and the din switched itself off. The five dogs cringed abjectly round my ankles, almost walking on their knees. The big greyhound got the best effect by drawing his lips back from his teeth in an apologetic grin.

I opened the door and looked into a round, eager face. Its owner, a plump man in wellington boots, leaned confidently against the railings.

'Hello, 'ello, Mr Farnon in?'

'Not at the moment. Can I help you?'

'Aye, give 'im a message when he comes in. Tell 'im Bert Sharpe of Barrow Hills has a cow wot wants borin' out?'

'Boring out?'

'That's right, she's nobbut going on three cylinders.'

'Three cylinders?'

'Aye and if we don't do summat she'll go wrang in 'er ewer, won't she?'

'Very probably.'

'Don't want felon, do we?'

'Certainly not.'

'O.K., you'll tell 'im, then. Ta-ta.'

I returned thoughtfully to the sitting-room. It was disconcerting but I had listened to my first case history without understanding a word of it.

I had hardly sat down when the bell rang again. This time I unleashed a frightening yell which froze the dogs when they were still in mid air; they took the point and returned, abashed, to their chairs.

This time it was a solemn gentleman with a straightly adjusted cloth cap resting on his ears, a muffler knotted precisely over his adam's apple and a clay pipe growing from the exact centre of his mouth. He removed the pipe and spoke with a rich, unexpected accent.

'Me name's Mulligan and I want Misther Farnon to make up some midicine for me dog.'

'Oh, what's the trouble with your dog, Mr Mulligan?'

He raised a questioning eyebrow and put a hand to his ear. I tried again with a full blooded shout.

'What's the trouble?'

He looked at me doubtfully for a moment. 'He's womitin, sorr. Womitin' bad.'

I immediately felt on secure ground now and my brain began to seethe with diagnostic procedures. 'How long after eating does he vomit?'

The hand went to the ear again. 'Phwhat's that?'

I leaned close to the side of his head, inflated my lungs and bawled: 'When does he womit – I mean vomit?'

Comprehension spread slowly across Mr Mulligan's face. He gave a gentle smile. 'Oh aye, he's womitin'. Womitin' bad, sorr.'

I didn't feel up to another effort so I told him I would see to it and asked him to call later. He must have been able to lipread me because he seemed satisfied and walked away.

Back in the sitting-room, I sank into a chair and poured a cup of tea. I had taken one sip when the bell rang again. This time, a wild glare from me was enough to make the dogs cower back in their chairs; I was relieved they had caught on so quickly.

Outside the front door a lovely, red-haired girl was standing. She smiled, showing a lot of very white teeth.

'Good afternoon,' she said in a loud, well-bred voice. 'I am Diana Brompton. Mr Farnon is expecting me for tea.'

I gulped and clung to the door handle. 'He's asked YOU to tea?'

The smile became fixed. 'Yes, that is correct,' she said, spelling the words out carefully, 'He asked me to tea.'

'I'm afraid Mr Farnon isn't at home. I can't say when he'll be back.'

The smile was plucked away. 'Oh,' she said, and she got a lot into the word. 'At any rate, perhaps I could come in.'

'Oh, certainly, do come in. I'm sorry.' I babbled, suddenly conscious that I had been staring, open mouthed, at her.

I held open the door and she brushed past me without a word. She knew her way about because, when I got to the first corner, she had

COCKER SPANIEL Although it is now nearly always a pet – a good-natured one inclined to put on weight – the cocker spaniel originated as a gundog, probably 500 years ago in Spain. It is diligent in quartering the ground close to its handler, using its keen scent to detect gamebirds which it then flushes out.

PIKELETS Freshly baked, bubbly pikelets oozing butter were a teatime delight to look forward to each autumn when the cold weather began. If any were left over – a rare event – they were just as enjoyable when toasted crisp and spread with butter or jam. To make 12 pikelets, mix ½ oz of fresh yeast and 1 teaspoon of salt with 8 oz of bread flour. Pour on ½ pint of mixed milk and water, heated until just warm, and beat well until free from lumps. Put to rise for about 30 minutes. When the mixture starts to drop, beat in ¼ teaspoon of bicarbonate of soda dissolved in 4 tablespoons of cold water. Fold in the lightly beaten white of an egg. Pour tablespoons of the batter on to a hot, greased griddle or heavy frying pan. Cook two or three at a time. When the surface is dry, flip them over to brown the other side.

disappeared into the room. I tiptoed past the door and broke into a gallop which took me along another thirty yards or so of twisting passage to a huge, stone-flagged kitchen. Mrs Hall was pottering about there and I rushed at her.

'There's a young lady here, a Miss Brompton. She's come to tea, too.' I had to fight an impulse to pluck at her sleeve.

Mrs Hall's face was expressionless. I thought she might have started to wave her arms about, but she didn't even seem surprised.

'You go through and talk to her and I'll bring a few more cakes,' she said.

'But what the heck am I going to talk to her about? How long is Mr Farnon going to be?'

'Oh, just chat to her for a bit. I shouldn't think he'll be very long,' she said calmly.

Slowly, I made my way back to the sitting-room and when I opened the door the girl turned quickly with the makings of another big smile. She made no attempt to hide her disgust when she saw it was only me.

'Mrs Hall thinks he should be back fairly soon. Perhaps you would join me in a cup of tea while you're waiting.'

She gave me a quick glance which raked me from my rumpled hair to my scuffed old shoes. I realised suddenly how grimy and sweaty I was after the long journey. Then she shrugged her shoulders and turned away. The dogs regarded her apathetically. A heavy silence blanketed the room.

I poured a cup of tea and held it out to her. She ignored me and lit a cigarette. This was going to be tough, but I could only try.

I cleared my throat and spoke lightly. 'I've only just arrived myself. I hope to be the new assistant.'

This time she didn't trouble to look round. She just said 'Oh' and again the monosyllable carried a tremendous punch.

'Lovely part of the world, this.' I said, returning to the attack.

'Yes.'

'I've never been in Yorkshire before, but I like what I've seen.'

'Oh.'

'Have you known Mr Farnon very long?'

'Yes.'

'I believe he's quite young – about thirty?'

'Yes.'

'Wonderful weather.'

'Yes.'

I kept at it with courage and tenacity for about five minutes, hunting for something original or witty, but finally, Miss Brompton, instead of answering, took the cigarette from her mouth, turned towards me and gave me a long, blank stare. I knew that was the end and shrank into silence.

After that, she sat staring out of the french window, pulling deeply at her cigarette, narrowing her eyes as the smoke trickled from her lips. As far as she was concerned, I just wasn't there.

I was able to observe her at will and she was interesting. I had never met a living piece of a society magazine before. Cool, linen dress, expensive-looking cardigan, elegant legs and glorious red hair falling on her shoulders.

And yet here was a fascinating thought. She was sitting there positively hungering for a little fat German vet. This Farnon must have something.

The tableau was finally broken up when Miss Brompton jumped to her feet. She hurled the cigarette savagely into the fireplace and marched from the room.

Wearily, I got out of my chair. My head began to ache as I shuffled through the french window into the garden. I flopped down among the knee deep grass on the lawn and rested my back against a towering acacia tree. Where the devil was Farnon? Was he really expecting me or had somebody played a horrible practical joke on me? I felt suddenly cold. I had spent my last few pounds getting here and if there was some mistake I was in trouble.

But, looking around me, I began to feel better. The sunshine beat back from the high old walls, bees droned among the bright masses of flowers. A gentle breeze stirred the withered blooms of a magnificent wistaria which almost covered the back of the house. There was peace here.

I leaned my head against the bark and closed my eyes. I could see Herr Farrenen, looking just as I had imagined him, standing over me. He wore a shocked expression.

'Wass is dis you haff done?' he spluttered, his fat jowls quivering with rage. 'You kom to my house under false pretences, you insult Fraulein Brompton, you trink my tea, you eat my food. Vat else you do, hein? Maybe you steal my spoons. You talk about assistant but I vant no assistant. Is best I telephone the police?'

Herr Farrenen seized the phone in a pudgy hand. Even in my dream, I wondered how the man could use such a completely corny accent. I heard the thick voice saying 'Hello, hello.'

And I opened my eyes. Somebody was saying 'Hello', but it wasn't Herr Farrenen. A tall, thin man was leaning against the wall, his hands in his pockets. Something seemed to be amusing him. As I struggled to my feet, he heaved himself away from the wall and held out his hand. 'Sorry you've had to wait. I'm Siegfried Farnon.'

He was just about the most English looking man I had ever seen. Long, humorous, strong-jawed face. Small, clipped moustache, untidy, sandy hair. He was wearing an old tweed jacket and shapeless flannel trousers. The collar of his check shirt was frayed and the tie carelessly knotted. He looked as though he didn't spend much time in front of a mirror.

Studying him, I began to feel better despite the ache in my neck where it had rested against the tree. I shook my head to get my eyes fully open

THE BUTTER CHURN The cream that rose to the top of the milk as it stood in bowls in the dairy went into the churn – usually an end-over-end churn turned by hand. It was invented in Yorkshire about 1880. Because the whole churn turned, the contents were agitated more thoroughly than in the older barrel churn where the handle turned wooden paddles inside the churn and the cream near the edges could lie undisturbed.

and tufts of grass fell from my hair. 'There was a Miss Brompton here.' I blurted out. 'She came to tea. I explained you had been called away.'

Farnon looked thoughtful, but not put out. He rubbed his chin slowly. 'Mm, yes – well, never mind. But I do apologise for being out when you arrived. I have a shocking memory and I just forgot.'

It was the most English voice, too.

Farnon gave me a long, searching look, then he grinned. 'Let's go inside. I want to show you round the place.'

2

Mr Farnon tests me out

The long offshoot behind the house had been the servants' quarters in grander days. Here, everything was dark and narrow and poky as if in deliberate contrast with the front.

Farnon led me to the first of several doors which opened off a passage where the smell of ether and carbolic hung on the air. 'This,' he said, with a secret gleam in his eye as though he were about to unveil the mysteries of Aladdin's cave, 'is the dispensary.'

The dispensary was an important place in the days before penicillin and the sulphonamides. Rows of gleaming Winchester bottles lined the white walls from floor to ceiling. I savoured the familiar names: Sweet Spirits of Nitre, Tincture of Camphor, Chlorodyne, Formalin, Salammoniac, Hexamine, Sugar of Lead, Linimentum Album, Perchloride of Mercury, Red Blister. The lines of labels were comforting.

I was an initiate among old friends. I had painfully accumulated their lore, ferreting out their secrets over the years. I knew their origins, actions and uses, and their maddeningly varied dosage. The examiner's voice – 'And what is the dose for the horse? – and the cow? and the sheep? – and the pig? – and the dog? – and the cat?'

These shelves held the vets' entire armoury against disease and, on a bench under the window, I could see the instruments for compounding them; the graduated vessels and beakers, the mortars and pestles. And underneath, in an open cupboard, the medicine bottles, piles of corks of all sizes, pill boxes, powder papers.

As we moved around, Farnon's manner became more and more animated. His eyes glittered and he talked rapidly. Often, he reached up and caressed a Winchester on its shelf; or he would lift out a horse ball or an electuary from its box, give it a friendly pat and replace it with tenderness.

'Look at this stuff, Herriot,' he shouted without warning. 'Adrevan! This is the remedy, par excellence, for red worms in horses. A bit

BALLING GUN Horses and other animals are usually given drugs by injection now, but in the 1930s it was usual to dose cattle with a liquid medicine and horses with a giant pill, or ball, that contained the drug mixed in a soft paste. A vet would use his hand to thrust the ball down the throat, but a farmer was more likely to use a balling gun. It was put well into the horse's mouth with the ball in the cavity, then the plunger was pressed to propel the ball into the throat.

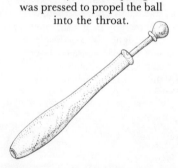

expensive, mind you – ten bob a packet. And these gentian violet pessaries. If you shove one of these into a cow's uterus after a dirty cleansing, it turns the discharges a very pretty colour. Really looks as though it's doing something. And have you seen this trick?'

He placed a few crystals of resublimated iodine on a glass dish and added a drop of turpentine. Nothing happened for a second then a dense cloud of purple smoke rolled heavily to the ceiling. He gave a great bellow of laughter at my startled face.

'Like witchcraft, isn't it? I use it for wounds in horses' feet. The chemical reaction drives the iodine deep into the tissues.'

'It does?'

'Well, I don't know, but that's the theory, and anyway, you must admit it looks wonderful. Impresses the toughest client.'

Some of the bottles on the shelves fell short of the ethical standards I had learned in college. Like the one labelled 'Colic Drench' and featuring a floridly drawn picture of a horse rolling in agony. The animal's face was turned outwards and wore an expression of very human anguish. Another bore the legend 'Universal Cattle Medicine' in ornate script – 'A sovereign Remedy for coughs, chills, scours, pneumonia, milk fever, gargett and all forms of indigestion. At the bottom of the label, in flaring black capitals was the assurance, 'Never Fails to Give Relief.'

Farnon had something to say about most of the drugs. Each one had its place in his five years' experience of practice; they all had their fascination, their individual mystique. Many of the bottles were beautifully shaped, with heavy glass stoppers and their Latin names cut deeply into their sides; names familiar to physicians for centuries, gathering fables through the years.

The two of us stood gazing at the gleaming rows without any idea that it was nearly all useless and that the days of the old medicines were nearly over. Soon they would be hustled into oblivion by the headlong rush of the new discoveries and they would never return.

'This is where we keep the instruments.' Farnon showed me into another little room. The small animal equipment lay on green baize shelves, very neat and impressively clean. Hypodermic syringes, whelping forceps, tooth scalers, probes, searchers, and, in a place of prominence, an ophthalmoscope.

Farnon lifted it lovingly from its black box. 'My latest purchase,' he murmured, stroking its smooth shaft. 'Wonderful thing. Here, have a peep at my retina.'

I switched on the bulb and gazed with interest at the glistening, coloured tapestry in the depths of his eye. 'Very pretty. I could write you a certificate of soundness.'

He laughed and thumped my shoulder. 'Good, I'm glad to hear it. I always fancied I had a touch of cataract in that one.'

He began to show me the large animal instruments which hung from hooks on the walls. Docking and firing irons, bloodless castrators,

BALLING GAG To open a horse's mouth wide enough to thrust in a ball, or large pill, containing a necessary drug, a vet or farmer might simply grasp its tongue. It was also common to use a balling gag, a device about 18 in. long including its handle. It was pushed horizontally into the horse's mouth and then the handle was swung down. The mouth was forced open, and the curled tips of the gag swung up outside the upper jaw. The ball was then placed far back in the throat by a hand or balling gun passed through the ring of the gag.

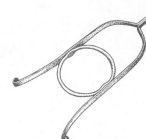

emasculators, casting ropes and hobbles, calving ropes and hooks. A new, silvery embryotome hung in the place of honour, but many of the instruments, like the drugs, were museum pieces. Particularly the blood stick and fleam, a relic of medieval times, but still used to bring the rich blood spouting into a bucket.

'You still can't beat it for laminitis,' Farnon declared seriously.

We finished up in the operating room with its bare white walls, high table, oxygen and ether anaesthetic outfit and a small steriliser.

'Not much small animal work in this district.' Farnon smoothed the table with his palm. 'But I'm trying to encourage it. It makes a pleasant change from lying on your belly in a cow house. The thing is, we've got to do the job right. The old castor oil and prussic acid doctrine is no good at all. You probably know that a lot of the old hands won't look at a dog or a cat, but the profession has got to change its ideas.'

He went over to a cupboard in the corner and opened the door. I could see glass shelves with a few scalpels, artery forceps, suture needles and bottles of catgut in spirit. He took out his handkerchief and flicked at an auroscope before closing the doors carefully.

'Well, what do you think of it all?' he asked as he went out into the passage.

'Great,' I replied. 'You've got just about everything you need here. I'm really impressed.'

He seemed to swell visibly. The thin cheeks flushed and he hummed softly to himself. Then he burst loudly into song in a shaky baritone, keeping time with our steps as we marched along.

Back in the sitting-room, I told him about Bert Sharpe. 'Something about boring out a cow which was going on three cylinders. He talked about her ewer and felon – I didn't quite get it.'

Farnon laughed. 'I think I can translate. He wants a Hudson's operation doing on a blocked teat. Ewer is the udder and felon the local term for mastitis.'

'Well, thanks. And there was a deaf Irishman, a Mr Mulligan ...'

'Wait a minute.' Farnon held up a hand. 'Let me guess – womitin?'

'Aye, womitin' bad, sorr.'

'Right, I'll put up another pint of bismuth carb for him. I'm in favour of long range treatment for this dog. He looks like an airedale but he's as big as a donkey and has a moody disposition. He's had Joe Mulligan on the floor a few times – just gets him down and worries him when he's got nothing better to do. But Joe loves him.'

'How about the womitin'?'

'Doesn't mean a thing. Natural reaction from eating every bit of rubbish he finds. Well, we'd better get out to Sharpe's. And there are one or two other visits – how about coming with me and I'll show you a bit of the district.'

Outside the house, Farnon motioned me towards a battered Hillman and, as I moved round to the passenger's side, I shot a startled glance at the treadless tyres, the rusty bodywork, the almost opaque windscreen with its network of fine cracks. What I didn't notice was that the passenger seat was not fixed to the floor but stood freely on its sledge-like runners. I dropped into it and went over backwards, finishing with my head on the rear seat and my feet against the roof. Farnon helped me up, apologising with great charm, and we set off.

Once clear of the market place, the road dipped quite suddenly and we could see all of the Dale stretching away from us in the evening sunshine. The outlines of the great hills were softened in the gentle light and a broken streak of silver showed where the Darrow wandered on the valley floor.

Farnon was an unorthodox driver. Apparently captivated by the scene, he drove slowly down the hill, elbows resting on the wheel, his chin cupped in his hands. At the bottom of the hill he came out of his reverie and spurted to seventy miles an hour. The old car rocked crazily along the narrow road and my movable seat slewed from side to side as I jammed my feet against the floor boards.

Then he slammed on the brakes, pointed out some pedigree Shorthorns in a field and jolted away again. He never looked at the road in front; all his attention was on the countryside around and behind him. It was that last bit that worried me, because he spent a lot of time driving fast and looking over his shoulder at the same time.

We left the road at last and made our way up a gated lane. My years of seeing practice had taught me to hop in and out very smartly as students were regarded primarily as gate-opening machines. Farnon, however, thanked me gravely every time and once I got over my surprise I found it refreshing.

We drew up in a farmyard. 'Lame horse here.' Farnon said. A

He never looked at the road in front; all his attention was on the countryside.

strapping Clydesdale gelding was brought out and we watched attentively as the farmer trotted him up and down.

'Which leg do you make it?' my colleague asked. 'Near fore? Yes, I think so, too. Like to examine it?'

I put my hand on the foot, feeling how much hotter it was than the other. I called for a hammer and tapped the wall of the hoof. The horse flinched, raised the foot and held it trembling for a few seconds before replacing it carefully on the ground. 'Looks like pus in the foot to me.'

'I'll bet you're right,' Farnon said. 'They call it gravel around here, by the way. What do you suggest we do about it?'

'Open up the sole and evacuate the pus.'

'Right.' He held out a hoof knife. 'I'll watch your technique.'

With the uncomfortable feeling that I was on trial, I took the knife, lifted the foot and tucked it between my knees. I knew what I had to do – find the dark mark on the sole where the infection had entered and follow it down till I reached the pus. I scraped away the caked dirt and found not one, but several marks. After more tapping to find the painful area I selected a likely spot and started to cut.

The horn seemed as hard as marble and only the thinnest little shaving came away with each twist of the knife. The horse, too, appeared to appreciate having his sore foot lifted off the ground and gratefully leaned his full weight on my back. He hadn't been so comfortable all day. I groaned and dug him in the ribs with my elbow and, though it made him change his position for a second, he was soon leaning on again.

The mark was growing fainter and, after a final gouge with the knife, it disappeared altogether. I swore quietly and started on another mark. With my back at breaking point and the sweat trickling into my eyes, I knew that if this one petered out, too, I would have to let the foot go and take a rest. And with Farnon's eye on me I didn't want to do that.

Agonisingly, I hacked away and, as the hole deepened, my knees began an uncontrollable trembling. The horse rested happily, his fifteen hundredweight cradled by this thoughtful human. I was wondering how it would look when I finally fell flat on my face when, under the knife blade, I saw a thin spurt of pus followed by a steady trickle.

'There it goes,' the farmer grunted. 'He'll get relief now.'

I enlarged the drainage hole and dropped the foot. It took me a long time to straighten up and when I stepped back, my shirt clung to my back.

'Well done, Herriot.' Farnon took the knife from me and slipped it into his pocket. 'It just isn't funny when the horn is as hard as that.'

He gave the horse a shot of tetanus antitoxin then turned to the farmer. 'I wonder if you'd hold up the foot for a second while I disinfect the cavity.' The stocky little man gripped the foot between his knees and looked down with interest as Farnon filled the hole with iodine crystals and added some turpentine. Then he disappeared behind a billowing purple curtain.

CLYDESDALE HORSE The major heavy horse in northern Britain is the Clydesdale. It is similar to the Shire, but its longer legs and less massive body make it more manoeuvrable and swifter moving. It has more white on its legs and belly. The brood mares usually foal in alternate years, in April or May, after carrying the foal for 11 months. There are still more than 6,000 Clydesdales in Britain.

I watched, fascinated, as the thick pall mounted and spread. I could locate the little man only by the spluttering noises from somewhere in the middle.

As the smoke began to clear, a pair of round, startled eyes came into view. 'By Gaw, Mr Farnon, I wondered what the 'ell had happened for a minute,' the farmer said between coughs. He looked down again at the blackened hole in the hoof and spoke reverently: 'It's wonderful what science can do nowadays.'

We did two more visits, one to a calf with a cut leg which I stitched, dressed and bandaged, then to the cow with the blocked teat.

Mr Sharpe was waiting, still looking eager. He led us into the byre and Farnon gestured towards the cow. 'See what you can make of it.'

I squatted down and palpated the teat, feeling the mass of thickened tissue half up. It would have to be broken down by a Hudson's instrument and I began to work the thin metal spiral up the teat. One second later, I was sitting gasping in the dung channel with the neat imprint of a cloven hoof on my shirt front, just over the solar plexus.

It was embarrassing, but there was nothing I could do but sit there fighting for breath, my mouth opening and shutting like a stranded fish.

Mr Sharpe held his hand over his mouth, his innate politeness at war with his natural amusement at seeing the vet come to grief. 'I'm sorry, young man, but I owt to 'ave told you that this is a very friendly cow. She allus likes to shake hands.' Then, overcome by his own wit, he rested his forehead on the cow's back and went into a long paroxysm of silent mirth.

I took my time to recover, then rose with dignity from the channel. With Mr Sharpe holding the nose and Farnon lifting up the tail, I managed to get the instrument past the fibrous mass and by a few downward tugs I cleared the obstruction; but, though the precautions cramped the cow's style a little, she still got in several telling blows on my arms and legs.

When it was over, the farmer grasped the teat and sent a long white jet frothing on the floor. 'Capital! She's going on four cylinders now!'

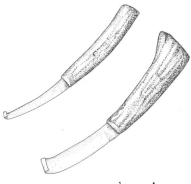

KNIVES FOR HORSES' FEET A lame horse is a frequent patient for a vet. The lameness is most often caused by a foot condition. Sometimes the hoof is overgrown, preventing the horse from walking properly. The vet uses a paring knife, traditionally with a sharp, curled-tipped, 4 in. steel blade in a horn handle (bottom), to trim away the excess hoof. Sometimes it is an infected wound on the sole of the foot that makes the horse lame.

With a narrow-bladed searching knife (top), also sharp and curled at the tip, the vet has to probe all the cracks in the hoof. After reaching the blind end of many cracks, he will find the one that penetrates right through to the wounded foot. Then he widens the opening to let the pus drain away from the infected spot.

3

Making friends

'We'll go home a different way.' Farnon leaned over the driving wheel and wiped the cracked windscreen with his sleeve. 'Over the Brenkstone Pass and down Sildale. It's not much further and I'd like you to see it.'

We took a steep, winding road, climbing higher and still higher with the hillside falling away sheer to a dark ravine where a rocky stream rushed headlong to the gentler country below. On the top, we got out of the car. In the summer dusk, a wild panorama of tumbling fells and peaks rolled away and lost itself in the crimson and gold ribbons of the Western sky. To the East, a black mountain overhung us, menacing in its naked bulk. Huge, square-cut boulders littered the lower slopes.

I whistled softly as I looked around. This was different from the friendly hill country I had seen on the approach to Darrowby.

Farnon turned towards me. 'Yes, one of the wildest spots in England. A fearsome place in winter. I've known this pass to be blocked for weeks on end.'

I pulled the clean air deeply into my lungs. Nothing stirred in the vastness, but a curlew cried faintly and I could just hear the distant roar of the torrent a thousand feet below.

It was dark when we got into the car and started the long descent into Sildale. The valley was a shapeless blur but points of light showed where the lonely farms clung to the hillsides.

We came to a silent village and Farnon applied his brakes violently. I tobogganed effortlessly across the floor on my mobile seat and collided with the windscreen. My head made a ringing sound against the glass but Farnon didn't seem to notice. 'There's a grand little pub here. Let's go in and have a beer.'

The pub was something new to me. It was, simply, a large kitchen, square and stone-flagged. An enormous fireplace and an old black cooking range took up one end. A kettle stood on the hearth and a single large log hissed and crackled, filling the room with its resinous scent.

About a dozen men sat on the high-backed settles which lined the walls. In front of them, rows of pint mugs rested on oak tables which were fissured and twisted with age.

There was a silence as we went in. Then somebody said 'Now then, Mr Farnon.' Not enthusiastically, but politely, and this brought some friendly grunts and nods from the company. They were mostly farmers or farm workers taking their pleasure without fuss or excitement. Most were burnt red by the sun and some of the younger ones were tieless, muscular necks and chests showing through the open shirt fronts. Soft murmurs and clicks rose from a peaceful domino game in the corner.

Farnon guided me to a seat, ordered two beers and turned to face me. 'Well, you can have this job if you want it. Four quid a week and full board. O.K.?'

The suddenness struck me silent. I was in. And four pounds a week! I remembered the pathetic entries in the *Record*. 'Veterinary surgeon, fully experienced, will work for keep.' The B.V.M.A. had had to put pressure on the editor to stop him printing these cries from the heart. It hadn't looked so good to see members of the profession offering their services free. Four pounds a week was affluence.

'Thank you,' I said, trying hard not to look triumphant. 'I accept.'

'Good.' Farnon took a hasty gulp at his beer. 'Let me tell you about the practice. I bought it a year ago from an old man of eighty. Still

FIREPLACE AND BAKING OVEN
Before the combined kitchen range was introduced into north Yorkshire in the 1860s, the baking oven was separate from the open fire and hot-water boiler. The chimney crane over the open fire had a reckon crook on which kettles and cauldrons were hung. Hot water was ladled out through the lid of the hob – on which pans could be kept warm. The baking oven had a separate fire beneath it which would be lit only on baking days. All the iron parts were kept black and gleaming by regular rubbing with blacklead, a graphite-based polish.

practising, mind you, a real tough old character. But he'd got past getting up in the middle of the night, which isn't surprising. And, of course, in lots of other ways he had let things slide – hanging on to all the old ideas. Some of those ancient instruments in the surgery were his. One way and another, there was hardly any practice left and I'm trying to work it up again now. There's very little profit in it so far, but if we stick in for a few years, I'm confident we'll have a good business. The farmers are pleased to see a younger man taking over and they welcome new treatments and operations. But I'm having to educate them out of the three and sixpenny consulting fee the old chap used to charge and it's been a hard slog. These Dalesmen are wonderful people and you'll like them, but they don't like parting with their brass unless you can prove they are getting something in return.'

He talked on enthusiastically of his plans for the future, the drinks kept coming and the atmosphere in the pub thawed steadily. The place filled up as the regulars from the village streamed in, the noise and heat increased and by near closing time I had got separated from my colleague and was in the middle of a laughing group I seemed to have known for years.

But there was one odd character who swam repeatedly into my field of vision. An elderly little man with a soiled white panama perched above a smooth, brown, time-worn face like an old boot. He was dodging round the edge of the group, beckoning and winking.

I could see there was something on his mind, so I broke away and allowed myself to be led to a seat in the corner. The old man sat opposite me, rested his hands and chin on the handle of his walking stick and regarded me from under drooping eyelids.

'Now then, young man, ah've summat to tell thee. Ah've been among beasts all me life and I'm going to tell tha summat.'

My toes began to curl. I had been caught this way before. Early in my college career I had discovered that all the older inhabitants of the agricultural world seemed to have the idea that they had something priceless to impart. And it usually took a long time. I looked around me in alarm but I was trapped. The old man shuffled his chair closer and began to talk in a conspiratorial whisper. Gusts of beery breath hit my face from six inches range.

There was nothing new about the old man's tales – just the usual recital of miraculous cures he had wrought, infallible remedies known only to himself and many little sidetracks about how unscrupulous people had tried in vain to worm his secrets from him. He paused only to take expert pulls at his pint pot; his tiny frame seemed to be able to accommodate a surprising amount of beer.

But he was enjoying himself and I let him ramble on. In fact I encouraged him by expressing amazement and admiration at his feats.

The little man had never had such an audience. He was a retired smallholder and it had been years since anybody had shown him the appreciation he deserved. His face wore a lopsided leer and his swimmy

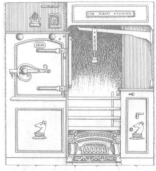

THE YORKSHIRE RANGE One of the first combined kitchen ranges – combining fireplace and oven – in Yorkshire was the Albert Kitchener, made by Walkers of York from the 1860s. Similar models, generally called Yorkshire ranges, were used all over the area until public gas and electricity supplies were available – which in remote areas was not until the 1950s. Smoke-control orders in the 1960s finally put them out of use. The combined range was about 4½ ft in height and width. It had an open fire, a boiler for heating water, an arm for supporting a kettle or stewpot, and an oven. Its cosy glow lit the farmhouse kitchen throughout the day and made it the heart of the family's home life.

DALES PONIES This sturdy, ancient breed native to the east side of the Pennines is known as a hard worker, and not only on farms. In the 19th century the powerful Dales ponies carried lead from mines to smelting works and coal to lime-kilns. On hill farms the pony pulled machinery, worked as a packhorse carrying wool, took the trap to market, delivered milk, and carried winter fodder to the sheep. Now it is finding a new role as a sure-footed mount for pony-trekkers. It is black or dark brown and stands about 4 ft 6 in. at the shoulder.

eyes were alight with friendship. But suddenly he became serious and sat up straight.

'Now, afore ye go, young man, I'm going to tell thee summat nobody knows but me. Ah could've made a lot o' money out o' this. Folks 'ave been after me for years to tell 'em but I never 'ave.'

He lowered the level in his glass by several inches then narrowed his eyes to slits. 'It's the cure for mallenders and sallenders in 'osses.'

I started up in my chair as though the roof had begun to fall in. 'You can't mean it,' I gasped. 'Not mallenders and sallenders.'

The old man looked smug. 'Ah, but ah do mean it. All you have to do is rub on this salve of mine and the 'oss walks away sound. He's better by that!' His voice rose to a thin shout and he made a violent gesture with his arm which swept his nearly empty glass to the floor.

I gave a low, incredulous whistle and ordered another pint. 'And you're really going to tell me the name of this salve?' I whispered.

'I am, young man, but only on one condition. Tha must tell no one. Tha must keep it to thaself, then nobody'll know but thee and me.' He effortlessly tipped half of his fresh pint down his throat. 'Just thee and me, lad.'

'All right, I promise you. I'll not tell a soul. Now what is this wonderful stuff?'

The old man looked furtively round the crowded room. Then he took a deep breath, laid his hand on my shoulder and put his lips close to my ear. He hiccuped once, solemnly, and spoke in a hoarse whisper. 'Marshmallow ointment.'

I grasped his hand and wrung it silently. The old man, deeply moved, spilled most of his final half pint down his chin.

But Farnon was making signals from the door. It was time to go. We surged out with our new friends, making a little island of noise and light in the quiet village street. A tow-haired young fellow in shirt sleeves opened the car door with natural courtesy and, waving a final good night, I plunged in. This time, the seat went over quicker than usual and I hurtled backwards, coming to rest with my head among some Wellingtons and my knees tucked underneath my chin.

A row of suprised faces peered in at me through the back window, but soon, willing hands were helping me up and the trick seat was placed upright on its rockers again. I wondered how long it had been like that and if my employer had ever thought of having it fixed.

We roared off into the darkness and I looked back at the waving group. I could see the little man, his panama gleaming like new in the light from the doorway. He was holding his finger to his lips.

4

Tristan gets the sack

I went over to the desk and got the day book. 'Here are this morning's calls. What would you like me to do?'

Farnon picked out a round of visits, scribbled the list on a scrap of paper and handed it over. 'Here you are,' he said. 'A few nice, trouble-free cases to get yourself worked in.'

I was turning to leave when he called me back. 'Oh, there's one other thing I'd like you to do. My young brother is hitching from Edinburgh today. He's at the Veterinary College there and the term finished yesterday. When he gets within striking distance he'll probably give us a ring. I wonder if you'd slip out and pick him up?'

'Certainly. Glad to.'

'His name is Tristan, by the way.'

'Tristan?'

'Yes. Oh, I should have told you. You must have wondered about my own queer name. It was my father. Great Wagnerian. It nearly ruled his life. It was music all the time – mainly Wagner.'

'I'm a bit partial myself.'

'Ah well, yes, but you didn't get it morning noon and night like we did. And then to be stuck with a name like Siegfried. Anyway, it could have been worse – Wotan, for instance.'

'Or Pogner.'

Farnon looked startled. 'By golly, you're right. I'd forgotten about old Pogner. I suppose I've got a lot to be thankful for.'

It was late afternoon before the expected call came. The voice at the other end was uncannily familiar.

'This is Tristan Farnon.'

'Gosh, you sound just like your brother.'

A pleasant laugh answered me. 'Everybody says that – oh, that's very good of you. I'd be glad of a lift. I'm at the Holly Tree Café on the Great North Road.'

After the voice I had been expecting to find a younger edition of my employer but the small, boyish-faced figure sitting on a rucksack could hardly have been less like him. He got up, pushed back the dark hair from his forehead and held out his hand. The smile was charming.

'Had much walking to do?' I asked.

'Oh, a fair bit, but I needed the exercise. We had a roughish end of term party last night.' He opened the car door and threw the rucksack into the back. As I started the engine he settled himself in the passenger seat as though it were a luxurious armchair, pulled out a paper packet of Woodbines, lit one with tender concentration and gulped the smoke

MAP FOR MOTORISTS The fourth series of Ordnance Survey ¼ in. maps began to be issued in 1933 and proved especially successful with motorists. Nineteen overlapping sheets covered England, Wales and Scotland at a scale of 4 miles to the inch. One of the series' values as a route-finder was that each road was identified by its Ministry of Transport road number, an innovation tried out in the 1928 series and carried on ever since. Motorists were never in the minds of the first Ordnance Survey map-makers. The survey was set up in 1791 to make maps of southern England for military use if Napoleon should invade the country.

down blissfully. He produced the *Daily Mirror* from a side pocket and shook it open with a sign of utter content. The smoke, which had been gone a long time, began to wisp from his nose and mouth.

I turned West off the great highway and the rumble of traffic faded rapidly behind us. I glanced round at Tristan. 'You'll have just finished exams?' I said.

'Yes, pathology and parasitology.'

I almost broke one of my steadfast rules by asking him if he had passed, but stopped myself in time. It is a chancy business. But in any case, there was no shortage of conversation. Tristan had something to say about most of the news items and now and then he read out an extract and discussed it with me. I felt a growing conviction that I was in the presence of a quicker and livelier mind than my own. It seemed no time at all before we pulled up outside Skeldale House.

Siegfried was out when we arrived and it was early evening when he returned. He came in through the french window, gave me a friendly greeting and threw himself into an armchair. He had begun to talk about one of his cases when Tristan walked in.

The atmosphere in the room changed as though somebody had clicked a switch. Siegfried's smile became sardonic and he gave his brother a long, appraising look. He grunted a 'hello', then reached up and began to run his finger along the titles of the books in the alcove. He seemed absorbed in this for a few minutes and I could feel the tension building up. Tristan's expression had changed remarkably; his face had gone completely deadpan but his eyes were wary.

Siegfried finally located the book he was looking for, took it down from the shelf and began to leaf through it unhurriedly. Then, without looking up, he said quietly: 'Well, how did the exams go?'

Tristan swallowed carefully and took a deep breath. 'Did all right in parasitology,' he replied in a flat monotone.

Siegfried didn't appear to have heard. He had found something interesting in his book and settled back to read. He took his time over it, then put the book back on the shelf. He began again the business of going along the titles; still with his back to his brother, he spoke again in the same soft voice.

'How about pathology?'

Tristan was on the edge of his chair now, as if ready to make a run for it. His eyes darted from his brother to the book shelves and back again. 'Didn't get it,' he said tonelessly.

There was no reaction from Siegfried. He kept up his patient search for his book, occasionally pulling a volume out, glancing at it and replacing it carefully. The he gave up the hunt, lay back in the chair with his arms dangling almost to the floor and looked at Tristan. 'So you failed pathology,' he said conversationally.

I was surprised to hear myself babbling with an edge of hysteria in my voice. 'Well now that's pretty good you know. It puts him in the final year and he'll be able to sit path. at Christmas. He won't lose any time

THE GATHERING STORM Military matters were already beginning to preoccupy the nation more than 18 months before the outbreak of the Second World War. About 1¼ million copies of the December 3, 1932 edition of the *Daily Mirror* were sold, carrying the news of the appointment of new army chiefs – and a threat from Japan. Ten editions of the paper were printed that day, all of them in London, for distribution during the night by train and van. The paper cost one old penny (less than ½p) then, and the price was not increased until 1951.

that way and, after all, it's a tough subject.'

Siegfried turned a cold eye on me. 'So you think it's pretty good, do you?' There was a pause and a long silence which was broken by a totally unexpected bellow as he rounded on his brother. 'Well, I don't! I think it is bloody awful! It's a damned disgrace, that's what it is. What the hell have you been doing all this term, anyway? Boozing, I should think, chasing women, spending my money, anything but working. And now you've got the bloody nerve to walk in here and tell me you've failed pathology. You're lazy, that's your trouble, isn't it? You're bloody bone idle!'

He was almost unrecognisable. His face was darkly flushed and his eyes glared. He yelled wildly again at his brother. 'But I've had enough this time. I'm sick of you. I'm not going to work my fingers to the bloody bone to keep you up there idling your time away. This is the end. You're sacked, do you hear me. Sacked once and for all. So get out of here – I don't want to see you around any more. Go on, get out!'

Tristan, who had preserved an air of injured dignity throughout, withdrew quietly.

Writhing with embarrassment, I looked at Siegfried. He was showing the strain of the interview. His complexion had gone blotchy; he muttered to himself and drummed his fingers on the arm of the chair.

I was aghast at having to witness this break-up and I was grateful when Siegfried sent me on a call and I was able to get out of the room.

It was nearly dark when I got back and I drove round to the back lane and into the yard at the foot of the garden. The creaking of the garage doors disturbed the rooks in the great elms which overhung the buildings. Far up in the darkness there was a faint fluttering, a muffled cawing then silence. As I stood listening, I became aware of a figure in the gloom, standing by the yard door, looking down the garden. As the face turned towards me I saw it was Tristan.

Again, I felt embarrassed. It was an unfortunate intrusion when the poor fellow had come up here to brood alone. 'Sorry about the way things turned out,' I said awkwardly.

The tip of the cigarette glowed brightly as Tristan took a long pull. 'No, no, that's all right. Could have been a lot worse, you know.'

'Worse? Well, it's bad enough, isn't it? What are you going to do?'

'Do? What do you mean?'

'Well, you've been kicked out, haven't you? Where are you going to sleep tonight?'

'I can see you don't understand,' Tristan said. He took his cigarette from his mouth and I saw the gleam of very white teeth as he smiled. 'You needn't worry, I'm sleeping here and I'll be down to breakfast in the morning.'

'But how about your brother?'

'Siegfried? Oh, he'll have forgotten all about it by then.'

'Are you sure?'

'Dead sure. He's always sacking me and he always forgets. Anyway,

BRITISH SAANEN GOAT The Berne region of Switzerland was the original home of the Saanen goat, from which the British breed was developed. It is a short-haired, all-white animal, short in the leg and rather slender in build. Females weigh about 140 lb and are prized for their high milk yield – more than 430 gallons in a year being given by one record-breaking animal. Most of the breed are naturally hornless. All goats are browsers, ready to feed on anything; and they give milk that some people find more digestible than cow's milk. An extra advantage is their docile disposition – an unusual characteristic in goats.

things turned out very well. The only tricky bit back there was getting him to swallow that bit about the parasitology.'

I stared at the shadowy form by my side. Again, there was a rustling as the rooks stirred in the tall trees then settled into silence.

'The parasitology?'

'Yes. If you think back, all I said was that I had done all right. I wasn't any more specific than that.'

'Then you mean ... ?'

Tristan laughed softly and thumped my shoulder.

'That's right, I didn't get parasitology. I failed in both. But don't worry, I'll pass them at Christmas.'

5

Mr Dean loses his only friend

I looked again at the slip of paper where I had written my visits. 'Dean, 3, Thompson's Yard. Old dog ill.'

There were a lot of these 'yards' in Darrowby. They were, in fact, tiny streets, like pictures from a Dickens novel. Some of them opened off the market place and many more were scattered behind the main thoroughfares in the old part of the town. From the outside you could see only an archway and it was always a surprise to me to go down a narrow passage and come suddenly upon the uneven rows of little houses with no two alike, looking into each other's windows across eight feet of cobbles.

In front of some of the houses a strip of garden had been dug out and marigolds and nasturtiums straggled over the rough stones; but at the far end the houses were in a tumbledown condition and some were abandoned with their windows boarded up.

Number three was down at this end and looked as though it wouldn't be able to hold out much longer.

The flakes of paint quivered on the rotten wood of the door as I knocked; above, the outer wall bulged dangerously on either side of a long crack in the masonry.

A small, white haired man answered. His face, pinched and lined, was enlivened by a pair of cheerful eyes; he wore a much-darned woollen cardigan, patched trousers and slippers.

'I've come to see your dog,' I said, and the old man smiled.

'Oh, I'm glad you've come, sir,' he said. 'I'm getting a bit worried about the old chap. Come inside, please.'

He led me into the tiny living-room. 'I'm alone now, sir. Lost my missus over a year ago. She used to think the world of the old dog.'

The grim evidence of poverty was everywhere. In the worn out lino,

the fireless hearth, the dank, musty smell of the place. The wallpaper hung away from the damp patches and on the table the old man's solitary dinner was laid; a fragment of bacon, a few fried potatoes and a cup of tea. This was life on the old age pension.

In the corner, on a blanket, lay my patient, a cross-bred labrador. He must have been a big, powerful dog in his time, but the signs of age showed in the white hairs round his muzzle and the pale opacity in the depth of his eyes. He lay quietly and looked at me without hostility.

'Getting on a bit, isn't he, Mr Dean?'

'Aye he is that. Nearly fourteen, but he's been like a pup galloping about until these last few weeks. Wonderful dog for his age, is old Bob and he's never offered to bite anybody in his life. Children can do anything with him. He's my only friend now – I hope you'll soon be able to put him right.'

'Is he off his food, Mr Dean?'

'Yes, clean off, and that's a strange thing because by gum, he could eat. He always sat by me and put his head on my knee at meal times, but he hasn't been doing it lately.'

I looked at the dog with growing uneasiness. The abdomen was grossly distended and I could read the tell-tale symptoms of pain; the catch in the respirations, the retracted commissures of the lips, the anxious, preoccupied expression in the eyes.

When his master spoke, the tail thumped twice on the blankets and a momentary interest showed in the white old eyes; but it quickly disappeared and the blank, inward look returned.

I passed my hand carefully over the dog's abdomen. Ascites was pronounced and the dropsical fluid had gathered till the pressure was intense. 'Come on, old chap,' I said, 'Let's see if we can roll you over.' The dog made no resistance as I eased him slowly on to his other side, but, just as the movement was completed, he whimpered and looked

In the corner, on a blanket, lay my patient, a cross-bred labrador.

31

round. The cause of the trouble was now only too easy to find.

I palpated gently. Through the thin muscle of the flank I could feel a hard, corrugated mass; certainly a splenic or hepatic carcinoma, enormous and completely inoperable. I stroked the old dog's head as I tried to collect my thoughts. This wasn't going to be easy.

'Is he going to be ill for long?' the old man asked, and again came the thump, thump of the tail at the sound of the loved voice. 'It's miserable when Bob isn't following me round the house when I'm doing my little jobs.'

'I'm sorry, Mr Dean, but I'm afraid this is something very serious. You see this large swelling. It is caused by an internal growth.'

'You mean ... cancer?' the little man said faintly.

'I'm afraid so, and it has progressed too far for anything to be done. I wish there was something I could do to help him, but there isn't.'

The old man looked bewildered and his lips trembled. 'Then he's going to die?'

I swallowed hard. 'We really can't just leave him to die, can we? He's in some distress now, but it will soon be an awful lot worse. Don't you think it would be kindest to put him to sleep? After all, he's had a good, long innings.' I always aimed at a brisk, matter-of-fact approach, but the old cliches had an empty ring.

The old man was silent, then he said, 'Just a minute,' and slowly and painfully knelt down by the side of the dog. He did not speak, but ran his hand again and again over the grey old muzzle and the ears, while the tail thump, thump, thumped on the floor.

He knelt there a long time while I stood in the cheerless room, my eyes taking in the faded pictures on the walls, the frayed, grimy curtains, the broken-springed arm chair.

At length the old man struggled to his feet and gulped once or twice. Without looking at me, he said huskily, 'All right, will you do it now?'

I filled the syringe and said the things I always said. 'You needn't worry, this is absolutely painless. Just an overdose of an anaesthetic. It is really an easy way out for the old fellow.'

The dog did not move as the needle was inserted, and, as the barbiturate began to flow into the vein, the anxious expression left his face and the muscles began to relax. By the time the injection was finished, the breathing had stopped.

'Is that it?' the old man whispered.

'Yes, that's it,' I said. 'He is out of his pain now.'

The old man stood motionless except for the clasping and unclasping of his hands. When he turned to face me his eyes were bright. 'That's right, we couldn't let him suffer, and I'm grateful for what you've done. And now, what do I owe you for your services, sir?'

'Oh, that's all right, Mr Dean,' I said quickly, 'It's nothing – nothing at all. I was passing right by here – it was no trouble.'

The old man was astonished. 'But you can't do that for nothing.'

'Now please say no more about it, Mr Dean. As I told you, I was

WOOL CART The 1940s was the last decade when a sheep farmer took his own fleeces to market or to a nearby mill. Since the early 1950s the Wool Marketing Board has collected and marketed wool. The Dales pony is pulling a cart with inflated rubber tyres, which gave a much smoother run than the iron tyres of previous decades. The centuries-old cart design has been adapted for the small pneumatic tyre. The cart body hangs much lower and the shafts are almost at the top of it.

passing right by your door.' I said goodbye and went out of the house, through the passage and into the street. In the bustle of people and the bright sunshine, I could still see only the stark, little room, the old man and his dead dog.

As I walked towards my car, I heard a shout behind me. The old man was shuffling excitedly towards me in his slippers. His cheeks were streaked and wet, but he was smiling. In his hand he held a small, brown object.

'You've been very kind, sir. I've got something for you.' He held out the object and I looked at it. It was tattered but just recognisable as a precious relic of a bygone celebration.

'Go on, it's for you,' said the old man. 'Have a cigar.'

6

The phoney war

MOWING BY HAND On difficult slopes and folds of land, hand-mowing of hay with a scythe continued long after horse-drawn mowers came into use about 1900. Each mower had a scythe to suit him in its length of shaft, angle of blade and the position of the two jutting nibs. He could cut a swathe 10 ft or more wide, advancing 2 or 3 ft with each cut, and would aim to mow an acre a day. He sharpened the blade frequently with his strickle – a piece of unseasoned oak pricked all over with holes. Before the day's work the mower worked grease into the strickle and coated it with sharp sand, making it in effect like a sanding block.

I was now comfortably settled into the way of life in Skeldale House. At first I wondered where Tristan fitted into the set up. Was he supposed to be seeing practice, having a holiday, working or what? But it soon became clear that he was a factotum who dispensed and delivered medicines, washed the cars, answered the phone and even, in an emergency, went to a case.

At least, that was how Siegfried saw him and he had a repertoire of tricks aimed at keeping him on his toes. Like returning unexpectedly or bursting into a room in the hope of catching him doing nothing. He never seemed to notice the obvious fact that the college vacation was over and Tristan should have been back there. I came to the conclusion over the next few months that Tristan must have had some flexible arrangement with the college authorities because, for a student, he seemed to spend a surprising amount of time at home.

He interpreted his role rather differently from his brother and, while resident in Darrowby, he devoted a considerable amount of his acute intelligence to the cause of doing as little as possible. Tristan did, in fact, spend much of his time sleeping in a chair. When he was left behind to dispense when we went out on our rounds he followed an unvarying procedure. He half filled a sixteen ounce bottle with water, added a few drachms of chlorodyne and a little epicacuanha, pushed the cork in and took it through to the sitting-room to stand by his favourite chair. It was a wonderful chair for his purpose; old fashioned and high backed with wings to support the head.

He would get out his *Daily Mirror*, light a Woodbine and settle down till sleep overcame him. If Siegfried rushed in on him he grabbed the

POPULAR TRANSPORT For £100 in 1936 a farmer could buy a saloon car to save much trudging up and down steep lanes, and make speedy work of a trip to the local market. *The Farmers Weekly* carried advertisements for cars, but in the Dales it was only the larger farmers who bought them. For the small farmer with an average yearly profit of under £500 on which to keep his family, a car was a luxury to be saved for. It was the late 1950s before most Dales farmers had a car, van or Land Rover.

bottle and started to shake it madly, inspecting the contents at intervals. Then he went through to the dispensary, filled up the bottle and labelled it.

It was a sound, workable system but it had one big snag. He never knew whether it was Siegfried or not when the door opened and often I walked in and found him half lying in his chair, staring up with startled, sleep-blurred eyes while he agitated his bottle.

Most evenings found him sitting on a high stool at the bar counter of the Drover's Arms, conversing effortlessly with the barmaid. At other times he would be out with one of the young nurses from the local hospital which he seemed to regard as an agency to provide him with female company. All in all, he managed to lead a fairly full life.

Saturday night, 10.30 p.m. and I was writing up my visits when the phone rang. I swore, crossed my fingers and lifted the receiver.

'Hello, Herriot speaking.'

'Oh, it's you is it,' growled a dour voice in broadest Yorkshire. 'Well, ah want Mr Farnon.'

'I'm sorry, Mr Farnon is out. Can I help you?'

'Well, I 'ope so, but I'd far raither 'ave your boss. This is Sims of Beal Close.'

(Oh no, please no, not Beal Close on a Saturday night. Miles up in the hills at the end of a rough lane with about eight gates.)

'Yes, Mr Sims, and what is the trouble?'

'Ah'll tell you, there is some trouble an' all. I 'ave a grand big show 'oss here. All of seventeen hands. He's cut 'isself badly on the hind leg, just above the hock. I want him stitched immediately.'

(Glory be! Above the hock! What a charming place to have to stitch a horse. Unless he's very quiet, this is going to be a real picnic.)

'How big is the wound, Mr Sims?'

'Big? It's a gurt big thing about a foot long and bleedin' like 'ell. And this 'oss is as wick as an eel. Could kick a fly's eye out. Ah can't get near 'im nohow. Goes straight up wall when he sees anybody. By gaw, I tell you I had 'im to t'blacksmith t'other day and feller was dead scared of 'im. Twiltin' gurt 'oss 'e is.'

(Damn you, Mr Sims, damn Beal Close and damn your twiltin' gurt 'oss.)

'Well, I'll be along straight away. Try to have some men handy just in case we have to throw him.'

'Throw 'im? Throw 'im? You'd never throw this 'oss. He'd kill yer first. Anyways, I 'ave no men here so you'll have to manage on your own. Ah know Mr Farnon wouldn't want a lot of men to help 'im.'

(Oh lovely, lovely. This is going to be one for the diary.)

'Very well, I'm leaving now, Mr Sims.'

'Oh, ah nearly forgot. My road got washed away in the floods yesterday. You'll 'ave to walk the last mile and a half. So get a move on and don't keep me waiting all night.'

(This is just a bit much.)

'Look here, Mr Sims, I don't like your tone. I said I would leave now and I will get there just as soon as I can.'

'You don't like ma tone, eh? Well, ah don't like useless young apprentices practising on my good stock, so ah don't want no cheek from you. You know nowt about t'damn job, any road.'

(That finally does it.)

'Now just listen to me, Sims. If it wasn't for the sake of the horse I'd refuse to come out at all. Who do you think you are, anyway? If you ever try to speak to me like that again ...'

'Now, now, Jim, get a grip on yourself. Take it easy old boy. You'll burst a blood vessel if you go on like this.'

'Who the devil ... ?'

'Ah, ah, Jim, calm yourself now. That temper of yours, you know. You'll really have to watch it.'

'Tristan! Where the hell are you speaking from?'

'The kiosk outside the Drovers. Five pints inside me and feeling a bit puckish. Thought I'd give you a ring.'

'By God, I'll murder you one of these days if you don't stop this game. It's putting years on me. Now and again isn't so bad, but this is the third time this week.'

'Ah, but this was by far the best, Jim. It was really wonderful. When you started drawing yourself up to your full height – it nearly killed me. Oh God, I wish you could have heard yourself.' He trailed off into helpless laughter.

And then my feeble attempts at retaliation; creeping, trembling, into some lonely phone box.

'Is that young Mr Farnon?' in a guttural croak. 'Well, this is Tilson of High Woods. Ah want you to come out here immediately I 'ave a terrible case of ...'

'Excuse me for interrupting, Jim, but is there something the matter with your tonsils? Oh, good. Well, go on with what you were saying, old lad. Sounds very interesting.'

There was only one time when I was not on the receiving end. It was Tuesday – my half day – and at 11.30 a.m. a call came in. An eversion of the uterus in a cow. This is a tough job in country practice and I felt the usual chill.

It happens when the cow, after calving, continues to strain until it pushes the entire uterus out and it hangs down as far as the animal's hocks. It is a vast organ and desperately difficult to replace, mainly because the cow, having once got rid of it, doesn't want it back. And in a straightforward contest between man and beast the odds were very much on the cow.

The old practitioners, in an effort to even things up a bit, used to sling the cow up by its hind limbs and the more inventive among them came up with all sorts of contraptions like the uterine valise which was

MOTORING COUNTRY There was plenty of motor traffic along the lanes of the Dales at summer week-ends and holiday times. Delivery vans and the shiny black saloons of local professional men formed some of it. But most of the motorists were visitors from industrial areas enjoying a day out. They drove down the green valleys and over the purple moors, parking in the pretty villages to pore over the route guide. The six old pence (2½p) this cost was well spent. With its help the day-trippers could enter with confidence the intricate network of winding lanes.

SHORTHORN COW The red, roan and white of Shorthorns dotted the green landscapes of the Dales almost without competition until the 1940s. Its versatility made it virtually the universal farmer's cow in the area – and in much of Britain. It is equally good for milk or beef, fattening quickly on good land but producing well as a milker on poor grazing. Most of the gentle-flavoured Wensleydale cheese was made from the milk of Dales-reared Shorthorns.

supposed to squeeze the organ into smaller bulk. But the result was usually the same – hours of back-breaking work.

The introduction of the epidural anaesthetic made everything easier by removing sensation from the uterus and preventing the cow from straining but, for all that, the words 'calf bed out' coming over the line were guaranteed to wipe the smile off any vet's face.

I decided to take Tristan in case I needed a few pounds of extra push. He came along but showed little enthusiasm for the idea. He showed still less when he saw the patient, a very fat shorthorn lying, quite unconcerned, in her stall. Behind her, a bloody mass of uterus, afterbirth, muck and straw spilled over into the channel.

She wasn't at all keen to get up, but after we had done a bit of shouting and pushing at her shoulder she rose to her feet, looking bored.

The epidural space was difficult to find among the rolls of fat and I wasn't sure if I had injected all the anaesthetic into the right place. I removed the afterbirth, cleaned the uterus and placed it on a clean sheet held by the farmer and his brother. They were frail men and it was all they could do to keep the sheet level. I wouldn't be able to count on them to help me much.

I nodded to Tristan; we stripped off our shirts, tied clean sacks round our waists and gathered the uterus in our arms.

It was badly engorged and swollen and it took us just an hour to get it back. There was a long spell at the beginning when we made no progress at all and the whole idea of pushing the enormous organ through a small hole seemed ludicrous, like trying to thread a needle with a sausage. Then there was a few minutes when we thought we were doing famously only to find we were feeding the thing down through a tear in the sheet (Siegfried once told me he had spent half a morning trying to stuff a uterus up a cow's rectum. What really worried him, he said, was that he nearly succeeded) and at the end when hope was fading, there was the blissful moment when the whole thing began to slip inside and incredibly disappeared from sight.

Somewhere half way through we both took a breather at the same time and stood panting, our faces almost touching. Tristan's cheeks were prettily patterned where a spouting artery had sprayed him; I was able to look deep into his eyes and I read there a deep distaste for the whole business.

Lathering myself in the bucket and feeling the ache in my shoulders and back, I looked over at Tristan. He was pulling his shirt over his head as though it cost him the last of his strength. The cow, chewing contentedly at a mouthful of hay, had come best out of the affair.

Out in the car, Tristan groaned. 'I'm sure that sort of thing isn't good for me. I feel as though I've been run over by a steam roller. Hell, what a life this is at times.'

After lunch I rose from the table. 'I'm off to Brawton now, Triss, and I think I'd better mention that you may not have seen the last of that cow. These bad cases sometimes recur and there's a chance that little lot may come out again. If it does, it's all yours because Siegfried won't be back for hours and nothing is going to stop me having my half day.'

For once Tristan's sense of humour failed him. He became haggard, he seemed to age suddenly. 'Oh God,' he moaned, 'don't even talk about it. I'm all in – another session like that would kill me. And on my own! It would be the end of me, I tell you.'

'Ah well,' I said sadistically, 'try not to worry. It may never happen.'

It was when I saw the phone box about ten miles along the Brawton road that the thought struck me. I slowed down and got out of the car. 'I wonder,' I muttered, 'I wonder if I could do it just once.'

Inside the box, inspiration was strong in me. I wrapped my handkerchief over the mouthpiece, dialled the practice number and when I heard Tristan on the line I shouted at the top of my voice. 'Are you t'young feller that put our cow's calf bed back this morning?'

'Yes, I'm one of them.' Tension sprang into Tristan's voice. 'Why, is there something wrong?'

'Aye, there is summat wrong,' I bawled. 'She's putten it out again.'

'Out again? Out again? All of it?' He was almost screaming.

'Aye, it's a terrible mess. Pourin' blood and about twice size it was this morning. You'll 'ave some job with 'er.'

There was a long silence and I wondered if he had fainted. Then I heard him again, hoarse but resolute. 'Very well, I'll come straight away.'

There was another pause then he spoke again almost in a whisper. 'Is it out completely?'

I broke down then. There was a wistful quality about the words which defeated me; a hint of a wild hope that the farmer may have been exaggerating and that there might be only a tiny piece peeping out. I began to laugh. I would have liked to toy with my victim a little longer but it was impossible. I laughed louder and took my handkerchief from the mouthpiece so that Tristan could hear me.

I listened for a few seconds to the frenzied swearing at the other end then gently replaced the receiver. It would probably never happen again but it was sweet, very sweet.

7

Tristan keeps the books

It was unfortunate that Siegfried ever had the idea of delegating the book-keeping to his brother, because Skeldale House had been passing through a period of peace and I found it soothing.

For nearly a fortnight there had been hardly a raised voice or an angry

SHORTHORN BULL The most common cattle breed of north Yorkshire was the Shorthorn until the Friesian began to replace it in the 1950s. Few Dales farmers had pure-bred herds, but they would send the in-season cows to a Shorthorn bull for mating to strengthen the Shorthorn characteristics in them. A bull is an expensive animal to buy and to feed; only larger farmers could afford one. Small farmers would pay for the use of the bull, or several would club together to hire a bull for a few weeks and have it sent to their farms.

word except for one unpleasant interlude when Siegfried had come in and found his brother cycling along the passage. Tristan found all the rage and shouting quite incomprehensible – he had been given the job of setting the table and it was a long way from kitchen to dining-room; it seemed the most natural thing in the world to bring his bike in.

Autumn had come with a sharpness in the air and at nights the log fire burned bright in the big room, sending shadows flickering over the graceful alcoves and up to the high, carved ceiling. It was always a good time when the work of the day was through and the three of us lay back in the shabby arm chairs and stretched our feet out to the blaze.

Tristan was occupied with *The Daily Telegraph* crossword which he did every night. Siegfried was reading and I was dozing. It embarrassed me to be drawn into the crossword; Siegfried could usually make a contribution after a minute's thought but Tristan could have the whole thing worked out while I wrestled with the first clue.

The carpet round our feet was hidden by the dogs, all five of them, draped over each other in heavy-breathing layers and adding to the atmosphere of camaraderie and content.

It seemed to me that a chill breath struck through the comfort of the room as Siegfried spoke. 'Market day tomorrow and the bills have just gone out. They'll be queueing up to give us their money so I want you, Tristan, to devote the entire day to taking it from them. James and I are going to be busy, so you'll be in sole charge. All you have to do is take their cheques, give them a receipt and enter their names in the receipt book. Now do you think you can manage that without making a bloody hash of it?'

I winced. It was the first discordant note for a long time and it struck deep.

'I think I might just about cope with that,' Tristan replied haughtily.

'Good. Let's get to bed then.'

But, next day, it was easy to see that the assignment was right up Tristan's street. Stationed behind the desk, he took in the money in handfuls; and all the time he talked. But he did not talk at random; each character got a personal approach.

With the upright Methodist, it was the weather, the price of cows and the activities of the village institute. The raffish type with his cap on one side, exhaling fumes of market ale, got the latest stories which Tristan kept on the backs of envelopes. But with the ladies he rose to his greatest heights. They were on his side from the first because of his innocent, boyish face, and when he turned the full blast of his charm on them their surrender was complete.

I was amazed at the giggles which came from behind the door. I was pleased the lad was doing well. Nothing was going wrong this time.

Tristan was smug at lunch time and cock-a-hoop at tea. Siegfried, too, was satisfied with the day's takings which his brother presented in the form of a column of neat figures accurately totalled at the bottom. 'Thank you, Tristan, very efficient.' All was sweetness.

PRIZE CROSSWORD Veterinary students, professional men, housewives at home or daily commuters to work have been challenged, captivated and maddened by *The Daily Telegraph* crossword since it was introduced on July 30, 1925. It appeared on each of the six weekdays that the paper was published. Prizes for the Saturday crossword were first offered in March, 1928. When Tristan attempted it in the late 1930s there were three prizes of books to the value of 2 guineas (£2.10) and 20 prizes of playing cards.

At the end of the day I was in the yard, throwing the used bottles from the boot of my car into a bin. It had been a busy day and I had accumulated a bigger than usual load of empties.

Tristan came panting in from the garden. 'Jim, I've lost the receipt book!'

'Always trying to pull my leg, always joking,' I said, 'Why don't you give your sense of humour a rest some time?' I laughed heartily and sent a liniment bottle crashing among the others.

He plucked at my sleeve. 'I'm not joking, Jim, believe me. I really have lost the bloody thing.' For once, his *sang froid* had deserted him. His eyes were wide, his face pale.

'But it can't just have disappeared,' I said. 'It's bound to turn up.'

'It'll never turn up.' Tristan wrung his hands and did a bit of pacing on the cobbles. 'Do you know I've spent about two hours searching for it. I've ransacked the house. It's gone, I tell you.'

'But it doesn't matter, does it? You'll have transferred all the names into the ledger.'

'That's just it. I haven't. I was going to do it tonight.'

'So that means that all the farmers who have been handing you money today are going to get the same bill next month?'

'Looks like it. I can't remember the names of more than two or three of them.'

I sat down heavily on the stone trough. 'Then God help us all, especially you. These Yorkshire lads don't like parting with their brass once, but when you ask them to do it twice – oh, brother!'

Another thought struck me and I said with a touch of cruelty: 'And how about Siegfried. Have you told him yet?'

A spasm crossed Tristan's face. 'No, he's just come in. I'm going to do it now.' He squared his shoulders and strode from the yard.

I decided not to follow him to the house. I didn't feel strong enough for the scene which was bound to follow. Instead, I went out into the back lane and round behind the house to the market place where the lighted entrance of the Drovers' Arms beckoned in the dusk.

I was sitting behind a pint when Tristan came in looking as though somebody had just drained half a gallon of blood from him.

'How did it go?' I asked.

'Oh, the usual, you know. Bit worse this time, maybe. But I can tell you this, Jim. I'm not looking forward to a month from today.'

The receipt book was never found and, a month later, all the bills were sent out again, timed, as usual, to arrive on market day morning.

The practice was quiet that particular day and I had finished my round by mid morning. I didn't go into the house, because through the waiting room window I could see rows of farmers sitting round the walls; they all wore the same offended, self-righteous expression.

I stole away to the market place. When I had time, I enjoyed moving among the stalls which crowded the ancient square. You could buy fruit,

PONY AND TRAP Developed from the ancient design of the cart, the trap had the same basic construction but was much lighter. Its two wheels were only about 2 in. wide at the rim and they were mounted on a metal instead of a wooden axle. The body was set on springs because the trap carried passengers – the farmer and his wife to market, the local carrier delivering goods, and many tradesmen such as the grocer and fishmonger. Traps were used until the 1940s.

This time, Billy wasn't so jocular.
'Hey, remember that bill you sent me
twice? Well, I've had it again.'

fish, second-hand books, cheeses, clothes, in fact nearly everything; but
the china stall was my favourite.

It was run by a Jewish gentleman from Leeds – fat, confident,
sweating, and with a hypnotic selling technique. I never got tired of
watching him. He fascinated me. He was in his best form today,
standing in a little clearing surrounded on all sides by heaps of crockery,
while beyond, the farmers' wives listened open-mouthed to his oratory.

'Ah'm not good lookin',' he was saying. 'Ah'm not clever, but by God
ah can talk. Ah can talk the hind leg off a donkey. Now look 'ere.' He
lifted a cheap cup and held it aloft, but tenderly, gripping it between his
thick thumb and forefinger, his little finger daintily outspread. 'Beautiful, isn't it? Now isn't that lovely?' Then he placed it reverently on the
palm of his hand and displayed it to the audience. 'Now I tell you ladies,
you can buy this self same tea-set in Conners in Bradford for three
pounds fifteen. I'm not jokin' nor jestin', it's there and that's the price.
But my price, ladies?' and here he fished out an old walking stick with a
splintered handle, 'My price for this beautiful tea-set?' He held the stick
by its end and brought it crashing down on an empty tea-chest. 'Never
mind three pound fifteen.' Crash! 'Never mind three pound.' Crash!
'Never mind two pound.' Crash! 'Never mind thirty bob.' Crash! ''ere,
'ere, come on, who'll give me a quid?' Not a soul moved. 'All right, all
right, I can see ah've met me match today. Go on, seventeen and a
tanner the lot.' A final devasting crash and the ladies began to make
signals and fumble in their handbags. A little man emerged from the
back of the stall and started to hand out the tea-sets. The ritual had been
observed and everybody was happy.

I was waiting, deeply content, for the next item from the virtuoso when I saw a burly figure in a check cap waving wildly at me from the edge of the crowd. He had his hand inside his jacket and I knew what he was feeling for. I didn't hesitate but dodged quickly behind a stall laden with pig troughs and wire netting. I had gone only a few steps before another farmer hailed me purposefully. He was brandishing an envelope.

I felt trapped, then I saw a way of escape. Rapidly skirting a counter displaying cheap jewellery, I plunged into the doorway of the Drovers' Arms and, avoiding the bar which was full of farmers, slipped into the manager's office. I was safe; this was one place where I was always welcome.

The manager looked up from his desk, but he did not smile. 'Look here,' he said sharply, 'I brought my dog in to see you some time ago and in due course I received an account from you.' I cringed inwardly. 'I paid by return and was extremely surprised this morning to find that another account had been rendered. I have here a receipt signed by . . .'

I couldn't stand any more. 'I'm very sorry, Mr Brooke, but there's been a mistake. I'll put it right. Please accept our apologies.'

This became a familiar refrain over the next few days, but it was Siegfried who had the most unfortunate experience. It was in the bar of his favourite pub, the Black Swan. He was approached by Billy Breckenridge, a friendly, jocular little character, one of Darrowby's worthies. 'Hey, remember that three and six I paid at your surgery? I've had another bill for it.'

Siegfried made a polished apology – he'd had a lot of practice – and bought the man a drink. They parted on good terms.

The pity of it was that Siegfried, who seldom remembered anything, didn't remember this. A month later, also in the Swan, he ran into Billy Breckenridge again. This time, Billy wasn't so jocular. 'Hey, remember that bill you sent me twice? Well, I've had it again.'

Siegfried did his best, but his charm bounced off the little man. He was offended. 'Right, I can see you don't believe I paid your bill. I had a receipt from your brother, but I've lost it.' He brushed aside Siegfried's protestations. 'No, no, there's only one way to settle this. I say I've paid the three and six, you say I haven't. All right, I'll toss you for it.'

Miserably, Siegfried demurred, but Billy was adamant. He produced a penny and, with great dignity, balanced it on his thumbnail. 'O.K., you call.'

'Heads,' muttered Siegfried and heads it was. The little man did not change expression. Still dignified, he handed the three and six to Siegfried. 'Perhaps we might be able to consider the matter closed.' He walked out of the bar.

Now there are all kinds of bad memories, but Siegfried's was of the inspired type. He somehow forgot to make a note of this last transaction and, at the end of the month, Billy Breckenridge received a fourth request for the amount which he had already paid twice. It was about then that Siegfried changed his pub and started going to the Cross Keys.

41

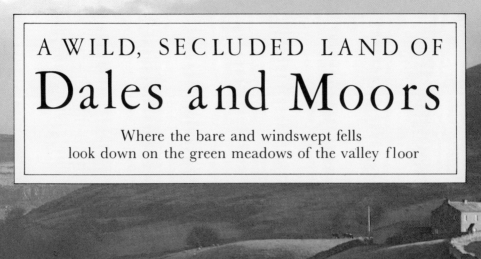

A WILD, SECLUDED LAND OF
Dales and Moors

Where the bare and windswept fells
look down on the green meadows of the valley floor

The pure air and hidden waterfalls of the Dales

His work as a vet has taken James Herriot into some of the wildest and loneliest parts of England. The high country at the top of Swaledale and Wensleydale is too bleak for many people; but it was up there on the empty moors, with the curlews crying, that the young vet found peace and tranquillity of mind.

It is a land of pure air, rocky streams and hidden waterfalls. On summer days the breeze carries the sweetness of warm grass and a thousand scents from the valley below.

This is one of the few areas of England where it is possible to be utterly alone.

STONESDALE Where Swaledale reaches up on to the Pennines, a small bridge carries a track over Stonesdale Beck.

HIGHEST The River Swale tumbles over Wain Wath Force, near Keld, the last and highest village in Swaledale.

PARK BRIDGE The Swale eddies towards Park Bridge near Keld (right).

The beauty and hardship of winter

When winter comes, the moors and dales of north Yorkshire can be covered by a wondrous white blanket, with the wind carving the piled snow into drifts of exquisite beauty.

To the country vet, however, it means walking long distances to isolated farms, hundreds of yards from the main roads, and a shovel may be the most useful item among his equipment.

The hardy Dales farmers have grown up to the snow and the knife-like wind driving in from the east. And the fiercest weather is likely to be met with the comment: 'Aye, it blows a bit thin this mornin'.'

WINTER'S GRIP Huddled below the towering heights of Sleddale, a farmhouse with its cluster of outbuildings rides out the winter.

SWALEDALE UNDER SNOW The drystone walls on the high land above Swaledale stand above the snow, but lower down they disappear under the drifts. For weather like this, the farmer needs the hardy Dales breeds of sheep, which can survive even though buried in snow.

BETWEEN THE DALES Oxnop Gill, a tributary of the Swale, winds down through Oxnop Common, the barren ridge betwee

waledale and Wensleydale. To be caught here in bad weather, even in summer, can be an unnerving experience.

The lake that hides the secret of a city

In a land where lakes are few, the long stretch of Semerwater comes as a delightful surprise. It covers about 100 acres, but in times of flood it can expand to twice that size. And when the wind rises, the placid lake becomes an inland sea with white-crested waves dashing themselves on the banks and swamping the trunks of the trees.

An old story tells that an opulent city lies beneath the surface of the lake – drowned by the spell of a magician who tried in vain to find food and shelter among the rich houses. Only the poorest tenant, living high on the hillside, would give him lodging for the night. The magician stood by the man's cottage and cursed the city, whereupon it was engulfed by a great flood of water.

LINES OF STONE Drystone walls march in straight lines almost from the banks of Semerwater to the top of the moors (left). And in a nearby dale, the colour of the land changes abruptly between the pasture of the valley floor and the rough grass on the moor above.

The waterfalls and rivulets of Wensleydale

Wensleydale is the second of the two main Pennine dales of North Yorkshire. It runs parallel to Swaledale, a few miles to the south.

Wensleydale's river is the Ure. While Swaledale takes its name from the River Swale, Wensleydale is named after the sleepy village of Wensley, once a busy market town.

WATERFALL At Hardraw Force, Fossdale Gill drops from the overhanging rock in a single narrow torrent.

NEAR SIMONSTONE Fossdale Gill is a small tributary of the Ure.

AYSGARTH FALLS The Ure is a gentle river until it reaches Aysgarth, where it goes wild and drops 200 ft in a series of boisterous falls (right).

COVERDALE In the secluded valley of Coverdale, sheep graze around an ancient stone pen which has partly collapsed into

y gulley. Coverdale has a stark beauty of treeless heights, where the silence is complete except for the bleating of sheep.

ARKENGARTHDALE A sunlit farmhouse stands in total isolation among the long stone walls of Arkengarthda

ore than a thousand years ago the dale was called Arkil's Garth, and local farmers still call their fields garths.

An airy land of gills and heather

A traveller starting at the top of the Pennines and heading towards the North Sea would descend one of the dales to the 30 mile wide Vale of York where every yard of the rich soil is farmed. He would then climb the steep escarpment of the Hambleton Hills back to a land of stone walls and moors.

This is the North York Moors, a spacious country of heather which sweeps for nearly 50 miles to the ocean. It is a different Yorkshire from the Pennine Dales, flat at first glance, but in fact cleft by a multitude of gills and valleys.

BRANSDALE One of the remotest valleys on the North York Moors is Bransdale, through which Hodge Beck flows from its source high on the moors to its junction with the River Dove south of Kirkbymoorside.

CHECKER PATTERN All year round the land is a checker pattern of fields, heather and trees, constantly changing colour with the seasons (above and right).

Looking down from Rudland Rigg

Rudland Rigg is a spine of land that runs between the twin dales of Bransdale and Farndale on the North York Moors.

This is splendid country for walking, cut through with soft clay paths. From the windy crest of the Rigg the walker looks down on a billowing ocean of heather, rolling away 30 or 40 miles to the skyline.

FARNDALE In spring, wild daffodils carpet the banks of the River Dove.

MOORLAND SIGN From Rudland Rigg, a solitary farmhouse is the only sign of habitation in Farndale (right). A stone signpost (above) directed drovers of long ago to Pickering and Stokesley, spelling the names as they were spoken.

SUTTON BANK On the edge of the Hambleton Hills, the sheer face of Sutton Bank falls away to the fertile Vale of Yor

the clear air of a frosty morning, the view extends right across the Vale into Wensleydale and the Pennines beyond.

SUNSET FROM SUTTON BANK As the weather changes, the view from Sutton Bank varies daily, almost by the hour. And when the sun sets behind the Pennines far off to the west, Sutton Bank witnesses a final vivid spectacle.

8

Tricki Woo shows his gratitude

As Autumn wore into Winter and the high tops were streaked with the first snows, the discomforts of practice in the Dales began to make themselves felt.

Driving for hours with frozen feet, climbing to the high barns in biting winds which seared and flattened the wiry hill grass. The interminable stripping off in draughty buildings and the washing of hands and chest in buckets of cold water, using scrubbing soap and often a piece of sacking for a towel.

I really found out the meaning of chapped hands. When there was a rush of work, my hands were never quite dry and the little red fissures crept up almost to my elbows.

This was when some small animal work came as a blessed relief. To step out of the rough, hard routine for a while; to walk into a warm drawing-room instead of a cow house and tackle something less formidable than a horse or a bull. And among all those comfortable drawing-rooms there was none so beguiling as Mrs Pumphrey's.

Mrs Pumphrey was an elderly widow. Her late husband, a beer baron whose breweries and pubs were scattered widely over the broad bosom of Yorkshire, had left her a vast fortune and a beautiful house on the outskirts of Darrowby. Here she lived with a large staff of servants, a gardener, a chauffeur and Tricki Woo. Tricki Woo was a Pekingese and the apple of his mistress's eye.

Standing now in the magnificent doorway, I furtively rubbed the toes of my shoes on the back of my trousers and blew on my cold hands. I could almost see the deep armchair drawn close to the leaping flames, the tray of cocktail biscuits, the bottle of excellent sherry. Because of the sherry, I was always careful to time my visits for half an hour before lunch.

A maid answered my ring, beaming on me as an honoured guest and led me to the room, crammed with expensive furniture and littered with glossy magazines and the latest novels. Mrs Pumphrey, in the high backed chair by the fire, put down her book with a cry of delight. 'Trick! Tricki! Here is your Uncle Herriot. I had been made an uncle very early and, sensing the advantages of the relationship, had made no objection.

Tricki, as always, bounded from his cushion, leaped on to the back of a sofa and put his paws on my shoulders. He then licked my face thoroughly before retiring, exhausted. He was soon exhausted because he was given roughly twice the amount of food needed for a dog of his size. And it was the wrong kind of food.

'Oh, Mr Herriot,' Mrs Pumphrey said, looking at her pet anxiously.

65

'I'm so glad you've come. Tricki has gone flop-bott again.'

This ailment, not to be found in any text book, was her way of describing the symptoms of Tricki's impacted anal glands. When the glands filled up, he showed discomfort by sitting down suddenly in mid walk and his mistress would rush to the phone in great agitation.

'Mr Herriot! Please come, he's going flop-bott again!'

I hoisted the little dog on to a table and, by pressure on the anus with a pad of cotton wool, I evacuated the glands.

It baffled me that the Peke was always so pleased to see me. Any dog who could still like a man who grabbed him and squeezed his bottom hard every time they met had to have an incredibly forgiving nature. But Tricki never showed any resentment; in fact he was an outstandingly equable little animal, bursting with intelligence, and I was genuinely attached to him. It was a pleasure to be his personal physician.

The squeezing over, I lifted my patient from the table, noticing the increased weight, the padding of extra flesh over the ribs. 'You know, Mrs Pumphrey, you're overfeeding him again. Didn't I tell you to cut out all those pieces of cake and give him more protein?'

'Oh yes, Mr Herriot,' Mrs Pumphrey wailed. 'But what can I do? He's so tired of chicken.'

I shrugged; it was hopeless. I allowed the maid to lead me to the palatial bathroom where I always performed a ritual handwashing after the operation. It was a huge room with a fully stocked dressing table, massive green ware and rows of glass shelves laden with toilet preparations. My private guest towel was laid out next to the slab of expensive soap.

Then I returned to the drawing-room, my sherry glass was filled and I settled down by the fire to listen to Mrs Pumphrey. It couldn't be called a conversation because she did all the talking, but I always found it rewarding.

Mrs Pumphrey was likeable, gave widely to charities and would help anybody in trouble. She was intelligent and amusing and had a lot of waffling charm; but most people have a blind spot and her's was Tricki Woo. The tales she told about her darling ranged far into the realms of fantasy and I waited eagerly for the next instalment.

'Oh Mr Herriot, I have the most exciting news. Tricki has a pen pal! Yes, he wrote a letter to the editor of *Doggy World* enclosing a donation, and told him that even though he was descended from a long line of Chinese emperors, he had decided to come down and mingle freely with the common dogs. He asked the editor to seek out a pen pal for him among the dogs he knew so that they could correspond to their mutual benefit. And for this purpose, Tricki said he would adopt the name of Mr Utterbunkum. And, do you know, he received the most beautiful letter from the editor' (I could imagine the sensible man leaping upon this potential gold mine) 'who said he would like to introduce Bonzo Fotheringham, a lonely Dalmatian who would be delighted to exchange letters with a new friend in Yorkshire.'

PEKINGESE This tiny aristocrat has 4,000 years of history behind it, although it was virtually unseen outside China until the late 19th century. The lion-maned Peke with its flat nose, huge, shining eyes and plumed tail has long enjoyed a life of luxury. It was a favourite at the Chinese court – and once a sacred creature there. Chinese mandarins used to carry their small Pekes about with them in their capacious sleeves.

I sipped the sherry. Tricki snored on my lap. Mrs Pumphrey went on.

'But I'm so disappointed about the new Summerhouse – you know I got it specially for Tricki so we could sit out together on warm afternoons. It's such a nice little rustic shelter, but he's taken a passionate dislike to it. Simply loathes it – absolutely refuses to go inside. You should see the dreadful expression on his face when he looks at it. And do you know what he called it yesterday? Oh, I hardly dare tell you.' She looked around the room before leaning over and whispering: 'He called it "the bloody hut"!'

The maid struck fresh life into the fire and refilled my glass. The wind hurled a handful of sleet against the window. This, I thought, was the life. I listened for more.

'And did I tell you, Mr Herriot, Tricki had another good win yesterday? You know, I'm sure he must study the racing columns, he's such a tremendous judge of form. Well, he told me to back Canny Lad in the three o'clock at Redcar yesterday and, as usual, it won. He put a shilling each way and got back nine shillings.'

These bets were always placed in the name of Tricki Woo and I thought with compassion of the reactions of the local bookies. The Darrowby turf accountants were a harassed and fugitive body of men. A board would appear at the end of some alley urging the population to invest with Joe Downs and enjoy perfect security. Joe would live for a few months on a knife edge while he pitted his wits against the knowledgeable citizens, but the end was always the same; a few favourites would win in a row and Joe would be gone in the night, taking his board with him. Once I had asked a local inhabitant about the sudden departure of one of these luckless nomads. He replied unemotionally: 'Oh, we brok 'im.'

DALMATIAN The round black or brown spots that spatter the hard, white coat of the Dalmatian give it a comic appearance, rather as if it had been the victim of a practical joke. But this belies the dog's intelligence. It was bred as a war dog to guard the chariots of archers who tried to keep out the Turks from Dalmatia on the eastern side of the Adriatic. In 18th and 19th-century Britain, Dalmatians were carriage dogs. They ran under the carriage just behind the horses, ready to repel highwaymen. Now they are pets, biddable and affectionate, but with the insatiable appetite for exercise that made them suitable for carriage work.

Losing a regular flow of shillings to a dog must have been a heavy cross for these unfortunate men to bear.

'I had such a frightening experience last week,' Mrs Pumphrey continued. 'I was sure I would have to call you out. Poor little Tricki – he went completely crackerdog!' I mentally lined this up with flop-bott among the new canine diseases and asked for more information.

'It was awful. I was terrified. The gardener was throwing rings for Tricki – you know he does this for half an hour every day.' I had witnessed this spectacle several times. Hodgkin, a dour, bent old Yorkshireman who looked as though he hated all dogs and Tricki in particular, had to go out on the lawn every day and throw little rubber rings over and over again. Tricki bounded after them and brought them back, barking madly till the process was repeated. The bitter lines on the old man's face deepened as the game progressed. His lips moved continually, but it was impossible to hear what he was saying.

Mrs Pumphrey went on: 'Well, he was playing his game, and he does adore it so, when suddenly, without warning, he went crackerdog. He forgot all about his rings and began to run around in circles, barking and yelping in such a strange way. Then he fell over on his side and lay like a little dead thing. Do you know, Mr Herriot, I really thought he was dead, he lay so perfectly still. And what hurt me most was that Hodgkin began to laugh. He has been with me for twenty-four years and I have never even seen him smile, and yet, when he looked down at that still form, he broke into a queer, high-pitched cackle. It was horrid. I was just going to rush to the telephone when Tricki got up and walked away – he seemed perfectly normal.'

Hysteria, I thought, brought on by wrong feeding and over-excitement. I put down my glass and fixed Mrs Pumphrey with a severe glare. 'Now look, this is just what I was talking about. If you persist in feeding all that fancy rubbish to Tricki you are going to ruin his health. You really must get him on to a sensible dog diet of one or, at the most, two small meals a day of meat and brown bread or a little biscuit. And nothing in between.'

Mrs Pumphrey shrank into her chair, a picture of abject guilt. 'Oh, please don't speak to me like that. I do try to give him the right things, but it is so difficult. When he begs for his little titbits, I can't refuse him.' She dabbed her eyes with a handkerchief.

But I was unrelenting. 'All right, Mrs Pumphrey, it's up to you, but I warn you that if you go on as you are doing, Tricki will go crackerdog more and more often.'

I left the cosy haven with reluctance, pausing on the gravelled drive to look back at Mrs Pumphrey waving and Tricki, as always, standing against the window, his wide-mouthed face apparently in the middle of a hearty laugh.

Driving home, I mused on the many advantages of being Tricki's uncle. When he went to the seaside he sent me boxes of oak-smoked kippers; and when the tomatoes ripened in his greenhouse, he sent a pound or two every week. Tins of tobacco arriving regularly, sometimes with a photograph carrying a loving inscription.

But it was when the Christmas hamper arrived from Fortnum and Mason's that I decided that I was on a really good thing which should be helped along a bit. Hitherto, I had merely rung up and thanked Mrs Pumphrey for the gifts, and she had been rather cool, pointing out that it was Tricki who had sent the things and he was the one who should be thanked.

With the arrival of the hamper it came to me, blindingly, that I had been guilty of a grave error of tactics. I set myself to compose a letter to Tricki. Avoiding Siegfried's sardonic eye, I thanked my doggy nephew for his Christmas gifts and for all his generosity in the past. I expressed my sincere hopes that the festive fare had not upset his delicate digestion and suggested that if he did experience any discomfort he should have recourse to the black powder his uncle always prescribed. A vague feeling of professional shame was easily swamped by floating visions of kippers, tomatoes and hampers. I addressed the envelope to Master Tricki Pumphrey, Barlby Grange and slipped it into the post box with only a slight feeling of guilt.

MAIL BY BICYCLE. In the 1940s and 1950s, rail and Post Office van still took mail to the Dales towns only. From there postmen had to take the mail on foot or by bicycle to the many small villages, and to farms that were long distances from even secondary roads. A daily route of 16 or even 21 miles was common for postmen. Here a letter is being delivered to the general store in West Tanfield, Wensleydale. Now most deliveries are made by van.

68

On my next visit, Mrs Pumphrey drew me to one side. 'Mr Herriot,' she whispered, 'Tricki adored your charming letter and he will keep it always, but he was very put out about one thing – you addressed it to Master Tricki and he does insist upon Mister. He was dreadfully affronted at first, quite beside himself, but when he saw it was from you he soon recovered his good temper. I can't think why he should have these little prejudices. Perhaps it is because he is an only dog – I do think an only dog develops more prejudices than one from a large family.'

Entering Skeldale House was like returning to a colder world. Siegfried bumped into me in the passage. 'Ah, who have we here? Why I do believe it's dear Uncle Herriot. And what have you been doing, Uncle? Slaving away at Barlby Grange, I expect. Poor fellow, you must be tired out. Do you really think it's worth it, working your fingers to the bone for another hamper?'

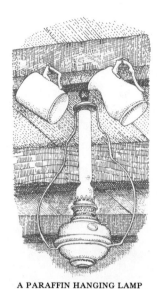

A PARAFFIN HANGING LAMP
Farming folk rose at dawn, went to bed soon after dusk, and spent almost all the hours between in hard physical labour. In the drowsy leisure hour after the evening meal round the kitchen table, the glow from the open fire in the range usually gave enough light, but a hanging lamp hooked on a beam would give extra light when it was needed for reading, sewing or preparing supper. The church, the inn, and perhaps a saddle-room where hands from neighbouring farms met for an evening game of cards were other places where hanging lamps were used.

9

The miracle that never grows stale

They didn't say anything about this in the books, I thought, as the snow blew in through the gaping doorway and settled on my naked back.

I lay face down on the cobbled floor in a pool of nameless muck, my arm deep inside the straining cow, my feet scrabbling for a toe hold between the stones. I was stripped to the waist and the snow mingled with the dirt and the dried blood on my body. I could see nothing outside the circle of flickering light thrown by the smoky oil lamp which the farmer held over me.

No, there wasn't a word in the books about searching for your ropes and instruments in the shadows; about trying to keep clean in a half bucket of tepid water; about the cobbles digging into your chest. Nor about the slow numbing of the arms, the creeping paralysis of the muscles as the fingers tried to work against the cow's powerful expulsive efforts.

There was no mention anywhere of the gradual exhaustion, the feeling of futility and the little far off voice of panic.

My mind went back to that picture in the obstetrics book. A cow standing in the middle of a gleaming floor while a sleek veterinary surgeon in a spotless parturition overall inserted his arm to a polite distance. He was relaxed and smiling, the farmer and his helpers were smiling, even the cow was smiling. There was no dirt or blood or sweat anywhere.

That man in the picture had just finished an excellent lunch and had moved next door to do a bit of calving just for the sheer pleasure of it, as a kind of dessert. He hadn't crawled shivering from his bed at two o'clock in the morning and bumped over twelve miles of frozen snow, staring sleepily ahead till the lonely farm showed in the headlights. He hadn't climbed half a mile of white fell-side to the doorless barn where his patient lay.

I tried to wriggle my way an extra inch inside the cow. The calf's head was back and I was painfully pushing a thin, looped rope towards its lower-jaw with my finger tips. All the time my arm was being squeezed between the calf and the bony pelvis. With every straining effort from the cow the pressure became almost unbearable, then she would relax and I would push the rope another inch. I wondered how long I would be able to keep this up. If I didn't snare that jaw soon I would never get the calf away. I groaned, set my teeth and reached forward again.

Another little flurry of snow blew in and I could almost hear the flakes sizzling on my sweating back. There was sweat on my forehead too, and it trickled into my eyes as I pushed.

There is always a time at a bad calving when you begin to wonder if you will ever win the battle. I had reached this stage.

Little speeches began to flit through my brain. 'Perhaps it would be better to slaughter this cow. Her pelvis is so small and narrow that I can't see a calf coming through.' or 'She's a good fat animal and really of the beef type, so don't you think it would pay you better to get the butcher?' or perhaps 'This is a very bad presentation. In a roomy cow it would be simple enough to bring the head round but in this case it is just about impossible.'

Of course, I could have delivered the calf by embryotomy – by passing a wire over the neck and sawing off the head. So many of these occasions ended with the floor strewn with heads, legs, heaps of intestines. There were thick text books devoted to the countless ways you could cut up a calf.

But none of it was any good here, because this calf was alive. At my furthest stretch I had got my finger as far as the commissure of the mouth and had been startled by a twitch of the little creature's tongue. It was unexpected because calves in this position are usually dead, asphyxiated by the acute flexion of the neck and the pressure of the dam's powerful contractions. But this one had a spark of life in it and if it came out it would have to be in one piece.

I went over to my bucket of water, cold now and bloody, and silently soaped my arms. Then I lay down again, feeling the cobbles harder than ever against my chest. I worked my toes between the stones, shook the sweat from my eyes and for the hundredth time thrust an arm that felt like spaghetti into the cow; alongside the little dry legs of the calf, like sandpaper tearing against my flesh, then to the bend in the neck and so to the ear and then, agonisingly, along the side of the face towards the lower jaw which had become my major goal in life.

It was incredible that I had been doing this for nearly two hours; fighting as my strength ebbed to push a little noose round that jaw. I had

TURNIP LOADING Like swedes, turnips provide winter fodder for sheep and cattle, but they do not keep as long as swedes. They could be carted back to the byre for cows, but for sheep they were often left lying in the fields, split open by a turnip cutter. Sheep would be penned on a small part of the field – a different part each day – to eat all the turnips there and also to manure the ground with their dung.

tried everything else – repelling a leg, gentle traction with a blunt hook in the eye socket, but I was back to the noose.

It had been a miserable session all through. The farmer, Mr Dinsdale, was a long, sad, silent man of few words who always seemed to be expecting the worst to happen. He had a long, sad, silent son with him and the two of them had watched my efforts with deepening gloom.

But worst of all had been Uncle. When I had first entered the hillside barn I had been surprised to see a little bright-eyed old man in a pork pie hat settling down comfortably on a bale of straw. He was filling his pipe and clearly looking forward to the entertainment.

'Now then, young man,' he cried in the nasal twang of the West Riding. 'I'm Mr Dinsdale's brother. I farm over in Listondale.'

I put down my equipment and nodded. 'How do you do? My name is Herriot.'

The old man looked me over, piercingly. 'My vet is Mr Broomfield. Expect you'll have heard of him – everybody knows him, I reckon. Wonderful man, Mr Broomfield, especially at calving. Do you know, I've never seen 'im beat yet.'

I managed a wan smile. Any other time I would have been delighted to hear how good my colleague was, but somehow not now, not now. In fact, the words set a mournful little bell tolling inside me.

'No, I'm afraid I don't know Mr Broomfield,' I said, taking off my jacket and, more reluctantly, peeling my shirt over my head. 'But I haven't been around these parts very long.'

Uncle was aghast. 'You don't know him! Well you're the only one as doesn't. They think the world of him in Listondale, I can tell you.' He lapsed into a shocked silence and applied a match to his pipe. Then he shot a glance at my goose-pimpled torso. 'Strips like a boxer does Mr Broomfield. Never seen such muscles on a man.'

A wave of weakness coursed sluggishly over me. I felt suddenly leaden-footed and inadequate. As I began to lay out my ropes and instruments on a clean towel the old man spoke again.

'And how long have you been qualified, may I ask?'

'Oh, about seven months.'

'Seven months!' Uncle smiled indulgently, tamped down his tobacco and blew out a cloud of rank, blue smoke. 'Well, there's nowt like a bit of experience, I always says. Mr Broomfield's been doing my work now for over ten years and he really knows what he's about. No, you can 'ave your book learning. Give me experience every time.'

I tipped some antiseptic into the bucket and lathered my arms carefully. I knelt behind the cow.

'Mr Broomfield always puts some special lubricating oils on his arms first,' Uncle said, pulling contentedly on his pipe. 'He says you get infection of the womb if you just use soap and water.'

I made my first exploration. It was the burdened moment all vets go through when they first put their hands into a cow. Within seconds I would know whether I would be putting on my jacket in fifteen minutes

CALVING ROPES AND HOOKS If a calf is wrongly positioned in the womb for an easy delivery, the vet will slip the loops of the cotton calving rope on its legs, or sometimes its head, and pull on them to manoeuvre the calf into a better position. Even when the calf is correctly positioned, the cow cannot always expel it and several men may have to pull on ropes to aid the delivery. It is not always possible to get a rope on the calf's head in the womb. Sometimes a blunt hook is placed in the eye socket to pull on the head, and it does the calf no harm. If the calf is dead in the womb, it must be removed as quickly as possible; sharp hooks are used to get a firm hold of it.

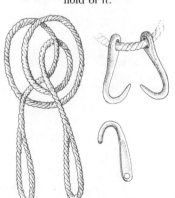

RED POLL COW Like the shorthorn, the red poll is a dual-purpose animal. It is reared to produce beef or milk. An annual agricultural fair at Thirsk, Richmond or Masham, would be the place for a farmer to buy a good beast. Rosettes on their halters indicated that cattle had been prizewinners at the show.

or whether I had hours of hard labour ahead of me.

I was going to be unlucky this time; it was a nasty presentation. Head back and no room at all; more like being inside an undeveloped heifer than a second calver. And she was bone dry – the 'waters' must have come away from her hours ago. She had been running out on the high fields and had started to calve a week before her time; that was why they had had to bring her into this half-ruined barn. Anyway, it would be a long time before I saw my bed again.

'Well now, what have you found, young man?' Uncle's penetrating voice cut through the silence. 'Head back, eh? You won't have much trouble, then. I've seen Mr Broomfield do 'em like that – he turns calf right round and brings it out back legs first.'

I had heard this sort of nonsense before. A short time in practice had taught me that all farmers were experts with other farmers' live stock. When their own animals were in trouble they tended to rush to the phone for the vet, but with their neighbours' they were confident, knowledgeable and full of helpful advice. And another phenomenon I had observed was that their advice was usually regarded as more valuable than the vet's. Like now, for instance; Uncle was obviously an accepted sage and the Dinsdales listened with deference to everything he said.

'Another way with a job like this,' continued Uncle, 'is to get a few strong chaps with ropes and pull the thing out, head back and all.'

I gasped as I felt my way around. 'I'm afraid it's impossible to turn a calf completely round in this small space. And to pull it out without bringing the head round would certainly break the mother's pelvis.'

The Dinsdales narrowed their eyes. Clearly they thought I was hedging in the face of Uncle's superior knowledge.

And now, two hours later, defeat was just round the corner. I was just about whacked. I had rolled and grovelled on the filthy cobbles while the Dinsdales watched me in morose silence and Uncle kept up a non-stop stream of comment. Uncle, his ruddy face glowing with delight, his little eyes sparkling, hadn't had such a happy night for years. His long trek up the hillside had been repaid a hundredfold. His vitality was undiminished; he had enjoyed every minute.

As I lay there, eyes closed, face stiff with dirt, mouth hanging open, Uncle took his pipe in his hand and leaned forward on his straw bale. 'You're about beat, young man,' he said with deep satisfaction. 'Well, I've never seen Mr Broomfield beat but he's had a lot of experience. And what's more, he's strong, really strong. That's one man you couldn't tire.'

Rage flooded through me like a draught of strong spirit. The right thing to do, of course, would be to get up, tip the bucket of bloody water over Uncle's head, run down the hill and drive away; away from Yorkshire, from Uncle, from the Dinsdales, from this cow.

Instead, I clenched my teeth, braced my legs and pushed with everything I had; and with a sensation of disbelief I felt my noose slide

72

over the sharp little incisor teeth and into the calf's mouth. Gingerly, muttering a prayer, I pulled on the thin rope with my left hand and felt the slipknot tighten. I had hold of that lower jaw.

At last I could start doing something. 'Now hold this rope, Mr Dinsdale, and just keep a gentle tension on it. I'm going to repel the calf and if you pull steadily at the same time, the head ought to come round.'

'What if the rope comes off? asked Uncle hopefully.

I didn't answer. I put my hand in against the calf's shoulder and began to push against the cow's contractions. I felt the small body moving away from me. 'Now a steady pull, Mr Dinsdale, without jerking.' And to myself, 'Oh God, don't let it slip off.'

The head was coming round. I could feel the neck straightening against my arm, then the ear touched my elbow. I let go the shoulder and grabbed the little muzzle. Keeping the teeth away from the vaginal wall with my hand, I guided the head till it was resting where it should be, on the fore limbs.

Quickly I extended the noose till it reached behind the ears. 'Now pull on the head as she strains.'

'Nay, you should pull on the legs now,' cried Uncle.

'Pull on the bloody head rope, I tell you!' I bellowed at the top of my voice and felt immediately better as Uncle retired, offended, to his bale.

With traction the head was brought out and the rest of the body followed easily. The little animal lay motionless on the cobbles, eyes glassy and unseeing, tongue blue and grossly swollen.

'It'll be dead. Bound to be,' grunted Uncle, returning to the attack.

I cleared the mucus from the mouth, blew hard down the throat and began artificial respiration. After a few pressures on the ribs, the calf gave a gasp and the eyelids flickered. Then it started to inhale and one leg jerked.

Uncle took off his hat and scratched his head in disbelief. 'By gaw, it's alive. I'd have thowt it'd sure to be dead after you'd messed about all that time.' A lot of the fire had gone out of him and his pipe hung down empty from his lips.

'I know what this little fellow wants,' I said. I grasped the calf by its fore legs and pulled it up to its mother's head. The cow was stretched out on her side, her head extended wearily along the rough floor. Her ribs heaved, her eyes were almost closed; she looked past caring about anything. Then she felt the calf's body against her face and there was a transformation; her eyes opened wide and her muzzle began a snuffling exploration of the new object. Her interest grew with every sniff and she struggled on to her chest, nosing and probing all over the calf, rumbling deep in her chest. Then she began to lick him methodically. Nature provides the perfect stimulant massage for a time like this and the little creature arched his back as the coarse papillae on the tongue dragged along his skin. Within a minute he was shaking his head and trying to sit up.

I grinned. This was the bit I liked. The little miracle. I felt it was

RED POLL BULL The hornless cattle of Suffolk and the dark blood-red horned cattle of Norfolk were separate breeds for centuries. In the mid-19th century the two were bred together to produce a new hornless red breed called the red poll. Since then they have been reared all over Britain and in Europe and America, but never in large numbers except in their native East Anglia. Calves cross-bred from red poll bulls are always hornless – a desirable feature because less stall space and yard space is needed for them and the animals are docile and easy to transport.

something that would never grow stale no matter how often I saw it. I cleaned as much of the dried blood and filth from my body as I could, but most of it had caked on my skin and not even my finger nails would move it. It would have to wait for the hot bath at home. Pulling my shirt over my head, I felt as though I had been beaten for a long time with a thick stick. Every muscle ached. My mouth was dried out, my lips almost sticking together.

A long, sad figure hovered near. 'How about a drink?' asked Mr Dinsdale.

I could feel my grimy face cracking into an incredulous smile. A vision of hot tea well laced with whisky swam before me. 'That's very kind of you, Mr Dinsdale, I'd love a drink. It's been a hard two hours.'

'Nay,' said Mr Dinsdale looking at me steadily, 'I meant for the cow.'

I began to babble. 'Oh yes, of course, certainly, by all means give her a drink. She must be very thirsty. It'll do her good. Certainly, certainly, give her a drink.'

I gathered up my tackle and stumbled out of the barn. On the moor it was still dark and a bitter wind whipped over the snow, stinging my eyes. As I plodded down the slope, Uncle's voice, strident and undefeated, reached me for the last time.

'Mr Broomfield doesn't believe in giving a drink after calving. Says it chills the stomach.'

10

'A bit of stock keeping'

There was little furniture in the dining-room but the noble lines and the very size of the place lent grace to the long sideboard and the modest mahogany table where Tristan and I sat at breakfast.

The single large window was patterned with frost and in the street outside, the footsteps of the passers-by crunched in the crisp snow. I looked up from my boiled egg as a car drew up. There was a stamping in the porch, the outer door banged shut and Siegfried burst into the room. Without a word he made for the fire and hung over it, leaning his elbows on the grey marble mantelpiece. He was muffled almost to the eyes in greatcoat and scarf but what you could see of his face was purplish blue.

He turned a pair of streaming eyes to the table. 'A milk fever up at old Heseltine's. One of the high buildings. God, it was cold up there. I could hardly breathe.'

As he pulled off his gloves and shook his numbed fingers in front of the flames, he darted sidelong glances at his brother. Tristan's chair was nearest the fire and he was enjoying his breakfast as he enjoyed everything, slapping the butter happily on to his toast and whistling as he applied the marmalade. His *Daily Mirror* was balanced against the coffee pot. You could almost see the waves of comfort and contentment coming from him.

Siegfried dragged himself unwillingly from the fire and dropped into a chair. 'I'll just have a cup of coffee, James. Heseltine was very kind – asked me to sit down and have breakfast with him. He gave me a lovely slice of home fed bacon – a bit fat, maybe, but what a flavour! I can taste it now.'

He put down his cup with a clatter. 'You know, there's no reason why we should have to go to the grocer for our bacon and eggs. There's a perfectly good hen house at the bottom of the garden and a pig sty in the yard with a boiler for the swill. All our household waste could go towards feeding a pig. We'd probably do it quite cheaply.'

He rounded on Tristan who had just lit a Woodbine and was shaking out his *Mirror* with the air of ineffable pleasure which was peculiar to him. 'And it would be a useful job for you. You're not producing much sitting around here on your arse all day. A bit of stock keeping would do you good.'

Tristan put down his paper as though the charm had gone out of it. 'Stock keeping? Well, I feed your mare as it is.' He didn't enjoy looking after Siegfried's new hunter because every time he turned her out to water in the yard she would take a playful kick at him in passing.

Siegfried jumped up. 'I know you do, and it doesn't take all day, does it? It won't kill you to take on the hens and pigs.

'Pigs?' Tristan looked startled. 'I thought you said pig?'

'Yes, pigs. I've just been thinking. If I buy a litter of weaners we can sell the others and keep one for ourselves. Won't cost a thing that way.'

'Not with free labour, certainly.'

'Labour? Labour? You don't know what it means! Look at you lying back there puffing your head off. You smoke too many of those bloody cigarettes!'

'So do you.'

'Never mind me, I'm talking about you!' Siegfried shouted.

I got up from the table with a sigh. Another day had begun.

When Siegfried got an idea he didn't muck about. Immediate action was his watchword. Within forty-eight hours a litter of ten little pigs had taken up residence in the sty and twelve Light Sussex pullets were pecking about behind the wire of the hen house. He was particularly pleased with the pullets. 'Look at them, James; just on point of lay and a very good strain, too. There'll be just a trickle of eggs at first, but once they get cracking we'll be snowed under. Nothing like a nice fresh egg warm from the nest.'

It was plain from the first that Tristan didn't share his brother's enthusiasm for the hens. I often found him hanging about outside the hen house, looking bored and occasionally throwing bread crusts over

LIGHT SUSSEX COCK AND HEN
Against the white plumage of the Light Sussex fowl the comb and wattle stand out brilliantly red. There is black speckling on the hackles – the feathers at the back of the neck – and the tail is black, with a green iridescent sheen on the cock's curling tail feathers. The egg is not white but a pale tint. This hardy, old English breed laid reasonably well but was prized mainly as a table bird. As it scratched for grain in the farmyard and under the hedges it fattened into a bird with a deep body and broad breast covered with plump, fine-textured and well-flavoured meat.

the wire. There was no evidence of the regular feeding, the balanced diet recommended by the experts. As egg producers, the hens held no appeal for him, but he did become mildly interested in them as personalities. An odd way of clucking, a peculiarity in gait – these things amused him.

But there were no eggs and as the weeks passed, Siegfried became increasingly irritable. 'Wait till I see the chap that sold me those hens. Damned scoundrel. Good laying strain my foot!' It was pathetic to see him anxiously exploring the empty nesting boxes every morning.

One afternoon, I was going down the garden when Tristan called to me. 'Come over here, Jim. This is something new. I bet you've never seen anything like it before.' He pointed upwards and I saw a group of unusually coloured large birds perched in the branches of the elms. There were more of them in the neighbour's apple trees.

I stared in astonishment. 'You're right, I've never seen anything like them. What are they?'

'Oh, come on,' said Tristan, grinning in delight, 'Surely there's

A group of unusually coloured large birds perched in the branches of the elms.

something familiar about them. Take another look.'

I peered upwards again. 'No, I've never seen birds as big as that and with such exotic plumage. What is it – a freak migration?'

Tristan gave a shout of laughter. 'They're our hens!'

'How the devil did they get up there?'

'They've left home. Hopped it.'

'But I can only see seven. Where are the rest of them?'

'God knows. Let's have a look over the wall.'

The crumbling mortar gave plenty of toe holds between the bricks and we looked down into the next garden. The other five hens were there, pecking contentedly among some cabbages.

It took a long time to get them all back into the hen house and the tedious business had to be repeated several times a day thereafter. For the hens had clearly grown tired of life under Tristan and decided that they would do better living off the country. They became nomads, ranging ever further afield in their search for sustenance.

At first the neighbours chuckled. They phoned to say their children were rounding up the hens and would we come and get them; but with the passage of time their jocularity wore thin. Finally Siegfried was involved in some painful interviews. His hens, he was told, were an unmitigated nuisance.

It was after one particularly unpleasant session that Siegfried decided that the hens must go. It was a bitter blow and as usual he vented his fury on Tristan. 'I must have been mad to think that any hens under your care would ever lay eggs. But really, isn't it just a bit hard? I give you this simple little job and one would have thought that even you would be hard put to it to make a mess of it. But look at the situation after only three weeks. Not one solitary egg have we seen. The bloody hens are flying about the countryside like pigeons. We are permanently estranged from our neighbours. You've done a thorough job haven't you?' All the frustrated egg producer in Siegfried welled out in his shrill tones.

Tristan's expression registered only wounded virtue, but he was rash enough to try to defend himself. 'You know, I thought there was something queer about those hens from the start,' he muttered.

Siegfried shed the last vestiges of his self control. 'Queer!' he yelled wildly, 'You're the one that's queer, not the poor bloody hens. You're the queerest bugger there is. For God's sake get out – get out of my sight!'

Tristan withdrew with quiet dignity.

It took some time for the last echoes of the poultry venture to die away but after a fortnight, sitting again at the dining-table with Tristan, I felt sure that all was forgotten. So that it was with a strange sense of the workings of fate that I saw Siegfried stride into the room and lean menacingly over his brother. 'You remember those hens, I suppose,' he said almost in a whisper, 'You'll recall that I gave them away to Mrs Dale, that old aged pensioner down Brown's Yard. Well, I've just been speaking to her. She's delighted with them. Gives them a hot mash night and morning and she's collecting ten eggs a day.' His voice rose almost to a scream. 'Ten eggs, do you hear, ten eggs!'

I hurriedly swallowed the last of my tea and excused myself. I trotted along the passage out the back door and up the garden to my car. On the way I passed the empty hen house. It had a forlorn look. It was a long way to the dining-room but I could still hear Siegfried.

'Jim! Come over here and look at these little beggars.' Tristan laughed excitedly as he leaned over the door of the pig sty.

I walked across the yard. 'What is it?'

'I've just given them their swill and it's a bit hot. Just look at them!'

The little pigs were seizing the food, dropping it and walking suspiciously round it. Then they would creep up, touch the hot potatoes with their muzzles and leap back in alarm. There was none of the usual meal time slobbering; just a puzzled grunting.

Right from the start Tristan had found the pigs more interesting than the hens which was a good thing because he had to retrieve himself after the poultry disaster. He spent a lot of time in the yard, sometimes feeding or mucking out but more often resting his elbows on the door watching his charges.

As with the hens, he was more interested in their characters than their ability to produce pork or bacon. After he poured the swill into the long trough he always watched, entranced, while the pigs made their first rush. Soon, in the desperate gobbling there would be signs of uneasiness. The tiny animals would begin to glance sideways till their urge to find out what their mates were enjoying so much became unbearable; they would start to change position frantically, climbing over each other's backs and falling into the swill.

Old Boardman was a willing collaborator, but mainly in an advisory capacity. Like all countrymen he considered he knew all about the husbandry and diseases of animals and, it turned out, pigs were his speciality. There were long conferences in the dark room under the Bairnsfather cartoons and the old man grew animated over his descriptions of the vast, beautiful animals he had reared in that very sty.

Tristan listened with respect because he had solid proof of Boardman's expertise in the way he handled the old brick boiler. Tristan could light the thing but it went out if he turned his back on it; but it was docile in Boardman's hands. I often saw Tristan listening wonderingly to the steady blub-blub while the old man rambled on and the delicious scent of cooking pig potatoes drifted over them both.

But no animal converts food more quickly into flesh than a pig and as the weeks passed the little pink creatures changed with alarming speed into ten solid, no-nonsense porkers. Their characters deteriorated, too. They lost all their charm. Meal times stopped being fun and became a battle with the odds growing heavier against Tristan all the time.

I could see that it brought a lot of colour into old Boardman's life and he always dropped whatever he was doing when he saw Tristan

BAIRNSFATHER CARTOONS In the dark cubby-hole where Boardman, the handyman and gardener, kept his tools in the yard at Skeldale House, there hung his collection of Bairnsfather cartoons, published during the First World War and reminders to Boardman of his own time in the trenches. Cynical Old Bill, the favourite character in the cartoons, was the seasoned survivor of the war, 'fed up' with its tedium and privation rather than its dangers. He was ever ready with ironic responses to the young and talkative new recruit, Bert – amiable, vacant, and innocent of the war and the world.

78

scooping the swill from the boiler.

He obviously enjoyed watching the daily contest from his seat on the stone trough. Tristan bracing himself, listening to the pigs squealing at the rattle of the bucket; giving a few fearsome shouts to encourage himself then shooting the bolt and plunging among the grunting, jostling animals; broad, greedy snouts forcing into the bucket, sharp feet grinding his toes, heavy bodies thrusting against his legs.

I couldn't help smiling when I remembered the light-hearted game it used to be. There was no laughter now. Tristan finally took to brandishing a heavy stick at the pigs before he dared to go in. Once inside his only hope of staying on his feet was to clear a little space by beating on the backs.

It was on a market day when the pigs had almost reached bacon weight that I came upon Tristan sprawled in his favourite chair. But there was something unusual about him; he wasn't asleep, no medicine bottle, no Woodbines, no *Daily Mirror*. His arms hung limply over the sides of the chair, his eyes were half closed and sweat glistened on his forehead.

'Jim,' he whispered. 'I've had the most hellish afternoon I've ever had in my life.'

I was alarmed at his appearance. 'What's happened.'

'The pigs,' he croaked. 'They escaped today.'

'Escaped! How the devil could they do that?'

Tristan tugged at his hair. 'It was when I was feeding the mare. I gave her her hay and thought I might as well feed the pigs at the same time. You know what they've been like lately – well, today they went berserk. Soon as I opened the door they charged out in a solid block. Sent me up in the air, bucket and all, then ran over the top of me.' He shuddered and looked up at me wide-eyed. 'I'll tell you this, Jim, when I was lying there on the cobbles, covered with swill and that lot trampling on me. I thought it was all over. But they didn't savage me. They belted out through the yard door at full gallop.'

'The yard door was open then?'

'Too true it was. I would just choose this one day to leave it open.'

Tristan sat up and wrung his hands. 'Well, you know, I thought it was all right at first. You see, they slowed down when they got into the lane and trotted quietly round into the front street with Boardman and I hard on their heels. They formed a group there. Didn't seem to know where to go next. I was sure we were going to be able to head them off, but just then one of them caught sight of itself in Robson's shop window.'

He gave a remarkable impression of a pig staring at its reflection for a few moments then leaping back with a startled grunt.

'Well, that did it, Jim. The bloody animal panicked and shot off into the market place at about fifty miles an hour with the rest after it.'

I gasped. Ten large pigs loose among the packed stalls and market day crowds was difficult even to imagine.

'Oh God, you should have seen it.' Tristan fell back wearily into his

FEEDING PIGS Dales farmers usually kept a dozen or so pigs, and cottagers, too, would keep a pig. Home-fed, home-killed and home-cured bacon and ham appeared often on the table – sweet-flavoured meat, but very fat to suit the local taste. Much labour went into rearing pigs, mostly in supplying them with food. Potatoes and barley were grown for them; the potatoes had to be washed and boiled, and the barley threshed and ground to make meal.

79

chair. 'Women and kids screaming. The stall holders, police and everybody else cursing me. There was a terrific traffic jam too – miles of cars tooting like hell while the policeman on point duty concentrated on browbeating me.' He wiped his brow. 'You know that fast talking merchant on the china stall – well, today I saw him at a loss for words. He was balancing a cup on his palm and in full cry when one of the pigs got its fore feet on his stall and stared him straight in the face. He stopped as if he'd been shot. Any other time it would have been funny but I thought the perishing animal was going to wreck the stall. The counter was beginning to rock when the pig changed its mind and made off.'

'What's the position now?' I asked. 'Have you got them back?'

'I've got nine of them back,' Tristan replied, leaning back and closing his eyes. 'With the help of almost the entire male population of the district I've got nine of them back. The tenth was last seen heading North at a good pace. God knows where it is now. Oh, I didn't tell you – one of them got into the post office. Spent quite some time in there.' He put his hands over his face. 'I'm for it this time, Jim. I'll be in the hands of the law after this lot. There's no doubt about it.'

I leaned over and slapped his leg. 'Oh, I shouldn't worry. I don't suppose there's been any serious damage done.'

Tristan replied with a groan. 'But there's something else. When I finally closed the door after getting the pigs back in their sty I was on the verge of collapse. I was leaning against the wall gasping for breath when I saw the mare had gone. Yes, gone. I'd gone straight out after the pigs

80

and forgot to close her box. I don't know where she is. Boardman said he'd look around – I haven't the strength.'

Tristan lit a trembling Woodbine. 'This is the end, Jim. Siegfried will have no mercy this time.'

As he spoke, the door flew open and his brother rushed in. 'What the hell is going on?' he roared. 'I've just been speaking to the vicar and he says my mare is in his garden eating his wallflowers. He's hopping mad and I don't blame him. Go on, you lazy young scoundrel. Don't lie there, get over to the vicarage this instant and bring her back!'

Tristan did not stir. He lay inert, looking up at his brother. His lips moved feebly.

'No,' he said.

'What's that?' Siegfried shouted incredulously. 'Get out of that chair immediately. Go and get that mare!'

'No,' replied Tristan.

I felt a chill of horror. This sort of mutiny was unprecedented. Siegfried had gone very red in the face and I steeled myself for an eruption; but it was Tristan who spoke.

'If you want your mare you can get her yourself.' His voice was quiet with no note of defiance. He had the air of a man to whom the future is of no account.

Even Siegfried could see that this was one time when Tristan had had enough. After glaring down at his brother for a few seconds he turned and walked. He got the mare himself.

Nothing more was said about the incident but the pigs were moved hurriedly to the bacon factory and were never replaced. The stock keeping project was at an end.

11

The perfect secretary

Looking back, I can scarcely believe we used to spend all those hours in making up medicines. But our drugs didn't come to us in proprietary packages and before we could get out on the road we had to fill our cars with a wide variety of carefully compounded and largely useless remedies.

When Siegfried came upon me that morning I was holding a twelve ounce bottle at eye level while I poured syrup of coccilana into it. Tristan was moodily mixing stomach powders with a mortar and pestle and he stepped up his speed of stroke when he saw his brother's eye on him. He was surrounded by packets of the powder and, further along the bench, were orderly piles of pessaries which he had made by filling

MORTAR AND PESTLE Ready-to-use preparations were beginning to come on the market from pharmaceutical companies by the late 1930s, but the mortar and pestle was still used – by vets, for example, to grind up stomach powders for wrapping in paper packets, and by chemists' assistants who had to pound large quantities of dentifrice to a powder. This mortar is carved from white marble, but it was more common to use one made from the extremely hard mortar porcelain introduced by Josiah Wedgwood in 1787.

cellophane cylinders with boric acid.

Tristan looked industrious; his elbow jogged furiously as he ground away at the ammon carb and nux vomica. Siegfried smiled benevolently.

I smiled too. I felt the strain badly when the brothers were at variance, but I could see that this was going to be one of the happy mornings. There had been a distinct improvement in the atmosphere since Christmas when Tristan had slipped casually back to college and, apparently without having done any work, had re-sat and passed his exams. And there was something else about my boss today; he seemed to glow with inner satisfaction as though he knew for certain that something good was on the way. He came in and closed the door.

'I've got a bit of good news.'

I screwed the cork into the bottle. 'Well, don't keep us in suspense. Let's have it.'

Siegfried looked from one of us to the other. He was almost smirking. 'You remember that bloody awful shambles when Tristan took charge of the bills?'

His brother looked away and began to grind still faster, but Siegfried laid a friendly hand on his shoulder. 'No, don't worry, I'm not going to ask you to do it again. In fact, you'll never have to do it again because, from now on, the job will be done by an expert.' He paused and cleared his throat. 'We're going to have a secretary.'

As we stared blankly at him he went on. 'Yes, I picked her myself and I consider she's perfect.' 'Well, what's she like?' I asked.

Siegfried pursed his lips. 'It's difficult to describe her. But just think – what do we want here? We don't want some flighty young thing hanging about the place. We don't want a pretty little blonde sitting behind that desk powdering her nose and making eyes at everybody.'

'We don't?' Tristan interrupted, plainly puzzled.

'No, we don't!' Siegfried rounded on him. 'She'd be day-dreaming about her boy friends half the time and just when we'd got her trained to our ways she'd be running off to get married.'

Tristan still looked unconvinced and it seemed to exasperate his brother. Siegfried's face reddened. 'And there's another thing. How could we have an attractive young girl in here with somebody like you in the house. You'd never leave her alone.'

Tristan was nettled. 'How about you?'

'I'm talking about you, not me!' Siegfried roared. I closed my eyes. The peace hadn't lasted long. I decided to cut in. 'All right, tell us about the new secretary.'

With an effort, he mastered his emotion. 'Well, she's in her fifties and she has retired after thirty years with Green and Moulton in Bradford. She was company secretary there and I've had the most wonderful reference from the firm. They say she is a model of efficiency and that's what we want in this practice – efficiency. We're far too slack. It's just a stroke of luck for us that she decided to come and live in Darrowby. Anyway, you'll be able to meet her in a few minutes – she's coming at ten o'clock this morning.'

The church clock was chiming when the door bell rang. Siegfried hastened out to answer it and led his great discovery into the room in triumph. 'Gentlemen, I want you to meet Miss Harbottle.'

She was a big, high-bosomed woman with a round healthy face and gold-rimmed spectacles. A mass of curls, incongruous and very dark, peeped from under her hat; they looked as if they might be dyed and they didn't go with her severe clothes and brogue shoes.

It occurred to me that we wouldn't have to worry about her rushing off to get married. It wasn't that she was ugly, but she had a jutting chin and an air of effortless command that would send any man running for his life.

I shook hands and was astonished at the power of Miss Harbottle's grip. We looked into each other's eyes and had a friendly trial of strength for a few seconds, then she seemed happy to call it a draw and turned away. Tristan was entirely unprepared and a look of alarm spread over his face as his hand was engulfed; he was released only when his knees started to buckle.

She began a tour of the office while Siegfried hovered behind her, rubbing his hands and looking like a shopwalker with his favourite customer. She paused at the desk, heaped high with in-coming and out-going bills, Ministry of Agriculture forms, circulars from drug firms with here and there stray boxes of pills and tubes of udder ointment.

Stirring distastefully between the mess, she extracted the dog-eared old ledger and held it up between finger and thumb. 'What's this?'

Siegfried trotted forward. 'Oh, that's our ledger. We enter the visits into it from our day book which is here somewhere.' He scrabbled about on the desk. 'Ah, here it is. This is where we write the calls as they come in.'

She studied the two books for a few minutes with an expression of amazement which gave way to a grim humour. 'You gentlemen will have to learn to write if I am going to look after your books. There are three different hands here, but this one is by far the worst. Quite dreadful. Whose is it?'

She pointed to an entry which consisted of a long, broken line with an occasional undulation.

'That's mine, actually,' said Siegfried, shuffling his feet. 'Must have been in a hurry that day.'

'But it's all like that, Mr Farnon. Look here and here and here. It won't do, you know.'

Siegfried put his hands behind his back and hung his head.

'I expect you keep your stationery and envelopes in here.' She pulled open a drawer in the desk. It appeared to be filled entirely with old seed packets, many of which had burst open. A few peas and french beans rolled gently from the top of the heap. The next drawer was crammed tightly with soiled calving ropes which somebody had forgotten to wash. They didn't smell so good and Miss Harbottle drew back hurriedly; but

ADVERTISER'S CHART Makers of veterinary medicines and instruments were diligent in promoting their products. General information on animal care and details of diseases were skilfully combined with advertising material on, for example, the series of illustrated wall-charts put out by this large firm which started in 1833. The charts were given away free to vets and farmers. Some firms produced small but comprehensive books for the same purpose.

SHEEP-DIPPING In 1905 it was made compulsory for sheep to be dipped at least once a year. They were usually dipped in both spring and autumn in a large dug-out pool with insecticide mixed in the water. Each animal's body was immersed for about a minute and its head was ducked briefly. The dipping rid the sheep of ticks, lice and the maggots of blowflies, but it was primarily to control scab, a notifiable disease similar to mange, which causes loss of fleece. When scab was eradicated in the early 1950s dipping was no longer compulsory, but it was enforced again when the disease re-emerged in 1973.

she was not easily deterred and tugged hopefully at the third drawer. It came open with a musical clinking and she looked down on a dusty row of empty pale ale bottles.

She straightened up slowly and spoke patiently. 'And where, may I ask, is your cash box?'

'Well, we just stuff it in there, you know.' Siegfried pointed to the pint pot on the corner of the mantelpiece. 'Haven't got what you'd call a proper cash box, but this does the job all right.'

Miss Harbottle looked at the pot with horror. 'You just stuff ...' Crumpled cheques and notes peeped over the brim at her; many of their companions had burst out on to the hearth below. 'And you mean to say that you go out and leave that money there day after day?'

'Never seems to come to any harm,' Siegfried replied.

'And how about your petty cash?'

Siegfried gave an uneasy giggle. 'All in there, you know. All cash – petty and otherwise.'

Miss Harbottle's ruddy face had lost some of its colour. 'Really, Mr Farnon, this is too bad. I don't know how you have gone on so long like this. I simply do not know. However, I'm confident I will be able to straighten things out very soon. There is obviously nothing complicated about your business – a simple card index system would be the thing for your accounts. The other little things' – she glanced back unbelievingly at the pot – 'I will put right very quickly.'

'Fine, Miss Harbottle, fine.' Siegfried was rubbing his hands harder than ever. 'We'll expect you on Monday morning.'

'Nine o'clock sharp, Mr Farnon.'

After she had gone there was a silence. Tristan had enjoyed her visit and was smiling thoughtfully, but I felt uncertain.

'You know, Siegfried,' I said, 'Maybe she is a demon of efficiency but isn't she just a bit tough?'

'Tough?' Siegfried gave a loud, rather cracked laugh. 'Not a bit of it. You leave her to me. I can handle her.'

When I came in, Miss Harbottle was sitting, head bowed, over the empty cash box; she looked bereaved. It was a new, shiny, black box with the words 'Petty Cash' printed on top in white letters. Inside was a red book with the incomings and outgoings recorded in neat columns. But there was no money.

Miss Harbottle's sturdy shoulders sagged. She listlessly took up the red book between finger and thumb and a lonely sixpence rolled from between its pages and tinkled into the box. 'He's been at it again,' she whispered.

A stealthy footstep sounded in the passage. 'Mr Farnon!' she called out. And to me: 'It's really absurd the way the man always tries to slink past the door.'

Siegfried shuffled in. He was carrying a stomach tube and pump, calcium bottles bulged from his jacket pockets and a bloodless castrator dangled from the other hand.

He smiled cheerfully but I could see he was uncomfortable, not only because of the load he carried, but because of his poor tactical position. Miss Harbottle had arranged her desk across the corner diagonally opposite the door and he had to walk across a long stretch of carpet to reach her. From her point of view it was strategically perfect. From her corner she could see every inch of the big room, into the passage when the door was open and out on to the front street from the window on her left. Nothing escaped her – it was a position of power.

Siegfried looked down at the square figure behind the desk. 'Good morning, Miss Harbottle, can I do anything for you?'

The grey eyes glinted behind the gold-rimmed spectacles. 'You can, indeed, Mr Farnon. You can explain why you have once more emptied my petty cash box.'

'Oh, I'm so sorry. I had to rush through to Brawton last night and I found myself a bit short. There was really nowhere else to turn to.'

'But Mr Farnon, in the two months I have been here, we must have been over this a dozen times. What is the good of my trying to keep an accurate record of the money in the practice if you keep stealing it and spending it?'

'Well, I suppose I got into the habit in the old pint pot days. It wasn't a bad system, really.'

'It wasn't a system at all. It was anarchy. You cannot run a business that way. But I've told you this so many times and each time you have promised to alter your ways. I feel almost at my wits' end.'

'Oh, never mind, Miss Harbottle. Get some more out of the bank and put it in your box. That'll put it right.' Siegfried gathered up the loose coils of the stomach tube from the floor and turned to go, but Miss Harbottle cleared her throat warningly.

'There are one or two other matters. Will you please try to keep your other promise to enter your visits in the book every day and to price them as you do so. Nearly a week has gone by since you wrote anything in. How can I possibly get the bills out on the first of the month? This is most important, but how do you expect me to do it when you impede me like this?'

'Yes, yes, I'm sorry, but I have a string of calls waiting. I really must go.' He was halfway across the floor and the tube was uncoiling itself again when he heard the ominous throat clearing behind him.

'And one more thing, Mr Farnon. I still can't decipher your writing. These medical terms are difficult enough, so please take a little care and don't scribble.'

'Very well, Miss Harbottle.' He quickened his pace through the door and into the passage where, it seemed, was safety and peace. He was clattering thankfully over the tiles when the familiar rumbling reached him. She could project that sound a surprising distance by giving it a bit of extra pressure, and it was a summons which had to be obeyed. I could hear him wearily putting the tube and pump on the floor; the calcium

bottles must have been digging into his ribs because I heard them go down too.

He presented himself again before the desk. Miss Harbottle wagged a finger at him. 'While I have you here I'd like to mention another point which troubles me. Look at this day book. You see all these slips sticking out of the pages? They are all queries – there must be scores of them – and I am at a standstill until you clear them for me. When I ask you you never have the time. Can you go over them with me now?'

Siegfried backed away hurriedly. 'No, no, not just now. As I said, I have some urgent calls waiting. I'm very sorry but it will have to be some other time. First chance I get I'll come in and see you.' He felt the door behind him and with a last glance at the massive, disapproving figure behind the desk, he turned and fled.

As I checked my list of calls it occurred to me that, this time, Siegfried didn't look so much like a schoolboy as he faced Miss Harbottle. For one thing, he hadn't marched straight in and stood in front of the desk; that was disastrous and he always looked beaten before he started. Instead, he had veered off over the last few yards till he stood with his back to the window. This way she had to turn her head slightly to face him and besides, he had the light at his back.

He thrust his hands into his pockets and leaned back against the window frame. He was wearing his patient look, his eyes were kind and his face was illumined by an almost saintly smile. Miss Harbottle's eyes narrowed.

'I just wanted a word with you, Miss Harbottle. One or two little points I'd like to discuss. First, about your petty cash box. It's a nice box and I think you were quite right to institute it, but I think you would be the first to agree that the main function of a cash box is to have cash in it.' He gave a light laugh. 'Now last night I had a few dogs in the surgery and the owners wanted to pay on the spot. I had no change and went for some to your box – it was quite empty. I had to say I would send them a bill, and that isn't good business, is it Miss Harbottle? It didn't look good, so I really must ask you to keep some cash in your cash box.'

Miss Harbottle's eyes widened incredulously. 'But Mr Farnon, you removed the entire contents to go to the hunt ball at ...'

Siegfried held up a hand and his smile took on an unearthly quality. 'Please hear me out. There is another very small thing I want to bring to your attention. It is now the tenth day of the month and the accounts have not gone out. Now this is a very undesirable state of affairs and there are several points to consider here.'

'But Mr Farnon ... !'

'Just one moment, Miss Harbottle, till I explain this to you. It is a known fact that farmers pay their bills more readily if they receive them on the first day of the month. And there is another, even more important factor.' The beautiful smile left his face and was replaced by an expression of sorrowing gravity. 'Have you ever stopped to work out just

Miss Harbottle wagged a finger at Siegfried. 'While I have you here I'd like to mention another point which troubles me . . .'

how much interest the practice is losing on all the money lying out there because you are late in sending out the accounts?'

'Mr Farnon . . . !'

'I am almost finished, Miss Harbottle, and, believe me, it grieves me to have to speak like this. But the fact is, I can't afford to lose money in this way.' He spread out his hands in a gesture of charming frankness. 'So if you will just apply yourself to this little matter I'm sure all will be well.'

'But will you tell me how I can possibly send the accounts when you refuse to write up the . . .'

'In conclusion, Miss Harbottle, let me say this. I have been very satisfied with your progress since you joined us, and I am sure that with time you will tighten up on those little points I have just mentioned.' A certain roguishness crept into his smile and he put his head on one side. Miss Harbottle's strong fingers closed tightly round a heavy ebony ruler.

'Efficiency,' he said, crinkling his eyes. 'That's what we must have – efficiency.'

I took the surgery steps at a jump and trotted along the passage, but as I rounded the corner my progress was halted. Siegfried was standing there, rigid, his back pressed against the wall. Over his shoulder dangled a long, flexible, leather probang. Between us was the half open door of the office with Miss Harbottle clearly visible at her desk.

I waved cheerfully. 'Hello, hello, off to a choke?'

Siegfried's face twisted in anguish and he held up a warning hand. Then he began to creep past the door, balancing on the balls of his feet like a tightrope walker. He was beyond the door and the tense lines of his body had begun to relax when the brass end of the swinging probang clattered against the wall and, as if in reply came the familiar rumble from Miss Harbottle's corner. Siegfried gave me a single despairing glance then, shoulders drooping, he went slowly into the room.

Watching him go, I thought wonderingly of how things had built up since the secretary's arrival. It was naked war now and it gave life an added interest to observe the tactics of the two sides.

At the beginning it seemed that Siegfried must run out an easy winner. He was the employer; he held the reins and it appeared that Miss Harbottle would be helpless in the face of his obstructive strategy. But Miss Harbottle was a fighter and a resourceful one and it was impossible not to admire the way she made use of the weapons at her command.

In fact, over the past week the tide had been running in her favour. She had been playing Siegfried like an expert fisherman with a salmon; bringing him repeatedly back to her desk to answer footling questions. Her throat clearing had developed into an angry bark which could penetrate the full extent of the house. And she had a new weapon; she had taken to writing Siegfried's clerical idiocies on slips of paper; mis-

continued on page 105

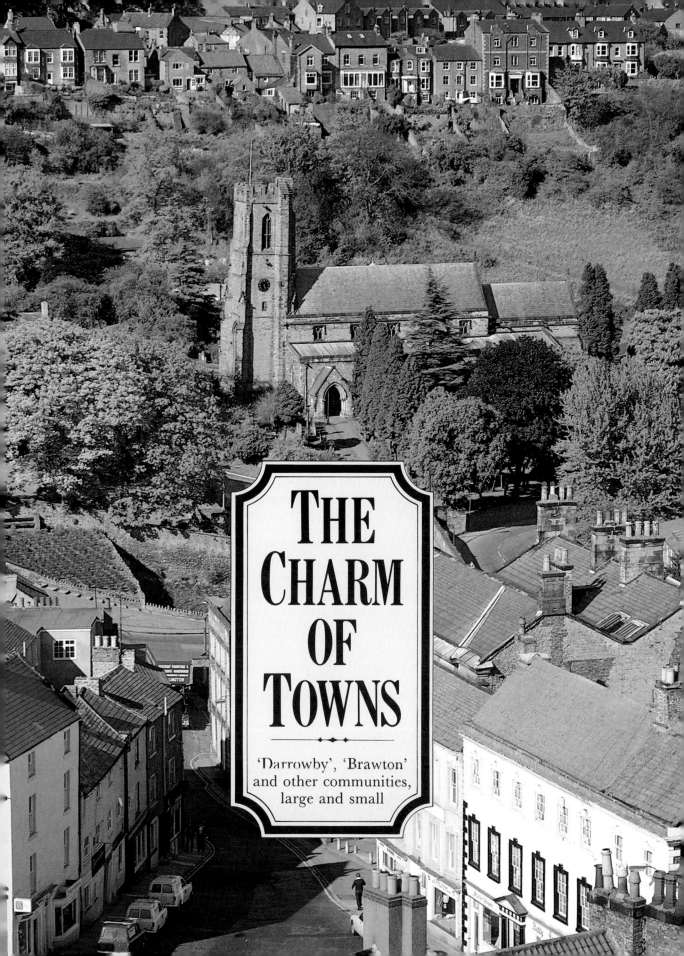

THE
CHARM
OF
TOWNS

'Darrowby', 'Brawton'
and other communities,
large and small

'DARROWBY'

James Herriot's Darrowby, the town high in the Yorkshire Dales where the young vet got his first job with the ebullient Siegfried Farnon, is not one but four places in north Yorkshire.

It is a composite of Richmond, at the foot of Swaledale, plus something borrowed from Thirsk, Leyburn and Middleham – and a little from the imagination.

The young James Herriot worked in or visited all four towns frequently in the late 1930s.

He and the real-life Siegfried had a partner in Leyburn, Frank Bingham, whose practice spread into the far corners of the Dales, and working with Bingham gave Herriot his deep love of the area.

CASTLE HILL Apart from the design of the cars, the view today of Castle Hill in Richmond has hardly changed since the 1930s (above).

MARKET PLACE Over the intervening years, a modern housing estate has sprouted on the hill behind the market place at Richmond (above). The view is from the castle keep.

THIRSK SQUARE The street lamp in
Thirsk's market square is less decorative
today. But the cobbles remain as a
parking place for shoppers' cars.

S SERVICE Richmond's ancient church,
ich sheltered plague victims in the late
th century, still stands foursquare in
chmond market place. But Maude's
Service has given way to red double-
kers.

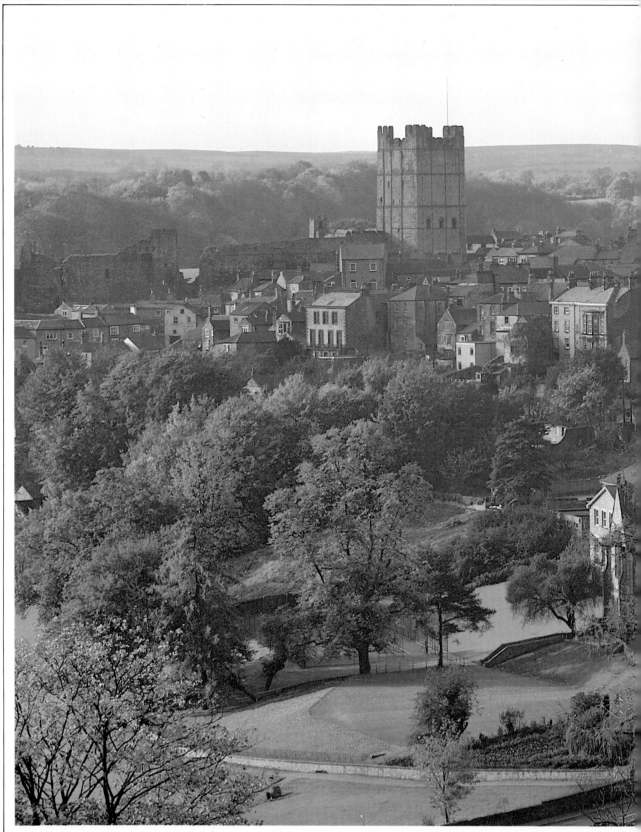

JEWEL OF SWALEDALE The ancient town of Richmond is the gateway to the wild beauty of Swaledale. It sits tranquilly

foot of the dale – a jewel in a perfect setting – with a network of cobbled alleys and streets twisting among the houses.

'BRAWTON'

The big town of Brawton, where James Herriot had his disastrous night out at the Reniston Hotel while courting Helen, is based on Harrogate. The 'La Scala' cinema at Brawton was the place, several years later, where Helen felt the imminent arrival of their second child Rosie and had to be driven swiftly back to Darrowby.

James and Helen spent their half-day off each week at Brawton. 'It was an oasis of relaxation in our busy lives,' he writes. 'For me it was an escape from the telephone and the mud and the Wellington boots, and for my wife it meant a rest from her hard slog plus the luxury of having meals cooked by someone else.'

PUMP ROOM In 1930 (above) the Pump Room still housed the evil-smelling sulphur well – used for drinking and bathing. Today it is a spa museum (left and below).

ROYAL BATHS Harrogate was a renowned spa town in Victorian and Edwardian times. At the Royal Baths 40 kinds of waters were available.

HARROGATE TOFFEE As the spa waters attracted wealthy patients, the town's shops developed, among them John Farrah, makers of Harrogate Toffee since 1840.

GARDENS Flowers bloom against a backdrop of Victorian ironwork.

MONTPELLIER PARADE The elegance recalls a time (in 1911) when the queens of England, Russia and Portugal visited Harrogate on the same day.

A magical strip where the sea meets the heather

'We were billeted in the Grand Hotel, the massive Victorian pile which dominated Scarborough in turreted splendour from its eminence above the sea, and the big dining-room was packed with several hundred shouting airmen.' It was from Scarborough that James Herriot went absent without leave to visit Helen when she gave birth to Jimmy during the war.

Scarborough is just one of the delights of the north Yorkshire coast. To the north stretch Robin Hood's Bay, Whitby, Runswick Bay and Staithes, all of them retaining the character of their fishing history, and just behind these coastal towns and villages lies the glorious backdrop of the North York Moors where the smells of sea and heather mingle.

GRAND HOTEL James Herriot, the airman, stood guard at the imposing entrance of the Grand Hotel, and whiled away the cold dark nights dreaming of the Dales.

SEA BATHING Scarborough became the birthplace of sea bathing in 1660, when Dr Wittie recommended sea water for 'drying up superfluous humours, and preserving them from putrefaction'.

SCARBOROUGH IN THE 1930s A railway poster of 1931 depicts Scarborough as a centre of fashionable night-life.

SCARBOROUGH 1931 BOOKLET FREE FROM TOWN CLERK TOWN HALL OR ANY L·N·E·R AGENCY

HARBOUR Whitby developed in the Middle Ages as a harbour on the Esk.

WHITBY Captain James Cook, who explored the world's oceans in the 18th century, learned his craft at Whitby. Its harbour with the 199 steps to Whitby Abbey (left and above) remains much as he knew it.

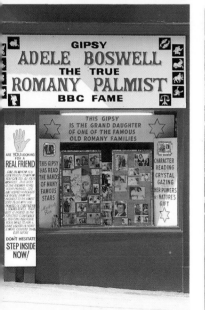

PALMIST A Gypsy fortune-teller – one of Scarborough's holiday attractions.

RUNSWICK BAY The north Yorkshire coast is dotted with picturesque fishing villages, sprawling at the base of high cliffs, the lowest house almost in the water.

Where a great sailor fell in love with the sea

The little harbour at Staithes typifies the fishing villages of the Yorkshire coast. Hugged in by two arms of crumbling cliffs, it breathes the very essence of the sea. The far blue water stretches away beyond the stone breakwaters, and gulls scream overhead.

It was at Staithes that young James Cook fell in love with the sea. The farmer's boy had been sent to be apprenticed to a grocer, whose shop was so close to the seafront that it has since been washed away.

Ships were built in Staithes in those days, and the seafaring spirit so captured James Cook that he chose to become a sailor with a firm of Whitby colliers.

In the years to come he went on to explore the Pacific Ocean from the bottom of the world to the top.

HOME-MADE TOFFEE One of Staithes' diverse little houses – with home-made toffee for sale in the porch.

HARBOUR AT DAWN The first sun of the morning glistens on the mud as the low tide leaves a fishing boat stranded on the harbour bottom.

York: a wondrous city where the past lives on

For those who enjoy the living remains of the past, York is a paradise. The Romans built the first city here, as the capital of the northern half of Roman Britain.

The Vikings overran the town in the 9th century, called it Jorvik, and made it their main base in England. Some of their timber houses were recently found in Coppergate, remarkably well preserved.

But it was medieval York that created the most wondrous sights of all – its circuit of walls, and the magnificent Minster, largest medieval church in England. It took more than 300 years to build, and still towers over the city as it did when it was completed in 1480.

YORK MINSTER A wooden church stood on the site of the great Minster as long ago as the 7th century, when a Saxon king was baptised there. It was followed by a stone Saxon church, a Norman church and, finally, the Minster, focal point of a network of medieval lanes such as the Shambles (above).

Farming villages with ancient origins

In the dales and moors of north Yorkshire nestles a treasure trove of tiny villages, many revealing in their names a Viking origin. As the Norsemen penetrated deep into Yorkshire in the two centuries before the Norman Conquest, they settled in farming communities with names such as Bradley (broad clearing), Caldbergh (cold hill) and Gunnerside (Gunnar's pasture).

In the Dales, typical villages will probably have a hump-backed bridge, stone houses clustered around a cobbled market place or village green, and an ancient church. They contain a self-sufficient breed of people who, after the summer visitors have left, may find themselves cut off for weeks by the winter snows.

STARTING POINT Helmsley, tucked in a hollow on the North York Moors, is the start the Cleveland Way, the second-longest footpath in the country.

VILLAGE GREEN Bainbridge in Wensleydale grew up around a spacious green where sheep graze and the stocks still stand.

SWALE HEAD At the top of Swaledale, the houses of Thwaite cluster together for protection against the bleak surroundings.

GUNNERSIDE Fields dotted with barns climb up the hillside from the old lead mining village of Gunnerside in Swaledale.

continued from page 88

spellings, errors in addition, wrong entries – they were all faithfully copied down.

Miss Harbottle used these slips as ammunition. She never brought one out when things were slack and her employer was hanging about the surgery. She saved them until he was under pressure, then she would push a slip under his nose and say 'How about this?'

She always kept an expressionless face at these times and it was impossible to say how much pleasure it gave her to see him cower back like a whipped animal. But the end was unvarying – mumbled explanations and apologies from Siegfried and Miss Harbottle, radiating self-righteousness, correcting the entry.

As Siegfried went into the room I watched through the partly open door. I knew my morning round was waiting but I was impelled by morbid curiosity. Miss Harbottle, looking brisk and businesslike, was tapping an entry in the book with her pen while Siegfried shuffled his feet and muttered replies. He made several vain attempts to escape and, as the time passed, I could see he was nearing breaking point. His teeth were clenched and his eyes had started to bulge.

The phone rang and the secretary answered it. Her employer was making again for the door when she called happily, 'Colonel Brent for you.' Like a man in a dream he turned back. The Colonel, a racehorse owner had been a thorn in our flesh for a long time with his complaints and his continual questioning and probing; a call from him was always liable to send up the blood pressure.

I could see it was that way this morning. The minutes ticked away and Siegfried's face got redder. He made his replies in a choked voice which finally rose almost to a shout. At the end he crashed the receiver down and leaned on the desk, breathing heavily.

Then, as I watched, unbelieving, Miss Harbottle began to open the drawer where she kept her slips. She fished one out, coughed and held it in Siegfried's face.

'How about this?' she asked.

I resisted the impulse to close my eyes and stared in horror. For a few seconds nothing happened and there was a tense interval while Siegfried stood quite motionless. Then his face seemed to break up and with a scything sweep of his arm he snatched the slip from the secretary's hand and began to tear at it with fierce intensity. He didn't say a word but as he tore, he leaned forward over the desk and his glaring eyes approached ever nearer to Miss Harbottle who slowly edged her chair back till it was jammed against the wall.

It was a weird picture. Miss Harbottle straining back, her mouth slightly opened, her tinted curls bobbing in alarm, and Siegfried, his ravaged features close to hers, still tearing with insane vigour at the piece of paper. The scene ended when Siegfried, putting every ounce of his strength into an action like a javelin thrower, hurled the torn up slip at the waste paper basket. It fell in a gentle shower, like confetti, in and

105

around the basket and Siegfried, still without speaking, wrapped his probang around him and strode from the room.

In the kitchen, Mrs Hall opened the parcel and extracted a pie, a chunk of liver and a cluster of the exquisite sausages. She turned a quizzical eye on me. 'You look kind of pleased with yourself this morning, Mr Herriot.'

I leaned back against the oak dresser. 'Yes, Mrs Hall, I've just been thinking. It must be very nice to be the principal of a practice but, you know, it's not such a bad life being an assistant.'

12

A lesson from a coalman's horse

I could look back now on six months of hard practical experience. I had treated cows, horses, pigs, dogs and cats seven days a week; in the morning, afternoon, evening and through the hours when the world was asleep. I had calved cows and farrowed sows till my arms ached and the skin peeled off. I had been knocked down, trampled on and sprayed liberally with every kind of muck. I had seen a fair cross section of the diseases of animals. And yet a little voice had begun to niggle at the back of my mind; it said I knew nothing, nothing at all.

This was strange, because those six months had been built upon five years of theory; a slow, painful assimilation of thousands of facts and a careful storage of fragments of knowledge like a squirrel with its nuts. Beginning with the study of plants and the lowest forms of life, working up to dissection in the anatomy lab and physiology and the vast, soulless territory of materia medica. Then pathology which tore down the curtain of ignorance and let me look for the first time into the deep secrets. And parasitology, the teeming other world of the worms and fleas and mange mites. Finally, medicine and surgery, the crystallisation of my learning and its application to the everyday troubles of animals.

And there were many others, like physics, chemistry, hygiene; they didn't seem to have missed a thing. Why then should I feel I knew nothing? Why had I begun to feel like an astronomer looking through a telescope at an unknown galaxy? This sensation that I was only groping about on the fringes of limitless space was depressing. It was a funny thing, because everybody else seemed to know all about sick animals. The chap who held the cow's tail, the neighbour from the next farm, men in pubs, jobbing gardeners; they all knew and were free and confident with their advice.

I tried to think back over my life. Was there any time when I had felt this supreme faith in my own knowledge. And then I remembered.

FOSTER PIG When a sow has a large litter, there is a danger that she will not be able to feed them all adequately. The weaker ones will do better with a 'foster mother' to bottle-feed them. One 1930s type of bottle was like an old-style earthenware hot-water bottle with a teat at each end and four down each side.

I was back in Scotland, I was seventeen and I was walking under the arch of the Veterinary College into Montrose Street. I had been a student for three days but not until this afternoon had I felt the thrill of fulfilment. Messing about with botany and zoology was all right but this afternoon had been the real thing; I had had my first lecture in animal husbandry.

The subject had been the points of the horse. Professor Grant had hung up a life size picture of a horse and gone over it from nose to tail, indicating the withers, the stifle, the hock, the poll and all the other rich, equine terms. And the professor had been wise; to make his lecture more interesting he kept throwing in little practical points like 'This is where we find curb,' or 'Here is the site for windgalls.' He talked of thoroughpins and sidebones, splints and quittor; things the students wouldn't learn about for another four years, but it brought it all to life.

The words were still spinning in my head as I walked slowly down the sloping street. This was what I had come for. I felt as though I had undergone an initiation and become a member of an exclusive club. I really knew about horses. And I was wearing a brand new riding mac with all sorts of extra straps and buckles which slapped against my legs as I turned the corner of the hill into busy Newton Road.

I could hardly believe my luck when I saw the horse. It was standing outside the library below Queen's Cross like something left over from another age. It drooped dispiritedly between the shafts of a coal cart which stood like an island in an eddying stream of cars and buses. Pedestrians hurried by, uncaring, but I had the feeling that fortune was smiling on me.

A horse. Not just a picture but a real, genuine horse. Stray words from the lecture floated up into my mind; the pastern, cannon bone, coronet and all those markings – snip, blaze, white sock near hind. I stood on the pavement and examined the animal critically.

I thought it must be obvious to every passer-by that here was a true expert. Not just an inquisitive onlooker but a man who knew and understood all. I felt clothed in a visible aura of horsiness.

I took a few steps up and down, hands deep in the pockets of the new riding mac, eyes probing for possible shoeing faults or curbs or bog spavins. So thorough was my inspection that I worked round to the off side of the horse and stood perilously among the racing traffic.

I glanced around at the people hurrying past. Nobody seemed to care, not even the horse. He was a large one, at least seventeen hands, and he gazed apathetically down the street, easing his hind legs alternatively in a bored manner. I hated to leave him but I had completed my examination and it was time I was on my way. But I felt that I ought to make a gesture before I left; something to communicate to the horse that I understood his problems and that we belonged to the same brotherhood. I stepped briskly forward and patted him on the neck.

Quick as a striking snake, the horse whipped downwards and seized my shoulder in his great strong teeth. He laid back his ears, rolled his

A FOLDING HOOF-PICK Soil and small stones become tightly packed into horses' hooves during a day's work. Part of the evening grooming is to clean them out. A simple, strong hook with a handle is used for this in most stables. A vet also needs to clean out the hoof before he examines a horse's foot, and for him a folding pick is more convenient for carrying in a pocket. This steel-alloy pick has a hook that swivels round to lock into the handle. When it is folded, a small screwdriver blade comes into the working position.

eyes wickedly and hoisted me up, almost off my feet. I hung there helplessly, suspended like a lopsided puppet. I wriggled and kicked but the teeth were clamped immovably in the material of my coat.

There was no doubt about the interest of the passers by now. The grotesque sight of a man hanging from a horse's mouth brought them to a sudden halt and a crowd formed with people looking over each other's shoulders and others fighting at the back to see what was going on.

A horrified old lady was crying: 'Oh, poor boy! Help him, somebody!' Some of the braver characters tried pulling at me but the horse whickered ominously and hung on tighter. Conflicting advice was shouted from all sides. With deep shame I saw two attractive girls in the

I hung there helplessly, suspended like a lopsided puppet.

front row giggling helplessly.

Appalled at the absurdity of my position, I began to thrash about wildly; my shirt collar tightened round my throat; a stream of the horse's saliva trickled down the front of my mac. I could feel myself choking and was giving up hope when a man pushed his way through the crowd.

He was very small. Angry eyes glared from a face blackened by coal dust. Two empty sacks were draped over an arm.

'Whit the hell's this?' he shouted. A dozen replies babbled in the air.

'Can ye no leave the bloody hoarse alone?' he yelled into my face. I made no reply, being pop-eyed, half throttled and in no mood for conversation.

The coalman turned his fury on the horse. 'Drop him, ya big bastard! Go on, let go, drop him!'

Getting no response he dug the animal viciously in the belly with his thumb. The horse took the point at once and released me like an obedient dog dropping a bone. I fell on my knees and ruminated in the gutter for a while till I could breathe more easily. As from a great distance I could still hear the little man shouting at me.

After some time I stood up. The coalman was still shouting and the crowd was listening appreciatively. 'Whit d'ye think you're playing at – keep yer hands off ma bloody hoarse – get the poliss tae ye.'

I looked down at my new mac. The shoulder was chewed to a sodden mass. I felt I must escape and began to edge my way through the crowd. Some of the faces were concerned but most were grinning. Once clear I started to walk away rapidly and as I turned the corner the last faint cry from the coalman reached me.

'Dinna meddle wi' things ye ken nuthin' aboot!'

13

The perils of Tricki Woo

I was really worried about Tricki this time. I had pulled up my car when I saw him in the street with his mistress and I was shocked at his appearance. He had become hugely fat, like a bloated sausage with a leg at each corner. His eyes, bloodshot and rheumy, stared straight ahead and his tongue lolled from his jaws.

Mrs Pumphrey hastened to explain. 'He was so listless, Mr Herriot. He seemed to have no energy. I thought he must be suffering from malnutrition, so I have been giving him some little extras between meals to build him up. Some calf's foot jelly and malt and cod liver oil and a bowl of Horlick's at night to make him sleep – nothing much really.'

'And did you cut down on the sweet things as I told you?'

'Oh, I did for a bit, but he seemed to be so weak. I had to relent. He does love cream cakes and chocolates so. I can't bear to refuse him.'

I looked down again at the little dog. That was the trouble. Tricki's only fault was greed. He had never been known to refuse food; he would tackle a meal at any hour of the day or night. And I wondered about all the things Mrs Pumphrey hadn't mentioned; the pate on thin biscuits, the fudge, the rich trifles – Tricki loved them all.

'Are you giving him plenty of exercise?'

'Well, he has his little walks with me as you can see, but Hodgkin has been down with lumbago, so there has been no ring-throwing lately.'

I tried to sound severe. 'Now I really mean this. If you don't cut his food right down and give him more exercise he is going to be really ill. You must harden your heart and keep him on a very strict diet.'

Mrs Pumphrey wrung her hands. 'Oh I will, Mr Herriot. I'm sure you are right, but it is so difficult, so very difficult.' She set off, head down, along the road, as if determined to put the new regime into practice immediately.

I watched their progress with growing concern. Tricki was tottering along in his little tweed coat; he had a whole wardrobe of these coats – warm tweed or tartan ones for the cold weather and macintoshes for the wet days. He struggled on, drooping in his harness. I thought it wouldn't be long before I heard from Mrs Pumphrey.

The expected call came within a few days. Mrs Pumphrey was distraught. Tricki would eat nothing. Refused even his favourite dishes; and besides, he had bouts of vomiting. He spent all his time lying on a rug, panting. Didn't want to go walks, didn't want to do anything.

I had made my plans in advance. The only way was to get Tricki out of the house for a period. I suggested that he be hospitalised for about a fortnight to be kept under observation.

The poor lady almost swooned. She had never been separated from her darling before; she was sure he would pine and die if he did not see her every day.

But I took a firm line. Tricki was very ill and this was the only way to save him; in fact, I thought it best to take him without delay and, followed by Mrs Pumphrey's wailings, I marched out to the car carrying the little dog wrapped in a blanket.

The entire staff was roused and maids rushed in and out bringing his day bed, his night bed, favourite cushions, toys and rubber rings, breakfast bowl, lunch bowl, supper bowl. Realising that my car would never hold all the stuff, I started to drive away. As I moved off, Mrs Pumphrey, with a despairing cry, threw an armful of little coats through the window. I looked in the mirror before I turned the corner of the drive; everybody was in tears.

Out on the road, I glanced down at the pathetic little animal gasping on the seat by my side. I patted the head and Tricki made a brave effort to wag his tail. 'Poor old lad,' I said, 'You haven't a kick in you but I think I know a cure for you.'

At the surgery, the household dogs surged round me. Tricki looked down at the noisy pack with dull eyes and, when put down, lay motionless on the carpet. The other dogs, after sniffing round him for a few seconds, decided he was an uninteresting object and ignored him.

I made up a bed for him in a warm loose box next to the one where the other dogs slept. For two days I kept an eye on him, giving him no food but plenty of water. At the end of the second day he started to show some interest in his surroundings and on the third he began to whimper when he heard the dogs in the yard.

When I opened the door, Tricki trotted out and was immediately engulfed by Joe the greyhound and his friends. After rolling him over and thoroughly inspecting him, the dogs moved off down the garden. Tricki followed them, rolling slightly with his surplus fat but obviously intrigued.

Later that day, I was present at feeding time. I watched while Tristan slopped the food into the bowls. There was the usual headlong rush followed by the sounds of high-speed eating; every dog knew that if he fell behind the others he was liable to have some competition for the last part of his meal.

When they had finished, Tricki took a walk round the shining bowls, licking casually inside one or two of them. Next day, an extra bowl was put out for him and I was pleased to see him jostling his way towards it.

From then on, his progress was rapid. He had no medicinal treatment of any kind but all day he ran about with the dogs, joining in their friendly scrimmages. He discovered the joys of being bowled over, trampled on and squashed every few minutes. He became an accepted member of the gang, an unlikely, silky little object among the shaggy crew, fighting like a tiger for his share at meal times and hunting rats in the old hen house at night. He had never had such a time in his life.

All the while, Mrs Pumphrey hovered anxiously in the background, ringing a dozen times a day for the latest bulletins. I dodged the questions about whether his cushions were being turned regularly or his correct coat worn according to the weather; but I was able to tell her that the little fellow was out of danger and convalescing rapidly.

The word 'convalescing' seemed to do something to Mrs Pumphrey. She started to bring round fresh eggs, two dozen at a time, to build up Tricki's strength. For a happy period there were two eggs each for breakfast, but when the bottles of sherry began to arrive, the real possibilities of the situation began to dawn on the household.

It was the same delicious vintage that I knew so well and it was to enrich Tricki's blood. Lunch became a ceremonial occasion with two glasses before and several during the meal. Siegfried and Tristan took turns at proposing Tricki's health and the standard of speech-making improved daily. As the sponsor, I was always called upon to reply.

We could hardly believe it when the brandy came. Two bottles of Cordon Bleu, intended to put a final edge on Tricki's constitution. Siegfried dug out some balloon glasses belonging to his mother. I had

GREYHOUND The greyhound hunts by sight rather than scent, and speed is essential to it in running down its natural quarry – small game such as hares. It has been known to reach 50 miles an hour, and the power and grace of its lean, muscular body alternately jack-knifing and stretching out are impressive. Despite thousands of years as a hunter, the greyhound is a gentle and sensitive dog that needs company. Nowadays it is more often a cog in the dog-racing business than a pet.

never seen them before, but for a few nights they saw constant service as the fine spirit was rolled around, inhaled and reverently drunk.

They were days of deep content, starting well with the extra egg in the morning, bolstered up and sustained by the midday sherry and finishing luxuriously round the fire with the brandy.

It was a temptation to keep Tricki on as a permanent guest, but I knew Mrs Pumphrey was suffering and after a fortnight, felt compelled to phone and tell her that the little dog had recovered and was awaiting collection.

Within minutes, about thirty feet of gleaming black metal drew up outside the surgery. The chauffeur opened the door and I could just make out the figure of Mrs Pumphrey almost lost in the interior. Her hands were tightly clasped in front of her; her lips trembled. 'Oh, Mr Herriot, do tell me the truth. Is he really better?'

'Yes, he's fine. There's no need for you to get out of the car – I'll go and fetch him.'

I walked through the house into the garden. A mass of dogs was

hurtling round and round the lawn and in their midst, ears flapping, tail waving, was the little golden figure of Tricki. In two weeks he had been transformed into a lithe, hard-muscled animal; he was keeping up well with the pack, stretching out in great bounds, his chest almost brushing the ground.

I carried him back along the passage to the front of the house. The chauffeur was still holding the car door open and when Tricki saw his mistress he took off from my arms in a tremendous leap and sailed into Mrs Pumphrey's lap. She gave a startled 'Ooh!' and then had to defend herself as he swarmed over her, licking her face and barking.

During the excitement, I helped the chauffeur to bring out the beds, toys, cushions, coats and bowls, none of which had been used. As the car moved away, Mrs Pumphrey leaned out of the window. Tears shone in her eyes. Her lips trembled.

'Oh, Mr Herriot,' she cried, 'How can I ever thank you? This is a triumph of surgery!'

I carried him to the front of the house. The chauffeur was still holding the car door open.

113

14

Fooled – by a cow

I could see that Mr Handshaw didn't believe a word I was saying. He looked down at his cow and his mouth tightened into a stubborn line.

'Broken pelvis? You're trying to tell me she'll never get up n'more? Why, look at her chewing her cud! I'll tell you this, young man – me dad would've soon got her up if he'd been alive today.'

I had been a veterinary surgeon for a year now and I had learned a few things. One of them was that farmers weren't easy men to convince – especially Yorkshire Dalesmen.

And that bit about his dad. Mr Handshaw was in his fifties and I suppose there was something touching about his faith in his late father's skill and judgement. But I could have done very nicely without it.

It had acted as an additional irritant in a case in which I felt I had troubles enough. Because there are few things which get more deeply under a vet's skin than a cow which won't get up. To the layman it may seem strange that an animal can be apparently cured of its original ailment and yet be unable to rise from the floor, but it happens. And it can be appreciated that a completely recumbent milk cow has no future.

The case had started when my boss, Siegfried Farnon, who owned the practice in the little Dales market town of Darrowby, sent me to a milk fever. This suddenly occurring calcium deficiency attacks high yielding animals just after calving and causes collapse and progressive coma. When I first saw Mr Handshaw's cow she was stretched out motionless on her side, and I had to look carefully to make sure she wasn't dead.

But I got out my bottles of calcium with an airy confidence because I had been lucky enough to qualify just about the time when the profession had finally got on top of this hitherto fatal condition. The breakthrough had come many years earlier with inflation of the udder and I still carried a little blowing-up outfit around with me (the farmers used bicycle pumps), but with the advent of calcium therapy one could bask in a cheap glory by jerking an animal back from imminent death within minutes. The skill required was minimal but it looked very very good.

By the time I had injected the two bottles – one into the vein, the other under the skin – and Mr Handshaw had helped me roll the cow on to her chest the improvement was already obvious; she was looking about her and shaking her head as if wondering where she had been for the last few hours. I felt sure that if I had had the time to hang about for a bit I could see her on her feet. But other jobs were waiting.

'Give me a ring if she isn't up by dinner time,' I said, but it was a formality. I was pretty sure I wouldn't be seeing her again.

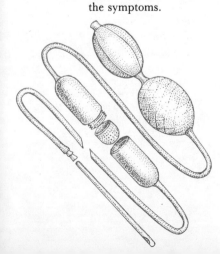

TREATING MILK FEVER Soon after calving, a dairy cow may become extremely weak and be unable to rise. The condition is called milk fever, although there are no symptoms of fever. Without treatment the cow will lapse into unconsciousness and die. From the late 19th century until the 1930s the standard treatment was to inflate the udder. The apparatus below had a set of bellows connected by tubing to a metal rod that was inserted in each teat in turn. The air was filtered during its passage along the tube by a box filled with cotton wool. The box unscrewed for clean wool to be put in. During the 1930s this treatment was replaced by injection of a calcium solution into the vein, because it had been established that a very low level of calcium in the blood was the cause of the symptoms.

114

When the farmer rang at midday to say she was still down it was just a pinprick. Some cases needed an extra bottle – it would be all right. I went out and injected her again.

I wasn't really worried when I learned she hadn't got up the following day, but Mr Handshaw, hands deep in pockets, shoulders hunched as he stood over his cow, was grievously disappointed at my lack of success.

'It's time t'awd bitch was up. She's doin' no good laid there. Surely there's summat you can do. I poured a bottle of water into her lug this morning but even that hasn't shifted her.'

'You what?'

'Poured some cold water down her lug 'ole. Me dad used to get 'em up that way and he was a very clever man with stock was me dad.'

'I've no doubt he was,' I said primly. 'But I really think another injection is more likely to help her.'

The farmer watched glumly as I ran yet another bottle of calcium under the skin. The procedure had lost its magic for him.

As I put the apparatus away I did my best to be hearty. 'I shouldn't worry. A lot of them stay down for a day or two – you'll probably find her walking about in the morning.'

The phone rang just before breakfast and my stomach contracted sharply as I heard Mr Handshaw's voice. It was heavy with gloom. 'Well, she's no different. Lyin' there eating her 'ead off, but never offers to rise. What are you going to do now?'

What indeed, I thought as I drove out to the farm. The cow had been down for forty-eight hours now – I didn't like it a bit.

The farmer went into the attack immediately. 'Me dad allus used to say they had a worm in the tail when they stayed down like this. He said if you cut tail end off it did the trick.'

My spirits sagged lower. I had had trouble with this myth before. The insidious thing was that the people who still practised this relic of barbarism could often claim that it worked because, after the end of the tail had been chopped off, the pain of the stump touching the ground forced many a sulky cow to scramble to her feet.

'There's no such thing as worm in the tail, Mr Handshaw,' I said. 'And don't you think it's a cruel business, cutting off a cow's tail? I hear the R.S.P.C.A. had a man in court last week over a job like that.'

The farmer narrowed his eyes. Clearly he thought I was hedging. 'Well, if you won't do that, what the hangment are you going to do? We've got to get this cow up somehow.'

I took a deep breath. 'Well, I'm sure she's got over the milk fever because she's eating well and looks quite happy. It must be a touch of posterior paralysis that's keeping her down. There's no point in giving her any more calcium so I'm going to try this stimulant injection.' I filled the syringe with a feeling of doom. I hadn't a scrap of faith in the stimulant injection but I just couldn't do nothing. I was scraping the barrel out now.

I was turning to go when Mr Handshaw called after me. 'Hey, Mister,

MILKING TO MUSIC Milking out of doors stopped during the 1930s, to avoid getting dust in the milk, and milkers began to wear almost clinical overalls. The 'wireless', which became common in the Dales in the 1930s, played music in some farm milking parlours because the farmer believed it made the cows relaxed. Cows must be contented if they are to give milk readily. Hand-milkers tried to imitate a calf's sucking. They squeezed the teats quickly and evenly without pulling. It took about nine minutes to milk each cow.

I remember summat else me dad used to do. Shout in their lugs. He got many a cow up that way. I'm not very strong in the voice – how about you having a go?'

It was a bit late to stand on my dignity. I went over to the animal and seized her by the ear. Inflating my lungs to the utmost I bent down and bawled wildly into the hairy depths. The cow stopped chewing for a moment and looked at me enquiringly, then her eyes drooped and she returned contentedly to her cudding. 'We'll give her another day,' I said wearily. 'And if she's still down tomorrow we'll have a go at lifting her. Could you get a few of your neighbours to give us a hand?'

Driving round my other cases that day I felt tied up inside with sheer frustration. Damn and blast the thing! What the hell was keeping her down? And what else could I do? This was 1938 and my resources were limited. Thirty years later there are still milk fever cows which won't get up but the vet has a much wider armoury if the calcium has failed to do the job. The excellent Bagshaw hoist which clamps on to the pelvis and raises the animal in a natural manner, the phosphorus injections, even the electric goad which administers a swift shock when applied to the rump and sends many a comfortably ensconced cow leaping to her feet with an offended bellow.

As I expected, the following day brought no change and as I got out of the car in Mr Handshaw's yard I was surrounded by a group of his neighbours. They were in festive mood, grinning, confident, full of helpful advice as farmers always are with somebody else's animals.

There was much laughter and legpulling as we drew sacks under the cow's body and a flood of weird suggestions to which I tried to close my ears. When we all finally gave a concerted heave and lifted her up, the result was predictable; she just hung there placidly with her legs dangling whilst her owner leaned against the wall watching us with deepening gloom.

After a lot of puffing and grunting we lowered the inert body and everybody looked at me for the next move. I was hunting round desperately in my mind when Mr Handshaw piped up again.

'Me dad used to say a strange dog would allus get a cow up.'

There were murmurs of assent from the assembled farmers and immediate offers of dogs. I tried to point out that one would be enough but my authority had dwindled and anyway everybody seemed anxious to demonstrate their dogs' cow-raising potential. There was a sudden excited exodus and even Mr Smedley the village shopkeeper pedalled off at frantic speed for his border terrier. It seemed only minutes before the byre was alive with snapping, snarling curs but the cow ignored them all except to wave her horns warningly at the ones which came too close.

The flash-point came when Mr Handshaw's own dog came in from the fields where he had been helping to round up the sheep. He was a skinny, hard-bitten little creature with lightning reflexes and a short temper. He stalked, stiff-legged and bristling, into the byre, took a single astounded look at the pack of foreigners on his territory and flew into action with silent venom.

Within seconds the finest dog fight I had ever seen was in full swing and I stood back and surveyed the scene with a feeling of being completely superfluous. The yells of the farmers rose above the enraged yapping and growling. One intrepid man leaped into the mêlée and reappeared with a tiny Jack Russell hanging on determinedly to the heel of his wellington boot. Mr Reynolds of Clover Hill was rubbing the cow's tail between two short sticks and shouting 'Cush! Cush!' and as I watched helplessly a total stranger tugged at my sleeve and whispered: 'Hasta tried a teaspoonful of Jeyes' Fluid in a pint of old beer every two hours?'

It seemed to me that all the forces of black magic had broken through and were engulfing me and that my slender resources of science had no chance of shoring up the dyke. I don't know how I heard the creaking sound above the din – probably because I was bending low over Mr Reynolds in an attempt to persuade him to desist from his tail rubbing. But at that moment the cow shifted her position slightly and I distinctly heard it. It came from the pelvis.

It took me some time to attract attention – I think everybody had forgotten I was there – but finally the dogs were separated and secured with innumerable lengths of binder twine, everybody stopped shouting,

It seemed only minutes before the byre was alive with snapping, snarling curs.

JACK RUSSELL TERRIER It was a Devon clergyman, the Reverend John Russell (1795–1883), who developed this small terrier. It stands about 12 in. high and has a wiry white coat, either smooth or rough, with some black or tan marking. Its jaws are very strong and its cheek muscles powerful to perform the work for which it was bred. Master of Foxhounds on Exmoor was the Rev. Russell's second occupation, and he developed the dog to run with the hounds and drive out foxes from bolt-holes which the hounds were too large to penetrate.

Mr Reynolds was pulled away from the tail and I had the stage.

I addressed myself to Mr Handshaw. 'Would you get me a bucket of hot water, some soap and a towel, please.'

He trailed off, grumbling, as though he didn't expect much from the new gambit. My stock was definitely low.

I stripped off my jacket, soaped my arms and pushed a hand into the cow's rectum until I felt the hard bone of the pubis. Gripping it through the wall of the rectum I looked up at my audience. 'Will two of you get hold of the hook bones and rock the cow gently from side to side.'

Yes, there it was again, no mistake about it. I could both hear and feel it – a looseness, a faint creaking, almost a grating.

I got up and washed my arm. 'Well, I know why your cow won't get up – she has a broken pelvis. Probably did it during the first night when she was staggering about with the milk fever. I should think the nerves are damaged, too. It's hopeless, I'm afraid.' Even though I was dispensing bad news it was a relief to come up with something rational.

Mr Handshaw stared at me. 'Hopeless? How's that?'

'I'm sorry,' I said, 'but that's how it is. The only thing you can do is get her off to the butcher. She has no power in her hind legs. She'll never get up again.'

That was when Mr Handshaw really blew his top and started a lengthy speech. He wasn't really unpleasant or abusive but firmly pointed out my shortcomings and bemoaned again the tragic fact that his dad was not there to put everything right. The other farmers stood in a wide-eyed ring, enjoying every word.

At the end of it I took myself off. There was nothing more I could do and anyway Mr Handshaw would have to come round to my way of thinking. Time would prove me right.

I thought of that cow as soon as I awoke next morning. It hadn't been a happy episode but at least I did feel a certain peace in the knowledge that there were no more doubts. I knew what was wrong, I knew that there was no hope. There was nothing more to worry about.

I was surprised when I heard Mr Handshaw's voice on the phone so soon. I had thought it would take him two or three days to realise he was wrong.

'Is that Mr Herriot? Aye, well, good mornin' to you. I'm just ringing to tell you that me cow's up on her legs and doing fine.'

I gripped the receiver tightly with both hands.

'What? What's that you say?'

'I said me cow's up. Found her walking about byre this morning, fit as a fiddle. You'd think there'd never been owt the matter with her.' He paused for a few moments then spoke with grave deliberation like a disapproving schoolmaster. 'And you stood there and looked at me and said she'd never get up n'more.'

'But ... but ...'

'Ah, you're wondering how I did it? Well, I just happened to remember another old trick of me dad's. I went round to t'butcher and got a fresh-killed sheep skin and put it on her back. Had her up in no time – you'll 'ave to come round and see her. Wonderful man was me dad.'

Blindly I made my way into the dining-room. I had to consult my boss about this. Siegfried's sleep had been broken by a 3 a.m. calving and he looked a lot older than his thirty-odd years. He listened in silence as he finished his breakfast then pushed away his plate and poured a last cup of coffee. 'Hard luck, James. The old sheep skin, eh? Funny thing – you've been in the Dales over a year now and never come across that one. Suppose it must be going out of fashion a bit now but you know it has a grain of sense behind it like a lot of these old remedies. You can imagine there's a lot of heat generated under a fresh sheep skin and it acts like a great hot poultice on the back – really tickles them up after a while, and if a cow is lying there out of sheer cussedness she'll often get up just to get rid of it.'

'But damn it, how about the broken pelvis? I tell you it was creaking and wobbling all over the place!'

'Well, James, you're not the first to have been caught that way. Sometimes the pelvic ligaments don't tighten up for a few days after calving and you get this effect.'

'Oh God,' I moaned, staring down at the table cloth. 'What a bloody mess I've made of the whole thing.'

'Oh, you haven't really.' Siegfried lit a cigarette and leaned back in his chair. 'That old cow was probably toying with the idea of getting up for a walk just when old Handshaw dumped the skin on her back. She could just as easily have done it after one of your injections and then you'd have got the credit. Don't you remember what I told you when you first came here? There's a very fine dividing line between looking a real smart vet on the one hand and an immortal fool on the other. This sort of thing happens to us all, so forget it, James.'

But forgetting wasn't so easy. That cow became a celebrity in the district. Mr Handshaw showed her with pride to the postman, the policeman, corn merchants, lorry drivers, fertiliser salesmen, Ministry of Agriculture officials and they all told me about it frequently with pleased smiles. Mr Handshaw's speech was always the same, delivered, they said, in ringing, triumphant tones:

'There's the cow that Mr Herriot said would never get up n'more!'

I'm sure there was no malice behind the farmer's actions. He had put one over on the young clever-pants vet and nobody could blame him for preening himself a little. And in a way I did that cow a good turn; I considerably extended her life span, because Mr Handshaw kept her long beyond her normal working period just as an exhibit. Years after she had stopped giving more than a couple of gallons of milk a day she was still grazing happily in the field by the roadside.

She had one curiously upturned horn and was easy to recognise. I often pulled up my car and looked wistfully over the wall at the cow that would never get up n'more.

HORN TRAINERS Cattle breeders who wanted their animals to win prizes in the show-ring at local and county agricultural shows paid great attention to every detail of their herd's appearance, including the horns. A perfectly symmetrical pair of horns was what the stockman aimed for, and to achieve this he would put a trainer on the horns of a calf. The iron set (top) and the lead and leather set (bottom) had cups to fit over the horn tips and bolts or straps for adjusting the pressure. The wooden set (centre) had flaps that fitted behind the horns and were adjusted by screws; this set could exert only forward pressure on the horns.

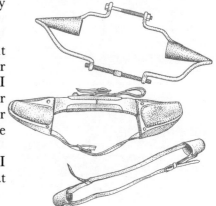

15

A lame calf leads me to Helen

A lot of the Dales farms were anonymous and it was a help to find this one so plainly identified. 'Heston Grange' it said on the gate in bold black capitals.

I got out of the car and undid the latch. It was a good gate, too, and swung easily on its hinges instead of having to be dragged round with a shoulder under the top spar. The farmhouse lay below me, massive, grey-stoned, with a pair of bow windows which some prosperous Victorian had added to the original structure.

KITCHEN BOWLS Farm kitchens were equipped with a variety of bowls, the oldest style among them being the wide, cone-shaped pancheons (top) of red earthenware with a cream, glazed interior. The large size was used for mixing dough and putting it to rise. Typical mixing bowls for cakes and puddings (right) were of buff, glazed stoneware with a white interior. The outside was decorated with rosettes in oval panels. Another popular range of bowls were of white, glazed earthenware decorated on the outside with blue bands (lower left). The smaller ones were used for beating eggs, for example.

It stood on a flat, green neck of land in a loop of the river and the lushness of the grass and the quiet fertility of the surrounding fields contrasted sharply with the stark hills behind. Towering oaks and beeches sheltered the house and a thick pine wood covered the lower slopes of the fell.

I walked round the buildings shouting as I always did, because some people considered it a subtle insult to go to the house and ask if the farmer was in. Good farmers are indoors only at meal times. But my shouts drew no reply, so I went over and knocked at the door set deep among the weathered stones.

A voice answered 'Come in,' and I opened the door into a huge, stone-flagged kitchen with hams and sides of bacon hanging from hooks in the ceiling. A dark girl in a check blouse and green linen slacks was kneading dough in a bowl. She looked up and smiled.

'Sorry I couldn't let you in. I've got my hands full.' She held up her arms, floury-white to the elbow.

'That's all right. My name is Herriot. I've come to see a calf. It's lame, I understand.'

'Yes, we think he's broken his leg. Probably got his foot in a hole when he was running about. If you don't mind waiting a minute, I'll come with you. My father and the men are in the fields. I'm Helen Alderson, by the way.'

She washed and dried her arms and pulled on a pair of short wellingtons. 'Take over this bread will you, Meg,' she said to an old woman who came through from an inner room. 'I have to show Mr Herriot the calf.'

Outside, she turned to me and laughed. 'We've got a bit of a walk, I'm afraid. He's in one of the top buildings. Look, you can just see it up there.' She pointed to a squat, stone barn, high on the fell-side. I knew all about these top buildings; they were scattered all over the high country and I got a lot of healthy exercise going round them. They were used for storing hay and other things and as shelters for the animals on the hill pastures.

I looked at the girl for a few seconds. 'Oh, that's all right, I don't mind. I don't mind in the least.'

We went over the field to a narrow bridge spanning the river, and, following her across, I was struck by a thought; this new fashion of women wearing slacks might be a bit revolutionary but there was a lot to be said for it. The path led upward through the pine wood and here the sunshine was broken up into islands of brightness among the dark trunks, the sound of the river grew faint and we walked softly on a thick carpet of pine needles. It was cool in the wood and silent except when a bird call echoed through the trees.

Ten minutes of hard walking brought us out again into the hot sun on the open moor and the path curved steeper still round a series of rocky outcrops. I was beginning to puff, but the girl kept up a brisk pace, swinging along with easy strides. I was glad when we reached the level ground on the top and the barn came in sight again.

When I opened the half door I could hardly see my patient in the dark interior which was heavy with the fragrance of hay piled nearly to the roof. He looked very small and sorry for himself with his dangling foreleg which trailed uselessly along the strawed floor as he tried to walk.

'Will you hold his head while I examine him, please?' I said.

The girl caught the calf expertly, one hand under its chin, the other holding an ear. As I felt my way over the leg the little creature stood trembling, his face a picture of woe.

'Well, your diagnosis was correct. Clean fracture of the radius and ulna, but there's very little displacement so it should do well with a plaster on it.' I opened my bag, took out some plaster bandages then filled a bucket with water from a near-by spring. I soaked one of the bandages and applied it to the leg, following it with a second and a third till the limb was encased in a rapidly hardening white sheath from elbow to foot.

'We'll just wait a couple of minutes till it hardens, then we can let him go.' I kept tapping the plaster till I was satisfied it was set like stone. 'All right,' I said finally. 'He can go now.'

The girl released the head and the little animal trotted away. 'Look,' she cried. 'He's putting his weight on it already! And doesn't he look a lot happier!' I smiled. I felt I had really done something. The calf felt no pain now that the broken ends of the bone were immobilised; and the fear which always demoralises a hurt animal had magically vanished.

'Yes,' I said. 'He certainly has perked up quickly.' My words were almost drowned by a tremendous bellow and the patch of blue above the half door was suddenly obscured by a large shaggy head. Two great liquid eyes stared down anxiously at the little calf and it answered with a high-pitched bawl. Soon a deafening duet was in progress.

'That's his mother,' the girl shouted above the din. 'Poor old thing, she's been hanging about here all morning wondering what we've done with her calf. She hates being separated from him.'

WING SWEEP FOR HAY For a smallholder without a wagon and farmhands to help him in the fields, a sweep was an easily made labour-saver. A wing sweep like a three-sided pen pulled by a pony or horse gathered up swathes of hay and dragged them to a corner of the field. There the hinged wings of the sweep could be swung back to leave the hay ready for building into a pike.

I straightened up and drew the bolt on the door. 'Well she can come in now.'

The big cow almost knocked me down as she rushed past me. Then she started a careful, sniffing inspection of her calf, pushing him around with her muzzle and making muffled lowing noises deep in her throat.

The little creature submitted happily to all the fuss and when it was over and his mother was finally satisfied, he limped round to her udder and began to suck heartily.

'Soon got his appetite back,' I said and we both laughed.

I threw the empty tins into my bag and closed it. 'He'll have to keep the plaster on for a month, so if you'll give me a ring then I'll come back and take it off. Just keep an eye on him and make sure his leg doesn't get sore round the top of the bandage.'

As we left the barn the sunshine and the sweet warm air met us like a high wave. I turned and looked across the valley to the soaring green heights, smooth, enormous, hazy in the noon heat. Beneath my feet the grassy slopes fell away steeply to where the river glimmered among trees. 'It's wonderful up here,' I said. 'Just look at that gorge over there. And that great hill – I suppose you could call it a mountain.' I pointed at a giant which heaved its heather-mottled shoulders high above the others.

'That's Heskit Fell – nearly two and a half thousand feet. And that's Eddleton just beyond, and Wedder Fell on the other side and Colver and Sennor.' The names with their wild, Nordic ring fell easily from her tongue; she spoke of them like old friends and I could sense the affection in her voice.

We sat down on the warm grass of the hillside, a soft breeze pulled at the heads of the moorland flowers, somewhere a curlew cried. Darrowby and Skeldale House and veterinary practice seemed a thousand miles away.

'You're lucky to live here,' I said. 'But I don't think you need me to tell you that.'

'No, I love this country. There's nowhere else quite like it.' She paused and looked slowly around her. 'I'm glad it appeals to you too – a lot of people find it too bare and wild. It almost seems to frighten them.'

I laughed. 'Yes, I know, but as far as I'm concerned I can't help feeling sorry for all the thousands of vets who don't work in the Yorkshire Dales.'

I began to talk about my work, then almost without knowing, I was going back over my student days, telling her of the good times, the friends I had made and our hopes and aspirations. I surprised myself with my flow of talk – I wasn't much of a chatterbox usually – and I felt I must be boring my companion. But she sat quietly looking over the valley, her arms around her green-clad legs, nodding at times at though she understood. And she laughed in all the right places.

I wondered too, at the silly feeling that I would like to forget all about the rest of the day's duty and stay up here on this sunny hillside. It came

CUTTING LING Farmers and besom-makers would make trips to the moors in late winter to harvest long, straight ling, or heather. It was used sometimes as an under-layer in thatching, but principally for making besoms, or brooms. A full day's work would yield 30 large sheaves, each tied with a ling band. Two uprooted plants made a band. With root ends together, the strands were bound, plaited, twisted and pulled tight to make the bond.

to me that it had been a long time since I had sat down and talked to a girl of my own age. I had almost forgotten what it was like.

I didn't hurry back down the path and through the scented pine wood but it seemed no time at all before we were walking across the wooden bridge and over the field to the farm.

I turned with my hand on the car door. 'Well, I'll see you in a month.' It sounded like an awful long time.

The girl smiled. 'Thank you for what you've done.' As I started the engine she waved and went into the house.

'Helen Alderson?' Siegfried said later over lunch. 'Of course I know her. Lovely girl.'

Tristan, across the table, made no comment, but he laid down his knife and fork, raised his eyes reverently to the ceiling and gave a long, low whistle. Then he started to eat again.

Siegfried went on. 'Oh yes, I know her very well. And I admire her. Her mother died a few years ago and she runs the whole place. Cooks and looks after her father and a younger brother and sister.' He spooned some mashed potatoes on to his plate. 'Any men friends? Oh, half the young bloods in the district are chasing her but she doesn't seem to be going steady with any of them. Choosy sort, I think.'

16

'Do dogs have souls?'

The card dangled above the old lady's bed. It read 'God is Near' but it wasn't like the usual religious text. It didn't have a frame or ornate printing. It was just a strip of cardboard about eight inches long with plain lettering which might have said 'No smoking' or 'Exit' and it was looped carelessly over an old gas bracket so that Miss Stubbs from where she lay could look up at it and read 'God is Near' in square black capitals.

There wasn't much more Miss Stubbs could see; perhaps a few feet of privet hedge through the frayed curtains but mainly it was just the cluttered little room which had been her world for so many years.

The room was on the ground floor and in the front of the cottage, and as I came up through the wilderness which had once been a garden I could see the dogs watching me from where they had jumped on to the old lady's bed. And when I knocked on the door the place almost erupted with their barking. It was always like this. I had been visiting regularly for over a year and the pattern never changed; the furious barking, then Mrs Broadwith who looked after Miss Stubbs would push all the animals but my patient into the back kitchen and open the door

REAPING SCYTHE AND SANDHORN
When a scythe was used for reaping corn, instead of for mowing hay, it was fitted with a slender bow of hazel at the lower end of the shaft. The bow collected the cut stems as they fell. At the end of one sweep with the scythe, the bow would be holding enough corn for a sheaf. A skilled reaper could tilt the corn into position on the sheafband ready for tying. A scythe was not properly balanced without a green oak strickle hooked at the top of the shaft. Over his shoulder the reaper kept his sandhorn or greasehorn, and when the scythe blade blunted he took a piece of pork fat from the broad end of the horn and rubbed it on the strickle. Then he sprinkled on sand from the tip of the horn and used the strickle as an emery board to sharpen the blade.

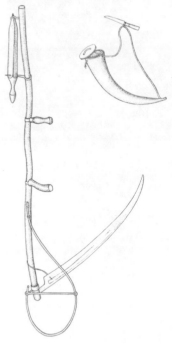

123

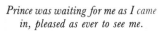

Prince was waiting for me as I came in, pleased as ever to see me.

and I would go in and see Miss Stubbs in the corner in her bed with the card hanging over it.

She had been there for a long time and would never get up again. But she never mentioned her illness and pain to me; all her concern was for her three dogs and two cats.

Today it was old Prince and I was worried about him. It was his heart – just about the most spectacular valvular incompetence I had ever heard. He was waiting for me as I came in, pleased as ever to see me, his long, fringed tail waving gently.

The sight of that tail used to make me think there must be a lot of Irish Setter in Prince but I was inclined to change my mind as I worked my way forward over the bulging black and white body to the shaggy head and upstanding Alsatian ears. Miss Stubbs often used to call him 'Mr Heinz' and though he may not have had 57 varieties in him his hybrid vigour had stood him in good stead. With his heart he should have been dead long ago.

'I thought I'd best give you a ring, Mr Herriot,' Mrs Broadwith said. She was a comfortable, elderly widow with a square, ruddy face contrasting sharply with the pinched features on the pillow. 'He's been coughing right bad this week and this morning he was a bit staggery. Still eats well, though.'

'I bet he does.' I ran my hands over the rolls of fat on the ribs. 'It

124

would take something really drastic to put old Prince off his grub.'

Miss Stubbs laughed from the bed and the old dog, his mouth wide, eyes dancing, seemed to be joining in the joke. I put my stethoscope over his heart and listened, knowing well what I was going to hear. They say the heart is supposed to go 'Lub-dup, lub-dup', but Prince's went 'swish-swoosh, swish-swoosh'. There seemed to be nearly as much blood leaking back as was being pumped into the circulatory system. And another thing, the 'swish-swoosh' was a good bit faster than last time; he was on oral digitalis but it wasn't quite doing its job.

Gloomily I moved the stethoscope over the rest of the chest. Like all old dogs with a chronic heart weakness he had an ever-present bronchitis and I listened without enthusiasm to the symphony of whistles, rales, squeaks and bubbles which signalled the workings of Prince's lungs. The old dog stood very erect and proud, his tail still waving slowly. He always took it as a tremendous compliment when I examined him and there was no doubt he was enjoying himself now. Fortunately his was not a very painful ailment.

Straightening up, I patted his head and he responded immediately by trying to put his paws on my chest. He didn't quite make it and even that slight exertion started his ribs heaving and his tongue lolling. I gave him an intramuscular injection of digitalin and another of morphine hydrochloride which he accepted with apparent pleasure as part of the game.

'I hope that will steady his heart and breathing, Miss Stubbs. You'll find he'll be a bit dopey for the rest of the day and that will help, too. Carry on with the tablets, and I'm going to leave you some more medicine for his bronchitis.' I handed over a bottle of my old standby mixture of ipecacuanha and ammonium acetate.

The next stage of the visit began now as Mrs Broadwith brought in a cup of tea and the rest of the animals were let out of the kitchen. There were Ben, a Sealyham, and Sally, a Cocker Spaniel, and they started a deafening barking contest with Prince. They were closely followed by the cats, Arthur and Susie, who stalked in gracefully and began to rub themselves against my trouser legs.

It was the usual scenario for the many cups of tea I had drunk with Miss Stubbs under the little card which dangled above her bed.

'How are you today?' I asked.

'Oh, much better,' she replied and immediately, as always, changed the subject.

Mostly she liked to talk about her pets and the ones she had known right back to her girlhood. She spoke a lot, too, about the days when her family were alive. She loved to describe the escapades of her three brothers and today she showed me a photograph which Mrs Broadwith had found at the bottom of a drawer.

I took it from her and three young men in the knee breeches and little round caps of the nineties smiled up at me from the yellowed old print; they all held long church warden pipes and the impish humour in their

LABRADOR RETRIEVER Beneath the Labrador's short yellow or black coat is a water-repellent undercoat that kept the dogs warm and active even in the icy seas round their original home, in eastern Canada. There, they were used by fishermen to swim from boat to shore, hauling in the end of the net with its catch of fish. In Britain they are indefatigable gundog retrievers, intelligent guide dogs for the blind, and energetic family pets.

expressions came down undimmed over the years.

'My word, they look really bright lads, Miss Stubbs,' I said.

'Oh, they were young rips!' she exclaimed. She threw back her head and laughed and for a moment her face was radiant, transfigured by her memories.

The things I had heard in the village came back to me; about the prosperous father and his family who lived in the big house many years ago. Then the foreign investments which crashed and the sudden change in circumstances. 'When t'owd feller died he was about skint,' one old man had said. 'There's not much brass there now.'

Probably just enough brass to keep Miss Stubbs and her animals alive and to pay Mrs Broadwith. Not enough to keep the garden dug or the house painted or for any of the normal little luxuries.

And, sitting there, drinking my tea, with the dogs in a row by the bedside and the cats making themselves comfortable on the bed itself, I felt as I had often felt before – a bit afraid of the responsibility I had. The one thing which brought some light into the life of the brave old woman was the transparent devotion of this shaggy bunch whose eyes were never far from her face. And the snag was that they were all elderly.

There had, in fact, been four dogs originally, but one of them, a truly ancient golden Labrador, had died a few months previously. And now I had the rest of them to look after and none of them less than ten years old.

They were perky enough but all showing some of the signs of old age; Prince with his heart, Sally beginning to drink a lot of water which made me wonder if she was starting with a pyometra, Ben growing steadily thinner with his nephritis. I couldn't give him new kidneys and I hadn't much faith in the hexamine tablets I had prescribed. Another peculiar thing about Ben was that I was always having to clip his claws; they grew at an extraordinary rate.

The cats were better, though Susie was a bit scraggy and I kept up a morbid kneading of her furry abdomen for signs of lymphosarcoma. Arthur was the best of the bunch; he never seemed to ail anything beyond a tendency for his teeth to tartar up.

This must have been in Miss Stubbs' mind because, when I had finished my tea, she asked me to look at him. I hauled him across the bedspread and opened his mouth.

'Yes, there's a bit of the old trouble there. Might as well fix it while I'm here.'

Arthur was a huge, grey, neutered Tom, a living denial of all those theories that cats are cold-natured, selfish and the rest. His fine eyes, framed in the widest cat face I have ever seen, looked out on the world with an all-embracing benevolence and tolerance. His every movement was marked by immense dignity.

As I started to scrape his teeth his chest echoed with a booming purr like a distant outboard motor. There was no need for anybody to hold him; he sat there placidly and moved only once – when I was using forceps to crack off a tough piece of tartar from a back tooth and accidentally nicked his gum. He casually raised a massive paw as if to say 'Have a care, chum', but his claws were sheathed.

My next visit was less than a month later and was in response to an urgent summons from Mrs Broadwith at six o'clock in the evening. Ben had collapsed. I jumped straight into my car and in less than ten minutes was threading my way through the overgrown grass in the front garden with the animals watching from their window. The barking broke out as I knocked, but Ben's was absent. As I went into the little room I saw the old dog lying on his side, very still, by the bed.

D.O.A. is what we write in the day book. Dead on arrival. Just three words but they covered all kinds of situations – the end of milk fever cows, bloated bullocks, calves in fits. And tonight they meant that I wouldn't be clipping old Ben's claws any more.

It wasn't often these nephritis cases went off so suddenly but his urine albumen had been building up dangerously lately.

'Well, it was quick, Miss Stubbs. I'm sure the old chap didn't suffer at all.' My words sounded lame and ineffectual.

The old lady was in full command of herself. No tears, only a fixity of expression as she looked down from the bed at her companion for so many years. My idea was to get him out of the place as quickly as possible and I pulled a blanket under him and lifted him up. As I was moving away, Miss Stubbs said, 'Wait a moment.' With an effort she turned on to her side and gazed at Ben. Still without changing expression, she reached out and touched his head lightly. Then she lay back calmly as I hurried from the room.

In the back kitchen I had a whispered conference with Mrs Broadwith. 'I'll run down t'village and get Fred Manners to come and bury him,' she said. 'And if you've got time could you stay with the old lady while I'm gone. Talk to her, like, it'll do her good.'

I went back and sat down by the bed. Miss Stubbs looked out of the window for a few moments then turned to me. 'You know, Mr Herriot,' she said casually. 'It will be my turn next.'

'What do you mean?'

'Well, tonight Ben has gone and I'm going to be the next one. I just know it.'

'Oh, nonsense! You're feeling a bit low, that's all. We all do when something like this happens.' But I was disturbed. I had never heard her even hint at such a thing before.

'I'm not afraid,' she said. 'I know there's something better waiting for me. I've never had any doubts.' There was silence between us as she lay calmly looking up at the card on the gas bracket.

Then the head on the pillow turned to me again. 'I have only one fear.' Her expression changed with startling suddenness as if a mask had dropped. The brave face was almost unrecognisable. A kind of terror flickered in her eyes and she quickly grasped my hand.

'It's my dogs and cats, Mr Herriot. I'm afraid I might never see them

SEALYHAM Named after the large Welsh estate at Haverfordwest where it was first bred only about 120 years ago, this small, white Welsh dog has the typical terrier qualities of energy, hardiness and enthusiasm for the chase. It was bred originally to hunt down foxes and badgers, and pursue them into their holes.

127

when I'm gone and it worries me so. You see, I know I'll be reunited with my parents and my brothers but ... but ...'

'Well, why not with your animals?'

'That's just it.' She rocked her head on the pillow and for the first time I saw tears on her cheeks. 'They say animals have no souls.'

'Who says?'

'Oh, I've read it and I know a lot of religious people believe it.'

'Well I don't believe it.' I patted the hand which still grasped mine. 'If having a soul means being able to feel love and loyalty and gratitude, then animals are better off than a lot of humans. You've nothing to worry about there.'

'Oh, I hope you're right. Sometimes I lie at night thinking about it.'

'I know I'm right, Miss Stubbs, and don't you argue with me. They teach us vets all about animals' souls.'

The tension left her face and she laughed with a return of her old spirit. 'I'm sorry to bore you with this and I'm not going to talk about it again. But before you go, I want you to be absolutely honest with me. I don't want reassurance from you – just the truth. I know you are very young but please tell me – what are your beliefs? Will my animals go with me?'

She stared intently into my eyes. I shifted in my chair and swallowed once or twice.

'Miss Stubbs, I'm afraid I'm a bit foggy about all this,' I said. 'But I'm absolutely certain of one thing. Wherever you are going, they are going too.'

She still stared at me but her face was calm again. 'Thank you, Mr Herriot, I know you are being honest with me. That is what you really believe, isn't it?'

'I do believe it,' I said. 'With all my heart I believe it.'

It must have been about a month later and it was entirely by accident that I learned I had seen Miss Stubbs for the last time. When a lonely, penniless old woman dies people don't rush up to you in the street to tell you. I was on my rounds and a farmer happened to mention that the cottage in Corby village was up for sale.

'But what about Miss Stubbs?' I asked.

'Oh, went off sudden about three weeks ago. House is in a bad state, they say – nowt been done at it for years.'

'Mrs Broadwith isn't staying on, then?'

'Nay, I hear she's staying at t'other end of village.'

'Do you know what's happened to the dogs and cats?'

'What dogs and cats?'

I cut my visit short. And I didn't go straight home though it was nearly lunch time. Instead I urged my complaining little car at top speed to Corby and asked the first person I saw where Mrs Broadwith was living. It was a tiny house but attractive and Mrs Broadwith answered my knock herself.

FUNERAL BISCUITS Caraway-flavoured shortcakes bearing a design that symbolised death were traditionally offered to funeral guests in Yorkshire's North Riding. The design of toothed circles enclosing a heart was stamped on the biscuits with a wooden mould about 4 in. across. The biscuits were handed round with glasses of wine after the funeral service.

'Oh, come in, Mr Herriot. It's right good of you to call.' I went inside and we sat facing each other across a scrubbed table top.

'Well, it was sad about the old lady,' she said.

'Yes, I've only just heard.'

'Any road, she had a peaceful end. Just slept away at finish.'

'I'm glad to hear that.'

Mrs Broadwith looked round the room. 'I was real lucky to get this place – it's just what I've always wanted.'

I could contain myself no longer. 'What's happened to the animals?' I blurted out.

'Oh, they're in t'garden,' she said calmly. 'I've got a grand big stretch at back.' She got up and opened the door and with a surge of relief I watched my old friends pour in.

Arthur was on my knee in a flash, arching himself ecstatically against my arm while his outboard motor roared softly above the barking of the dogs. Prince, wheezy as ever, tail fanning the air, laughed up at me delightedly between barks.

'They look great, Mrs Broadwith. How long are they going to be here?'

'They're here for good. I think just as much about them as t'old lady ever did and I couldn't be parted from them. They'll have a good home with me as long as they live.'

I looked at the typical Yorkshire country face, at the heavy cheeks with their grim lines belied by the kindly eyes. 'This is wonderful,' I said. 'But won't you find it just a bit . . . er . . . expensive to feed them?'

'Nay, you don't have to worry about that. I 'ave a bit put away.'

'Well fine, fine, and I'll be looking in now and then to see how they are. I'm through the village every few days.' I got up and started for the door.

Mrs Broadwith held up her hand. 'There's just one thing I'd like you to do before they start selling off the things at the cottage. Would you please pop in and collect what's left of your medicines. They're in t'front room.'

I took the key and drove along to the other end of the village. As I pushed open the rickety gate and began to walk through the tangled grass the front of the cottage looked strangely lifeless without the faces of the dogs at the window; and when the door creaked open and I went inside the silence was like a heavy pall.

Nothing had been moved. The bed with its rumpled blankets was still in the corner. I moved around, picking up half empty bottles, a jar of ointment, the cardboard box with old Ben's tablets – a lot of good they had done him.

When I had got everything I looked slowly round the little room. I wouldn't be coming here any more and at the door I paused and read for the last time the card which hung over the empty bed.

IRISH SETTER This strikingly beautiful dog with its silky chestnut coat, tall and slender build and shapely head has a curiously mixed character. It is known as a playful, skittish pet, but as a gundog it excels in its role as a pointer. It is quick to cover the ground, and uses its keen sight and smell to detect gamebirds. It does not approach close enough to alarm them once it has located them, but stays completely still, pointing towards the game until its handler catches up.

129

17

A grand night out

I was spending Tuesday evening as I spent all the Tuesday evenings – staring at the back of Helen Alderson's head at the Darrowby Music Society. It was a slow way of getting to know her better but I had been unable to think of a better idea.

Since the morning on the high moor when I had set the calf's leg, I had scanned the day book regularly in the hope of getting another visit to the farm. But the Aldersons seemed to have lamentably healthy stock. I had to be content with the thought that there was the visit at the month end to take off the plaster. The really crushing blow came when Helen's father rang up to say that, since the calf was going sound he had removed the plaster himself. He was pleased to say that the fracture had knitted perfectly and there was no sign of lameness.

I had come to admire the self-reliance and initiative of the Dalesmen but I cursed it now at great length; and I joined the Music Society. I had seen Helen going into the schoolroom where the meetings were held and, with the courage of desperation, had followed her inside.

That was weeks ago and, I reflected miserably, I had made no progress at all. I couldn't remember how many tenors, sopranos and male voice choirs had come and gone and on one occasion the local brass band had packed themselves into the little room and almost burst my ear drums; but I was no further forward.

Tonight a string quartet was scraping away industriously, but I hardly heard them. My eyes, as usual, were focused on Helen, several rows in front of me, sitting between the two old ladies she always seemed to bring with her. That was part of the trouble; those two old girls were always there, cutting out any chance of private conversation, even at the half-time break for tea. And there was the general atmosphere of the place; the members were nearly all elderly, and over everything hung the powerful schoolroom scent of ink and exercise books and chalk and lead pencils. It was the sort of place where you just couldn't say without warning 'Are you doing anything on Saturday night?'

The scraping stopped and everybody clapped. The vicar got up from the front row and beamed on the company. 'And now, ladies and gentlemen, I think we might stop for fifteen minutes as I see our willing helpers have prepared tea. The price, as usual, is threepence.' There was laughter and a general pushing back of chairs.

I went to the back of the hall with the others, put my threepence on the plate and collected a cup of tea and a biscuit. This was when I tried to get near Helen in the blind hope that something might happen. It wasn't always easy, because I was often buttonholed by the school headmaster and others who regarded a vet who liked music as an

A MEDICINE CHEST Drenches and dressings, powders and pills were remedies that many farmers kept by them and tried before paying for the services of the vet. The wooden Stockbreeders' Medicine Chest was similar to several others sold to farmers by agricultural merchants or commercial travellers. Its contents were effective in a limited way – and, indeed, were much the same as those used by the vet until modern drugs became available in the 1930s.

130

interesting curiosity, but tonight I managed to edge myself as if by accident into her group. She looked at me over the top of her cup. 'Good evening, Mr Herriot, are you enjoying it?' Oh God, she always said that. And Mr Herriot! But what could I do? 'Call me Jim', would sound great. I replied, as always, 'Good evening, Miss Alderson. Yes, it's very nice, isn't it.' Things were going with a bang again.

I munched my biscuit while the old ladies talked about Mozart. It was going to be the same as all the other Tuesdays. It was about time I gave up the whole thing. I felt beaten.

The vicar approached our group, still beaming. 'I'm afraid I have to call on somebody for the washing-up rota. Perhaps our two young friends would take it on tonight.' His friendly gaze twinkled from Helen to me and back again.

The idea of washing up teacups had never held much attraction for me but suddenly it was like sighting the promised land. 'Yes, certainly, delighted – that is if it's all right with Miss Alderson.' Helen smiled. 'Of course it's all right. We all have to take a turn, don't we?'

I wheeled the trolley of cups and saucers into the scullery. It was a cramped, narrow place with a sink and a few shelves and there was just about room for the two of us to get inside.

'Would you like to wash or dry?' Helen asked.

'I'll wash,' I replied and began to run the hot water into the sink. It shouldn't be too difficult now, I thought, to work the conversation round to where I wanted it. I'd never have a better chance than now, jammed into this little room with Helen.

But it was surprising how the time went by. Five whole minutes and we hadn't talked about anything but music. With mounting frustration I saw that we had nearly got through the pile of crockery and I had achieved nothing. The feeling changed to near panic when I lifted the last cup from the soapy water.

It had to be now. I held out the cup to Helen and she tried to take it from me; but I kept a grip on the handle while I waited for inspiration. She pulled gently but I clung to it tenaciously. It was developing into a tug of war. Then I heard a hoarse croak which I only just recognised as my own voice. 'Can I see you some time?' For a moment she didn't answer and I tried to read her face. Was she surprised, annoyed, even shocked? She flushed and replied, 'If you like.' I heard the croak again. 'Saturday evening?' She nodded, dried the cup and was gone.

I went back to my seat with my heart thudding. The strains of mangled Haydn from the quartet went unheeded. I had done it at last. But did she really want to come out? Had she been hustled into it against her will? My toes curled with embarrassment at the thought, but I consoled myself with the knowledge that for better or for worse it was a step forward. Yes, I had done it at last.

'The Reniston, eh?' I fidgeted uneasily. 'Bit grand, isn't it?'

Tristan lay rather than sat in his favourite chair and peered up

DOSING FOR WORMS Farmers were using an automatic dosing gun by the 1950s to give drugs that would previously have been poured as a medicine from a drenching bottle down the sheep's throat. The worming drug is in a container strapped to the man's back, and passes into the gun down a tube. The gun delivers a measured dose from its nozzle each time the handle is squeezed.

SMOOTHING IRONS Mrs Potts's cold-handle sad-irons were patented in the 1870s, sold for 3 shillings and 10 pence (19p) in 1907, and were so satisfactory that some Dales wives used them until mains electricity was brought to them in the late 1940s and allowed them to use electric irons. The sad-irons, or solid irons, came in a set of three, two of which were kept hot on the fireside hob while the third was being used. The handle, of wood so that it did not conduct heat from the metal, clipped quickly on to the iron that was to be used.

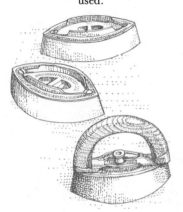

through a cloud of cigarette smoke. 'Of course it's grand. It's the most luxurious hotel in the country outside of London, but for your purpose it's the only possible place. Look, tonight is your big chance isn't it? You want to impress this girl, don't you? Well, ring her up and tell her you're taking her to the Reniston. The food is wonderful and there's a dinner dance every Saturday night. And today is Saturday.' He sat up suddenly and his eyes widened. 'Can't you see it, Jim? The music oozing out of Benny Thornton's trombone and you, full of lobster thermidor, floating round the floor with Helen snuggling up to you. The only snag is that it will cost you a packet, but if you are prepared to spend about a fortnight's wages you can have a really good night.'

I hardly heard the last part, I was concentrating on the blinding vision of Helen snuggling up to me. It was an image which blotted out things like money and I stood with my mouth half open listening to the trombone. I could hear it quite clearly.

Tristan broke in. 'There's one thing – have you got a dinner-jacket? You'll need one.'

'Well, I'm not very well off for evening-dress. In fact, when I went to Mrs Pumphrey's party I hired a suit from Brawton, but I wouldn't have time for that now.' I paused and thought for a moment. 'I do have my first and only dinner-suit but I got it when I was about seventeen and I don't know whether I'd be able to get into it.'

Tristan waved this aside. He dragged the Woodbine smoke into the far depths of his lungs and released it reluctantly in little wisps and trickles as he spoke. 'Doesn't matter in the least, Jim. As long as you're wearing the proper gear they'll let you in, and with a big, good-looking chap like you the fit of the suit is unimportant!'

We went upstairs and extracted the garment from the bottom of my trunk. I had cut quite a dash in this suit at the college dances and though it had got very tight towards the end of the course it had still been a genuine evening-dress outfit and as such had commanded a certain amount of respect.

But now it had a pathetic, lost look. The fashion had changed and the trend was towards comfortable jackets and soft, unstarched shirts. This one was rigidly of the old school and included an absurd little waistcoat with lapels and a stiff, shiny-fronted shirt with a tall, winged collar.

My problems really started when I got the suit on. Hard work, Pennine air and Mrs Hall's good food had filled me out and the jacket failed to meet across my stomach by six inches. I seemed to have got taller, too, because there was a generous space between the bottom of the waistcoat and the top of the trousers. The trousers themselves were skin tight over the buttocks, yet seemed foolishly baggy lower down.

Tristan's confidence evaporated as I paraded before him and he decided to call on Mrs Hall for advice. She was an unemotional woman and endured the irregular life at Skeldale House without noticeable reaction, but when she came into the bedroom and looked at me her facial muscles went into a long, twitching spasm. She finally overcame

132

the weakness, however, and became very businesslike.

'A little gusset at the back of your trousers will work wonders, Mr Herriot, and I think if I put a bit of silk cord across the front of your jacket it'll hold it nicely. Mind you, there'll be a bit of space, like, but I shouldn't think that'll worry you. And I'll give the whole suit a good press – makes all the difference in the world.'

I had never gone in much for intensive grooming, but that night I really went to work on myself, scrubbing and anointing and trying a whole series of different partings in my hair before I was satisfied. Tristan seemed to have appointed himself master of the wardrobe and carried the suit tenderly upstairs, still warm from Mrs Hall's ironing board. Then, like a professional valet, he assisted in every step of the robing. The high collar gave most trouble and he drew strangled oaths from me as he trapped the flesh of my neck under the stud.

When I was finally arrayed he walked around me several times, pulling and patting the material and making delicate adjustments here and there.

Eventually he stopped his circling and surveyed me from the front. I had never seen him look so serious. 'Fine, Jim, fine – you look great. Distinguished, you know. It's not everybody who can wear a dinner-jacket – so many people look like conjurers, but not you. Hang on a minute and I'll get your overcoat.'

I had arranged to pick up Helen at seven o'clock and as I climbed from the car in the darkness outside her house a strange unease crept over me. This was different. When I had come here before it had been as a veterinary surgeon – the man who knew, who was wanted, who came to render assistance in time of need. It had never occurred to me how much this affected my outlook every time I walked on to a farm. This wasn't the same thing at all. I had come to take this man's daughter out. He might not like it, might positively resent it.

Standing outside the farmhouse door I took a deep breath. The night was very dark and still. No sound came from the great trees near by and only the distant roar of the Darrow disturbed the silence. The recent heavy rains had transformed the leisurely, wandering river into a rushing torrent which in places overflowed its banks and flooded the surrounding pastures.

I was shown into the large kitchen by Helen's young brother. The boy had a hand over his mouth in an attempt to hide a wide grin. He seemed to find the situation funny. His little sister sitting at a table doing her homework was pretending to concentrate on her writing but she, too, wore a fixed smirk as she looked down at her book.

Mr Alderson was reading the *Farmer and Stockbreeder*, his breeches unlaced, his stockinged feet stretched out towards a blazing pile of logs. He looked up over his spectacles.

'Come in, young man, and sit by the fire,' he said absently. I had the uncomfortable impression that it was a frequent and boring experience for him to have young men calling for his eldest daughter.

FARMING PAPERS The routine of the farm year followed a traditional, unalterable pattern, but the methods changed and most farmers liked to learn of advances that could reduce their labour or make it more profitable. Agricultural shows, the local market and above all the weekly farming papers kept them informed about food supplements, fertility drugs and foot-rot cures – and, just as important, offered bargains in machine parts, fencing, creosote, and other necessities for maintaining their farms.

I had the uncomfortable impression that it was a frequent and boring experience for him to have young men calling for his eldest daughter.

I sat down at the other side of the fire and Mr Alderson resumed his study of the *Farmer and Stockbreeder*. The ponderous tick-tock of a large wall clock boomed out into the silence. I stared into the red depths of the fire till my eyes began to ache, then I looked up at a big oil painting in a gilt frame hanging above the mantelpiece. It depicted shaggy cattle standing knee-deep in a lake of an extraordinary bright blue; behind them loomed a backcloth of fearsome, improbable mountains, their jagged summits wreathed in a sulphurous mist.

134

Averting my eyes from this, I examined, one by one, the sides of bacon and the hams hanging from the rows of hooks in the ceiling. Mr Alderson turned over a page. The clock ticked on. Over by the table, spluttering noises came from the children.

After about a year I heard footsteps on the stairs, then Helen came into the room. She was wearing a blue dress – the kind, without shoulder straps, that seems to stay up by magic. Her dark hair shone under the single pressure lamp which lit the kitchen, shadowing the soft curves of her neck and shoulders. Over one white arm she held a camel-hair coat.

I felt stunned. She was like a rare jewel in the rough setting of stone flags and whitewashed walls. She gave me her quiet, friendly smile and walked towards me. 'Hello, I hope I haven't kept you waiting too long.'

I muttered something in reply and helped her on with her coat. She went over and kissed her father who didn't look up but waved his hand vaguely. There was another outburst of giggling from the table. We went out.

In the car I felt unusually tense and for the first mile or two had to depend on some inane remarks about the weather to keep a conversation going. I was beginning to relax when I drove over a little hump-backed bridge into a dip in the road. Then the car suddenly stopped. The engine coughed gently and then we were sitting silent and motionless in the darkness. And there was something else; my feet and ankles were freezing cold.

'My God!' I shouted. 'We've run into a bit of flooded road. The water's right into the car.' I looked round at Helen. 'I'm terribly sorry about this – your feet must be soaked.'

But Helen was laughing. She had her feet tucked up on the seat, her knees under her chin. 'Yes, I am a bit wet, but it's no good sitting about like this. Hadn't we better start pushing?'

Wading out into the black icy waters was a nightmare but there was no escape. Mercifully it was a little car and between us we managed to push it beyond the flooded patch. Then by torchlight I dried the plugs and got the engine going again.

Helen shivered as we squelched back into the car. 'I'm afraid I'll have to go back and change my shoes and stockings. And so will you. There's another road back through Fensley. You take the first turn on the left.'

Back at the farm, Mr Alderson was still reading the *Farmer and Stockbreeder* and kept his finger on the list of pig prices while he gave me a baleful glance over his spectacles. When he learned that I had come to borrow a pair of his shoes and socks he threw the paper down in exasperation and rose, groaning, from his chair. He shuffled out of the room and I could hear him muttering to himself as he mounted the stairs.

Helen followed him and I was left alone with the two young children. They studied my sodden trousers with undisguised delight. I had wrung most of the surplus water out of them but the final result was remarkable. Mrs Hall's knife-edge crease reached to just below the knee,

GILLAMOOR SUN-DIAL The sun and the seasons were the only timekeepers that farmers needed in their daily work, but a number of north Yorkshire villages, including Gillamoor, had fine sun-dials. The dials were probably for showing the times of church services. Churches and grand houses began to have mechanical clocks from the 17th century – but a sun-dial was still used to correct them. It was only with the coming of the railway at the end of the 19th century that standardised time became important for the village halts along the railway line.

but then there was chaos. The trousers flared out at that point in a crumpled, shapeless mass and as I stood by the fire to dry them a gentle steam rose about me. The children stared at me, wide-eyed and happy. This was a big night for them.

Mr Alderson reappeared at length and dropped some shoes and rough socks at my feet. I pulled on the socks quickly but shrank back when I saw the shoes. They were a pair of dancing slippers from the early days of the century and their cracked patent leather was topped by wide, black silk bows.

I opened my mouth to protest but Mr Alderson had dug himself deep into his chair and had found his place again among the pig prices. I had the feeling that if I asked for another pair of shoes Mr Alderson would attack me with the poker. I put the slippers on.

We had to take a roundabout road to avoid the floods but I kept my foot down and within half-an-hour we had left the steep sides of the Dale behind us and were heading out on to the rolling plain. I began to feel better. We were making good time and the little car, shuddering and creaking, was going well. I was just thinking that we wouldn't be all that late when the steering-wheel began to drag to one side.

I had a puncture most days and recognised the symptoms immediately. I had become an expert at changing wheels and with a word of apology to Helen was out of the car like a flash. With my rapid manipulation of the rusty jack and brace the wheel was off within three minutes. The surface of the crumpled tyre was quite smooth except for the lighter, frayed parts where the canvas showed through. Working like a demon, I screwed on the spare, cringing inwardly as I saw that this tyre was in exactly the same condition as the other. I steadfastly refused to think of what I would do if its frail fibres should give up the struggle.

By day, the Reniston dominated Brawton like a vast mediaeval fortress, bright flags fluttering arrogantly from its four turrets, but tonight it was like a dark cliff with a glowing cavern at street level where the Bentleys discharged their expensive cargoes. I didn't take my vehicle to the front entrance but tucked it away quietly at the back of the car park. A magnificent commissionaire opened the door for us and we trod noiselessly over the rich carpeting of the entrance hall.

We parted there to get rid of our coats, and in the men's cloakroom I scrubbed frantically at my oily hands. It didn't do much good; changing that wheel had given my finger nails a border of deep black which defied ordinary soap and water. And Helen was waiting for me.

I looked up in the mirror at the white-jacketed attendant hovering behind me with a towel. The man, clearly fascinated by my ensemble, was staring down at the wide-bowed pierrot shoes and the rumpled trouser bottoms. As he handed over the towel he smiled broadly as if in gratitude for this little bit of extra colour in his life.

I met Helen in the reception hall and we went over to the desk. 'What time does the dinner dance start?' I asked.

The girl at the desk looked surprised. 'I'm sorry, sir, there's no dance tonight. We only have them once a fortnight.'

I turned to Helen in dismay but she smiled encouragingly. 'It doesn't matter,' she said. 'I don't really care what we do.'

'We can have dinner, anyway,' I said. I tried to speak cheerfully but a little black cloud seemed to be forming just above my head. Was anything going to go right tonight? I could feel my morale slumping as I padded over the lush carpet and my first sight of the dining-room didn't help.

It looked as big as a football field with great marble pillars supporting a carved, painted ceiling. The Reniston had been built in the late Victorian period and all the opulence and ornate splendour of those days had been retained in this tremendous room. Most of the tables were occupied by the usual clientele, a mixture of the county aristocracy and industrialists from the West Riding. I had never seen so many beautiful women and masterful-looking men under one roof and I noticed with a twinge of alarm that, though the men were wearing everything from dark lounge suits to hairy tweeds, there wasn't another dinner-jacket in sight.

A majestic figure in white tie and tails bore down on us. With his mane of white hair falling back from the lofty brow, the bulging waistline, the hooked nose and imperious expression he looked exactly like a Roman emperor. His eyes flickered expertly over me and he spoke tonelessly.

'You want a table, sir?'

'Yes please,' I mumbled, only just stopping myself saying 'sir' to the man in return. 'A table for two.'

'Are you staying, sir?'

This question baffled me. How could I possibly have dinner here if I wasn't staying.

'Yes, I am staying.'

The emperor made a note on a pad. 'This way, sir.'

He began to make his way with great dignity among the tables while I followed abjectly in his wake with Helen. It was a long way to the table and I tried to ignore the heads which turned to have a second look at me as I passed. It was Mrs Hall's gusset that worried me most and I imagined it standing out like a beacon below the short jacket. It was literally burning my buttocks by the time we arrived.

The table was nicely situated and a swarm of waiters descended on us, pulling out our chairs and settling us into them, shaking out our napkins and spreading them on our laps. When they had dispersed the emperor took charge again. He poised a pencil over his pad.

'May I have your room number, sir?'

I swallowed hard and stared up at him over my dangerously billowing shirt front. 'Room number? Oh, I'm not living in the hotel.'

'Ah, NOT staying.' He fixed me for a moment with an icy look before crossing out something on the pad with unnecessary violence. He muttered something to one of the waiters and strode away.

RIPLEY STOCKS IN NIDDERDALE
From mediaeval times almost every village in Britain had a pair of stocks, sometimes near the church, often by the market cross. Here, minor offenders were clamped by the ankles for a few hours or all day to suffer the ridicule, and missiles, of the villagers. The offender was clamped into the stocks by the parish constable, frequently on a market day when he would get more public notice. Drunkenness was the most common cause of being put in the stocks. The punishment died out after about 1830, when the constable had cells to put criminals in for a night or two.

It was about then that the feeling of doom entered into me. The black cloud over my head spread and descended, enveloping me in a dense cloud of misery. The whole evening had been a disaster and would probably get worse. I must have been mad to come to this sumptuous place dressed up like a knockabout comedian. I was as hot as hell inside this ghastly suit and the stud was biting viciously into my neck.

I took a menu card from a waiter and tried to hold it with my fingers curled inwards to hide my dirty nails. Everything was in French and in my numbed state the words were largely meaningless, but somehow I ordered the meal and, as we ate, I tried desperately to keep a conversation going. But long deserts of silence began to stretch between us; it seemed that only Helen and I were quiet among all the surrounding laughter and chatter.

Worst of all was the little voice which kept telling me that Helen had never really wanted to come out with me anyway. She had done it out of politeness and was getting through a boring evening as best she could.

The journey home was a fitting climax. We stared straight ahead as the headlights picked out the winding road back into the Dales. We made stumbling remarks then the strained silence took over again. By the time we drew up outside the farm my head had begun to ache.

We shook hands and Helen thanked me for a lovely evening. There was a tremor in her voice and in the moonlight her face was anxious and withdrawn. I said goodnight, got into the car and drove away.

18

Old John and his 'pensioners'

As I sat at breakfast I looked out at the autumn mist dissolving in the early sunshine. It was going to be another fine day but there was a chill in the old house this morning, a shiveriness as though a cold hand had reached out to remind us that summer had gone and the hard months lay just ahead.

'It says here,' Siegfried said, adjusting his copy of the *Darrowby and Houlton Times* with care against the coffee-pot, 'that farmers have no feeling for their animals.'

I buttered a piece of toast and looked across at him.

'Cruel, you mean?'

'Well, not exactly, but this chap maintains that to a farmer, livestock are purely commercial – there's no sentiment in his attitude towards them, no affection.'

'Well, it wouldn't do if they were all like poor Kit Bilton, would it? They'd all go mad.'

PLOUGH-MAKERS Horse-drawn ploughs were being made until the early 1950s for some small Yorkshire farmers whose irregular fields on awkward folds of land made a tractor an extravagant investment. Local joiners and blacksmiths fashioned the ploughs, tailoring the height to suit different heights of farmer and the mould-board to suit different purposes. There were ploughs for light soils and heavy soils, for shallow ploughing or deeper digging, for crumbling the furrows or for turning them unbroken. The lightest plough would weigh 10 stones and the heaviest twice as much.

Kit was a lorry driver who, like so many of the working men of Darrowby, kept a pig at the bottom of his garden for family consumption. The snag was that when killing time came, Kit wept for three days. I happened to go into his house on one of these occasions and found his wife and daughter hard at it cutting up the meat for pies and brawn while Kit huddled miserably by the kitchen fire, his eyes swimming with tears. He was a huge man who could throw a twelve stone sack of meal on to his wagon with a jerk of his arms, but he seized my hand in his and sobbed at me 'I can't bear it, Mr Herriot. He was like a Christian was that pig, like a Christian.'

'No, I agree,' Siegfried leaned over and sawed off a slice of Mrs Hall's home-baked bread. 'But Kit isn't a real farmer. This article is about people who own large numbers of animals. The question is, is it possible for such men to become emotionally involved? Can the dairy farmer milking maybe fifty cows become really fond of any of them or are they just milk producing units?'

'It's an interesting point,' I said. 'And I think you've put your finger on it with the numbers. You know there are a lot of our farmers up in the high country who have only a few stock. They always have names for their cows – Daisy, Mabel, I even came across one called Kipperlugs the other day. I do think these small farmers have an affection for their animals but I don't see how the big men can possibly have.'

Siegfried rose from the table and stretched luxuriously. 'You're probably right. Anyway, I'm sending you to see a really big man this morning. John Skipton of Dennaby Close – he's got some tooth rasping to do. Couple of horses losing condition. You'd better take all the instruments, it might be anything.'

I went through to the little room down the passage and surveyed the tooth instruments. I always felt at my most mediaeval when I was caught up in large animal dentistry and in the days of the draught horse it was a regular task. One of the commonest jobs was knocking the wolf teeth out of young horses. I have no idea how it got its name but you found the little wolf tooth just in front of the molars and if a young horse was doing badly it always got the blame.

It was no good the vets protesting that such a minute, vestigial object couldn't possibly have any effect on the horse's health and that the trouble was probably due to worms. The farmers were adamant; the tooth had to be removed.

We did this by having the horse backed into a corner, placing the forked end of a metal rod against the tooth and giving a sharp tap with an absurdly large wooden mallet. Since the tooth had no proper root the operation was not particularly painful, but the horse still didn't like it. We usually had a couple of fore-feet waving around our ears at each tap.

And the annoying part was that after we had done the job and pointed out to the farmer that we had only performed this bit of black magic to humour him, the horse would take an immediate turn for the better and thrive consistently from then on. Farmers are normally reticent about

BACON AND EGG PIE Many Dales cottagers kept a pig for killing and curing in November to provide pork, hams and bacon for the winter. Bacon was preferred sweet-flavoured, unsmoked and very fat. There were countless recipes for using it. A bacon and egg pie was a filling dish for eating hot at tea-time or for taking into the fields for a midday meal in summer.

To prepare the pie, roll out 1 lb of shortcrust pastry to make a base and a lid for an 8 in. flan tin. Fit in the base and lay on 4 oz of thin bacon rashers. Break 4 whole eggs over the rashers, and season with salt and pepper. Put another 4 oz of bacon rashers in the pie and then cover it with the pastry lid. Bake for 30 minutes at 450°F (230°C), gas mark 8.

CARRYING HAY IN CREELS In the district round Hawes, a bundle of hay taken from the barn stack to supplement the winter food supply for cattle and sheep was carried in a pair of creels when it was being moved only a short distance. If it had to go to far-off hill sheep, a pony or a sled would carry it. The creels, for carrying on a man's back, were made from arch-shaped hazel rods linked by a mesh of tarred rope. About 30–40 lb of loosely packed hay filled the space between the creels, but twice as much could be packed in tightly if necessary.

our successful efforts for fear we might put a bit more on the bill but in these cases they cast aside all caution. They would shout at us across the market place: 'Hey, remember that 'oss you knocked wolf teeth out of? Well he never looked back. It capped him.'

I looked again with distaste at the tooth instruments; the vicious forceps with two-feet-long arms, sharp-jawed shears, mouth gags, hammers and chisels, files and rasps; it was rather like a quiet corner in the Spanish Inquisition. We kept a long wooden box with a handle for carrying the things and I staggered out to the car with a fair selection.

Dennaby Close was not just a substantial farm, it was a monument to a man's endurance and skill. The fine old house, the extensive buildings, the great sweep of lush grass land along the lower slopes of the fell were all proof that old John Skipton had achieved the impossible; he had started as an uneducated farm labourer and he was now a wealthy landowner.

The miracle hadn't happened easily; old John had a lifetime of grinding toil behind him that would have killed most men, a lifetime with no room for a wife or family or creature comforts, but there was more to it than that; there was a brilliant acumen in agricultural matters that had made the old man a legend in the district. 'When all t'world goes one road, I go t'other' was one of his quoted sayings and it is true that the Skipton farms had made money in the hard times when others were going bankrupt. Dennaby was only one of John's farms; he had two large arable places of about 400 acres each lower down the Dale.

He had conquered, but to some people it seemed that he had himself been conquered in the process. He had battled against the odds for so many years and driven himself so fiercely that he couldn't stop. He could be enjoying all kinds of luxuries now but he just hadn't the time; they said that the poorest of his workers lived in better style than he did.

I paused as I got out of the car and stood gazing at the house as though I had never seen it before; and I marvelled again at the elegance which had withstood over three hundred years of the harsh climate. People came a long way to see Dennaby Close and take photographs of the graceful manor with its tall, leaded windows, the massive chimneys towering over the old moss-grown tiles; or to wander through the neglected garden and climb up the sweep of steps to the entrance with its wide stone arch over the great studded door.

There should have been a beautiful woman in one of those pointed hats peeping out from that mullioned casement or a cavalier in ruffles and hose pacing beneath the high wall with its pointed copings. But there was just old John stumping impatiently towards me, his tattered, buttonless coat secured only by a length of binder twine round his middle.

'Come in a minute, young man,' he cried. 'I've got a little bill to pay you.' He led the way round to the back of the house and I followed, pondering on the odd fact that it was always a 'little bill' in Yorkshire. We went in through a flagged kitchen to a room which was graceful and spacious but furnished only with a table, a few wooden chairs and a collapsed sofa.

The old man bustled over to the mantelpiece and fished out a bundle of papers from behind the clock. He leafed through them, threw an envelope on to the table then produced a cheque book and slapped it down in front of me. I did the usual – took out the bill, made out the amount on the cheque and pushed it over for him to sign. He wrote with a careful concentration, the small-featured, weathered face bent low, the peak of the old cloth cap almost touching the pen. His trousers had ridden up his legs as he sat down showing the skinny calves and bare ankles. There were no socks underneath the heavy boots.

When I had pocketed the cheque, John jumped to his feet. 'We'll have to walk down to t'river; 'osses are down there.' He left the house almost at a trot.

I eased my box of instruments from the car boot. It was a funny thing but whenever I had heavy equipment to lug about, my patients were always a long way away. This box seemed to be filled with lead and it wasn't going to get any lighter on the journey down through the walled pastures.

The old man seized a pitch fork, stabbed it into a bale of hay and hoisted it effortlessly over his shoulder. He set off again at the same brisk pace. We made our way down from one gateway to another, often walking diagonally across the fields. John didn't reduce speed and I stumbled after him, puffing a little and trying to put away the thought that he was at least fifty years older than me.

About half way down we came across a group of men at the age-old task of 'walling' – repairing a gap in one of the dry stone walls which trace their patterns everywhere on the green slopes of the Dales. One of the men looked up. 'Nice mornin', Mr Skipton,' he sang out cheerfully.

'Bugger t'mornin'. Get on wi' some work,' grunted old John in reply and the man smiled contentedly as though he had received a compliment.

I was glad when we reached the flat land at the bottom. My arms seemed to have been stretched by several inches and I could feel a trickle of sweat on my brow. Old John appeared unaffected; he flicked the fork from his shoulder and the bale thudded on to the grass.

The two horses turned towards us at the sound. They were standing fetlock deep in the pebbly shallows just beyond a little beach which merged into the green carpet of turf; nose to tail, they had been rubbing their chins gently along each other's back, unconscious of our approach. A high cliff overhanging the far bank made a perfect wind break while on either side of us clumps of oak and beech blazed in the autumn sunshine.

'They're in a nice spot, Mr Skipton,' I said.

'Aye, they can keep cool in the hot weather and they've got the barn when winter comes.' John pointed to a low, thick-walled building with a single door. 'They can come and go as they please.'

The sound of his voice brought the horses out of the river at a stiff trot

MAKING HAY CREELS Straight and slender hazel branches about 6 ft long were cut when they were still young and pliable for making the frames for creels. Each branch was bent, tied into an arch and kept like that for at least a year so that it would hold its shape. Then a pair of arches was set upright, about as far apart as the width of a man's shoulders, and tarred rope was wound and tied round the four branch ends to form a square. Ropes were knotted vertically and horizontally across each arch to make a network, and another mesh of ropes was made between the two arches.

SHEARS FOR HORSE'S TEETH If a horse grinds its teeth down unevenly when it chews its food, sharp spikes will be left on some teeth. These have to be cut off or they will damage the cheek or tongue, and may prevent the horse from eating properly. The vet needs steel shears to clip off the spike. He cannot force the blades together by hand, so while he holds them in place a helper turns the screw attached to the shear handles.

and as they came near you could see they really were old. The mare was a chestnut and the gelding was a light bay but their coats were so flecked with grey that they almost looked like roans. This was most pronounced on their faces where the sprinkling of white hairs, the sunken eyes and the deep cavity above the eyes gave them a truly venerable appearance.

For all that, they capered around John with a fair attempt at skittishness, stamping their feet, throwing their heads about, pushing his cap over his eyes with their muzzles.

'Get by, leave off!' he shouted. 'Daft awd beggars.' But he tugged absently at the mare's forelock and ran his hand briefly along the neck of the gelding.

'When did they last do any work?' I asked.

'Oh, about twelve years ago, I reckon.'

I stared at John. 'Twelve years! And have they been down here all that time?'

'Aye, just lakin' about down here, retired like. They've earned it an' all.' For a few moments he stood silent, shoulders hunched, hands deep in the pockets of his coat, then he spoke quietly as if to himself. 'They were two slaves when I was a slave.' He turned and looked at me and for a revealing moment I read in the pale blue eyes something of the agony and struggle he had shared with the animals.

'But twelve years! How old are they, anyway?'

John's mouth twisted up at one corner. 'Well you're t'vet. You tell me.'

I stepped forward confidently, my mind buzzing with Galvayne's groove, shape of marks, degree of slope and the rest; I grasped the unprotesting upper lip of the mare and looked at her teeth.

'Good God!' I gasped, 'I've never seen anything like this.' The incisors were immensely long and projecting forward till they met at an angle of about forty-five degrees. There were no marks at all – they had long since gone.

I laughed and turned back to the old man. 'It's no good, I'd only be guessing. You'll have to tell me.'

'Well she's about thirty and gelding's a year or two younger. She's had fifteen grand foals and never ailed owt except a bit of teeth trouble. We've had them rasped a time or two and it's time they were done again, I reckon. They're both losing ground and dropping bits of half chewed hay from their mouths. Gelding's the worst – has a right job champin' his grub.'

I put my hand into the mare's mouth, grasped her tongue and pulled it out to one side. A quick exploration of the molars with my other hand revealed what I suspected; the outside edges of the upper teeth were overgrown and jagged and were irritating the cheeks while the inside edges of the lower molars were in a similar state and were slightly excoriating the tongue.

'I'll soon make her more comfortable, Mr Skipton. With those sharp edges rubbed off she'll be as good as new.' I got the rasp out of my vast

142

box, held the tongue in one hand and worked the rough surface along the teeth, checking occasionally with my fingers till the points had been sufficiently reduced.

'That's about right,' I said after a few minutes. 'I don't want to make them too smooth or she won't be able to grind her food.'

John grunted. 'Good enough. Now have a look at t'other. There's summat far wrong with him.'

I had a feel at the gelding's teeth. 'Just the same as the mare. Soon put him right, too.'

But pushing at the rasp, I had an uncomfortable feeling that something was not quite right. The thing wouldn't go fully to the back of his mouth; something was stopping it. I stopped rasping and explored again, reaching with my fingers as far as I could. And I came upon something very strange, something which shouldn't have been there at all. It was like a great chunk of bone projecting down from the roof of the mouth.

It was time I had a proper look. I got out my pocket torch and shone it over the back of the tongue. It was easy to see the trouble now; the last upper molar was overlapping the lower one resulting in a gross overgrowth of the posterior border. The result was a sabre-like barb about three inches long stabbing down into the tender tissue of the gum.

That would have to come off – right now. My jauntiness vanished and I suppressed a shudder; it meant using the horrible shears – those great long-handled things with the screw operated by a cross bar. They gave me the willies because I am one of those people who can't bear to watch anybody blowing up a balloon and this was the same sort of thing only worse. You fastened the sharp blades of the shears on to the tooth and began to turn the bar slowly, slowly. Soon the tooth began to groan and creak under the tremendous leverage and you knew that any second it would break off and when it did it was like somebody letting off a rifle in your ear. That was when all hell usually broke loose but mercifully this was a quiet old horse and I wouldn't expect him to start dancing around on his hind legs. There was no pain for the horse because the overgrown part had no nerve supply – it was the noise that caused the trouble.

Returning to my crate I produced the dreadful instrument and with it a Haussman's gag which I inserted on the incisors and opened the ratchet till the mouth gaped wide. Everything was easy to see then, and, of course, there it was – a great prong at the other side of the mouth exactly like the first. Great, great, now I had two to chop off.

The old horse stood patiently, eyes almost closed, as though he had seen it all and nothing in the world was going to bother him. I went through the motions with my toes curling and when the sharp crack came, the white-bordered eyes opened wide, but only in mild surprise. He never even moved. When I did the other side he paid no attention at all; in fact, with the gag prising his jaws apart he looked exactly as though he was yawning with boredom.

As I bundled the tools away, John picked up the bony spicules from

143

CUTTING A TOOTH The vet holds the horse's mouth open with a metal-and-rubber gag. A screwed rod is turned to force the gag's jaws apart and a ratchet holds them open. One helper then steadies the horse's head while another stands by with the screw that will be used to force the shear blades together on the very hard tooth. The horse feels no pain, but may be upset by the noise.

the grass and studied them with interest. 'Well, poor awd beggar. Good job I got you along, young man. Reckon he'll feel a lot better now.'

On the way back, old John, relieved of his bale, was able to go twice as fast and he stumped his way up the hill at a furious pace, using the fork as a staff. I panted along in the rear, changing the box from hand to hand every few minutes.

About half way up, the thing slipped out of my grasp and it gave me a chance to stop for a breather. As the old man muttered impatiently I looked back and could just see the two horses; they had returned to the shallows and were playing together, chasing each other jerkily, their feet splashing in the water. The cliff made a dark backcloth to the picture – the shining river, the trees glowing bronze and gold and the sweet green of the grass.

Back in the farm yard, John paused awkwardly. He nodded once or twice, said 'Thank ye, young man,' then turned abruptly and walked away.

I was dumping the box thankfully into the boot when I saw the man who had spoken to us on the way down. He was sitting, cheerful as ever, in a sunny corner, back against a pile of sacks, pulling his dinner packet from an old army satchel.

'You've been down to see t'pensioners, then? By gaw, awd John should know the way.'

'Regular visitor, is he?'

'Regular? Every day God sends you'll see t'awd feller ploddin' down there. Rain, snow or blow, never misses. And allus has summat with him – bag o' corn, straw for their bedding.'

'And he's done that for twelve years?'

The man unscrewed his thermos flask and poured himself a cup of black tea. 'Aye, them 'osses haven't done a stroke o' work all that time and he could've got good money for them from the horse flesh merchants. Rum 'un, isn't it?'

'You're right,' I said, 'it is a rum 'un.'

Just how rum it was occupied my thoughts on the way back to the surgery. I went back to my conversation with Siegfried that morning; we had just about decided that the man with a lot of animals couldn't be expected to feel affection for individuals among them. But those buildings back there were full of John Skipton's animals – he must have hundreds.

Yet what made him trail down that hillside every day in all weathers? Why had he filled the last years of those two old horses with peace and beauty? Why had he given them a final ease and comfort which he had withheld from himself?

It could only be love.

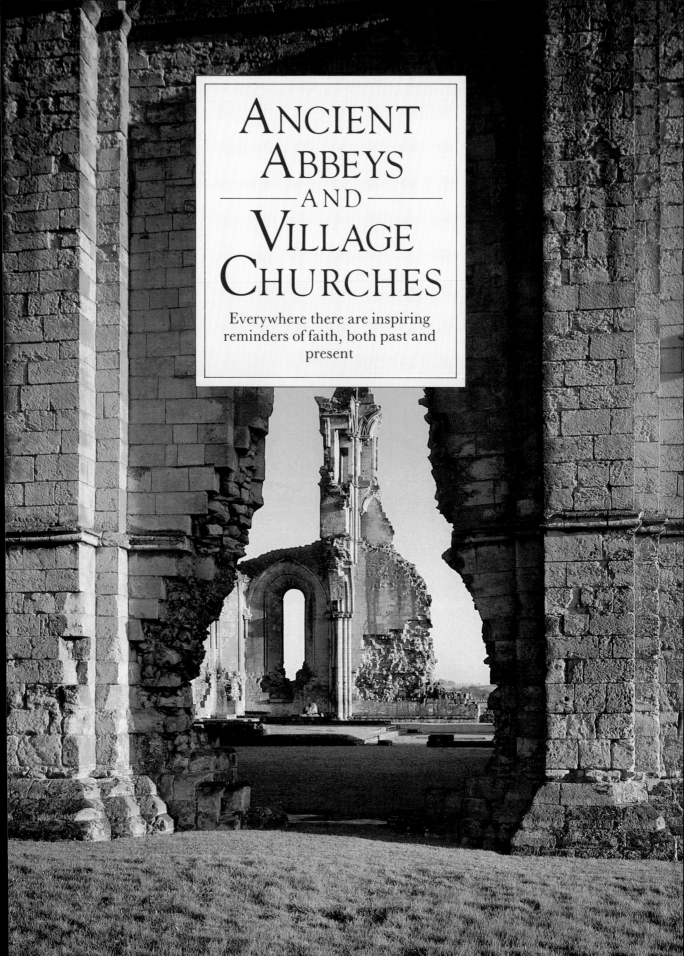

ANCIENT
ABBEYS
—AND—
VILLAGE
CHURCHES

Everywhere there are inspiring
reminders of faith, both past and
present

The sheltered spot where monks made their home

Near Coxwold in the Hambleton Hills, stand the noble ruins of Byland Abbey, warmly sheltered from the east wind by the hillside above Wass village. The Cistercian monks who built it in the 12th century originally settled in the village of Old Byland, high on the moors. But later they left that windswept spot for the greater comfort of the valley.

This glorious building once housed about 36 monks with probably 100 lay brethren.

It was at Byland that Edward II was resting in 1322 when an invading Scottish force fell upon his army and defeated it at Shaws Moor near by. Edward was forced to flee to York.

PAVED INTERIOR The abbey church was 330 ft long and 140 ft wide at the transepts. Practically all of this huge area was paved with green and yellow tiles, which still exist in two of the chapels (above). The whole interior was white-washed, with patterns on the walls picked out in red masonry.

Sublime ruins from an age of monastic riches

Yorkshire is rich in the dramatic ruins of mediaeval abbeys. The most historic is probably Whitby; the most beautiful are almost certainly Rievaulx and Fountains.

King Oswy of Northumbria, grateful for a military victory, built the first Whitby Abbey in AD 675. It was later rebuilt as a Benedictine monastery in the 11th century, on the same exposed cliff-top site, overlooking the cold North Sea.

Rievaulx and Fountains were both founded in the 1130s, nestling in river valleys out of the biting east wind. They housed monks of the Cistercian Order, who created self-sufficient communities through their skill as farmers. By the end of the 13th century, Fountains had acquired vast estates that stretched across the Yorkshire dales into Lancashire. It was the largest wool producer in the North, with a flock of 15,000 sheep.

Rievaulx, however, eventually fell into debt, and declined until it was dissolved by Henry VIII in 1538, leaving the most sublime monastic ruin in all of England.

RIEVAULX The stone-ribbed choir of Rievaulx Abbey was built in the 13th century, and remains as one of the most beautiful examples of Gothic architecture in England

FOUNTAINS A superb vaulted building, running for 300 ft along the cloisters at Fountains (above and right), contained the abbey's storehouse. It also housed the refectory, or dining room, for the uneducated monks known as lay brothers, 500 of whom did the manual work on the abbey's farms.

WHITBY The ruins of Whitby Abbey are from the third church on the site – the first Saxon, the second Norman, the third Gothic.

A church built as a tomb for a Saxon saint

A group of monks from Whitby Abbey moved, in 1078, to Lastingham, an already ancient village on the North York Moors. Their intention was to rebuild a ruined Saxon monastery, and they began with a crypt to house the sacred remains of St Cedd, the Saxon founder of the old monastery.

The monks abandoned their work to set up St Mary's Abbey at York, but their crypt remains, a church beneath a church. It has hardly been altered for nearly a thousand years, and to descend the few steps into it is to enter another age.

ANCIENT STONES The crypt at Lastingham was built less than 20 years after the Norman Conquest. It contains even older remains, including Saxon and Danish carvings.

WHERE SHEEP SAFELY GRAZE Sheep explore the green grass around the old gravestones at Lastingham church.

WENSLEY CHURCH Wensley was the capital of Wensleydale, until plague ravaged the population in 1563. It is now a village.

AYSGARTH CHURCH The stately church, founded in the 12th century, is set in trees by the River Ure.

19

If at first you don't succeed

'Could Mr Herriot see my dog, please?'

Familiar enough words coming from the waiting-room but it was the voice that brought me to a slithering halt just beyond the door.

It couldn't be, no of course it couldn't, but it sounded just like Helen. I tiptoed back and applied my eye without hesitation to the crack in the door. Tristan was standing there looking down at somebody just beyond my range of vision. All I could see was a hand resting on the head of a patient sheep dog, the hem of a tweed skirt and two silk stockinged legs.

They were nice legs – not skinny – and could easily belong to a big girl like Helen. My cogitations were cut short as a head bent over to speak to the dog and I had a close up in profile of the small straight nose and the dark hair falling across the milky smoothness of the cheek.

I was still peering, bemused, when Tristan shot out of the room and collided with me. Stifling an oath, he grabbed my arm and hauled me along the passage into the dispensary. He shut the door and spoke in a hoarse whisper.

'It's her! The Alderson woman! And she wants to see you! Not Siegfried, not me, but you, Mr Herriot himself!'

He looked at me wide-eyed for a few moments then, as I stood hesitating he opened the door and tried to propel me into the passage.

'What the hell are you waiting for?' he hissed.

'Well, it's a bit embarrassing, isn't it? After that dance, I mean. Last time she saw me I was a lovely sight – so pie-eyed I couldn't even speak.'

Tristan struck his forehead with his hand. 'God help us! You worry about details, don't you? She's asked to see you – what more do you want? Go on, get in there!'

I was shuffling off irresolutely when he raised a hand. 'Just a minute. Stay right there.' He trotted off and returned in a few seconds holding out a white lab coat.

'Just back from the laundry,' he said as he began to work my arms into the starched sleeves. 'You'll look marvellous in this, Jim – the immaculate young surgeon.'

I stood unresisting as he buttoned me into the garment but struck away his hand when he started to straighten my tie. As I left him he gave me a final encouraging wave before heading for the back stairs.

I didn't give myself any more time to think but marched straight into the waiting-room. Helen looked up and smiled. And it was just the same smile. Nothing behind it. Just the same friendly, steady-eyed smile as when I first met her.

We faced each other in silence for some moments then when I didn't

BORDER COLLIE The farmer's best friend is his working dog, and none is better than the tireless Border collie. It herds sheep and cattle not only to spoken and whistled commands, but with an uncanny initiative of its own. With a low, crouching run, it rounds up stragglers that are separated from the herd then, once they have been driven to the right spot, it presses its black and white, slightly shaggy body motionless on the ground and dominates the animals with an unwavering stare to hold them in place. The farmer's Border collie usually lives outside in the yard, tethered on a long rope to its kennel, and acts as guard dog between its periods of work.

say anything she looked down at the dog.

'It's Dan in trouble this time,' she said. 'He's our sheep dog but we're so fond of him that he's more like one of the family.'

The dog wagged his tail furiously at the sound of his name but yelped as he came towards me. I bent down and patted his head. 'I see he's holding up a hind leg.'

'Yes, he jumped over a wall this morning and he's been like that ever since. I think it's something quite bad – he can't put any weight on the leg.'

'Right bring him through to the other room and I'll have a look at him. But take him on in front of me, will you, and I'll be able to watch how he walks.'

I held the door open and she went through ahead of me with the dog.

Watching how Helen walked distracted me over the first few yards, but it was a long passage and by the time we had reached the second bend I managed to drag my attention back to my patient.

And glory be, it was a dislocated hip. It had to be with that shortening of the limb and the way he carried it underneath his body with the paw just brushing the ground.

My feelings were mixed. This was a major injury but on the other hand the chances were I could put it right quickly and look good in the process. Because I had found, in my brief experience, that one of the most spectacular procedures in practice was the reduction of a dislocated hip. Maybe I had been lucky, but with the few I had seen I had been able to convert an alarmingly lame animal into a completely sound one as though by magic.

In the operating room I hoisted Dan on to the table. He stood without moving as I examined the hip. There was no doubt about it at all – the head of the femur was displaced upwards and backwards, plainly palpable under my thumb.

The dog looked round only once – when I made a gentle attempt to flex the limb – but turned away immediately and stared resolutely ahead. His mouth hung open a little as he panted nervously but like a lot of the placid animals which arrived on our surgery table he seemed to have resigned himself to his fate. I had the strong impression that I could have started to cut his head off and he wouldn't have made much fuss.

'Nice, good-natured dog,' I said. 'And a bonny one, too.'

Helen patted the handsome head with the broad blaze of white down the face; the tail waved slowly from side to side.

'Yes,' she said. 'He's just as much a family pet as a working dog. I do hope he hasn't hurt himself too badly.'

'Well, he has a dislocated hip. It's a nasty thing but with a bit of luck I ought to be able to put it back.'

'What happens if it won't go back?'

'He'd have to form a false joint up there. He'd be very lame for several weeks and probably always have a slightly short leg.'

154

'Oh dear, I wouldn't like that,' Helen said. 'Do you think he'll be all right?'

I looked at the docile animal still gazing steadfastly to his front. 'I think he's got a good chance, mainly because you haven't hung about for days before bringing him in. The sooner these things are tackled the better.'

'Oh good. When will you be able to start on him?'

'Right now.' I went over to the door. 'I'll just give Tristan a shout. This is a two man job.'

'Couldn't I help?' Helen said. 'I'd very much like to if you wouldn't mind.'

I looked at her doubtfully. 'Well I don't know. You mightn't like playing tug of war with Dan in the middle. He'll be anaesthetised of course but there's usually a lot of pulling.'

Helen laughed. 'Oh, I'm quite strong. And not a bit squeamish. I'm used to animals, you know, and I like working with them.'

'Right,' I said. 'Slip on this spare coat and we'll begin.'

The dog didn't flinch as I pushed the needle into his vein and as the Nembutal flowed in, his head began to slump against Helen's arm and his supporting paw to slide along the smooth top of the table. Soon he was stretched unconscious on his side.

I held the needle in the vein as I looked down at the sleeping animal. 'I might have to give him a bit more. They have to be pretty deep to overcome the muscular resistance.'

Another cc. and Dan was as limp as any rag doll. I took hold of the affected leg and spoke across the table. 'I want you to link your hands underneath his thigh and try to hold him there when I pull. O.K.? Here we go, then.'

It takes a surprising amount of force to pull the head of a displaced femur over the rim of the acetabulum. I kept up a steady traction with my right hand, pressing on the head of the femur at the same time with my left. Helen did her part efficiently, leaning back against the pull, her lips pushed forward in a little pout of concentration.

I suppose there must be a foolproof way of doing this job – a method which works the very first time – but I have never been able to find it. Success has always come to me only after a fairly long period of trial and error and it was the same today. I tried all sorts of angles, rotations and twists on the flaccid limb, trying not to think of how it would look if this just happened to be the one I couldn't put back. I was wondering what Helen, still hanging on determinedly to her end, must be thinking of this wrestling match when I heard the muffled click. It was a sweet and welcoming sound.

I flexed the hip joint once or twice. No resistance at all now. The femoral head was once more riding smoothly in its socket.

'Well that's it,' I said. 'Hope it stays put – we'll have to keep our fingers crossed. The odd one does pop out again but I've got a feeling this is going to be all right.'

WOOL WEIGHTS Since the late 17th century, wool has been weighed in stones (standard 14 lb units). Farmers in the Yorkshire Dales literally used stones for weighing. They would collect boulders, have them weighed and marked and keep them in the barn. Here at clipping time the wrapped fleeces were weighed in the huge iron scales, at least 6 ft high, that were suspended from one of the building's beams. A typical dressed and ringed weighing boulder was 60 lb, and four times this weight made up a woolpack for one horse to carry to the local mill or wool merchant. During the Second World War, the government took over the selling and pricing of wool, which farmers had settled independently until then.

CARRYING A HILL SHEEP A shepherd walking the hills and moors to inspect his flock needs to take an ailing sheep back to the farm quickly without walking all the way back for transport. Slinging the animal across his shoulders and holding it firmly by the legs, he can carry it with him at once.

Helen ran her hand over the silky ears and neck of the sleeping dog. 'Poor old Dan. He wouldn't have jumped over that wall this morning if he'd known what was in store for him. How long will it be before he comes round?'

'Oh, he'll be out for the rest of the day. When he starts to wake up tonight I want you to be around to steady him in case he falls and puts the thing out again. Perhaps you'd give me a ring. I'd like to know how things are.'

I gathered Dan up in my arms and was carrying him along the passage, staggering under his weight, when I met Mrs Hall. She was carrying a tray with two cups.

'I was just having a drink of tea, Mr Herriot,' she said. 'I thought you and the young lady might fancy a cup.'

I looked at her narrowly. This was unusual. Was it possible she had joined Tristan in playing Cupid? But the broad, dark-skinned face was as unemotional as ever. It told me nothing.

'Well, thanks very much, Mrs Hall. I'll just put this dog outside first.' I went out and settled Dan on the back seat of Helen's car; with only his eyes and nose sticking out from under a blanket he looked at peace with the world.

Helen was already sitting with a cup in her lap and I thought of the other time I had drunk tea in this room with a girl. On the day I had arrived in Darrowby. She had been one of Siegfried's followers and surely the toughest of them all.

This was a lot different. During the struggle in the operating room I had been able to observe Helen at close range and I had discovered that her mouth turned up markedly at the corners as though she was just going to smile or had just been smiling; also that the deep warm blue of the eyes under the smoothly arching brows made a dizzying partnership with the rich black-brown of her hair.

And this time the conversation didn't lag. Maybe it was because I was on my own ground – perhaps I never felt fully at ease unless there was a sick animal involved somewhere, but at any rate I found myself prattling effortlessly just as I had done up on that hill when we had first met.

Mrs Hall's teapot was empty and the last of the biscuits gone before I finally saw Helen off and started on my round.

The same feeling of easy confidence was on me that night when I heard her voice on the phone.

'Dan is up and walking about,' she said. 'He's still a bit wobbly but he's perfectly sound on that leg.'

'Oh great, he's got the first stage over. I think everything's going to be fine.'

There was a pause at the other end of the line, then: 'Thank you so much for what you've done. We were terribly worried about him, especially my young brother and sister. We're very grateful.'

'Not at all, I'm delighted too. He's a grand dog.' I hesitated for a moment – it had to be now. 'Oh, you remember we were talking about

Scotland today. Well, I was passing the Plaza this afternoon and I see they're showing a film about the Hebrides. I thought maybe ... I wondered if perhaps, er ... you might like to come and see it with me.'

Another pause and my heart did a quick thud-thud.

'All right,' Helen said. 'Yes, I'd like that. When? Friday night? Well, thank you – goodbye till then.'

I replaced the receiver with a trembling hand. Why did I make such heavy weather of these things? But it didn't matter – I was back in business.

Tristan was unpacking the U.C.M.'s These bottles contained a rich red fluid which constituted our last line of defence in the battle with animal disease. Its full name, Universal Cattle Medicine, was proclaimed on the label in big black type and underneath it pointed out that it was highly efficacious for coughs, chills, scours, garget, milk fever, pneumonia, felon and bloat. It finished off on a confident note with the assurance: 'Never Fails to Give Relief' and we had read the label so often that we half believed it.

It was a pity it didn't do any good because there was something compelling about its ruby depths when you held it up to the light and about the solid camphor-ammonia jolt when you sniffed at it and which made the farmers blink and shake their heads and say 'By gaw, that's powerful stuff,' with deep respect. But our specific remedies were so few and the possibilities of error so plentiful that it was comforting in cases of doubt to be able to hand over a bottle of the old standby. Whenever an entry of Siegfried's or mine appeared in the day book stating 'Visit attend cow, advice, 1 U.C.M.' it was a pretty fair bet we didn't know what was wrong with the animal.

The bottles were tall and shapely and they came in elegant white cartons, so much more impressive than the unobtrusive containers of the antibiotics and steriods which we use today. Tristan was lifting them out of the tea chest and stacking them on the shelves in deep rows. When he saw me he ceased his labours, sat on the chest and pulled out a packet of Woodbines. He lit one, pulled the smoke a long way down and then fixed me with a non-committal stare.

'You're taking her to the pictures then?'

Feeling vaguely uneasy under his eye, I tipped a pocketful of assorted empties into the waste basket. 'Yes, that's right. In about an hour.'

'Mm.' He narrowed his eyes against the slowly escaping smoke. 'Mm, I see.'

'Well what are you looking like that for?' I said defensively. 'Anything wrong with going to the pictures?'

'No-no. No-no-no. Nothing at all, Jim. Nothing, nothing. A very wholesome pursuit.'

'But you don't think I should be taking Helen there.'

'I never said that. No, I'm sure you'll have a nice time. It's just that ...' He scratched his head. 'I thought you might have gone in

CORN DOLLIES Today's decorative plaited token is a relic of a primitive custom by which the goddess of harvest was honoured and won over. At harvest time when her spirit remained in only the last few standing stems of the crop, these were plaited into an image or idol (of which the term dolly seems to be a corruption). The dolly represented the goddess. It was kept safe in the farmhouse until spring, and then broken over the sown field to make the seed prosper. In recent years many different dollies have been evolved from the goddess figure – bells, horseshoes, spindles, sickles, lanterns and candlesticks, for example.

157

LEMON PUDDING Families who rose at dawn and did hard farm labour were ready for a hearty meal at mid-day. In winter a stew with vegetables and afterwards a filling pudding would restore a man for work until dusk. Cheap, sustaining and infinitely varied puddings were made with suet. Lemon gave a welcome, sharp flavour. The pudding would be tied in a cloth and boiled for at least two hours – and come to no harm if it was left to boil for much longer.

To make lemon pudding, grate the rind of a lemon into 2 oz of flour and mix in 2 oz of fine breadcrumbs, 4 oz of shredded suet and 2 oz of sugar. Work in 1 beaten egg, 2 tablespoons of syrup, the juice of the lemon and 5 tablespoons of milk. Mix thoroughly and turn into a buttered basin. Cover and steam for at least 2 hours. Turn out and serve with custard, cream or a sweetened, lemon-flavoured white sauce.

for something a bit more ... well ... enterprising.'

I gave a bitter laugh. 'Look, I tried enterprise at the Reniston. Oh, I'm not blaming you, Triss, you meant well, but as you know it was a complete shambles. I just don't want anything to go wrong tonight. I'm playing safe.'

'Well, I won't argue with you there,' Tristan said. 'You couldn't get much safer than the Darrowby Plaza.'

And later, shivering in the tub in the vast, draughty bathroom, I couldn't keep out the thought that Tristan was right. Taking Helen to the local cinema was a form of cowardice, a shrinking away from reality into what I hoped would be a safe, dark intimacy. But as I towelled myself, hopping about to keep warm, and looked out through the fringe of wistaria at the darkening garden there was comfort in the thought that it was another beginning, even though a small one.

And as I closed the door of Skeldale House and looked along the street to where the first lights of the shops beckoned in the dusk I felt a lifting of the heart. It was as though a breath from the near-by hills had touched me. A fleeting fragrance which said winter had gone. It was still cold – it was always cold in Darrowby until well into May – but the promise was there, of sunshine and warm grass and softer days.

You had to look closely or you could easily miss the Plaza, tucked in as it was between Pickersgills the ironmongers and Howarths the chemists. There had never been much attempt at grandeur in its architecture and the entrance was hardly wider than the average shop front. But what puzzled me as I approached was that the place was in darkness. I was in good time but the show was due to start in ten minutes or so and there was no sign of life.

I hadn't dared tell Tristan that my precautions had extended as far as arranging to meet Helen here. With a car like mine there was always an element of doubt about arriving anywhere in time or indeed at all and I had thought it prudent to eliminate all transport hazards.

'Meet you outside the cinema.' My God, it wasn't very bright was it? It took me back to my childhood, to the very first time I had taken a girl out. I was just fourteen and on my way to meet her I tendered my only half-crown to a bloody-minded Glasgow tram conductor and asked for a penny fare. He vented his spleen on me by ransacking his bag and giving me my change entirely in halfpennies. So when the cinema queue reached the pay box I had to stand there with my little partner and everybody else watching while I paid for our shilling tickets with great handfuls of copper. The shame of it left a scar – it was another four years before I took out a girl again.

But the black thoughts were dispelled when I saw Helen picking her way across the market-place cobbles. She smiled and waved cheerfully as if being taken to the Darrowby Plaza was the biggest treat a girl could wish for, and when she came right up to me there was a soft flush on her cheeks and her eyes were bright.

Everything was suddenly absolutely right. I felt a surging conviction that this was going to be a good night – nothing was going to spoil it. After we had said hello she told me that Dan was running about like a puppy with no trace of a limp and the news was another wave on the high tide of my euphoria.

The only thing that troubled me was the blank, uninhabited appearance of the cinema entrance.

'Strange there's nobody here,' I said. 'It's nearly starting time. I suppose the place is open?'

'Must be,' Helen said. 'It's open every night but Sunday. Anyway, I'm sure these people are waiting too.'

I looked around. There was no queue as such but little groups were standing here and there; a few couples, mostly middle-aged, a bunch of small boys rolling and fighting on the pavement. Nobody seemed worried.

And indeed there was no cause. Exactly two minutes before the picture was due to start a figure in a mackintosh coat pedalled furiously round the corner of the street, head down, legs pistoning, the bicycle lying over at a perilous angle with the ground. He came to a screeching halt outside the entrance, inserted a key in the lock and threw wide the doors. Reaching inside, he flicked a switch and a single neon strip flickered fitfully above our heads and went out. It did this a few times and seemed bent on mischief till he stood on tiptoe and beat it into submission with a masterful blow of his fist. Then he whipped off the mackintosh revealing faultless evening-dress. The manager had arrived.

While this was going on a very fat lady appeared from nowhere and wedged herself into the pay box. The show was ready to roll.

We all began to shuffle inside. The little boys put down their ninepences and punched each other as they passed through a curtain into the stalls, while the rest of us proceeded decorously upstairs to the one-and-sixpenny seats in the balcony. The manager, his white shirt front and silk lapels gleaming, smiled and bowed with great courtesy as we passed.

We paused at a row of pegs at the top of the stairs while some people hung up their coats. I was surprised to see Maggie Robinson the blacksmith's daughter there, taking the tickets, and she appeared to be intrigued by the sight of us. She simpered and giggled, darted glances at Helen and did everything but dig me in the ribs. Finally she parted the curtains and we went inside.

It struck me immediately that the management were determined that their patrons wouldn't feel cold because if it hadn't been for the all-pervading smell of old sofas we might have been plunging into a tropical jungle. Maggie steered us through the stifling heat to our places and as I sat down I noticed that there was no arm between the two seats.

'Them's the courting seats,' she blurted out and fled with her hand to her mouth.

The lights were still on and I looked round the tiny balcony. There were only about a dozen people dotted here and there sitting in patient

GOING TO THE PICTURES The self-sufficient, local world of Dalesfolk – most of their hours filled by farm work with a few leisure hours for home-made entertainment – was breached in the 1930s. The radio brought national entertainment into the home and the cinema brought international entertainment to the local towns. In the suburbs and towns around Leeds there were more than 30 cinemas in the late 1930s. It was an occasional rather than a regular treat for village dwellers to go to the cinema, but once there they saw William Powell, Jeanette MacDonald, Spencer Tracey, Clark Gable, Irene Dunne or Shirley Temple, and shared in a popular culture that was attracting 200 million people a week worldwide by the 1940s.

silence under the plain distempered walls. By the side of the screen the hands of a clock stood resolutely at twenty-past four.

But it was all right sitting there with Helen. I felt fine except for a tendency to gasp like a goldfish in the airless atmosphere. I was settling down cosily when a little man seated in front of us with his wife turned slowly round. The mouth in the haggard face was pursed grimly and he fixed his eyes on mine in a long, challenging stare. We faced each other for several silent moments before he finally spoke.

'She's dead,' he said.

A thrill of horror shot through me. 'Dead?'

'Aye, she is. She's dead.' He dragged the word out slowly with a kind of mournful satisfaction while his eyes still stared into mine.

I swallowed a couple of times. 'Well, I'm sorry to hear that. Truly sorry.'

He nodded grimly and continued to regard me with a peculiar intensity as though he expected me to say more. Then with apparent reluctance he turned away and settled in his seat.

I looked helplessly at the rigid back, at the square, narrow shoulders muffled in a heavy overcoat. Who in God's name was this? And what

was he talking about? I knew the face from somewhere – must be a client. And what was dead? Cow? Ewe? Sow? My mind began to race over the cases I had seen during the past week but the face didn't seem to fit in anywhere.

Helen was looking at me questioningly and I managed a wan smile. But the spell was shattered. I started to say something to her when the little man began to turn again with menacing deliberation.

A figure in a mackintosh coat
pedalled furiously round the corner
of the street.

161

He fixed me once more with a hostile glare. 'Ah don't think there was ever owt wrong with her stomach,' he declared.

'You don't, eh?'

'No, young man, ah don't.' He dragged his eyes unwillingly from my face and turned towards the screen again.

The effect of this second attack was heightened because the lights went off suddenly and an incredible explosion of noise blasted my ear drums. It was the Gaumont News. The sound machine, like the heating system, had apparently been designed for something like the Albert Hall and for a moment I cowered back under the assault. As a voice bellowed details of fortnight-old events I closed my eyes and tried again to place the man in front of me.

I often had trouble identifying people outside their usual environment and had once discussed the problem with Siegfried.

He had been airy. 'There's an easy way, James. Just ask them how they spell their names. You'll have no trouble at all.'

I had tried this on one occasion and the farmer had looked at me strangely, replied 'S-M-I-T-H' and hurried away. So there seemed nothing to do now but sit sweating with my eyes on the disapproving back and search through my memory. When the news finished with a raucous burst of music I had got back about three weeks without result.

There was a blessed respite of a few seconds before the uproar broke out again. This was the main feature – the film about Scotland was on later – and was described outside as a tender love story. I can't remember the title but there was a lot of embracing which would have been all right except that every kiss was accompanied by a chorus of long-drawn sucking noises from the little boys downstairs. The less romantic blew raspberries.

And all the time it got hotter. I opened my jacket wide and unbuttoned my shirt collar but I was beginning to feel decidedly light-headed. The little man in front, still huddled in his heavy coat, seemed unperturbed. Twice the projector broke down and we stared for several minutes at a blank screen while a storm of whistling and stamping came up from the stalls.

Maggie Robinson, standing in the dim light by the curtain, still appeared to be fascinated by the sight of Helen and me. Whenever I looked up I found her eyes fixed upon us with a knowing leer. About half-way through the film, however, her concentration was disturbed by a commotion on the other side of the curtain and she was suddenly brushed aside as a large form burst through.

With a feeling of disbelief I recognised Gobber Newhouse. I had had previous experience of his disregard of the licensing laws and it was clear he had been at it again. He spent most afternoons in the back rooms of the local pubs and here he was, come to relax after a rough session.

He reeled up the aisle, turned, to my dismay, into our row, rested briefly on Helen's lap, trod on my toe and finally spread his enormous carcass over the seat on my left. Fortunately it was another courting seat

THE HORSE-DEALER This was the business card of John Dickinson, a Yorkshire horse-dealer who died in 1938. He travelled all over the country and sometimes abroad. He undertook commissions to find any type of horse for agricultural or town use, broke in young horses, and usually kept eight or nine horses that were for immediate sale.

JOHN DICKINSON,
COMMISSION ◆ AGENT,
AND
Dealer in Horses,
17½, Ogleforth, York.
Telegrams receive prompt attention.

162

with no central arm rest to get in his way but for all that he had great difficulty in finding a comfortable position. He heaved and squirmed about and the wheezing and snuffling and grunting in the darkness might have come from a pen of bacon pigs. But at last he found a spot and with a final cavernous belch composed himself for slumber.

The tender love story never did have much of a chance but Gobber sounded its death knell. With his snores reverberating in my ear and a dense pall of stale beer drifting over me I was unable to appreciate any of the delicate nuances.

It was a relief when the last close-up came to an end and the lights went up. I was a bit worried about Helen. I had noticed as the evening wore on that her lips had a tendency to twitch occasionally and now and then she drew her brows down in a deep frown. I wondered if she was upset. But Maggie appeared providentially with a tray round her neck and stood over us, still leering, while I purchased two chocolate ices.

I had taken only one bite when I noticed a stirring under the overcoat in front of me. The little man was returning to the attack. The eyes staring from the grim mask were as chilling as ever.

'Ah knew,' he said. 'Right from start, that you were on the wrong track.'

'Is that so?'

'Aye, I've been among beasts for fifty years and they never go on like that when it's the stomach.'

'Don't they? You're probably right.'

The little man twisted higher in his seat and for a moment I thought he was going to climb over at me. He raised a forefinger. 'For one thing a beast wi' a bad stomach is allus hard in its muck.'

'I see.'

'And if you think back, this un's muck was soft, real soft.'

'Yes, yes, quite,' I said hastily, glancing across at Helen. This was great – just what I needed to complete the romantic atmosphere.

He sniffed and turned away and once again, as if the whole thing had been stage-managed, we were plunged into blackness and the noise blasted out again. I was lying back quivering when it came through to me that something was wrong. What was this strident Western music? Then the title flashed on the screen. Arizona Guns.

I turned to Helen in alarm. 'What's going on? This is supposed to be the Scottish film, isn't it? The one we came to see?'

'It's supposed to be.' Helen paused and looked at me with a half-smile. 'But I'm afraid it isn't going to be. The thing is they often change the supporting film without warning. Nobody seems to mind.'

I slumped wearily in my seat. Well I'd done it again. No dance at the Reniston, wrong picture tonight. I was a genius in my own way.

'I'm sorry,' I said. 'I hope you don't mind too much.'

She shook her head. 'Not a bit. Anyway, let's give this one a chance. It may be all right.'

But as the ancient horse opera crackled out its cliché-ridden message I

MIDDLEHAM SWINE CROSS
Standing in the Upper Market Place of Middleham is the Old Swine Cross. It marks the site where a market was held from 1388, when Ralph Neville obtained a market charter from his cousin Richard II. At the back of the cross are carved two beasts which may represent bears, emblem of the earls of Warwick. Middleham has a second market place, also with an old cross. The small town of steep streets on the slopes of Wensleydale was a centre of importance in the 14th century. Warwick 'the Kingmaker', head of the Neville family and the country's most powerful nobleman during the Wars of the Roses, had his stronghold there.

MAKING HAY PIKES Hay dragged to the field corner by a horse-drawn sweep or sled was stacked into circular pikes, straight-sided to a height of about 4 ft and then domed. So that it would throw off rain-water, the dome was well 'combed' with a rake to give it a smooth finish with the stalks of hay pointing down towards the base. Once the pikes were built, strands of hay were drawn out from the base with a twisting action that formed a rope. The rope was cast over the dome and secured by a stone on the other side.

gave up hope. This was going to be another of those evenings. I watched apathetically as the posse galloped for the fourth time past the same piece of rock and I was totally unprepared for the deafening fusillade of shots which rang out. It made me jump and it even roused Gobber from his sleep.

''Ellow! 'ellow! 'ellow!' he bawled jerking upright and thrashing around him with his arms. A backhander on the side of the head drove me violently against Helen's shoulder and I was beginning to apologise when I saw that her twitching and frowning had come on again. But this time it spread and her whole faced seemed to break up. She began to laugh, silently and helplessly.

I had never seen a girl laugh like this. It was as though it was something she had wanted to do for a long time. She abandoned herself utterly to it, lying back with her head on the back of the seat, legs stretched out in front of her, arms dangling by her side. She took her time and waited until she had got it all out of her system before she turned to me.

She put her hand on my arm. 'Look,' she said faintly. 'Next time, why don't we just go for a walk?'

I settled down. Gobber was asleep again and his snores, louder than ever, competed with the bangs and howls from the screen. I still hadn't the slightest idea who that little man in front could be and I had the feeling he wasn't finished with me yet. The clock still stood at twenty-past four. Maggie was still staring at us and a steady trickle of sweat ran down my back.

The environment wasn't all I could have desired, but never mind. There was going to be a next time.

PART TWO
The vet finds a wife

This was my second spring in the Dales: the din of
the lambing pens, the bass rumble of the ewes and the
high, insistent bawling of the lambs. This, for me, has
always heralded the end of winter and the beginning
of something new.

1

A tactful remedy

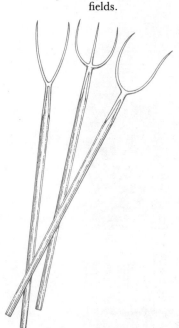

FARM FORKS Local blacksmiths at one time made all the iron heads of the various forks farmers needed, and fitted them on shafts prepared by joiners. By the 1930s, markets and agricultural supply shops sold factory-made tools. The pitchfork (left) had a long handle – about 6 ft – and was for forking hay from field to wagon and from wagon to stack or hayloft. The straw fork (right) was for spreading straw bedding for the animals. A farmer might have one or other of these forks and use it for many different tasks. Sometimes the prongs were blunted for safety. The three-pronged fork (centre) was used for spreading manure in the fields.

'Them masticks,' said Mr Pickersgill judicially, 'is a proper bugger.'

I nodded my head in agreement that his mastitis problem was indeed giving cause for concern; and reflected at the same time that while most farmers would have been content with the local word 'felon' it was typical that Mr Pickersgill should make a determined if somewhat inaccurate attempt at the scientific term.

Sometimes he got very wide of the mark as one time long after this when Artificial Insemination or A.I. was gaining a foothold in the Dales he made my day by telling me he had a cow in calf to the I.C.I.

However he usually did better than this – most of his efforts were near misses or bore obvious evidence of their derivation – but I could never really fathom where he got the masticks. I did know that once he fastened on to an expression it never changed; mastitis had always been 'them masticks' with him and it always would be. And I knew, too, that nothing would ever stop him doggedly trying to be right.

Because Mr Pickersgill had what he considered to be a scholastic background. He was a man of about sixty and when in his teens he had attended a two-week course of instruction for agricultural workers at Leeds University. This brief glimpse of the academic life had left an indelible impression on his mind, and it was as if the intimation of something deep and true behind the facts of his everyday work had kindled a flame in him which had illumined his subsequent life.

No capped and gowned don ever looked back to his years among the spires of Oxford with more nostalgia than did Mr Pickersgill to his fortnight at Leeds, and his conversation was usually laced with references to a godlike Professor Malleson who had apparently been in charge of the course.

'Ah don't know what to make of it,' he continued. 'In ma college days I was allus told that you got a big swollen bag and dirty milk with them masticks but this must be another kind. Just little bits of flakes in the milk off and on – neither nowt nor something, but I'm right fed up with it, I'll tell you.'

I took a sip from the cup of tea which Mrs Pickersgill had placed in front of me on the kitchen table. 'Yes, it's very worrying the way it keeps going on and on. I'm sure there's a definite factor behind it all – I wish I could put my finger on it.'

But in fact I had a good idea what was behind it. I had happened in at the little byre late one afternoon when Mr Pickersgill and his daughter Olive were milking their ten cows. I had watched the two at work as they crouched under the row of roan and red backs, and one thing was immediately obvious; while Olive drew the milk by almost imperceptible movements of her fingers and with a motionless wrist, her father hauled away at the teats as though he was trying to ring in the new year.

This insight coupled with the fact that it was always the cows Mr Pickersgill milked that gave trouble was enough to convince me that the chronic mastitis was of traumatic origin.

But how to tell the farmer that he wasn't doing his job right and that the only solution was to learn a more gentle technique or let Olive take over all the milking?

It wouldn't be easy because Mr Pickersgill was an impressive man. I don't suppose he had a spare penny in the world, but even as he sat there in the kitchen in his tattered, collarless flannel shirt and braces he looked, as always, like an industrial tycoon. You could imagine that massive head with its fleshy cheeks, noble brow and serene eyes looking out from the financial pages of *The Times*. Put him in a bowler and striped trousers and you'd have the perfect chairman of the board.

I was very chary of affronting such natural dignity and anyway, Mr Pickersgill was fundamentally a fine stocksman. His few cows, like all the animals of that fast-dying breed of small farmer, were fat and sleek and clean. You had to look after your beasts when they were your only source of income and somehow Mr Pickersgill had brought up a family by milk production eked out by selling a few pigs and the eggs from his wife's fifty hens.

I could never quite work out how they did it but they lived, and they lived graciously. All the family but Olive had married and left home but there was still a rich decorum and harmony in that house. The present scene was typical. The farmer expounding gravely, Mrs Pickersgill bustling about in the background, listening to him with quiet pride. Olive too, was happy. Though in her late thirties, she had no fears of spinsterhood because she had been assiduously courted for fifteen years by Charlie Hudson from the Darrowby fish shop and though Charlie was not a tempestuous suitor there was nothing flighty about him and he was confidently expected to pop the question over the next ten years or so.

Mr Pickersgill offered me another buttered scone and when I declined he cleared his throat a few times as though trying to find words. 'Mr Herriot,' he said at last, 'I don't like to tell nobody his job, but we've tried all your remedies for them masticks and we've still got trouble. Now when I studied under Professor Malleson I noted down a lot of good cures and I'd like to try this 'un. Have a look at it.'

He put his hand in his hip pocket and produced a yellowed slip of paper almost falling apart at the folds. 'It's an udder salve. Maybe if we gave the bags a good rub with it it'd do t'trick.'

I read the prescription in the fine copperplate writing. Camphor, eucalyptus, zinc oxide – a long list of the old familiar names. I couldn't help feeling a kind of affection for them but it was tempered by a growing disillusion. I was about to say that I didn't think rubbing anything on

TURF CAKES Before every kitchen had its own oven, cooking was done over a fire. Meat was roasted on a spit or simmered in a cauldron, and oatbread and scones were baked on a griddle. Turf cakes were cooked in a large, flat, iron pan over a turf fire with hot turves piled on the lid to give extra heat. By about 1900, turf cakes were sweetened with sugar and dried fruit and were being cooked in ovens.
To make about 24 turf cakes, add a pinch of salt to 8 oz of self-raising flour and rub in 4 oz of lard. Mix in 3 oz of sugar, 2 oz of currants and 1 oz of sultanas. Mix to a soft dough with combined milk and water. Roll out to ½ in. thick and cut into 2 in. rounds. Bake on a greased baking sheet for 15 minutes at 400°F (200°C), gas mark 6.

MILK FOR THE CHEESE FACTORY
Wensleydale Dairy Products,
one of the Dales cheese-making
factories of the late 1930s,
collected a daily total of 500
gallons of milk from many
small farmers. The farmers
took their full churns to the
nearest road and stood them
high on a stone or wooden
platform at the roadside so that
the lorry driver could drag
them aboard without lifting.

the udder would make the slightest difference when the farmer groaned loudly.

The action of reaching into his hip pocket had brought on a twinge of his lumbago and he sat very upright, grimacing with pain.

'This bloody old back of mine! By gaw, it does give me some stick, and doctor can't do nowt about it. I've had enough pills to make me rattle but ah get no relief.'

I'm not brilliant but I do get the odd blinding flash and I had one now.

'Mr Pickersgill,' I said solemnly, 'you've suffered from that lumbago ever since I've known you and I've just thought of something. I believe I know how to cure it.'

The farmer's eyes widened and he stared at me with a childlike trust in which there was no trace of scepticism. This could be expected, because just as people place more reliance on the words of knacker men and meal travellers than their vets' when their animals are concerned it was natural that they would believe the vet rather than their doctor with their own ailments.

'You know how to put me right?' he said faintly.

'I think so, and it has nothing to do with medicine. You'll have to stop milking.'

'Stop milking! What the 'ell ...?'

'Of course. Don't you see, it's sitting crouched on that little stool night and morning every day of the week that's doing it. You're a big chap and you've got to bend to get down there – I'm sure it's bad for you.'

Mr Pickersgill gazed into space as though he had seen a vision. 'You really think ...'

'Yes, I do. You ought to give it a try, anyway. Olive can do the milking. She's always saying she ought to do it all.'

'That's right, Dad,' Olive chimed in. 'I like milking, you know I do, and it's time you gave it up – you've done it ever since you were a lad.'

'Dang it, young man, I believe you're right! I'll pack it in, now – I've made my decision!' Mr Pickersgill threw up his fine head, looked imperiously around him and crashed his fist on the table as though he had just concluded a merger between two oil companies.

I stood up, 'Fine, fine. I'll take this prescription with me and make up the udder salve. It'll be ready for you tonight and I should start using it immediately.'

It was about a month later that I saw Mr Pickersgill. He was on a bicycle, pedalling majestically across the market place and he dismounted when he saw me.

'Now then, Mr Herriot,' he said, puffing slightly. 'I'm glad I've met you. I've been meaning to come and tell you that we don't have no flakes in the milk now. Ever since we started with t'salve they began to disappear and milk's as clear as it can be now.'

'Oh, great. And how's your lumbago?'

'Well I'll tell you, you've really capped it and I'm grateful. Ah've

168

never milked since that day and I hardly get a twinge now.' He paused and smiled indulgently. 'You gave me some good advice for me back, but we had to go back to awd Professor Malleson to cure them masticks, didn't we?'

My next encounter with Mr Pickersgill was on the telephone.

'I'm speaking from the cossack,' he said in a subdued shout.

'From the what?'

'The cossack, the telephone cossack in t'village.'

'Yes, indeed,' I said, 'and what can I do for you?'

'I want you to come out as soon as possible, to treat a calf for semolina.'

'I beg your pardon?'

'I 'ave a calf with semolina.'

'Semolina?'

'Aye, that's right. A feller was on about it on t'wireless the other morning.'

'Oh! Ah yes, I see.' I too had heard a bit of the farming talk on Salmonella infection in calves. 'What makes you think you've got this trouble?'

'Well it's just like that feller said. Me calf's bleeding from the rectrum.'

'From the . . . ? Yes, yes, of course. Well I'd better have a look at him – I won't be long.'

The calf was pretty ill when I saw him and he did have rectal bleeding, but it wasn't like Salmonella.

'There's no diarrhoea, you see, Mr Pickersgill,' I said. 'In fact, he seems to be constipated. This is almost pure blood coming away from him. And he hasn't got a very high temperature.'

The farmer seemed a little disappointed. 'Dang, I thowt it was just same as that feller was talking about. He said you could send samples off to the labrador.'

'Eh? To the what?'

'The investigation labrador – you know.'

'Oh yes, quite, but I don't think the lab would be of any help in this case.'

'Aye well, what's wrong with him, then? Is something the matter with his rectrum?'

'No, no,' I said. 'But there seems to be some obstruction high up his bowel which is causing this haemorrhage.' I looked at the little animal standing motionless with his back up. He was totally preoccupied with some internal discomfort and now and then he strained and grunted softly.

And of course I should have known straight away – it was so obvious. But I suppose we all have blind spells when we can't see what is pushed in front of our eyes, and for a few days I played around with that calf in a haze of ignorance, giving it this and that medicine which I'd rather not

SCREW-PRESS FOR CHEESE To make cheese, milk is first curdled with rennet – an acid liquid prepared from a calf's stomach. The curds are strained and then crumbled into a vat to drain. Afterwards they are pressed. This press from Ryedale exerts force on the cheese by means of a screw-down sinker-board. The vat, about 10 in. across, is made of oak strips held by three iron hoops and pierced by holes for the whey to drain out. The screw that forces down the sinker is threaded through the arched iron crossbar.

LARGE BLACK BOAR The original
Large Blacks came from south-
west England and East Anglia,
but the breed was widespread
all over England in the early
1900s. One of its virtues was its
extremely docile nature, which
meant that it could be safely
put out in the fields. It is
entirely black with ears
drooping forwards, right over
the eyes. It is a hardy breed
that matures early for both
bacon and pork.

talk about.

But I was lucky. He recovered in spite of my treatment. It wasn't until
Mr Pickersgill showed me the little roll of necrotic tissue which the calf
had passed that the thing dawned on me.

I turned, shamefaced, to the farmer. 'This is a bit of dead bowel all
telescoped together – an intussusception. It's usually a fatal condition
but fortunately in this case the obstruction has sloughed away and your
calf should be all right now.'

'What was it you called it?'

'An intussusception.'

Mr Pickersgill's lips moved tentatively and for a moment I thought he
was going to have a shot at it. But he apparently decided against it. 'Oh,'
he said. 'That's what it was, was it?'

'Yes, and it's difficult to say just what caused it.'

The farmer sniffed. 'I'll bet I know what was behind it. I always said
this one 'ud be a weakly calf. When he was born he bled a lot from his
biblical cord.'

Mr Pickersgill hadn't finished with me yet. It was only a week later that
I heard him on the phone again.

'Get out here, quick. There's one of me pigs going bezique.'

'Bezique?' With an effort I put away from me a mental picture of two
porkers facing each other over a green baize table. 'I'm afraid I don't
quite . . .'

'Aye, ah gave him a dose of worm medicine and he started jumpin'
about and rollin' on his back. I tell you he's going proper bezique.'

'Ah! Yes, yes I see, right. I'll be with you in a few minutes.'

The pig had quietened down a bit when I arrived but was still in
considerable pain, getting up, lying down, trotting in spurts round the
pen. I gave him half a grain of morphine hydrochloride as a sedative and
within a few minutes he began to relax and finally curled up in the straw.

'Looks as though he's going to be all right,' I said. 'But what's this
worm medicine you gave him?'

Mr Pickersgill produced the bottle sheepishly.

'Bloke was coming round sellin' them. Said it would shift any worms
you cared to name.'

'It nearly shifted your pig, didn't it?' I sniffed at the mixture. 'And no
wonder. It smells almost like pure turpentine.'

'Turpentine! Well by gaw is that all it is? And bloke said it was
summat new. Charged me an absorbent price for it too.'

I gave him back the bottle. 'Well never mind, I don't think there's any
harm done, but I think the dustbin's the best place for that.'

As I was getting into my car I looked up at the farmer. 'You must be
about sick of the sight of me. First the mastitis, then the calf and now
your pig. You've had a bad run.'

Mr Pickersgill squared his shoulders and gazed at me with massive
composure. Again I was conscious of the sheer presence of the man.

'Young feller,' he said. 'That don't bother me. Where there's stock there's trouble and ah know from experience that trouble allus comes in cyclones.'

2

Making an impression

'Well, it's a good sign.' Tristan reluctantly expelled a lungful of Woodbine smoke and looked at me with wide, encouraging eyes.

'You think so?' I said doubtfully.

Tristan nodded. 'Sure of it. Helen just rang you up, did she?'

'Yes, out of the blue. I haven't seen her since I took her to the pictures that night and it's been hectic ever since with the lambing – and suddenly there she was asking me to tea on Sunday.'

'I like the sound of it,' Tristan said. 'But of course you don't want to get the idea you're home and dry or anything like that. You know there are others in the field?'

'Hell, yes, I suppose I'm one of a crowd.'

'Not exactly, but Helen Alderson is really something. Not just a looker but ... mm-mm, very nice. There's a touch of class about that girl.'

'Oh I know, I know. There's bound to be a mob of blokes after her. Like young Richard Edmundson – I hear he's very well placed.'

'That's right,' Tristan said. 'Old friends of the family, big farmers, rolling in brass. I understand old man Alderson fancies Richard strongly as a son-in-law.'

I dug my hands into my pockets. 'Can't blame him. A ragged-arsed young vet isn't much competition.'

'Well, don't be gloomy, old lad, you've made a bit of progress, haven't you?'

'In a way,' I said with a wry smile. 'I've taken her out twice – to a dinner dance which wasn't on and to a cinema showing the wrong film. A dead loss the first time and not much better the second. I just don't seem to have any luck there – something goes wrong every time. Maybe this invitation is just a polite gesture – returning hospitality or something like that.'

'Nonsense!' Tristan laughed and patted me on the shoulder. 'This is the beginning of better things. You'll see – nothing will go wrong this time.'

And on Sunday afternoon as I got out of the car to open the gate to Heston Grange it did seem as if all was right with the world. The rough track snaked down from the gate through the fields to Helen's home

THE CULTIVATOR Before seeds are sown on the ploughed land, the furrows have to be broken down into a finer, more crumbly texture. The tractor is pulling a five-pronged cultivator which acts as a giant rake, crumbling the soil and at the same time uprooting weeds. The handle within reach of the tractor driver raises and lowers the cultivator's prongs. Sometimes a harrow is used instead of or after the cultivator. The harrow does the same work but does not penetrate the soil as deeply as a cultivator.

slumbering in the sunshine by the curving river, and the grey-stoned old building was like a restful haven against the stark backcloth of the fells beyond.

I leaned on the gate for a moment, breathing in the sweet air. There had been a change during the last week; the harsh winds had dropped, everything had softened and greened and the warming land gave off its scents. On the lower slopes of the fell, in the shade of the pine woods, a pale mist of bluebells drifted among the dead bronze of the bracken and their fragrance came up to me on the breeze.

I drove down the track among the cows relishing the tender young grass after their long winter in the byres and as I knocked on the farmhouse door I felt a surge of optimism and well-being. Helen's younger sister answered and it wasn't until I walked into the big flagged kitchen that I experienced a qualm. Maybe it was because it was so like that first disastrous time I had called for Helen; Mr Alderson was there by the fireside, deep in the *Farmer and Stockbreeder* as before, while above his head the cows in the vast oil painting still paddled in the lake of startling blue under the shattered peaks. On the whitewashed wall the clock still tick-tocked inexorably.

Helen's father looked up over his spectacles just as he had done before. 'Good afternoon, young man, come and sit down.' And as I dropped into the chair opposite to him he looked at me uncertainly for a few seconds. 'It's a better day,' he murmured, then his eyes were drawn back irresistibly to the pages on his knee. As he bent his head and started to read again I gained the strong impression that he hadn't the slightest idea who I was.

It came back to me forcibly that there was a big difference in coming to a farm as a vet and visiting socially. I was often in farm kitchens on my rounds, washing my hands in the sink after kicking my boots off in the porch, chatting effortlessly to the farmer's wife about the sick beast. But here I was in my good suit sitting stiffly across from a silent little man whose daughter I had come to court. It wasn't the same at all.

I was relieved when Helen came in carrying a cake which she placed on the big table. This wasn't easy as the table was already loaded; ham and egg pies rubbing shoulders with snowy scones, a pickled tongue cheek by jowl with a bowl of mixed salad, luscious-looking custard tarts jockeying for position with sausage rolls, tomato sandwiches, fairy cakes. In a clearing near the centre a vast trifle reared its cream-topped head. It was a real Yorkshire tea.

Helen came over to me. 'Hello, Jim, it's nice to see you – you're quite a stranger.' She smiled her slow, friendly smile.

'Hello, Helen. Yes, you know what lambing time's like. I hope things will ease up a bit now.'

'Well I hope so too. Hard work's all right up to a point but you need a break some time. Anyway, come and have some tea. Are you hungry?'

'I am now,' I said, gazing at the packed foodstuffs. Helen laughed. 'Well come on, sit in. Dad, leave your precious *Farmer and Stockbreeder* and come over here. We were going to sit you in the dining room, Jim, but Dad won't have his tea anywhere but in here, so that's all about it.'

I took my place along with Helen, young Tommy and Mary her brother and sister, and Auntie Lucy, Mr Alderson's widowed sister who had recently come to live with the family. Mr Alderson groaned his way over the flags, collapsed on to a high-backed wooden chair and began to saw phlegmatically at the tongue.

As I accepted my laden plate I can't say I felt entirely at ease. In the course of my work I had eaten many meals in the homes of the hospitable Dalesmen and I had discovered that light chatter was not welcomed at table. The accepted thing, particularly among the more old-fashioned types, was to put the food away in silence and get back on the job, but maybe this was different. Sunday tea might be a more social occasion; I looked round the table, waiting for somebody to lead the way.

Helen spoke up. 'Jim's had a busy time among the sheep since we saw him last.'

'Oh yes?' Auntie Lucy put her head on one side and smiled. She was a little bird-like woman, very like her brother, and the way she looked at me made me feel she was on my side.

The young people regarded me fixedly with twitching mouths. The only other time I had met them they had found me an object of some

Mr Alderson collapsed on to a high-backed wooden chair and began to saw phlegmatically at the tongue.

amusement and things didn't seem to have changed. Mr Alderson sprinkled some salt on a radish, conveyed it to his mouth and crunched it impassively.

'Did you have much twin lamb disease this time, Jim?' Helen asked, trying again.

'Quite a bit,' I replied brightly. 'Haven't had much luck with treatment, though. I tried dosing the ewes with glucose this year and I think it did a bit of good.'

Mr Alderson swallowed the last of his radish. 'I think nowt to glucose,' he grunted. 'I've had a go with it and I think nowt to it.'

'Really?' I said. 'Well now that's interesting. Yes ... yes ... quite.'

I buried myself in my salad for a spell before offering a further contribution.

'There's been a lot of sudden deaths in the lambs,' I said. 'Seems to be more Pulpy Kidney about.'

'Fancy that,' said Auntie Lucy, smiling encouragingly.

'Yes,' I went on, getting into my stride. 'It's a good job we've got a vaccine against it now.'

'Wonderful things, those vaccines,' Helen chipped in. 'You'll soon be able to prevent a lot of the sheep diseases that way.' The conversation was warming up.

Mr Alderson finished his tongue and pushed his plate away. 'I think nowt to the vaccines. And those sudden deaths you're on about – they're caused by wool ball on t'stomach. Nowt to do wi' the kidneys.'

'Ah yes, wool ball eh? I see, wool ball.' I subsided and decided to concentrate on the food.

And it was worth concentrating on. As I worked my way through I was aware of a growing sense of wonder that Helen had probably baked the entire spread. It was when my teeth were sinking into a poem of a curd tart that I really began to appreciate the miracle that somebody of Helen's radiant attractiveness should be capable of this.

I looked across at her. She was a big girl, nothing like her little wisp of a father. She must have taken after her mother. Mrs Alderson had been dead for many years and I wondered if she had had that same wide, generous mouth that smiled so easily, those same warm blue eyes under the same mass of black-brown hair.

A spluttering from Tommy and Mary showed that they had been appreciatively observing me gawping at their sister.

'That's enough, you two,' Auntie Lucy reproved. 'Anyway you can go now, we're going to clear the table.'

Helen and she began to move the dishes to the scullery beyond the door while Mr Alderson and I returned to our chairs by the fireside.

The little man ushered me to mine with a vague wave of the hand. 'Here ... take a seat, er ... young man.'

A clattering issued from the kitchen as the washing-up began. We were alone.

Mr Alderson's hand strayed automatically towards his *Farmer and*

A LAMB TAKES ITS MEDICINE To make sure that a lamb took its liquid dose of anti-worm drug, a shepherd would hold up the animal's lower jaw to straighten the throat, then push a small drenching bottle into the corner of the mouth and empty the medicine straight down the gullet. When the whole flock was being treated, a helper to measure out the doses made the process faster.

Stockbreeder, but he withdrew it after a single hunted glance in my direction and began to drum his fingers on the arm of the chair, whistling softly under his breath.

I groped desperately for an opening gambit but came up with nothing. The ticking of the clock boomed out into the silence. I was beginning to break out into a sweat when the little man cleared his throat.

'Pigs were a good trade on Monday,' he vouchsafed.

'They were, eh? Well, that's fine – jolly good.'

Mr Alderson nodded, fixed his gaze somewhere above my left shoulder and started drumming his fingers again. Once more the heavy silence blanketed us and the clock continued to hammer out its message.

After several years Mr Alderson stirred in his seat and gave a little cough. I looked at him eagerly.

'Store cattle were down, though,' he said.

'Ah, too bad, what a pity,' I babbled. 'But that's how it goes, I suppose, eh?'

Helen's father shrugged and we settled down again. This time I knew it was hopeless. My mind was a void and my companion had the defeated look of a man who has shot his conversational bolt. I lay back and studied the hams and sides of bacon hanging from their hooks in the ceiling, then I worked my way along the row of plates on the big oak dresser to a gaudy calendar from a cattle cake firm which dangled from a nail on the wall. I took a chance then and stole a glance at Mr Alderson out of the corner of my eye and my toes curled as I saw he had chosen that precise moment to have a sideways peep at me. We both looked away hurriedly.

By shifting round in my seat and craning my neck I was able to get a view of the other side of the kitchen where there was an old-fashioned roll top desk surmounted by a wartime picture of Mr Alderson looking very stern in the uniform of the Yorkshire Yeomanry, and I was proceeding along the wall from there when Helen opened the door and came quickly into the room.

'Dad,' she said, a little breathlessly. 'Stan's here. He says one of the cows is down with staggers.'

Her father jumped up in obvious relief. I think he was delighted he had a sick cow and I, too, felt like a released prisoner as I hurried out with him.

Stan, one of the cowmen, was waiting in the yard.

'She's at t'top of t'field, boss,' he said. 'I just spotted 'er when I went to get them in for milkin'.'

Mr Alderson looked at me questioningly and I nodded at him as I opened the car door.

'I've got the stuff with me,' I said. 'We'd better drive straight up.'

The three of us piled in and I set course to where I could see the stretched-out form of a cow near the wall in the top corner. My bottles and instruments rattled and clattered as we bumped over the rig and furrow.

CAKE-CRUSHER A common piece of equipment in a 1930s barn was a hand-turned machine that fed oil-cake from a hopper between rotating bars, usually spiked, to crumble it for fodder or reduce it to a powder for a soil dressing. The thin, hard cakes are made from compressed linseed and rape seed after the oil has been extracted. It is a rich fertiliser and a concentrated food for fattening beef cattle and sheep.

CRAWLER TRACTOR When grass was turned in to prepare a field for a cereal crop, only shallow ploughing was needed and the tractor could easily turn five furrows at once. This tractor, used in Farndale in 1939, had crawler tracks. Pneumatic tyres were only then coming into use on British tractors. Previously tractors had iron wheels with cleats or spade lugs to gain traction.

This was something every vet gets used to in early summer; the urgent call to milk cows which have collapsed suddenly a week or two after being turned out to grass. The farmers called it grass staggers and as its scientific name of hypomagesaemia implied it was associated with lowered magnesium level in the blood. An alarming and highly fatal condition but fortunately curable by injection of magnesium in most cases.

Despite the seriousness of the occasion I couldn't repress a twinge of satisfaction. It had got me out of the house and it gave me a chance to prove myself by doing something useful. Helen's father and I hadn't established anything like a rapport as yet, but maybe when I gave his unconscious cow my magic injection and it leaped to its feet and walked away he might look at me in a different light. And it often happened that way; some of the cures were really dramatic.

'She's still alive, any road,' Stan said as we roared over the grass. 'I saw her legs move then.'

He was right, but as I pulled up and jumped from the car I felt a tingle of apprehension. Those legs were moving too much.

This was the kind that often died; the convulsive type. The animal, prone on her side, was pedalling frantically at the air with all four feet, her head stretched backwards, eyes staring, foam bubbling from her mouth. As I hurriedly unscrewed the cap from the bottle of magnesium lactate she stopped and went into a long, shuddering spasm, legs stiffly extended, eyes screwed tightly shut; then she relaxed and lay inert for a frightening few seconds before recommencing the wild thrashing with her legs.

My mouth had gone dry. This was a bad one. The strain on the heart during these spasms was enormous and each one could be her last.

I crouched by her side, my needle poised over the milk vein. My usual practice was to inject straight into the bloodstream to achieve the quickest possible effect, but in this case I hesitated. Any interference with the heart's action could kill this cow; best to play safe – I reached over and pushed the needle under the skin of the neck.

As the fluid ran in, bulging the subcutaneous tissues and starting a widening swelling under the roan-coloured hide, the cow went into another spasm. For an agonising few seconds she lay there, the quivering limbs reaching desperately out at nothing, the eyes disappearing deep down under tight-twisted lids. Helplessly I watched her, my heart thudding, and this time as she came out of the rigor and started to move again it wasn't with the purposeful pedalling of before; it was an aimless laboured pawing and as even this grew weaker her eyes slowly opened and gazed outwards with a vacant stare.

I bent and touched the cornea with my finger, there was no response.

The farmer and cowman looked at me in silence as the animal gave a final jerk then lay still.

'I'm afraid she's dead, Mr Alderson,' I said.

The farmer nodded and his eyes moved slowly over the still form, over the graceful limbs, the fine dark roan flanks, the big, turgid udder that would give no more milk.

'I'm sorry,' I said. 'I'm afraid her heart must have given out before the magnesium had a chance to work.'

'It's a bloody shame,' grunted Stan. 'She was a right good cow, that 'un.'

Mr Alderson turned quietly back to the car. 'Aye well, these things happen,' he muttered.

We drove down the field to the house.

Inside, the work was over and the family was collected in the parlour. I sat with them for a while but my overriding emotion was an urgent desire to be elsewhere. Helen's father had been silent before but now he sat hunched miserably in an armchair taking no part in the conversation. I wondered whether he thought I had actually killed his cow. It certainly hadn't looked very good, the vet walking up to the sick animal, the quick injection and hey presto, dead. No, I had been blameless but it hadn't looked good.

On an impulse I jumped to my feet.

'Thank you very much for the lovely tea,' I said, 'but I really must be off. I'm on duty this evening.'

Helen came with me to the door. 'Well it's been nice seeing you again, Jim.' She paused and looked at me doubtfully. 'I wish you'd stop worrying about that cow. It's a pity but you couldn't help it. There was nothing you could do.'

'Thanks, Helen, I know. But it's a nasty smack for your father isn't it?'

She shrugged and smiled her kind smile. Helen was always kind.

Driving back through the pastures up to the farm gate I could see the motionless body of my patient with her companions sniffing around her curiously in the gentle evening sunshine. Any time now the knacker man would be along to winch the carcase on to his wagon. It was the grim epilogue to every vet's failure.

I closed the gate behind me and looked back at Heston Grange. I had thought everything would be all right this time but it hadn't worked out that way.

The jinx was still on.

CAMBRIDGE ROLLER After ploughing, soil needs to be broken down to a crumbly texture before it is ready for sowing. A cultivator and a harrow will do this, but the ground may also need working with a Cambridge roller to crush any clods. The roller's axle carries a row of separate discs, each one ridged to exert maximum pressure on the clods. The seat on this 1940 roller shows that it was made to be drawn by a horse, but it has been adapted for use behind a tractor.

3

Wine-tasting with Mr Crump

'Monday morning disease' they used to call it. The almost unbelievably gross thickening of the hind limb in cart horses which had stood in the stable over the weekend. It seemed that the sudden suspension of their

SHIRE HORSE The biggest breed of heavy horse in Britain – in build and in number – is the Shire. This is England's horse, the descendant of the Great Horse that William the Conqueror introduced in 1066 as transport for his armoured knights. It is a powerful but slow-moving animal that sometimes weighs more than a ton and is often 17 hands (6 ft) high at the shoulder. It can be black, brown or grey, and its beautiful 'feathered' feet are often white.

normal work and exercise produced the massive lymphangitis and swelling which gave many a farmer a nasty jolt right at the beginning of the week.

But it was Wednesday evening now and Mr Crump's big Shire gelding was greatly improved.

'That leg's less than half the size it was,' I said, running my hand over the inside of the hock feeling the remains of the oedema pitting under my fingers. 'I can see you've put in some hard work here.'

'Aye, ah did as you said.' Mr Crump's reply was typically laconic, but I knew he must have spent hours fomenting and massaging the limb and forcibly exercising the horse as I had told him when I gave the arecoline injection on Monday.

I began to fill the syringe for a repeat injection. 'He's having no corn, is he?'

'Nay, nowt but bran.'

'That's fine. I think he'll be back to normal in a day or two if you keep up the treatment.'

The farmer grunted and no sign of approval showed in the big, purple-red face with its perpetually surprised expression. But I knew he was pleased all right; he was fond of the horse and had been unable to hide his concern at the animal's pain and distress on my first visit.

I went into the house to wash my hands and Mr Crump led the way into the kitchen, his big frame lumbering clumsily ahead of me. He proffered soap and towel in his slow-moving way and stood back in silence as I leaned over the long shallow sink of brown earthenware.

As I dried my hands he cleared his throat and spoke hesitantly. 'Would you like a drink of ma wine?'

Before I could answer, Mrs Crump came bustling through from an inner room. She was pulling on her hat and behind her her teenage son and daughter followed, dressed ready to go out.

'Oh, Albert, stop it!' she snapped, looking up at her husband. 'Mr Herriot doesn't want your wine. I wish you wouldn't pester people so with it!'

The boy grinned. 'Dad and his wine, he's always looking for a victim.' His sister joined in the general laughter and I had an uncomfortable feeling that Mr Crump was the odd man out in his own home.

'We're going down t'village institute to see a school play, Mr Herriot,' the wife said briskly. 'We're late now so we must be off.' She hurried away with her children, leaving the big man looking after her sheepishly.

There was a silence while I finished drying my hands, then I turned to the farmer. 'Well, how about that drink, Mr Crump?'

He hesitated for a moment and the surprised look deepened. 'Would you ... you'd really like to try some?'

'I'd love to. I haven't had my evening meal yet – I could just do with an aperitif.'

'Right, I'll be back in a minute.' He disappeared into the large pantry at the end of the kitchen and came back with a bottle of amber liquid and glasses.

'This is ma rhubarb,' he said, tipping out two good measures.

I took a sip and then a good swallow, and gasped as the liquid blazed a fiery trail down to my stomach.

'It's strong stuff,' I said a little breathlessly, 'but the taste is very pleasant. Very pleasant indeed.'

Mr Crump watched approvingly as I took another drink. 'Aye, it's just right. Nearly two years old.'

I drained the glass and this time the wine didn't burn so much on its way down but seemed to wash around the walls of my empty stomach and send glowing tendrils creeping along my limbs.

'Delicious,' I said. 'Absolutely delicious.'

The farmer expanded visibly. He refilled the glasses and watched with rapt attention as I drank. When we had finished the second glass he jumped to his feet.

'Now for a change I want you to try summat different.' He almost trotted to the pantry and produced another bottle, this time of colourless fluid. 'Elderflower,' he said, panting slightly.

When I tasted it I was amazed at the delicate flavour, the bubbles sparkling and dancing on my tongue.

'Gosh, this is terrific! It's just like champagne. You know, you really have a gift – I never thought home-made wines could taste like this.'

Mr Crump stared at me for a moment then one corner of his mouth began to twitch and incredibly a shy smile spread slowly over his face. 'You're about fust I've heard say that. You'd think I was trying to poison folks when I offer them ma wine – they always shy off but they can sup plenty of beer and whisky.'

'Well they don't know what they're missing, Mr Crump.' I watched while the farmer replenished my glass. 'I wouldn't have believed you could make stuff as good as this at home.' I sipped appreciatively at the elderflower. It still tasted like champagne.

I hadn't got more than half way down the glass before Mr Crump was clattering and clinking inside the pantry again. He emerged with a bottle with contents of a deep blood red. 'Try that,' he gasped.

I was beginning to feel like a professional taster and rolled the first mouthful around my mouth with eyes half closed. 'Mm, mm, yes. Just like an excellent port, but there's something else here – a fruitiness in the background – something familiar about it – it's ... it's ...'

'Blackberry!' shouted Mr Crump triumphantly. 'One of t'best I've done. Made it two back-ends since – it were a right good year for it.'

Leaning back in the chair I took another drink of the rich, dark wine; it was round-flavoured, warming, and behind it there was always the elusive hint of the brambles. I could almost see the heavy-hanging clusters of berries glistening black and succulent in the autumn sunshine. The mellowness of the image matched my mood which was becoming more expansive by the minute and I looked round with leisurely appreciation at the rough comfort of the farmhouse kitchen; at

ELDERFLOWER WINE Flower wines need six months to mature, so in country kitchens June was the time for making the elderflower wine with which guests were made welcome at Christmas.

To make the wine, fill a 1 pint jug tightly with the flower heads, free of stalks. Wash and drain them well and put them in a large bowl with the thinly pared rind of 2 lemons. Pour on 1 gallon of boiling water, cover with a cloth and leave for 3 days, stirring occasionally. Strain the liquid into a large pan, add 3 lb of granulated sugar and heat until the sugar has dissolved. Simmer for 10 minutes, then strain the liquid into an 8 pint fermentation jar. Add the juice of the lemons and sprinkle on ½ oz of wine or baking yeast. Fit the airlock on the jar and leave at room temperature for weeks or months until fermentation stops. Siphon off the clear wine from the sediment once or twice during this time into a clean jar. Bottle the wine and store it in a cool, dark place.

Mr Crump threw back his head and laughed delightedly before hurriedly refilling both of our tumblers.

the hams and sides of bacon hanging from their hooks in the ceiling, and at my host sitting across the table, watching me eagerly. He was, I noticed for the first time, still wearing his cap.

'You know,' I said, holding the glass high and studying its ruby depths against the light, 'I can't make up my mind which of your wines I like best. They're all excellent and yet so different.'

Mr Crump, too, had relaxed. He threw back his head and laughed delightedly before hurriedly refilling both of our tumblers. 'But you haven't started yet. Ah've got dozens of bottles in there – all different. You must try a few more.' He shambled again over to the pantry and this time when he reappeared he was weighed down by an armful of bottles of differing shapes and colours.

What a charming man he was, I thought. How wrong I had been in my previous assessment of him; it had been so easy to put him down as lumpish and unemotional but as I looked at him now his face was alight with friendship, hospitality, understanding. He had cast off his inhibitions and as he sat down surrounded by the latest batch he began to talk rapidly and fluently about wines and wine making.

180

Wide-eyed and impassioned he ranged at length over the niceties of fermentation and sedimentation, of flavour and bouquet. He dealt learnedly with the relative merits of Chambertin and Nuits St George, Montrachet and Chablis. Enthusiasts are appealing but a fanatic is irresistible and I sat spellbound while Mr Crump pushed endless samples of his craft in front of me, mixing and adjusting expertly.

'How did you find that 'un?'

'Very nice ...'

'But sweet, maybe?'

'Well, perhaps ...'

'Right, try some of this with it.' The meticulous addition of a few drops of nameless liquid from the packed rows of bottles. 'How's that?'

'Marvellous!'

'Now this 'un. Perhaps a bit sharpish, eh?'

'Possibly ... yes ...'

Again the tender trickling of a few mysterious droplets into my drink and again the anxious enquiry.

'Is that better?'

'Just right.'

The big man drank with me, glass by glass. We tried parsnip and dandelion, cowslip and parsley, clover, gooseberry, beetroot and crab apple. Incredibly we had some stuff made from turnips which was so exquisite that I insisted on a refill.

Everything gradually slowed down as we sat there. Time slowed down till it was finally meaningless. Mr Crump and I slowed down and our speech and actions became more and more deliberate. The farmer's visits to the pantry developed into laboured, unsteady affairs; sometimes he took a roundabout route to reach the door and on one occasion there was a tremendous crash from within and I feared he had fallen among his bottles. But I couldn't be bothered to get up to see and in due course he reappeared, apparently unharmed.

It was around nine o'clock that I heard the soft knocking on the outer door. I ignored it as I didn't want to interrupt Mr Crump who was in the middle of a deep exposition.

'Thish,' he was saying, leaning close to me and tapping a bulbous flagon with his forefinger. 'Thish is, in my 'pinion, comp'rable to a fine Moselle. Made it lash year and would 'preciate it if you'd tell me what you think.' He went low over the glass, blinking, heavy-eyed as he poured.

'Now then, wha' d'you say? Ish it or ishn't it?'

I took a gulp and paused for a moment. It all tasted the same now and I had never drunk Moselle anyway, but I nodded and hiccuped solemnly in reply.

The farmer rested a friendly hand on my shoulder and was about to make a further speech when he, too, heard the knocking. He made his way across the floor with some difficulty and opened the door. A young lad was standing there and I heard a few muttered words.

LEICESTER SHEEP This large, placid sheep was bred by Robert Bakewell in the 18th century for the arable countryside of Leicestershire, but by the 20th century it was kept on the Yorkshire Wolds more than anywhere else. Now it is very rare. Rams and ewes are hornless with a smooth white face and legs. They are often known as Leicester longwools, a name that reveals the breed's chief virtue – its heavy, high-quality fleece. The wool hangs in tightly corkscrewed locks, and the clipped fleece weighs about 12 lb.

'We 'ave a cow on calving and we 'phoned surgery and they said vitnery might still be here.'

Mr Crump turned to face me. 'It's the Bamfords of Holly Bush. They wan' you to go there – jush a mile along t'road.'

'Right,' I heaved myself to my feet then gripped the table tightly as the familiar objects of the room began to whirl rapidly around me. When they came to rest Mr Crump appeared to be standing at the head of a fairly steep slope. The kitchen floor had seemed perfectly level when I had come in but now it was all I could do to fight my way up the gradient.

When I reached the door Mr Crump was staring owlishly into the darkness.

''Sraining,' he said. ''Sraining like 'ell.'

I peered out at the steady beat of the dark water on the cobbles of the yard, but my car was just a few yards away and I was about to set out when the farmer caught my arm.

'Jus' minute, can't go out like that.' He held up a finger then went over and groped about in a drawer. At length he produced a tweed cap which he offered me with great dignity.

I never wore anything on my head whatever the weather but I was deeply touched and wrung my companion's hand in silence. It was understandable that a man like Mr Crump who wore his cap at all times, indoors and out, would recoil in horror from the idea of anybody venturing uncovered into the rain.

The tweed cap which I now put on was the biggest I had ever seen; a great round flat pancake of a thing which even at that moment I felt would keep not only my head but my shoulders and entire body dry in the heaviest downpour.

I took my leave of Mr Crump with reluctance and as I settled in the seat of the car trying to remember where first gear was situated I could see his bulky form silhouetted against the light from the kitchen; he was waving his hand with gentle benevolence and it struck me as I at length drove away what a deep and wonderful friendship had been forged that night.

Driving at walking pace along the dark narrow road, my nose almost touching the windscreen, I was conscious of some unusual sensations. My mouth and lips felt abnormally sticky as though I had been drinking liquid glue instead of wine, my breath seemed to be whistling in my nostrils like a strong wind blowing under a door, and I was having difficulty focusing my eyes. Fortunately I met only one car and as it approached and flashed past in the other direction I was muzzily surprised by the fact that it had two complete sets of headlights which kept merging into each other and drawing apart again.

In the yard at Holly Bush I got out of the car, nodded to the shadowy group of figures standing there, fumbled my bottle of antiseptic and calving ropes from the boot and marched determinedly into the byre. One of the men held an oil lamp over a cow lying on a deep bed of straw in one of the standings; from the vulva a calf's foot protruding a few inches and as the cow strained a little muzzle showed momentarily then disappeared as she relaxed.

Far away inside me a stone cold sober veterinary surgeon murmured: 'Only a leg back and a big roomy cow. Shouldn't be much trouble.' I turned and looked at the Bamfords for the first time. I hadn't met them before but it was easy to classify them; simple, kindly, anxious-to-please people – two middle-aged men, probably brothers, and two young men who would be the sons of one or the other. They were all staring at me in the dim light, their eyes expectant, their mouths slightly open as though ready to smile or laugh if given half a chance.

I squared my shoulders, took a deep breath and said in a loud voice: 'Would you please bring me a bucket of hot water, some soap and a towel.' Or at least that's what I meant to say, because what actually issued from my lips was a torrent of something that sounded like Swahili. The Bamfords, poised, ready to spring into action to do my bidding, looked at me blankly. I cleared my throat, swallowed, took a few seconds' rest and tried again. I cleared my throat, swallowed, another volley of gibberish echoing uselessly round the cow house.

Clearly I had a problem. It was essential to communicate in some way, particularly since these people didn't know me and were waiting for some action. I suppose I must have appeared a strange and enigmatic figure standing there, straight and solemn, surmounted and dominated by the vast cap. But through the mists a flash of insight showed me where I was going wrong. It was over-confidence. It wasn't a bit of good trying to speak loudly like that. I tried again in the faintest of whispers.

'Could I have a bucket of hot water, some soap and a towel, please.' It came out beautifully though the oldest Mr Bamford didn't quite get it first time. He came close, cupped an ear with his hand and watched my lips intently. Then he nodded eagerly in comprehension, held up a forefinger at me, tiptoed across the floor like a tight rope walker to one of the sons and whispered in his ear. The young man turned and crept out noiselessly, closing the door behind him with the utmost care; he was back in less than a minute, padding over the cobbles daintily in his heavy boots and placing the bucket gingerly in front of me.

I managed to remove my jacket, tie and shirt quite efficiently and they were taken from me in silence and hung upon nails by the Bamfords who were moving around as though in church. I thought I was doing fine till I started to wash my arms, The soap kept shooting from my arms, slithering into the dung channel, disappearing into the dark corners of the byre with the Bamfords in hot pursuit. It was worse still when I tried to work up to the top of my arms. The soap flew over my shoulders like a live thing, at times cannoning off the walls, at others gliding down my back. The farmers never knew where the next shot was going and they took on the appearance of a really sharp fielding side crouching around me with arms outstretched waiting for a catch.

SCALING MANURE The straw and bracken bedding of farm livestock was gathered with their dung and heaped on the vast farmyard midden to rot down into manure. After a cereal crop had been harvested, cartloads of manure were slowly hauled up and down the field while a man followed with a muckrake. He drew out the manure and scaled, or spread, it on the field, to be ploughed in during the early autumn.

LONK SHEEP The large-boned, agile Lonk lives on the high moorlands of Yorkshire. Its legs and face are free of wool and are patterned black and white. The ewe has flat horns and the ram downward-curving ones. The Lonk's short but very dense fleece is well-suited to the climate. The animal can quickly shake off rain and has no low-dangling coat to become a solid, dragging weight of ice from trailing on the snow-covered winter ground. The Lonk's lambs stay beside the mother right through their first winter, and only begin to venture off to an independent life when the new April lambs are born.

However I did finally work up a lather and was ready to start, but the cow refused firmly to get to her feet, so I had to stretch out behind her face down on the unyielding cobbles. It wasn't till I got down there that I felt the great cap dropping over my ears; I must have put it on again after removing my shirt though it was difficult to see what purpose it might serve.

Inserting a hand gently into the vagina I pushed along the calf's neck, hoping to come upon a flexed knee or even a foot, but I was disappointed; the leg really was right back, stretching from the shoulder away flat against the calf's side. Still, I would be all right – it just meant a longer reach.

And there was one reassuring feature; the calf was alive. As I lay, my face was almost touching the rear end of the cow and I had a close up of the nose which kept appearing every few seconds; it was good to see the little nostrils twitching as they sought the outside air. All I had to do was get that leg round.

But the snag was that as I reached forward the cow kept straining, squeezing my arm cruelly against her bony pelvis, making me groan and roll about in agony for a few seconds till the pressure went off. Quite often in these crises my cap fell on to the floor and each time gentle hands replaced it immediately on my head.

At last the foot was in my hand – there would be no need for ropes this time – and I began to pull it round. It took me longer than I thought and it seemed to me that the calf was beginning to lose patience with me because when its head was forced out by the cow's contractions we were eye to eye and I fancied the little creature was giving me a disgusted 'For heaven's sake get on with it' look.

When the leg did come round it was with a rush and in an instant everything was laid as it should have been.

'Get hold of the feet,' I whispered to the Bamfords and after a hushed consultation they took up their places. In no time at all a fine heifer calf was wriggling on the cobbles shaking its head and snorting the placental fluid from its nostrils.

In response to my softly hissed instructions the farmers rubbed the little creature down with straw wisps and pulled it round for its mother to lick.

It was a happy ending to the most peaceful calving I have ever attended. Never a voice raised, everybody moving around on tiptoe. I got dressed in a cathedral silence, went out to the car, breathed a final goodnight and left with the Bamfords waving mutely.

To say I had a hangover next morning would be failing even to hint at the utter disintegration of my bodily economy and personality. Only somebody who had consumed two or three quarts of assorted home-made wines at a sitting could have an inkling of the quaking nausea, the raging inferno within, the jangling nerves, the black despairing outlook.

Tristan had seen me in the bathroom running the cold tap on my tongue and had intuitively administered a raw egg, aspirins and brandy which, as I came downstairs, lay in a cold, unmoving blob in my outraged stomach.

'What are you walking like that for, James?' asked Siegfried in what sounded like a bull's bellow as I came in on him at breakfast. 'You look as though you'd pee'd yourself.'

'Oh it's nothing much.' It was no good telling him I was treading warily across the carpet because I was convinced that if I let my heels down too suddenly it would jar my eyeballs from their sockets. 'I had a few glasses of Mr Crump's wine last night and it seems to have upset me.'

'A few glasses! You ought to be more careful – that stuff's dynamite. Could knock anybody over.' He crashed his cup into its saucer then began to clatter about with knife and fork as if trying to give a one man rendering of the Anvil Chorus. 'I hope you weren't any the worse to go to Bamford's.'

I listlessly crumbled some dry toast on my plate. 'Well I did the job all right, but I'd had a bit too much – no use denying it.'

Siegfried was in one of his encouraging moods. 'By God, James, those Bamfords are very strict Methodists. They're grand chaps but absolutely dead nuts against drink – if they thought you were under the influence of alcohol they'd never have you on the place again.' He ruthlessly bisected an egg yolk. 'I hope they didn't notice anything. Do you think they knew?'

'Oh maybe not. No, I shouldn't think so.' I closed my eyes and shivered as Siegfried pushed a forkful of sausage and fried bread into his mouth and began to chew briskly. My mind went back to the gentle hands replacing the monstrous cap on my head and I groaned inwardly.

Those Bamfords knew all right. Oh yes, they knew.

TEESWATER SHEEP The original home of this now rare breed was the northern edge of Yorkshire, in Teesdale. The Teeswater is hornless with a white or grey face topped by a woolly forelock. Its fleece and its birthrate are its outstanding characteristics. The fleece is fine with very long fibres – 12 in. on average – and is extremely dense. The Teeswater is only a medium-size animal but its fleece weighs 15 lb, compared with only 4 lb for the Dalesbred. Triplet lambs are common in Teeswaters, but the extra work sometimes involved in feeding the third lamb – since ewes have only two teats – is made worthwhile by the valuable wool.

4

A case of cruelty

The silvery haired old gentleman with the pleasant face didn't look the type to be easily upset but his eyes glared at me angrily and his lips quivered with indignation.

'Mr Herriot,' he said. 'I have come to make a complaint. I strongly object to your callousness in subjecting my dog to unnecessary suffering.'

'Suffering? What suffering?' I was mystified.

'I think you know, Mr Herriot. I brought my dog in a few days ago. He was very lame and I am referring to your treatment on that occasion.'

I nodded. 'Yes, I remember it well ... but where does the suffering come in?'

'Well, the poor animal is going around with his leg dangling and I have it on good authority that the bone is fractured and should have been put in plaster immediately.' The old gentleman stuck his chin out fiercely.

'All right, you can stop worrying,' I said. 'Your dog has a radial paralysis caused by a blow on the ribs and if you are patient and follow my treatment he'll gradually improve. In fact I think he'll recover completely.'

'But he trails his leg when he walks.'

'I know – that's typical, and to the layman it does give the appearance of a broken leg. But he shows no sign of pain, does he?'

'No, he seems quite happy, but this lady seemed to be absolutely sure of her facts. She was adamant.'

'Lady?'

'Yes,' said the old gentleman. 'She is very clever with animals and she came round to see if she could help in my dog's convalescence. She brought some excellent condition powders with her.'

'Ah!' A blinding shaft pierced the fog in my mind. All was suddenly clear. 'It was Mrs Donovan, wasn't it?'

'Well ... er, yes. That was her name.'

Old Mrs Donovan was a woman who really got around. No matter what was going on in Darrowby – weddings, funerals, house-sales – you'd find the dumpy little figure and walnut face among the spectators, the darting, black-button eyes taking everything in. And always, on the end of its lead, her terrier dog.

When I say 'old', I'm only guessing, because she appeared ageless; she seemed to have been around a long time but she could have been anything between fifty-five and seventy-five. She certainly had the vitality of a young woman because she must have walked vast distances in her dedicated quest to keep abreast of events. Many people took an uncharitable view of her acute curiosity, but whatever the motivation her activities took her into almost every channel of life in the town. One of these channels was our veterinary practice.

Because Mrs Donovan, among her other widely ranging interests, was an animal doctor. In fact I think it would be safe to say that this facet of her life transcended all the others.

She could talk at length on the ailments of small animals and she had a whole armoury of medicines and remedies at her command, her two specialities being her miracle working condition powders and a dog shampoo of unprecedented value for improving the coat. She had an uncanny ability to sniff out a sick animal and it was not uncommon when I was on my rounds to find Mrs Donovan's dark, gipsy face poised intently over what I had thought was my patient while she administered calf's foot jelly or one of her own patent nostrums.

I suffered more than Siegfried because I took a more active part in the

BORDER TERRIER A working dog with workaday looks, this is one of the oldest terriers in the counties where England and Scotland meet. The tan or grey rough coat of the Border terrier always has a shaggy, unkempt look, and the broad, short head with drooping ears has a bristling moustache. The dog was a hard worker at hunting foxes to earth, and now as a pet it is an active, loyal and friendly companion.

small animal side of our practice. I was anxious to develop this aspect and to improve my image in this field and Mrs Donovan didn't help at all. 'Young Mr Herriot,' she would confide to my clients, 'is all right with cattle and such like, but he don't know nothing about dogs and cats.'

And of course they believed her and had implicit faith in her. She had the irresistible mystic appeal of the amateur and on top of that there was her habit, particularly endearing in Darrowby, of never charging for her advice, her medicines, her long periods of diligent nursing.

Older folk in the town told how her husband, an Irish farm worker, had died many years ago and how he must have had a 'bit put away' because Mrs Donovan had apparently been able to indulge all her interests over the years without financial strain. Since she inhabited the streets of Darrowby all day and every day I often encountered her and she always smiled up at me sweetly and told me how she had been sitting up all night with Mrs So-and-so's dog that I'd been treating. She felt sure she'd be able to pull it through.

There was no smile on her face, however, on the day when she rushed into the surgery while Siegfried and I were having tea.

'Mr Herriot!' she gasped. 'Can you come? My little dog's been run over!'

I jumped up and ran out to the car with her. She sat in the passenger seat with her head bowed, her hands clasped tightly on her knees.

'He slipped his collar and ran in front of a car,' she murmured. 'He's lying in front of the school half way up Cliffend Road. Please hurry.'

I was there within three minutes but as I bent over the dusty little body stretched on the pavement I knew there was nothing I could do. The fast-glazing eyes, the faint, gasping respirations, the ghastly pallor of the mucous membranes all told the same story.

'I'll take him back to the surgery and get some saline into him, Mrs Donovan,' I said. 'But I'm afraid he's had a massive internal haemorrhage. Did you see what happened exactly?'

She gulped. 'Yes, the wheel went right over him.'

Ruptured liver, for sure. I passed my hands under the little animal and began to lift him gently, but as I did so the breathing stopped and the eyes stared fixedly ahead.

Mrs Donovan sank to her knees and for a few moments she gently stroked the rough hair of the head and chest. 'He's dead, isn't he?' she whispered at last.

'I'm afraid he is,' I said.

She got slowly to her feet and stood bewilderedly among the little group of bystanders on the pavement. Her lips moved but she seemed unable to say any more.

I took her arm, led her over to the car and opened the door. 'Get in and sit down,' I said. 'I'll run you home. Leave everything to me.'

I wrapped the dog in my calving overall and laid him in the boot before driving away. It wasn't until we drew up outside Mrs Donovan's

TYING SHEAVES The tyer held a sheaf against his knee while he wound a straw band round it. With one hand he twisted the band ends together, then tucked them under the band to secure them. This was a Wolds method of tying which did away with back-breaking crouching to tie a sheaf on the ground. The bands were made from strands of straw twisted and knotted together. They were often made by children and laid out at intervals along the field for the tyer to have within reach as he needed them.

house that she began to weep silently. I sat there without speaking till she had finished. Then she wiped her eyes and turned to me.

'Do you think he suffered at all?'

'I'm certain he didn't. It was all so quick – he wouldn't know a thing about it.'

She tried to smile. 'Poor little Rex, I don't know what I'm going to do without him. We've travelled a few miles together, you know.'

'Yes, you have. He had a wonderful life, Mrs Donovan. And let me give you a bit of advice – you must get another dog. You'd be lost without one.'

She shook her head. 'No. I couldn't. That little dog meant too much to me. I couldn't let another take his place.'

'Well I know that's how you feel just now but I wish you'd think about it. I don't want to seem callous – I tell everybody this when they lose an animal and I know it's good advice.'

'Mr Herriot, I'll never have another one.' She shook her head again, very decisively. 'Rex was my faithful friend for many years and I just want to remember him. He's the last dog I'll ever have.'

I often saw Mrs Donovan around the town after this and I was glad to see she was still as active as ever, though she looked strangely incomplete without the little dog on its lead. But it must have been over a month before I had the chance to speak to her.

It was on the afternoon that Inspector Halliday of the R.S.P.C.A. rang me.

'Mr Herriot,' he said, 'I'd like you to come and see an animal with me. A cruelty case.'

'Right, what is it?'

'A dog, and it's pretty grim. A dreadful case of neglect.' He gave me the name of a row of old brick cottages down by the river and said he'd meet me there.

Halliday was waiting for me, smart and business-like in his dark uniform, as I pulled up in the back lane behind the houses. He was a big, blond man with cheerful blue eyes but he didn't smile as he came over to the car.

'He's in here,' he said, and led the way towards one of the doors in the long, crumbling wall. A few curious people were hanging around and with a feeling of inevitability I recognised a gnome-like brown face. Trust Mrs Donovan, I thought, to be among those present at a time like this.

We went through the door into the long garden. I had found that even the lowliest dwellings in Darrowby had long strips of land at the back as though the builders had taken it for granted that the country people who were going to live in them would want to occupy themselves with the pursuits of the soil; with vegetable and fruit growing, even stock keeping in a small way. You usually found a pig there, a few hens, often pretty beds of flowers.

Halliday was waiting for me, smart and business-like in his dark uniform.

But this garden was a wilderness. A chilling air of desolation hung over the few gnarled apple and plum trees standing among a tangle of rank grass as though the place had been forsaken by all living creatures.

Halliday went over to a ramshackle wooden shed with peeling paint and a rusted corrugated iron roof. He produced a key, unlocked the padlock and dragged the door partly open. There was no window and it wasn't easy to identify the jumble inside; broken gardening tools, an ancient mangle, rows of flower pots and partly used paint tins. And right at the back, a dog sitting quietly.

I didn't notice him immediately because of the gloom and because the smell in the shed started me coughing, but as I drew closer I saw that he was a big animal, sitting very upright, his collar secured by a chain to a ring in the wall. I had seen some thin dogs but this advanced emaciation reminded me of my textbooks on anatomy; nowhere else did the bones of pelvis, face and rib cage stand out with such horrifying clarity. A deep, smoothed out hollow in the earth floor showed where he had lain, moved about, in fact lived, for a very long time.

The sight of the animal had a stupefying effect on me; I only half took in the rest of the scene – the filthy shreds of sacking scattered nearby, the bowl of scummy water.

'Look at his back end,' Halliday muttered.

I carefully raised the dog from his sitting position and realised that the

189

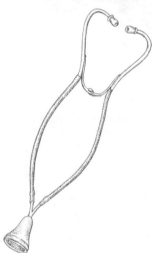

stench in the place was not entirely due to the piles of excrement. The hindquarters were a welter of pressure sores which had turned gangrenous and strips of sloughing tissue hung down from them. There were similar sores along the sternum and ribs. The coat, which seemed to be a dull yellow, was matted and caked with dirt.

The Inspector spoke again. 'I don't think he's ever been out of here. He's only a young dog – about a year old – but I understand he's been in this shed since he was an eight-week-old pup. Somebody out in the lane heard a whimper or he'd never have been found.'

I felt a tightening of the throat and a sudden nausea which wasn't due to the smell. It was the thought of this patient animal sitting starved and forgotten in the darkness and filth for a year. I looked again at the dog and saw in his eyes only a calm trust. Some dogs would have barked their heads off and soon been discovered, some would have become terrified and vicious, but this was one of the totally undemanding kind, the kind which had complete faith in people and accepted all their actions without complaint. Just an occasional whimper perhaps as he sat interminably in the empty blackness which had been his world and at times wondered what it was all about.

'Well, Inspector, I hope you're going to throw the book at whoever's responsible,' I said.

Halliday grunted. 'Oh, there won't be much done. It's a case of diminished responsibility. The owner's definitely simple. Lives with an aged mother who hardly knows what's going on either. I've seen the fellow and it seems he threw in a bit of food when he felt like it and that's about all he did. They'll fine him and stop him keeping an animal in the future but nothing more than that.'

'I see.' I reached out and stroked the dog's head and he immediately responded by resting a paw on my wrist. There was a pathetic dignity about the way he held himself erect, the calm eyes regarding me, friendly and unafraid. 'Well, you'll let me know if you want me in court.'

'Of course, and thank you for coming along.' Halliday hesitated for a moment. 'And now I expect you'll want to put this poor thing out of his misery right away.'

I continued to run my hand over the head and ears while I thought for a moment. 'Yes . . . yes, I suppose so. We'd never find a home for him in this state. It's the kindest thing to do. Anyway, push the door wide open will you so that I can get a proper look at him.'

In the improved light I examined him more thoroughly. Perfect teeth, well-proportioned limbs with a fringe of yellow hair. I put my stethoscope on his chest and as I listened to the slow, strong thudding of the heart the dog again put his paw on my hand.

I turned to Halliday, 'You know, Inspector, inside this bag of bones there's a lovely healthy Golden Retriever. I wish there was some way of letting him out.'

As I spoke I noticed there was more than one figure in the door opening. A pair of black pebble eyes were peering intently at the big dog from behind the Inspector's broad back. The other spectators had remained in the lane but Mrs Donovan's curiosity had been too much for her. I continued conversationally as though I hadn't seen her.

'You know, what this dog needs first of all is a good shampoo to clean up his matted coat.'

'Huh?' said Halliday.

'Yes. And then he wants a long course of some really strong condition powders.'

'What's that?' The Inspector looked startled.

'There's no doubt about it,' I said. 'It's the only hope for him, but where are you going to find such things? Really powerful enough, I mean.' I sighed and straightened up. 'Ah well, I suppose there's nothing else for it. I'd better put him to sleep right away. I'll get the things from my car.'

When I got back to the shed Mrs Donovan was already inside examining the dog despite the feeble remonstrances of the big man.

'Look!' she said excitedly, pointing to a name roughly scratched on the collar. 'His name's Roy.' She smiled up at me. 'It's a bit like Rex, isn't it, that name?'

'You know, Mrs Donovan, now you mention it, it is. It's very like Rex, the way it comes off your tongue.' I nodded seriously.

She stood silent for a few moments, obviously in the grip of a deep emotion, then she burst out.

'Can I have 'im? I can make him better, I know I can. Please, please let me have 'im!'

'Well I don't know,' I said. 'It's really up to the Inspector. You'll have to get his permission.'

Halliday looked at her in bewilderment, then he said: 'Excuse me, Madam,' and drew me to one side. We walked a few yards through the long grass and stopped under a tree.

'Mr Herriot,' he whispered, 'I don't know what's going on here, but I can't just pass over an animal in this condition to anybody who has a casual whim. The poor beggar's had one bad break already – I think it's enough. This woman doesn't look a suitable person ...'

I held up a hand. 'Believe me, Inspector, you've nothing to worry about. She's a funny old stick but she's been sent from heaven today. If anybody in Darrowby can give this dog a new life it's her.'

Halliday still looked very doubtful. 'But I still don't get it. What was all that stuff about him needing shampoos and condition powders?'

'Oh never mind about that. I'll tell you some other time. What he needs is lots of good grub, care and affection and that's just what he'll get. You can take my word for it.'

'All right, you seem very sure.' Halliday looked at me for a second or two then turned and walked over to the eager little figure by the shed.

I had never before been deliberately on the look out for Mrs Donovan: she had just cropped up wherever I happened to be, but now I scanned

DRYING HAY After the mowing, the swathes of hay were strewn, or lightly tossed, with wide, wooden-toothed rakes to let the air in. On the following day the hay was turned over with the rakes to let the sun and air dry the other side. Wooden teeth in the rakes made sure that the grass roots were not damaged. Many joiners earned a living by making the rakes. One Wensleydale specialist in the 1930s made up to 12,000 rakes a year. They were sold at markets.

191

the streets of Darrowby anxiously day by day without sighting her. I didn't like it when Gobber Newhouse got drunk and drove his bicycle determinedly through a barrier into a ten-foot hole where they were laying the new sewer and Mrs Donovan was not in evidence among the happy crowd who watched the council workmen and two policemen trying to get him out; and when she was nowhere to be seen when they had to fetch the fire engine to the fish and chip shop the night the fat burst into flames I became seriously worried.

Maybe I should have called round to see how she was getting on with that dog. Certainly I had trimmed off the necrotic tissue and dressed the sores before she took him away, but perhaps he needed something more than that. And yet at the time I had felt a strong conviction that the main thing was to get him out of there and clean him and feed him and nature would do the rest. And I had a lot of faith in Mrs Donovan – far more than she had in me – when it came to animal doctoring; it was hard to believe I'd been completely wrong.

It must have been nearly three weeks and I was on the point of calling at her home when I noticed her stumping briskly along the far side of the market place, peering closely into every shop window exactly as before. The only difference was that she had a big yellow dog on the end of the lead.

I turned the wheel and sent my car bumping over the cobbles till I was abreast of her. When she saw me getting out she stopped and smiled impishly but she didn't speak as I bent over Roy and examined him. He was still a skinny dog but he looked bright and happy, his wounds were healthy and granulating and there was not a speck of dirt in his coat or on his skin. I knew then what Mrs Donovan had been doing all this time; she had been washing and combing and teasing at that filthy tangle till she had finally conquered it.

As I straightened up she seized my wrist in a grip of surprising strength and looked up into my eyes.

'Now, Mr Herriot,' she said. 'Haven't I made a difference to this dog!'

'You've done wonders, Mrs Donovan,' I said. 'And you've been at him with that marvellous shampoo of yours, haven't you?'

She giggled and walked away and from that day I saw the two of them frequently but at a distance and something like two months went by before I had a chance to talk to her again. She was passing by the surgery as I was coming down the steps and again she grabbed my wrist.

'Mr Herriot,' she said, just as she had done before. 'Haven't I made a difference to this dog!'

I looked down at Roy with something akin to awe. He had grown and filled out and his coat, no longer yellow but a rich gold, lay in luxuriant shining swathes over the well-fleshed ribs and back. A new, brightly studded collar glittered on his neck, and his tail, beautifully fringed, fanned the air gently. He was now a Golden Retriever in full magnificence. As I stared at him he reared up, plunked his forepaws on my chest and looked into my face, and in his eyes I read plainly the same

CASH REGISTER In most village stores, each transaction was meticulously rung up on the cash register kept on or behind the counter. The register was most commonly the glistening, sumptuously embossed, 'brassbound' model made by the National Cash Register Company. The machine recorded each transaction on a paper roll so that the shopkeeper was able to balance his cash against the record after each day's business.

calm affection and trust I had seen in that black, noisome shed.

'Mrs Donovan,' I said softly, 'he's the most beautiful dog in Yorkshire.' Then, because I knew she was waiting for it. 'It's those wonderful condition powders. Whatever do you put in them?'

'Ah, wouldn't you like to know!' She bridled and smiled up at me coquettishly and indeed she was nearer being kissed at that moment than for many years.

I suppose you could say that that was the start of Roy's second life. And as the years passed I often pondered on the beneficent providence which had decreed that an animal which had spent his first twelve months abandoned and unwanted, staring uncomprehendingly into that unchanging, stinking darkness, should be whisked in a moment into an existence of light and movement and love. Because I don't think any dog had it quite so good as Roy from then on.

His diet changed dramatically from odd bread crusts to best stewing steak and biscuit, meaty bones and a bowl of warm milk every evening. And he never missed a thing. Garden fêtes, school sports, evictions, gymkhanas – he'd be there. I was pleased to note that as time went on Mrs Donovan seemed to be clocking up an even greater daily mileage. Her expenditure on shoe leather must have been phenomenal, but of course it was absolute pie for Roy – a busy round in the morning, home for a meal then straight out again; it was all go.

Mrs Donovan didn't confine her activities to the town centre; there was a big stretch of common land down by the river where there were seats, and people used to take their dogs for a gallop and she liked to get down there fairly regularly to check on the latest developments on the domestic scene. I often saw Roy loping majestically over the grass among a pack of assorted canines, and when he wasn't doing that he was submitting to being stroked or patted or generally fussed over. He was handsome and he just liked people; it made him irresistible.

It was common knowledge that his mistress had bought a whole selection of brushes and combs of various sizes with which she laboured over his coat. Some people said she had a little brush for his teeth, too, and it might have been true, but he certainly wouldn't need his nails clipped – his life on the roads would keep them down.

Mrs Donovan, too, had her reward; she had a faithful companion by her side every hour of the day and night. But there was more to it than that; she had always had the compulsion to help and heal animals and the salvation of Roy was the high point of her life – a blazing triumph which never dimmed.

I know the memory of it was always fresh because many years later I was sitting on the sidelines at a cricket match and I saw the two of them; the old lady glancing keenly around her, Roy gazing placidly out at the field of play, apparently enjoying every ball. At the end of the match I watched them move away with the dispersing crowd; Roy would be about twelve then and heaven only knows how old Mrs Donovan must

GOLDEN RETRIEVER The blunt, broad muzzle, wide 'smiling' mouth and feathered creamy-gold coat of the retriever give it a look of soft amiability. It is a good-natured dog, but tough.

It was bred as a powerful gundog. The retriever does not hunt the game like a spaniel or setter, but seeks it out when it has been shot and carries it back to the gun in its large, soft mouth.

AYRSHIRE COW Only a few Dales farmers kept an Ayrshire herd in the 1930s, when Shorthorns were the area's favourite breed. The farmer who kept Ayrshires was a dairy specialist, for this fairly small white cow marked with red or black is renowned for its high milk yield.

have been, but the big golden animal was trotting along effortlessly and his mistress, a little more bent perhaps and her head rather nearer the ground, was going very well.

When she saw me she came over and I felt the familiar tight grip on my wrist.

'Mr Herriot,' she said, and in the dark probing eyes the pride was still as warm, the triumph still as bursting new as if it had all happened yesterday.

'Mr Herriot, haven't I made a difference to this dog!'

5

Newton Montmorency the Sixth

Ben Ashby the cattle dealer looked over the gate with his habitual deadpan expression. It always seemed to me that after a lifetime of buying cows from farmers he had developed a terror of showing any emotion which might be construed as enthusiasm. When he looked at a beast his face registered nothing beyond, occasionally, a gentle sorrow.

This was how it was this morning as he leaned on the top spar and directed a gloomy stare at Harry Sumner's heifer. After a few moments he turned to the farmer.

'I wish you'd had her in for me, Harry. She's too far away. I'm going to have to get over the top.' He began to climb stiffly upwards and it was then that he spotted Monty. The bull hadn't been so easy to see before as he cropped the grass among the group of heifers but suddenly the great head rose high above the others, the nose ring gleamed, and an ominous, strangled bellow sounded across the grass. And as he gazed at us he pulled absently at the turf with a fore foot.

Ben Ashby stopped climbing, hesitated for a second then returned to ground level.

'Aye well,' he muttered, still without changing expression. 'It's not that far away. I reckon I can see all right from here.'

Monty had changed a lot since the first day I saw him about two years ago. He had been a fortnight old then, a skinny, knock-kneed little creature, his head deep in a calf bucket.

'Well, what do you think of me new bull?' Harry Sumner had asked, laughing. 'Not much for a hundred quid is he?'

I whistled. 'As much as that?'

'Aye, it's a lot for a new-dropped calf, isn't it? But I can't think of any other way of getting into the Newton strain. I haven't the brass to buy a big 'un.'

Not all the farmers of those days were as farseeing as Harry and some of them would use any type of male bovine to get their cows in calf.

One such man produced a gaunt animal for Siegfried's inspection and asked him what he thought of his bull. Siegfried's reply of 'All horns and balls' didn't please the owner but I still treasure it as the most graphic description of the typical scrub bull of that period.

Harry was a bright boy. He had inherited a little place of about a hundred acres on his father's death and with his young wife had set about making it go. He was in his early twenties and when I first saw him I had been deceived by his almost delicate appearance into thinking that he wouldn't be up to the job; the pallid face, the large, sensitive eyes and slender frame didn't seem fitted for the seven days a week milking, feeding, mucking-out slog that was dairy farming. But I had been wrong.

The fearless way he plunged in and grabbed at the hind feet of kicking cows for me to examine and his clenched-teeth determination as he hung on to the noses of the big loose beasts at testing time made me change my mind in a hurry. He worked endlessly and tirelessly and it was natural that his drive should have taken him to the south of Scotland to find a bull.

Harry's was an Ayrshire herd – unusual among the almost universal shorthorns in the Dales – and there was no doubt an injection of the famous Newton blood would be a sure way of improving his stock.

'He's got prize winners on both his sire and dam's side,' the young farmer said. 'And a grand pedigree name, too. Newton Montmorency the Sixth – Monty for short.'

As though recognising his name, the calf raised his head from the bucket and looked at us. It was a comic little face – wet-muzzled, milk slobbered half way up his cheeks and dribbling freely from his mouth. I bent over into the pen and scratched the top of the hard little head, feeling the tiny horn buds no bigger than peas under my fingers. Limpid-eyed and unafraid, Monty submitted calmly to the caress for a few moments then sank his head again in the bucket.

I saw quite a bit of Harry Sumner over the next few weeks and usually had a look at his expensive purchase. And as the calf grew you could see why he had cost £100. He was in a pen with three of Harry's own calves and his superiority was evident at a glance; the broad forehead and wide-set eyes; the deep chest and short, straight legs; the beautifully even line of the back from shoulder to tail head. Monty had class; and small as he was he was all bull.

He was about three months old when Harry rang to say he thought the calf had pneumonia. I was surprised because the weather was fine and warm and I knew Monty was in a draught-free building. But when I saw him I thought immediately that his owner's diagnosis was right. The heaving of the rib cage, the temperature of 105 degrees – it looked fairly straightforward. But when I got my stethoscope on his chest and listened for the pneumonic sounds I heard nothing. His lungs were perfectly clear. I went over him several times but there was not a squeak,

AYRSHIRE BULL Few farmers in the Dales reared pedigree herds, but when they wanted to improve their cross-bred milking herd they would sometimes introduce a pure Ayrshire bull. A good strain of bull calf would cost a 1930s farmer at least £100. The native cattle of Ayrshire were the origin of the pedigree breed. In their home county the herds supplied the milk for the famed soft Ayrshire cheese.

not a râle, not the slightest sign of consolidation.

This was a facer. I turned to the farmer. 'It's a funny one, Harry. He's sick, all right, but his symptoms don't add up to anything recognisable.'

I was going against my early training because the first vet I ever saw practice with in my student days told me once: 'If you don't know what's wrong with an animal for God's sake don't admit it. Give it a name – call it McLuskie's Disease or Galloping Dandruff – anything you like, but give it a name.' But no inspiration came to me as I looked at the panting, anxious-eyed little creature.

Treat the symptoms. That was the thing to do. He had a temperature so I'd try to get that down for a start. I brought out my pathetic armoury of febrifuges; the injection of non-specific antiserum, the 'fever drink' of sweet spirit of nitre; but over the next two days it was obvious that the time-honoured remedies were having no effect.

On the fourth morning, Harry Sumner met me as I got out of my car. 'He's walking funny, this morning, Mr Herriot – and he seems to be blind.'

Blind! An unusual form of lead-poisoning – could that be it? I hurried into the calf pen and began to look round the walls, but there wasn't a scrap of paint anywhere and Monty had spent his entire life in there.

And anyway, as I looked at him I realised that he wasn't really blind; his eyes were staring and slightly upturned and he blundered unseeingly around the pen, but he blinked as I passed my hand in front of his face. To complete my bewilderment he walked with a wooden, stiff-legged gait almost like a mechanical toy and my mind began to snatch at diagnostic straws – tetanus, no – meningitis – no, no; I always tried to maintain the calm, professional exterior but I had to fight an impulse to scratch my head and stand gaping.

I got off the place as quickly as possible and settled down to serious thought as I drove away. My lack of experience didn't help, but I did have a knowledge of pathology and physiology and when stumped for a diagnosis I could usually work something out on rational grounds. But this thing didn't make sense.

That night I got out my books, notes from college, back numbers of the Veterinary Record and anything else I could find on the subject of calf diseases. Somewhere here there would surely be a clue. But the volumes on medicine and surgery were barren of inspiration and I had about given up hope when I came upon the passage in a little pamphlet on calf diseases. 'Peculiar, stilted gait, staring eyes with a tendency to gaze upwards, occasionally respiratory symptoms with high tempera-ture.' The words seemed to leap out at me from the printed page and it was as though the unknown author was patting me on the shoulder and murmuring reassuringly: 'This is it, you see. It's all perfectly clear.'

I grabbed the phone and rang Harry Sumner. 'Harry, have you ever noticed Monty and those other calves in the pen licking each other?'

'Aye, they're allus at it, the little beggars. It's like a hobby with them. Why?'

A DRENCHING HORN Drugs which are now given to cattle by injection were in the 1930s given in liquid doses called drenches. Usually the vet would dispense the medicine and the farmer would give the drenches to his animals. He would use a horn with its wide end cut off obliquely – the vessel that had been used for centuries. It would be almost a foot long, cheap to obtain, easy to prepare and not easily damaged if the cow bit it.

'Well I know what's wrong with your bull. He's got a hair-ball.'

'A hair-ball? Where?'

'In the abomasum – the fourth stomach. That's what's setting up all those strange symptoms.'

'Well I'll go to hell. What do we do about it, then?'

'It'll probably mean an operation, but I'd like to try dosing him with liquid paraffin first. I'll put a pint bottle on the step for you if you'll come and collect it. Give him half a pint now and the same first thing in the morning. It might just grease the thing through. I'll see you tomorrow.'

I hadn't a lot of faith in the liquid paraffin. I suppose I suggested it for the sake of doing something while I played nervously with the idea of operating. And next morning the picture was as I expected; Monty was still rigid-limbed, still staring sightlessly ahead of him, and an oiliness round his rectum and down his tail showed that the paraffin had by-passed the obstruction.

'He hasn't had a bite now for three days,' Harry said. 'I doubt he won't stick it much longer.'

I looked from his worried face to the little animal trembling in the pen. 'You're right. We'll have to open him up straight away to have any hope of saving him. Are you willing to let me have a go?'

'Oh, aye, let's be at t'job – sooner the better.' He smiled at me. It was a confident smile and my stomach gave a lurch. His confidence could be badly misplaced because in those days abdominal surgery in the bovine was in a primitive state. There were a few jobs we had begun to tackle fairly regularly but removal of a hair-ball wasn't one of them and my knowledge of the procedure was confined to some rather small-print reading in the textbooks.

But this young farmer had faith in me. He thought I could do the job so it was no good letting him see my doubts. It was at times like this that I envied our colleagues in human medicine. When a surgical case came up they packed their patient off to a hospital but the vet just had to get his jacket off on the spot and make an operating theatre out of the farm buildings.

Harry and I busied ourselves in boiling up the instruments, setting out buckets of hot water and laying a clean bed of straw in an empty pen. Despite his weakness the calf took nearly sixty c.c.'s of Nembutal into his vein before he was fully anaesthetised but finally he was asleep, propped on his back between two straw bales, his little hooves danging above him. I was ready to start.

It's never the same as it is in the books. The pictures and diagrams look so simple and straightforward, but it is a different thing when you are cutting into a living, breathing creature with the abdomen rising and falling gently and the blood oozing beneath your knife. The abomasum, I knew, was just down there, slightly to the right of the sternum but as I cut through the peritoneum there was this slippery mass of fat-streaked omentum obscuring everything; and as I pushed it aside one of the bales moved and Monty tilted to his left causing a sudden gush of intestines

DRENCHING A COW To give a drench to a cow, the cowman pulled up its head by the jaw and slipped the drenching horn into the corner of the mouth behind the tongue. He then poured the measured dose straight down its throat. If a cow bit on the horn, it would not do itself any harm, but a glass drenching bottle would have been dangerous.

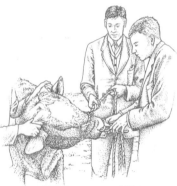

RINGING A BULL With farmhands holding the young bull's head steady by its horns and with a halter, the vet can use his nose-punch to clip a hole in the septum which divides the nostrils. The ring is for leading a bull safely at arm's length. A hooked pole is slipped through it – or a length of rope can be used if the bull is sufficiently docile.

into the wound. I put the flat of my hand against the shining pink loops – it would be just great if my patient's insides started spilling out on to the straw before I had started.

'Pull him upright, Harry, and shove that bale back into place,' I gasped. The farmer quickly complied but the intestines weren't at all anxious to return to their place and kept intruding coyly as I groped for the abomasum. Frankly I was beginning to feel just a bit lost and my heart was thudding when I came upon something hard. It was sliding about beyond the wall of one of the stomachs – at the moment I wasn't sure which. I gripped it and lifted it into the wound. I had hold of the abomasum and that hard thing inside must be the hair-ball.

Repelling the intestines which had made another determined attempt to push their way into the act, I incised the stomach and had my first look at the cause of the trouble. It wasn't a ball at all, rather a flat plaque of densely matted hair mixed freely with strands of hay, sour curd and a shining covering of my liquid paraffin. The whole thing was jammed against the pyloric opening.

Gingerly I drew it out through the incision and dropped it in the straw. It wasn't till I had closed the stomach wound with the gut, stitched up the muscle layer and had started on the skin that I realised that the sweat was running down my face. As I blew away a droplet from my nose end Harry broke the silence.

'It's a hell of a tricky job, isn't it?' he said. Then he laughed and thumped my shoulder. 'I bet you felt a bit queer the first time you did one of these!'

I pulled another strand of suture silk through and knotted it. 'You're right, Harry,' I said. 'How right you are.'

When I had finished we covered Monty with a horse rug and piled straw on top of that, leaving only his head sticking out. I bent over and touched a corner of the eye. Not a vestige of a corneal reflex. God, he was deep – had I given him too much anaesthetic? And of course there'd be surgical shock, too. As I left I glanced back at the motionless little animal. He looked smaller than ever and very vulnerable under the bare walls of the pen.

I was busy for the rest of the day but that evening my thoughts kept coming back to Monty. Had he come out of it yet? Maybe he was dead. I hadn't the experience of previous cases to guide me and I simply had no idea of how a calf reacted to an operation like that. And I couldn't rid myself of the nagging consciousness of how much it all meant to Harry Sumner. The bull is half the herd, they say, and half of Harry's future herd was lying there under the straw – he wouldn't be able to find that much money again.

I jumped suddenly from my chair. It was no good, I had to find out what was happening. Part of me rebelled at the idea of looking amateurish and unsure of myself by going fussing back, but, I thought, I could always say I had returned to look for an instrument.

The farm was in darkness as I crept into the pen. I shone my torch on the mound of straw and saw with a quick thump of the heart that the calf had not moved. I dropped to my knees and pushed a hand under the rug; he was breathing anyway. But there was still no eye reflex – either he was dying or he was taking a hell of a time to come out.

In the shadows of the yard I looked across at the soft glow from the farmhouse kitchen. Nobody had heard me. I slunk over to the car and drove off with the sick knowledge that I was no further forward. I still didn't know how the job was going to turn out.

Next morning I had to go through the same thing again and as I walked stiffly across to the calf pen I knew for sure I'd see something this time. Either he'd be dead or better. I opened the outer door and almost ran down the passage. It was the third pen along and I stared hungrily into it.

Monty was sitting up on his chest. He was still under the rug and straw and he looked sorry for himself but when a bovine animal is on its chest I always feel hopeful. The tensions flowed from me in a great wave. He had survived the operation – the first stage was over; and as I knelt rubbing the top of his head I had the feeling that we were going to win.

And, in fact, he did get better, though I have always found it difficult to explain to myself scientifically why the removal of that pad of tangled fibres could cause such a dramatic improvement in so many directions. But there it was. His temperature did drop and his breathing returned to normal, his eyes did stop staring and the weird stiffness disappeared from his limbs.

But though I couldn't understand it, I was none the less delighted. Like a teacher with his favourite pupil I developed a warm proprietary affection for the calf and when I happened to be on the farm I found my feet straying unbidden to his pen. He always walked up to me and regarded me with friendly interest; it was as if he had a fellow feeling for me, too.

He was rather more than a year old when I noticed the change. The friendly interest gradually disappeared from his eyes and was replaced by a thoughtful, speculative look; and he developed a habit of shaking his head at me at the same time.

'I'd stop going in there, Mr Herriot, if I were you,' Harry said one day. 'He's getting big and I reckon he's going to be a cheeky bugger before he's finished.'

But cheeky was the wrong word. Harry had a long, trouble-free spell and Monty was nearly two years old when I saw him again. It wasn't a case of illness this time. One or two of Harry's cows had been calving before their time and it was typical of him that he should ask me to blood test his entire herd for Brucellosis.

We worked our way easily through the cows and I had a long row of glass tubes filled with blood in just over an hour.

'Well, that's the lot in here,' the farmer said. 'We only have bull to do and we're finished.' He led the way across the yard through the door into the calf pens and along a passage to the bull box at the end. He opened

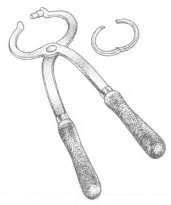

NOSE-PUNCH AND BULL-RING
The pincer-like nose-punch is about 10 in. long with a sharp-edged ring protruding from one jaw and a soft lead or copper knob on the other jaw for it to close against. The punch clips a small hole, and through it the vet slips the ring, which is usually copper. It is made in two halves pivoted together so that it can be opened up for slipping through the hole. Once the ring is in place, the two free ends are joined with a small screw.

the half door and as I looked inside I felt a sudden sense of shock.

Monty was enormous. The neck with its jutting humps of muscle supported a head so huge that the eyes looked tiny. And there was nothing friendly in those eyes now; no expression at all, in fact, only a cold black glitter. He was standing sideways to me, facing the wall, but I knew he was watching me as he pushed his head against the stones, his great horns scoring the whitewash with slow, menacing deliberation. Occasionally he snorted from deep in his chest but apart from that he remained ominously still. Monty wasn't just a bull – he was a vast, brooding presence.

Harry grinned as he saw me staring over the door. 'Well, do you fancy popping inside to scratch his head? That's what you allus used to do.'

'No thanks.' I dragged my eyes away from the animal. 'But I wonder what my expectation of life would be if I did go in.'

'I reckon you'd last about minute,' Harry said thoughtfully. 'He's a grand bull – all I ever expected – but by God he's a mean 'un. I never trust him an inch.'

'And how,' I asked without enthusiasm, 'am I supposed to get a sample of blood from him?'

'Oh I'll trap his head in yon corner.' Harry pointed to a metal yoke above a trough in an opening into the yard at the far side of the box. 'I'll give him some meal to 'tice him in.' He went back down the passage and soon I could see him out in the yard scooping meal into the trough.

The bull at first took no notice and continued to prod at the wall with his horns, then he turned with awesome slowness, took a few unhurried steps across the box and put his nose down to the trough. Harry, out of sight in the yard, pulled the lever and the yoke crashed shut on the great neck.

'All right,' the farmer cried, hanging on to the lever, 'I have 'im. You can go in now.'

I opened the door and entered the box and though the bull was held fast by the head there was still the uneasy awareness that he and I were alone in that small space together. And as I passed along the massive body and put my hand on the neck I sensed a quivering emanation of pent up power and rage. Digging my fingers into the jugular furrow I watched the vein rise up and poised my needle. It would take a good hard thrust to pierce that leathery skin.

The bull stiffened but did not move as I plunged the needle in and with relief I saw the blood flowing darkly into the syringe. Thank God I had hit the vein first time and didn't have to start poking around. I was withdrawing the needle and thinking that the job had been so simple after all when everything started to happen. The bull gave a tremendous bellow and whipped round at me with no trace of his former lethargy. I saw that he had got one horn out of the yoke and though he couldn't reach me with his head his shoulder knocked me on my back with a terrifying revelation of unbelievable strength. I heard Harry shouting from outside and as I scrambled up and headed for the box door I saw

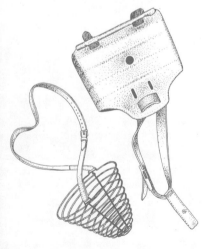

BULL BLIND AND CALF MUZZLE
An aggressive bull could be fitted with a metal blind, or face mask (top), which prevented it from seeing objects and being provoked by them into charging. Stockmen disagreed on how effective a blind was. It was fastened on by leather straps, and sometimes the blind itself was leather, not metal. The wire calf muzzle (bottom) is a device that was occasionally used to stop newly weaned calves from sucking. Some try to suck parts of their stall, each other or anything they can get hold of. They were muzzled for about a week to break the habit. The muzzle was taken off to let the calves eat and drink.

that the madly plunging creature had almost got his second horn clear and when I reached the passage I heard the clang of the yoke as he finally freed himself.

Anybody who has travelled a narrow passage a few feet ahead of about a ton of snorting, pounding death will appreciate that I didn't dawdle. I was spurred on by the certain knowledge that if Monty caught me he would plaster me against the wall as effortlessly as I would squash a ripe plum, and though I was clad in a long oilskin coat and wellingtons I doubt whether an Olympic sprinter in full running kit would have bettered my time.

I made the door at the end with a foot to spare, dived through and crashed it shut. The first thing I saw was Harry Sumner running round from the outside of the box. He was very pale. I couldn't see my face but it felt pale; even my lips were cold and numb.

'God, I'm sorry!' Harry said hoarsely. 'The yoke couldn't have closed properly – that bloody great neck of his. The lever just jerked out of my hand. Damn, I'm glad to see you – I thought you were a goner!'

I looked down at my hand. The blood-filled syringe was still tightly clutched there. 'Well I've got my sample anyway, Harry. And it's just as well, because it would take some fast talking to get me in there to try for another. I'm afraid you've just seen the end of a beautiful friendship.'

'Aye, the big sod!' Harry listened for a few moments to the thudding of Monty's horns against the door. 'And after all you did for him. That's gratitude for you.'

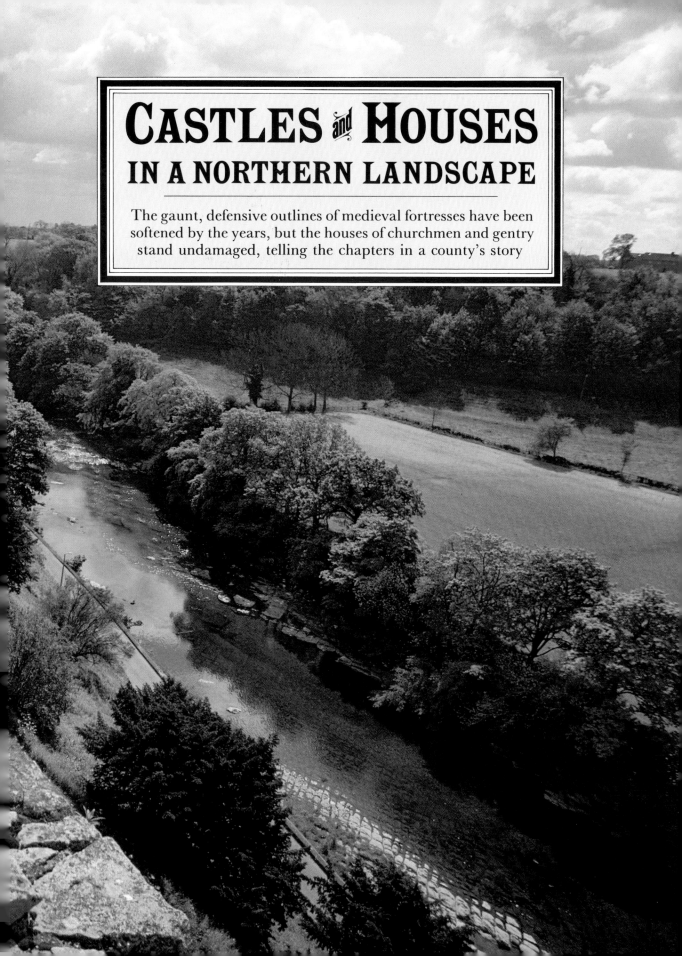

CASTLES & HOUSES
IN A NORTHERN LANDSCAPE

The gaunt, defensive outlines of medieval fortresses have been
softened by the years, but the houses of churchmen and gentry
stand undamaged, telling the chapters in a county's story

Seats of power for the friends of the monarch

In north Yorkshire, guarding the fringe of the secure kingdom, the Normans had by 1200 already built nine castles. In these and later castles familiar names from history's pages knew ambition, tragedy and pleasure.

Warwick the Kingmaker, who created and destroyed monarchs during the Wars of the Roses, lived lavishly and feasted his noble guests at Middleham.

The Scropes, Chief Justices and Lord Chancellors of England, built the 14th-century fortress Castle Bolton. At its windows in 1586 sat a prisoner, Mary, Queen of Scots, numb to Wensleydale's beauty, hoping to avoid execution.

Pickering was a royal castle which William I and King John visited to enjoy their favourite sport, hunting.

BASTION BYPASSED BY HISTORY Norman lords built Richmond Castle's walls within 2 years of the Conquest, and its 100 ft high keep a century later. Only a few Scottish raiders tested the defences, for north Yorkshire's main routes bypassed Richmond.

KEEPING WATCH From the 13th-century keep on its man-made mound, Pickering Castle's commander watched over the royal forest domain in the vale below.

RULING HOUSE The fate of 15th-century kings was plotted here at Middleham by assemblies of lords brought to his Norman stronghold by the Earl of Warwick.

PAST POWER Massive in placid Wensleydale, Castle Bolton speaks of times when kings had rivals and needed strong friends.

Homes between cottage and castle

Between the lowly cottagers and farmers and the proud nobles were tiers of gentry whose homes reflected their status. Parsonage, mansion, farm and castle alike often revealed in their design the early style of a single, large room.

The humble 15th-century brick cottage that became Shandy Hall was an open hall, but in the late 16th century the area entered a period of prosperity and soon the hall was enlarged with gables, divided into rooms. and given a stone-slate roof.

The gracefully curling gables that lighten the rendered brick at Norton Conyers were 17th-century additions. The main door opens into the original Tudor hall, where an arched ceiling conceals the earlier beamed roof.

The battlemented towers of Grinton Lodge and many sturdy mansions were survivals of the castle keep, which held the entire living space.

PARSON'S HOUSE For 350 years the vicars of Coxwold lived here. It was named Shandy Hall after one vicar, Laurence Sterne, wrote his comic novel *Tristram Shandy* in it.

GRINTON LODGE From this mock castle on the open moor above the Swaledale village of Grinton, war was waged on the game. It was built as a shooting lodge.

NORTON CONYERS Serene Stuart façades face tranquil meadows at Wath. But its owners, opposing Elizabeth I and then the Puritans, suffered failure and death.

MOAT The 14th-century moat remains at Markenfield Hall, near Ripon, built when a landowner needed his own defences.

6

A change of horse power for Cliff

Probably the most dramatic occurrence in the history of veterinary practice was the disappearance of the draught horse. It is an almost incredible fact that this glory and mainstay of the profession just melted quietly away within a few years. And I was one of those who were there to see it happen.

When I first came to Darrowby the tractor had already begun to take over, but tradition dies hard in the agricultural world and there were still a lot of horses around. Which was just as well because my veterinary education had been geared to things equine with everything else a poor second. It had been a good scientific education in many respects but at times I wondered if the people who designed it still had a mental picture of the horse doctor with his top hat and frock coat busying himself in a world of horse-drawn trams and brewers' drays.

We learned the anatomy of the horse in great detail then, that of the other animals much more superficially. It was the same with the other subjects; from animal husbandry with such insistence on a thorough knowledge of shoeing that we developed into amateur blacksmiths – right up to medicine and surgery where it was much more important to know about glanders and strangles than canine distemper. Even as we were learning, we youngsters knew it was ridiculous, with the draught horse already cast as a museum piece and the obvious potential of cattle and small animal work.

Still, after we had absorbed a vast store of equine lore it was a certain comfort that there were still a lot of patients on which we could try it out. I should think in my first two years I treated farm horses nearly every day and though I never was and never will be an equine expert there was a strange thrill in meeting with the age-old conditions whose names rang down almost from mediaeval times. Quittor, fistulous withers, poll evil, thrush, shoulder slip – vets had been wrestling with them for hundreds of years using very much the same drugs and procedures as myself. Armed with my firing iron and box of blister I plunged determinedly into what had always been the surging mainstream of veterinary life.

And now, in less than three years, the stream had dwindled, not exactly to a trickle but certainly to the stage where the final dry-up was in sight. This meant, in a way, a lessening of the pressures on the veterinary surgeon because there is no doubt that horse work was the roughest and most arduous part of our life.

So that today, as I looked at the three-year-old gelding, it occurred to me that this sort of thing wasn't happening as often as it did. He had a long tear in his flank where he had caught himself on barbed wire and it

209

gaped open whenever he moved. There was no getting away from the fact that it had to be stitched.

The horse was tied by the head in his stall, his right side against the tall wooden partition. One of the farm men, a hefty six footer, took a tight hold of the head collar and leaned back against the manger as I puffed some iodoform into the wound. The horse didn't seem to mind, which was a comfort because he was a massive animal emanating an almost tangible vitality and power. I threaded my needle with a length of silk, lifted one of the lips of the wound and passed it through. This was going to be no trouble, I thought as I lifted the flap at the other side and pierced it, but as I was drawing the needle through, the gelding made a convulsive leap and I felt as though a great wind had whistled across the front of my body. Then, strangely, he was standing there against the wooden boards as if nothing had happened.

On the occasions when I have been kicked I have never seen it coming. It is surprising how quickly those great muscular legs can whip out. But there was no doubt he had had a good go at me because my needle and silk was nowhere to be seen, the big man at the head was staring at me with wide eyes in a chalk white face and the front of my clothing was in an extraordinary state. I was wearing a gaberdine mac and it looked as if somebody had taken a razor blade and painstakingly cut the material into narrow strips which hung down in ragged strips to ground level. The great iron-shod hoof had missed my legs by an inch or two but my mac was a write-off.

I was standing there looking around me in a kind of stupor when I heard a cheerful hail from the doorway.

'Now then, Mr Herriot, what's he done at you?' Cliff Tyreman, the old horseman, looked me up and down with a mixture of amusement and asperity.

'He's nearly put me in hospital, Cliff,' I replied shakily. 'About the closest near miss I've ever had. I just felt the wind of it.'

'What were you tryin' to do?'

'Stitch that wound, but I'm not going to try any more. I'm off to the surgery to get a chloroform muzzle.'

The little man looked shocked. 'You don't need no chloroform. I'll haud him and you'll have no trouble.'

'I'm sorry, Cliff.' I began to put away my suture materials, scissors and powder. 'You're a good bloke, I know, but he's had one go at me and he's not getting another chance. I don't want to be lame for the rest of my life.'

The horseman's small, wiry frame seemed to bunch into a ball of aggression. He thrust forward his head in a characteristic posture and glared at me. 'I've never heard owt as daft in me life.' Then he swung round on the big man who was still hanging on to the horse's head, the ghastly pallor of his face now tinged with a delicate green. 'Come on out o' there, Bob! You're that bloody scared you're upsetting t'oss. Come on out of it and let me have 'im!'

Bob gratefully left the head and, grinning sheepishly, moved with care along the side of the horse. He passed Cliff on the way and the little man's head didn't reach his shoulder.

Cliff seemed thoroughly insulted by the whole business. He took hold of the head collar and regarded the big animal with the disapproving stare of a schoolmaster at a naughty child. The horse, still in the mood for trouble, laid back his ears and began to plunge about the stall, his huge feet clattering ominously on the stone floor, but he came to rest quickly as the little man uppercutted him furiously in the ribs.

'Get stood up straight there, ye big bugger. What's the matter with ye?' Cliff barked and again he planted his tiny fist against the swelling barrel of the chest, a puny blow which the animal could scarcely have felt but which reduced him to quivering submission. 'Try to kick, would you, eh? I'll bloody fettle you!' He shook the head collar and fixed the horse with a hypnotic stare as he spoke. Then he turned to me. 'You can come and do your job, Mr Herriot, he won't hurt tha.'

I looked irresolutely at the huge, lethal animal.

I looked irresolutely at the huge, lethal animal. Stepping open-eyed into dangerous situations is something vets are called upon regularly to do and I suppose we all react differently. I know there were times when an over-vivid imagination made me acutely aware of the dire possibilities and now my mind seemed to be dwelling voluptuously on the frightful power in those enormous shining quarters, on the unyielding flintiness of the spatulate feet with their rims of metal. Cliff's voice cut into my musings.

'Come on, Mr Herriot, I tell ye he won't hurt tha.'

I reopened my box and tremblingly threaded another needle. I didn't seem to have much option; the little man wasn't asking me, he was telling me. I'd have to try again.

I couldn't have been a very impressive sight as I shuffled forwards, almost tripping over the tattered hula-hula skirt which dangled in front of me, my shaking hands reaching out once more for the wound, my heart thundering in my ears. But I needn't have worried. It was just as the little man had said; he didn't hurt me. In fact he never moved. He seemed to be listening attentively to the muttering which Cliff was directing into his face from a few inches' range. I powdered and stitched and clipped as though working on an anatomical specimen. Chloroform couldn't have done it any better.

As I retreated thankfully from the stall and began again to put away my instruments the monologue at the horse's head began to change its character. The menacing growl was replaced by a wheedling, teasing chuckle.

'Well, ye see, you're just a daft awd bugger, getting yourself all airigated over nowt. You're a good lad, really, aren't ye, a real good lad.' Cliff's hand ran caressingly over the neck and the towering animal began to nuzzle his cheek, as completely in his sway as any Labrador puppy.

When he had finished he came slowly from the stall, stroking the back, ribs, belly and quarters, even giving a playful tweak at the tail on parting while what had been a few minutes ago an explosive mountain of bone and muscle submitted happily.

I pulled a packet of Gold Flake from my pocket. 'Cliff, you're a marvel. Will you have a cigarette?'

'It 'ud be like givin' a pig a strawberry,' the little man replied, then he thrust forth his tongue on which reposed a half-chewed gobbet of tobacco. 'It's allus there. Ah push it in fust thing every mornin' soon as I get out of bed and there it stays. You'd never know, would you?'

I must have looked comically surprised because the dark eyes gleamed and the rugged little face split into a delighted grin. I looked at that grin – boyish, invincible – and reflected on the phenomenon that was Cliff Tyreman.

In a community in which toughness and durability was the norm he stood out as something exceptional. When I had first seen him nearly three years ago barging among cattle, grabbing their noses and hanging

MOWING THE HAY Before a mower started cutting the hayfields in June, he made sure his scythe was set up properly for him. The length of the light, willow shaft, the positioning of the two nibs, or projecting handles, and the angle at which the sharp, curved blade was set affected his rate and precision of work. He could mow at least an acre a day, sweeping each blade stroke smoothly across so that the cut grass lay in a neat swathe or line all the way up the field. After completing each swathe, he walked back down the field to mow in the same direction again so that the swathes were evenly spaced and all the cut grass was lying the same way.

on effortlessly, I had put him down as an unusually fit middle-aged man; but he was in fact nearly seventy. There wasn't much of him but he was formidable; with his long arms swinging, his stumping, pigeon-toed gait and his lowered head he seemed always to be butting his way through life.

'I didn't expect to see you today,' I said. 'I heard you had pneumonia.'

He shrugged. 'Aye, summat of t'sort. First time I've ever been off work since I was a lad.'

'And you should be in your bed now, I should say.' I looked at the heaving chest and partly open mouth. 'I could hear you wheezing away when you were at the horse's head.'

'Nay, I can't stick that nohow. I'll be right in a day or two.' He seized a shovel and began busily clearing away the heap of manure behind the horse, his breathing loud and stertorous in the silence.

TURNIP CUTTER Getting the first bite from the hard globes of turnips or swedes is no easy matter for the sheep or cow that is feeding on them. This stamp cutter uses a lever action to bring down a stepped block on the turnip and force it through blades below, which divide it into slices.

Harland Grange was a large, mainly arable farm in the low country at the foot of the Dale, and there had been a time when this stable had had a horse standing in every one of the long row of stalls. There had been over twenty with at least twelve regularly at work, but now there were only two, the young horse I had been treating and an ancient grey called Badger.

Cliff had been head horseman and when the revolution came he turned to tractoring and other jobs around the farm with no fuss at all. This was typical of the reaction of thousands of other farm workers throughout the country; they didn't set up a howl at having to abandon the skills of a lifetime and start anew – they just got on with it. In fact, the younger men seized avidly upon the new machines and proved themselves natural mechanics.

But to the old experts like Cliff, something had gone. He would say: 'It's a bloody sight easier sitting on a tractor – it used to play 'ell with me feet walking up and down them fields all day.' But he couldn't lose his love of horses; the fellow feeling between working man and working beast which had grown in him since childhood and was in his blood for ever.

My next visit to the farm was to see a fat bullock with a piece of turnip stuck in his throat, but while I was there, the farmer, Mr Gilling, asked me to have a look at old Badger.

'He's had a bit of a cough lately. Maybe it's just his age, but see what you think.'

The old horse was the sole occupant of the stable now. 'I've sold the three-year-old,' Mr Gilling said. 'But I'll still keep the old 'un – he'll be useful for a bit of light carting.'

I glanced sideways at the farmer's granite features. He looked the least sentimental of men but I knew why he was keeping the old horse. It was for Cliff.

'Cliff will be pleased, anyway,' I said.

Mr Gilling nodded. 'Aye, I never knew such a feller for 'osses. He was

HORSE BRASSES The oldest-surviving horse brasses are from the late 18th century. They first became popular about 1850 and were made in imitation of the silver decorations used on the fine harness of aristocrats' carriages and state coaches. These bore heraldic designs which the horse brasses copied. Many traditional good-luck emblems have since been used on brasses. Common among the designs are suns, crescent moons, crosses, wheatsheaves, tinkling bells and horseshoes.

never happier than when he was with them.' He gave a short laugh. 'Do you know, I can remember years ago when he used to fall out with his missus he'd come down to this stable of a night and sit among his 'osses. Just sit here for hours on end looking at 'em and smoking. That was before he started chewing tobacco.'

'And did you have Badger in those days?'

'Aye, we bred him. Cliff helped at his foaling – I remember the little beggar came arse first and we had a bit of a job pullin' him out.' He smiled again. 'Maybe that's why he was always Cliff's favourite. He always worked Badger himself – year in year out – and he was that proud of 'im that if he had to take him into the town for any reason he'd plait ribbons into his mane and hang all his brasses on him first.' He shook his head reminiscently.

The old horse looked round with mild interest as I went up to him. He was in his late twenties and everything about him suggested serene old age; the gaunt projection of the pelvic bones, the whiteness of face and muzzle, the sunken eye with its benign expression. As I was about to take his temperature he gave a sharp, barking cough and it gave me the first clue to his ailment. I watched the rise and fall of his breathing for a minute or two and the second clue was there to be seen; further examination was unnecessary.

'He's broken winded, Mr Gilling,' I said. 'Or he's got pulmonary emphysema to give it its proper name. Do you see that double lift of the abdomen as he breathes out? That's because his lungs have lost their elasticity and need an extra effort to force the air out.'

'What's caused it, then?'

'Well it's to do with his age, but he's got a bit of cold on him at the moment and that's brought it out.'

'Will he get rid of it in time?' the farmer asked.

'He'll be a bit better when he gets over his cold, but I'm afraid he'll never be quite right. I'll give you some medicine to put in his drinking water which will alleviate his symptoms.' I went out to the car for a bottle of the arsenical expectorant mixture which we used then.

It was about six weeks later that I heard from Mr Gilling again. He rang me about seven o'clock one evening.

'I'd like you to come out and have a look at old Badger,' he said.

'What's wrong? Is it his broken wind again?'

'No, it's not that. He's still got the cough but it doesn't seem to bother him much. No, I think he's got a touch of colic. I've got to go out but Cliff will attend to you.'

The little man was waiting for me in the yard. He was carrying an oil lamp. As I came up to him I exclaimed in horror.

'Good God, Cliff, what have you been doing to yourself?' His face was a patchwork of cuts and scratches and his nose, almost without skin, jutted from between two black eyes.

He grinned through the wounds, his eyes dancing with merriment. 'Came off me bike t'other day. Hit a stone and went right over handlebars, arse over tip.' He burst out laughing at the very thought.

'But damn it, man, haven't you been to a doctor? You're not fit to be out in that state.'

'Doctor? Nay, there's no need to bother them fellers. It's nowt much.' He fingered a gash on his jaw. 'Ah lapped me chin up for a day in a bit o' bandage, but it's right enough now.'

I shook my head as I followed him into the stable. He hung up the oil lamp then went over to the horse.

'Can't reckon t'awd feller up,' he said. 'You'd think there wasn't much ailing him but there's summat.'

There were no signs of violent pain but the animal kept transferring his weight from one hind foot to the other as if he did have a little abdominal discomfort. His temperature was normal and he didn't show symptoms of anything else.

I looked at him doubtfully. 'Maybe he has a bit of colic. There's nothing else to see, anyway. I'll give him an injection to settle him down.'

'Right you are, maister, that's good.' Cliff watched me get my syringe out then he looked around him into the shadows at the far end of the stable.

'Funny seeing only one 'oss standing here. I remember when there was a great row of 'em and the barfins and bridles hangin' there on the stalls and the rest of the harness behind them all shinin' on t'wall.' He transferred his plug of tobacco to the other side of his mouth and smiled. 'By gaw, I were in here at six o'clock every morning feedin' them and gettin' them ready for work and ah'll tell you it was a sight to see us all goin' off ploughing at the start o' the day. Maybe six pairs of 'osses setting off with their harness jinglin' and the ploughmen sittin' sideways on their backs. Like a regular procession it was.'

I smiled. 'It was an early start, Cliff.'

'Aye, by Gaw, and a late finish. We'd bring the 'osses home at night and give 'em a light feed and take their harness off, then we'd go and have our own teas and we'd be back 'ere again afterwards, curry-combing and dandy-brushin' all the sweat and dirt off 'em. Then we'd give them a right good stiff feed of chop and oats and hay to set 'em up for the next day.'

'There wouldn't be much left of the evening then, was there?'

'Nay, there wasn't. It was about like work and bed, I reckon, but it never bothered us.'

I stepped forward to give Badger the injection, then paused. The old horse had undergone a slight spasm, a barely perceptible stiffening of the muscles, and as I looked at him he cocked his tail for a second then lowered it.

'There's something else here,' I said. 'Will you bring him out of his stall, Cliff, and let me see him walk across the yard.'

And watching him clop over the cobbles I saw it again; the stiffness, the raising of the tail. Something clicked in my mind, I walked over and

TOOTH CHISELS A horse quickly loses condition if it cannot chew its food properly. It used to be thought that 'wolf teeth' hindered chewing. These were extra, small teeth in front of the first premolars. Chisels about 18 in. long were used to knock off the projections. The horse's mouth was held open by a gag, and the chisel was hammered against the tooth. Some chisels had rounded lugs and some a serrated cutting edge to stop the blade from slipping sideways when the chisel was struck.

215

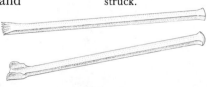

rapped him under the chin and as the membrana nictitans flicked across his eye then slid slowly back I knew.

I paused for a moment. My casual little visit had suddenly become charged with doom.

'Cliff,' I said. 'I'm afraid he's got tetanus.'

'Lockjaw, you mean?'

'That's right. I'm sorry, but there's no doubt about it. Has he had any wounds lately – especially in his feet?'

'Well he were dead lame about a fortnight ago and blacksmith let some matter out of his hoof. Made a right big 'ole.'

There it was. 'It's a pity he didn't get an anti-tetanus shot at the time,' I said. I put my hand into the animal's mouth and tried to prise it open but the jaws were clamped tightly together. 'I don't suppose he's been able to eat today.'

'He had a bit this morning but nowt tonight. What's the lookout for him, Mr Herriot?'

What indeed? If Cliff had asked me the same question today I would have been just as troubled to give him an answer. The facts are that seventy to eighty per cent of tetanus cases die and whatever you do to them in the way of treatment doesn't seem to make a whit of difference to those figures. But I didn't want to sound entirely defeatist.

'It's a very serious condition as you know, Cliff, but I'll do all I can. I've got some antitoxin in the car and I'll inject that into his vein and if the spasms get very bad I'll give him a sedative. As long as he can drink there's a chance for him because he'll have to live on fluids – gruel would be fine.'

For a few days Badger didn't get any worse and I began to hope. I've seen tetanus horses recover and it is a wonderful experience to come in one day and find that the jaws have relaxed and the hungry animal can once more draw food into its mouth.

But it didn't happen with Badger. They had got the old horse into a big loose box where he could move around in comfort and each day as I looked over the half door I felt myself willing him to show some little sign of improvement; but instead, after that first few days, he began to deteriorate. A sudden movement or the approach of any person would throw him into a violent spasm so that he would stagger stiff-legged round the box like a big wooden toy, his eyes terrified, saliva drooling from between his fiercely clenched teeth. One morning I was sure he would fall and I suggested putting him in slings. I had to go back to the surgery for the slings and it was just as I was entering Skeldale House that the phone rang.

It was Mr Gilling. 'He's beat us to it, I'm afraid. He's flat out on the floor and I doubt it's a bad job, Mr Herriot. We'll have to put him down, won't we?'

'I'm afraid so.'

'There's just one thing. Mallock will be taking him away but old Cliff says he doesn't want Mallock to shoot 'im. Wants you to do it. Will you

THE STANDARD FORDSON
Tractors found a place only slowly on British farms because there was ample cheap labour, and slumps in the 1920s and 1930s made the tractor an extravagance. By 1939 there were about 55,000; by the end of the Second World War the shortage of labour and the need to produce food at home, rather than importing it, had increased the number to over 200,000. The most numerous by far was the Standard Fordson, also called the Fordson Model N. The product of Henry Ford's mass-production methods, it was made at Dagenham in Essex from 1933. Increasing numbers had the new pneumatic tyres, which made them usable on roads as well as much faster over the ground.

come?'

I got out the humane killer and drove back to the farm, wondering at the fact that the old man should find the idea of my bullet less repugnant than the knacker man's. Mr Gilling was waiting in the box and by his side Cliff, shoulders hunched, hands deep in his pockets. He turned to me with a strange smile.

'I was just saying to t'boss how grand t'awd lad used to look when I got 'im up for a show. By Gaw you should have seen him with 'is coat polished and the feathers on his legs scrubbed as white as snow and a big blue ribbon round his tail.'

'I can imagine it, Cliff,' I said. 'Nobody could have looked after him better.'

He took his hands from his pockets, crouched by the prostrate animal and for a few minutes stroked the white-flecked neck and pulled at the ears while the old sunken eye looked at him impassively.

He began to speak softly to the old horse but his voice was steady, almost conversational, as though he was chatting to a friend.

'Many's the thousand miles I've walked after you, awd lad, and many's the talk we've had together. But I didn't have to say much to tha, did I? I reckon you knew every move I made, everything I said. Just one little word and you always did what ah wanted you to do.'

He rose to his feet. 'I'll get on with me work now, boss,' he said firmly, and strode out of the box.

I waited awhile so that he would not hear the bang which signalled the end of Badger, the end of the horses of Harland Grange and the end of the sweet core of Cliff Tyreman's life.

As I was leaving I saw the little man again. He was mounting the iron seat of a roaring tractor and I shouted to him above the noise.

'The boss says he's going to get some sheep in and you'll be doing a bit of shepherding. I think you'll enjoy that.'

Cliff's undefeated grin flashed out as he called back to me.

'Aye, I don't mind learnin' summat new. I'm nobbut a lad yet!'

7

I grasp the nettle of life

The big room at Skeldale House was full. It seemed to me that this room with its graceful alcoves, high, carved ceiling and french windows lay at the centre of our life in Darrowby. It was where Siegfried, Tristan and I gathered when the day's work was done, toasting our feet by the white wood fireplace with the glass-fronted cupboard on top, talking over the day's events. It was the heart of our bachelor existence, sitting there in a

DRESSING HORSES Daily grooming, up to four daily feeds – the first at half-past five in the morning – and five or six hours' work in the fields was the normal pattern of life for farm horses. Extra attention was given to grooming when the horse was going on a public road or into town. The tail would be plaited or rolled up, and the mane plaited. Each small plait along the mane was tied at the end with horsehair. The plaited-rope bridle was also part of the special dressing for shows.

THE WIRELESS AGE The largely self-contained life of a Dales farm family ended in the 1930s when the outside world broke in daily through the wireless, which was becoming a widespread household item. It provided daytime company for the farmer's wife, who was often alone, and was the centre of evening interest. The radios were powered by heavy, glass-cased batteries – which could be recharged at the hardware or grocery shop – before there was a mains electricity supply.

happy stupor, reading, listening to the radio, Tristan usually flipping effortlessly through the *Daily Telegraph* crossword.

It was where Siegfried entertained his friends and there was a constant stream of them – old and young, male and female. But tonight it was Tristan's turn and the pack of young people with drinks in their hands were there at his invitation. And they wouldn't need much persuasion. Though just about the opposite of his brother in many ways he had the same attractiveness which brought the friends running at the crook of a finger.

The occasion was the Daffodil Ball at the Drovers' Arms and we were dressed in our best. This was a different kind of function from the usual village institute hop with the farm lads in their big boots and music from a scraping fiddle and piano. It was a proper dance with a popular local band – Lenny Butterfield and his Hot Shots – and was an annual affair to herald the arrival of spring.

I watched Tristan dispensing the drinks. The bottles of whisky, gin and sherry which Siegfried kept in the fireplace cupboard had taken some severe punishment but Tristan himself had been abstemious. An occasional sip from a glass of light ale perhaps, but nothing more. Drinking, to him, meant the bulk intake of draught bitter; all else was mere vanity and folly. Dainty little glasses were anathema and even now when I see him at a party where everybody is holding small drinks Tristan somehow contrives to have a pint in his hand.

'Nice little gathering, Jim,' he said, appearing at my elbow. 'A few more blokes than girls but that won't matter much.'

I eyed him coldly. I knew why there were extra men. It was so that Tristan wouldn't have to take the floor too often. It fitted in with his general dislike of squandering energy that he was an unenthusiastic dancer; he didn't mind walking a girl round the floor now and again during the evening but he preferred to spend most of the time in the bar.

So, in fact, did a lot of the Darrowby folk. When we arrived at the Drovers the bar was congested while only a dedicated few circled round the ballroom. But as time went on more and more couples ventured out and by ten o'clock the dance floor was truly packed.

And I soon found I was enjoying myself. Tristan's friends were an effervescent bunch; likeable young men and attractive girls; I just couldn't help having a good time.

Butterfield's famed band in their short red jackets added greatly to the general merriment. Lenny himself looked about fifty-five and indeed all four of the Hot Shots ensemble were rather elderly, but they made up for their grey hairs by sheer vivacity. Not that Lenny's hair was grey; it was dyed a determined black and he thumped the piano with dynamic energy, beaming out at the company through his horn-rimmed glasses, occasionally bawling a chorus into the microphone by his side, announcing the dances, making throaty wisecracks. He gave value for money.

There was no pairing off in our party and I danced with all the girls in turn. At the peak of the evening I was jockeying my way around the floor with Daphne and the way she was constructed made it a rewarding experience. I never have been one for skinny women but I suppose you could say that Daphne's development had strayed a little too far in the other direction. She wasn't fat, just lavishly endowed.

Battling through the crush, colliding with exuberant neighbours, bouncing deliciously off Daphne, with everybody singing as they danced and the Hot Shots pouring out an insistent boom-boom beat, I felt I hadn't a care in the world. And then I saw Helen.

She was dancing with the inevitable Richard Edmundson, his shining gold head floating above the company like an emblem of doom. And it was uncanny how in an instant my cosy little world disintegrated leaving a chill gnawing emptiness.

When the music stopped I returned Daphne to her friends and went to find Tristan. The comfortable little bar in the Drovers was overflowing and the temperature like an oven. Through an almost impenetrable fog of cigarette smoke I discerned my colleague on a high stool holding court with a group of perspiring revellers. Tristan himself looked cool and, as always, profoundly content. He drained his glass, smacked his lips gently as though it had been the best pint of beer he'd ever tasted, then, as he reached across the counter and courteously requested a refill, he spotted me struggling towards him.

When I reached his stool he laid an affable hand on my shoulder, 'Ah, Jim, nice to see you. Splendid dance, this, don't you think?'

I didn't bring up the fact that I hadn't seen him on the floor yet, but making my voice casual I mentioned that Helen was there.

Tristan nodded benignly. 'Yes, saw her come in. Why don't you go and dance with her?'

'I can't do that. She's with a partner – young Edmundson.'

'Not at all.' Tristan surveyed his fresh pint with a critical eye and took an exploratory sip. 'She's with a party, like us. No partner.'

'How do you know that?'

'I watched all the fellows hang their coats out there while the girls went upstairs. No reason at all why you shouldn't have a dance with her.'

'I see.' I hesitated for a few moments then made my way back to the ballroom.

But it wasn't as easy as that. I had to keep doing my duty with the girls in our group and whenever I headed for Helen she was whisked away by one of her men friends before I got near her. At times I fancied she was looking over at me but I couldn't be sure; the only thing I knew for certain was that I wasn't enjoying myself any more; the magic and gaiety had gone and I felt a rising misery at the thought that this was going to be another of my frustrating contacts with Helen when all I could do was look at her hopelessly. Only this time was worse – I hadn't even spoken to her.

I was almost relieved when the manager came up and told me there

A VET'S WARDROBE Working clothes for a young vet in a country practice were not worn to impress, for he spent much of his time trudging across muddy fields and crouching in cowsheds. Corduroy trousers and an old tweed jacket made a typical outfit. But for church or chapel on Sundays, or for trips to town, he needed a suit. Near at hand in Leeds there was by the 1930s the largest clothing factory in the world – Montague Burton's – and all the larger Dales towns had a Burton shop with a black and silver façade. Here, James Herriot would be able to buy a ready-made suit for 55 shillings (£2.75).

was a call for me. I went to the phone and spoke to Mrs Hall. There was a bitch in trouble whelping and I had to go. I looked at my watch – after midnight, so that was the end of the dance for me.

I stood for a moment listening to the muffled thudding from the dance floor then slowly pulled on my coat before going in to say goodbye to Tristan's friends. I exchanged a few words with them, waved, then turned back and pushed the swing door open.

Helen was standing there, about a foot away from me. Her hand was on the door, too. I didn't wonder whether she was going in or out but stared dumbly into her smiling blue eyes.

'Leaving already, Jim?' she said.

'Yes, I've got a call, I'm afraid.'

'Oh what a shame. I hope it's nothing very serious.'

I opened my mouth to speak, but her dark beauty and the very nearness of her suddenly filled my world and a wave of hopeless longing swept over and submerged me. I slid my hand a few inches down the door and gripped hers as a drowning man might, and wonderingly I felt her fingers come round and entwine themselves tightly in mine.

And in an instant there was no band, no noise, no people, just the two of us standing very close in the doorway.

'Come with me,' I said.

Helen's eyes were very large as she smiled that smile I knew so well.

'I'll get my coat,' she murmured.

This wasn't really me, I thought, standing on the hall carpet watching Helen trotting quickly up the stairs, but I had to believe it as she reappeared on the landing pulling on her coat. Outside, on the cobbles of the market place my car, too, appeared to be taken by surprise because it roared into life at the first touch of the starter.

I had to go back to the surgery for my whelping instruments and in the silent moonlit street we got out and I opened the big white door to Skeldale House.

And once in the passage it was the most natural thing in the world to take her in my arms and kiss her gratefully and unhurriedly. I had waited a long time for this and the minutes flowed past unnoticed as we stood there, our feet on the black and red eighteenth-century tiles, our heads almost touching the vast picture of the Death of Nelson which dominated the entrance.

We kissed again at the first bend of the passage under the companion picture of the Meeting of Wellington and Blucher at Waterloo. We kissed at the second bend by the tall cupboard where Siegfried kept his riding coats and boots. We kissed in the dispensary in between searching for my instruments. Then we tried it out in the garden and this was the best of all with the flowers still and expectant in the moonlight and the fragrance of the moist earth and grass rising about us.

I have never driven so slowly to a case. About ten miles an hour with Helen's head on my shoulder and all the scents of spring drifting in through the open window. And it was like sailing from stormy seas into a

PARAFFIN PILLAR-LAMP From the mid-19th century, oil lamps were replacing the tallow candles of the previous centuries but, except in the grander homes, one lamp often served the whole house. Many lamps were elegant in design, and in farming families they were often used for special occasions when there was company, not for regular use. This pillar-lamp has a brass base and fluted column with a translucent glass shade and an amethyst glass reservoir for the paraffin.

sweet, safe harbour, like coming home.

The light in the cottage window was the only one showing in the sleeping village, and when I knocked at the door Bert Chapman answered. Bert was a council roadman – one of the breed for whom I felt an abiding affinity.

The council men were my brethren of the roads. Like me they spent most of their lives on the lonely by-ways around Darrowby and I saw them most days of the week, repairing the tarmac, cutting back the grass verges in the summer, gritting and snow ploughing in the winter. And when they spotted me driving past they would grin cheerfully and wave as if the very sight of me had made their day. I don't know whether they were specially picked for good nature but I don't think I have ever met a more equable body of men.

One old farmer remarked sourly to me once. 'There's no wonder the buggers are 'appy, they've got nowt to do.' An exaggeration, of course, but I knew how he felt; compared with farming every other job was easy.

I had seen Bert Chapman just a day or two ago, sitting on a grassy bank, his shovel by his side, a vast sandwich in his hand. He had raised a corded forearm in salute, a broad smile bisecting his round, sun-reddened face. He had looked eternally carefree but tonight his smile was strained.

'I'm sorry to bother you this late, Mr Herriot,' he said as he ushered us into the house, 'but I'm gettin' a bit worried about Susie. Her pups are due and she's been making a bed for them and messing about all day but nowt's happened. I was goin' to leave her till morning but about midnight she started panting like 'ell – I don't like the look of her.'

Susie was one of my regular patients. Her big, burly master was always bringing her to the surgery, a little shamefaced at his solicitude, and when I saw him sitting in the waiting room looking strangely out of place among the ladies with their pets, he usually said 'T'missus asked me to bring Susie.' But it was a transparent excuse.

'She's nobbut a little mongrel, but very faithful,' Bert said, still apologetic, but I could understand how he felt about Susie, a shaggy little ragamuffin whose only wile was to put her paws on my knees and laugh up into my face with her tail lashing. I found her irresistible.

But she was a very different character tonight. As we went into the living room of the cottage the little animal crept from her basket, gave a single indeterminate wag of her tail then stood miserably in the middle of the floor, her ribs heaving. As I bent to examine her she turned a wide, panting mouth and anxious eyes up to me.

I ran my hands over her abdomen. I don't think I have ever felt a more bloated little dog; she was as round as a football, absolutely bulging with pups, ready to pop, but nothing was happening.

'What do you think?' Bert's face was haggard under his sunburn, and he touched the dog's head briefly with a big calloused hand.

'I don't know yet, Bert,' I said. 'I'll have to have a feel inside. Bring me some hot water, will you?'

PARAFFIN HAND-LAMP With bright light flooding a room at the touch of a switch, it is hard now to imagine the inconveniences of moving round the house in the pre-electric age. The glow of the kitchen or parlour fire threw a flickering light as far as the door, but beyond that all was dark. Traditionally it was candles in holders that were carried along passages, up the staircase and into the bedroom. Paraffin hand-lamps replaced these after the mid-19th century and were used until electricity was laid on – in the 1950s in some parts of the Dales. This brass lamp has a wide, flat base to stand securely, a handle large enough to grasp with the whole hand, and a clear glass shade.

I added some antiseptic to the water, soaped my hand and with one finger carefully explored the vagina. There was a pup there, all right; my finger tip brushed across the nostrils, the tiny mouth and tongue; but he was jammed in that passage like a cork in a bottle.

Squatting back on my heels I turned to the Chapmans.

'I'm afraid there's a big pup stuck fast. I have a feeling that if she could get rid of this chap the others would come away. They'd probably be smaller.'

'Is there any way of shiftin' him, Mr Herriot?' Bert asked.

I paused for a moment. 'I'm going to put forceps on his head and see if he'll move. I don't like using forceps but I'm going to have one careful try and if it doesn't work I'll have to take her back to the surgery for a caesarian.'

'An operation?' Bert said hollowly. He gulped and glanced fearfully at his wife. Like many big men he had married a tiny woman and at this moment Mrs Chapman looked even smaller than her four foot eleven inches as she huddled in her chair and stared at me with wide eyes.

'Oh I wish we'd never had her mated,' she wailed, wringing her hands. 'I told Bert five year old was too late for a first litter but he wouldn't listen. And now we're maybe going to lose 'er.'

I hastened to reasssure her. 'No, she isn't too old, and everything may be all right. Let's just see how we get on.'

I boiled the instrument for a few minutes on the stove then kneeled behind my patient again. I poised the forceps for a moment and at the flash of steel a grey tinge crept under Bert's sunburn and his wife coiled herself into a ball in her chair. Obviously they were non-starters as assistants so Helen held Susie's head while I once more reached in towards the pup. There was desperately little room but I managed to direct the forceps along my finger till they touched the nose. Then very gingerly I opened the jaws and pushed them forward with the very gentlest pressure until I was able to clamp them on either side of the head.

I'd soon know now. In a situation like this you can't do any pulling, you can only try to ease the thing along. This I did and I fancied I felt just a bit of movement; I tried again and there was no doubt about it, the pup was coming towards me. Susie, too, appeared to sense that things were taking a turn for the better. She cast off her apathy and began to strain lustily.

It was no trouble after that and I was able to draw the pup forth almost without resistance.

'I'm afraid this one'll be dead,' I said, and as the tiny creature lay across my palm there was no sign of breathing. But, pinching the chest between thumb and forefinger I could feel the heart pulsing steadily and I quickly opened his mouth and blew softly down into his lungs.

I repeated this a few times then laid the pup on his side in the basket. I was just thinking it was going to be no good when the little rib cage gave a sudden lift, then another and another.

WHELPING FORCEPS If a puppy is large or awkwardly placed in the womb, the bitch has difficulty in giving birth to it and the vet has to help. There are several designs of forceps which he can use to insert into the vagina or the womb and draw the puppy out. They all have jaws shaped to grasp the puppy's head securely without injuring it. Forceps are made in various sizes from 7 in. to 2 ft long for treating different breeds. They are now made of stainless steel which does not deteriorate as the earlier nickel-plated forceps did from much use and repeated boiling.

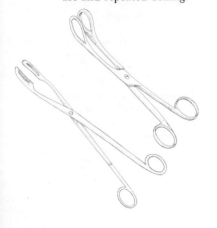

'He's off!' Bert exclaimed happily. 'That's champion! We want these puppies alive tha knows. They're by Jack Dennison's terrier and he's a grand 'un.'

'That's right,' Mrs Chapman put in. 'No matter how many she has, they're all spoken for. Everybody wants a pup out of Susie.'

'I can believe that,' I said. But I smiled to myself. Jack Dennison's terrier was another hound of uncertain ancestry, so this lot would be a right mixture. But none the worse for that.

I gave Susie half a c.c. of pituitrin. 'I think she needs it after pushing against that fellow for hours. We'll wait and see what happens now.'

And it was nice waiting. Mrs Chapman brewed a pot of tea and began to slap butter on to home-made scones. Susie, partly aided by my pituitrin, pushed out a pup in a self-satisfied manner about every fifteen minutes. The pups themselves soon set up a bawling of surprising volume for such minute creatures. Bert, relaxing visibly with every minute, filled his pipe and regarded the fast-growing family with a grin of increasing width.

'Ee, it is kind of you young folks to stay with us like this.' Mrs Chapman put her head on one side and looked at us worriedly. 'I should think you've been dying to get back to your dance all this time.'

I thought of the crush at the Drovers. The smoke, the heat, the non-stop boom-boom of the Hot Shots and I looked around the peaceful little room with the old-fashioned black grate, the low, varnished beams, Mrs Chapman's sewing box, the row of Bert's pipes on the wall. I took a firmer grasp of Helen's hand which I had been holding under the table for the last hour.

'Not at all, Mrs Chapman,' I said. 'We haven't missed it in the least.' And I have never been more sincere.

It must have been about half past two when I finally decided that Susie had finished. She had six fine pups which was a good score for a little thing like her and the noise had abated as the family settled down to feast on her abundant udder.

I lifted the pups out one by one and examined them. Susie didn't mind in the least but appeared to be smiling with modest pride as I handled her brood. When I put them back with her she inspected them and sniffed them over busily before rolling on to her side again.

'Three dogs and three bitches,' I said. 'Nice even litter.'

Before leaving I took Susie from her basket and palpated her abdomen. The degree of deflation was almost unbelievable; a pricked balloon could not have altered its shape more spectacularly and she had made a remarkable metamorphosis to the lean, scruffy little extrovert I knew so well.

When I released her she scurried back and curled herself round her new family who were soon sucking away with total absorption.

Bert laughed. 'She's fair capped wi' them pups.' He bent over and prodded the first arrival with a horny forefinger. 'I like the look o' this big dog pup. I reckon we'll keep this 'un for ourselves, mother. He'll be

THE SEWING MACHINE On the weekly trip to the local market a farmer's wife would look for bargains among the 'fents', or ends of rolls of fabric from the mills – woollens from the West Riding and cottons from the Lancashire towns just over the heads of the valleys. It could also be at the market, or from a travelling salesman, that she bought a sewing machine – perhaps paid for in instalments. With the hand-turned Singer machine, enamelled black and gilt on the body and set on a polished wooden base, she could run up curtains, chair covers and bedspreads as well as many of the family's clothes.

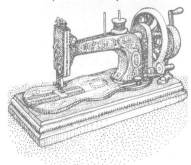

company for t'awd lass.'

It was time to go. Helen and I moved over to the door and little Mrs Chapman with her fingers on the handle looked up at me.

'Well, Mr Herriot,' she said, 'I can't thank you enough for comin' out and putting our minds at rest. I don't know what I've done wi' this man of mine if anything had happened to his little dog.'

Bert grinned sheepishly. 'Nay,' he muttered. 'Ah was never really worried.'

His wife laughed and opened the door and as we stepped out into the silent, scented night she gripped my arm and looked up at me roguishly.

'I suppose this is your young lady,' she said.

I put my arm round Helen's shoulders.

'Yes,' I said firmly, 'this is my young lady.'

After the night of the Daffodil Ball I just seemed to drift naturally into the habit of dropping in to see Helen on an occasional evening. And before I knew what was happening I had developed a pattern; around eight o'clock my feet began to make of their own accord for Heston Grange. Of course I fought the impulse – I didn't go every night; there was my work which often occupied me round the clock, there was a feeling of propriety, and there was Mr Alderson.

Helen's father was a vague little man who had withdrawn into himself to a great extent since his wife's death a few years ago. He was an expert stocksman and his farm could compare with the best, but a good part of his mind often seemed to be elsewhere. And he had acquired some little peculiarities; when things weren't going well he carried on long muttered conversations with himself, but when he was particularly pleased about something he was inclined to break into a loud, tuneless humming. It was a penetrating sound and on my professional visits I could often locate him by tracking down this characteristic droning among the farm buildings.

At first when I came to see Helen I'm sure he never even noticed me – I was just one of the crowd of young men who hung around his daughter; but as time went on and my visits became more frequent he suddenly seemed to become conscious of me and began to regard me with an interest which deepened rapidly into alarm. I couldn't blame him, really. He was devoted to Helen and it was natural that he should desire a grand match for her. Richard Edmundson represented just that. His family were rich, powerful people and Richard was very keen indeed. Compared to him, an unknown, impecunious young vet was a poor bargain.

When Mr Alderson was around, my visits were uncomfortable affairs, and it was a pity because I instinctively liked him. He had an amiable, completely inoffensive nature which was very appealing and under other conditions we would have got along very well. But there was no getting round the fact that he resented me. And it wasn't because he wanted to hang on to Helen – he was an unselfish man and, anyway, he had an

THE HUB OF THE FARM The principal workshop of a farm has always been the barn in the farmyard. The wide, high, main doorway was designed to let loaded harvest and hay wagons enter. As much as possible of the hay and the corn crop was stacked in the barn. During the winter, sheaves of corn were unstacked for threshing and winnowing inside the barn. The horses' trappings and the machines they pulled were housed in the barn, and at one end of the building were the stalls for the cows. The floor of the stalls was often lower than the rest of the barn so that the dung did not spread beyond the stalls. it was convenient to have an opening in the wall for shovelling the dung out directly on to the dung-heap in a walled enclosure against the outside wall of the barn.

excellent housekeeper in his sister who had been recently widowed and had come to live with the Aldersons. Auntie Lucy was a redoubtable character and was perfectly capable of running the household and looking after the two younger children. It was just that he had got used to the comfortable assumption that one day his daughter would marry the son of his old friend and have a life of untroubled affluence; and he had a stubborn streak which rebelled fiercely against any prospect of change.

So it was always a relief when I got out of the house with Helen. Everything was right then; we went to the little dances in the village institutes, we walked for miles along the old grassy mine tracks among the hills, or sometimes she came on my evening calls with me. There wasn't anything spectacular to do in Darrowby but there was a complete lack of strain, a feeling of being self-sufficient in a warm existence of our own that made everything meaningful and worthwhile.

Things might have gone on like this indefinitely but for a conversation I had with Siegfried. We were sitting in the big room at Skeldale House as we often did before bedtime, talking over the day's events, when he laughed and slapped his knee.

'I had old Harry Forster in tonight paying his bill. He was really funny – sat looking round the room and saying "It's a nice little nest you have here, Mr Farnon, a nice little nest" and then, very sly "It's time there was a bird in this nest, you know, there should be a little bird in here."'

I laughed too. 'Well, you should be used to it by now. You're the most eligible bachelor in Darrowby. People are always having a dig at you – they won't be happy till they've got you married off.'

'Wait a minute, not so fast.' Siegfried eyed me thoughtfully. 'I don't think for a moment that Harry was talking about me, it was you he had in mind.'

'What do you mean?'

'Well just think. Didn't you say you had run into the old boy one night when you were walking over his land with Helen. He'd be on to a thing like that in a flash. He thinks it's time you were hitched up, that's all.'

I lay back in my chair and gave myself over to laughter. 'Me! Married! That'll be the day. Can you imagine it? Poor old Harry.'

Siegfried leaned forward. 'What are you laughing at, James? He's quite right – it's time you were married.'

'What's that?' I looked at him incredulously. 'What are you on about now?'

'It's quite simple,' he said. 'I'm saying you ought to get married, and soon.'

'Oh come on Siegfried, you're joking!'

'Why should I be?'

'Well damn it, I'm only starting my career, I've no money, no nothing, I've never even thought about it.'

'You've never even ... well tell me this, are you courting Helen

225

Alderson or aren't you?'

'Well I'm ... I've been ... oh I suppose you could call it that.'

Siegfried settled back comfortably on his chair, put his finger tips together and assumed a judicial expression. 'Good, good. You admit you're courting the girl. Now let us take it a step further. She is, from my own observation, extremely attractive – in fact she nearly causes a traffic pile-up when she walks across the cobbles on market day. It's common knowledge that she is intelligent, equable and an excellent cook. Perhaps you would agree with this?'

'Of course I would,' I said, nettled at his superior air. 'But what's this all about? Why are you going on like a High Court judge?'

'I'm only trying to establish my point, James, which is that you seem to have an ideal wife lined up and you are doing nothing about it. In fact, not to put a too fine point on it, I wish you'd stop playing around and let us see a little action.'

'But it's not as simple as that,' I said, my voice rising, 'I've told you already I'd have to be a lot better off, and, anyway, give me a chance, I've only been going to the house for a few weeks – surely you don't start thinking of getting married as soon as that. And there's another thing – her old man doesn't like me.'

Siegfried put his head on one side and I gritted my teeth as a saintly expression began to settle on his face. 'Now, my dear chap, don't get angry, but there's something I have to tell you for your own good. Caution is often a virtue, but in your case you carry it too far. It's a little flaw in your character and it shows in a multitude of ways. In your wary approach to problems in your work, for instance – you are always too apprehensive, proceeding fearfully step by step when you should be plunging boldly ahead. You keep seeing dangers when there aren't any – you've got to learn to take a chance, to lash out a bit. As it is, you are confined to a narrow range of activity by your own doubts.'

'The original stick-in-the-mud in fact, eh?'

'Oh come now, James, I didn't say that, but while we're talking, there's another small point I want to bring up. I know you won't mind my saying this. Until you get married I'm afraid I shall fail to get the full benefit of your assistance in the practice because frankly you are becoming increasingly besotted and bemused to the extent that I'm sure you don't know what you're doing half the time.'

'What the devil are you talking about? I've never heard such ...'

'Kindly hear me out, James. What I'm saying is perfectly true – you're walking about like a man in a dream and you've developed a disturbing habit of staring into space when I'm talking to you. There's only one cure, my boy.'

'And it's a simple little cure, isn't it!' I shouted. 'No money, no home, but leap into matrimony with a happy cry. There's not a thing to worry about!'

'Ah-ah, you see, there you go again, looking for difficulties.' He gave a little laugh and gazed at me with pitying affection. 'No money you say.

GOATHLAND SHEEP SALE For north Yorkshire sheep farmers some of the major annual livestock auction markets were at Reeth, Malham, Kilnsey and Goathland. From early dawn on market day the lanes and streets were swarming with flocks being driven to market. There they were penned in lots by movable gates for prospective buyers to have a good look at them. This was the place to convert the year's surplus into money by selling to larger breeders or for slaughter. At Yorkshire's 50 livestock markets more than a million sheep and lambs changed hands each year in the 1930s.

Well one of these days you'll be a partner here. Your plate will be out on those railings in front of the house, so you'll never be short of your daily bread. And as regards a home – look at all the empty rooms in this house. You could set up a private suite upstairs without any trouble. So that's just a piffling little detail.'

I ran my hand distractedly through my hair. My head was beginning to swim. 'You make it all sound easy.'

'But it IS easy!' Siegfried shot upright in his chair. 'Go out and ask that girl without further delay and get her into church before the month is out!' He wagged a finger at me. 'Learn to grasp the nettle of life, James. Throw off your hesitant ways and remember:' He clenched his fist and struck an attitude. 'There is a tide in the affairs of men which, taken at the flood ...'

'O.K., O.K.,' I said, rising wearily from my chair, 'that's enough, I get the message. I'm going to bed now.'

And I don't suppose I am the first person to have had his life fundamentally influenced by one of Siegfried's chance outbursts. I thought his opinions ridiculous at the time but he planted a seed which germinated and flowered almost overnight. There is no doubt he is responsible for the fact that I was the father of a grown-up family while I was still a young man, because when I brought the subject up with Helen she said yes she'd like to marry me and we set our eyes on an early date. She seemed surprised at first – maybe she had the same opinion of me as Siegfried and expected it would take me a few years to get off the ground.

Anyway, before I had time to think much more about it everything was neatly settled and I found I had made a magical transition from jeering at the whole idea to making plans for furnishing our prospective bedsitter at Skeldale House.

It was a blissful time with only one cloud on the horizon; but that cloud bulked large and forbidding. As I walked hand in hand with Helen, my thoughts in the air, she kept bringing me back to earth with an appealing look.

'You know, Jim, you'll really have to speak to Dad. It's time he knew.'

I had been warned long before I qualified that country practice was a dirty, stinking job. I had accepted the fact and adjusted myself to it but there were times when this side of my life obtruded itself and became almost insupportable. Like now, when even after a long hot, bath I still smelt.

As I hoisted myself from the steaming water I sniffed at my arm and there it was; the malodorous memory of that horrible cleansing at Tommy Dearlove's striking triumphantly through all the soap and antiseptic almost as fresh and pungent as it had been at four o'clock this afternoon. Nothing but time would move it.

But something in me rebelled at the idea of crawling into bed in this

GATE HURDLES Split poles of ash, or sometimes willow, make gate hurdles. The two spiked uprights are about 6 ft apart. The six crossbars, strengthened by a centre rib and two diagonals, are set closer at the bottom. This is to prevent a sheep's head or an inquisitive lamb from passing through. The hurdles are used to make movable sheep pens at market or for shearing, and to contain sheep in one section of a field so that they clear it of food before being allowed on to another section.

227

HOME BUTTER-MAKER Small dairy farms stopped processing their milk into butter and cheese in the 1930s, and began sending it to factories instead. But the farmer's wife would still keep back enough to supply her own family's needs – not only for milk but also for butter. This glass churn, used from the 1930s to 1950s, would hold about a gallon of cream.

state and I looked with something like desperation along the row of bottles on the bathroom shelf. I stopped at Mrs Hall's bath salts, shining violent pink in their big glass jar. This was something I'd never tried before and I tipped a small handful into the water round my feet. For a moment my head swam as the rising steam was suddenly charged with an aggressive sweetness then on an impulse I shook most of the jar's contents into the bath and lowered myself once more under the surface.

For a long time I lay there smiling to myself in triumph as the oily liquid lapped around me. Not even Tommy Dearlove's cleansing could survive this treatment.

The whole process had a stupefying effect on me and I was half asleep even as I sank back on the pillow. There followed a few moments of blissful floating before a delicious slumber claimed me. And when the bedside phone boomed in my ear the sense of injustice and personal affront was even stronger than usual. Blinking sleepily at the clock which said 1.15 a.m. I lifted the receiver and mumbled into it, but I was jerked suddenly wide awake when I recognised Mr Alderson's voice. Candy was calving and something was wrong. Would I come right away.

There has always been a 'this is where I came in' feeling about a night call. And as my lights swept the cobbles of the deserted market place it was there again; a sense of returning to fundamentals, of really being me. The silent houses, the tight drawn curtains, the long, empty street giving way to the stone walls of the country road flipping endlessly past on either side. At these times I was usually in a state of suspended animation, just sufficiently awake to steer the car in the right direction, but tonight I was fully alert, my mind ticking over anxiously.

Because Candy was something special. She was the house cow, a pretty little Jersey and Mr Alderson's particular pet. She was the sole member of her breed in the herd but whereas the milk from the Shorthorns went into the churns to be collected by the big dairy, Candy's rich yellow offering found its way on to the family porridge every morning or appeared heaped up on trifles and fruit pies or was made into butter, a golden creamy butter to make you dream.

But apart from all that, Mr Alderson just liked the animal. He usually stopped opposite her on his way down the byre and began to hum to himself and gave her tail head a brief scratch as he passed. And I couldn't blame him because I sometimes wish all cows were Jerseys; small, gentle, doe-eyed creatures you could push around without any trouble; with padded corners and fragile limbs. Even if they kicked you it was like a love tap compared with the clump from a craggy Friesian.

I just hoped it would be something simple with Candy, because my stock wasn't high with Mr Alderson and I had a nervous conviction that he wouldn't react favourably if I started to make a ham-fisted job of calving his little favourite. I shrugged away my fears; obstetrics in the Jersey were usually easy.

Helen's father was an efficient farmer. As I pulled up in the yard I could see into the lighted loose box where two buckets of water were steaming in readiness for me. A towel was draped over the half door and Stan and Bert, the two long-serving cowmen, were standing alongside their boss. Candy was lying comfortably in deep straw. She wasn't straining and there was nothing visible at the vulva but the cow had a preoccupied, inward look as though all was not well with her.

I closed the door behind me. 'Have you had a feel inside her, Mr Alderson?'

'Aye, I've had me hand in and there's nowt there.'

'Nothing at all?'

'Not a thing. She'd been on for a few hours and not showing so I popped me hand in and there's no head, no legs, nowt. And not much room, either. That's when I rang you.'

This sounded very strange. I hung my jacket on a nail and began thoughtfully to unbutton my shirt. It was when I was pulling it over my head that I noticed Mr Alderson's nose wrinkling. The farm men, too, began to sniff and look at each other wonderingly. Mrs Hall's bath salts, imprisoned under my clothing had burst from their bondage in a sickly wave, filling the enclosed space with their strident message. Hurriedly I began to wash my arms in the hope that the alien odour might pass away but it seemed to get worse, welling from my warm skin, competing incongruously with the honest smells of cow, hay and straw. Nobody said anything. These men weren't the type to make the ribald remark which would have enabled me to laugh the thing off. There was no ambiguity about this scent; it was voluptuously feminine and Bert and Stan stared at me open mouthed. Mr Alderson, his mouth turned down at the corners, his nostrils still twitching, kept his eyes fixed on the far wall.

Cringing inwardly I knelt behind the cow and in a moment my embarrassment was forgotten. The vagina was empty; a smooth passage narrowing rapidly to a small, ridged opening just wide enough to admit my hand. Beyond I could feel the feet and head of a calf. My spirits plummeted. Torsion of the uterus. There was going to be no easy victory for me here.

I sat back on my heels and turned to the farmers. 'She's got a twisted calf bed. There's a live calf in there all right but there's no way out for it – I can barely get my hand through.'

'Aye, I thought it was something peculiar.' Mr Alderson rubbed his chin and looked at me doubtfully. 'What can we do about it, then?'

'We'll have to try to correct the twist by rolling the cow over while I keep hold of the calf. It's a good job there's plenty of us here.'

'And that'll put everything right, will it?'

I swallowed. I didn't like these jobs. Sometimes rolling worked and sometimes it didn't and in those days we hadn't quite got round to performing caesarians on cows. If I was unsuccessful I had the prospect of telling Mr Alderson to send Candy to the butcher. I banished the thought quickly.

'It'll put everything right,' I said. It had to. I stationed Bert at the

BRITISH FRIESIAN COW More than half Britain's cows now are British Friesians, developed from Dutch cattle imported during the late 19th century. The Friesian cow, a large beast weighing half a ton or more, is a supreme milker. It is always black and white but infinitely varied in marking, has a long, level back and a very large, white udder. A fully grown cow needs 35–40 lb of food a day, and is found more on lowland farms than rough hillsides. In return the cow will be giving 6 gallons a day, and it is common to give 2,000 gallons during the 305-day lactation period.

'Mr Alderson,' I said. 'I would like to marry your daughter.'

front legs, Stan at the hind and the farmer holding the cow's head on the floor. Then I stretched myself on the hard concrete, pushed in a hand and grasped the calf's foot.

'Now roll her,' I gasped, and the men pulled the legs round in a clockwise direction. I held fiercely to the little feet as the cow flopped on to her other side. Nothing seemed to be happening inside.

'Push her on to her chest,' I panted.

Stan and Bert expertly tucked the legs under the cow and rolled her on to her brisket and as she settled there I gave a yell of pain.

'Get her back, quick! We're going the wrong way!' The smooth band of tissue had tightened on my wrist in a numbing grip of frightening power. For a moment I had the panicky impression that I'd never get out of there again.

But the men worked like lightning. Within seconds Candy was stretched out on her original side, the pressure was off my arm and we were back where we started.

I gritted my teeth and took a fresh grip on the calf's foot. 'O.K., try her the other way.'

This time the roll was anti-clockwise and we went through 180 degrees without anything happening. I only just kept my grasp on the foot – the resistance this time was tremendous. Taking a breather for a few seconds I lay face down while the sweat sprang out on my back, sending out fresh exotic vapours from the bath salts.

'Right. One more go!' I cried and the men hauled the cow further

over. And oh it was beautiful to feel everything magically unravelling and my arm lying free in a wide uterus with all the room in the world and the calf already beginning to slide towards me.

Candy summed up the situation immediately and for the first time gave a determined heaving strain. Sensing victory just round the corner she followed up with another prolonged effort which popped the calf wet and wriggling into my arms.

'By gum, it was quick at t'finish,' Mr Alderson murmured wonderingly. He seized a wisp of hay and began to dry off the little creature.

Thankfully I soaped my arms in one of the buckets. After every delivery there is a feeling of relief but in this case it was overwhelming. It no longer mattered that the loose box smelt like a ladies' hairdressing salon, I just felt good. I said good night to Bert and Stan as they returned to their beds, giving a final incredulous sniff as they passed me. Mr Alderson was pottering about, having a word with Candy then starting again on the calf which he had already rubbed down several times. He seemed fascinated by it. And I couldn't blame him because it was like something out of Disney; a pale gold faun, unbelievably tiny with large dark limpid eyes and an expression of trusting innocence. It was a heifer, too.

The farmer lifted it as if it were a whippet dog and laid it by the mother's head. Candy nosed the little animal over, rumbling happily in her throat, then she began to lick it. I watched Mr Alderson. He was standing, hands clasped behind him, rocking backwards and forwards on his heels, obviously enchanted by the scene. Any time now, I thought.

231

And I was right; the tuneless humming broke out, even louder than usual, like a joyful paean.

I stiffened in my wellingtons. There would never be a better time. After a nervous cough I spoke up firmly.

'Mr Alderson,' I said, and he half turned his head. 'I would like to marry your daughter.'

The humming was switched off abruptly and he turned slowly till he was facing me. He didn't speak but his eyes searched my face unhappily. Then he bent stiffly, picked up the buckets one by one, tipped out the water and made for the door.

'You'd better come in the house,' he said.

The farmhouse kitchen looked lost and forsaken with the family abed. I sat in a high-backed wooden chair by the side of the empty hearth while Mr Alderson put away his buckets, hung up the towel and washed his hands methodically at the sink, then he pottered through to the parlour and I heard him bumping and clinking about in the sideboard. When he reappeared he bore a tray in front of him on which a bottle of whisky and two glasses rattled gently. The tray lent the simple procedure an air of formality which was accentuated by the heavy cut crystal of the glasses and the virgin, unopened state of the bottle.

Mr Alderson set the tray down on the kitchen table which he dragged nearer to us before settling in the chair at the other side of the fireplace. Nobody said anything. I waited in the lengthening silence while he peered at the cap of the bottle like a man who had never seen one before then unscrewed it with slow apprehension as though he feared it might blow up in his face.

Finally he poured out two measures with the utmost gravity and precision, ducking his head frequently to compare the levels in the two glasses, and with a last touch of ceremony proffered the laden tray.

I took my drink and waited expectantly.

Mr Alderson looked into the lifeless fireplace for a minute or two then he directed his gaze upwards at the oil painting of the paddling cows which hung above the mantelpiece. He pursed his lips as though about to whistle but appeared to change his mind and without salutation took a gulp of his whisky which sent him into a paroxysm of coughing from which it took him some time to recover. When his breathing had returned to normal he sat up straight and fixed me with streaming eyes. He cleared his throat and I felt a certain tension.

'Aye well,' he said, 'it's grand hay weather.'

I agreed with him and he looked round the kitchen with the interested stare of a total stranger. Having completed his inspection he took another copious swallow from his glass, grimaced, closed his eyes, shook his head violently a few times, then leaned forward.

'Mind you,' he said, 'a night's rain would do a lot o' good.'

I gave my opinion that it undoubtedly would and the silence fell again. It lasted even longer this time and my host kept drinking his whisky as though he was getting used to it. And I could see that it was

GATHERING HAY On the third day of haymaking in June the dry hay was raked into footcocks, or small mounds. The bow curving from the rake shaft to the head helped to keep together a rakeful of hay. Some farmers forked the cocks on to the wagon and took them back to the farm, while others built them into pikes to stand in the field for a longer time.

232

having a relaxing effect; the strained lines on his face were beginning to smooth out and his eyes were losing their hunted look.

Nothing more was said until he had replenished our glasses, balancing the amounts meticulously again. He took a sip at his second measure then he looked down at the rug and spoke in a small voice.

'James,' he said, 'I had a wife in a thousand.'

I was so surprised I hardly knew what to say. 'Yes, I know,' I murmured. 'I've heard a lot about her.'

Mr Alderson went on, still looking down, his voice full of gentle yearning.

'Yes, she was the grandest lass for miles around and the bonniest.' He looked up at me suddenly with the ghost of a smile. 'Nobody thought she'd ever have a feller like me, you know. But she did.' He paused and looked away. 'Aye, she did.'

He began to tell me about his dead wife. He told me calmly, without self-pity, but with a wistful gratitude for the happiness he had known. And I discovered that Mr Alderson was different from a lot of the farmers of his generation because he said nothing about her being a 'good worker'. So many of the women of those times seemed to be judged mainly on their working ability and when I had first come to Darrowby I had been shocked when I commiserated with a newly widowed old man. He had brushed a tear from his eye and said, 'Aye, she was a grand worker.'

But Mr Alderson said only that his wife had been beautiful, that she had been kind, and that he had loved her very much. He talked about Helen, too, about the things she had said and done when she was a little girl, about how very like her mother she was in every way. He never said anything about me but I had the feeling all the time that he meant it to concern me; and the very fact that he was talking so freely seemed a sign that the barriers were coming down.

Actually he was talking a little too freely. He was half way down his third huge whisky, and in my experience Yorkshiremen just couldn't take the stuff. I had seen burly ten pint men from the local pub keel over after a mere sniff at the amber fluid and little Mr Alderson hardly drank at all. I was getting worried.

But there was nothing I could do, so I let him ramble on happily. He was lying right back in his chair now, completely at ease, his eyes, alight with his memories, gazing somewhere above my head. In fact I am convinced he had forgotten I was there because after one long passage he dropped his eyes, caught sight of me and stared for a moment without recognition. When he did manage to place me it seemed to remind him of his duties as a host. But as he reached again for the bottles he caught sight of the clock on the wall.

'Well dang it, it's four o'clock. We've been here long enough. It's hardly worth goin' to bed, but I suppose we'd better have an hour or two's sleep.' He tipped the last of the whisky down his throat, jumped briskly to his feet, looked around him for a few moments in a business-

BANDAGING A FARMHOUSE CHEESE From May to October the wife of a small Dales dairy farmer would make one or two cheeses a day. Heating, renneting and moulding took short periods of work throughout the day. Before she set a cheese on the shelf to mature she sewed a cotton strip round it to hold it in shape. In the traditional farmhouse method of cheese-making, the moulded curd was pickled in brine for two or three days before bandaging, but from the 1890s another method was to mix salt into the curd and bandage the cheese straight after moulding.

ROLLER MARKERS After butter had been churned, squeezed free of buttermilk, and salted, it was divided into pounds or half pounds and stamped with a pattern to attract the buyer at the market stall. Butter that was shaped into long rolls was marked with wooden rollers. Most rollers were made of sycamore with a wheel 1–1½ in. across. The style of handle varied, and so did the pattern on the wheels. The leaves and flowers on these three rollers were frequently seen, as were acorns, cows and thistles.

like sort of way then pitched head first with a sickening clatter among the fire-irons.

Frozen with horror, I started forward to help the small figure scrabbling on the hearth but I needn't have worried because he bounced back to his feet in a second or two and looked me in the eye as if nothing had happened.

'Well, I'd better be off,' I said. 'Thanks for the drink.' There was no point in staying longer as I realised that the chances of Mr Alderson saying 'Bless you, my son' or anything like that were remote. But I had a comforting impression that all was going to be well.

As I made my way to the door the farmer made a creditable attempt to usher me out but his direction was faulty and he tacked helplessly away from me across the kitchen floor before collapsing against a tall dresser. From under a row of willow pattern dinner plates his face looked at me with simple bewilderment.

I hesitated then turned back. 'I'll just walk up the stairs with you, Mr Alderson,' I said in a matter of fact voice, and the little man made no resistance as I took his arm and guided him towards the door in the far corner.

As we creaked our way upstairs he stumbled and would have gone down again had I not grabbed him round the waist. As I caught him he looked up at me and grunted 'Thanks, lad,' and we grinned at each other for a moment before restarting the climb.

I supported him across the landing to his bedroom door and he stood hesitating as though about to say something. But finally he just nodded to me a couple of times before ducking inside.

I waited outside the door, listening in some anxiety to the bumps and thumps from within; but I relaxed as a loud, tuneless humming came through the panels. Everything most certainly was going to be all right.

Considering we spent our honeymoon tuberculin testing it was a big success. It compared favourably, at any rate, with the experiences of a lot of people I know who celebrated this milestone in their lives by cruising for a month on sunny seas and still wrote it off as a dead loss. For Helen and me it had all the ingredients; laughter, fulfilment and camaraderie, and yet it only lasted a week. And, as I say, we spent it tuberculin testing.

The situation had its origins one morning at the breakfast table when Siegfried, red-eyed after a bad night with a colicky mare, was opening the morning mail. He drew his breath in sharply as a thick roll of forms fell from an official envelope.

'God almighty! Look at all that testing!' He smoothed out the forms on the table cloth and read feverishly down the long list of farm premises. 'And they want us to start this lot around Ellerthorpe next week without fail – it's very urgent.' He glanced at me for a moment. 'That's when you're getting married, isn't it?'

I shifted uncomfortably in my chair. 'Yes, I'm afraid it is.'

Siegfried snatched a piece of toast from the rack and began to slap butter on it. 'Well this is just great isn't it? The practice going mad, a week's testing right at the top of the Dale, away in the back of beyond, and your wedding smack in the middle of it. You'll be drifting gaily off on your honeymoon without a care in the world while I'm rushing around here nearly disappearing up my own backside!' He bit a piece from the toast and began to chew it worriedly.

'I'm sorry, Siegfried,' I said. 'I didn't mean to land you in the cart like this. I couldn't know the practice was going to get so busy right now and I never expected them to throw all this testing at us.'

Siegfried paused in his chewing and pointed a finger at me. 'That's just it, James, that's your trouble – you don't look ahead. You just go belting straight on without a thought. Even when it comes to a bloody wedding you're not worried – oh no, let's get on with it, to hell with the consequences.' He paused to cough up a few crumbs which he had inhaled in his agitation. 'In fact I can't see what all the hurry is – you've got all the time in the world to get married, you're just a boy. And another thing – you hardly know this girl, you've only been seeing her regularly for a few weeks.'

'But wait a minute, you said ...'

'No, let me finish, James. Marriage is a very serious step, not to be embarked upon without long and serious thought. Why in God's name does it have to be next week? Next year would have been soon enough and you could have enjoyed a nice long engagement. But no, you've got to rush in and tie the knot and it isn't so easily untied you know.'

'Oh hell, Siegfried, this is too bad! You know perfectly well it was you who ...'

'One moment more. Your precipitate marital arrangements are going to cause me a considerable headache but believe me I wish you well. I hope all turns out for the best despite your complete lack of foresight, but at the same time I must remind you of the old saying, "Marry in haste, repent at leisure."'

I could stand no more. I leaped to my feet, thumped a fist on the table and yelled at him.

'But damn it, it was your idea! I was all for leaving it for a bit but you ...'

Siegfried wasn't listening. He had been cooling off all the time and now his face broke into a seraphic smile. 'Now, now, now, James, you're getting excited again. Sit down and calm yourself. You mustn't mind my speaking to you like this – you are very young and it's my duty. You haven't done anything wrong at all; I suppose it's the most natural thing in the world for people of your age to act without thinking ahead, to jump into things with never a thought of the morrow. It's just the improvidence of youth.' Siegfried was about six years older than me but he had donned the mantle of the omniscient greybeard without effort.

I dug my fingers into my knees and decided not to pursue the matter. I had no chance anyway, and besides I was beginning to feel a bit

BUTTER PRINTS The pound and half-pound pats weighed out from the finished butter were often shaped into rounds. Each was stamped with a wooden mould, usually of sycamore. Intricate designs surrounded by fluted borders were carved on the prints – usually by skilled craftsmen, although some prints were roughly made. Birds, fruits, thistles, acorns, cows, leaves and wheatsheaves were among the many traditional designs. Quartered designs belonged particularly to the North York Moors. The print was moistened with cold water before being pressed on to the butter.

worried about clearing off and leaving him snowed under with work. I got up and walked to the window where I watched old Will Varley pushing a bicycle up the street with a sack of potatoes balanced on the handlebars as I had watched him a hundred times before. Then I turned back to my employer. I had had one of my infrequent ideas.

'Look, Siegfried, I wouldn't mind spending my honeymoon round Ellerthorpe. It's wonderful up there at this time of the year and we could stay at the Wheat Sheaf. I could do the testing from there.'

He looked at me in astonishment. 'Spend it at Ellerthorpe? And testing? It's impossible – what would Helen say?'

'She wouldn't mind. In fact she could do the writing for me. We were only going off touring in the car so we haven't made any plans, and anyway it's funny, but Helen and I have often said we'd like to stay at the Wheaf Sheaf some time – there's something about that little pub.'

Siegfried shook his head decisively. 'No, James, I won't hear of it. In fact you're beginning to make me feel guilty. I'll get through the work all right so forget about it and go away and have a good time.'

'No, I've made up my mind. I'm really beginning to like the idea.' I scanned the list quickly. 'I can start testing at Allen's and do all those smaller ones around there on Tuesday, get married on Wednesday and go back for the second injection and readings on Thursday and Friday. I can knock hell out of that list by the end of the week.'

Siegfried looked at me as though he was seeing me for the first time. He argued and protested but for once I got my way. I fished the Ministry notification cards from the desk drawer and began to make the arrangements for my honeymoon.

On Tuesday at 12 noon I had finished testing the Allen's huge herd scattered for miles over the stark fells at the top of the Dale and was settling down with the hospitable folk for the inevitable 'bit o' dinner.' Mr Allen was at the head of the scrubbed table and facing me were his two sons, Jack, aged about twenty, and Robbie, about seventeen. The young men were superbly fit and tough and I had been watching all morning in something like awe as they man-handled the wild, scattered beasts, chasing and catching tirelessly hour after hour. I had stared incredulously as Jack had run down a galloping heifer on the open moor, seized its horns and borne it slowly to the ground for me to inject; it struck me more than once that it was a pity that an Olympic selector was unlikely to stray into this remote corner of high Yorkshire – he would have found some world-beating material.

I always had to stand a bit of leg-pulling from Mrs Allen, a jolly talkative woman; on previous visits she had ribbed me mercilessly about being a slowcoach with the girls, the disgrace of having nothing better than a housekeeper to look after me. I knew she would start on me again today but I bided my time; I had a devastating riposte up my sleeve. She had just opened the oven door, filling the room with a delectable fragrance, and as she dumped a huge slab of roast ham on the table she

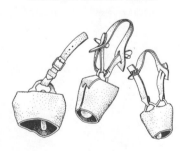

CATTLE BELLS Many of the sheep and cows that grazed freely over wide stretches of moor and fell wore bells so the herdsman could hear them if they were out of sight. The bells were made in various sizes by local blacksmiths out of thin iron, with clappers of iron or bone, and leather straps to go round the animals' necks.

looked down at me with a smile.

'Now then, Mr Herriot, when are we going to get you married off? It's time you found a nice girl, you know I'm always at you but you take not a bit o' notice.' She giggled as she bustled back to the cooking range for a bowl of mashed potatoes.

I waited until she returned before I dropped my bombshell. 'Well, as a matter of fact, Mrs Allen,' I said airily, 'I've decided to accept your advice. I'm getting married tomorrow.'

The good woman, mounding mashed potatoes on to my plate, stopped with her spoon in mid-air. 'Married tomorrow?' Her face was a study in blank astonishment.

'That's right. I thought you'd be pleased.'

'But ... but ... you're coming back here to read the test on Thursday and Friday.'

'Well, of course. I have to finish the test, haven't I? I'll be bringing my wife with me – I'm looking forward to introducing her to you.'

There was a silence. The young men stared at me, Mr Allen stopped sawing at the ham and regarded me stolidly, then his wife gave an uncertain laugh.

'Oh come on, I don't believe it. You're kidding us. You'd be off on your honeymoon if you were getting married tomorrow.'

'Mrs Allen,' I said with dignity, 'I wouldn't joke about a serious matter like that. Let me repeat – tomorrow is my wedding day and I'll be bringing my wife along on Thursday to see you.'

Completely deflated, she heaped our plates and we all fell to in silence. But I knew she was in agony; she kept darting little glances at me and it was obvious she was dying to ask me more. The boys, too, seemed intrigued; only Mr Allen, a tall, quiet man who, I'm sure wouldn't have cared if I'd been going to rob a bank tomorrow, ploughed calmly through his food.

Nothing more was said until I was about to leave, then Mrs Allen put a hand on my arm.

'You really don't mean it, do you?' Her face was haggard with strain.

I got into the car and called out through the window. 'Goodbye and thank you, Mrs Allen. Mrs Herriot and I will be along first thing on Thursday.'

I can't remember much about the wedding. It was a 'quiet do' and my main recollection is of desiring to get it all over with as soon as possible. I have only one vivid memory; of Siegfried, just behind me in the church, booming 'Amen' at regular intervals throughout the ceremony – the only time I have ever heard a best man do this.

It was an incredible relief when Helen and I were ready to drive away and when we were passing Skeldale House Helen grasped my hand.

'Look!' she cried excitedly. 'Look over there!'

Underneath Siegfried's brass plate which always hung slightly askew on the iron railings was a brand new one. It was of the modern bakelite

YOUNG HIGHLAND CATTLE
Outside their native area, north-west Scotland, Highland cattle are often regarded as curiosities. Their long, brown or black coats, broad, fringed faces, and wide spread of horn give them the look of a primitive bovine ancestor. But the cattle have valuable characteristics. They thrive in the harshest weather and on the scantiest grazing, the sort of conditions found in parts of the Pennines. Sturdy legs and sure feet carry them to ground that is difficult to reach. They are not milkers, but produce the highest-quality beef.

type with a black background and bold white letters which read 'J. Herriot M.R.C.V.S. Veterinary Surgeon', and it was screwed very straight and level on the metal.

Siegfried had said something about 'You'll see my wedding present on the way out.' And here it was. Not many people got a partnership as a gift, but it had happened to me and was the crowning point of three years of magnanimity.

I looked back down the street to try to see Siegfried but we had said our goodbyes and I would have to thank him later. So I drove out of Darrowby with a feeling of swelling pride because I knew what the plate meant – I was a man with a real place in the world. The thought made me slightly breathless. In fact we were both a little dizzy and we cruised for hours around the countryside, getting out when we felt like it, walking among the hills, taking no account of time. It must have been nine o'clock in the evening and darkness coming in fast when we realised we had gone far out of our way.

We had to drive ten miles over a desolate moor on the fell top and it was very dark when we rattled down the steep, narrow road into Ellerthorpe. The Wheat Sheaf was an unostentatious part of the single, long village street, a low grey stone building with no light over the door, and as we went into the slightly musty-smelling hallway the gentle clink of glasses came from the public bar on our left. Mrs Burn, the elderly widow who owned the place, appeared from a back room and scrutinised us unemotionally.

'We've met before, Mrs Burn,' I said, and she nodded. I apologised for our lateness and was wondering whether I dare ask for a few sandwiches at this time of night when the old lady spoke up, quite unperturbed.

'Nay,' she said, 'it's all right. We've been expecting you and your supper's waiting.' She led us to the dining room where her niece, Beryl, served a hot meal in no time. Thick lentil soup, followed by what would probably be called a goulash these days but which was in fact simply a delicious stew with mushrooms and vegetables obviously concocted by a culinary genius. We had to say no to the gooseberry pie and cream.

It was like that all the time at the Wheat Sheaf. The whole place was aggressively unfashionable; needing a lick of paint, crammed with hideous Victorian furniture, but it was easy to see how it had won its reputation. It didn't have stylish guests, but fat, comfortable men from the industrial West Riding brought their wives at the weekends and did a bit of fishing or just took in the incomparable air between the mealtimes which were the big moments of the day. There was only one guest while we were there and he was a permanent one – a retired draper from Darlington who was always at the table in good time, a huge white napkin tucked under his chin, his eyes gleaming as he watched Beryl bring in the food.

But it wasn't just the home-fed ham, the Wensleydale cheese, the succulent steak and kidney pies, the bilberry tarts and mountainous Yorkshire puddings which captivated Helen and me. There was a peace,

BILBERRY PIE A week-end walk on a brilliant August day, following the tracks that thread the peaty moor-tops of north Yorkshire, is the time to pick bilberries for a pie. It is a task to take time over. The small, purple-black berries with a waxy bloom hide among the leaves of the ankle-high shrubs. But a bilberry pie is worth all the stooping – rich and sharp in flavour, copiously juicy and marking its devotees with tell-tale blue-stained lips.

To make the pie, roll out 12 oz of shortcrust pastry to make a base and lid for a shallow 9 in. pie plate. Fit in the base and fill with 8 oz of bilberries. Sprinkle liberally with sugar and seal on the pie lid. Make a slit in the top and bake for 40 minutes, starting at 425°F (220°C), gas mark 7, and reducing after 10 minutes to 350°F (180°C), gas mark 4.

a sleepy insinuating charm about the old pub which we always recalled with happiness. I still often pass the Wheat Sheaf, and as I look at its ancient stone frontage, quite unaltered by the passage of a mere thirty years, the memories are still fresh and warm; our footsteps echoing in the empty street when we took our last walk at night, the old brass bedstead almost filling the little room, the dark rim of the fells bulking against the night sky beyond our window, faint bursts of laughter from the farmers in the bar downstairs.

I particularly enjoyed, too, our very first morning when I took Helen to do the test at Allen's. As I got out of the car I could see Mrs Allen peeping round the curtains in the kitchen window. She was soon out in the yard and her eyes popped when I brought my bride over to her. Helen was one of the pioneers of slacks in the Dales and she was wearing a bright purple pair this morning which would in modern parlance knock your eye out. The farmer's wife was partly shocked, partly fascinated but she soon found that Helen was of the same stock as herself and within seconds the two women were chattering busily. I judged from Mrs Allen's vigorous head-nodding and her ever widening smile that Helen was putting her out of her pain by explaining all the circumstances. It took a long time and finally Mr Allen had to break into the conversation.

'If we're goin', we'll have to go,' he said gruffly and we set off to start the second day of the test.

We began on a sunny hillside where a group of young animals had been penned. Jack and Robbie plunged in among the beasts while Mr Allen took off his cap and courteously dusted the top of the wall.

'Your missus can sit 'ere,' he said.

I paused as I was about to start measuring. My missus! It was the first time anybody had said that to me. I looked over at Helen as she sat cross-legged on the rough stones, her notebook on her knee, pencil at the ready, and as she pushed back the shining, dark hair from her forehead she caught my eye and smiled; and as I smiled back at her I became aware suddenly of the vast, swelling glory of the Dales around us, and of the Dales scent of clover and warm grass, more intoxicating than any wine. And it seemed that my first three years at Darrowby had been leading up to this moment; that the first big step of my life was being completed right here with Helen smiling at me and the memory, fresh in my mind, of my new plate hanging in front of Skeldale House.

I might have stood there indefinitely, in a sort of trance, but Mr Allen cleared his throat in a marked manner and I turned back to the job in hand.

'Right,' I said, placing my calipers against the beast's neck. 'Number thirty-eight, seven millimetres and circumscribed,' I called out to Helen. 'Number thirty-eight, seven, C.'

'Thirty-eight, seven, C,' my wife repeated as she bent over her book and started to write.

COMBINED SOWING It used to be common in the 1930s and later to sow grass or clover at the same time as cereal seed, or a week or two afterwards. It was believed that the cereal acted as a 'nurse crop' and brought along the lower crop, which then had plenty of time to make a good hay crop for the summer following the cereal harvest. The horse-drawn drill is sowing the corn while the hand-pushed machine follows on, broadcasting grass and clover. The practice died out as it was established that the cereal robs the lower crop of light and water, and that just as much hay would come from sowing after the cereal had been harvested.

8

Just a song ... at midnight!

As I crawled into bed and put my arm around Helen it occurred to me, not for the first time, that there are few pleasures in this world to compare with snuggling up to a nice woman when you are half frozen.

There weren't any electric blankets in the thirties. Which was a pity because nobody needed the things more than country vets. It is surprising how deeply bone-marrow cold a man can get when he is dragged from his bed in the small hours and made to strip off in farm buildings when his metabolism is at a low ebb. Often the worst part was coming back to bed; I often lay exhausted for over an hour, longing for sleep but kept awake until my icy limbs and feet had thawed out.

But since my marriage such things were but a dark memory. Helen stirred in her sleep – she had got used to her husband leaving her in the night and returning like a blast from the North Pole – and instinctively moved nearer to me. With a sigh of thankfulness I felt the blissful warmth envelop me and almost immediately the events of the last two hours began to recede into unreality.

It had started with the aggressive shrilling of the bedside phone at one a.m. And it was Sunday morning, a not unusual time for some farmers after a late Saturday night to have a look round their stock and decide to send for the vet.

This time it was Harold Ingledew. And it struck me right away that he would have just about had time to get back to his farm after his ten pints at the Four Horse Shoes where they weren't too fussy about closing time.

And there was a significant slur in the thin croak of his voice.

'I 'ave a ewe amiss. Will you come?'

'Is she very bad?' In my semi-conscious state I always clung to the faint hope that one night somebody would say it would wait till morning. It had never happened yet and it didn't happen now: Mr Ingledew was not to be denied.

'Aye, she's in a bad way. She'll have to have summat done for 'er soon.'

Not a minute to lose, I thought bitterly. But she had probably been in a bad way all the evening when Harold was out carousing.

Still, there were compensations. A sick sheep didn't present any great threat. It was worst when you had to get out of bed facing the prospect of a spell of sheer hard labour in your enfeebled state. But in this case I was confident that I would be able to adopt my half-awake technique; which meant simply that I would be able to go out there and deal with the emergency and return between the sheets while still enjoying many of

THE FARM SLED Hummocky fields, rutted tracks and snowbound winters were severe tests for wheeled vehicles, and sleds had several advantages over them. A stout timber sled with metal runners ran easily over hard-frozen ground and over grass. It was cheaper than a cart or wagon, needed only a pony to pull it, and was at ground level for loading and unloading. It carried loads of bracken, hay, manure or stones, or could be used to collect sick animals.

the benefits of sleep.

There was so much night work in country practice that I had been compelled to perfect this system as, I suspect, had many of my fellow practitioners. I had done some sterling work while in a somnambulistic limbo.

So, eyes closed, I tiptoed across the carpet and pulled on my working clothes. I effortlessly accomplished the journey down the long flights of stairs but when I opened the side door the system began to crumble, because even in the shelter of the high-walled garden the wind struck at me with savage force. It was difficult to stay asleep. In the yard as I backed out of the garage the high branches of the elms groaned in the darkness as they bent before the blast.

Driving from the town I managed to slip back into my trance and my mind played lazily with the phenomenon of Harold Ingledew. This drinking of his was so out of character. He was a tiny mouse of a man about seventy years old and when he came into the surgery on an occasional market day it was difficult to extract more than a few muttered words from him. Dressed in his best suit, his scrawny neck protruding from a shirt collar several sizes too big for him, he was the very picture of a meek and solid citizen; the watery blue eyes and fleshless cheeks added to the effect and only the brilliant red colouration of the tip of his nose gave any hint of other possibilities.

His fellow smallholders in Therby village were all steady characters and did not indulge beyond a social glass of beer now and then, and his next door neighbour had been somewhat bitter when he spoke to me a few weeks ago.

'He's nowt but a bloody nuisance is awd Harold.'

'How do you mean?'

'Well, every Saturday night and every market night he's up roarin' and singin' till four o'clock in the mornin'.'

'Harold Ingledew? Surely not! He's such a quiet little chap.'

'Aye, he is for the rest of t'week.'

'But I can't imagine him singing!'

'You should live next door to 'im, Mr Herriot. He makes a 'ell of a racket. There's no sleep for anybody till he settles down.'

Since then I had heard from another source that this was perfectly true and that Mrs Ingledew tolerated it because her husband was entirely submissive at all other times.

The road to Therby had a few sharp little switchbacks before it dipped to the village and looking down I could see the long row of silent houses curving away to the base of the fell which by day hung in peaceful green majesty over the huddle of roofs but now bulked black and menacing under the moon.

As I stepped from the car and hurried round to the back of the house the wind caught at me again, jerking me to wakefulness as though somebody had thrown a bucket of water over me. But for a moment I forgot the cold in the feeling of shock as the noise struck me. Singing . . .

DALESBRED SHEEP One of the most easily recognised sheep of north Yorkshire is the Dalesbred, because of its black face with a white patch on each side. The patch is known locally as a smit. Both ram and ewe are horned. The long, rough fleece is crimped with a thick, short undercoat well able to withstand the 70 in. annual rainfall that is common on the hills where the Dalesbred lives the year round. The sheep thrive on the rough grazing and, once they have stopped suckling their April lambs, they fatten quickly during the late summer to build up reserves that carry them through the scant grazing of the hard winter.

Dressed in his best suit, he was the very picture of a meek and solid citizen.

loud raucous singing echoing around the old stones of the yard.

It was coming from the lighted kitchen window.

'JUST A SONG AT TWILIGHT, WHEN THE LIGHTS ARE LOW!'

I looked inside and saw little Harold sitting with his stockinged feet extended towards the dying embers of the fire while one hand clutched a bottle of brown ale.

'AND THE FLICKERING SHADOWS SOFTLY COME AND GO!' He was really letting it rip, head back, mouth wide.

I thumped on the kitchen door.

'THOUGH THE HEART BE WEARY, SAD THE DAY AND LONG!' replied Harold's reedy tenor and I banged impatiently at the woodwork again.

The noise ceased and I waited an unbelievably long time till I heard the key turning and the bolt rattling back. The little man pushed his nose out and gave me a questioning look.

'I've come to see your sheep,' I said.

'Oh aye.' He nodded curtly with none of his usual diffidence. 'Ah'll put me boots on.' He banged the door in my face and I heard the bolt shooting home.

242

Taken aback as I was I realised that he wasn't being deliberately rude. Bolting the door was proof that he was doing everything mechanically. But for all that he had left me standing in an uncharitable spot. Vets will tell you that there are corners in farmyards which are colder than any hill top and I was in one now. Just beyond the kitchen door was a stone archway leading to the open fields and through this black opening there whistled a Siberian draught which cut effortlessly through my clothes.

I had begun to hop from one foot to the other when the singing started again.

'THERE'S AN OLD MILL BY THE STREAM, NELLIE DEAN!'

Horrified, I rushed back to the window. Harold was back in his chair, pulling on a vast boot and taking his time about it. As he bellowed he poked owlishly at the lace holes and occasionally refreshed himself from the bottle of brown ale.

I tapped on the window. 'Please hurry, Mr Ingledew.'

'WHERE WE USED TO SIT AND DREAM, NELLIE DEAN!' bawled Harold in response.

My teeth had begun to chatter before he got both boots on but at last he reappeared in the doorway.

'Come on then,' I gasped. 'Where is this ewe? Have you got her in one of these boxes?'

The old man raised his eyebrows. 'Oh, she's not 'ere.'

'Not here?'

'Nay, she's up at t'top buildings.'

'Right back up the road, you mean?'

'Aye, ah stopped off on t'way home and had a look at 'er.'

I stamped and rubbed my hands. 'Well, we'll have to drive back up. But there's no water, is there? You'd better bring a bucket of warm water, some soap and a towel.'

'Very good.' He nodded solemnly and before I knew what was happening the door was slammed shut and bolted and I was alone again in the darkness. I trotted immediately to the window and was not surprised to see Harold seated comfortably again. He leaned forward and lifted the kettle from the hearth and for a dreadful moment I thought he was going to start heating the water on the ashes of the fire. But with a gush of relief I saw him take hold of a ladle and reach into the primitive boiler in the old black grate.

'AND THE WATERS AS THEY FLOW SEEM TO MURMUR SWEET AND LOW!' he warbled, happy at his work, as he unhurriedly filled a bucket.

I think he had forgotten I was there when he finally came out because he looked at me blankly as he sang.

'YOU'RE MY HEART'S DESIRE, I LOVE YOU, NELLIE DEAN!' he informed me at the top of his voice.

'All right, all right,' I grunted. 'Let's go.' I hurried him into the car and we set off on the way I had come.

Harold held the bucket at an angle on his lap, and as we went over the

MARKS TO IDENTIFY LAMBS
Before a lamb is weaned it is
dependent on its mother and
stays close to her. By the time it
is ready to leave the ewe, a
lamb must bear the registered
mark of its farm so that it can
be identified and reclaimed if it
wanders. This lamb is being
marked on the ear – a more
permanent mark than a wool-
mark or a horn-brand. Wool-
marks have to be renewed after
shearing, and sheep sometimes
lose their horns as they age.
Slits, semi-circles, squares, V-
shapes, holes, lopped tips and
other notches, doubled or
combined, on left ear or right,
on the upper edge or the lower,
give a huge number of possible
ear-marks.

switchbacks the water slopped gently on to my knee. The atmosphere in the car soon became so highly charged with beer fumes that I began to feel lightheaded.

'In 'ere!' the old man barked suddenly as a gate appeared in the headlights. I pulled on to the grass verge and stood on one leg for a few moments till I had shaken a surplus pint or two of water from my trousers. We went through the gate and I began to hurry towards the dark bulk of the hillside barn, but I noticed that Harold wasn't following me. He was walking aimlessly around the field.

'What are you doing, Mr Ingledew?'

'Lookin' for t'ewe.'

'You mean she's outside?' I repressed an impulse to scream.

'Aye, she lambed this afternoon and ah thowt she'd be right enough out 'ere.' He produced a torch, a typical farmer's torch – tiny and with a moribund battery – and projected a fitful beam into the darkness. It made not the slightest difference.

As I stumbled across the field a sense of hopelessness assailed me. Above, the ragged clouds scurried across the face of the moon but down here I could see nothing. And it was so cold. The recent frosts had turned the ground to iron and the crisp grass cowered under the piercing wind. I had just decided that there was no way of finding an animal in this black waste land when Harold piped up.

'She's over 'ere.'

And sure enough when I groped my way towards the sound of his voice he was standing by an unhappy looking ewe. I don't know what instinct had brought him to her but there she was. And she was obviously in trouble; her head hung down miserably and when I put my hand on her fleece she took only a few faltering steps instead of galloping off as a healthy sheep would. Beside her, a tiny lamb huddled close to her flank.

I lifted her tail and took her temperature. It was normal. There were no signs of the usual post-lambing ailments; no staggering to indicate a deficiency, no discharge or accelerated respirations. But there was something very far wrong.

I looked again at the lamb. He was an unusually early arrival in this high country and it seemed unfair to bring the little creature into the inhospitable world of a Yorkshire March. And he was so small ... yes ... yes ... it was beginning to filter through to me. He was too damn small for a single lamb.

'Bring me that bucket, Mr Ingledew!' I cried. I could hardly wait to see if I was right. But as I balanced the receptacle on the grass the full horror of the situation smote me. I was going to have to strip off.

They don't give vets medals for bravery but as I pulled off my overcoat and jacket and stood shivering in my shirt sleeves on that black hillside I felt I deserved one.

'Hold her head,' I gasped and soaped my arm quickly. By the light of the torch I felt my way into the vagina and I didn't have to go very far

244

before I found what I expected; a woolly little skull. It was bent downwards with the nose under the pelvis and the legs were back.

'There's another lamb in here,' I said. 'It's laid wrong or it would have been born with its mate this afternoon.'

Even as I spoke my fingers had righted the presentation and I drew the little creature gently out and deposited him on the grass. I hadn't expected him to be alive after his delayed entry but as he made contact with the cold ground his limbs gave a convulsive twitch and almost immediately I felt his ribs heaving under my hand.

For a moment I forgot the knife-like wind in the thrill which I always found in new life, the thrill that was always fresh, always warm. The ewe, too, seemed stimulated because in the darkness I felt her nose pushing interestedly at the new arrival.

But my pleasant ruminations were cut short by a scuffling from behind me and some muffled words.

'Bugger it!' mumbled Harold.

'What's the matter?'

'Ah've kicked bucket ower.'

'Oh no! Is the water all gone?'

'Aye, nowt left.'

Well this was great. My arm was smeared with mucus after being inside the ewe. I couldn't possibly put my jacket on without a wash.

Harold's voice issued again from the darkness. 'There's some watter ower at building.'

'Oh good. We've got to get this ewe and lambs over there anyway.' I threw my clothes over my shoulder, tucked a lamb under each arm and began to blunder over the tussocks of grass to where I thought the barn lay. The ewe, clearly feeling better without her uncomfortable burden, trotted behind me.

It was Harold again who had to give me directions.

'Ower 'ere!' he shouted.

When I reached the barn I cowered thankfully behind the massive stones. It was no night for a stroll in shirt sleeves. Shaking uncontrollably I peered at the old man. I could just see his form in the last faint radiance of the torch and I wasn't quite sure what he was doing. He had lifted a stone from the pasture and was bashing something with it; then I realised he was bending over the water trough, breaking the ice.

When he had finished he plunged the bucket into the trough and handed it to me.

'There's your watter,' he said triumphantly.

I thought I had reached the ultimate in frigidity but when I plunged my hands into the black liquid with its floating icebergs I changed my mind. The torch had finally expired and I lost the soap very quickly. When I found I was trying to work up a lather with one of the pieces of ice I gave it up and dried my arms.

Somewhere nearby I could hear Harold humming under his breath, as comfortable as if he was by his own fireside. The vast amount of

CORN PIKES Until the 1930s a characteristic feature of the Dales was each farm's cluster of corn pikes – circular stacks, each topped by a neatly thatched dome. Each pike was built on a base of wood raised on support stones called hemmells to keep vermin out of the corn. There might be up to 1,000 sheaves, arranged grain end inwards, in a pike. The side of the pike was shaved smooth with a sharp knife. Every week or two weeks a pike was dismantled and taken to the barn for threshing.

alcohol surging through his bloodstream must have made him impervious to the cold.

We pushed the ewe and lambs into the barn which was piled high with hay and before leaving I struck a match and looked down at the little sheep and her new family settled comfortably among the fragrant clover. They would be safe and warm in there till morning.

My journey back to the village was less hazardous because the bucket on Harold's knee was empty. I dropped him outside his house then I had to drive to the bottom of the village to turn; and as I came past the house again the sound forced its way into the car.

'IF YOU WERE THE ONLY GIRL IN THE WORLD AND I WERE THE ONLY BOY!'

I stopped, wound the window down and listened in wonder. It was incredible how the noise reverberated around the quiet street and if it went on till four o'clock in the morning as the neighbours said, then they had my sympathy.

'NOTHING ELSE WOULD MATTER IN THE WORLD TODAY!'

It struck me suddenly that I could soon get tired of Harold's singing. His volume was impressive but for all that he would never be in great demand at Covent Garden; he constantly wavered off key and there was a grating quality in his top notes which set my teeth on edge.

'WE WOULD GO ON LOVING IN THE SAME OLD WAY!'

Hurriedly I wound the window up and drove off. As the heaterless car picked its way between the endless flitting pattern of walls I crouched in frozen immobility behind the wheel. I had now reached the state of total numbness and I can't remember much about my return to the yard at Skeldale House, nor my automatic actions of putting away the car, swinging shut the creaking doors of what had once been the old coach house, and trailing slowly down the long garden.

But a realisation of my blessings began to return when I slid into bed and Helen, instead of shrinking away from me as it would have been natural to do, deliberately draped her feet and legs over the human ice block that was her husband. The bliss was unbelievable. It was worth getting out just to come back to this.

I glanced at the luminous dial of the alarm clock. It was three o'clock and as the warmth flowed over me and I drifted away, my mind went back to the ewe and lambs, snug in their scented barn. They would be asleep now, I would soon be asleep, everybody would be asleep.

Except, that is, Harold Ingledew's neighbours. They still had an hour to go.

THE CLOVER CROP Clover serves a double purpose in the farming cycle. Grown as a crop in the four-year rotation system, its roots make soil more fertile by increasing the nitrogen content. The crop itself can be grazed by stock, whose droppings also fertilise the land, or it can be gathered for a winter fodder as good as hay. It was a common sight in the 1930s and 1940s to see a horse-drawn reaper mowing clover, with a raker following on pulling the crop into swathes, or rows.

9

Jock sees off all challengers

I had only to sit up in bed to look right across Darrowby to the hills beyond.

I got up and walked to the window. It was going to be a fine morning and the early sun glanced over the weathered reds and greys of the jumbled roofs, some of them sagging under their burden of ancient tiles, and brightened the tufts of green where trees pushed upwards from the gardens among the bristle of chimney pots. And behind everything the calm bulk of the fells.

It was my good fortune that this was the first thing I saw every morning; after Helen, of course, which was better still.

Following our unorthodox tuberculin testing honeymoon we had set up our first home on the top of Skeldale House. Siegfried, my boss up to my wedding and now my partner, had offered us free use of these empty rooms on the third storey and we had gratefully accepted; and though it was a makeshift arrangement there was an airy charm, an exhilaration in our high perch that many would have envied.

It was makeshift because everything at that time had a temporary complexion and we had no idea how long we would be there. Siegfried and I had both volunteered for the RAF and were on deferred service but that is all I am going to say about the war. This book is not about such things which in any case were so very far from Darrowby; it is the story of the months I had with Helen between our marriage and my call-up and is about the ordinary things which have always made up our lives; my work, the animals, the Dales.

This front room was our bed-sitter and though it was not luxuriously furnished it did have an excellent bed, a carpet, a handsome side table which had belonged to Helen's mother and two armchairs. It had an ancient wardrobe, too, but the lock didn't work and the only way we kept the door closed was by jamming one of my socks in it. The toe always dangled outside but it never seemed of any importance.

I went out and across a few feet of landing to our kitchen-dining room at the back. This apartment was definitely spartan. I clumped over bare boards to a bench we had rigged against the wall by the window. This held a gas ring and our crockery and cutlery. I seized a tall jug and began my long descent to the main kitchen downstairs because one minor snag was that there was no water at the top of the house. Down two flights to the three rooms on the first storey then down two more and a final gallop along the passage to the big stone-flagged kitchen at the end.

I filled the jug and returned to our eyrie two steps at a time. I

GAS-HEATED KETTLES It was the coming of the railway to north Yorkshire that led to the public supply of gas. In the late 19th century the railway followed Wensleydale and crossed the southern edge of the North York Moors, and along it came trucks of coal. Within a few years companies had been set up to convert the coal into gas for the towns and villages along the line – Masham, Bedale and Kirkbymoorside, for example. Cleaner, more controllable gas cookers began to oust the solid-fuel range, and the kettle boiled quickly over the gas ring instead of hanging over the fire and then standing simmering on the hob.

wouldn't like to do this now whenever I needed water but at that time I didn't find it the least inconvenience.

Helen soon had the kettle boiling and we drank our first cup of tea by the window looking down on the long garden. From up here we had an aerial view of the unkempt lawns, the fruit trees, the wistaria climbing the weathered brick towards our window, and the high walls with their old stone copings stretching away to the cobbled yard under the elms. Every day I went up and down that path to the garage in the yard but it looked so different from above.

'Wait a minute, Helen,' I said. 'Let me sit on that chair.'

She had laid the breakfast on the bench where we ate and this was where the difficulty arose. Because it was a tall bench and our recently acquired high stool fitted it but our chair didn't.

'No, I'm all right, Jim, really I am.' She smiled at me reassuringly from her absurd position, almost at eye level with her plate.

'You can't be all right,' I retorted. 'Your chin's nearly in among your cornflakes. Please let me sit there.'

She patted the seat of the stool. 'Come on, stop arguing. Sit down and have your breakfast.'

This, I felt, just wouldn't do. I tried a different tack.

'Helen!' I said severely. 'Get off that chair!'

'No!' she replied without looking at me, her lips pushed forward in a characteristic pout which I always found enchanting but which also meant she wasn't kidding.

I was at a loss. I toyed with the idea of pulling her off the chair, but she was a big girl. We had had a previous physical try-out when a minor disagreement had escalated into a wrestling match and though I thoroughly enjoyed the contest and actually won in the end I had been surprised by her sheer strength. At this time in the morning I didn't feel up to it. I sat on the stool.

After breakfast Helen began to boil water for the washing-up, the next stage in our routine. Meanwhile I went downstairs, collected my gear, including suture material for a foal which had cut its leg and went out the side door into the garden. Just about opposite the rockery I turned and looked up at our window. It was open at the bottom and an arm emerged holding a dishcloth. I waved and the dishcloth waved back furiously. It was the start to every day.

And, driving from the yard, it seemed a good start. In fact everything was good. The raucous cawing of the rooks in the elms above as I closed the double doors, the clean fragrance of the air which greeted me every morning, and the challenge and interest of my job.

The injured foal was at Robert Corner's farm and I hadn't been there long before I spotted Jock, his sheepdog. And I began to watch the dog because behind a vet's daily chore of treating his patients there is always the fascinating kaleidoscope of animal personality and Jock was an interesting case.

continued on page 257

248

THE COUNTRY

· PUB ·

Homely comforts give
local pubs a special
place in a rural
way of life

An atmosphere that inspires far-flung loyalties

For centuries Yorkshire inns attracted their customers from an area no greater than could be reached by foot or horse. Now people living 30 miles from a country inn may regard it as their local, and holidaymakers come on pilgrimages of hundreds of miles. But the qualities that arouse these loyalties remain little changed.

By tradition, Yorkshire inns were judged by four standards: the fires, the food, the company and, of course, the beer. Intense loyalties were felt for Tetley's of Leeds, Cameron's of Hartlepool, and the Tadcaster rivals, Samuel Smith and John Smith.

Most of these still flourish; but old-timers like to pay wistful tribute to vanished brews such as the legendary Russell and Rangham's of Malton, lost in a merger in 1961.

HIGHEST INN Little has changed in 40 years at the Tan Hill Inn, at 1,732 ft possibly the highest, and the loneliest, public house in England.

BREWERY TOWN Taddy Ale takes its name from Tadcaster, the small Yorkshire town which is dominated by its two breweries, Samuel Smith and Bass.

UNDYING FIRE A cauldron and several blackened kettles cluster over the peat fire in this old photograph of the Saltersgate Inn. Another block of peat waits in the hearth. Standing beside the old coach road between York and Whitby, the inn – which is reputed to be haunted – is famous for its fire, said to have burned continuously for nearly 200 years, and for a particular kind of scone, known as a turf cake, baked in the oven and served hot to hungry travellers.

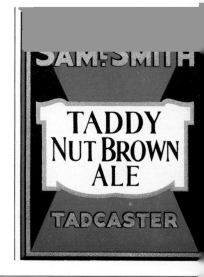

SAM SMITH

TADDY NUT BROWN ALE

TADCASTER

FARM AND INN Landlords of the Hare at Scawton used to augment their small income by keeping cows, pigs and hens.

ROYAL SIGN The Royal Oak at Thirsk recalls the tree that sheltered Charles after the Battle of Worcester.

SIMPLE FARE The menu at the White Lion, Cray, near Kettlewell.

Menu
Pie & Peas 45p
Soup 35p
Sandwiches
Cheese 35p
Ham 40p
Egg 35p

FOREIGN IMPORT Brought to England by French prisoners in the Napoleonic Wars, dominoes are particularly popular in the remote Yorkshire dales.

PUB GAME Darts began in the late 19th century and grew after World War I.

251

Signs of welcome over well worn doorways

The stone-built pubs of north Yorkshire invite custom with a single main feature: their wide, low doors surmounted by a simple sign. Often an inscription records a date, a reminder that these buildings have been fulfilling their humbler purpose for almost as long as the local churches.

From medieval times there were two kinds of country pub: the alehouse set in the heart of a village for the use of local people, and the roadside inn, built on a moor, far from any community. These remote hostelries catered for such travellers as pilgrims, packhorsemen and drovers bringing Scottish cattle to English markets.

Many have found a new purpose, providing refreshments for tourists. But others, such as Limekiln House, high on the old drovers' road skirting the Hambleton Hills, are now only heaps of stones, almost lost in besieging bracken and heather.

FLOWERY ENTRY Daffodils and a tangle of honeysuckle front a 17th-century pub in Low Row, Swaledale.

FARM PUB Cobbles and rings for tying horses and dogs provide an appropriat entry to the Farmer's Arms at Muker.

PROGRAMME Business-like announcements outside a West Witton hotel include the programme of the Royal British Legion.

MOORS PUB The Birch Hall Inn stands by a stream near the moors town of Goathlar

  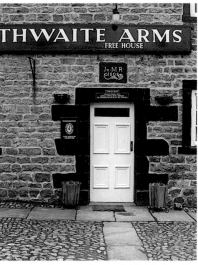

LOCAL HISTORY A Wensleydale landlord uses beneath an inscription recording predecessor of 1698.

HORSEMEN'S REST A mounting block outside a West Burton pub recalls past generations of horse-riding customers.

ELEGANCE Stark paintwork highlights the charming flourishes of an 1808 inscription at Horsehouse, Coverdale.

ES TOPIC The Wensleydale Heifer at West Witton dates from a period when farm stock was the main local interest.

Tranquil comforts of a Yorkshireman's home from home

Yorkshire inns provided their customers with the familiar solid comforts they knew at home. By tradition, there were no bars – only bare, stone-flagged kitchen-like rooms, with high-backed settles, pitted oak tables, and a single main feature: the range, with its black ovens and hanging kettles and its ever-burning fire of peat, coal or wood. Pint mugs were provided for men, and a few half pints were kept for rare women visitors.

The beer was brought up in a tall white jug from barrels in the cellar. It was to this cellar that favoured drinkers might be invited to retreat, closing the trapdoor behind them, for amiable after-hours drinking sessions with the landlord.

LOCAL INTERESTS An accumulation of local mementoes decorates an inviting corner of the White Bear, Masham.

SHEPHERD LANDLORD The landlord of the Victoria Arms, Worton, who keeps a small flock of sheep, shares his fireside with an orphan lamb.

A BEAR RE-BORN Modern stained glass decorates the White Bear, Masham, which was hit by a German bomb in 1942.

continued from page 248

A lot of farm dogs are partial to a little light relief from their work. They like to play and one of their favourite games is chasing cars off the premises. Often I drove off with a hairy form galloping alongside and the dog would usually give a final defiant bark after a few hundred yards to speed me on my way. But Jock was different.

He was really dedicated. Car chasing to him was a deadly serious art which he practised daily without a trace of levity. Corner's farm was at the end of a long track, twisting for nearly a mile between its stone walls down through the gently sloping fields to the road below and Jock didn't consider he had done his job properly until he had escorted his chosen vehicle right to the very foot. So his hobby was an exacting one.

I watched him now as I finished stitching the foal's leg and began to tie on a bandage. He was slinking about the buildings, a skinny little creature who, without his mass of black and white hair would have been an almost invisible mite, and he was playing out a transparent charade of pretending he was taking no notice of me – wasn't the least bit interested in my presence, in fact. But his furtive glances in the direction of the stable, his repeated criss-crossing of my line of vision gave him away. He was waiting for his big moment.

When I was putting on my shoes and throwing my wellingtons into the boot I saw him again. Or rather part of him; just a long nose and one eye protruding from beneath a broken door. It wasn't till I had started the engine and begun to move off that he finally declared himself, stealing out from his hiding place, body low, tail trailing, eyes fixed intently on the car's front wheels, and as I gathered speed and headed down the track he broke into an effortless lope.

I had been through this before and was always afraid he might run in front of me so I put my foot down and began to hurtle downhill. This was where Jock came into his own. I often wondered how he'd fare against a racing greyhound because by golly he could run. That sparse frame housed a perfect physical machine and the slender limbs reached and flew again and again, devouring the stony ground beneath, keeping up with the speeding car with joyful ease.

There was a sharp bend about half way down and here Jock invariably sailed over the wall and streaked across the turf, a little dark blur against the green, and having craftily cut off the corner he reappeared like a missile zooming over the grey stones lower down. This put him into a nice position for the run to the road and when he finally saw me on to the tarmac my last view of him was of a happy panting face looking after me. Clearly he considered it was a job well done and he would wander contentedly back up to the farm to await the next session, perhaps with the postman or the baker's van.

And there was another side to Jock. He was an outstanding performer at the sheepdog trials and Mr Corner had won many trophies with him. In fact the farmer could have sold the little animal for a lot of money but couldn't be persuaded to part with him. Instead he purchased a bitch, a

257

By golly he could run. That sparse frame housed a perfect physical machine.

scrawny little female counterpart of Jock and a trial winner in her own right. With this combination Mr Corner thought he could breed some world-beating types for sale. On my visits to the farm the bitch joined in the car-chasing but it seemed as though she was doing it more or less to humour her new mate and she always gave up at the first bend leaving Jock in command. You could see her heart wasn't in it.

When the pups arrived, seven fluffy black balls tumbling about the yard and getting under everybody's feet. Jock watched indulgently as they tried to follow him in his pursuit of my vehicle and you could almost see him laughing as they fell over their feet and were left trailing far behind.

It happened that I didn't have to go there for about ten months but I saw Robert Corner in the market occasionally and he told me he was training the pups and they were shaping well. Not that they needed much training; it was in their blood and he said they had tried to round up the cattle and sheep nearly as soon as they could walk. When I finally saw them they were like seven Jocks – meagre, darting little creatures flitting noiselessly about the buildings – and it didn't take me long to find out that they had learned more than sheep herding from their

258

father. There was something very evocative about the way they began to prowl around in the background as I prepared to get into my car, peeping furtively from behind straw bales, slinking with elaborate nonchalance into favourable positions for a quick getaway. And as I settled in my seat I could sense they were all crouched in readiness for the off.

I revved my engine, let in the clutch with a bump and shot across the yard and in a second the immediate vicinity erupted in a mass of hairy forms. I roared on to the track and put my foot down and on either side of me the little animals pelted along shoulder to shoulder, their faces all wearing the intent fanatical expression I knew so well. When Jock cleared the wall the seven pups went with him and when they reappeared and entered the home straight I noticed something different. On past occasions Jock had always had one eye on the car – this was what he considered his opponent; but now on that last quarter mile as he hurtled along at the head of a shaggy phalanx he was glancing at the pups on either side as though they were the main opposition.

And there was no doubt he was in trouble. Superbly fit though he was, these stringy bundles of bone and sinew which he had fathered had all his speed plus the newly minted energy of youth and it was taking every shred of his power to keep up with them. Indeed there was one terrible moment when he stumbled and was engulfed by the bounding creatures around him; it seemed that all was lost but there was a core of steel in Jock. Eyes popping, nostrils dilated, he fought his way through the pack until by the time we reached the road he was once more in the lead.

But it had taken its toll. I slowed down before driving away and looked down at the little animal standing with lolling tongue and heaving flanks on the grass verge. It must have been like this with all the other vehicles and it wasn't a merry game any more. I suppose it sounds silly to say you could read a dog's thoughts but everything in his posture betrayed the mounting apprehension that his days of supremacy were numbered. Just round the corner lay the unthinkable ignominy of being left trailing in the rear of that litter of young upstarts and as I drew away Jock looked after me and his expression was eloquent.

'How long can I keep this up?'

I felt for the little dog and on my next visit to the farm about two months later I wasn't looking forward to witnessing the final degradation which I felt was inevitable. But when I drove into the yard I found the place strangely unpopulated.

Robert Corner was forking hay into the cow's racks in the byre. He turned as I came in.

'Where are all your dogs?' I asked.

He put down his fork. 'All gone. By gaw, there's a market for good workin' sheepdogs. I've done right well out of t'job.'

'But you've still got Jock?'

'Oh aye, ah couldn't part with t'awd lad. He's over there.'

And so he was, creeping around as of old, pretending he wasn't

259

watching me. And when the happy time finally arrived and I drove away it was like it used to be with the lean, little animal haring along by the side of the car, but relaxed, enjoying the game, winging effortlessly over the wall and beating the car down to the tarmac with no trouble at all.

I think I was as relieved as he was that he was left alone with his supremacy unchallenged; that he was still top dog.

10

The biggest small-animal expert

This was one for Granville Bennett. I liked a bit of small animal surgery and was gradually doing more as time went on but this one frightened me. A twelve-year-old spaniel bitch in the last stages of pyometritis, pus dripping from her vulva on to the surgery table, temperature a hundred and four, panting, trembling, and as I held my stethoscope against her chest I could hear the classical signs of valvular insufficiency. A dicky heart was just what I needed on top of everything else.

'Drinking a lot of water, is she?' I asked.

Old Mrs Barker twisted the strings of her shopping bag anxiously. 'Aye, she never seems to be away from the water bowl. But she won't eat – hasn't had a bite for the last four days.'

'Well I don't know' I took off my stethoscope and stuffed it in my pocket. 'You should have brought her in long ago. She must have been ill for weeks.'

'Not rightly ill, but a bit off it. I thought there was nothing to worry about as long as she was eating.'

I didn't say anything for a few moments. I had no desire to upset the old girl but she had to be told.

'I'm afraid this is rather serious, Mrs Barker. The condition has been building up for a long time. It's in her womb, you see, a bad infection, and the only cure is an operation.'

'Well will you do it, please?' The old lady's lips quivered.

I came round the table and put my hand on her shoulder.

'I'd like to, but there are snags. She's in poor shape and twelve years old. Really a poor operation risk. I'd like to take her through to the Veterinary Hospital at Hartington and let Mr Bennett operate on her.'

'All right,' she said, nodding eagerly. 'I don't care what it costs.'

'Oh we'll keep it down as much as possible.' I walked along the passage with her and showed her out of the door. 'Leave her with me – I'll look after her, don't worry. What's her name, by the way?'

'Dinah,' she replied huskily, still peering past me down the passage.

I went through and lifted the phone. Thirty years ago country

SENTRY DOG A small wooden kennel beside a moorland road was the workspot for many sheepdogs. If sheep grazing the moor reached the road, some would follow it for miles, straying far from their own area. A dog chained to his kennel would bark to drive the wanderers back. Cattle-grids across roads have now made sentry dogs unnecessary.

practitioners had to turn to the small animal experts when anything unusual cropped up in that line. It is different nowadays when our practices are more mixed. In Darrowby now we have the staff and equipment to tackle any type of small animal surgery but it was different then. I had heard it said that sooner or later every large animal man had to scream for help from Granville Bennett and now it was my turn.

'Hello, is that Mr Bennett?'

'It is indeed.' A big voice, friendly, full of give.

'Herriot here. I'm with Farnon in Darrowby.'

'Of course! Heard of you, laddie, heard of you.'

'Oh ... er ... thanks. Look, I've got a bit of a sticky job here. I wonder if you'd take it on for me.'

'Delighted, laddie, what is it?'

'A real stinking pyo.'

'Oh lovely!'

'The bitch is twelve years old!'

'Splendid!'

'And toxic as hell.'

'Excellent!'

'And one of the worst hearts I've heard for a long time.'

'Fine, fine! When are you coming through?'

'This evening, if it's OK with you. About eight.'

'Couldn't be better laddie. See you.'

Hartington was a fair-sized town – about 200,000 inhabitants – but as I drove into the centre the traffic had thinned and only a few cars rolled past the rows of shop fronts. I hoped my twenty-five-mile journey had been worth it. Dinah, stretched out on a blanket in the back looked as if she didn't care either way. I glanced behind me at the head drooping over the edge of the seat, at the white muzzle and the cataracts in her eyes gleaming palely in the light from the dash. She looked so old. Maybe I was wasting my time, placing too much faith in this man's reputation.

There was no doubt Granville Bennett had become something of a legend in northern England. In those days when specialisation was almost unknown he had gone all out for small animal work – never looked at farm stock – and had set a new standard by the modern procedures in his animal hospital which was run as nearly as possible on human lines. It was, in fact, fashionable for veterinary surgeons of that era to belittle dog and cat work; a lot of the older men who had spent their lives among the teeming thousands of draught horses in city and agriculture would sneer, 'Oh I've no time to bother with those damn things.' Bennett had gone dead in the opposite direction.

I had never met him but I knew he was a young man in his early thirties. I had heard a lot about his skill, his business acumen, and about his reputation as a *bon viveur*. He was, they said, a dedicated devotee of the work-hard-play-hard school.

The Veterinary Hospital was a long, low building near the top of a

CLEVELAND BAY The native horse of Yorkshire, the Cleveland bay, was highly prized by farmers for its stamina, ability to carry heavy weights and speedy gait. It was not used on heavy land; on light soils it could do the same type of work as a Shire or a Clydesdale. It was faster, did not need as much fodder and did not wear through shoes as often as the heavier horses.

Outside Yorkshire the Cleveland bay was much used as a carriage horse – and still is in the Royal Mews. It is any shade of bay with a black mane and tail. Its short legs are free of any feathering.

PEAT CUTTING When spring lambing finished, it was time to collect fuel from the moors for the next winter. Peat, dug out of moist, brown bogs, or turf pared from the surface was gathered according to which was most available locally. At a deep peat breast, or face, the cutter stood at the bottom and sliced horizontally into the peat. At a shallow breast he would stand at the top and cut downwards.

busy street. I drove into a yard and knocked at a door in the corner. I was looking with some awe at a gleaming Bentley dwarfing my own battered little Austin when the door was opened by a pretty receptionist.

'Good evening,' she murmured with a dazzling smile which I thought must be worth another half crown on the bill for a start. 'Do come in, Mr Bennett is expecting you.'

I was shown into a waiting room with magazines and flowers on a corner table and many impressive photographs of dogs and cats on the walls – taken, I learned later, by the principal himself. I was looking closely at a superb study of two white poodles when I heard a footstep behind me. I turned and had my first view of Granville Bennett.

He seemed to fill the room. Not over tall but of tremendous bulk. Fat, I thought at first, but as he came nearer it seemed to me that the tissue of which he was composed wasn't distributed like fat. He wasn't flabby, he didn't stick out in any particular place, he was just a big wide, solid, hard-looking man. From the middle of a pleasant blunt-featured face the most magnificent pipe I had ever seen stuck forth shining and glorious, giving out delicious wisps of expensive smoke. It was an enormous pipe, in fact it would have looked downright silly with a smaller man, but on him it was a thing of beauty. I had a final impression of a beautifully cut dark suit and sparkling shirt cuffs as he held out a hand.

'James Herriot!' He said it as somebody else might have said 'Winston Churchill', or 'Stanley Matthews'.

'That's right.'

'Well, this is grand. Jim, is it?'

'Well yes, usually.'

'Lovely. We've got everything laid on for you, Jim. The girls are waiting in the theatre.'

'That's very kind of you, Mr Bennett.'

'Granville, Granville please!' He put his arm through mine and led me to the operating room.

Dinah was already there, looking very woebegone. She had had a sedative injection and her head nodded wearily. Bennett went over to her and gave her a swift examination.

'Mm, yes, let's get on, then.'

The two girls went into action like cogs in a smooth machine. Bennett kept a large lay staff and these animal nurses, both attractive, clearly knew what they were about. While one of them pulled up the anaesthetic and instrument trolleys the other seized Dinah's foreleg expertly above the elbow, raised the radial vein by pressure and quickly clipped and disinfected the area.

The big man strolled up with a loaded needle and effortlessly slipped the needle into the vein.

'Pentothal,' he said as Dinah slowly collapsed and lay unconscious on the table. It was one of the new short-acting anaesthetics which I had never seen used.

While Bennett scrubbed up and donned sterilised gown and cap the girls rolled Dinah on her back and secured her there with ties to loops on the operating table. They applied the ether and oxygen mask to her face then shaved and swabbed the operation site. The big man returned in time to have a scalpel placed in his hand.

With almost casual speed he incised skin and muscle layers and when he went through the peritoneum the horns of the uterus which in normal health would have been two slim pink ribbons now welled into the wound like twin balloons, swollen and turgid with pus. No wonder Dinah had felt ill, carrying that lot around with her.

The stubby fingers tenderly worked round the mass, ligated the ovarian vessels and uterine body then removed the whole thing and dropped it into an enamel bowl. It wasn't till he had begun to stitch that I realised that the operation was nearly over though he had been at the table for only a few minutes. It would all have looked childishly easy except that his total involvement showed in occasional explosive commands to the nurses.

And as I watched him working under the shadowless lamp with the white tiled walls around him and the rows of instruments gleaming by his side it came to me with a rush of mixed emotions that this was what I had always wanted to do myself. My dreams when I had first decided on veterinary work had been precisely of this. Yet here I was, a somewhat shaggy cow doctor; or perhaps more correctly a farm physician, but certainly something very different. The scene before me was a far cry from my routine of kicks and buffets, of muck and sweat. And yet I had no regrets; the life which had been forced on me by circumstances had turned out to be a thing of magical fulfilment. It came to me with a flooding certainty that I would rather spend my days driving over the unfenced roads of the high country than stooping over that operating table.

And anyway I couldn't have been a Bennett. I don't think I could have matched his technique and this whole set up was eloquent of a lot of things like business sense, foresight and driving ambition which I just didn't possess.

My colleague was finished now and was fitting up an intravenous saline drip. He taped the needle down in the vein then turned to me.

'That's it, then, Jim. It's up to the old girl now.' He began to lead me from the room and it struck me how very pleasant it must be to finish your job and walk away from it like this. In Darrowby I'd have been starting now to wash the instruments, scrub the table, and the final scene would have been of Herriot the great surgeon swilling the floor with mop and bucket. This was a better way.

Back in the waiting room Bennett pulled on his jacket and extracted from a side pocket the immense pipe which he inspected with a touch of anxiety as if he feared mice had been nibbling at it in his absence. He wasn't satisfied with his examination because he brought forth a soft yellow cloth and began to polish the briar with intense absorption. Then he held the pipe high, moving it slightly from side to side, his eyes

LOADING PEAT Slices were cut in the soft peat by pressing down a winged spade vertically. Then the peat cutter could push his spade under about six slices at once and cast them straight on to the sturdy wooden barrow. The barrow loads were wheeled to the drying ground to be set in neat rows for a week or two before being propped together in small heaps, or rickles. The rickles were left to dry until after the June haymaking and then carted back to the farm.

YORKSHIRE TERRIER Pampered lap-dog is the role this diminutive dog frequently fills. Doting matrons cuddle it, brush the glossy, steel-blue coat that falls right down to its feet, and comb the golden face hair that conceals its features, or tie it up with a ribbon to reveal the mischievous bright eyes. The Yorkshire terrier has become Britain's most numerous toy breed of dog since it was developed in the 19th century, but it was bred for a practical purpose. Yorkshire wool workers used it for killing vermin in the mills and for the now-illegal rat-baiting. The dainty lap-dog, put in a pit with 20 rats and urged on by those who had wagers on it, could kill the rats with swift bites within 3 minutes.

softening at the play of the light on the exquisite grain. Finally he produced a pouch of mammoth proportions, filled the bowl, applied a match with a touch of reverence and closed his eyes as a fragrant mist drifted from his lips.

'That baccy smells marvellous,' I said. 'What is it?'

'Navy Cut De Luxe.' He closed his eyes again. 'You know, I could eat the smoke.'

I laughed. 'I use the ordinary Navy Cut myself.'

He gazed at me like a sorrowing Buddha, 'Oh you mustn't, laddie, you mustn't. This is the only stuff. Rich ... fruity ...' His hand made languid motions in the air. 'Here, you can take some away with you.'

He pulled open a drawer. I had a brief view of a stock which wouldn't have disgraced a fair-sized tobacconist's shop; innumerable tins, pipes, cleaners, reamers, cloths.

'Try this,' he said, 'and tell me if I'm not right.'

I looked down at the first container in my hand. 'Oh but I can't take all this. It's a four-ounce tin!'

'Rubbish, my boy. Put it in your pocket.' He became suddenly brisk. 'Now I expect you'll want to hang around till old Dinah comes out of the anaesthetic so why don't we have a quick beer? I'm a member of a nice little club just across the road.'

'Well fine, sounds great.'

He moved lightly and swiftly for a big man and I had to hurry to keep up with him as he left the surgery and crossed to a building on the other side of the street.

Inside the club was masculine comfort, hails of welcome from some prosperous looking members and a friendly greeting from the man behind the bar.

'Two pints, Fred,' murmured Bennett absently, and the drinks appeared with amazing speed. My colleague poured his down apparently without swallowing and turned to me.

'Another, Jim?'

I had just tried a sip at mine and began to gulp anxiously at the bitter ale. 'Right, but let me get this one.'

'No can do, laddie.' He glanced at me with mild severity. 'Only members can buy drinks. Same again, Fred.'

I found I had two glasses at my elbow and with a tremendous effort I got the first one down. Gasping slightly I was surveying the second one timidly when I noticed that Bennett was three-quarters down his. As I watched he drained it effortlessly.

'You're slow, Jim,' he said, smiling indulgently. 'Just set them up again will you, Fred.'

In some alarm I watched the barman ply his handle and attacked my second pint resolutely. I surprised myself by forcing it over my tonsils' then, breathing heavily, I got hold of the third one just as Bennett spoke again.

'We'll just have one for the road, Jim,' he said pleasantly. 'Would you be so kind, Fred?'

This was ridiculous but I didn't want to appear a piker at our first meeting. With something akin to desperation I raised the third and began to suck feebly at it. When my glass was empty I almost collapsed against the counter. My stomach was agonisingly distended and a light perspiration had broken out on my brow. As I almost lay there I saw my colleague moving across the carpet towards the door.

'Time we were off, Jim,' he said. 'Drink up.'

It's wonderful what the human frame can tolerate when put to the test. I would have taken bets that it was impossible for me to drink that fourth pint without at least half an hour's rest, preferably in the prone position, but as Bennett's shoe tapped impatiently I tipped the beer a little at a time into my mouth, feeling it wash around my back teeth before incredibly disappearing down my gullet. I believe the water torture was a favourite with the Spanish Inquisition and as the pressure inside me increased I knew just how their victims felt.

When I at last blindly replaced my glass and splashed my way from the bar the big man was holding the door open. Outside in the street he placed an arm across my shoulder.

'The old Spaniel won't be out of it yet,' he said. 'We'll just slip to my house and have a bite – I'm a little peckish.'

Sunk in the deep upholstery of the Bentley, cradling my swollen abdomen in my arms I watched the shop fronts flicker past the windows and give way to the darkness of the open countryside. We drew up outside a fine grey stone house in a typical Yorkshire village and Bennett ushered me inside.

He pushed me towards a leather armchair. 'Make yourself at home, laddie. Zoe's out at the moment but I'll get some grub.' He bustled through to the kitchen and reappeared in seconds with a deep bowl which he placed on a table by my side.

'You know, Jim,' he said, rubbing his hands. 'There's nothing better after beer than a few pickled onions.'

I cast a timorous glance into the bowl. Everything in this man's life seemed to be larger than life, even the onions. They were bigger than golf balls, brownish-white, glistening.

'Well thanks, Mr Ben ... Granville.' I took one of them, held it between finger and thumb and stared at it helplessly. The beer hadn't even begun to sort itself out inside me; the idea of starting on this potent-looking vegetable was unthinkable.

Granville reached into the bowl, popped an onion into his mouth, crunched it quickly, swallowed and sank his teeth into a second. 'By God, that's good. You know, my little wife's a marvellous cook. She even makes pickled onions better than anyone.'

Munching happily he moved over to the sideboard and clinked around for a few moments before placing in my hand a heavy cut glass tumbler about two-thirds full of neat whisky. I couldn't say anything

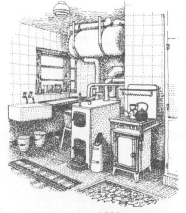

A LABOUR-SAVING 1937 KITCHEN
In the more prosperous houses and farms of north Yorkshire in the 1930s, the kitchen was no longer dominated by the open-fired range but housed a hygienic collection of labour-saving devices. A closed, enamelled boiler and an enamelled gas cooker ousted the range with its smoke and dirt. A porcelain-glazed sink replaced the stone type. A washing machine and soap powder or flakes did away with the wooden tub, the rubbing board and soft soap. Kitchen units were built in to hold brooms, cutlery and baking ingredients.

because I had taken the plunge and put the onion in my mouth; and as I bit boldly into it the fumes rolled in a volatile wave into my nasal passages, making me splutter. I took a gulp at the whisky and looked up at Granville with watering eyes.

He was holding out the onion bowl again and when I declined he regarded it for a moment with hurt in his eyes. 'It's funny you don't like them, I always thought Zoe did them marvellously.'

'Oh you're wrong, Granville, they're delicious. I just haven't finished this one.'

He didn't reply but continued to look at the bowl with gentle sorrow. I realised there was nothing else for it; I took another onion.

Immensely gratified, Granville hurried through to the kitchen again. This time when he came back he bore a tray with an enormous cold roast, a loaf of bread, butter and mustard.

'I think a beef sandwich would go down rather nicely, Jim,' he murmured, as he stropped his carving knife on a steel. Then he noticed my glass of whisky still half full.

'C'mon, c'mon, c'mon!' he said with some asperity. 'You're not touching your drink.' He watched me benevolently as I drained the glass then he refilled it to its old level. 'That's better. And have another onion.'

I stretched my legs out and rested my head on the back of the chair in an attempt to ease my internal turmoil. My stomach was a lake of volcanic lava bubbling and popping fiercely in its crater with each additional piece of onion, every sip of whisky setting up a fresh violent reaction. Watching Granville at work, a great wave of nausea swept over me. He was sawing busily at the roast, carving off slices which looked to be an inch thick, slapping mustard on them and enclosing them in the bread. He hummed with contentment as the pile grew. Every now and then he had another onion.

'Now then, laddie,' he cried at length, putting a heaped plate at my elbow. 'Get yourself round that lot.' He took his own supply and collapsed with a sigh into another chair.

He took a gargantuan bite and spoke as he chewed. 'You know, Jim, this is something I enjoy – a nice little snack. Zoe always leaves me plenty to go at when she pops out.' He engulfed a further few inches of sandwich. 'And I'll tell you something, though I say it myself, these are bloody good, don't you think so?'

'Yes indeed.' Squaring my shoulders I bit, swallowed and held my breath as another unwanted foreign body slid down to the ferment below.

Just then I heard the front door open.

'Ah, that'll be Zoe,' Granville said, and was about to rise when a disgracefully fat Staffordshire Bull Terrier burst into the room, waddled across the carpet and leapt into his lap.

'Phoebles, my dear, come to daddykins!' he shouted. 'Have you had a nice walkies with mummy?'

The Staffordshire was closely followed by a Yorkshire Terrier which was also enthusiastically greeted by Granville.

'Yoo-hoo, Victoria, Yoo-hoo!'

The Yorkie, an obvious smiler, did not jump up but contented herself with sitting at her master's feet, baring her teeth ingratiatingly every few seconds.

I smiled through my pain. Another myth exploded; the one about these specialist small animal vets not being fond of dogs themselves. The big man crooned over the two little animals. The fact that he called Phoebe 'Phoebles' was symptomatic.

I heard light footsteps in the hall and looked up expectantly. I had Granville's wife taped neatly in my mind; domesticated, devoted, homely; many of these dynamic types had wives like that, willing slaves

Gasping slightly I was surveying the second one timidly.

267

content to lurk in the background. I waited confidently for the entrance of a plain little hausfrau.

When the door opened I almost let my vast sandwich fall. Zoe Bennett was a glowing warm beauty who would make any man alive stop for another look. A lot of soft brown hair, large grey-green friendly eyes, a tweed suit sitting sweetly on a slim but not too slim figure; and something else, a wholesomeness, an inner light which made me wish suddenly that I was a better man or at least that I looked better than I did.

In an instant I was acutely conscious of the fact that my shoes were dirty, that my old jacket and corduroy trousers were out of place here. I hadn't troubled to change but had rushed straight out in my working clothes, and they were different from Granville's because I couldn't go round the farms in a suit like this.

'My love, my love!' he carolled joyously as his wife bent over and kissed him fondly. 'Let me introduce Jim Herriot from Darrowby.'

The beautiful eyes turned on me.

'How d'you do, Mr Herriot!' She looked as pleased to see me as her husband had done and again I had the desperate wish that I was more presentable; that my hair was combed, that I didn't have this mounting conviction that I was going to explode into a thousand pieces at any moment.

'I'm going to have a cup of tea, Mr Herriot. Would you like one?'

'No-no, no no, thank you very much but no, no, not at the moment.' I backed away slightly.

'Ah well, I see you've got one of Granville's little sandwiches.' She giggled and went to get her tea.

When she came back she handed a parcel to her husband. 'I've been shopping today, darling. Picked up some of those shirts you like so much.'

'My sweet! how kind of you!' He began to tear at the brown paper like a schoolboy and produced three elegant shirts in cellophane covers. 'They're marvellous, my pet, you spoil me.' He looked up at me. 'Jim! These are the most wonderful shirts, you must have one.' He flicked a shining package across the room on to my lap.

I looked down at it in amazement. 'No, really I can't ...'

'Of course you can. You keep it.'

'But, Granville, not a shirt ... it's too ...'

'It's a very good shirt.' He was beginning to look hurt again.

I subsided.

They were both so kind. Zoe sat right by me with her tea cup, chatting pleasantly, while Granville beamed at me from his chair as he finished the last of the sandwiches and started again on the onions.

The proximity of the attractive woman was agreeable but embarrassing. My corduroys in the warmth of the room had begun to give off the unmistakable bouquet of the farmyard where they spent most of their time. And though it was one of my favourite scents there was no doubt it

POTTED BEEF An economical spread for bread and butter at teatime was made from a cheap cut of beef. At the teas in the local chapel which followed the anniversary service or the Sunday School procession at Whitsuntide, there would always be sandwiches or teacakes filled with this savoury paste.

To make potted beef, cut up 1 lb of stewing beef into small pieces and put it in a stoneware or glass jar with a teaspoon of salt and 6 tablespoons of water. Cover the jar with kitchen foil and stand it in a pan of hot water. Boil for 2½ hours, topping up the pan with hot water from time to time, then turn out the beef, season it liberally and mince it finely or pound it to a paste. Press it into small pots and seal them with a thin covering of melted butter.

didn't go with these elegant surroundings.

And worse still, I had started a series of internal rumblings and musical tinklings which resounded only too audibly during every lull in the conversation. The only other time I have heard such sounds was in a cow with an advanced case of displacement of the abomasum. My companions delicately feigned deafness even when I produced a shameful, explosive belch which made the little fat dog start up in alarm, but when another of these mighty borborygmi escaped me and almost made the windows rattle I thought it was time to go.

In any case I wasn't contributing much else. The alcohol had taken hold and I was increasingly conscious that I was just sitting there with a stupid leer on my face. In striking contrast to Granville who looked just the same as when I first met him back at the surgery. He was cool and possessed, his massive urbanity unimpaired. It was a little hard.

So, with the tin of tobacco bumping against my hip and the shirt tucked under my arm I took my leave.

Back at the hospital I looked down at Dinah. The old dog had come through wonderfully well and she lifted her head and gazed at me sleepily. Her colour was good and her pulse strong. The operative shock had been dramatically minimised by my colleague's skilful, speedy technique and by the intravenous drip.

I knelt down and stroked her ears. 'You know, I'm sure she's going to make it, Granville.'

Above me the great pipe nodded with majestic confidence.

'Of course, laddie, of course.'

And he was right. Dinah was rejuvenated by her hysterectomy and lived to delight her mistress for many more years.

On the way home that night she lay by my side on the passenger seat, her nose poking from a blanket. Now and then she rested her chin on my hand as it gripped the gear lever and occasionally she licked me lazily.

I could see she felt better than I did.

11

The piccalilli saves my bacon

I had never been married before so there was nothing in my past experience to go by but it was beginning to dawn on me that I was very nicely fixed.

I am talking, of course, of material things. It would have been enough for me or anybody else to be paired with a beautiful girl whom I loved and who loved me. I hadn't reckoned on the other aspects.

This business of studying my comfort, for instance. I thought such

STAFFORDSHIRE BULL TERRIER
Strength, courage, intelligence, speed and a need for extensive exercise are the characteristics of the Staffordshire bull terrier, which was developed in the 19th century from crosses between the bulldog and the old English terrier. The stocky bull terrier, white with brown, red or black – or sometimes brindled – has great loyalty to its owner's family and is fiercely protective of them. Ferocity is bred in it, for it was developed to fight other dogs. Dog-fights became popular when bull-baiting was made illegal in the 1830s, and they were held in London even after 1900 although they were officially banned by then. Crowds would stand round the fighting-pit for up to two hours until one of the dogs was killed or too exhausted to continue.

things had gone out of fashion, but not so with Helen. It was brought home to me again as I walked in to breakfast this morning. We had at last acquired a table – I had bought it at a farm sale and brought it home in triumph tied to the roof of my car – and now Helen had vacated the chair on which she used to sit at the bench and had taken over the high stool. She was perched away up there now, transporting her food from far below, while I was expected to sit comfortably in the chair. I don't think I am a selfish swine by nature but there was nothing I could do about it.

And there were other little things. The neat pile of clothing laid out for me each morning; the clean, folded shirt and handkerchief and socks so different from the jumble of my bachelor days. And when I was late for meals, which was often, she served me with my food but instead of going off and doing something else she would down tools and sit watching me while I ate. It made me feel like a sultan.

It was this last trait which gave me a clue to her behaviour. I suddenly remembered that I had seen her sitting by Mr Alderson while he had a late meal; sitting in the same pose, one arm on the table, quietly watching him. And I realised I was reaping the benefit of her lifetime attitude to her father. Mild little man though he was she had catered gladly to his every wish in the happy acceptance that the man of the house was number one; and the whole pattern was rubbing off on me now.

In fact it set me thinking about the big question of how girls might be expected to behave after marriage. One old farmer giving me advice about choosing a wife once said; 'Have a bloody good look at the mother first, lad', and I'm sure he had a point. But if I may throw in my own little word of counsel it would be to have a passing glance at how she acts towards her father.

Watching her now as she got down and started to serve my breakfast the warm knowledge flowed through me as it did so often that my wife was the sort who just liked looking after a man and that I was so very lucky.

And I was certainly blooming under the treatment. A bit too much, in fact, and I was aware I shouldn't be attacking this plateful of porridge and cream; especially with all that material sizzling in the frying pan. Helen had brought with her to Skeldale House a delicious dowry in the shape of half a pig and there hung from the beams of the topmost attic a side of bacon and a majestic ham; a constant temptation. Some samples were in the pan now and though I had never been one for large breakfasts I did not demur when she threw in a couple of big brown eggs to keep them company. And I put up only feeble resistance when she added some particularly tasty smoked sausage which she used to buy in a shop in the market place.

When I had got through it all I rose rather deliberately from the table and as I put on my coat I noticed it wasn't so easy to button as it used to be.

BAKING UTENSILS Tinplate, fluted pastry cutters (top) had many uses – and still have, but they are frequently made of aluminium or plastic now. They stamp out biscuits, scones and pastry for small tarts and pies. The 5 in. long boxwood pastry jigger (centre) with its zig-zagged bone wheel, trimmed off the pastry round a pie dish, pressing on a decorative mark and at the same time sealing the pastry to the dish, or a pastry lid to the pastry base of a covered tart. The sycamore biscuit pricker (bottom), 2 in. across and fitted with iron spikes, was pressed on to biscuits just before they were baked to prevent them from bubbling in the centre. It was also used to mark Yorkshire teacakes – flat circles of bread similar to baps.

'Here are your sandwiches, Jim,' Helen said, putting a parcel in my hand. I was spending a day in the Scarburn district, tuberculin testing for Ewan Ross, and my wife was always concerned lest I grow faint from lack of nourishment on the long journey.

I kissed her, made a somewhat ponderous descent of the long flights of stairs and went out the side door. Half way up the garden I stopped as always and looked up at the window under the tiles. An arm appeared and brandished a dishcloth vigorously. I waved back and continued my walk to the yard. I found I was puffing a little as I got the car out and I laid my parcel almost guiltily on the back seat. I knew what it would contain; not just sandwiches but meat and onion pie, buttered scones, ginger cake to lead me into further indiscretions.

There is no doubt that in those early days I would have grown exceedingly gross under Helen's treatment. But my job saved me; the endless walking between the stone barns scattered along the hillsides, the climbing in and out of calf pens, pushing cows around, and regular outbursts of hard physical effort in calving and foaling. So I escaped with only a slight tightening of my collar and the occasional farmer's remark, 'By gaw, you've been on a good pasture, young man!'

Driving away, I marvelled at the way she indulged my little whims, too. I have always had a pathological loathing of fat, so Helen carefully trimmed every morsel from my meat. This feeling about fat, which almost amounted to terror, had been intensified since coming to Yorkshire, because back in the thirties the farmers seemed to live on the stuff. One old man, noticing my pop-eyed expression as I viewed him relishing his lunch of roast fat bacon, told me he had never touched lean meat in his life.

'Ah like to feel t'grease runnin' down ma chin!' he chuckled. He pronounced it 'grayus' which made it sound even worse. But he was a ruddy-faced octogenarian, so it hadn't done him any harm; and this held good for hundreds of others just like him. I used to think that the day in day out hard labour of farming burned it up in their systems but if I had to eat the stuff it would kill me very rapidly.

The latter was, of course, a fanciful notion as was proved to me one day.

It was when I was torn from my bed one morning at 6 a.m. to attend a calving heifer at old Mr Horner's small farm and when I got there I found there was no malpresentation of the calf but that it was simply too big. I don't like a lot of pulling but the heifer, lying on her bed of straw, was obviously in need of assistance. Every few seconds she strained to the utmost and a pair of feet came into view momentarily then disappeared as she relaxed.

'Is she getting those feet out any further?' I asked.

'Nay, there's been no change for over an hour,' the old man replied.

'And when did the water bag burst?'

'Two hours since.'

There was no doubt the calf was well and truly stuck and getting drier

MIDDLE WHITE SOW Developed from a cross between the Large White and the now extinct Small White, this breed was reared as a quick-maturing porker, but it is now rare. It is shorter in the body and face than the Large White and has a heavier jowl – a pointer to the characteristic that put it out of favour, its tendency to put on fat. This greatly reduced the breed's numbers as the demand for lean pork became predominant.

THE KITCHEN SINK A wide, shallow 'slapestone', or sink, shaped from one slab of stone and raised on brick piers was a feature of every Yorkshire farm kitchen until porcelain-glazed sinks became widely available in the 1930s and 1940s. Soap and scrubbing brushes were kept in the holders on the wall behind the sink. Water came from the iron pump installed at the side. The kitchen served also as the bathroom, and hot water would be ladled from the boiler of the kitchen range to warm the icy water that came from the pump.

all the time, and if the labouring mother had been able to speak I think she would have said: 'For Pete's sake get this thing away from me!'

I could have done with a big strong man to help me but Mr Horner, apart from his advanced age, was a rather shaky lightweight. And since the farm was perched on a lonely eminence miles from the nearest village there was no chance of calling in a neighbour. I would have to do the job myself.

It took me nearly an hour. With a thin rope behind the calf's ears and through his mouth to stop the neck from telescoping I eased the little creature inch by inch into the world. Not so much pulling but rather leaning back and helping the heifer as she strained. She was a rather undersized little animal and she lay patiently on her side, accepting the situation with the resignation of her kind. She could never have calved without help and all the time I had the warm conviction that I was doing what she wanted and needed. I felt I should be as patient as she was so I didn't hurry but let things come in their normal sequence; the little nose with the nostrils twitching reassuringly, then the eyes wearing a preoccupied light during the tight squeeze, then the ears and with a final rush the rest of the calf.

The young mother was obviously none the worse because she rolled on to her chest almost immediately and began to sniff with the utmost interest at the new arrival. She was in better shape than myself because I discovered with some surprise that I was sweating and breathless and my arms and shoulders were aching.

The farmer, highly pleased, rubbed my back briskly with the towel as I bent over the bucket, then he helped me on with my shirt.

'Well that's champion, lad. You'll come in and have a cup of tea now, won't you?'

In the kitchen Mrs Horner placed a steaming mug on the table and smiled across at me.

'Will you sit down along o' my husband and have a bit o' breakfast?' she asked.

There is nothing like an early calving to whet the appetite and I nodded readily. 'That's very kind of you, I'd love to.'

It is always a good feeling after a successful delivery and I sighed contentedly as I sank into a chair and watched the old lady set out bread, butter and jam in front of me. I sipped my tea and as I exchanged a word with the farmer I didn't see what she was doing next. Then my toes curled into a tight ball as I found two huge slices of pure white fat lying on my plate.

Shrinking back in my seat I saw Mrs Horner sawing at a great hunk of cold boiled bacon. But it wasn't ordinary bacon, it was one hundred per cent fat without a strip of lean anywhere. Even in my shocked state I could see it was a work of art; cooked to a turn, beautifully encrusted with golden crumbs and resting on a spotless serving dish ... but fat.

She dropped two similar slices on her husband's plate and looked at me expectantly.

My position was desperate. I could not possibly offend this sweet old person but on the other hand I knew beyond all doubt that there was no way I could eat what lay in front of me. Maybe I could have managed a tiny piece if it had been hot and fried crisp, but cold, boiled and clammy … never. And there was an enormous quantity; two slices about six inches by four and at least half an inch thick with the golden border of crumbs down one side. The thing was impossible.

Mrs Horner sat down opposite me. She was wearing a flowered mob cap over her white hair and for a moment she reached out, bent her head to one side and turned the dish with the slab of bacon a little to the left to show it off better. Then she turned to me and smiled. It was a kind, proud smile.

There have been times in my life when, confronted by black and hopeless circumstances, I have discovered in myself undreamed-of resources of courage and resolution. I took a deep breath, seized knife and fork and made a bold incision in one of the slices, but as I began to transport the greasy white segment to my mouth I began to shudder and my hand stayed frozen in space. It was at that moment I spotted the jar of piccalilli.

Feverishly I scooped a mound of it on to my plate. It seemed to contain just about everything; onions, apples, cucumber and other assorted vegetables jostling each other in a powerful mustard-vinegar sauce. It was the work of a moment to smother my loaded fork with the mass, then I popped it into my mouth, gave a couple of quick chews and swallowed. It was a start and I hadn't tasted a thing except the piccalilli.

'Nice bit of bacon,' Mr Horner murmured.

'Delicious!' I replied, munching desperately at the second forkful. 'Absolutely delicious!'

'And you like ma piccalilli too!' The old lady beamed at me. 'Ah can tell by the way you're slappin' it on!' She gave a peal of delighted laughter.

'Yes, indeed.' I looked at her with streaming eyes. 'Some of the best I've ever tasted.'

Looking back, I realise it was one of the bravest things I have ever done. I stuck to my task unwaveringly, dipping again and again into the jar, keeping my mind a blank, refusing grimly to think of the horrible thing that was happening to me. There was only one bad moment, when the piccalilli, which packed a tremendous punch and was never meant to be consumed in large mouthfuls, completely took my breath away and I went into a long coughing spasm. But at last I came to the end. A final heroic crunch and swallow, a long gulp at my tea and the plate was empty. The thing was accomplished.

And there was no doubt it had been worth it. I had been a tremendous success with the old folks. Mr Horner slapped my shoulder.

'By gaw, it's good to see a young feller enjoyin' his food! When I were a lad I used to put it away sharpish, like that, but ah can't do it now.' Chuckling to himself, he continued with his breakfast.

PICCALILLI Some of the best high teas begin with cold meats, accompanied by relishes such as piccalilli.

To make piccalilli, prepare and cut into small pieces 6 lb of mixed vegetables – for example cucumber, marrow, green beans, onions, cauliflower and green tomatoes. Spread them on a dish and sprinkle on 1 lb of cooking salt. Cover and leave for 24 hours, then rinse thoroughly and drain. Warm almost 2 pints of white wine vinegar, having set aside 3–4 tablespoons. Stir 6 oz of sugar, ½ oz of turmeric, 1 oz of dry mustard and 1 oz of ground ginger into the warm vinegar, then add the vegetables and simmer for 15 minutes. Blend 1½ oz of flour with the reserved vinegar, add to the pan and stir until it boils. Simmer for 3 minutes. Ladle the piccalilli into jars and seal them.

His wife showed me the door. 'Aye, it was a real compliment to me.' She looked at the table and giggled. 'You've nearly finished the jar!'

'Yes, I'm sorry, Mrs Horner,' I said, smiling through my tears and trying to ignore the churning in my stomach. 'But I just couldn't resist it.'

Contrary to my expectations I didn't drop down dead soon afterwards but for a week I was oppressed by a feeling of nausea which I am prepared to believe was purely psychosomatic.

At any rate, since that little episode I have never knowingly eaten fat again. My hatred was transformed into something like an obsession from then on.

And I haven't been all that crazy about piccalilli either.

12

Gyp finds his voice

SUGAR CUTTERS Until granulated sugar became common in the 1930s, every kitchen needed sugar cutters. Sugar was sold in very hard conical loaves, up to 3 ft high and more than 1 ft across at the base. A small hammer broke the loaf into sections, and these were cut into smaller pieces for dissolving in drinks or crushing for baking. Pincer-like iron cutters about 9 in. long (left) were common, but the cutting was easier if they were mounted on a wooden base and operated by a single long handle that could exert greater pressure than cutters gripped in the hand.

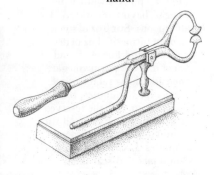

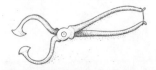

'Is this the thing you've been telling me about?' I asked.

Mr Wilkin nodded. 'Aye, that's it, it's always like that.'

I looked down at the helpless convulsions of the big dog lying at my feet; the staring eyes, the wildly pedalling limbs. The farmer had told me about the periodic attacks which had begun to affect his sheepdog, Gyp, but it was coincidence that one should occur when I was on the farm for another reason.

'And he's all right afterwards, you say?'

'Right as a bobbin. Seems a bit dazed, maybe, for about an hour then he's back to normal.' The farmer shrugged. 'I've had lots o' dogs through my hands as you know and I've seen plenty of dogs with fits. I thought I knew all the causes – worms, wrong feeding, distemper – but this has me beat. I've tried everything.'

'Well you can stop trying, Mr Wilkin,' I said. 'You won't be able to do much for Gyp. He's got epilepsy.'

'Epilepsy? But he's a grand, normal dog most of t'time.'

'Yes, I know. That's how it goes. There's nothing actually wrong with his brain – it's a mysterious condition. The cause is unknown but it's almost certainly hereditary.'

Mr Wilkin raised his eyebrows. 'Well that's a rum 'un. If it's hereditary why hasn't it shown up before now? He's nearly two years old and he didn't start this till a few weeks ago.'

'That's typical,' I replied. 'Eighteen months to two years is about the time it usually appears.'

Gyp interrupted us by getting up and staggering towards his master, wagging his tail. He seemed untroubled by his experience. In fact the whole thing had lasted less than two minutes.

Mr Wilkin bent and stroked the rough head briefly. His craggy features were set in a thoughtful cast. He was a big powerful man in his forties and now as his eyes narrowed in that face which rarely smiled he looked almost menacing. I had heard more than one man say he wouldn't like to get on the wrong side of Sep Wilkin and I could see what they meant. But he had always treated me right and since he farmed nearly a thousand acres I saw quite a lot of him.

His passion was sheepdogs. A lot of farmers liked to run dogs at the trials but Mr Wilkin was one of the top men. He bred and trained dogs which regularly won at the local events and occasionally at the national trials. And what was troubling me was that Gyp was his main hope.

He had picked out the two best pups from a litter – Gyp and Sweep – and had trained them with the dedication that had made him a winner. I don't think I have ever seen two dogs enjoy each other quite as much; whenever I was on the farm I would see them together, sometimes peeping nose by nose over the half door of the loose box where they slept, occasionally slinking devotedly round the feet of their master but usually just playing together. They must have spent hours rolling about in ecstatic wrestling matches, growling and panting, gnawing gently at each other's limbs.

A few months ago George Crossley, one of Mr Wilkin's oldest friends and a keen trial man, had lost his best dog with nephritis and Mr Wilkin had let him have Sweep. I was surprised at the time because Sweep was shaping better than Gyp in his training and looked like turning out a real champion. But it was Gyp who remained. He must have missed his friend but there were other dogs on the farm and if they didn't quite make up for Sweep he was never really lonely.

As I watched, I could see the dog recovering rapidly. It was extraordinary how soon normality was restored after that frightening convulsion. And I waited with some apprehension to hear what his master would say.

The cold, logical decision for him to make would be to have Gyp put down and, looking at the friendly, tail-wagging animal I didn't like the idea at all. There was something attractive about him. The big-boned, well-marked body was handsome but his most distinctive feature was his head where one ear somehow contrived to stick up while the other lay flat, giving him a lop-sided, comic appeal. Gyp, in fact, looked a bit of a clown. But a clown who radiated goodwill and camaraderie.

Mr Wilkin spoke at last. 'Will he get any better as he grows older?'

'Almost certainly not,' I replied.

'Then he'll always 'ave these fits?'

'I'm afraid so. You say he has them every two or three weeks – well it will probably carry on more or less like that with occasional variations.'

'But he could have one any time?'

'Yes.'

'In the middle of a trial, like.' The farmer sunk his head on his chest

SHEEPDOG'S KENNEL The usual place for a farm dog to live is out in the yard. There is no grand provision for a kennel, since the dog is not often in it. Frequently the kennel is simply the space under the short, outside flight of stone steps leading up to a hayloft or barn over a byre. The space is built up, leaving an opening for a door. The dog is tethered to the kennel by a long rope so that it can wander about the farmyard acting as a guard dog.

and his voice rumbled deep. 'That's it, then.'

In the long silence which followed, the fateful words became more and more inevitable. Sep Wilkin wasn't the man to hesitate in a matter which concerned his ruling passion. Ruthless culling of any animal which didn't come up to standard would be his policy. When he finally cleared his throat I had a sinking premonition of what he was going to say.

But I was wrong.

'If I kept him, could you do anything for him?' he asked.

'Well I could give you some pills for him. They might decrease the frequency of the fits.' I tried to keep the eagerness out of my voice.

'Right . . . right . . . I'll come into t'surgery and get some,' he muttered.

'Fine. But . . . er . . . you won't ever breed from him, will you?' I said.

'Naw, naw, naw,' the farmer grunted with a touch of irritability as though he didn't want to pursue the matter further.

And I held my peace because I felt intuitively that he did not want to be detected in a weakness; that he was prepared to keep the dog simply as a pet. It was funny how events began to slot into place and suddenly make sense. That was why he had let Sweep, the superior trial dog, go. He just liked Gyp. In fact Sep Wilkin, hard man though he may be, had succumbed to that off-beat charm.

So I shifted to some light chatter about the weather as I walked back to the car, but when I was about to drive off the farmer returned to the main subject.

'There's one thing about Gyp I never mentioned,' he said, bending to the window. 'I don't know whether it has owt to do with the job or not. He has never barked in his life.'

I looked at him in surprise. 'You mean never, ever?'

'That's right. Not a single bark. T'other dogs make a noise when strangers come on the farm but I've never heard Gyp utter a sound since he was born.'

'Well that's very strange,' I said. 'But I can't see that it is connected with his condition in any way.'

And as I switched on the engine I noticed for the first time that while a bitch and two half grown pups gave tongue to see me on my way Gyp merely regarded me in his comradely way, mouth open, tongue lolling, but made no noise. A silent dog.

The thing intrigued me. So much so that whenever I was on the farm over the next few months I made a point of watching the big sheepdog at whatever he was doing. But there was never any change. Between the convulsions which had settled down to around three-week intervals he was a normal, active, happy animal. But soundless.

I saw him, too, in Darrowby when his master came in to market. Gyp was often seated comfortably in the back of the car, but if I happened to speak to Mr Wilkin on these occasions I kept off the subject because, as I said, I had the feeling that he more than most farmers would hate to be exposed in keeping a dog for other than working purposes.

STOOKING THE CORN Once sheaves of corn were bound, they were set up in stooks and left to dry before being taken back to the farm. The farmhands, or family, stooked in pairs. First they propped two sheaves against each other, setting the cut ends firmly into the stubble. Then they leaned eight or ten more sheaves against them in two rows, but not set too close to one another. Air had to pass up through the stook to dry the crop.

276

And yet I have always entertained a suspicion that most farm dogs were more or less pets. The dogs on sheep farms were of course indispensable working animals and on other establishments they no doubt performed a function in helping to bring in the cows. But watching them on my daily rounds I often wondered. I saw them rocking along on carts at haytime, chasing rats among the stooks at harvest, pottering around the buildings or roaming the fields at the side of the farmer; and I wondered ... what did they really do?

My suspicions were strengthened at other times – as when I was trying to round up some cattle into a corner and the dog tried to get into the act by nipping at a hock or tail. There was invariably a hoarse yell of 'Siddown, dog!' or 'Gerrout, dog!'

So right up to the present day I still stick to my theory; most farm dogs are pets and they are there mainly because the farmer just likes to have them around. You would have to put a farmer on the rack to get him to admit it but I think I am right. And in the process those dogs have a wonderful time. They don't have to beg for walks, they are out all day long, and in the company of their masters. If I want to find a man on a farm I look for his dog, knowing the man won't be far away. I try to give my own dogs a good life but it cannot compare with the life of the average farm dog.

There was a long spell when Sep Wilkin's stock stayed healthy and I didn't see either him or Gyp, then I came across them both by accident at a sheepdog trial. It was a local event run in conjunction with the Mellerton Agricultural Show and since I was in the district I decided to steal an hour off.

I took Helen with me, too, because these trials have always fascinated us. The wonderful control of the owners over their animals, the intense involvement of the dogs themselves, the sheer skill of the whole operation always held us spellbound.

She put her arm through mine as we went in at the entrance gate to where a crescent of cars was drawn up at one end of a long field. The field was on the river's edge and through a fringe of trees the afternoon sunshine glinted on the tumbling water of the shallows and turned the long beach of bleached stones to a dazzling white. Groups of men, mainly competitors, stood around chatting as they watched. They were quiet, easy, bronzed men and as they seemed to be drawn from all social strata from prosperous farmers to working men their garb was varied; cloth caps, trilbies, deerstalkers or no hat at all; tweed jackets, stiff best suits, open-necked shirts, fancy ties, sometimes neither collar nor tie. Nearly all of them leaned on long crooks with the handles fashioned from rams' horns.

Snatches of talk reached us as we walked among them.

'You got 'ere, then, Fred.' 'That's a good gather.' 'Nay, 'e's missed one, 'e'll get nowt for that.' 'Them sheep's a bit flighty.' 'Aye they're buggers.' And above it all the whistles of the man running a dog; every

SWALEDALE SHEEP Ideal for high bleak moorlands is the Swaledale sheep. Its dark head, grey muzzle and grey fleece are seen all over England's northern counties, where it is the most numerous breed. It is a sheep that fends for itself in the poorest conditions, foraging with great persistence and always providing enough milk for its lamb, even in the worst spring. Both ewes and rams are horned, the rams with spectacular corkscrews of horn curling downwards and forwards – giving a wealth of raw material for craftsmen who make sticks and shepherds' crooks.

conceivable level and pitch of whistle with now and then a shout. 'Sit!' 'Get by!' Every man had his own way with his dog.

The dogs waiting their turn were tied up to a fence with a hedge growing over it. There were about seventy of them and it was rather wonderful to see that long row of waving tails and friendly expressions. They were mostly strangers to each other but there wasn't even the semblance of disagreement, never mind a fight. It seemed that the natural obedience of these little creatures was linked to an amicable disposition.

This appeared to be common to their owners, too. There was no animosity, no resentment at defeat, no unseemly display of triumph in victory. If a man overran his time he ushered his group of sheep quietly in the corner and returned with a philosophical grin to his colleagues. There was a little quiet leg-pulling but that was all.

We came across Sep Wilkin leaning against his car at the best vantage point about thirty yards away from the final pen. Gyp, tied to the bumper, turned and gave me his crooked grin while Mrs Wilkin on a camp stool by his side rested a hand on his shoulder. Gyp, it seemed, had got under her skin too.

Helen went over to speak to her and I turned to her husband. 'Are you

Groups of men, mainly competitors, stood around chatting as they watched.

running a dog today, Mr Wilkin?'

'No, not this time, just come to watch. I know a lot o' the dogs.'

I stood near him for a while watching the competitors in action, breathing in the clean smell of trampled grass and plug tobacco. In front of us next to the pen the judge stood by his post.

I had been there for about ten minutes when Mr Wilkin lifted a pointing finger. 'Look who's there!'

George Crossley with Sweep trotting at his heels was making his way unhurriedly to the post. Gyp suddenly stiffened and sat up very straight, his cocked ears accentuating his lop-sided look. It was many months since he had seen his brother and companion; it seemed unlikely, I thought, that he would remember him. But his interest was clearly intense, and as the judge waved his white handkerchief and the three sheep were released from the far corner he rose slowly to his feet.

A gesture from Mr Crossley sent Sweep winging round the perimeter of the field in a wide, joyous gallop and as he neared the sheep a whistle dropped him on his belly. From then on it was an object lesson in the cooperation of man and dog. Sep Wilkin had always said Sweep would be a champion and he looked the part, darting and falling at his master's commands. Short piercing whistles, shrill plaintive whistles; he was in tune with them all.

No dog all day had brought his sheep through the three lots of gates as effortlessly as Sweep did now and as he approached the pen near us it was obvious that he would win the cup unless some disaster struck. But this was the touchy bit; more than once with other dogs the sheep had broken free and gone bounding away within feet of the wooden rails.

George Crossley held the gate wide and extended his crook. You could see now why they all carried those long sticks. His commands to Sweep, huddled flat along the turf, were now almost inaudible but the quiet words brought the dog inching first one way then the other. The sheep were in the entrance to the pen now but they still looked around them irresolutely and the game was not over yet. But as Sweep wriggled towards them almost imperceptibly they turned and entered and Mr Crossley crashed the gate behind them.

As he did so he turned to Sweep with a happy cry of '*Good lad!*' and the dog responded with a quick jerking wag of his tail.

At that, Gyp, who had been standing very tall, watching every move with the most intense concentration raised his head and emitted a single resounding bark.

'*Woof!*' went Gyp as we all stared at him in astonishment.

'Did you hear that?' gasped Mrs Wilkin.

'Well, by gaw!' her husband burst out, looking open-mouthed at his dog.

Gyp didn't seem to be aware that he had done anything unusual. He was too preoccupied by the reunion with his brother and within seconds the two dogs were rolling around, chewing playfully at each other as of old.

I suppose the Wilkins as well as myself had the feeling that this event might start Gyp barking like any other dog, but it was not to be.

Six years later I was on the farm and went to the house to get some hot water. As Mrs Wilkin handed me the bucket she looked down at Gyp who was basking in the sunshine outside the kitchen window.

'There you are, then, funny fellow,' she said to the dog.

I laughed. 'Has he ever barked since that day?'

Mrs Wilkin shook her head. 'No he hasn't, not a sound. I waited a long time but I know he's not going to do it now.'

'Ah well, it's not important. But still, I'll never forget that afternoon at the trial,' I said.

'Nor will I!' She looked at Gyp again and her eyes softened in reminiscence. 'Poor old lad, eight years old and only one woof!'

13

An effortless miracle

I suppose there was a wry humour in the fact that my call-up papers arrived on my birthday, but I didn't see the joke at the time.

The event is preserved in my memory in a picture which is as clear to me today as when I walked into our 'dining-room' that morning. Helen perched away up on her high stool at the end of the table, very still, eyes downcast. By the side of my plate my birthday present, a tin of Dobie's Blue Square tobacco, and next to it a long envelope. I didn't have to ask what it contained.

I had been expecting it for some time but it still gave me a jolt to find I had only a week before presenting myself at Lord's Cricket Ground, St John's Wood, London. And that week went by at frightening speed as I made my final plans, tidying up the loose ends in the practice, getting my Ministry of Agriculture forms sent off, arranging for our few possessions to be taken to Helen's old home where she would stay while I was away.

Having decided that I would finish work at teatime on Friday I had a call from old Arthur Summergill at about three o'clock that afternoon; and I knew that would be my very last job because it was always an expedition rather than a visit to his smallholding which clung to a bracken strewn slope in the depths of the hills. I didn't speak directly to Arnold but to Miss Thompson the postmistress in Hainby village.

'Mr Summergill wants you to come and see his dog,' she said over the phone.

'What's the trouble?' I asked.

I heard a muttered consultation at the far end.

THE BRACKEN HARVEST The apparently sparse vegetation of the moors yielded several useful 'crops' – turf, peat, bilberries, heather, moss and bracken. Common rights allow people to gather most of these free. Bracken, dried crisp and russet by the time autumn came, was carted back to farms and cottages to use as bedding for animals and as thatching material.

'He says its leg's gone funny.'

'Funny? What d'you mean, funny?'

Again the quick babble of voices. 'He says it's kind of stickin' out.'

'All right,' I said. 'I'll be along very soon.'

It was no good asking for the dog to be brought in. Arnold had never owned a car. Nor had he ever spoken on a telephone – all our conversations had been carried on through the medium of Miss Thompson. Arnold would mount his rusty bicycle, pedal to Hainby and tell his troubles to the postmistress. And the symptoms; they were typically vague and I didn't suppose there would be anything either 'funny' or 'sticking out' about that leg when I saw it.

Anyway, I thought, as I drove out of Darrowby, I wouldn't mind having a last look at Benjamin. It was a fanciful name for a small farmer's dog and I never really found out how he had acquired it. But after all he was an unlikely breed for such a setting, a massive Old English Sheep Dog who would have looked more in place decorating the lawns of a stately home than following his master round Arnold's stony pastures. He was a classical example of the walking hearthrug and it took a second look to decide which end of him was which. But when you did manage to locate his head you found two of the most benevolent eyes imaginable glinting through the thick fringe of hair.

Benjamin was in fact too friendly at times, especially in winter when he had been strolling in the farmyard mud and showed his delight at my arrival by planting his huge feet on my chest. He did the same thing to my car, too, usually just after I had washed it, smearing clay lavishly over windows and bodywork while exchanging pleasantries with Sam inside. When Benjamin made a mess of anything he did it right.

But I had to interrupt my musings when I reached the last stage of my journey. And as I hung on to the kicking, jerking wheel and listened to the creaking and groaning of springs and shock absorbers, the thought forced its way into my mind as it always did around here that it cost us money to come to Mr Summergill's farm. There could be no profit from the visit because this vicious track must knock at least five pounds off the value of the car on every trip. Since Arnold did not have a car himself he saw no reason why he should interfere with the primeval state of his road.

It was simply a six-foot strip of earth and rock and it wound and twisted for an awful long way. The trouble was that to get to the farm you had to descend into a deep valley before climbing through a wood towards the house. I think going down was worse because the vehicle hovered agonisingly on the top of each ridge before plunging into the yawning ruts beyond; and each time, listening to the unyielding stone grating on sump and exhaust, I tried to stop myself working out the damage in pounds shillings and pence.

And when at last, mouth gaping, eyes popping, tyres sending the sharp pebbles flying, I ground my way upwards in bottom gear over the last few yards leading to the house I was surprised to see Arnold waiting

MAIL PONY A Dales pony was an efficient method of transport for a rural north Yorkshire postman in the 1920s and 1930s. It could carry him along the tracks and lanes that led to out-of-the-way farms – and carry the mail satchel. The volume of mail could be large because many farmers had their newspapers posted directly to them. Newsagents could not offer as good a service. A postman was useful for passing on spoken messages as well as mail.

for me there alone. It was unusual to see him without Benjamin.

He must have read my questioning look because he jerked his thumb over his shoulder.

'He's in t'house,' he grunted, and his eyes were anxious.

I got out of the car and looked at him for a moment as he stood there in a typical attitude, wide shoulders back, head high. I have called him 'old' and indeed he was over seventy, but the features beneath the woollen tammy which he always wore pulled down over his ears were clean and regular and the tall figure lean and straight. He was a fine-looking man and must have been handsome in his youth, yet he had never married. I often felt there was a story there but he seemed content to live here alone, a 'bit of a 'ermit' as they said in the village. Alone, that is, except for Benjamin.

As I followed him into the kitchen he casually shooed out a couple of hens who had been perching on a dusty dresser. Then I saw Benjamin and pulled up with a jerk.

The big dog was sitting quite motionless by the side of the table and this time the eyes behind the overhanging hair were big and liquid with fright. He appeared to be too terrified to move and when I saw his left foreleg I couldn't blame him. Arnold had been right after all; it was indeed sticking out with a vengeance, at an angle which made my heart give a quick double thud; a complete lateral dislocation of the elbow, the radius projecting away out from the humerus at an almost impossible obliquity.

I swallowed carefully. 'When did this happen, Mr Summergill?'

'Just an hour since.' He tugged worriedly at his strange headgear. 'I was changing the cows into another field and awd Benjamin likes to have a nip at their heels when he's behind 'em. Well he did it once ower often and one of them lashed out and got 'im on the leg.'

'I see.' My mind was racing. This thing was grotesque. I had never seen anything like it, in fact thirty years later I still haven't seen anything like it. How on earth was I going to reduce the thing away up here in the hills? By the look of it I would need general anaesthesia and a skilled assistant.

'Poor old lad,' I said, resting my hand on the shaggy head as I tried to think. 'What are we going to do with you?'

The tail whisked along the flags in reply and the mouth opened in a nervous panting, giving a glimpse of flawlessly white teeth.

Arnold cleared his throat. 'Can you put 'im right?'

Well it was a good question. An airy answer might give the wrong impression yet I didn't want to worry him with my doubts. It would be a mammoth task to get the enormous dog down to Darrowby; he nearly filled the kitchen, never mind my little car. And with that leg sticking out and with Sam already in residence. And would I be able to get the joint back in place when I got him there? And even if I did manage it I would still have to bring him all the way back up here. It would just about take care of the rest of the day.

OLD ENGLISH SHEEPDOG The shaggy, grey and white formless heap of the Old English sheepdog is unmistakable – as is its unusual swinging walk. It is the way the dog moves both legs on the same side forward together that gives the swinging movement.

Hidden beneath its heavy fringe the dog frequently has eyes that do not match in colour. The breed was being used to herd sheep more than 500 years ago, but then it had a shorter coat and a longer tail – the natural tail, which is now customarily docked.

282

Gently I passed my fingers over the dislocated joint and searched my memory for details of the anatomy of the elbow. For the leg to be in this position the processus anconeus must have been completely disengaged from the supracondyloid fossa where it normally lay; and to get it back the joint would have to be flexed until the anconeus was clear of the epicondyles.

'Now let's see,' I murmured to myself. 'If I had this dog anaesthetised and on the table I would have to get hold of him like this.' I grasped the leg just above the elbow and began to move the radius slowly upwards. Benjamin gave me a quick glance then turned his head away, a gesture typical of good-natured dogs, conveying the message that he was going to put up with whatever I thought it necessary to do.

I flexed the joint still further until I was sure the anconeus was clear, then carefully rotated the radius and ulna inwards.

'Yes ... yes ...' I muttered again. 'This must be about the right position ...' But my soliloquy was interrupted by a sudden movement of the bones under my hand; a springing, flicking sensation.

I looked incredulously at the leg. It was perfectly straight.

Benjamin, too, seemed unable to take it in right away, because he peered cautiously through his shaggy curtain before lowering his nose and sniffing around the elbow. Then he seemed to realise all was well and ambled over to his master.

And he was perfectly sound. Not a trace of a limp.

A slow smile spread over Arnold's face. 'You've mended him, then.'

'Looks like it, Mr Summergill.' I tried to keep my voice casual, but I felt like cheering or bursting into hysterical laughter. I had only been making an examination, feeling things out a little, and the joint had popped back into place. A glorious accident.

'Aye well, that's grand,' the farmer said. 'Isn't it, awd lad?' He bent and tickled Benjamin's ear.

I could have been disappointed by this laconic reception of my performance, but I realised it was a compliment to me that he wasn't surprised that I, James Herriot, his vet, should effortlessly produce a miracle when it was required.

A theatre-full of cheering students would have rounded off the incident or it would be nice to do this kind of thing to some millionaire's animal in a crowded drawing room, but it never happened that way. I looked around the kitchen, at the cluttered table, the pile of unwashed crockery in the sink, a couple of Arnold's ragged shirts drying before the fire, and I smiled to myself. This was the sort of setting in which I usually pulled off my spectacular cures. The only spectators here, apart from Arnold, were the two hens who had made their way back on to the dresser and they didn't seem particularly impressed.

'Well, I'll be getting back down the hill,' I said. And Arnold walked with me across the yard to the car.

'I hear you're off to join up,' he said as I put my hand on the door.

'Yes, I'm away tomorrow, Mr Summergill.'

RHODE ISLAND RED This American breed of fowl, now widespread throughout the world, is a deep chestnut-red with a lustrous green-black fall of feathers on the cock's tail. A cock usually weighs 8–9 lb and a hen about 6 lb. The Rhode Island Red is a hardy, free-range, dual-purpose bird, long in the back and plump in the breast for the table, but also a good layer of brown eggs.

'Tomorrow, eh?' he raised his eyebrows.

'Yes, to London. Ever been there?'

'Nay, nay, be damned!' The woollen cap quivered as he shook his head. 'That'd be no good to me.'

I laughed. 'Why do you say that?'

'Well now, I'll tell ye.' He scratched his chin ruminatively. 'Ah nobbut went once to Brawton and that was enough. Ah couldn't walk on t'street!'

'Couldn't walk?'

'Nay. There were that many people about. I 'ad to take big steps and little 'uns, then big steps and little 'uns again. Couldn't get goin'.'

I had often seen Arnold stalking over his fields with the long, even stride of the hillman with nothing in his way and I knew exactly what he meant. 'Big steps and little 'uns.' That put it perfectly.

I started the engine and waved and as I moved away the old man raised a hand.

'Tek care, lad,' he murmured.

I spotted Benjamin's nose peeping round the kitchen door. Any other time he would have been out with his master to see me off the premises but it had been a strange day for him culminating with my descending on him and mauling his leg about. He wasn't taking any more chances.

I drove gingerly down through the wood and before starting up the track on the other side I stopped the car and got out with Sam leaping eagerly after me.

This was a little, lost valley in the hills, a green cleft cut off from the wild country above. One of the bonuses in a country vet's life is that he sees these hidden places. Apart from old Arnold nobody ever came down here, not even the postman who left the infrequent mail in a box at the top of the track, and nobody saw the blazing scarlets and golds of the autumn trees nor heard the busy clucking and murmuring of the beck among its clean-washed stones.

I walked along the water's edge watching the little fish darting and flitting in the cool depths. In the spring these banks were bright with primroses and in May a great sea of bluebells flowed among the trees but today, though the sky was an untroubled blue, the clean air was touched with the sweetness of the dying year.

I climbed a little way up the hillside and sat down among the bracken now fast turning to bronze. Sam, as was his way, flopped by my side and I ran a hand over the silky hair of his ears. The far side of the valley rose steeply to where, above the gleaming ridge of limestone cliffs, I could just see the sunlit rim of the moor.

I looked back to where the farm chimney sent a thin tendril of smoke from behind the brow of the hill, and it seemed that the episode with Benjamin, my last job in veterinary practice before I left Darrowby, was a fitting epilogue. A little triumph, intensely satisfying but by no means world shaking; like all the other little triumphs and disasters which make up a veterinary surgeon's life but go unnoticed by the world.

The clean air was touched with the sweetness of the dying year.

Last night, after Helen had packed my bag, I had pushed Black's Veterinary Dictionary in among the shirts and socks. It was a bulky volume but I had been gripped momentarily by a fear that I might forget the things I had learned, and conceived on an impulse the scheme of reading a page or two each day to keep my memory fresh. And here among the bracken the thought came back to me; that it was the greatest good fortune not only to be fascinated by animals but to know about them. Suddenly the knowing became a precious thing.

I went back and opened the car door. Sam jumped on to the seat and before I got in I looked away down in the other direction from the house to the valley's mouth where the hills parted to give a glimpse of the plain below. And the endless wash of pale tints, the gold of the stubble, the dark smudges of wood, the mottled greens of the pastureland were like a perfect watercolour. I found myself staring greedily as if for the first time at the scene which had so often lifted my heart, the great, wide, clean-blown face of Yorkshire.

I would come back to it all, I thought as I drove away; back to my work ... how was it that book had described it ... my hard, honest and fine profession.

I had to catch the early train and Bob Cooper was at the door with his ancient taxi before eight o'clock next morning.

Sam followed me across the room expectantly as he always did but I closed the door gently against his puzzled face. Clattering down the long flight of stairs I caught a glimpse through the landing window of the garden with the sunshine beginning to pierce the autumn mist, turning the dewy grass into a glittering coverlet, glinting on the bright colours of the apples and the last roses.

In the passage I paused at the side door where I had started my day's work so many times since coming to Darrowby, but then I hurried past. This was one time I went out the front.

Bob pushed open the taxi door and I threw my bag in before looking up over the ivy-covered brick of the old house to our little room under the tiles. Helen was in the window. She was crying. When she saw me she waved gaily and smiled, but it was a twisted smile as the tears flowed. And as we drove round the corner and I swallowed the biggest lump in my throat a fierce resolve welled in me; men all over the country were leaving their wives and I had to leave Helen now, but nothing, nothing, nothing would ever get me away from her again.

The shops were still closed and nothing stirred in the market place. As we left I turned and looked back at the cobbled square with the old clock tower and the row of irregular roofs with the green fells quiet and peaceful behind, and it seemed that I was losing something for ever.

I wish I had known then that it was not the end of everything. I wish I had known it was only the beginning. But at that moment I knew only that soon I would be far from here; in London, pushing my way through the crowds. Taking big steps and little 'uns.

CUSTOM BUILT One Swaledale farmer of the 1930s had his own custom-built, wheel-less carriage. A wooden chair and footrest, a pram hood and one of the farm sleds combined to make a transport curiosity. Ropes through the iron stays at the front were attached to the horse or pony that provided the power, and the iron-shod runners slid quickly, if roughly, over short grass as well as snow.

PART THREE
Memories of a wartime vet

News of the posting seemed too good to be true – I was
going to Scarborough. I knew it as a beautiful seaside
resort, but that wasn't why I was so delighted. It was
because it was in Yorkshire.

1

Blossom comes home

'Move!' bawled the drill corporal. 'Come on, speed it up!' He sprinted effortlessly to the rear of the gasping, panting column of men and urged us on from there.

I was somewhere in the middle, jog-trotting laboriously with the rest and wondering how much longer I could keep going. And as my ribs heaved agonisingly and my leg muscles protested I tried to work out just how many miles we had run.

I had suspected nothing when we lined up outside our billets. We weren't clad in PT kit but in woollen pullovers and regulation slacks and it seemed unlikely that anything violent was imminent. The corporal, too, a cheerful little cockney, appeared to regard us as his brothers. He had a kind face.

'Awright, lads,' he had cried, smiling over the fifty new airmen. 'We're just going to trot round to the park, so follow me. Le-eft turn! At the double, qui-ick march! 'eft-ight, 'eft-ight, 'eft-ight!'

That had been a long, long time ago and we were still reeling through the London streets with never a sign of a park anywhere. The thought hammered in my brain that I had been under the impression that I was fit. A country vet, especially in the Yorkshire Dales, never had the chance to get out of condition; he was always on the move, wrestling with the big animals, walking for miles between the fell-side barns; he was hard and tough. That's what I thought.

But now other reflections began to creep in. My few months of married life with Helen had been so much lotus eating. She was too good a cook and I was too faithful a disciple of her art. Just lounging by our bed-sitter's fireside was the sweetest of all occupations. I had tried to ignore the disappearance of my abdominal muscles, the sagging of my pectorals, but it was all coming home to me now.

'It's not far now, lads,' the corporal chirped from the rear, but he struck no responsive chords in the toiling group. He had said it several times before and we had stopped believing him.

But this time it seemed he really meant it, because as we turned into yet another street I could see iron railings and trees at the far end. The relief was inexpressible. I would just about have the strength to make it through the gates – to the rest and smoke which I badly needed because my legs were beginning to seize up.

We passed under an arch of branches which still bore a few autumn leaves and stopped as one man, but the corporal was waving us on.

'Come on, lads, round the track!' he shouted and pointed to a broad earthen path which circled the park.

BARREL STILE A Wensleydale perfectionist made this stile, which displays precise workmanship and the waller's essential – an eye for matching stones. The courses of neatly dressed stones run level, and carefully rounded wall ends guard the narrow slit where a man's leg could pass but not sheep or cattle. The wide, barrel-shaped opening above for a man's body to pass through is shaped with careful symmetry.

We stared at him. He couldn't be serious! A storm of protest broke out.

'Aw no, corp ...!' 'Have a heart, corp ...!'

The smile vanished from the little man's face. 'Get movin', I said! Faster, faster ... one-two, one-two.'

As I stumbled forward over the black earth, between borders of sooty rhododendrons and tired grass, I just couldn't believe it. It was all too sudden. Three days ago I was in Darrowby and half of me was still back there, back with Helen. And another part was still looking out of the rear window of the taxi at the green hills receding behind the tiled roofs into the morning sunshine; still standing in the corridor of the train as the flat terrain of southern England slid past and a great weight built up steadily in my chest.

My first introduction to the RAF was at Lord's Cricket Ground. Masses of forms to fill, medicals, then the issue of an enormous pile of kit. I was billeted in a block of flats in St John's Wood – luxurious before the lush fittings had been removed. But they couldn't take away the heavy bathroom ware and one of our blessings was the unlimited hot water gushing at our touch into the expensive surroundings.

After that first crowded day I retired to one of those green-tiled sanctuaries and lathered myself with a new bar of a famous toilet soap which Helen had put in my bag. I have never been able to use that soap since. Scents are too evocative and the merest whiff jerks me back to that first night away from my wife, and to the feeling I had then. It was a dull, empty ache which never really went away.

On the second day we marched endlessly; lectures, meals, inoculations. I was used to syringes but the very sight of them was too much for many of my friends. Especially when the doctor took the blood samples; one look at the dark fluid flowing from their veins and the young men toppled quietly from their chairs, often four or five in a row, while the orderlies, grinning cheerfully, bore them away.

We ate in the London Zoo and our meals were made interesting by the chatter of monkeys and the roar of lions in the background. But in between it was march, march, march, with our new boots giving us hell.

And on this third day the whole thing was still a blur. We had been wakened as on my first morning by the hideous 6 a.m. clattering of dustbins lids; I hadn't really expected a bugle but I found this noise intolerable. However, at the moment my only concern was that we had completed the circuit of the park. The gates were only a few yards ahead and I staggered up to them and halted among my groaning comrades.

'Round again, lads!' the corporal yelled, and as we stared at him aghast he smiled affectionately. 'You think this is tough? Wait till they get hold of you at ITW. I'm just kinda breakin' you in gently. You'll thank me for this later. Right, at the double! One-two, one-two!'

Bitter thoughts assailed me as I lurched forward once more. Another round of the park would kill me – there was not a shadow of a doubt about that. You left a loving wife and a happy home to serve king and

STEPPED STILE The simplest stile is often the most effective for the purpose of letting men and dogs through but not sheep and cattle. Where an opening widens at the top to let a man's body pass with ease, there is a possibility that agile, scrambling sheep will find a way over. No sheep could make its way up and down stairways made by four long stones passing right through a drystone wall and projecting on both sides.

WALKING STICKS A simple, straight hazel shoot with a projecting shoot or root trimmed to make a handle helped the farmer as he climbed steep fields or drove livestock along farm tracks. Craftsman-made sticks appealed to some, and were displayed on market days and at shows. They are still made, with a polished shaft of seasoned hazel topped by a handle made from a tup's, or ram's, horn. Tups' horns are used instead of ewes' because they are larger and more substantial. The horn was softened by boiling, bent and filed into shape, bored to receive the shaft, and often elaborately carved with a bird, fox or some other design.

country and this was how they treated you. It wasn't fair.

The night before I had dreamed of Darrowby. I was back in old Mr Dakin's cow byre. The farmer's patient eyes in the long, drooping-moustached face looked down at me from his stooping height.

'It looks as though it's over wi' awd Blossom, then,' he said, and rested his hand briefly on the old cow's back. It was an enormous, work-swollen hand. Mr Dakin's gaunt frame carried little flesh but the grossly thickened fingers bore testimony to a life of toil.

I dried off the needle and dropped it into the metal box where I carried my suture materials, scalpels and blades. 'Well, it's up to you of course, Mr Dakin, but this is the third time I've had to stitch her teats and I'm afraid it's going to keep on happening.'

'Aye, it's just the shape she is.' The farmer bent and examined the row of knots along the four-inch scar. 'By gaw, you wouldn't believe it could mek such a mess – just another cow standin' on it.'

'A cow's hoof is sharp,' I said. 'It's nearly like a knife coming down.'

That was the worst of very old cows. Their udders dropped and their teats became larger and more pendulous so that when they lay down in their stalls the vital milk-producing organ was pushed away to one side into the path of the neighbouring animals. If it wasn't Mabel on the right standing on it, it was Buttercup on the other side.

There were only six cows in the little cobbled byre with its low roof and wooden partitions and they all had names. You don't find cows with names any more and there aren't any farmers like Mr Dakin, who somehow scratched a living from a herd of six milkers plus a few calves, pigs and hens.

'Aye, well,' he said. 'Ah reckon t'awd lass doesn't owe me anythin'. Ah remember the night she was born, twelve years ago. She was out of awd Daisy and ah carried her out of this very byre on a sack and the snow was comin' down hard. Sin' then ah wouldn't like to count how many thousand gallons o' milk she's turned out – she's still givin' four a day. Naw, she doesn't owe me a thing.'

As if she knew she was the topic of conversation Blossom turned her head and looked at him. She was the classical picture of an ancient bovine; as fleshless as her owner, with jutting pelvic bones, splayed, overgrown feet and horns with a multitude of rings along their curving length. Beneath her, the udder, once high and tight, drooped forlornly almost to the floor.

She resembled her owner, too, in her quiet, patient demeanour. I had infiltrated her teat with a local anaesthetic before stitching but I don't think she would have moved if I hadn't used any. Stitching teats puts a vet in the ideal position to be kicked, with his head low down in front of the hind feet, but there was no danger with Blossom. She had never kicked anybody in her life.

Mr Dakin blew out his cheeks. 'Well, there's nowt else for it. She'll have to go. I'll tell Jack Dodson to pick 'er up for the fatstock market on

290

Thursday. She'll be a bit tough for eatin' but ah reckon she'll make a few steak pies.'

He was trying to joke but he was unable to smile as he looked at the old cow. Behind him, beyond the open door, the green hillside ran down to the river and the spring sunshine touched the broad sweep of the shallows with a million dancing lights. A beach of bleached stones gleamed bone-white against the long stretch of grassy bank which rolled up to the pastures lining the valley floor.

I had often felt that this smallholding would be an ideal place to live; only a mile outside Darrowby, but secluded, and with this heart-lifting vista of river and fell. I remarked on this once to Mr Dakin and the old man turned to me with a wry smile.

'Aye, but the view's not very sustainin',' he said.

It happened that I was called back to the farm on the following Thursday to 'cleanse' a cow and was in the byre when Dodson the drover called to pick up Blossom. He had collected a group of fat bullocks and cows from other farms and they stood, watched by one of his men, on the road high above.

'Nah then, Mr Dakin,' he cried as he bustled in. 'It's easy to see which one you want me to tek. It's that awd screw over there.'

He pointed at Blossom, and in truth the unkind description seemed to fit the bony creature standing between her sleek neighbours.

The farmer did not reply for a moment, then he went up between the cows and gently rubbed Blossom's forehead. 'Aye, this is the one, Jack.' He hesitated, then undid the chain round her neck. 'Off ye go, awd lass,' he murmured, and the old animal turned and made her way placidly from the stall.

'Aye, come on with ye!' shouted the dealer, poking his stick against the cow's rump.

'Doan't hit 'er!' barked Mr Dakin.

Dodson looked at him in surprise. 'Ah never 'it 'em, you know that. Just send 'em on, like.'

'Ah knaw, ah knaw, Jack, but you won't need your stick for this 'un. She'll go wherever ye want – allus has done.'

Blossom confirmed his words as she ambled through the door and, at a gesture from the farmer, turned along the track.

The old man and I stood watching as the cow made her way unhurriedly up the hill, Jack Dodson in his long khaki smock sauntering behind her. As the path wound behind a clump of sparse trees man and beast disappeared but Mr Dakin still gazed after them, listening to the clip-clop of the hooves on the hard ground.

When the sound died away he turned to me quickly. 'Right, Mr Herriot, we'll get on wi' our job, then. I'll bring your hot watter.'

The farmer was silent as I soaped my arm and inserted it into the cow. If there is one thing more disagreeable than removing the bovine afterbirth it is watching somebody else doing it, and I always try to maintain a conversation as I grope around inside. But this time it was

ELECTRIC MILKER This milking machine exhibited at the Great Yorkshire Show at Halifax in July 1939 was just a curiosity, not only to schoolboys but also to farmers from the Dales who had made a day trip to the show. It was powered by electricity, which did not reach Dales farmers until the late 1940s, the 1950s – or even later. This machine imitated the action of a sucking calf. The teat cups intermittently squeezed the teats while a pump created a vacuum in the pipes so that milk was drawn from the udder into the sealed can. The machine took about eight minutes to milk, virtually the same time as hand-milking, but five cans would operate at the same time.

THE MILK LORRY In the 1920s and 1930s a network of milk-lorry routes probed further and further into the Dales until almost every village was on a collecting route. The lorries picked up full churns from roadside platforms and took them to local cheese and butter factories, and to railway stations where dawn 'milk trains' carried them on to industrial Teesside or the West Riding mill towns to satisfy the demand for liquid milk. Now a milk tanker visits dairy farms and uses a pipeline to suck in their milk from a tank at each farm.

hard work. Mr Dakin responded to my sallies on the weather, cricket and the price of milk with a series of grunts.

Holding the cow's tail he leaned on the hairy back and, empty-eyed, blew smoke from the pipe which like most farmers at a cleansing he had prudently lit at the outset. And of course, since the going was heavy, it just would happen that the job took much longer than usual. Sometimes a placenta simply lifted out but I had to peel this one away from the cotyledons one by one, returning every few minutes to the hot water and antiseptic to re-soap my aching arms.

But at last it was finished. I pushed in a couple of pessaries, untied the sack from my middle and pulled my shirt over my head. The conversation had died and the silence was almost oppressive as we opened the byre door.

Mr Dakin paused, his hand on the latch. 'What's that?' he said softly.

From somewhere on the hillside I could hear the clip-clop of a cow's feet. There were two ways to the farm and the sound came from a narrow track which joined the main road half a mile beyond the other entrance. As we listened a cow rounded a rocky outcrop and came towards us.

It was Blossom, moving at a brisk trot, great udder swinging, eyes fixed purposefully on the open door behind us.

'What the hangment...?' Mr Dakin burst out, but the old cow brushed past us and marched without hesitation into the stall which she had occupied for all those years. She sniffed enquiringly at the empty hay rack and looked round at her owner.

Mr Dakin stared back at her. The eyes in the weathered face were expressionless but the smoke rose from his pipe in a series of rapid puffs.

Heavy boots clattered suddenly outside and Jack Dodson panted his way through the door.

'Oh, you're there, ye awd beggar!' he gasped. 'Ah thought I'd lost ye!'

He turned to the farmer. 'By gaw, I'm sorry, Mr Dakin. She must 'ave turned off at t'top of your other path. Ah never saw her go.'

The farmer shrugged. 'It's awright, Jack. It's not your fault, ah should've told ye.'

'That's soon mended anyway.' The drover grinned and moved towards Blossom. 'Come on, lass, let's have ye out o' there again.'

But he halted as Mr Dakin held an arm in front of him.

There was a long silence as Dodson and I looked in surprise at the farmer who continued to gaze fixedly at the cow. There was a pathetic dignity about the old animal as she stood there against the mouldering timber of the partition, her eyes patient and undemanding. It was a dignity which triumphed over the unsightliness of the long upturned hooves, the fleshless ribs, the broken-down udder almost brushing the cobbles.

Then, still without speaking, Mr Dakin moved unhurriedly between the cows and a faint chink of metal sounded as he fastened the chain around Blossom's neck. Then he strolled to the end of the byre and returned with a forkful of hay which he tossed expertly into the rack.

This was what Blossom was waiting for. She jerked a mouthful from between the spars and began to chew with quiet satisfaction.

'What's to do, Mr Dakin?' the drover cried in bewilderment. 'They're waiting for me at t'mart!'

The farmer tapped out his pipe on the half door and began to fill it with black shag from a battered tin. 'Ah'm sorry to waste your time, Jack, but you'll have to go without 'er.'

'Without 'er ...?' But ...?'

'Aye, ye'll think I'm daft, but that's how it is. T'awd lass has come 'ome and she's stoppin' 'ome.' He directed a look of flat finality at the drover.

Dodson nodded a couple of times then shuffled from the byre. Mr Dakin followed and called after him,

'Ah'll pay ye for your time, Jack. Put it down on ma bill.'

He returned, applied a match to his pipe and drew deeply.

'Mr Herriot,' he said as the smoke rose around his ears, 'do you ever feel when summat happens that it was meant to happen and that it was for t'best?'

'Yes, I do, Mr Dakin. I often feel that.'

'Aye well, that's how I felt when Blossom came down that hill.' He reached out and scratched the root of the cow's tail. 'She's allus been a favourite and by gaw I'm glad she's back.'

'But how about those teats? I'm willing to keep stitching them up, but ...'

'Nay, lad, ah've had an idea. Just came to me when you were tekkin' away that cleansin' and I thowt I was ower late.'

'An idea?'

'Aye.' The old man nodded and tamped down the tobacco with his thumb. 'I can put two or three calves on to 'er instead of milkin' 'er. The old stable is empty – she can live in there where there's nobody to stand on 'er awd tits.'

I laughed. 'You're right, Mr Dakin. She'd be safe in the stable and she'd suckle three calves easily. She could pay her way.'

'Well, as ah said, it's matterless. After all them years she doesn't owe me a thing.' A gentle smile spread over the seamed face. 'Main thing is, she's come 'ome.'

My eyes were shut most of the time now as I blundered round the park and when I opened them a red mist swirled. But it is incredible what the human frame will stand and I blinked in disbelief as the iron gates appeared once more under their arch of sooty branches.

I had survived the second lap but an ordinary rest would be inadequate now. This time I would have to lie down. I felt sick.

'Good lads!' the corporal called out, cheerful as ever. 'You're doin' fine. Now we're just going to 'ave a little hoppin' on the spot.'

Incredulous wails rose from our demoralised band but the corporal

SHARPENING A SCYTHE Among the many skills of the village blacksmith were shoeing horses, making locks, hinges and cooking utensils, tyring wheels – for the blacksmith was often the wheelwright also – and making the metal parts of harness, shepherds' crooks, forks, hoes, harrows and scythes. After the scythe blade was forged, it was sharpened on the grindstone. Once it was in use the scythe was sharpened at least once a day by the mower's strickle, and at the beginning of the mowing season by a stone.

was unabashed.

'Feet together now. Up! Up! Up! That's no good, come on, get some height into it! Up! Up!'

This was the final absurdity. My chest was a flaming cavern of agony. These people were supposed to be making us fit and instead they were doing irreparable damage to my heart and lungs.

'You'll thank me for this later, lads. Take my word for it. GET YOURSELVES OFF THE GROUND. UP! UP!'

Through my pain I could see the corporal's laughing face. The man was clearly a sadist. It was no good appealing to him.

And as, with the last of my strength, I launched myself into the air it came to me suddenly why I had dreamed about Blossom last night.

I wanted to go home, too.

2

The odd couple

I like women better than men.

Mind you, I have nothing against men – after all, I am one myself – but in the RAF there were too many of them. Literally thousands, jostling, shouting, swearing; you couldn't get away from them. Some of them became my friends and have remained so until the present day, but the sheer earthy mass of them made me realise how my few months of married life had changed me.

Women are gentler, softer, cleaner, altogether nicer things and I, who always considered myself one of the boys, had come to the surprising conclusion that the companion I wanted most was a woman.

My impression that I had been hurled into a coarser world was heightened at the beginning of each day, particularly one morning when I was on fire-picket duty and had the sadistic pleasure of rattling the dustbin lids and shouting 'Wakey-wakey!' along the corridors. It wasn't the cursing and the obscene remarks which struck deepest, it was the extraordinary abdominal noises issuing from the dark rooms. They reminded me of my patient, Cedric, and in an instant I was back in Darrowby answering the telephone.

The voice at the other end was oddly hesitant.

'Mr Herriot ... I should be grateful if you would come and see my dog.' It was a woman, obviously upper class.

'Certainly. What's the trouble?'

'Well ... he ... er ... he seems to suffer from ... a certain amount of flatus.'

'I beg your pardon?'

IN FOR THE NIGHT These calves are being brought in to spend the night in the byre. Since they are not yet milkers and are hardy creatures, they would be perfectly comfortable outside all night, but the farmer can collect their manure in the byre and use it to fertilise the land where he needs it most. It is traditional to house cattle in winter – again for the manure, as well as to give them shelter.

There was a long pause. 'He has ... excessive flatus.'

'In what way, exactly?'

'Well ... I suppose you'd describe it as ... windiness.' The voice had begun to tremble.

I thought I could see a gleam of light. 'You mean his stomach ...?'

'No, not his stomach. He passes ... er ... a considerable quantity of ... wind from his ... his ...' A note of desperation had crept in.

'Ah, yes!' All became suddenly clear. 'I quite understand. But that doesn't sound very serious. Is he ill?'

'No, he's very fit in other ways.'

'Well, then, do you think it's necessary for me to see him?'

'Oh yes, indeed, Mr Herriot. I wish you would come as soon as possible. It has become quite ... quite a problem.'

'All right,' I said. 'I'll look in this morning. Can I have your name and address, please?'

'It's Mrs Rumney, The Laurels.'

The Laurels was a very nice house on the edge of the town standing back from the road in a large garden. Mrs Rumney herself let me in and I felt a shock of surprise at my first sight of her. It wasn't just that she was strikingly beautiful; there was an unworldly air about her. She would be around forty but had the appearance of a heroine in a Victorian novel – tall, willowy, ethereal. And I could understand immediately her hesitation on the 'phone. Everything about her suggested fastidiousness and delicacy.

'Cedric is in the kitchen,' she said. 'I'll take you through.'

I had another surprise when I saw Cedric. An enormous Boxer hurled himself on me in delight, clawing at my chest with the biggest, horniest feet I had seen for a long time. I tried to fight him off but he kept at me, panting ecstatically into my face and wagging his entire rear end.

'Sit down, boy!' the lady said sharply, then, as Cedric took absolutely no notice, she turned to me nervously. 'He's so friendly.'

'Yes,' I said breathlessly, 'I can see that.' I finally managed to push the huge animal away and backed into a corner for safety. 'How often does this ... excessive flatus occur?'

As if in reply an almost palpable sulphurous wave arose from the dog and eddied around me. It appeared that the excitement of seeing me had activated Cedric's weakness. I was up against the wall and unable to obey my first instinct to run for cover so I held my hand over my face for a few moments before speaking.

'Is that what you meant?'

Mrs Rumney waved a lace handkerchief under her nose and the faintest flush crept into the pallor of her cheeks.

'Yes,' she replied almost inaudibly. 'Yes ... that is it.'

'Oh well,' I said briskly. 'There's nothing to worry about. Let's go into the other room and we'll have a word about his diet and a few other things.'

BOXER This short-faced, quizzical German relative of the bulldog was, like its British counterpart, bred for the cruel medieval sport of bull-baiting. When the sport declined, so did the number of boxers – until the German police began to train the dog for police work. It is intelligent and has a strong urge to protect its own territory. Its unwavering adherence to the rules it has been trained by make it exceptionally reliable, whether as a police dog, a guard or an even-tempered companion for children.

It turned out that Cedric was getting rather a lot of meat and I drew up a little chart cutting down the protein and adding extra carbohydrates. I prescribed a kaolin antacid mixture to be given night and morning and left the house in a confident frame of mind.

It was one of those trivial things and I had entirely forgotten it when Mrs Rumney 'phoned again.

'I'm afraid Cedric is no better, Mr Herriot.'

'Oh I'm sorry to hear that. He's still ... er ... still ... yes ... yes ...' I spent a few moments in thought. 'I tell you what – I don't think I can do any more by seeing him at the moment, but I think you should cut out his meat completely for a week or two. Keep him on biscuits and brown bread rusked in the oven. Try him with that and vegetables and I'll give you some powder to mix in his food. Perhaps you'd call round for it.'

The powder was a pretty strong absorbent mixture and I felt sure it would do the trick, but a week later Mrs Rumney was on the 'phone again.

'There's absolutely no improvement, Mr Herriot.' The tremble was back in her voice. 'I ... I do wish you'd come and see him again.'

I couldn't see much point in viewing this perfectly healthy animal again but I promised to call. I had a busy day and it was after six o'clock before I got round to The Laurels. There were several cars in the drive and when I went into the house I saw that Mrs Rumney had a few people in for drinks; people like herself – upper class and of obvious refinement. In fact I felt rather a lout in my working clothes among the elegant gathering.

Mrs Rumney was about to lead me through to the kitchen when the door burst open and Cedric bounded delightedly into the midst of the company. Within seconds an aesthetic-looking gentleman was frantically beating off the attack as the great feet ripped down his waistcoat. He got away at the cost of a couple of buttons and the Boxer turned his attention to one of the ladies. She was in imminent danger of losing her dress when I pulled the dog off her.

Pandemonium broke out in the graceful room. The hostess's plaintive appeals rang out above the cries of alarm as the big dog charged around, but very soon I realised that a more insidious element had crept into the situation. The atmosphere in the room became rapidly charged with an unmistakable effluvium and it was clear that Cedric's unfortunate malady had reasserted itself.

I did my best to shepherd the animal out of the room but he didn't seem to know the meaning of obedience and I chased him in vain. And as the embarrassing minutes ticked away I began to realise for the first time the enormity of the problem which confronted Mrs Rumney. Most dogs break wind occasionally but Cedric was different; he did it all the time. And while his silent emanations were perhaps more treacherous there was no doubt that the audible ones were painfully distressing in a company like this.

continued on page 305

296

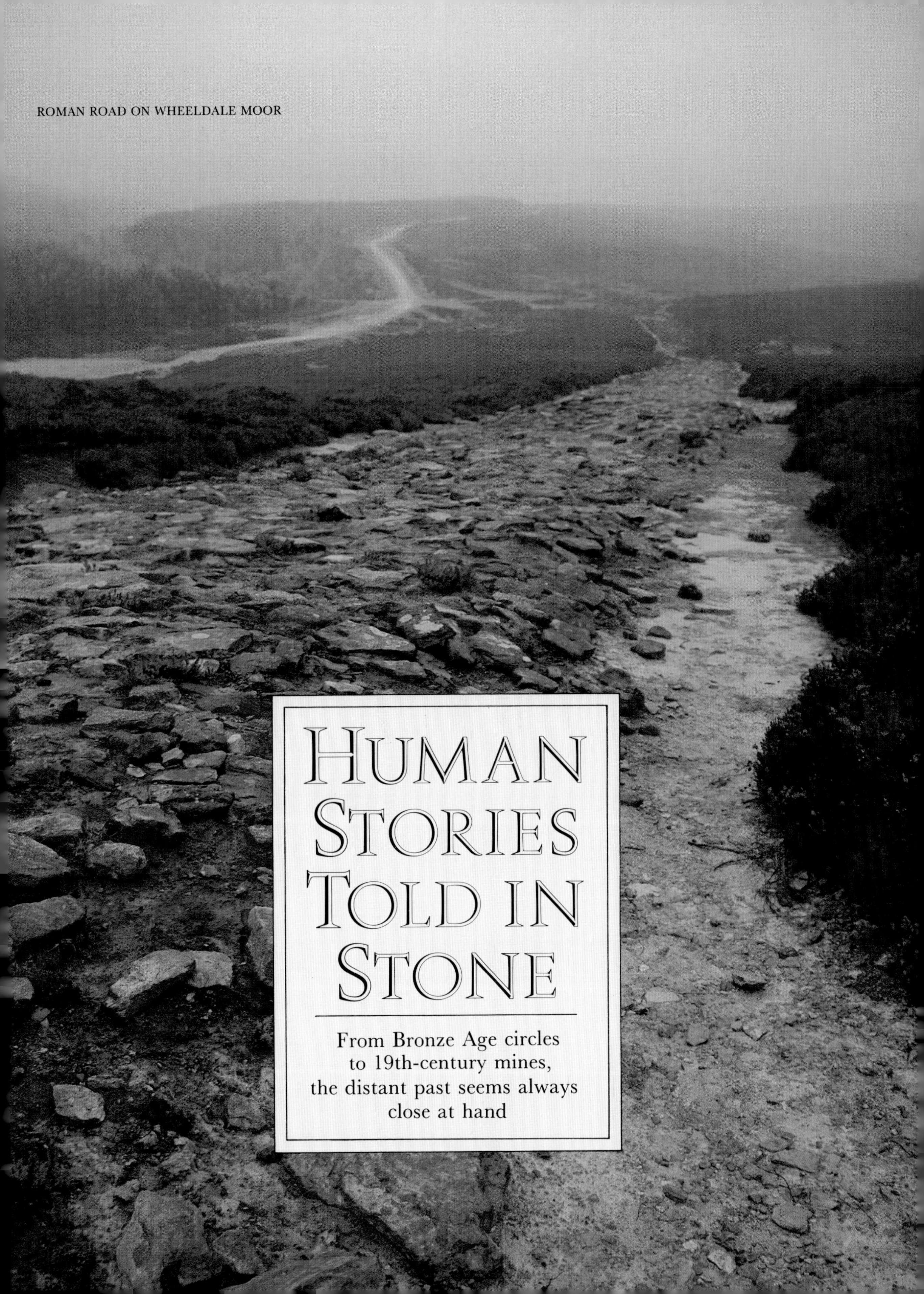

ROMAN ROAD ON WHEELDALE MOOR

Human Stories Told in Stone

From Bronze Age circles to 19th-century mines, the distant past seems always close at hand

Early settlers build for war and worship

The first marks of man in the dales and moors came with the rising population of the Bronze Age, which began about 1700 BC. In the warm, dry climate, more people lived there then than ever again, even today.

They changed the look of the land for ever. They began to denude it of its woods, by clearing patches for crops and by letting their stock graze freely. Their ritual stone circles are numerous and perhaps 10,000 burial sites still show on the open land – both round barrows and the later stone cairns.

The Iron Age, starting about 500 BC, was a cold era, when life was hard. Hill-forts were common – not all as grand as Stanwick, usually small earthworks round 5–10 acres. Every dominant hill-top and spur seems to have its fort, where wary tribesmen gathered with their stock for shelter from marauders.

NATIVE FORTRESS A 15 ft ditch round a bank retained by a drystone wall enclosed a 750 acre hill-fort at Stanwick, near Richmond. Here the Brigantes opposed the Roman army, but the fort fell about AD 74.

RITUAL RING The peaceful folk of the Bronze Age lavished time and labour over their sacred rites and burials. Close to the Wharfe at Yockenthwaite, they set 20 stones in a ring 25 ft across. Here they prayed, and perhaps buried a chief.

DEVIL'S ARROWS Three ghostly stone figures at Boroughbridge were set up by Bronze Age men. Later they were called Devil's Arrows from fears that Satan had hurled them into the ground.

Roman conquerors briefly show an advanced culture

TOWN FINDS Low remnants are left of the red sandstone wall (right) that enclosed 3rd-century Aldborough. Shops and houses, temples and baths made up the oblong grid pattern of the 55 acre town. Pottery and glass, pins and needles, combs and dice were found there – and intact in one house, a mosaic floor (above).

For 350 years Rome ruled the dales and moors but the soldiers and governors remained apart from the natives. Rome's skills did not spread much beyond their forts and the network of roads that connected them.

But in a few villas and in the three civilian towns at Aldborough, Catterick and York, there were comforts unknown to the native chiefs – tables, cushioned couches and chairs set on mosaic floors in rooms with frescoed walls. They did not survive for long after the Romans left in 407.

EXTRA DEFENCES Powerful catapults armed the ten-sided tower added in the 4th century to the fortress walls at York.

Saxons establish Christianity and write in English

Saxon pirates began raiding eastern Britain before the Romans left, and by the late 6th century raiders and immigrants had founded the Saxon kingdom of Deira in Yorkshire.

Deira was conquered by its neighbour in 605 and the two formed Northumbria. Deira's King Edwin fled south and married a Christian in Kent before he returned and took Northumbria. In 625 his queen, Ethelberga, brought north Paulinus, a missionary, who converted Edwin and thousands of others.

Northumbria became a centre of Christian learning. At Whitby a monk, Caedmon, had a vision and wrote a hymn to creation. The historian Bede quoted it in its original form – the earliest written English. Few Saxon churches have survived because they were wooden, but there are some intricately carved stone crosses.

The first Vikings attacked Northumbria in 793. It was a dreadful foretaste of 80 years of violence before Christian Saxons and pagan Danes lived side by side.

KIRKDALE'S CHURCH The sundial over the door tells the church's tale: 'Orm, Gamal's son, bought St Gregory's Minster when it was broken and fallen and he had it rebuilt from the ground to Christ and St Gregory when Edward was king and Tosti earl.'

DOORWAY A Saxon doorway was part of the church built at Kirkdale about 1055 when Edward the Confessor was king. Crosses and grave slabs from the 7th-century church the Danes destroyed are built into the walls.

MERGING CULTURES On a 10th-century cross at Middleton church the interlaced pattern on the wheel-head is typically Anglo-Saxon. But below it, as if laid out for burial, there is carved a Viking warrior wearing his battle-helmet, with his weapons at his side.

TIME TELLS The sundial put over the door of Kirkdale Church when it was rebuilt about 1055 is proudly inscribed, 'This is day's sun marker at every time. I Hawarth made it and Brand the priest.'

Heavy industry marks the remote dales and moors

Machinery and science gave better access to the inches-wide lead veins of Swaledale and Nidderdale which had been mined from Roman times. Gunpowder, steam-pumps, drills and hydraulic engines kept a huge industry active from 1700 until cheap imports killed it in the 1800s.

Miners breathed lead-laden air in wet tunnels and walked for miles over the moors to the mine – all for low pay that varied with the unpredictable output of the mine.

They used picks, hammers and drills, and sent the ore to the surface in sacks or rail-trucks for crushing and sorting on the dressing-floor. Metal-rich ore was smelted in the furnace.

TIP OF AN ICEBERG Below the mine buildings, ten miles or more of tunnels radiate off at many levels.

INDUSTRIAL DECAY All the derelict surface works of Old Gang lead mine sprawl in Swaledale – smelt-mill, dressing-floor, fuel store, powder house, spoil heaps and, leading up the hill to a short chimney, the long furnace-flue.

ROSEDALE REMAINS On the silent, spacious moor sprinkled with ruffled pools, a tumbling ruin hints at a differ

:. A century ago shifts of men were mining ironstone that rattled away in rail-trucks to the Teesside smelt-mills.

LIME-KILN Stone kilns in the Pennine dales recall a time when local limestone was burned to a powder to feed the soil.

continued from page 296

Cedric made it worse, because at each rasping expulsion he would look round enquiringly at his back end then gambol about the room as though the fugitive zephyr was clearly visible to him and he was determined to corner it.

It seemed a year before I got him out of there. Mrs Rumney held the door wide as I finally managed to steer him towards it but the big dog wasn't finished yet. On his way out he cocked a leg swiftly and directed a powerful jet against an immaculate trouser leg.

After that night I threw myself into the struggle on Mrs Rumney's behalf. I felt she desperately needed my help, and I made frequent visits and tried innumerable remedies. I consulted my colleague Siegfried on the problem and he suggested a diet of charcoal biscuits. Cedric ate them in vast quantities and with evident enjoyment but they, like everything else, made not the slightest difference to his condition.

And all the time I pondered upon the enigma of Mrs Rumney. She had lived in Darrowby for several years but the townsfolk knew little about her. It was a matter of debate whether she was a widow or separated from her husband. But I was not interested in such things; the biggest mystery to me was how she ever got involved with a dog like Cedric.

It was difficult to think of any animal less suited to her personality. Apart from his regrettable affliction he was in every way the opposite to herself; a great thick-headed rumbustious extrovert totally out of place in her gracious menage. I never did find out how they came together but on my visits I found that Cedric had one admirer at least.

He was Con Fenton, a retired farm worker, who did a bit of jobbing gardening and spent an average of three days a week at The Laurels. The Boxer romped down the drive after me as I was leaving and the old man looked at him with undisguised admiration.

'By gaw,' he said. 'He's a fine dog, is that!'

'Yes, he is, Con, he's a good chap, really.' And I meant it. You couldn't help liking Cedric when you got to know him. He was utterly amiable and without vice and he gave off a constant aura not merely of noxious vapours but of bonhomie. When he tore off people's buttons or sprinkled their trousers he did it in a spirit of the purest amity.

'Just look at them limbs!' breathed Con, staring rapturously at the dog's muscular thighs. 'By heck, 'e can jump over that gate as if it weren't there. He's what ah call a dog!'

As he spoke it struck me that Cedric would be likely to appeal to him because he was very like the Boxer himself; not over-burdened with brains, built like an ox with powerful shoulders and a big constantly-grinning face – they were two of a kind.

'Aye, ah allus likes it when t'missus let's him out in t'garden,' Con went on. He always spoke in a peculiar snuffling manner. 'He's grand company.'

I looked at him narrowly. No, he wouldn't be likely to notice Cedric's

305

*The old man looked at him with
undisguised admiration.*

complaint since he always saw him out of doors.

On my way back to the surgery I brooded on the fact that I was achieving absolutely nothing with my treatment. And though it seemed ridiculous to worry about a case like this, there was no doubt the thing had began to prey on my mind. In fact I began to transmit my anxieties to Siegfried. As I got out of the car he was coming down the steps of Skeldale House and he put a hand on my arm.

'You've been to The Laurels, James? Tell me,' he enquired solicitously, 'how is your farting Boxer today.'

'Still at it, I'm afraid,' I replied, and my colleague shook his head in commiseration.

We were both defeated. Maybe if chlorophyll tablets had been available in those days they might have helped but as it was I had tried everything. It seemed certain that nothing would alter the situation. And it wouldn't have been so bad if the owner had been anybody else but Mrs Rumney; I found that even discussing the thing with her had become almost unbearable.

Siegfried's student brother Tristan didn't help, either. When seeing practice he was very selective in the cases he wished to observe, but he was immediately attracted to Cedric's symptoms and insisted on coming with me on one occasion. I never took him again because as we went in the big dog bounded from his mistress' side and produced a particularly sonorous blast as if in greeting.

Tristan immediately threw out a hand in a dramatic gesture and declaimed: 'Speak on, sweet lips that never told a lie!' That was his only visit. I had enough trouble without that.

I didn't know it at the time but a greater blow awaited me. A few days later Mrs Rumney was on the 'phone again.

'Mr Herriot, a friend of mine has such a sweet little Boxer bitch. She wants to bring her along to be mated with Cedric.'

'Eh?'

'She wants to mate her bitch with my dog.'

'With Cedric ...?' I clutched at the edge of the desk. It couldn't be true! 'And ... and are you agreeable?'

'Yes, of course.'

I shook my head to dispel the feeling of unreality. I found it incomprehensible that anyone should want to reproduce Cedric, and as I gaped into the receiver a frightening vision floated before me of eight little Cedrics all with his complaint. But of course such a thing wasn't hereditary. I took a grip of myself and cleared my throat.

'Very well, then, Mrs Rumney, you'd better go ahead.'

There was a pause. 'But, Mr Herriot, I want you to supervise the mating.'

'Oh really, I don't think that's necessary.' I dug my nails into my palm. 'I think you'll be all right without me.'

'Oh but I would be much happier if you were there. Please come,' she said appealingly.

Instead of emitting a long-drawn groan I took a deep breath.

'Right,' I said. 'I'll be along in the morning.'

All that evening I was obsessed by a feeling of dread. Another acutely embarrassing session was in store with this exquisite woman. Why was it I always had to share things like this with her? And I really feared the worst. Even the daftest dog, when confronted with a bitch in heat, knows instinctively how to proceed, but with a really ivory-skulled animal like Cedric I wondered....

And next morning all my fears were realised. The bitch, Trudy, was a trim little creature and showed every sign of willingness to cooperate. Cedric, on the other hand, though obviously delighted to meet her, gave no hint of doing his part. After sniffing her over, he danced around her a few times, goofy-faced, tongue lolling. Then he had a roll on the lawn before charging at her and coming to a full stop, big feet out-splayed, head down, ready to play. I sighed. It was as I thought. The big chump didn't know what to do.

This pantomime went on for some time and, inevitably, the emotional strain brought on a resurgence of his symptoms. Frequently he paused to inspect his tail as though he had never heard noises like that before.

He varied his dancing routine with occasional headlong gallops round the lawn and it was after he had done about ten successive laps that he seemed to decide he ought to do something about the bitch. I held my breath as he approached her but unfortunately he chose the wrong end

307

SADDLEBACK SOW The distinctive marking of this pig varies slightly depending on which of the two strains it belongs to, the Essex or the Wessex. The Essex Saddleback's black body has a rather broader hoop of white round the shoulders, its hind feet as well as its front are white, and its tail and nose have some white. Despite its southern origins, the breed was hardy enough for the Dales, and until the Large White and Landrace ousted it, it was reared there widely for both pork and bacon.

to commence operations. Trudy had put up with his nonsense with great patience but when she found him busily working away in the region of her left ear it was too much. With a shrill yelp she nipped him in the hind leg and he shot away in alarm.

After that whenever he came near she warned him off with bared teeth. Clearly she was disenchanted with her bridegroom and I couldn't blame her.

'I think she's had enough, Mrs Rumney,' I said.

I certainly had had enough and so had the poor lady, judging by her slight breathlessness, flushed cheeks and waving handkerchief.

'Yes . . . yes . . . I suppose you're right,' she replied.

So Trudy was taken home, and that was the end of Cedric's career as a stud dog.

This last episode decided me. I had to have a talk with Mrs Rumney and a few days later I called in at The Laurels.

'Maybe you'll think it's none of my business,' I said. 'But I honestly don't think Cedric is the dog for you. In fact he's so wrong for you that he is upsetting your life.'

Mrs Rumney's eyes widened. 'Well . . . he is a problem in some ways . . . but what do you suggest?'

'I think you should get another dog in his place. Maybe a poodle or a corgi – something smaller, something you could control.'

'But, Mr Herriot, I couldn't possibly have Cedric put down.' Her eyes filled quickly with tears. 'I really am fond of him despite his . . . despite everything.'

'No, no, of course not!' I said. 'I like him too. He has no malice in him. But I think I have a good idea. Why not let Con Fenton have him?'

'Con . . . ?'

'Yes, he admires Cedric tremendously and the big fellow would have a good life with the old man. He has a couple of fields behind his cottage and keeps a few beasts. Cedric could run to his heart's content out there and Con would be able to bring him along when he does the garden. You'd still see him three times a week.'

Mrs Rumney looked at me in silence for a few moments and I saw in her face the dawning of relief and hope.

'You know, Mr Herriot, I think that could work very well. But are you sure Con would take him?'

'I'd like to bet on it. An old bachelor like him must be lonely. There's only one thing worries me. Normally they only meet outside and I wonder how it would be when they were indoors and Cedric started to . . . when the old trouble . . .'

'Oh, I think that would be all right,' Mrs Rumney broke in quickly. 'When I go on holiday Con always takes him for a week or two and he has never mentioned any . . . anything unusual . . . in that way.'

I got up to go. 'Well, that's fine. I should put it to the old man right away.'

Mrs Rumney rang within a few days. Con had jumped at the chance of taking on Cedric and the pair had apparently settled in happily together. She had also taken my advice and acquired a poodle puppy.

I didn't see the new dog till it was nearly six months old and its mistress asked me to call to treat it for a slight attack of eczema. As I sat in the graceful room looking at Mrs Rumney, cool, poised, tranquil, with the little white creature resting on her knee I couldn't help feeling how right and fitting the whole scene was. The lush carpet, the trailing velvet curtains, the fragile tables with their load of expensive china and framed miniatures. It was no place for Cedric.

Con Fenton's cottage was less than half a mile away and on my way back to the surgery on an impulse I pulled up at the door. The old man answered my knock and his big face split into a delighted grin when he saw me.

'Come in, young man!' he cried in his strange snuffly voice. 'I'm right glad to see tha!'

I had hardly stepped into the tiny living room when a hairy form hurled itself upon me. Cedric hadn't changed a bit and I had to battle my way to the broken armchair by the fireside. Con settled down opposite and when the Boxer leaped to lick his face he clumped him companionably on the head with his fist.

'Siddown, ye great daft bugger,' he murmured with affection. Cedric sank happily on to the tattered hearthrug at his feet and gazed up adoringly at his new master.

'Well, Mr Herriot,' Con went on as he cut up some villainous-looking plug tobacco and began to stuff it into his pipe. 'I'm right grateful to ye for gettin' me this grand dog. By gaw, he's a topper and ah wouldn't sell 'im for any money. No man could ask for a better friend.'

'Well, that's great, Con,' I said. 'And I can see that the big chap is really happy here.'

The old man ignited his pipe and a cloud of acrid smoke rose to the low, blackened beams. 'Aye, he's 'ardly ever inside. A gurt strong dog like 'im wants to work 'is energy off, like.'

But just at that moment Cedric was obviously working something else off because the familiar pungency rose from him even above the billowings of the pipe. Con seemed oblivious of it but in the enclosed space I found it overpowering.

'Ah well,' I gasped. 'I just looked in for a moment to see how you were getting on together. I must be on my way.' I rose hurriedly and stumbled towards the door but the redolence followed me in a wave. As I passed the table with the remains of the old man's meal I saw what seemed to be the only form of ornament in the cottage, a cracked vase holding a magnificent bouquet of carnations. It was a way of escape and I buried my nose in their fragrance.

Con watched me approvingly. 'Aye, they're lovely flowers, aren't they? T'missus at Laurels lets me bring 'ome what I want and I reckon them carnations is me favourite.'

'Yes, they're a credit to you.' I still kept my nose among the blooms.

HAY KNIVES While hay was standing in the stack it became compressed. When it was needed during the winter for feeding to the cattle or sheep, it could not be pulled out in handfuls or bundles, but had to be cut out in blocks with a sharp knife. Hay knives differed in their style of handle and shape of blade. The one most commonly used in Yorkshire (top left) had its handle projecting from one side of the shaft and its 15 in. long steel blade broadened out before the tip.

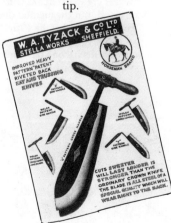

'There's only one thing,' the old man said pensively. 'Ah don't get t'full benefit of 'em.'

'How's that, Con?'

He pulled at his pipe a couple of times. 'Well, you can hear ah speak a bit funny, like?'

'No ... no ... not really.'

'Oh aye, ye know ah do. I've been like it since I were a lad. I 'ad a operation for adenoids and summat went wrong.'

'Oh, I'm sorry to hear that,' I said.

'Well, it's nowt serious, but it's left me lackin' in one way.'

'You mean ...?' A light was beginning to dawn in my mind, an elucidation of how man and dog had found each other, of why their relationship was so perfect, of the certainty of their happy future together. It seemed like fate.

'Aye,' the old man went on sadly. 'I 'ave no sense of smell.'

3

The hard life of Wesley Binks

I think it was when I saw the London policeman wagging a finger at a scowling urchin that I thought of Wesley Binks and the time he put the firework through the surgery letter box.

It was what they used to call a 'banger' and it exploded at my feet as I hurried along the dark passage in answer to the door bell's ring, making me leap into the air in terror.

I threw open the front door and looked into the street. It was empty, but at the corner where the lamplight was reflected in Robson's shop window I had a brief impression of a fleeing form and a faint echo of laughter. I couldn't do anything about it but I knew Wes was out there somewhere.

Wearily I trailed back into the house. Why did this lad persecute me? What could a ten-year-old boy possibly have against me? I had never done him any harm, yet I seemed to be the object of a deliberate campaign.

Or maybe it wasn't personal. It could be that he felt I represented authority or the establishment in some way, or perhaps I was just convenient.

I was certainly the ideal subject for his little tricks of ringing the door bell and running away, because I dared not ignore the summons in case it might be a client, and also the consulting and operating rooms were such a long way from the front of the house. Sometimes I was dragged down from our bed-sitter under the tiles. Every trip to the door was an

ON-THE-SPOT REPAIR An old way of fitting the metal tyre on to a cartwheel was to nail several separate iron arcs to the wooden felloes, or sections of rim. The arcs were called strakes. A farmer could replace one himself in an emergency. The slight unevenness where strakes met could give the wheel greater purchase on steep land, but the method died out at the end of the 19th century. After that all wheels were fitted with one-piece iron hoops.

expedition and it was acutely exasperating to arrive there and see only a little figure in the distance dancing about and grimacing at me.

He varied this routine by pushing rubbish through the letter box, pulling the flowers from the tiny strip of garden we tried to cultivate between the flagstones and chalking rude messages on my car.

I knew I wasn't the only victim because I had heard complaints from others; the fruiterer who saw his apples disappear from the box in front of the shop, the grocer who unwillingly supplied him with free biscuits.

He was the town naughty boy all right, and it was incongruous that he should have been named Wesley. There was not the slightest sign in his behaviour of any strict Methodist upbringing. In fact I knew nothing of his family life – only that he came from the poorest part of the town, a row of 'yards' containing tumbledown cottages, some of them evacuated because of their condition.

I often saw him wandering about in the fields and lanes or fishing in quiet reaches of the river when he should have been in school. When he spotted me on these occasions he invariably called out some mocking remark and if he happened to be with some of his cronies they all joined in the laughter at my expense. It was annoying but I used to tell myself that there was nothing personal in it. I was an adult and that was enough to make me a target.

Wes's greatest triumph was undoubtedly the time he removed the grating from the coal cellar outside Skeldale House. It was on the left of the front steps and underneath it was a steep ramp down which the coalmen tipped their bags.

I don't know whether it was inspired intuition but he pinched the grating on the day of the Darrowby Gala. The festivities started with a parade through the town led by the Houlton Silver Band and as I looked down from the windows of our bed-sitter I could see them all gathering in the street below.

'Look, Helen,' I said. 'They must be starting the march from Trengate. Everybody I know seems to be down there.'

Helen leaned over my shoulder and gazed at the long lines of boy scouts, girl guides, ex-servicemen, with half the population of the town packed on the pavements, watching. 'Yes, it's quite a sight, isn't it? Let's go down and see them move off.'

We trotted down the long flight of stairs and I followed her out through the front door. And as I appeared in the entrance I was suddenly conscious that I was the centre of attention. The citizens on the pavements, waiting patiently for the parade to start, had something else to look at now. The little brownies and wolf cubs waved at me from their ranks and there were nods and smiles from the people across the road and on all sides.

I could divine their thoughts. 'There's t'young vitnery coming out of his house. Not long married, too. That's his missus next to him.'

A feeling of well-being rose in me. I don't know whether other newly married men feel the same, but in those early days I was aware of a calm

THE WHEELWRIGHT'S SHOP
When he has prepared a metal-lined nave, or hub, of elm the wheelwright fits oak spokes into it. The rim is made in several sections, called felloes, of ash, elm or beech. A spoke dog – a long-handled lever device – pulls two spokes closer together as each felloe is being fitted on. All the jointing – mortises, tenons and dowels – must be precisely made for a sound wheel. Once the felloes are in place, the wheel is ready for its iron tyre.

satisfaction and fulfilment. And I was proud to be the 'vitnery' and part of the life of the town. There was my plate on the wall beside me, a symbol of my solid importance. I was a man of substance now, I had arrived.

Looking around me, I acknowledged the greeting with a few dignified little smiles, raising a gracious hand now and then rather like a royal personage on view. Then I noticed that Helen hadn't much room by my side, so I stepped to the left to where the grating should have been and slid gracefully down into the cellar.

It would be a dramatic touch to say I disappeared from view; in fact I wish I had, because I would have stayed down there and avoided further embarrassment. But as it was I travelled only so far down the ramp and stuck there with my head and shoulders protruding into the street.

My little exhibition caused a sensation among the spectators. Nothing in the Gala parade could compete with this. One or two of the surrounding faces expressed alarm but loud laughter was the general response. The adults were almost holding each other up but the little brownies and wolf cubs made my most appreciative audience, breaking their ranks and staggering about helplessly in the roadway while their leaders tried to restore order.

I caused chaos, too, in the Houlton Silver Band, who were hoisting

The little brownies and wolf cubs
made my most appreciative audience.

their instruments prior to marching off. If they had any ideas about bursting into tune they had to abandon them temporarily because I don't think any of them had breath to blow.

It was, in fact, two of the bandsmen who extricated me by linking their hands under my armpits. My wife was of no service at all in the crisis and I could only look up at her reproachfully as she leaned against the doorpost dabbing at her eyes.

It all became clear to me when I reached street level. I was flicking the coal dust from my trousers and trying to look unconcerned when I saw Wesley Binks doubled up with mirth, pointing triumphantly at me and at the hole over the cellar. He was quite near, jostling among the spectators, and I had my first close look at the wild-eyed little goblin who had plagued me. I may have made an unconscious movement towards him because he gave me a last malevolent grin and disappeared into the crowd.

Later I asked Helen about him. She could only tell me that Wesley's father had left home when he was about six years old, that his mother had remarried and the boy now lived with her and his stepfather.

Strangely, I had another opportunity to study him quite soon afterwards. It was about a week later and my feathers were still a little ruffled after the grating incident when I saw him sitting all alone in the waiting room. Alone, that is, except for a skinny black dog in his lap.

I could hardly believe it. I had often rehearsed the choice phrases which I would use on this very occasion but the sight of the animal restrained me; if he had come to consult me professionally I could hardly start pitching into him right away. Maybe later.

I pulled on a white coat and went in.

'Well, what can I do for you?' I asked coldly.

The boy stood up and his expression of mixed defiance and desperation showed that it had cost him something to enter this house.

'Summat matter wi' me dog,' he muttered.

'Right, bring him through.' I led the way along the passage to the consulting room.

'Put him on the table please,' I said, and as he lifted the little animal I decided that I couldn't let this opportunity pass. While I was carrying out my examination I would quite casually discuss recent events. Nothing nasty, no clever phrases, just a quiet probe into the situation. I was just about to say something like 'What's the idea of all those tricks you play on me?' when I took my first look at the dog and everything else fled from my mind.

He wasn't much more than a big puppy and an out-and-out mongrel. His shiny black coat could have come from a labrador and there was a suggestion of terrier in the pointed nose and pricked ears, but the long string-like tail and the knock-kneed fore-limbs baffled me. For all that he was an attractive little creature with a sweetly expressive face.

But the things that seized my whole attention were the yellow blobs of pus in the corners of the eyes, the muco-purulent discharge from the

PEAT SPADES Each dale had its own model of peat spade, but all models shared the essential features. A flange at a right-angle to the steel blade cut the side of the peat while the main blade was cutting the base. The wooden handle was broad where it met the blade so that it supported the cut peat as it was swung round to the barrow. With such a spade an experienced man could cut 2,000 peats a day.

nostrils and the photophobia which made the dog blink painfully at the light from the surgery window.

Classical canine distemper is so easy to diagnose but there is never any satisfaction in doing so.

'I didn't know you had a dog,' I said. 'How long have you had him?'

'A month. Feller got 'im from t'dog and cat home at Hartington and sold 'im to me.'

'I see.' I took the temperature and was not surprised to find it was 104°F.

'How old is he?'

'Nine months.'

I nodded. Just about the worst age.

I went ahead and asked all the usual questions but I knew the answers already.

Yes, the dog had been slightly off colour for a week or two. No, he wasn't really ill, but listless and coughing occasionally. And of course it was not until the eyes and nose began to discharge that the boy became worried and brought him to see me. That was when we usually saw these cases – when it was too late.

Wesley imparted the information defensively, looking at me under lowered brows as though he expected me to clip his ear at any moment. But as I studied him any aggressive feelings I may have harboured evaporated quickly. The imp of hell appeared on closer examination to be a neglected child. His elbows stuck out through holes in a filthy jersey, his shorts were similarly ragged, but what appalled me most was the sour smell of his unwashed little body. I hadn't thought there were children like this in Darrowby.

When he had answered my questions he made an effort and blurted out one of his own.

'What's matter with 'im?'

I hesitated a moment. 'He's got distemper, Wes.'

'What's that?'

'Well, it's a nasty infectious disease. He must have got it from another sick dog.'

'Will 'e get better?'

'I hope so. I'll do the best I can for him.' I couldn't bring myself to tell a small boy of his age that his pet was probably going to die.

I filled a syringe with a 'mixed macterin' which we used at that time against the secondary invaders of distemper. It never did much good and even now with all our antibiotics we cannot greatly influence the final outcome. If you can catch a case in the early viral phase then a shot of hyperimmune serum is curative, but people rarely bring their dogs in until that phase is over.

As I gave the injection the dog whimpered a little and the boy stretched out a hand and patted him.

'It's awright, Duke,' he said.

'That's what you call him, is it – Duke?'

314

'Aye.' He fondled the ears and the dog turned, whipped his strange long tail about and licked the hand quickly. Wes smiled and looked up at me and for a moment the tough mask dropped from the grubby features and in the dark wild eyes I read sheer delight. I swore under my breath. This made it worse.

I tipped some boracic crystals into a box and handed it over. 'Use this dissolved in water to keep his eyes and nose clean. See how his nostrils are all caked and blocked up – you can make him a lot more comfortable.'

He took the box without speaking and almost with the same movement dropped three and sixpence on the table. It was about our average charge and resolved my doubts on that score.

'When'll ah bring 'im back?' he asked.

I looked at him doubtfully for a moment. All I could do was repeat the injections, but was it going to make the slightest difference?

The boy misread my hesitation.

'Ah can pay!' he burst out. 'Ah can get t'money!'

'Oh I didn't mean that, Wes. I was just wondering when it would be suitable. How about bringing him in on Thursday?'

He nodded eagerly and left with his dog.

As I swabbed the table with disinfectant I had the old feeling of helplessness. The modern veterinary surgeon does not see nearly as many cases of distemper as we used to, simply because most people immunise their puppies at the earliest possible moment. But back in the thirties it was only the few fortunate dogs who were inoculated. The disease is so easy to prevent but almost impossible to cure.

The next three weeks saw an incredible change in Wesley Binks's character. He had built up a reputation as an idle scamp but now he was transferred into a model of industry, delivering papers in the mornings, digging people's gardens, helping to drive the beasts at the auction mart. I was perhaps the only one who knew he was doing it for Duke.

He brought the dog in every two or three days and paid on the nail. I naturally charged him as little as possible but the money he earned went on other things – fresh meat from the butcher, extra milk and biscuits.

'Duke's looking very smart today,' I said on one of the visits. 'I see you've been getting him a new collar and lead.'

The boy nodded shyly then looked up at me, dark eyes intent. 'Is 'e any better?'

'Well, he's about the same, Wes. That's how it goes – dragging on without much change.'

'When ... when will ye know?'

I thought for a moment. Maybe he would worry less if he understood the situation. 'The thing is this. Duke will get better if he can avoid the nervous complications of distemper.'

'Wot's them?'

'Fits, paralysis and a thing called chorea which makes the muscles twitch.'

GEESE AT THE MARKET Geese were auctioned in lots at markets and bought by farmers, who let them feed on the stubble fields to fatten up for the table. Traditionally geese were driven to market in large flocks by dealers who bought them from many farms and had their feet coated with tar and sand for the walk of 20 miles or more to a major market, perhaps at Richmond. Villagers also kept a few geese on the green or on stream verges and sold the goslings to dealers for about 3 shillings (15 pence).

'Wot if he gets them?'

'It's a bad lookout in that case. But not all dogs develop them.' I tried to smile reassuringly. 'And there's one thing in Duke's favour – he's not a pure bred. Cross-bred dogs have a thing called hybrid vigour which helps them to fight disease. After all, he's eating fairly well and he's quite lively, isn't he?'

'Aye, not bad.'

'Well then, we'll carry on. I'll give him another shot now.'

The boy was back in three days and I knew by his face he had momentous news.

'Duke's a lot better – 'is eyes and nose 'ave dried up and he's eatin' like a 'oss!' He was panting with excitement.

I lifted the dog on to the table. There was no doubt he was enormously improved and I did my best to join in the rejoicing.

'That's great, Wes,' I said, but a warning bell was tinkling in my mind. If nervous symptoms were going to supervene, this was the time – just when the dog was apparently recovering.

I forced myself to be optimistic. 'Well now, there's no need to come back any more but watch him carefully and if you see anything unusual bring him in.'

The ragged little figure was overjoyed. He almost pranced along the passage with his pet and I hoped fervently that I would not see them in there again.

That was on the Friday evening and by Monday I had put the whole thing out of my head and into the category of satisfying memories when the boy came in with Duke on the lead.

I looked up from the desk where I was writing in the day book. 'What is it, Wes?'

'He's dotherin'.'

I didn't bother going through to the consulting room but hastened from behind the desk and crouched on the floor, studying the dog intently. At first I saw nothing, then as I watched I could just discern a faint nodding of the head. I placed my hand on the top of the skull and waited. And it was there; the slight but regular twitching of the temporal muscles which I had dreaded.

'I'm afraid he's got chorea, Wes,' I said.

'What's that?'

'It's one of the things I was telling you about. Sometimes they call it St Vitus' Dance. I was hoping it wouldn't happen.'

The boy looked suddenly small and forlorn and he stood there silent, twisting the new leather lead between his fingers. It was such an effort for him to speak that he almost closed his eyes.

'Will 'e die?'

'Some dogs do get over it, Wes.' I didn't tell him that I had seen it happen only once. 'I've got some tablets which might help him. I'll get you some.'

I gave him a few of the arsenical tablets I had used in my only cure. I

POTATO PIE The autumn potato harvest used to be made into a clamp, called a 'tatie pie' in Yorkshire, for keeping during the winter. Here, the last load of the crop is being raked from the cart to complete the long heap, and sheaves of straw set ready in the field are laid over as a thatch to keep the heap frostproof and watertight but ventilated. Potatoes would be taken out as they were needed for the market. Now, potato crops are usually stored indoors.

316

didn't even know if they had been responsible but I had nothing more to offer.

Duke's chorea pursued a textbook course over the next two weeks. All the things which I had feared turned up in a relentless progression. The twitching spread from his head to his limbs, then his hindquarters began to sway as he walked.

His young master brought him in repeatedly and I went through the motions, trying at the same time to make it clear that it was all hopeless. The boy persisted doggedly, rushing about meanwhile with his paper deliveries and other jobs, insisting on paying though I didn't want his money. Then one afternoon he called in.

'Ah couldn't bring Duke,' he muttered. 'Can't walk now. Will you come and see 'im?'

We got into my car. It was a Sunday, about three o'clock and the streets were quiet. He led me up the cobbled yard and opened the door of one of the houses.

The stink of the place hit me as I went in. Country vets aren't easily sickened but I felt my stomach turning. Mrs Binks was very fat and a filthy dress hung shapelessly on her as she slumped, cigarette in mouth, over the kitchen table. She was absorbed in a magazine which lay in a clearing among mounds of dirty dishes and her curlers nodded as she looked up briefly at us.

On a couch under the window her husband sprawled asleep, open-mouthed, snoring out the reek of beer. The sink, which held a further supply of greasy dishes, was covered in a revolting green scum. Clothes, newspapers and nameless rubbish littered the floor and over everything a radio blasted away at full strength.

The only clean new thing was the dog basket in the corner. I went across and bent over the little animal. Duke was now prostrate and helpless, his body emaciated and jerking uncontrollably. The sunken eyes had filled up again with pus and gazed apathetically ahead.

'Wes,' I said. 'You've got to let me put him to sleep.'

He didn't answer, and as I tried to explain the blaring radio drowned my words. I looked over at his mother.

'Do you mind turning the radio down?' I asked.

She jerked her head at the boy and he went over and turned the knob. In the ensuing silence I spoke to him again.

'It's the only thing, believe me. You can't let him die by inches like this.'

He didn't look at me. All his attention was fixed desperately on his dog. Then he raised a hand and I heard his whisper.

'Awright.'

I hurried out to the car for the Nembutal.

'I promise you he'll feel no pain,' I said as I filled the syringe. And indeed the little creature merely sighed before lying motionless, the fateful twitching stilled at last.

I put the syringe in my pocket. 'Do you want me to take him away,

BAGGING POTATOES During the winter, potatoes were taken from the straw-covered storage clamp, or pie, as they were needed for supplying to the market. They were put through the potato-screening machine which graded them according to size, then sorted them into sacks for transporting to market. Few would be left when spring came, and some of these would begin to shoot and become too soft for selling.

317

SPICE BREAD At Christmas the weekly baking-day output of loaves, plain and currant teacakes, biscuits and cakes was increased and a special festive bread was made – spice bread. It was enriched with butter, eggs, dried fruit, and spices such as nutmeg, cinnamon and allspice. Some families called it Yule Cake. It was sliced and buttered for supper on Christmas Eve.

To make spice bread, mix ½ teaspoon of salt, 1 teaspoon of grated nutmeg and 1 teaspoon of ground cinnamon into 2 lb of bread flour. Rub in 12 oz of butter and mix in 12 oz of sugar. Pour ¾ pint of warm milk on to 2 beaten eggs and use a little of the mixture to mix 1½ oz of fresh yeast to a paste. Stir the paste into the flour and mix in the rest of the egg and milk. Work up a dough and put it to rise for an hour. Knead the dough until springy, working in 1 lb of currants, 8 oz of sultanas and 4 oz of chopped candied peel. Divide the dough between three 1 lb loaf tins and put to rise for 30 minutes. Bake for 50 minutes at 400°F (200°C), gas mark 6.

Wes?'

He looked at me bewilderedly and his mother broke in.

'Aye, get 'im out. Ah never wanted t'bloody thing 'ere in t'first place.' She resumed her reading.

I quickly lifted the little body and went out. Wes followed me and watched as I opened the boot and laid Duke gently on top of my black working coat.

As I closed the lid he screwed his knuckles into his eyes and his body shook. I put my arm across his shoulders, and as he leaned against me for a moment and sobbed I wondered if he had ever been able to cry like this – like a little boy with somebody to comfort him.

But soon he stood back and smeared the tears across the dirt on his cheeks.

'Are you going back into the house, Wes?' I asked.

He blinked and looked at me with a return of his tough expression.

'Naw!' he said and turned and walked away. He didn't look back and I watched him cross the road, climb a wall and trail away across the fields towards the river.

And it has always seemed to me that at that moment Wes walked back into his old life. From then on there were no more odd jobs or useful activities. He never played any more tricks on me but in other ways he progressed into more serious misdemeanours. He set barns on fire, was up before the magistrates for theft and by the time he was thirteen he was stealing cars.

Finally he was sent to an approved school and then he disappeared from the district. Nobody knew where he went and most people forgot him. One person who didn't was the police sergeant.

'That young Wesley Binks,' he said to me ruminatively. 'He was a wrong 'un if ever I saw one. You know, I don't think he ever cared a damn for anybody or any living thing in his life.'

'I know how you feel, sergeant,' I replied. 'But you're not entirely right. There was one living thing....'

4

A Christmas kitten

I had plenty of company for Christmas that year. We were billeted in the Grand Hotel, the massive Victorian pile which dominated Scarborough in turreted splendour from its eminence above the sea, and the big dining room was packed with several hundred shouting airmen. The iron discipline was relaxed for a few hours to let the Yuletide spirit run free. It was so different from other Christmases I had known that it ought to have remained like a beacon in my mind, but I know that my strongest memory of Christmas will always be bound up with a certain little cat.

I first saw her when I was called to see one of Mrs Ainsworth's dogs, and I looked in some surprise at the furry black creature sitting before the fire.

'I didn't know you had a cat,' I said.

The lady smiled. 'We haven't, this is Debbie.'

'Debbie?'

'Yes, at least that's what we call her. She's a stray. Comes here two or three times a week and we give her some food. I don't know where she lives but I believe she spends a lot of her time around one of the farms along the road.'

'Do you ever get the feeling that she wants to stay with you?'

'No.' Mrs Ainsworth shook her head. 'She's a timid little thing. Just creeps in, has some food then flits away. There's something so appealing about her but she doesn't seem to want to let me or anybody into her life.'

I looked again at the little cat. 'But she isn't just having food today.'

'That's right. It's a funny thing but every now and again she slips through here into the lounge and sits by the fire for a few minutes. It's as though she was giving herself a treat.'

'Yes ... I see what you mean.' There was no doubt there was something unusual in the attitude of the little animal. She was sitting bolt upright on the thick rug which lay before the fireplace in which the coals glowed and flamed. She made no effort to curl up or wash herself or do anything other than gaze quietly ahead. And there was something in the dusty black of her coat, the half-wild scrawny look of her, that gave me a clue. This was a special event in her life, a rare and wonderful thing; she was lapping up a comfort undreamed of in her daily existence.

As I watched she turned, crept soundlessly from the room and was gone.

'That's always the way with Debbie,' Mrs Ainsworth laughed. 'She never stays more than ten minutes or so, then she's off.'

She was a plumpish, pleasant-faced woman in her forties and the kind of client veterinary surgeons dream of; well off, generous, and the owner of three cosseted Basset hounds. And it only needed the habitually mournful expressions of one of the dogs to deepen a little and I was round there post-haste. Today one of the Bassets had raised its paw and scratched its ear a couple of times and that was enough to send its mistress scurrying to the 'phone in great alarm.

So my visits to the Ainsworth home were frequent but undemanding, and I had ample opportunity to look out for the little cat which had intrigued me. On one occasion I spotted her nibbling daintily from a saucer at the kitchen door. As I watched she turned and almost floated on light footsteps into the hall then through the lounge door.

The three Bassets were already in residence, draped snoring on the

BASSET HOUND Nose-to-the-ground is the characteristic pose of the Basset, and this accentuates the dog's habitual downcast expression – sad eyes under a furrowed velvet brow with great drooping ears set low on the long head. The Basset's short legs are deceptive, for it is quite a large dog with an ample head and a long, hefty body. It trails patiently and slowly by scent, and has been used on the Continent since the 1500s to work in packs with huntsmen on foot seeking out badgers, wild boar and vermin. It was introduced into Britain in the late 19th century, and used for hunting hares in open country.

fireside rug, but they seemed to be used to Debbie because two of them sniffed her in a bored manner and the third merely cocked a sleepy eye at her before flopping back on the rich pile.

Debbie sat among them in her usual posture; upright, intent, gazing absorbedly into the glowing coals. This time I tried to make friends with her. I approached her carefully but she leaned away as I stretched out my hand. However, by patient wheedling and soft talk I managed to touch her and gently stroked her cheek with one finger. There was a moment when she responded by putting her head on one side and rubbing back against my hand but soon she was ready to leave. Once outside the house she darted quickly along the road then through a gap in a hedge and the last I saw was the little black figure flitting over the rain-swept grass of a field.

'I wonder where she goes,' I murmured half to myself.

Mrs Ainsworth appeared at my elbow. 'That's something we've never been able to find out.'

It must have been nearly three months before I heard from Mrs Ainsworth, and in fact I had begun to wonder at the Bassets' long symptomless run when she came on the 'phone.

It was Christmas morning and she was apologetic. 'Mr Herriot, I'm so sorry to bother you today of all days. I should think you want a rest at Christmas like anybody else.' But her natural politeness could not hide the distress in her voice.

'Please don't worry about that,' I said. 'Which one is it this time?'

'It's not one of the dogs. It's ... Debbie.'

'Debbie? She's at your house now?'

'Yes ... but there's something wrong. Please come quickly.'

Driving through the market place I thought again that Darrowby on Christmas Day was like Dickens come to life; the empty square with the snow thick on the cobbles and hanging from the eaves of the fretted lines of roofs; the shops closed and the coloured lights of the Christmas trees winking at the windows of the clustering houses, warmly inviting against the cold white bulk of the fells behind.

Mrs Ainsworth's home was lavishly decorated with tinsel and holly, rows of drinks stood on the sideboard and the rich aroma of turkey and sage and onion stuffing wafted from the kitchen. But her eyes were full of pain as she led me through to the lounge.

Debbie was there all right, but this time everything was different. She wasn't sitting upright in her usual position; she was stretched quite motionless on her side, and huddled close to her lay a tiny black kitten.

I looked down in bewilderment. 'What's happened here?'

'It's the strangest thing,' Mrs Ainsworth replied. 'I haven't seen her for several weeks then she came in about two hours ago – sort of staggered into the kitchen, and she was carrying the kitten in her mouth. She took it through to the lounge and laid it on the rug and at first I was amused. But I could see all was not well because she sat as she usually

Darrowby on Christmas Day was like Dickens come to life.

does, but for a long time – over an hour – then she lay down like this and she hasn't moved.'

I knelt on the rug and passed my hand over Debbie's neck and ribs. She was thinner than ever, her fur dirty and mud-caked. She did not resist as I gently opened her mouth. The tongue and mucous membranes were abnormally pale and the lips ice-cold against my fingers. When I pulled down her eyelid and saw the dead white conjunctiva a knell sounded in my mind.

I palpated the abdomen with a grim certainty as to what I would find and there was no surprise, only a dull sadness as my fingers closed around a hard lobulated mass deep among the viscera. Massive lymphosarcoma. Terminal and hopeless. I put my stethoscope on her heart and listened to the increasingly faint, rapid beat then I straightened up and sat on the rug looking sightlessly into the fireplace, feeling the warmth of the flames on my face.

Mrs Ainsworth's voice seemed to come from afar. 'Is she ill, Mr Herriot?'

I hesitated. 'Yes ... yes, I'm afraid so. She has a malignant growth.' I stood up. 'There's absolutely nothing I can do. I'm sorry.'

'Oh!' Her hand went to her mouth and she looked at me wide-eyed. When at last she spoke her voice trembled. 'Well, you must put her to sleep immediately. It's the only thing to do. We can't let her suffer.'

'Mrs Ainsworth,' I said. 'There's no need. She's dying now – in a coma – far beyond suffering.'

She turned quickly away from me and was very still as she fought with her emotions. Then she gave up the struggle and dropped on her knees beside Debbie.

'Oh, poor little thing!' she sobbed and stroked the cat's head again and again as the tears fell unchecked on the matted fur. 'What she must have come through. I feel I ought to have done more for her.'

For a few moments I was silent, feeling her sorrow, so discordant among the bright seasonal colours of this festive room. Then I spoke gently.

'Nobody could have done more than you,' I said. 'Nobody could have been kinder.'

'But I'd have kept her here – in comfort. It must have been terrible out there in the cold when she was so desperately ill – I daren't think about it. And having kittens, too – I ... I wonder how many she did have?'

I shrugged. 'I don't suppose we'll ever know. Maybe just this one. It happens sometimes. And she brought it to you, didn't she?'

'Yes ... that's right ... she did ... she did.' Mrs Ainsworth reached out and lifted the bedraggled black morsel. She smoothed her finger along the muddy fur and the tiny mouth opened in a soundless miaow. 'Isn't it strange? She was dying and she brought her kitten here. And on Christmas Day.'

I bent and put my hand on Debbie's heart. There was no beat.

I looked up. 'I'm afraid she's gone.' I lifted the small body, almost feather light, wrapped it in the sheet which had been spread on the rug and took it out to the car.

When I came back Mrs Ainsworth was still stroking the kitten. The tears had dried on her cheeks and she was bright-eyed as she looked at me.

'I've never had a cat before,' she said.

I smiled. 'Well it looks as though you've got one now.'

And she certainly had. That kitten grew rapidly into a sleek handsome cat with a boisterous nature which earned him the name of Buster. In every way he was the opposite of his timid little mother. Not for him the privations of the secret outdoor life; he stalked the rich carpets of the Ainsworth home like a king and the ornate collar he always wore added something more to his presence.

On my visits I watched his development with delight but the occasion which stays in my mind was the following Christmas Day, a year from his arrival.

I was out on my rounds as usual. I can't remember when I haven't had to work on Christmas Day because the animals have never got round to recognising it as a holiday; but with the passage of the years the vague resentment I used to feel has been replaced by philosophical acceptance. After all, as I tramped around the hillside barns in the frosty air I was working up a better appetite for my turkey than all the millions lying in bed or slumped by the fire; and this was aided by the innumerable aperitifs I received from the hospitable farmers.

I was on my way home, bathed in a rosy glow. I had consumed several whiskies – the kind the inexpert Yorkshiremen pour as though it was ginger ale – and I had finished with a glass of old Mrs Earnshaw's rhubarb wine which has seared its way straight to my toenails. I heard the cry as I was passing Mrs Ainsworth's house.

'Merry Christmas, Mr Herriot!' She was letting a visitor out of the front door and she waved at me gaily. 'Come in and have a drink to warm you up.'

I didn't need warming up but I pulled in to the kerb without hesitation. In the house there was all the festive cheer of last year and the same glorious whiff of sage and onion which set my gastric juices surging. But there was not the sorrow; there was Buster.

He was darting up to each of the dogs in turn, ears pricked, eyes blazing with devilment, dabbing a paw at them then streaking away.

Mrs Ainsworth laughed. 'You know, he plagues the life out of them. Gives them no peace.'

She was right. To the Bassets, Buster's arrival was rather like the intrusion of an irreverent outsider into an exclusive London club. For a long time they had led a life of measured grace; regular sedate walks with their mistress, superb food in ample quantities and long snoring sessions on the rugs and armchairs. Their days followed one upon another in unruffled calm. And then came Buster.

He was dancing up to the youngest dog again, sideways this time, head on one side, goading him. When he started boxing with both paws it was too much even for the Basset. He dropped his dignity and rolled over with the cat in a brief wrestling match.

'I want to show you something.' Mrs Ainsworth lifted a hard rubber ball from the sideboard and went out to the garden, followed by Buster. She threw the ball across the lawn and the cat bounded after it over the frosted grass, the muscles rippling under the black sheen of his coat. He seized the ball in his teeth, brought it back to his mistress, dropped it at her feet and waited expectantly. She threw it and he brought it back again.

I gasped incredulously. A feline retriever!

The Bassets looked on disdainfully. Nothing would ever have induced them to chase a ball, but Buster did it again and again as though he would never tire of it.

Mrs Ainsworth turned to me. 'Have you ever seen anything like that?'

'No,' I replied. 'I never have. He is a most remarkable cat.'

She snatched Buster from his play and we went back into the house where she held him close to her face, laughing as the big cat purred and arched himself ecstatically against her cheek.

Looking at him, a picture of health and contentment, my mind went back to his mother. Was it too much to think that that dying little creature with the last of her strength had carried her kitten to the only haven of comfort and warmth she had ever known in the hope that it would be cared for there? Maybe it was.

But it seemed I wasn't the only one with such fancies. Mrs Ainsworth turned to me and though she was smiling her eyes were wistful.

'Debbie would be pleased,' she said.

I nodded. 'Yes, she would.... It was just a year ago today she brought

PEPPER CAKE A carol singer or any other Christmas-time visitor to a north Yorkshire house would be offered pepper cake and cheese. Some families made a round cake and served it on top of a large cheese, some made a square cake, and some served it with a specially made cheese marked with a cross.

Ground cloves became the most common 'pepper' spicing the cake, but originally a blend of ginger, caraway, coriander and allspice was used.

To make pepper cake, mix 1 teaspoon of baking powder and 1 oz of ground cloves with 12 oz of plain flour. Melt 12 oz of treacle with 4 oz of brown sugar and 4 oz of butter. Combine this with the flour then mix in thoroughly 3 beaten eggs. Bake in a deep, greased and lined 9 in. cake tin at 325°F (170°C), gas mark 3, for about 1½ hours or until firm in the centre.

him, wasn't it?' 'That's right.' She hugged Buster to her again. 'The best Christmas present I ever had.'

5

What a beautiful boy!

WELSH SOW The white breed developed from the ancient, hardy pigs of the Welsh hills is very similar to the Landrace, with a long body and a long face hidden by forward-drooping ears. Like other breeds of sow, it will produce two litters a year, with about ten piglets to a litter, and suckle the piglets for two months. By-products of the dairy industry, especially whey, are the main part of a pig's diet while it is being fattened for the market.

My stint in London was nearing its end. Our breaking-in weeks were nearly over and we waited for news of posting to Initial Training Wing.

The air was thick with rumours. We were going to Aberystwyth in Wales; too far away for me. I wanted the north. Then we were going to Newquay in Cornwall; worse still. I was aware that the impending birth of AC2 Herriot's child did not influence the general war strategy but I still wanted to be as near to Helen as possible at the time.

The whole London phase is blurred in my memory. Possibly because everything was so new and different that the impressions could not be fully absorbed, and also perhaps because I was tired most of the time. I think we were all tired. Few of us were used to being jerked from slumber at 6 a.m. every morning and spending the day in continual physical activity. If we weren't being drilled we were being marched to meals, to classes, to talks. I had lived in a motor car for a few years and the re-discovery of my legs was painful.

There were times, too, when I wondered what it was all about. Like all the other young men I had imagined that after a few brisk pre-liminaries I would be sitting in an aeroplane, learning to fly, but it turned out that this was so far in the future that it was hardly mentioned. At the ITW we would spend months learning navigation, principles of flight, morse and many other things.

I was thankful for one blessing. I had passed the mathematics exam. I have always counted on my fingers and still do and I had been so nervous about this that I went to classes with the ATC in Darrowby before my call-up, dredging from my schooldays horrific calculations about trains passing each other at different speeds and water running in and out of bath tubs. But I had managed to scrape through and felt ready to face anything.

There were some unexpected shocks in London. I didn't anticipate spending days mucking out some of the dirtiest piggeries I had ever seen. Somebody must have had the idea of converting all the RAF waste food into pork and bacon and of course there was plenty of labour at hand. I had a strong feeling of unreality as, with other aspiring pilots, I threw muck and swill around hour after hour.

There was another time I had the same feeling. One night three of us decided to go to the cinema. We took pains to get to the front of the queue for the evening meal so that we would be in time for the start of the picture. When the doors of the huge dining room at the Zoo were thrown open we were first in, but a sergeant cook met us in the entrance with: 'I want three volunteers for dishwashing – you, you and you,' and marched us away. He probably had a kind heart because he patted our shoulders as we climbed miserably into greasy dungarees.

'Never mind, lads,' he said. 'I'll see you get a real good meal afterwards.'

My friends were taken somewhere else and I found myself alone in a kind of dungeon at the end of a metal chute. Very soon dirty plates began to cascade down the chute and my job was to knock the food remains off them and transfer them to a mechanical washer.

The menu that night was cottage pie and chips, a combination which has remained engraved on my memory. For more than two hours I stood at bay while a non-stop torrent of crockery poured down on me; thousands and thousands of plates, every one bearing a smear of cottage pie, a blob of cold gravy, a few adhering chips.

As I reeled around in the meaty steam a little tune tinkled repetitively in my mind; it was the song Siegfried and I were forever singing as we waited to enter the RAF, the popular jingle which in our innocence we thought typified the new life ahead.

> 'If I only had wings.
> Oh what a difference it would make to things,
> All day long I'd be in the sky, up on high,
> Talking to the birdies that pass me by.'

But in this reeking cavern with my hands, face, hair and every pore of my skin impregnated with cottage pie and chips, those birdies seemed far away.

At last, however, the plates began to slow down and finally stopped coming. The sergeant came in beaming and congratulated me on doing a fine job. He led me back to the dining hall, vast and empty save for my two friends. They both wore bemused, slightly stunned expressions and I am pretty sure I looked the same.

'Sit down here, lads,' the sergeant said. We took our places side by side in a corner with the bare boards of the table stretching away into the distance. 'I told you you'd get a real good meal, didn't I? Well, here it is.' He slid three heaped platefuls in front of us.

'There y'are,' he said. 'Cottage pie and chips, double helpin's!'

The following day I might have felt more disenchanted than ever, but news of the posting blotted out all other feelings. It seemed too good to be true – I was going to Scarborough. I had been there and I knew it as a beautiful seaside resort, but that wasn't why I was so delighted. It was because it was in Yorkshire.

I suppose once you embark on a life of crime it gets easier all the time. Making a start is the only hard bit.

WARTIME DELIVERY WAGON
When petrol was rationed during the Second World War, horse-drawn vehicles were seen in the streets again. This LNER wagon pulled by a pair of Shires was working from a railway goods yard in 1942. The price of horses rose with the new demand for them, from £40 to about £60.

At any rate, that is how it seemed to me as I sat in the bus, playing hookey again. There had been absolutely no trouble about dodging out of the Grand, the streets of Scarborough had been empty of SPs and nobody had given me a second look as I strolled casually into the bus station.

It was Saturday, 13 February. Helen was expecting our baby this week-end. It could happen any time and I just didn't see how I could sit here these few miles away and do nothing. I had no classes today or tomorrow so I would miss nothing and nobody would miss me. It was, I told myself, a mere technical offence, and anyway I had no option. Like the first time, I just had to see Helen.

And it wouldn't be long now, I thought, as I hurried up to the familiar doorway of her home. I went inside and gazed disappointedly at the empty kitchen – somehow I had been sure she would be standing there waiting for me with her arms wide. I shouted her name but nothing stirred in the house. I was still there, listening, when her father came through from an inner room.

'You've got a son,' he said.

I put my hand on the back of a chair. 'What ...?'

'You've got a son.' He was so calm.

'When ...?'

'Few minutes ago. Nurse Brown's just been on the 'phone. Funny you should walk in.'

As I leaned on the chair he gave me a keen look. 'Would you like a drop of whisky?'

'Whisky? No – why?'

'Well you've gone a bit white, lad, that's all. Anyway, you'd better have something to eat.'

'No, no, no thanks, I've got to get out there.'

He smiled. 'There's no hurry, lad. Anyway, they won't want anybody there too soon. Better eat something.'

'Sorry, I couldn't. Would you – would you mind if I borrowed your car?'

I was still trembling a little as I drove away. If only Mr Alderson had led up to it gradually – he might have said, 'I've got some news for you,' or something like that, but his direct approach had shattered me. When I pulled up outside Nurse Brown's it still hadn't got through to me that I was a father.

Greenside Nursing Home sounded impressive, but it was in fact Nurse Brown's dwelling house. She was State Registered and usually had two or three of the local women in at a time to have their babies.

She opened the door herself and threw up her hands. 'Mr Herriot! It hasn't taken you long! Where did you spring from?' She was a cheerfully dynamic little woman with mischievous eyes.

I smiled sheepishly. 'Well, I just happened to drop in on Mr Alderson and got the news.'

'You might have given us time to get the little fellow properly

THE WOMEN'S LAND ARMY All over the Dales green-jerseyed, dungareed girls worked 50 hour weeks throughout the Second World War, milking, ploughing, harvesting, haymaking and coping with all the other work of a farm. They were Land Girls, members of the Women's Land Army which numbered 80,000 by 1943 and took over the work of farmhands who had been called up for the forces. More than one-third of them were city girls – volunteers and call-up recruits without farming experience, but trained briefly or having to learn on the job. They had to go where they were sent, but remained a civil force paid by the individual farmers who had asked for them.

washed,' she said. 'But never mind, come up and see him. He's a fine baby – nine pounds.'

Still in a dreamlike state I followed her up the stairs of the little house into a small bedroom. Helen was there, in the bed, looking flushed.

'Hello,' she said.

I went over and kissed her.

'What was it like?' I enquired nervously.

'Awful,' Helen replied without enthusiasm. Then she nodded towards the cot beside her.

I took my first look at my son. Little Jimmy was brick-red in colour and his face had a bloated, dissipated look. As I hung over him he twisted his tiny fists under his chin and appeared to be undergoing some mighty internal struggle. His face swelled and darkened as he contorted his features then from deep among the puffy flesh his eyes fixed me with a baleful glare and he stuck his tongue out of the corner of his mouth.

'My God!' I exclaimed.

The nurse looked at me, startled. 'What's the matter?'

'Well, he's a funny-looking little thing, isn't he?'

'What!' She stared at me furiously. 'Mr Herriot, how can you say such a thing? He's a beautiful baby!'

I peered into the cot again. Jimmy greeted me with a lopsided leer, turned purple and blew a few bubbles.

'Are you sure he's all right?' I said. There was a tired giggle from the bed but Nurse Brown was not amused.

'All right! What exactly do you mean?' She drew herself up stiffly.

I shuffled my feet. 'Well, er – is there anything wrong with him?'

I thought she was going to strike me. 'Anything ... how dare you! Whatever are you talking about? I've never heard such nonsense!' She turned appealingly towards the bed, but Helen, a weary smile on her face, had closed her eyes.

I drew the enraged little woman to one side. 'Look, Nurse, have you by chance got any others on the premises?'

'Any other what?' she asked icily.

'Babies – new babies. I want to compare Jimmy with another one.'

Her eyes widened. 'Compare him! Mr Herriot, I'm not going to listen to you any longer – I've lost patience with you!'

'I'm asking you, Nurse,' I repeated. 'Have you any more around?'

There was a long pause as she looked at me as though I was something new and incredible. 'Well – there's Mrs Dewburn in the next room. Little Sidney was born about the same time as Jimmy.'

'Can I have a look at him?' I gazed at her appealingly.

She hesitated then a pitying smile crept over her face. 'Oh you ... you ... just a minute, then.'

She went into the other room and I heard a mumble of voices. She reappeared and beckoned to me.

Mrs Dewburn was the butcher's wife and I knew her well. The face on the pillow was hot and tired like Helen's.

PARKIN The staple cereal crop of Britain's colder and wetter northern half is oats, not wheat. Parkin combines the chewy texture of oatmeal with the sweetness of treacle and the spicy bite of ginger. It is the traditional snack for munching round November 5th bonfires.

To make parkin, mix together 4 oz of self-raising flour, 1 teaspoon of ground ginger, 1 teaspoon of bicarbonate of soda and a good pinch of salt. Stir in 4 oz of fine oatmeal. Melt 4 oz of treacle gently in a pan with 2 oz of butter and 2 oz of sugar. Pour on to the dry ingredients, add 1 egg and stir well, adding about 2 tablespoons of milk to soften the mixture. Pour into a well-greased tin about 6 in. square and bake at 325°F (170°C), gas mark 3, for an hour or until firm in the centre. Cut the parkin into squares when it has cooled.

'Eee, Mr Herriot, I didn't expect to see you. I thought you were in the Army.'

'RAF, actually, Mrs Dewburn. I'm on – er – leave at the moment.'

I looked in the cot. Sidney was dark red and bloated, too, and he, also, seemed to be wrestling with himself. The inner battle showed in a series of grotesque facial contortions culminating in a toothless snarl.

I stepped back involuntarily. 'What a beautiful child,' I said.

'Yes, isn't he lovely,' said his mother fondly.

'He is indeed, gorgeous.' I took another disbelieving glance into the cot. 'Well, thank you very much, Mrs Dewburn. It was kind of you to let me see him.'

'Not at all, Mr Herriot, it's nice of you to take an interest.'

Outside the door I took a long breath and wiped my brow. The relief was tremendous. Sidney was even funnier than Jimmy.

When I returned to Helen's room Nurse Brown was sitting on the bed and the two women were clearly laughing at me. And of course, looking back, I must have appeared silly. Sidney Dewburn and my son are now two big, strong, remarkably good-looking young men, so my fears were groundless.

The little nurse looked at me quizzically. I think she had forgiven me.

'I suppose you think all your calves and foals are beautiful right from the moment they are born?'

'Well, yes,' I replied. 'I have to admit it – I think they are.'

As I have said before, ideas do not come readily to me, but on the bus journey back to Scarborough a devilish scheme began to hatch in my brain.

I was due for compassionate leave, but why should I take it now? Helen would be in the Nursing Home for a fortnight and there didn't seem any sense in my mooning round Darrowby on my own. The thing to do would be to send myself a telegram a fortnight from now announcing the birth, and we would be able to spend my leave together.

It was interesting how my moral scruples dissolved in the face of this attraction, but anyway, I told myself, where was the harm? I wasn't scrounging anything extra, I was just altering the time. The RAF or the war effort in general would suffer no mortal blow. Long before the darkened vehicle had rolled into the town I had made up my mind and on the following day I wrote to a friend in Darrowby and arranged about the telegram.

But I wasn't such a hardened criminal as I thought, because as the days passed doubts began to creep in. The rules at ITW were rigidly strict. I would be in trouble if I was found out. But the prospect of a holiday with Helen blotted out all other considerations.

When the fateful day arrived my room-mates and I were stretched on our beds after lunch when a great voice boomed along the corridor.

'AC2 Herriot! Come on, let's have you, Herriot!'

My stomach lurched. Somehow I hadn't reckoned on Flight Sergeant

Blackett coming into this. I had thought maybe an LAC or a corporal, even one of the sergeants might have handled it, not the great man himself.

Flight Sergeant Blackett was an unsmiling martinet of immense natural presence which a gaunt six feet two inch frame, wide bony shoulders and a craggy countenance did nothing to diminish. It was usually the junior NCOs who dealt with our misdemeanours, but if Flight Sergeant Blackett ever took a hand it was a withering experience.

I heard it again. The same bull bellow which echoed over our heads on the square every morning.

'Herriot! Let's be having you, Herriot!'

I was on my way at a brisk trot out of the room and along the polished surface of the corridor. I came to a halt stiffly in front of the tall figure.

'Yes, Flight Sergeant.'

'You Herriot?'

'Yes, Flight Sergeant.'

The telegram between his fingers scuffed softly against the blue serge of his trousers as he swung his hand to and fro. My pulse rate accelerated painfully as I waited.

'Well now, lad, I'm pleased to tell you that your wife has had her baby safely.' He raised the telegram to his eyes. 'It says 'ere, "A boy, both well. Nurse Brown." Let me be the first to congratulate you.' He held out his hand and as I took it he smiled. Suddenly he looked very like Gary Cooper.

'Now you'll want to get off right away and see them both, eh?'

I nodded dumbly. He must have thought I was an unemotional character.

He put a hand on my shoulder and guided me into the orderly room.

'Come on, you lot, get movin'!' The organ tones rolled over the heads of the airmen seated at the tables. 'This is important. Got a brand new father 'ere. Leave pass, railway warrant, pay, double quick!'

'Right, Flight. Very good, Flight.' The typewriters began to tap.

The big man went over to a railway timetable on the wall. 'You haven't far to go, anyway. Let's see – Darrowby, Darrowby ... yes, there's a train out of here for York at three twenty.' He looked at his watch. 'You ought to make that if you get your skates on.'

A deepening sense of shame threatened to engulf me when he spoke again.

'Double back to your room and get packed. We'll have your documents ready.'

I changed into my best blue, filled my kit bag and threw it over my shoulder, then hurried back to the orderly room.

The Flight Sergeant was waiting. He handed me a long envelope. 'It's all there, son, and you've got plenty of time.' He looked me up and down, walked round me and straightened the white flash of my cap. 'Yes, very smart. We've got to have you lookin' right for your missus, haven't we?' He gave me the Gary Cooper smile again. He was a

BUTTER WORKER An easy method of squeezing buttermilk out of newly churned butter was to pass it through a butter worker. This 40 in. long, arched tray has a hand-turned, grooved, wooden roller that moves back and forth along the tray crushing the butter. As the buttermilk is released, it trickles down the slopes to collect at both ends. It would be added to the buttermilk left in the churn and used in the pig-feed, or on baking day in scones or oatmeal bread.

handsome, kind-eyed man and I'd never noticed it.

He strolled with me along the corridor. 'This'll be your first 'un, of course?'

'Yes, Flight.'

He nodded. 'Well, it's a great day for you. I've got three of 'em, meself. Getting big now but I miss 'em like hell with this ruddy war. I really envy you, walking in that door tonight and seeing your son for the very first time.'

Guilt drove through me in a searing flood and as we halted at the top of the stairs I was convinced my shifty eyes and furtive glances would betray me. But he wasn't really looking at me.

'You know, lad,' he said softly, gazing somewhere over my head. 'This is the best time of your life coming up.'

We weren't allowed to use the main stairways and as I clattered down the narrow stone service stairs I heard the big voice again.

'Give my regards to them both.'

I had a wonderful time with Helen, walking for miles, discovering the delights of pram pushing, with little Jimmy miraculously improved in appearance. Everything was so much better than if I had taken my leave at the official time and there is no doubt my plan was a success.

But I was unable to gloat about it. The triumph was dimmed and to this day I have reservations about the whole thing.

Flight Sergeant Blackett spoiled it for me.

6

Mrs Beck drives a hard bargain

A tender nerve twinged as the old lady passed me the cup of tea. She looked just like Mrs Beck.

One of the local churches was having a social evening to entertain us lonely airmen and as I accepted the cup and sat down I could hardly withdraw my eyes from the lady's face.

Mrs Beck! I could see her now standing by the surgery window.

'Oooh, I never thought you were such a 'eartless man, Mr Herriot.' Her chin trembled and she looked up at me reproachfully.

'But, Mrs Beck,' I said. 'I assure you I am not being in the least heartless. I just cannot carry out a major operation on your cat for ten shillings.'

'Well, I thought you would've done it for a poor widder woman like me.'

I regarded her thoughtfully, taking in the small compact figure, the

healthy cheeks, the neat helmet of grey hair pulled tightly into a bun. Was she really a poor widow? There was cause for doubt. Her next-door neighbour in Rayton village was a confirmed sceptic.

'It's all a tale, Mr Herriot,' he had said. 'She tries it on wi' everybody, but I'll tell you this – she's got a long stockin'. Owns property all over t'place.'

I took a deep breath. 'Mrs Beck. We often do work at reduced rates for people who can't afford to pay, but this is what we call a luxury operation.'

'Luxury!' The lady was aghast. 'Eee, ah've been tellin' you how Georgina keeps havin' them kittens. She's at it all the time and it's gettin' me down. Ah can't sleep for worryin' when t'next lot's comin'.' She dabbed her eyes.

'I understand and I'm sorry. I can only tell you again that the only way to prevent this trouble is to spay your cat and the charge is one pound.'

'Nay, I can't afford that much!'

I spread my hands. 'But you are asking me to do it for half the price. That's ridiculous. This operation involves the removal of the uterus and ovaries under a general anaesthetic. You just can't do a job like that for ten shillings.'

'Oh, you are cruel!' She turned and looked out of the window and her shoulders began to shake. 'You won't even take pity on a poor widder.'

This had been going on for ten minutes and it began to dawn on me that I was in the presence of a stronger character than myself. I glanced at my watch – I should have been on my round by now and it was becoming increasingly obvious that I wasn't going to win this argument.

I sighed. Maybe she really was a poor widow. 'All right, Mrs Beck, I'll do it for ten shillings, just this once. Will Tuesday afternoon be all right for you?'

She swung round from the window, her face crinkling magically into a smile. 'That'll suit me grand! Eee, that's right kind of you.' She tripped past me and I followed her along the passage.

'Just one thing,' I said as I held the front door open for her. 'Don't give Georgina any food from midday on Monday. She must have an empty stomach when you bring her in.'

'Bring 'er in?' She was a picture of bewilderment. 'But I 'aven't got no car. I thought you'd be collectin' her.'

'Collecting! But Rayton's five miles away!'

'Yes, and bring 'er back afterwards, too. I 'ave no transport.'

'Collect ... operate on her ... take her back! All for ten shillings!'

She was still smiling but a touch of steel glinted in her eyes. 'Well, that's what you agreed to charge – ten shillings.'

'But ... but ...'

'Oh now you're startin' again.' The smile faded and she put her head on one side. 'And I'm only a poor ...'

'Okay, okay,' I said hastily. 'I'll call on Tuesday.'

TEACAKES Home baking with yeast had its regular weekly slot in Yorkshire's farm and cottage kitchens until the 1950s or later. Teacakes, soft in crumb and crust, were split open and spread with dripping or potted beef, or filled with cold meat and pickle. They made a substantial start to tea.

To make teacakes, mix 2 teaspoons of salt into 2 lb of bread flour and rub in 4 oz of lard. Warm 1 pint of mixed milk and water and use a little to mix 2 oz of yeast with 2 teaspoons of sugar to a paste. Stir the paste into the flour and gradually add the remaining liquid to work up a dough. Put it to rise until doubled in bulk, then knead it until smooth and springy and divide it into 12 pieces. Shape them into flat discs and space them out on greased baking trays. Leave to rise again until doubled in size. Bake for 15 minutes at 450°F (230°C), gas mark 8.

SEED PACKETS On the packets of seeds bought for the vegetable garden, the familiar names of seedsmen and the proven varieties of vegetables are seen still, as they were in the 1950s and before. Then, Dales cottagers could buy their seeds for six old pence (2½p) a packet. The blue-tinged January King is one of the hardiest cabbages, well able to stand in the frozen winter ground of north Yorkshire. Parsnip seed is the earliest to be sown when the gardening season starts.

And when Tuesday afternoon came round I cursed my softness. If that cat had been brought in I could have operated on her at two o'clock and been out on the road doing my farm calls by two thirty. I didn't mind working at a loss for half an hour, but how long was this business going to take?

On my way out I glanced through the open door of the sitting room. Tristan was supposed to be studying but was sleeping soundly in his favourite chair. I went in and looked down at him, marvelling at the utter relaxation, seen only in a dedicated sleeper. His face was as smooth and untroubled as a baby's, the *Daily Mirror*, open at the comic strips, had fallen across his chest and a burnt-out Woodbine hung from one dangling hand.

I shook him gently. 'Like to come with me, Triss? I've got to pick up a cat.'

He came round slowly, stretching and grimacing, but his fundamental good nature soon reasserted itself.

'Certainly, Jim,' he said with a final yawn. 'It will be a pleasure.'

Mrs Beck lived half way down the left side of Rayton village. I read 'Jasmine Cottage' on the brightly painted gate, and as we went up the garden path the door opened and the little woman waved gaily.

'Good afternoon, gentlemen, I'm right glad to see you both.' She ushered us into the living room among good, solid-looking furniture which showed no sign of poverty. The open cupboard of a mahogany sideboard gave me a glimpse of glasses and bottles. I managed to identify Scotch, cherry brandy and sherry before she nudged the door shut with her knee.

I pointed to a cardboard box loosely tied with string. 'Ah, good, you've got her in there, have you?'

'Nay, bless you, she's in t'garden. She allus has a bit of play out there of an afternoon.'

'In the garden, eh?' I said nervously. 'Well, please get her in, we're in rather a hurry.'

We went through a tiled kitchen to the back door. Most of these cottages had a surprising amount of land behind them and Mrs Beck's patch was in very nice order. Flower-beds bordered a smooth stretch of lawn and the sunshine drew glittering colours from the apples and pears among the branches of the trees.

'Georgina,' carolled Mrs Beck. 'Where are you, my pet?'

No cat appeared and she turned to me with a roguish smile. 'I think the little imp's playin' a game with us. She does that, you know.'

'Really?' I said without enthusiasm. 'Well, I wish she'd show herself. I really don't have much ...'

At that moment a very fat tabby darted from a patch of chrysanthemums and flitted across the grass into a clump of rhododendrons with Tristan in close pursuit. The young man dived among the greenery and the cat emerged from the other end at top speed, did a couple of laps of the lawn then shot up a gnarled tree.

Tristan, eyes gleaming in anticipation, lifted a couple of windfall apples from the turf. 'I'll soon shift the bugger from there, Jim,' he whispered and took aim.

I grabbed his arm. 'For heaven's sake, Triss!' I hissed. 'You can't do that. Put those things down.'

'Oh ... all right.' He dropped the apples and made for the tree. 'I'll get hold of her for you, anyway.'

'Wait a minute.' I seized his coat as he passed. 'I'll do it. You stay down here and try to catch her if she jumps.'

Tristan looked disappointed but I gave him a warning look. The way the cat had moved, it struck me that it only needed a bit of my colleague's ebullience to send the animal winging into the next county. I began to climb the tree.

I like cats, I've always liked them, and since I feel that animals recognise this in a person I have usually been able to approach and handle the most difficult types. It is not too much to say that I prided myself on my cat technique; I didn't foresee any trouble here.

Puffing slightly, I reached the top branch and extended a hand to the crouching animal.

'Pooss-pooss,' I cooed, using my irresistible cat tone.

Georgina eyed me coldly and gave no answering sign other than a higher arching of the back.

I lean further along the branch. 'Pooss-pooss, pooss-pooss.' My voice was like molten honey, my finger near her face. I would rub her cheek ever so gently and she would be mine. It never failed.

'Pah!' replied Georgina warningly but I took no heed and touched the fur under her chin.

'Pah-pah!' Georgina spat and followed with a lightning left hook which opened a bloody track across the back of my hand.

Muttering fervently, I retreated and nursed my wounds. From below Mrs Beck gave a tinkling laugh.

'Oh, isn't she a little monkey! She's that playful, bless her.'

I snorted and began to ease my way along the branch again. This time, I thought grimly, I would dispense with finesse. The quick grab was indicated here.

As though reading my thoughts the little creature tripped to the end of the branch and as it bent low under her weight she dropped lightly to the grass.

Tristan was on her in a flash, throwing himself full length and seizing her by the hind leg. Georgina whipped round and unhesitatingly sank her teeth into his thumb but Tristan's core of resilience showed. After a single howl of agony he changed his grip at lightning speed to the scruff of the neck.

A moment later he was standing upright holding a dangling fighting fury high in the air.

'Right, Jim,' he called happily. 'I have her.'

'Good lad! Hang on!' I said breathlessly and slithered down the tree

PLANT LABELS In the cottage gardens of the Dales the vegetables and flowers were old varieties needing no identification. In a large garden, however, the lady of the house or her gardener would regularly be trying new and exotic varieties. They would mark each row of seeds with a push-in label, and tie or strap tags to the flowers or shrubs, with the variety name written in indelible ink. Sets of marking equipment such as this could be bought from the seedsman or at the local market.

as quickly as I could. Too quickly, in fact, as an ominous ripping sound announced the removal of a triangular piece of my jacket elbow.

But I couldn't bother with trifles. Ushering Tristan at a gallop into the house I opened the cardboard box. There were no sophisticated cat containers in those days and it was a tricky job to enclose Georgina, who was lashing out in all directions and complaining bitterly in a bad-tempered wail.

It took a panting ten minutes to imprison the cat but even with several yards of rough twine round the floppy cardboard I still didn't feel very secure as I bore it to the car.

Mrs Beck raised a finger as we were about to drive away. I carefully explored my lacerated hand and Tristan sucked his thumb as we waited for her to speak.

'Mr Herriot, I 'ope you'll be gentle with 'er,' she said anxiously. 'She's very timid, you know.'

We had covered barely half a mile before sounds of strife arose from the back.

'Get back! Get in there. Get back, you bugger!'

I glanced behind me. Tristan was having trouble. Georgina clearly didn't care for the motion of the car and from the slits in the box clawed feet issued repeatedly; on one occasion an enraged spitting face got free as far as the neck. Tristan kept pushing everything back with great resolution but I could tell from the rising desperation of his cries that he was fighting a losing battle.

I heard the final shout with a feeling of inevitability.

'She's out, Jim! The bugger's out!'

Well this was great. Anybody who has driven a car with a hysterical cat hurtling around the interior will appreciate my situation. I crouched low over the wheel as the furry creature streaked round the sides or leaping clawing at the roof or windscreen with Tristan lunging vainly after her.

But cruel fate had not finished with us yet. My colleague's gasps and grunts from the rear ceased for a moment to be replaced by a horrified shriek.

'The bloody thing's shitting, Jim! She's shitting everywhere!'

The cat was obviously using every weapon at her disposal and he didn't have to tell me. My nose was way ahead of him, and I frantically wound down the window. But I closed it just as quickly at the rising image of Georgina escaping and disappearing into the unknown.

I don't like to think of the rest of that journey. I tried to breathe through my mouth and Tristan puffed out dense clouds of Woodbine smoke but it was still pretty terrible. Just outside Darrowby I stopped the car and we made a concerted onslaught on the animal; at the cost of a few more wounds, including a particularly painful scratch on my nose, we cornered her and fastened her once more in the box.

Even on the operating table Georgina had a few tricks left. We were using ether and oxygen as anaesthetic and she was particularly adept at

DOCKING IRON A minor operation was performed on each lamb by the shepherd rather than the vet. He docked, or shortened, the lamb's tail to about 2 in. long. A long tail became soiled and attracted flies which laid eggs in the wool. The developing maggots could burrow through and destroy the lamb's skin, causing severe illness. To dock the tail, the shepherd heated the iron or steel head of the 12 in. long docking iron before pressing it on to the tail, which was laid along a piece of wood. The hot metal rapidly seared through the tail.

holding her breath while the mask was on her face then returning suddenly to violent life when we thought she was asleep. We were both sweating when she finally went under.

I suppose it was inevitable, too, that she should be a difficult case. Ovaro-hysterectomy in the cat is a fairly straightforward procedure and nowadays we do innumerable cases uneventfully, but in the thirties, particularly in country practice, it was infrequently done and consequently a much larger undertaking.

I personally had my own preferences and aversions in this field. For instance, I found thin cats easy to do and fat cats difficult. Georgina was extremely fat.

When I opened her abdomen an ocean of fat welled up at me, obscuring everything, and I spent a long nerve-racking period lifting out portions of bowel or omentum with my forceps, surveying them gloomily and stuffing them back in again. A great weariness had begun to creep over me by the time I at last managed to grip the pink ovary between the metallic jaws and drew forth the slender string of uterus. After that it was routine, but I still felt a strange sense of exhaustion as I inserted the last stitch.

I put the sleeping cat into the box and beckoned to Tristan. 'Come on, let's get her home before she comes round.' I was starting along the passage when he put his hand on my arm.

'Jim,' he said gravely. 'You know I'm your friend.'

'Yes, Triss, of course.'

'I'd do anything for you, Jim.'

'I'm sure you would.'

He took a deep breath. 'Except one thing. I'm not going back in that bloody car.'

I nodded dully. I really couldn't blame him.

'That's all right,' I said. 'I'll be off, then.'

Before leaving I sprinkled the interior with pine-smelling disinfectant but it didn't make much difference. In any case my main emotion was the hope that Georgina wouldn't wake up before I got to Rayton, and that was shattered before I had crossed Darrowby market place. The hair prickled on the back of my neck as an ominous droning issued from the box on the rear seat. It was like the sound of a distant swarm of bees but I knew what it meant; the anaesthetic was wearing off.

Once clear of the town I put my foot on the boards. This was something I rarely did because whenever I pushed my vehicle above forty miles an hour there was such a clamour of protest from engine and body that I always feared the thing would disintegrate around me. But at this moment I didn't care. Teeth clenched, eyes staring, I hurtled forward, but I didn't see the lonely strip of tarmac or the stone walls flitting past; all my attention was focused behind me, where the swarm of bees was getting nearer and the tone angrier.

When it developed into a bad-tempered yowling and was accompanied by the sound of strong claws tearing at cardboard I began to

SMOUT HOLES Near the base of a drystone wall, the waller would leave holes that passed right through the structure – which was about 2½ ft thick at the foundation. Each hole was immediately above one of the through-stones that keyed together the two sloping outside layers of the wall. The main purpose of a smout hole was to let water run away on sloping land, instead of collecting against the wall and seeping through all along it. Small animals used the holes as passages; traps set beside the holes caught many a rabbit.

tremble. As I thundered into Rayton village I glanced behind me. Georgina was half out of the box. I reached back and grasped her scruff and when I stopped at the gate of Jasmine Cottage I pulled on the brake with one hand and lifted her on to my lap with the other.

I sagged in the seat, my breath escaping in a great explosion of relief; and my stiff features almost bent into a smile as I saw Mrs Beck pottering in her garden.

She took Georgina from me with a cry of joy but gasped in horror when she saw the shaven area and the two stitches on the cat's flank.

'Oooh, my darlin'! What 'ave those nasty men been doin' to you?' She hugged the animal to her and glared at me.

'She's all right, Mrs Beck, she's fine,' I said. 'You can give her a little milk tonight and some solid food tomorrow. There's nothing to worry about.'

She pouted. 'Oh, very well. And now ...' She gave me a sidelong glance. 'I suppose you'll want your money?'

'Well, er ...'

'Wait there, then. I'll get it.' She turned and went into the house.

Standing there, leaning against the reeking car, feeling the sting of the scratches on my hands and nose and examining the long tear on my jacket elbow I felt physically and emotionally spent. All I had done this afternoon was spay a cat but I had nothing more to offer.

Apathetically I watched the lady coming down the path. She was carrying a purse. At the gate she stopped and faced me.

'Ten shillin's, wasn't it?'

'That's right.'

She rummaged in the purse for some time before pulling out a ten-shilling note which was regarded sadly.

'Oh, Georgina, Georgina, you *are* an expensive pussy,' she soliloquised.

Tentatively I began to extend my hand but she pulled the note away. 'Just a minute, I'm forgettin'. You 'ave to take the stitches out, don't you?'

'Yes, in ten days.'

She set her lips firmly. 'Well there's plenty of time to pay ye then – ye'll be here again.'

'Here again ...? But you can't expect ...'

'I allus think it's unlucky to pay afore a job's finished,' she said. 'Summat terrible might happen to Georgina.'

'But ... but ...'

'Nay, ah've made up me mind,' she said. She replaced the money and snapped the purse shut with an air of finality before turning towards the house. Halfway up the path she looked over her shoulder and smiled.

'Aye, that's what I'll do. I'll pay ye when ye come back.'

336

A FARMER'S WORLD

The horses have mostly gone now, but in many other ways work and life on the hill farms of 'Herriot country' remain as they were centuries ago

Citadels against winter's siege

Built to last, the stone farmhouses and barns of the Yorkshire dales are mementoes of yesteryear's way of life. They evolved over many centuries to house all the varied activities of mixed hill farming.

By a tradition dating back to the Norse settlers of the 9th century, the farmhouse and the main barn were built under a single roof as a longhouse, sometimes with a door through from the kitchen to the barn so the farmer could visit his cattle without having to go outdoors. The house provided space for a dairy, a cooling room for the cheese and a beef loft where hams and pickled carcases were hung through the winter. Pigs were housed near by, as they were fed on swill from the dairy. Within this secure and self-contained citadel, the people and their stock could ride out the long siege of winter.

TWO FLOORS A field barn can house cattle below and their fodder above.

ONE LEVEL In a one-storey cowhouse, fodder is kept in a Dutch (open) barn.

PROSPERITY AND DECLINE With washing billowing in the breeze and hens enjoying the sunshine, a spring scene in Wensleydale evokes prosperity and content. But a century of depopulation in the moors and dales has left a sad legacy of abandoned farms, such as the one on the right.

A NEW DAY As the first rays of the rising sun reach up the valley, a Swaledale farm awakes to an A

rning. Already the sheep are grazing in their frosty fields, and in the yard a sheepdog awaits its master.

The farmyard: home for creatures great and small

Farmers of the Yorkshire dales and moors still work their land in ways that recall the 1930s. Their farmland often ranges from rich streamside meadows to rough moorland high up on the fells.

A traditional balance of mixed farming is needed to give an economic return. A single farm may contain both sheep and dairy cattle, some pigs and hens, and perhaps some geese and goats. The living heart of the small farm is the yard, where an untidy range of ancient stone-built barns shelters a nursery-book abundance of creatures great and small.

HARDY SURVIVORS Goats, which are kept for their milk, can survive in conditions too bleak and sparse even for the local Swaledale sheep.

THE PORKER Pigs, killed in November, provide ham and bacon all year.

HARDY TRADITION Yorkshire farmers thrive on long hours of hard work. Many of them have never taken holidays and have no intention of retiring.

IN MONEY By Yorkshire tradition, the farm hens are the property of the farmer's wife and the sale of eggs provides her with pin money.

ON THE PROWL In the ever-active life of the farm, even the barnyard cats keep busy, prowling for rats and mice.

ON THE ALERT Border Collies are trained to work with sheep and bring in the cows. They also warn a farmer when strangers arrive on the farm.

RARE SURVIVOR One of the main changes in farming in the past 50 years has been the disappearance of the horse. But a few remain, and farmers take pride in harnessing them the traditional way.

Changing times in the cowhouse

While dairy farms in the grazing lands of lowland England become fewer and larger, some of the mixed farms of north Yorkshire retain their small herds of a dozen or so cows. But the cattle themselves have changed. The brown and white shorthorns – the popular breed of the 1930s – are bowing out to the black and white friesians which give more milk – an average of 3 gallons a day, and sometimes more than 6 gallons a day.

All milk now must be sold through the local Milk Marketing Board, where once a farmer might sell his milk to a local town dairy or cheesemaker.

FEEDING As well as hay in winter, cows are fed on concentrates, such as oats, barley, bran and oil cake.

CALVES A source of income for the farmer are the calves born each year. Most are sold to be reared for beef.

A DYING SKILL From November until May the cows live under cover, in the cowhouse (or byre). They give more milk there than in the open, and their straw bedding (above) makes manure for the farm's arable fields. Few farmers persist with hand-milking (right). Machines will milk several cows at once, making the job much faster.

The arrival of a new spring

Where the dales rise towards the Pennines, sheep become the most numerous animals on the farms. The hardy Swaledale and Dalesbred ewes can carry their unborn lambs through the snowbound winter, when other animals would perish.

As the warmth of spring creeps over the hills, and the grass begins to grow again, the lambs are born.

NEW-BORN Only 30 minutes old, a new lamb is nuzzled by its mother.

BOTTLE-FED When a ewe has triplets, one of the lambs must be fed by hand.

TWINS Satisfaction at the end of a year's work – a ewe with her new-born twins.

WORK TEAM A shepherd and his dog walk miles a day tending their flock. Every season brings its work – mating, lambing, dipping, shearing.

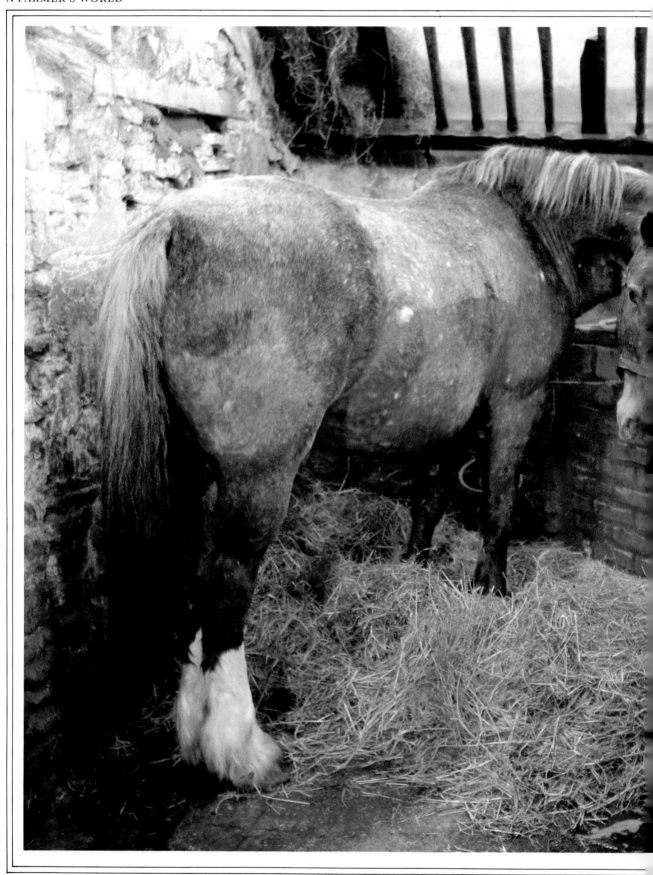

Dales ponies: reminders of a past age

North Yorkshire farmers stuck loyally to their horses long after most of Britain had moved into the age of the tractor. Even today a few of the farms in the dales and moors continue to maintain horses. The area even has its own breed, the strong and very hardy Dales ponies which require less winter fodder than other work horses and can live out in all types of weather. In addition to pulling carts and all manner of farm implements, a Dales pony could be harnessed to a trap to trot to market with a load of butter, eggs and cheese. Most important of all, they can struggle through winter blizzards with bales of hay tied to their backs to feed the snowbound and starving sheep.

OFF TO WORK A Dales crossbred is led out to be harnessed at a farm on the edge of the North York Moors where horses are now used mainly for carrying fodder to sheep.

VET'S LIVELIHOOD Farm horses are groomed with brushes and combs kept near at hand (above). The decline of the horse in the '30s and '40s sent shock waves through the veterinary world, which lost a major source of livelihood.

END OF A DAY Electricity now brings light to the most isolated farms of north Yorkshire, and power for radio a

...vision. In the 1930s, sunset brought little choice but supper and then sleep in preparation for the day to come.

COMFORT An old Yorkshire range, no longer used for cooking, still warms the kitchen on a winter's evening.

7

Shouts and whispers

There was a lot of shouting in the RAF. The NCOs always seemed to be shouting at me or at somebody else and a lot of them had impressively powerful voices. But for sheer volume I don't think any of them could beat Len Hampson.

I was on the way to Len's farm and on an impulse I pulled up the car and leaned for a moment on the wheel. It was a hot still day in late summer and this was one of the softer corners of the Dales, sheltered by the enclosing fells from the harsh winds which shrivelled all but the heather and the tough moorland grass.

Here, great trees, oak, elm and sycamore in full rich leaf, stood in gentle majesty in the green dips and hollows, their branches quite still in the windless air.

In all the grassy miles around me I could see no movement, nor could I hear anything except the fleeting hum of a bee and the distant bleating of a sheep.

Through the open window drifted the scents of summer; warm grass, clover and the sweetness of hidden flowers. But in the car they had to compete with the all-pervading smell of cow. I had spent the last hour injecting fifty wild cattle and I sat there in soiled breeches and sweat-soaked shirt looking out sleepily at the tranquil landscape.

I opened the door and Sam jumped out and trotted into a nearby wood. I followed him into the cool shade, into the damp secret fragrance of pine needles and fallen leaves which came from the dark heart of the crowding boles. From somewhere in the branches high above I could hear that most soothing of sounds, the cooing of a wood pigeon.

Then, although the farm was two fields away, I heard Len Hampson's voice. He wasn't calling the cattle home or anything like that. He was just conversing with his family as he always did in a long tireless shout.

I drove on to the farm and he opened the gate to let me into the yard.

'Good morning, Mr Hampson,' I said.

'NOW THEN, MR HERRIOT,' he bawled. 'IT'S A GRAND MORNIN'.'

The blast of sound drove me back a step but his three sons smiled contentedly. No doubt they were used to it.

I stayed at a safe distance. 'You want me to see a pig.'

'AYE, A GOOD BACON PIG. GONE RIGHT OFF. IT HASN'T ATE NOWT FOR TWO DAYS.'

We went into the pig pen and it was easy to pick out my patient. Most of the big white occupants careered around at the sight of a stranger, but one of them stood quietly in a corner.

It isn't often a pig will stand unresisting as you take its temperature

353

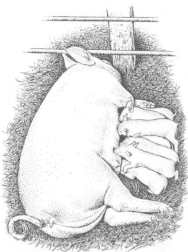

LARGE WHITE PIGS The Large White was originally bred in Yorkshire and by far the most numerous pig kept there. It became common in other parts of Britain, and abroad, and was often known as the Yorkshire pig. The Large White and the Landrace are the basis of the modern pig industry, while other breeds are dying out. A long-bodied pig that puts on meat at the hind end is what the breeder wants, and what the Large White can produce. It satisfies consumer demand for lean back rashers of bacon and lean legs of pork.

but this one never stirred as I slipped the thermometer into its rectum. There was only a slight fever but the animal had the look of doom about it; back slightly arched, unwilling to move, eyes withdrawn and anxious.

I looked up at Len Hampson's red-faced bulk leaning over the wall of the pen.

'Did this start suddenly or gradually?' I asked.

'RIGHT SUDDEN!' In the confined space the full-throated yell was deafening. 'HE WERE AS RIGHT AS NINEPENCE ON MONDAY NIGHT AND LIKE THIS ON TUESDAY MORNIN'.'

I felt my way over the pig's abdomen. The musculature was tense and boardlike and the abdominal contents were difficult to palpate because of this, but the whole area was tender to the touch.

'I've seen them like this before,' I said. 'This pig has a ruptured bowel. They do it when they are fighting or jostling each other, especially when they are full after a meal.'

'WHAT'S GOIN' TO 'APPEN THEN?'

'Well, the food material has leaked into the abdomen, causing peritonitis. I've opened up pigs like this and they are a mass of adhesions – the abdominal organs all growing together. I'm afraid the chances of recovery are very small.'

He took off his cap, scratched his bald head and replaced the tattered headgear. 'THAT'S A BUGGER. GOOD PIG AN' ALL. IS IT 'OPELESS?' He still gave tongue at the top of his voice despite his disappointment.

'Yes, I'm afraid it's pretty hopeless. They usually eat very little and just waste away. It would really be best to slaughter him.'

'NAY, AH DON'T LIKE THAT MUCH! AH ALLUS LIKE TO 'AVE A GO. ISN'T THERE SUMMAT WE CAN DO? WHERE THERE'S LIFE THERE'S 'OPE, THA KNAWS.'

I smiled. 'I suppose there's always some hope, Mr Hampson.'

'WELL THEN, LET'S GET ON. LET'S TRY!'

'All right.' I shrugged. 'He's not really in acute pain – more discomfort – so I suppose there's no harm in treating him. I'll leave you a course of powders.'

As I pushed my way from the pen I couldn't help noticing the superb sleek condition of the other pigs.

'My word,' I said. 'These pigs are in grand fettle. I've never seen a better lot. You must feed them well.'

It was a mistake. Enthusiasm added many decibels to his volume.

'AYE!' he bellowed. 'YOU'VE GOT TO GIVE STOCK A BIT O' GOOD STUFF TO MEK 'EM DO RIGHT!'

My head was still ringing when I reached the car and opened the boot. I handed over a packet of my faithful sulphonamide powders. They had done great things for me but I didn't expect much here.

It was strange that I should go straight from the chief shouter of the practice to the chief whisperer. Elijah Wentworth made all his communications *sotto voce*.

I found Mr Wentworth hosing down his cow byre and he turned and looked at me with his habitual serious expression. He was a tall, thin man, very precise in his speech and ways, and though he was a hard-working farmer he didn't look like one. This impression was heightened by his clothes which were more suited to office work than his rough trade.

A fairly new trilby hat sat straight on his head as he came over to me. I was able to examine it thoroughly because he came so close that we were almost touching noses.

He took a quick look around him. 'Mr Herriot,' he whispered, 'I've got a real bad case.' He spoke always as though every pronouncement was of the utmost gravity and secrecy.

'Oh I'm sorry to hear that. What's the trouble?'

'Fine big bullock, Mr Herriot. Goin' down fast.' He moved in closer till he could murmur directly into my ear. 'I suspect TB.' He backed away, face drawn.

'That's doesn't sound so good,' I said. 'Where is he?'

The farmer crooked a finger and I followed him into a loose box. The bullock was a Hereford Cross and should have weighed about ten hundredweight, but was gaunt and emaciated. I could understand Mr Wentworth's fears, but I was beginning to develop a clinical sense and it didn't look like TB to me.

'Is he coughing?' I asked.

'No, never coughs, but he's a bit skittered.'

I went over the animal carefully and there were a few things – the submaxillary oedema, the pot-bellied appearance, the pallor of the mucous membranes – which made diagnosis straightforward.

'I think he's got liver fluke, Mr Wentworth. I'll take a dung sample and have it examined for fluke eggs but I want to treat him right away.'

'Liver fluke? Where would he pick that up?'

'Usually from a wet pasture. Where has he been running lately?'

The farmer pointed through the door. 'Over yonder. I'll show you.'

I walked with him a few hundred yards and through a couple of gates into a wide flat field lying at the base of the fell. The squelchy feel of the turf and the scattered tufts of bog grass told the whole story.

'This is just the place for it,' I said. 'As you know, it's a parasite which infests the liver, but during its life cycle it has to pass through a snail and that snail can only live where there is water.'

He nodded slowly and solemnly several times then began to look around him and I knew he was going to say something. Again he came very close then scanned the horizon anxiously. In all directions the grassland stretched empty and bare for miles but he still seemed worried he might be overheard.

We were almost cheek to cheek as he breathed the words into my ear. 'Ah know who's to blame for this.'

'Really? Who is that?'

He made another swift check to ensure that nobody had sprung up

ADVERTISING MACHINERY There was keen competition among firms that made agricultural machines. They would set enamelled metal sheets bearing colourful advertisements in places where they would catch a farmer's eye – near the market-place for example. The mowing machine for the hay crop (left) and the reaper and binder for corn (right) were seen everywhere during 1930s summers, but a decade later tractors had taken over the work of the horses that pulled the machines. The tractor firms were also taking over the machine-making companies and adapting their products for towing behind tractors.

through the ground then I felt his hot breath again. 'It's me landlord.'

'How do you mean?'

'Won't do anything for me.' He brought his face round and looked at me wide-eyed before taking up his old position by my ear. 'Been goin' to drain this field for years but done nowt.'

I moved back. 'Ah well, I can't help that, Mr Wentworth. In any case there's other things you can do. You can kill the snails with copper sulphate – I'll tell you about that later – but in the meantime I want to dose your bullock.'

I had some hexachlorethane with me in the car and I mixed it in a bottle of water and administered it to the animal. Despite his bulk he offered no resistance as I held his lower jaw and poured the medicine down his throat.

'He's very weak, isn't he?' I said.

The farmer gave me a haggard look. 'He is that. I doubt he's a goner.'

'Oh don't give up hope, Mr Wentworth. I know he looks terrible but if it is fluke then the treatment will do a lot for him. Let me know how he goes on.'

It was about a month later, on a market day, and I was strolling among the stalls which packed the cobbles. In front of the entrance to the Drovers' Arms the usual press of farmers stood chatting among themselves, talking business with cattle dealers and corn merchants, while the shouts of the stallholders sounded over everything.

I was particularly fascinated by the man in charge of the sweet stall. He held up a paper bag and stuffed into it handfuls of assorted sweetmeats while he kept up a non-stop brazen-voiced commentary.

'Lovely peppermint drops! Delicious liquorice allsorts! How about some sugar candies! A couple o' bars o' chocolate! Let's 'ave some butterscotch an' all! Chuck in a beautiful slab o' Turkish Delight!' Then holding the bulging bag aloft in triumph ''ere! 'ere! Who'll give me a tanner for the lot?'

Amazing, I thought as I moved on. How did he do it? I was passing the door of the Drovers when a familiar voice hailed me.

'HEY! MR HERRIOT!' There was no mistaking Len Hampson. He hove in front of me, red-faced and cheerful. 'REMEMBER THAT PIG YE DOCTORED FOR ME?' He had clearly consumed a few market-day beers and his voice was louder than ever.

The packed mass of farmers pricked up their ears. There is nothing so intriguing as the ailments of another farmer's livestock.

'Yes, of course, Mr Hampson,' I replied.

'WELL 'E NEVER DID NO GOOD!' bawled Len.

I could see the farmers' faces lighting up. It is more interesting still when things go wrong.

'Really? Well I'm sorry.'

'NAW 'E DIDN'T. AH'VE NEVER SEEN A PIG GO DOWN AS FAST!'

'Is that so?'

CHOCOLATE BOYS After 150 years of chocolate-making, Fry's of Bristol introduced their Five Boys bar in 1902. Generations of children loved it and spent their pocket money on it. In 1937, 40 million bars were sold at one old penny (less than ½p) each. The joy for children was to see their own moods mirrored in the faces moulded on the bar and to arrange and rearrange the boys before deciding the order in which they were to be munched. The last Five Boys bars were made in 1970.

'AYE, FLESH JUST MELTED OFF 'IM!'

'Oh, what a pity. But if you recall I rather expected ...'

'WENT DOWN TO SKIN AND BONE 'E DID!' The great bellow rolled over the market place, drowning the puny cries of the stallholders. In fact the man with the sweets had suspended operations and was listening with as much interest as the others.

I looked around me uneasily. 'Well, Mr Hampson, I did warn you at the time ...'

'LIKE A WALKIN' SKELETON 'E WERE! NEVER SEEN SUCH A OBJECK!'

I realised Len wasn't in the least complaining. He was just telling me, but for all that I wished he would stop.

'Well, thank you for letting me know,' I said. 'Now I really must be off ...'

'AH DON'T KNOW WHAT THEM POWDERS WERE YOU GAVE 'IM.'

I cleared my throat. 'Actually they were ...'

'THEY DID 'IM NO BLOODY GOOD ANY ROAD!'

'I see. Well as I say, I have to run ...'

'AH GOT MALLOCK TO KNOCK 'IM ON T'HEAD LAST WEEK.'

'Oh dear ...'

'FINISHED UP AS DOG MEAT, POOR BUGGER!'

'Quite ... quite ...'

'WELL, GOOD DAY TO YE, MR HERRIOT.' He turned and walked away, leaving a quivering silence behind him.

With an uncomfortable feeling that I was the centre of attention I was about to retreat hastily when I felt a gentle hand on my arm. I turned and saw Elijah Wentworth.

'Mr Herriot,' he whispered. 'About that bullock.'

I stared at him, struck by the coincidence. The farmers stared, too, but expectantly.

'Yes, Mr Wentworth?'

'Well now, I'll tell you.' He came very near and breathed into my ear. 'It was like a miracle. He began to pick up straight away after you treated him.'

I stepped back. 'Oh marvellous! But speak up, will you, I can't quite hear you.' I looked around hopefully.

He came after me again and put his chin on my shoulder. 'Yes, I don't know what you gave 'im but it was wonderful stuff. I could hardly believe it. Every day I looked at 'im he had put on a bit more.'

'Great! But do speak a little louder,' I said eagerly.

'He's as fat as butter now.' The almost inaudible murmur wafted on my cheek. 'Ah'm sure he'll get top grade at the auction mart.'

I backed away again. 'Yes ... yes ... what was that you said?'

'I was sure he was dyin', Mr Herriot, but you saved him by your skill,' he said, but every word was pianissimo, sighed against my face.

The farmers had heard nothing and, their interest evaporating, they began to talk among themselves. Then as the man with the sweets started to fill his bags and shout again Mr Wentworth moved in and

HEREFORD BULL The broad, yellow-horned white head, slightly waved red coat, and white under-belly of Hereford beef cattle are seen all over Britain – where they are the most numerous beef breed. They are also bred in Canada, Australia, Argentina and on the cattle ranches of the American West. No breed can outdo the Hereford for hardiness. It originated centuries ago in Welsh border country, lives out of doors the year round, undefeated by cold or drought, and fattens early and well on grass without needing extra food. These qualities are transmitted to any Hereford bull's offspring and, no matter what breed of cow is the mother, the calf will be stocky and white-faced.

confided softly and secretly into my private ear.

'That was the most brilliant and marvellous cure I 'ave ever seen.'

8

Sweet revenge

'That young Herriot's a bloody thick-'ead.'

It wasn't the sort of statement to raise one's morale and for a moment the good ale turned to vinegar in my mouth. I was having a quiet pint all alone in the 'snug' of the Crown and Anchor on my way home from an evening colic case, and the words came clearly through the hatch from the public bar.

I suppose it was the fact that I had come to the conclusion that my flying instructor, F.O. Woodham, considered me to be a person of low intelligence that brought the incident back to my mind.

I shifted my position slightly so that I could see into the brightly lit room. The speaker was Seth Pilling, a casual labourer and a well known character in Darrowby. He was designated a labourer, but in truth he didn't labour unduly and his burly frame and red meaty face was a common sight around the Labour Exchange where he signed for his unemployment pay.

'Aye, 'e's got no idea. Knaws nowt about dogs.' The big man tipped about half a pint over his throat in one swallow.

'He's not a bad hand wi' cows,' another voice broke in.

'Aye, maybe, but I'm not talkin' about bloody awd cows,' Seth retorted witheringly. 'I'm talkin' about dogs. Ye need skill to doctor dogs.'

A third man spoke up. 'Well, 'e's a vitnery, isn't he?'

'Aye, a knaw he is, but there's all kind o' vitneries and this 'un's a dead loss. Ah could tell ye some tales about this feller.'

They say an eavesdropper never hears anything good about himself, and I knew the sensible thing would be to get out of there immediately rather than hear this man vilifying me in a crowded bar. But of course I didn't get out. I stayed, morbidly fascinated, listening with every nerve and fibre.

'What sort o' tales, Seth?' The company was as interested as I was.

'Well,' he replied. 'There's many a time folks 'ave brought dogs to me that he's made a mess of.'

'Tha knaws all about dogs, doesn't tha, Seth?'

It was perhaps wishful thinking that made me imagine a touch of sarcasm in the last remark, but if it were so it was lost on Mr Pilling. His big, stupid face creased into a self-satisfied smirk.

'Ah'll tell ye there's not a lot ah don't know about 'em. I've been among 'em all me life and I've studied t'job, too.' He slurped down more beer. 'I've got a houseful o' books and read 'em all. Ah ken everythin' about them diseases and the remedies.'

Another of the men in the bar spoke. 'Have ye never been beat wi' a dog job, Seth?'

There was a pause. 'Well ah'm not goin' to say I never 'ave,' he said judicially. 'It's very rare I'm beat, but if I am I don't go to Herriot.' He shook his head. 'Nay, nay, ah slip through to Brawton and consult wi' Dennaby Broome. He's a big friend o' mine.'

In the quiet of the snug I sipped at my glass. Dennaby Broome was one of the many 'quacks' who flourished in those days. He had started in the building trade – as a plasterer to be exact – and had gravitated mysteriously and without formal training into the field of veterinary science where he now made a comfortable living.

I had nothing against him for that – we all have to live. In any case he rarely bothered me because Brawton was mainly outside our practice orbit, but my colleagues around there used some unkind words about him. I had a private conviction that a lot of his success was due to his resounding name. To me, the very words 'Dennaby Broome' were profoundly imposing.

The speaker was Seth Pilling, a casual labourer and well-known character.

KEESHOUND Guarding Dutch barges was the job of this handsome dog for hundreds of years. Its grey coat is thick and harsh and it has a large ruff framing its neat, fox-like face. Bushy 'trousers' clothe its legs, and a feathered tail curls over its back. Energy pulsates from its 18 in. high body. It moves busily, looks watchful and gives out a commanding bark. It was introduced into Britain about 1900, but as a pet and show dog, not a worker.

'Aye, that's what ah do,' Seth continued. 'Dennaby and me's big friends and we oft consult about dogs. Matter of fact ah took me own dog to 'im once – he looks well, eh?'

I stood on tiptoe and peered into the bar. I could just see Seth's keeshound sitting at his feet. A handsome creature with a luxuriant glossy coat. The big man leaned over and patted the fox-like head. 'He's a vallible animal is that. Ah couldn't trust 'im to a feller like Herriot.'

'What's the matter wi' Herriot, any road?' somebody asked.

'Well, ah'll tell tha.' Seth tapped his head. 'He hasn't got over much up 'ere.'

I didn't want to hear any more. I put down my glass and stole out into the night.

After that experience I took more notice of Seth Pilling. He was often to be seen strolling round the town because, despite his vast store of knowledge on many subjects, he was frequently out of work. He wasn't an expert only on dogs – he pontificated in the Crown and Anchor on politics, gardening, cage birds, agriculture, the state of the economy, cricket, fishing and many other matters. There were few topics which his wide intellect did not effortlessly embrace, so that it was surprising that employers seemed to dispense with his services after a very brief period.

He usually took his dog with him on his strolls, and the attractive animal began to appear to me as a symbol of my shortcomings. Instinctively I kept out of his way but one morning I came right up against him.

It was at the little shelter in the market place and a group of people were waiting for the Brawton bus. Among them was Seth Pilling and the keeshound, and as I passed within a few feet of them on my way to the post office I stopped involuntarily and stared. The dog was almost unrecognisable.

The dense, off-standing ash-grey coat I knew so well had become sparse and lustreless. The thick ruff, so characteristic of the breed, had shrunk to nothing.

'You're lookin' at me dog?' Mr Pilling tightened the lead and pulled the little animal towards him protectively as though he feared I might put my contaminating hand on him.

'Yes ... I'm sorry, but I couldn't help noticing. He has a skin condition ...?'

The big man looked down his nose at me. 'Aye, 'e has, a bit. I'm just takin' him through to Brawton to see Dennaby Broome.'

'I see.'

'Yes, ah thought ah'd better take 'im to somebody as knows summat about dogs.' He smirked as he looked around at the people in the shelter who were listening with interest. 'He's a vallible dog is that.'

'I'm sure he is,' I said.

He raised his voice further. 'Mind you, ah've been givin' him some of me own treatment.' He didn't have to tell me. There was a strong smell of tar, and the dog's hair was streaked with some oily substance. 'But it's maybe better to make sure. We're lucky to 'ave a man like Dennaby Broome to turn to.'

'Quite.'

He looked around his audience appreciatively. 'Especially with a vallible dog like this. You can't 'ave any Tom, Dick or Harry muckin' around with 'im.'

'Well,' I said. 'I hope you get him put right.'

'Oh, ah will.' The big man was enjoying the interlude, and he laughed. 'Don't *you* worry about *that*.'

This little session did not enliven my day, but it gave me more reason to watch out for Mr Pilling. For the next two weeks I observed his movements with the deepest interest because his dog was losing its hair at an alarming rate. Not only that, but the animal's whole demeanour had changed and instead of tripping along in his old sprightly way he dragged one foot after another as though he were on the point of death.

Towards the end of the period I was horrified to see the big man with something like a shorn ewe on the end of the lead. It was all that was left of the beautiful keeshound, but as I started to walk towards him his master spotted me and hurried off in the opposite direction, dragging the unfortunate animal behind him.

I did, however, succeed in having a look at the dog a few days afterwards. He was in the waiting room at Skeldale House, and this time he was accompanied by his mistress instead of his master.

Mrs Pilling was sitting very upright, and when I asked her to come through to the consulting room she jumped to her feet, marched past me and stumped quickly along the passage in front of me.

She was quite small, but broad hipped and stocky, and she always walked rapidly, her head nodding forward aggressively at each step, her jaw thrust out. She never smiled.

I had heard it said that Seth Pilling was a big talker outside, but under his own roof he was scared to death of his little wife. And as the tight-mouthed fiery-eyed face turned to me I could believe it.

She bent, pushed powerful arms under the keeshound and hoisted him on to the table.

'Just look at me good dog, Mr Herriot!' She rapped out.

I looked. 'Good heavens!' I gasped.

The little animal was almost completely bald. His skin was dry, scaly and wrinkled, and his head hung down as though he were under sedation.

'Aye, you're surprised, aren't you?' she barked. 'And no wonder. He's in a terrible state, isn't he?'

'I'm afraid so. I wouldn't have known him.'

'No, nobody would. Ah think the world 'o this dog and just look at 'im!' She paused and snorted a few times. 'And I know who's responsible, don't you?'

'Well. . . .'

'Oh, you do. It's that husband o' mine.' She paused and glared at me,

THE BUS SERVICE The steep, narrow lanes and their poor surfaces made regular bus services slow to penetrate north Yorkshire villages, but in 1926 the Wensleydale Bus Service started operating and by 1930 United Automobile Services ran buses in large areas of the Dales. From then on, week-end excursions from the industrial West Riding brought many visitors into the villages, and Dalesfolk could reach the market towns more easily – and go further afield to Richmond, Ripon, Harrogate and even Leeds for special shopping.

361

CUTTING TURF Supplies of fuel for winter were gathered in the previous spring when lambing had finished. Turf or peat was gathered according to which was plentiful locally. A turf cutter wore a leather apron that held in place wooden bars to protect him from too much bruising. He pushed with his body against the spade cross-handle to pare off pieces of turf. He turned the pieces over to lie soil-side up, waiting to be stacked. If the turves were wet, they were propped up three together on their sides for a week before being stacked. The stacks, or rooks, were left to dry out for about three weeks before the turves were taken back to the farm or cottage.

breathing rapidly. 'What d'you think of my husband, Mr Herriot?'

'I really don't know him very well. I ...'

'Well ah know 'im and he's a gawp. He's a great gawp. Knows everything and knows nowt. He's played around wi' me good dog till he's ruined 'im.'

I didn't say anything. I was studying the keeshound. It was the first time I had been able to observe him closely and I was certain I knew the cause of his trouble.

Mrs Pilling stuck her jaw out further and continued.

'First me husband said it was eczema. Is it?'

'No.'

'Then 'e said it was mange. Is it?'

'No.'

'D'you know what it is?'

'Yes.'

'Well, will you tell me please?'

'It's myxoedema.'

'Myx ...?'

'Wait a minute,' I said. 'I'll just make absolutely sure.' I reached for my stethoscope and put it on the dog's chest. And the bradycardia was there as I expected, the slow, slow heartbeat of hypothyroidism. 'Yes, that's it. Not a shadow of a doubt about it.'

'What did you call it?'

'Myxoedema. It's a thyroid deficiency – there's a gland in his neck which isn't doing its job properly.'

'And that makes 'is hair fall out?'

'Oh yes. And it also causes this typical scaliness and wrinkling of the skin.'

'Aye, but he's half asleep all t'time. How about that?'

'Another classical symptom. Dogs with this condition become very lethargic – lose all their energy.'

She reached out and touched the dog's skin, bare and leathery where once the coat had grown in bushy glory. 'And can you cure it?'

'Yes.'

'Now Mr Herriot, don't take this the wrong way, but could you be mistaken? Are ye positive it's this myxi-whatever-it-is?'

'Of course I am. It's a straightforward case.'

'Straightforward to you, maybe.' She flushed and appeared to be grinding her teeth. 'But not straightforward to that clever husband o' mine. The great lubbert! When ah think what he's put me good dog through – ah could kill 'im.'

'Well, I suppose he thought he was acting for the best, Mrs Pilling.'

'Ah don't care what he thought, he's made this poor dog suffer, the big fool. Wait till ah get hold of 'im.'

I gave her a supply of tablets. 'These are thyroid extract, and I want you to give him one night and morning.' I also handed her a bottle of potassium iodide which I had found helpful in these cases.

She looked at me doubtfully. 'But surely he'll want summat rubbed on 'is skin.'

'No,' I replied. 'Applications to the skin do no good at all.'

'Then you mean.' She turned a dark purple colour and began snorting again. 'You mean all them bottles o' filthy stuff me husband put on 'im were a waste o' time?'

'Afraid so.'

'Oh ah'll murder 'im!' she burst out. 'Mucky, oily rubbish, it was. And that fancy feller in Brawton sent some 'orrible lotion – yeller it was, and stank the place out. Ruined me carpets and good chair covers an' all!'

Sulphur, whale oil and creosote, I thought. Splendid old fashioned ingredients, but quite useless in this case and definitely antisocial.

Mrs Pilling heaved the keeshound to the floor and strode along the passage, head down, powerful shoulders hunched. I could hear her muttering to herself as she went.

'By gaw, just wait till ah get home. Ah'll sort 'im, by gaw ah will!'

I was naturally interested in the progress of my patient, and when I failed to see him around for the next fortnight I could only conclude that Seth Pilling was keeping out of my way. Indeed there was one occasion when I thought I saw him and the dog disappearing down an alley, but I couldn't be sure.

When I did see them both it was by accident. I was driving round the corner into the market place and I came upon a man and dog coming away from one of the stalls on the cobbles.

And as I peered through the window I caught my breath. Even in that short space of time the animal's skin was covered with a healthy down of new hair, and he was stepping out with something very like his old vitality.

His master swung round as I slowed down. He gave me a single hunted look then tugged on the lead and scuttled away.

I could only imagine the turmoil in his mind, the conflict of emotions. No doubt he wanted to see his dog recover, but not this way. And as it turned out, the dice were loaded against the poor man because this was an unbelievably rapid recovery. I have seen some spectacular cures in myxoedema, but none so dramatic as that keeshound.

Mr Pilling's sufferings were communicated to me in various ways. For instance I heard he had changed his pub and now went to the Red Bear of an evening. In a little place like Darrowby, news fairly crackles around and I had a good idea that the farm men in the Crown and Anchor would have had a bit of quiet Yorkshire sport with the expert.

But his main martyrdom was at home. It was about six weeks after I had finished treating the dog that Mrs Pilling brought him to the surgery.

As before, she lifted him easily on to the table and looked at me, her face as always grim and unsmiling.

TURF SPADES AND RAKE Steel blades made for spades by local blacksmiths varied in style, and joiners made wooden handles to suit the height of the man who was going to use the spade. A cock blade had one right-angled flange so that it cut the base and one side of the turf. The less common hen blade had two curved flanges and cut the base and both sides. It was used where there was not an unbroken carpet of turf. Two-pronged rakes were used to pull turves from a rook.

RESTRAINING SHEEP An ungainly but effective device for restricting the movement of a sheep that is inclined to wander is made from three slender branches fixed round its neck as a triangular frame with the six ends sticking out. This prevents the animal from going through slit stiles, wriggling out of a pen, or forcing its way through any small gap in a fence or hedge.

'Mr Herriot,' she said. 'Ah've just come to say thank ye, and ah thought you'd be interested to see me dog now.'

'I am indeed, Mrs Pilling. It's nice of you to come.' I gazed wonderingly at the thick coat, bushy, shining and new, and at the sparkling eyes and alert expression. 'I think you can say he's about back to normal.'

She nodded. 'That's what I thought and ah'm grateful to ye for what you've done.'

I walked with her to the front door and as she led her dog onto the street she turned her tough little face to me again. As the stern eyes met mine she looked very menacing.

'There's one thing,' she said. 'Ah'll never forgive that man o' mine for what he did to me dog. By gum, I've given 'im some stick, the great goof! He'll never hear the last of it from me.'

As she made off down the street, the little animal trotting briskly by her side, I brimmed with pleasant emotions. It is always warming to see a case recover so well, but in this instance there was an additional bonus.

For a long time little Mrs Pilling was going to give her husband pure hell.

9

Night of the Hunt Ball

To me there are few things more appealing than a dog begging. This one was tied to a lamp post outside a shop in Windsor. Its eyes were fixed steadfastly on the shop doorway, willing its owner to come out, and every now and then it sat up in mute entreaty.

Flying had been suspended for an afternoon. It gave us all a chance to relax and no doubt it eased the frayed nerves of our instructors, but as I looked at that dog all the pressures of the RAF fell away and I was back in Darrowby.

It was when Siegfried and I were making one of our market day sorties that we noticed the little dog among the stalls.

When things were quiet in the surgery we often used to walk together across the cobbles and have a word with the farmers gathered round the doorway of the Drovers' Arms. Sometimes we collected a few outstanding bills or drummed up a bit of work for the forthcoming week – and if nothing like that happened we still enjoyed the fresh air.

The thing that made us notice the dog was that he was sitting up begging in front of the biscuit stall.

'Look at that little chap,' Siegfried said. 'I wonder where he's sprung from.'

As he spoke, the stallholder threw a biscuit which the dog devoured eagerly but when the man came round and stretched out a hand the little animal trotted away.

He stopped, however, at another stall which sold produce; eggs, cheese, butter, cakes and scones. Without hesitation he sat up again in the begging position, rock steady, paws dangling, head pointing expectantly.

I nudged Siegfried. 'There he goes again.'

My colleague nodded. 'Yes, he's an engaging little thing, isn't he? What breed would you call him?'

'A cross, I'd say. He's like a little brown sheepdog, but there's a touch of something else – maybe terrier.'

It wasn't long before he was munching a bun, and this time we walked over to him. And as we drew near I spoke gently.

'Here, boy,' I said, squatting down a yard away. 'Come on, let's have a look at you.'

He faced me and for a moment two friendly brown eyes gazed at me from a singularly attractive little face. The fringed tail waved in response to my words but as I inched nearer he turned and ambled unhurriedly among the market day crowd till he was lost to sight. I didn't want to make a thing out of the encounter because I could never quite divine Siegfried's attitude to the small animals. He was eminently wrapped up in his horse work and often seemed amused at the way I rushed around after dogs and cats.

At that time, in fact, Siegfried was strongly opposed to the whole idea of keeping animals as pets. He was quite vociferous on the subject – said it was utterly foolish – despite the fact that five assorted dogs travelled everywhere with him in his car. Now, thirty-five years later, he is just as strongly in favour of keeping pets, though he now carries only one dog in his car. So, as I say, it was difficult to assess his reactions in this field and I refrained from following the little animal.

I was standing there when a young policeman came up to me.

'I've been watching that little dog begging among the stalls all morning,' he said. 'But like you, I haven't been able to get near him.'

'Yes, it's strange. He's obviously friendly, yet he's afraid. I wonder who owns him.'

'I reckon he's a stray, Mr Herriot. I'm interested in dogs myself and I fancy I know just about all of them around here. But this 'un's a stranger to me.'

I nodded. 'I bet you're right. So anything could have happened to him. He could have been ill-treated by somebody and run away, or he could have been dumped from a car.'

'Yes,' he replied. 'There's some lovely people around. It beats me how anybody can leave a helpless animal to fend for itself like that. I've had a few goes at catching him myself but it's no good.'

The memory stayed with me for the rest of the day and even when I lay in bed that night I was unable to dispel the disturbing image of the

CHEESE TRAVES Cheeses were put on traves, or loose shelves, to dry out. At first they were turned twice a day, then once a day for a fortnight and afterwards on alternate days until they were sent to market or sold to the factor in October or November ready for the Christmas trade. Moisture oozed from the maturing cheeses, in large amounts at first, and the traves needed frequent wiping down until the cheese had dried.

little brown creature wandering in a strange world, sitting up asking for help in the only way he knew.

I was still a bachelor at that time and on the Friday night of the same week Siegfried and I were arraying ourselves in evening dress in preparation for the Hunt Ball at East Hirdsley, about ten miles away.

It was a tortuous business because those were the days of starched shirt fronts and stiff high collars and I kept hearing explosions of colourful language from Siegfried's room as he wrestled with his studs.

I was in an even worse plight because I had outgrown my suit and even when I had managed to secure the strangling collar I had to fight my way into the dinner jacket which nipped me cruelly under the arms. I had just managed to don the complete outfit and was trying out a few careful breaths when the phone rang.

It was the same young policeman I had been speaking to earlier in the week. 'We've got that dog round here, Mr Herriot. You know – the one that was begging in the market place.'

'Oh yes? Somebody's managed to catch him, then?'

There was a pause. 'No, not really. One of our men found him lying by the roadside about a mile out of town and brought him in. He's been in an accident.'

I told Siegfried. He looked at his watch. 'Always happens, doesn't it, James. Just when we're ready to go out. It's nine o'clock now and we should be on our way.' He thought for a moment. 'Anyway, slip round there and have a look and I'll wait for you. It would be better if we could go to this affair together.'

As I drove round to the Police Station I hoped fervently that there wouldn't be much to do. This Hunt Ball meant a lot to my boss because it would be a gathering of the horse-loving fraternity of the district and he would have a wonderful time just chatting and drinking with so many kindred spirits even though he hardly danced at all. Also, he maintained, it was good for business to meet the clients socially.

The kennels were at the bottom of a yard behind the Station and the policeman led me down and opened one of the doors. The little dog was lying very still under the single electric bulb and when I bent and stroked the brown coat his tail stirred briefly among the straw of his bed.

'He can still manage a wag, anyway,' I said.

The policeman nodded. 'Aye, there's no doubt he's a good-natured little thing.'

I tried to examine him as much as possible without touching. I didn't want to hurt him and there was no saying what the extent of his injuries might be. But even at a glance certain things were obvious; he had multiple lacerations, one hind leg was crooked in the unmistakable posture of a fracture and there was blood on his lips.

This could be from damaged teeth and I gently raised the head with a view to looking into his mouth. He was lying on his right side and as the head came round it was as though somebody had struck me in the face.

MAKING BESOMS Thin strips of ash peeled from a log 3½ ft long made the lappings, or bands, that held a bundle of ling, or heather, together for a besom. The bundle was held by foot-operated metal nippers while four to nine lappings were bound round it. Some farmers made their own besoms, but cottagers earned money by making them in large quantities – more than 200 a day in some families. On the farm, besoms were for cleaning boots and brushing out the cow byre and stable. The foundries of shipyards also used them to skim the scum off molten metal.

366

The right eye had been violently dislodged from its socket and it sprouted like some hideous growth from above the cheek bone, a great glistening orb with the eyelids tucked behind the white expanse of sclera.

I seemed to squat there for a long time, stunned by the obscenity, and as the seconds dragged by I looked into the little dog's face and he looked back at me – trustingly from one soft brown eye, glaring meaninglessly from the grotesque ball on the other side.

The policeman's voice broke my thoughts. 'He's a mess, isn't he?'

'Yes ... yes ... must have been struck by some vehicle – maybe dragged along by the look of all those wounds.'

'What d'you think, Mr Herriot?'

I knew what he meant. It was the sensible thing to ease this lost unwanted creature from the world. He was grievously hurt and he didn't seem to belong to anybody. A quick overdose of anaesthetic – his troubles would be over and I'd be on my way to the dance.

But the policeman didn't say anything of the sort. Maybe, like me, he was looking into the soft depths of that one trusting eye.

I stood up quickly. 'Can I use your phone?'

At the other end of the line Siegfried's voice crackled with impatience. 'Hell, James, it's half-past nine! If we're going to this thing we've got to go now or we might as well not bother. A stray dog, badly injured. It doesn't sound such a great problem.'

'I know, Siegfried. I'm sorry to hold you up but I can't make up my mind. I wish you'd come round and tell me what you think.'

There was a silence then a long sigh. 'All right, James. See you in five minutes.'

He created a slight stir as he entered the Station. Even in his casual working clothes Siegfried always managed to look distinguished, but as he swept into the station newly bathed and shaved, a camel coat thrown over the sparkling white shirt and black tie there was something ducal about him.

He drew respectful glances from the men sitting around, then my young policeman stepped forward.

'This way, sir,' he said, and we went back to the kennels.

Siegfried was silent as he crouched over the dog, looking him over as I had done without touching him. Then he carefully raised the head and the monstrous eye glared.

'My God!' he said softly, and at the sound of his voice the long fringed tail moved along the ground.

For a few seconds he stayed very still looking fixedly at the dog's face while in the silence, the whisking tail rustled the straw.

Then he straightened up. 'Let's get him round there,' he murmured.

In the surgery we anaesthetised the little animal and as he lay unconscious on the table we were able to examine him thoroughly. After a few minutes Siegfried stuffed his stethoscope into the pocket of his white coat and leaned both hands on the table.

PIECING A TYRE To prepare the iron tyre for a wagon wheel, the wheelwright bends the measured strip in a roller machine. Then the ends are heated to piece, or weld, them together. The whole tyre is made red hot for dropping over the wooden wheel, which is clamped on the ground. A drenching with water makes the tyre contract tightly on to the wooden rim.

'Luxated eyeball, fractured femur, umpteen deep lacerations, broken claws. There's enough here to keep us going till midnight, James.'

I didn't say anything.

My boss pulled the knot from his black tie and undid the front stud. He peeled off the stiff collar and hung it on the cross bar of the surgery lamp.

'By God, that's better,' he muttered, and began to lay out suture materials.

I looked at him across the table. 'How about the Hunt Ball?'

'Oh bugger the Hunt Ball,' Siegfried said. 'Let's get busy.'

We were busy, too, for a long time. I hung up my collar next to my colleague's and we began on the eye. I know we both felt the same – we wanted to get rid of that horror before we did anything else.

I lubricated the great ball and pulled the eyelids apart while Siegfried gently manoeuvred it back into the orbital cavity. I sighed as everything slid out of sight, leaving only the cornea visible.

Siegfried chuckled with satisfaction. 'Looks like an eye again, doesn't it.' He seized an ophthalmoscope and peered into the depths.

'And there's no major damage – could be as good as new again. But we'll just stitch the lids together to protect it for a few days.'

The broken ends of the fractured tibia were badly displaced and we had a struggle to bring them into apposition before applying the plaster of paris. But at last we finished and started on the long job of stitching the many cuts and lacerations.

We worked separately for this, and for a long time it was quiet in the operating room except for the snip of scissors as we clipped the brown hair away from the wounds. I knew and Siegfried knew that we were almost certainly working without payment, but the most disturbing thought was that after all our efforts we might still have to put him down. He was still in the care of the police and if nobody claimed him within ten days it meant euthanasia. And if his late owners were really interested in his fate, why hadn't they tried to contact the police before now . . .

By the time we had completed our work and washed the instruments it was after midnight. Siegfried dropped the last suture needle into its tray and looked at the sleeping animal.

'I think he's beginning to come round,' he said. 'Let's take him through to the fire and we can have a drink while he recovers.'

We stretchered the dog through to the sitting-room on a blanket and laid him on the rug before the brightly burning coals. My colleague reached a long arm up to the glass-fronted cabinet above the mantel-piece and pulled down the whisky bottle and two glasses. Drinks in hand, collarless, still in shirt sleeves, with our starched white fronts and braided evening trousers to remind us of the lost dance we lay back in our chairs on either side of the fireplace and between us our patient stretched peacefully.

He was a happier sight now. One eye was closed by the protecting

MECHANICAL SWATHE-TURNER
Horse-drawn equipment for turning the hay cut out the laborious process of turning with a hand-rake. The turner was used, when the top of the cut swathes had dried, to lift the swathes and flick them sideways for the other side to dry. The machine is often called a side-delivery rake. It came into use soon after 1900 and is still used, but since the 1940s has been tractor-drawn rather than horse-drawn.

stitches and his hind leg projected stiffly in its white cast, but he was tidy, cleaned up, cared for. He looked as though he belonged to somebody – but then there was a great big doubt about that.

It was nearly one o'clock in the morning and we were getting well down the bottle when the shaggy brown head began to move.

Siegfried leaned forward and touched one of the ears and immediately the tail flapped against the rug and a pink tongue lazily licked his fingers.

'What an absolutely grand little dog,' he murmured, but his voice had a distant quality. I knew he was worried too.

I took the stitches out of the eyelids in two days and was delighted to find a normal eye underneath.

The young policeman was as pleased as I was. 'Look at that!' he exclaimed. 'You'd never know anything had happened there.'

'Yes, it's done wonderfully well. All the swelling and inflammation has gone.' I hesitated for a moment. 'Has anybody enquired about him?'

He shook his head. 'Nothing yet. But there's another eight days to go and we're taking good care of him here.'

I visited the Police Station several times and the little animal greeted me with undisguised joy, all his fear gone, standing upright against my legs on his plastered limb, his tail swishing.

But all the time my sense of foreboding increased, and on the tenth day I made my way almost with dread to the police kennels. I had heard nothing. My course of action seemed inevitable. Putting down old or hopelessly ill dogs was often an act of mercy but when it was a young healthy dog it was terrible. I hated it, but it was one of the things veterinary surgeons had to do.

The young policeman was standing in the doorway.

'Still no news?' I asked, and he shook his head.

I went past him into the kennel and the shaggy little creature stood up against my legs as before, laughing into my face, mouth open, eyes shining.

I turned away quickly. I'd have to do this right now or I'd never do it.

'Mr Herriot.' The policeman put his hand on my arm. 'I think I'll take him.'

'You?' I stared at him.

'Aye, that's right. We get a lot o' stray dogs in here and though I feel sorry for them you can't give them all a home, can you?'

'No, you can't,' I said. 'I have the same problem.'

He nodded slowly. 'But somehow this 'un's different, and it seems to me he's just come at the right time. I have two little girls and they've been at me for a bit to get 'em a dog. This little bloke looks just right for the job.'

Warm relief began to ebb through me. 'I couldn't agree more. He's the soul of good nature. I bet he'll be wonderful with children.'

'Good. That's settled then. I thought I'd ask your advice first.' He

THE SWING PLOUGH A strong, skilled man was needed to guide and balance a swing plough, which had no wheels to assist him – but neither did it have wheels to get stuck in heavy land. Generally it made ploughing harder work for man and horse, particularly on steep Dales fields. Two horses were usually harnessed to it abreast.

The triangular blade of the ploughshare made a horizontal cut below the surface, the knife-like coulter above it made a vertical cut, and the curving mouldboard behind the ploughshare lifted and turned over the furrow.

smiled happily.

I looked at him as though I had never seen him before. 'What's your name?'

'Phelps,' he replied. 'P.C. Phelps.'

He was a good-looking young fellow, clear-skinned, with cheerful blue eyes and a solid dependable look about him. I had to fight against an impulse to wring his hand and thump him on the back. But I managed to preserve the professional exterior.

'Well, that's fine.' I bent and stroked the little dog. 'Don't forget to bring him along to the surgery in ten days for removal of the stitches, and we'll have to get that plaster off in about a month.'

It was Siegfried who took out the stitches, and I didn't see our patient again until four weeks later.

P.C. Phelps had his little girls, aged four and six, with him as well as the dog.

'You said the plaster ought to come off about now,' he said, and I nodded.

He looked down at the children. 'Well, come on, you two, lift him on the table.'

Eagerly the little girls put their arms around their new pet and as they hoisted him the tail wagged furiously and the wide mouth panted in delight.

'Looks as though he's been a success,' I said.

He smiled. 'That's an understatement. He's perfect with these two. I can't tell you what pleasure he's given us. He's one of the family.'

I got out my little saw and began to hack at the plaster.

'It's worked both ways, I should say. A dog loves a secure home.'

'Well, he couldn't be more secure.' He ran his hand along the brown coat and laughed as he addressed the little dog. 'That's what you get for begging among the stalls on market day, my lad. You're in the hands of the law now.'

10

A word with Mr Harcourt

When I entered the RAF I had a secret fear. All my life I have suffered from vertigo and even now I have only to look down from the smallest height to be engulfed by that dreadful dizziness and panic. What would I feel, then, when I started to fly?

As it turned out, I felt nothing. I could gaze downwards from the open cockpit through thousands of feet of space without a qualm, so my fear

A TIP-CART In its sturdy oak frame, box-like plank body and single axle with large wheels, the tip-cart or tumbril was much the same as other farm carts. What distinguished it was the rod-and-pin or ratchet mechanism at the front end. When this was released, the front of the cart rose without the horse having to be taken out of the shafts. The load – of manure, hay, turnips or animals – was easily taken out from the rear. Carts were cheaper than wagons and, being shorter, were more suitable for steep and winding lanes. In the Dales, carts were much more common than wagons.

was groundless.

I had my fears in veterinary practice, too, and in the early days the thing which raised the greatest terror in my breast was the Ministry of Agriculture.

An extraordinary statement, perhaps, but true. It was the clerical side that scared me – all those forms. As to the practical Ministry work itself, I felt in all modesty that I was quite good at it. My thoughts often turned back to all the tuberculin testing I used to do – clipping a clean little area from just the right place in the cow's neck, inserting the needle into the thickness of the skin and injecting one tenth of a c.c. of tuberculin.

It was on Mr Hill's farm, and I watched the satisfactory intradermal 'pea' rise up under my needle. That was the way it should be, and when it came up like that you knew you were really doing your job and testing the animal for tuberculosis.

'That 'un's number 65,' the farmer said, then a slightly injured look spread over his face as I checked the number in the ear.

'You're wastin' your time, Mr Herriot. I 'ave the whole list, all in t'correct order. Wrote it out special for you so you could take it away with you.'

I had my doubts. All farmers were convinced that their herd records were flawless but I had been caught out before. I seemed to have the gift of making every possible clerical mistake and I didn't need any help from the farmers.

But still … it was tempting. I looked at the long list of figures dangling from the horny fingers. If I accepted it I would save a lot of time. There were still more than fifty animals to test here and I had to get through two more herds before lunch time.

I looked at my watch. Damn! I was well behind my programme and I felt the old stab of frustration.

'Right, Mr Hill, I'll take it and thank you very much.' I stuffed the sheet of paper into my pocket and began to move along the byre, clipping and injecting at top speed.

A week later the dread words leaped out at me from the open day book. 'Ring Min.' The cryptic phrase in Miss Harbottle's writing had the power to freeze my blood quicker than anything else. It meant simply that I had to telephone the Ministry of Agriculture office, and whenever our secretary wrote those words in the book it meant that I was in trouble again. I extended a trembling hand towards the receiver.

As always, Kitty Pattison answered my call and I could detect the note of pity in her voice. She was the attractive girl in charge of the office staff and she knew all about my misdemeanours. In fact when it was something very trivial she sometimes brought it to my attention herself, but when I had really dropped a large brick I was dealt with by the boss, Charles Harcourt the Divisional Inspector.

'Ah, Mr Herriot,' Kitty said lightly. I knew she sympathised with me but she couldn't do a thing about it. 'Mr Harcourt wants a word with you.'

TESTING FOR TUBERCULOSIS
Some vets act as Local Veterinary Inspectors for the Ministry of Agriculture, and one of their duties is to test cattle for bovine tuberculosis – which is dangerous not only to cattle but also to people who drink infected milk. The test consists of injecting separately a small amount of two types of tuberculin, extracted from tubercle bacilli, into the animal's skin. The reaction is judged after 72 hours by measuring any swelling round the injection sites. By making comparisons with the original skin thickness and following strict rules of interpretation, the inspector can identify any animals that have tuberculosis. All infected cattle must be slaughtered.

There it was. The terrible sentence that always set my heart thumping.

'Thank you,' I said huskily, and waited an eternity as the phone was switched through.

'Herriot!' The booming voice made me jump.

I swallowed. 'Good morning, Mr Harcourt. How are you?'

'I'll tell you how I am, I'm bloody annoyed!' I could imagine vividly the handsome, high-coloured, choleric face flushing deeper, the greenish eyes glaring. 'In fact I'm hopping bloody mad!'

'Oh.'

'It's no use saying "oh". That's what you said the last time when you tested that cow of Frankland's that had been dead for two years! That was very clever – I don't know how you managed it. Now I've been going over your test at Hill's of High View and there are two cows here that you've tested – numbers 74 and 103. Now our records show that he sold both of them at Brawton Auction Mart six months ago, so you've performed another miracle.'

'I'm sorry ...'

'Please don't be sorry, it's bloody marvellous how you do it. I have all the figures here – skin measurements, the lot. I see you found they were both thin-skinned animals even though they were about fifteen miles away at the time. Clever stuff!'

'Well I ...'

'All right, Herriot, I'll dispense with the comedy. I'm going to tell you once more, for the last time, and I hope you're listening.' He paused and I could almost see the big shoulders hunching as he barked into the phone. '*Look in the bloody ears in future!*'

I broke into a rapid gabble. 'I will indeed, Mr Harcourt, I assure you from now on ...'

'All right, all right, but there's something else.'

'Something else?'

'Yes, I'm not finished yet.' The voice took on a great weariness. 'Can I ask you to cast your mind back to that cow you took under the T.B. order from Wilson of Low Parks?'

I dug my nails into my palm. We were heading for deep water. 'Yes – I remember it.'

'Well now, Herriot, lad, do you remember a little chat we had about the forms?' Charles was trying to be patient, because he was a decent man, but it was costing him dearly. 'Didn't anything I told you sink in?'

'Well, yes, of course.'

'Then why, why didn't you send me a receipt for slaughter?'

'Receipt for ... didn't I ...?'

'No, you didn't,' he said. 'And honestly I can't understand it. I went over it with you step by step last time when you forgot to forward a copy of the valuation agreement.'

'Oh dear, I really am sorry.'

A deep sigh came from the other end. 'And there's nothing to it.' He

BOROUGHBRIDGE CATTLE SALE The weekly auction market of cattle at Boroughbridge – and at Yarm – grew on one of the ancient drove roads along which stock was moved about the country. Dairy farmers sold off their bull calves and bought heifers; beef farmers bought animals for fattening or breeding; and butchers bought for slaughtering. Other large markets were at Leyburn, York, Hawes, Northallerton and Thirsk. At the 50 or so Yorkshire markets in the 1930s more than half a million cattle a year were bought and sold.

paused. 'Tell you what we'll do. Let's go over the procedure once more, shall we?'

'Yes, by all means.'

'Very well,' he said. 'First of all, when you find an infected animal you serve B. 205 D.T., Form A, which is the notice requiring detention and isolation of the animal. Next,' and I could hear the slap of finger on palm as he enumerated his points, 'next, there is B. 207 D.T., Form C, Notice of intended slaughter. Then B. 208 D.T., Form D, Post Mortem Certificate. Then B. 196 D.T., Veterinary Inspector's report. Then B. 209 D.T., Valuation agreement, and in cases where the owner objects, there is B. 213 D.T., Appointment of valuer. Then we have B. 212 D.T., Notice to owner of time and place of slaughter, followed by B. 227 D.T., Receipt for animal for slaughter, and finally B. 230 D.T., Notice requiring cleansing and disinfection. Dammit, a child could understand that. It's perfectly simple, isn't it?'

'Yes, yes, certainly, absolutely.' It wasn't simple to me, but I didn't mention the fact. He had calmed down nicely and I didn't want to inflame him again.

'Well thank you, Mr Harcourt,' I said. 'I'll see it doesn't happen again.' I put down the receiver with the feeling that things could have turned out a lot worse, but for all that my nerves didn't stop jangling for some time. The trouble was that the Ministry work was desperately important to general practitioners. In fact, in those precarious days it was the main rent payer.

This business of the Tuberculosis Order. When a veterinary surgeon came upon a cow with open T.B. it was his duty to see that the animal was slaughtered immediately because its milk could be a danger to the public. That sounds easy, but unfortunately the law insisted that the demise of each unhappy creature be commemorated by a confetti-like shower of the doom-laden forms.

It wasn't just that there were so many of these forms, but they had to be sent to an amazing variety of people. Sometimes I used to think that there were very few people in England who didn't get one. Apart from Charles Harcourt, other recipients included the farmer concerned, the police, the Head Office of the Ministry, the knacker man, the local authority. I nearly always managed to forget one of them. I used to have nightmares about standing in the middle of the market place, throwing the forms around me at the passers-by and laughing hysterically.

Looking back, I can hardly believe that for all this wear and tear on the nervous system the payment was one guinea plus ten and sixpence for the post mortem.

It was a mere two days after my interview with the Divisional Inspector that I had to take another cow under the T.B. Order. When I came to fill in the forms I sat at the surgery desk in a dither of apprehension, going over them again and again, laying them out side by side and enclosing them one by one in their various envelopes. This time there must be no mistake.

AUTUMN PLOUGHING The laborious job of guiding a single-furrow, horse-drawn plough was one for fine autumn days. The stubble from the summer grain crop is being ploughed in to prepare the land for the following year's root crop. The pair of plough horses usually worked side by side, and each had its preferred side – land side or furrow side.

FOOT AND MOUTH INFECTION A virus, usually brought into this country by infected meat, causes foot and mouth disease. It is not fatal, but it causes suffering to all cloven-hoofed animals – cattle, sheep, pigs and goats – and is highly infectious. There is no cure for it, and Britain's policy is to isolate farms where the disease occurs, slaughter all the infected animals and their contacts, and stop hunting and movement of livestock over the affected area. The police or the Ministry of Agriculture must be notified at once of any suspected case, and the police enforce the restrictions.

I took them over to the post myself and uttered a silent prayer as I dropped them into the box. Charles would have them the following morning, and I would soon know if I had done it again. When two days passed without incident I felt I was safe, but midway through the third morning I dropped in at the surgery and read the message in letters of fire. 'RING MIN!'

Kitty Pattison sounded strained. She didn't even try to appear casual. 'Oh yes, Mr Herriot,' she said hurriedly. 'Mr Harcourt asked me to call you. I'm putting you through now.'

My heart almost stopped as I waited for the familiar bellow, but when the quite voice came on the line it frightened me even more.

'Good morning, Herriot.' Charles was curt and impersonal. 'I'd like to discuss that last cow you took under the Order.'

'Oh yes?' I croaked.

'But not over the telephone. I want to see you here in the office.'

'In the . . . the office?'

'Yes, right away if you can.'

I put down the phone and went out to the car with my knees knocking. Charles Harcourt was really upset this time. There was a kind of restrained fury in his words, and this business of going to the office – that was reserved for serious transgressions.

Twenty minutes later my footsteps echoed in the corridor of the Ministry building. Marching stiffly like a condemned man I passed the windows where I could see the typists at work, then I read 'Divisional Inspector' on the door at the end.

I took one long shuddering breath, then knocked.

'Come in.' The voice was still quiet and controlled.

Charles looked up unsmilingly from his desk as I entered. He motioned me to a chair and directed a cold stare at me.

'Herriot,' he said unemotionally. 'You're really on the carpet this time.'

Charles had been a major in the Punjabi Rifles and he was very much the Indian Army officer at this moment. A fine looking man, clear-skinned and ruddy, with massive cheek bones above a powerful jaw. Looking at the dangerously glinting eyes it struck me that only a fool would trifle with somebody like him – and I had a nasty feeling that I had been trifling.

Dry-mouthed, I waited.

'You know, Herriot,' he went on. 'After our last telephone conversation about T.B. forms I thought you might give me a little peace.'

'Peace . . .?'

'Yes, yes, it was silly of me, I know, but when I took all that time to go over the procedure with you I actually thought you were listening.'

'Oh I was, I was!'

'You were? Oh good.' He gave me a mirthless smile. 'Then I suppose it was even more foolish of me to expect you to act upon my instructions. In my innocence I thought you cared about what I was telling you.'

'Mr Harcourt, believe me, I do care, I ...'

'*Then why,*' he bawled without warning, bringing his great hand flailing down on the desk with a crash that made pens and inkwells dance. '*Why the bloody hell do you keep making a balls of it?*'

I resisted a strong impulse to run away. 'Making a ... I don't quite understand.'

'You don't?' He kept up his pounding on the desk. 'Well I'll tell you. One of my veterinary officers was on that farm, and he found that you hadn't served a Notice of Cleansing and Disinfection!'

'Is that so?'

'Yes, it bloody well is so! You didn't give one to the farmer but you sent one to me. Maybe you want me to go and disinfect the place, is that it? Would you like me to slip along there and get busy with a hosepipe – I'll go now if it'll make you feel any happier!'

'Oh no, no, no ... no.'

He was apparently not satisfied with the thunderous noise he was making because he began to use both hands, bringing them down simultaneously with sickening force on the wood while he glared wildly.

'Herriot!' he shouted. 'There's just one thing I want to know from you – do you want this bloody work or don't you? Just say the word and I'll give it to another practice and then maybe we'd both be able to live a quiet life!'

'Please, Mr Harcourt, I give you my word, I ... we ... we do want the work very much.' And I meant it with all my heart.

The big man slumped back in his chair and regarded me for a few moments in silence. Then he glanced at his wrist watch.

'Ten past twelve,' he murmured. 'Just time to have a beer at the Red Lion before lunch.'

In the pub lounge he took a long pull at his glass, placed it carefully on the table in front of him, then turned to me with a touch of weariness.

'You know, Herriot, I do wish you'd stop doing this sort of thing. It takes it out of me.'

I believed him. His face had lost a little of its colour and his hand trembled slightly as he raised his glass again.

'I'm truly sorry, Mr Harcourt, I don't know how it happened. I did try to get it right this time and I'll do my best to avoid troubling you in future.'

He nodded a few times then clapped me on the shoulder. 'Good, good – let's just have one more.'

He moved over to the bar, brought back the drinks then fished out a brown paper parcel from his pocket.

'Little wedding present, Herriot. Understand you're getting married soon – this is from my missus and me with our best wishes.'

I didn't know what to say. I fumbled the wrapping away and uncovered a small square barometer.

Shame engulfed me as I muttered a few words of thanks. This man was the head of the Ministry in the area while I was the newest and

PRECAUTIONS AGAINST INFECTION If foot and mouth disease infects a farm, all the other farms in the area operate strict measures to try to keep it out. Vehicles are not allowed in until their wheels have been washed down with disinfectant such as Jeyes fluid. The precautions are willingly observed, because an outbreak of foot and mouth is costly. Severe epidemics in Britain in 1922, 1923 and 1924 cost about £3 million, and a catastrophic outbreak in 1967–8 cost £27 million and the slaughter of hundreds of thousands of cattle.

lowest of his minions. Not only that, but I was pretty sure I caused him more trouble than all the others put together – I was like a hair shirt to him. There was no earthly reason why he should give me a barometer.

This last experience deepened my dread of form filling to the extent that I hoped it would be a long time before I encountered another tuberculous animal, but fate decreed that I had some concentrated days of clinical inspections and it was with a feeling of inevitability that I surveyed Mr Moverley's Ayrshire cow.

It was the soft cough which made me stop and look at her more closely, and as I studied her my spirits sank. This was another one. The skin stretched tightly over the bony frame, the slightly accelerated respirations and that deep careful cough. Mercifully you don't see cows like that now, but in those days they were all too common.

I moved along her side and examined the wall in front of her. The tell-tale blobs of sputum were clearly visible on the rough stones and I quickly lifted a sample and smeared it on a glass slide.

Back at the surgery I stained the smear by Ziehl-Nielson's method and pushed the slide under the microscope. The red clumps of tubercle bacilli lay among the scattered cells, tiny, iridescent and deadly. I hadn't really needed the grim proof but it was there.

Mr Moverley was not amused when I told him next morning that the animal would have to be slaughtered.

'It's nobbut got a bit of a chill,' he grunted. The farmers were never pleased when one of their milk producers was removed by a petty bureaucrat like me. 'But ah suppose it's no use arguin'.'

'I assure you, Mr Moverley, there's no doubt about it. I examined that sample last night, and ...'

'Oh never mind about that.' The farmer waved an impatient hand. 'If t'bloody government says me cow's got to go she's got to go. But ah get compensation, don't I?'

'Yes, you do.'

'How much?'

I thought rapidly. The rules stated that the animal be valued as if it were up for sale in the open market in its present condition. The minimum was five pounds and there was no doubt that this emaciated cow came into that category.

'The statutory value is five pounds,' I said.

'Shit!' replied Mr Moverley.

'We can appoint a valuer if you don't agree.'

'Oh 'ell, let's get t'job over with.' He was clearly disgusted and I thought it imprudent to tell him that he would only get a proportion of the five pounds, depending on the post mortem.

'Very well,' I said. 'I'll tell Jeff Mallock to collect her as soon as possible.'

The fact that I was unpopular with Mr Moverley didn't worry me as

HALTING FOOT AND MOUTH
During an outbreak of the highly infectious foot and mouth disease, for which there is no treatment, all farms in the area take precautions to keep out the virus. Footwear can be disinfected, but the incurable virus could still be carried in by the wind. If his farm becomes infected a farmer has to slaughter all his cloven-hoofed animals, have his premises thoroughly cleaned and disinfected, and have no replacement stock for six weeks. There are now compensatory payments, but the loss of output and the destruction of many years' work is crippling.

376

much as the prospect of dealing with the dreaded forms. The very thought of sending another batch winging hopefully on its way to Charles Harcourt brought me out in a sweat.

Then I had a flash of inspiration. Such things don't often happen to me, but this struck me as brilliant. I wouldn't send off the forms till I'd had them vetted by Kitty Pattison.

I couldn't wait to get the plan under way. Almost gleefully I laid the papers out in a long row, signed them and laid them by their envelopes, ready for their varied journeys. Then I phoned the Ministry office.

Kitty was patient and kind. I am sure she realised that I did my work conscientiously but that I was a clerical numbskull and she sympathised.

When I had finished going through the list she congratulated me. 'Well done, Mr Herriot, you've got them right this time! All you need now is the knacker man's signature and your post mortem report and you're home and dry.

'Bless you, Kitty,' I said. 'You've made my day.'

And she had. The airy sensation of relief was tremendous. The knowledge that there would be no come-back from Charles this time was like the sun bursting through dark clouds. I felt like singing as I went round to Mallock's yard and arranged with him to pick up the cow.

'Have her ready for me to inspect tomorrow, Jeff,' I said, and went on my way with a light heart.

I couldn't understand it when Mr Moverley waved me down from his farm gate next day. As I drew up I could see he was extremely agitated.

'Hey!' he cried. 'Ah've just got back from the market and my missus tells me Mallock's been!'

I smiled. 'That's right, Mr Moverley. Remember I told you I was going to send him round for your cow.'

'Aye, ah know all about that!' He paused and glared at me. 'But he's took the wrong one!'

'Wrong ... wrong what?'

'Wrong cow, that's what! He's off wi' the best cow in me herd. Pedigree Ayrshire – ah bought 'er in Dumfries last week and they only delivered 'er this mornin'.'

Horror drove through me in a freezing wave. I had told the knacker man to collect the Ayrshire which would be isolated in the loose box in the yard. The new animal would be in a box, too, after her arrival. I could see Jeff and his man leading her up the ramp into his wagon with a dreadful clarity.

'This is your responsibility, tha knaws!' The farmer waved a threatening finger. 'If he kills me good cow you'll 'ave to answer for it!'

He didn't have to tell me. I'd have to answer for it to a lot of people, including Charles Harcourt.

'Get on the phone to the knacker yard right away!' I gasped.

The farmer waved his arms about 'Ah've tried that and there's no reply. Ah tell ye he'll shoot 'er afore we can stop 'im. Do you know how

THATCHING A PIKE Thatching a pike, or stack, of corn sheaves was necessary to protect the crop from rain and wind. The thatching material was oat or wheat straw, sometimes rushes.

It was laid thinly and, traditionally, held with bands which old men and boys had spent days twisting together from oat straw; string made of coconut fibre replaced these. Hazel prods, or pins, held the bands in place while thatching progressed. The finished pike was topped by a straw ornament called a dozzle. It could be more than a day's work to thatch a pike for some pikes were very large.

SEED-DRILL From the mid-19th century it became common to sow seed by a horse-drawn machine, the drill. In this double-row drill, two shallow channels, or drills, are scraped out and seed is dropped into them down tubes from the hopper. Gears driven by the rear wheels turn discs in the hopper that scoop up seed on tiny spoons and drop it into the tubes. The flow of seed could be adjusted for different grain and root crops.

much ah paid for that cow?'

'Never mind about that! Which way did he go?'

'T'missus said he went towards Grampton – about ten minutes ago.'

I started my engine. 'He'll maybe be picking up other beasts – I'll go after him.'

Teeth clenched, eyes popping, I roared along the Grampton road. The enormity of this latest catastrophe was almost more than I could assimilate. The wrong form was bad enough, but the wrong cow was unthinkable. But it had happened. Charles would crucify me this time. He was a good bloke but he would have no option, because the higher-ups in the Ministry would get wind of an immortal boner like this and they would howl for blood.

Feverishly but vainly I scanned each farm entrance in Grampton village as I shot through, and when I saw the open countryside ahead of me again the tension was almost unbearable. I was telling myself that the whole thing was hopeless when in the far distance above a row of trees I spotted the familiar top of Mallock's wagon.

It was a high, wooden-sided vehicle and I couldn't mistake it. Repressing a shout of triumph I put my foot on the boards and set off in that direction with the fanatical zeal of the hunter. But it was a long way off and I hadn't travelled a mile before I realised I had lost it.

Over the years many things have stayed in my memory, but the Great Cow Chase is engraven deeper than most. The sheer terror I felt is vivid to this day. I kept sighting the wagon among the maze of lanes and side roads but by the time I had cut across country my quarry had disappeared behind a hillside or dipped into one of the many hollows in the wide vista. I was constantly deceived by the fact that I expected him to be turning towards Darrowby after passing through a village, but he never did. Clearly he had other business on the way.

The whole thing seemed to last a very long time and there was no fun in it for me. I was gripped throughout by a cold dread, and the violent swings – the alternating scents of hope and despair – were wearing to the point of exhaustion. I was utterly drained when at last I saw the tall lorry rocking along a straight road in front of me.

I had him now! Forcing my little car to the limit, I drew abreast of him, sounding my horn repeatedly till he stopped. Breathlessly I pulled up in front of him and ran round to offer my explanations. But as I looked up into the driver's cab my eager smile vanished. It wasn't Jeff Mallock at all. I had been following the wrong man.

It was the 'ket feller'. He had exactly the same type of wagon as Mallock and he went round a wide area of Yorkshire picking up the nameless odds and ends of the dead animals which even the knacker men didn't want. It was a strange job and he was a strange-looking man. The oddly piercing eyes glittered uncannily from under a tattered army peaked cap.

'Wot's up, guvnor?' He removed a cigarette from his mouth and spat companionably into the roadway.

My throat was tight. 'I – I'm sorry. I thought you were Jeff Mallock.'

The eyes did not change expression, but the corner of his mouth twitched briefly. 'If tha wants Jeff he'll be back at his yard now, ah reckon.' He spat again and replaced his cigarette.

I nodded dully. Jeff would be there now all right – long ago. I had been chasing the wrong wagon for about an hour and that cow would be dead and hanging up on hooks at this moment. The knacker man was a fast and skilful worker and wasted no time when he got back with his beasts.

'Well, ah'm off 'ome now,' the ket feller said. 'So long, boss.' He winked at me, started his engine and the big vehicle rumbled away.

I trailed back to my car. There was no hurry now. And strangely, now that all was lost my mood relaxed. In fact, as I drove away, a great calm settled on me and I began to assess my future with cool objectivity. I would be drummed out of the Ministry's service for sure, and idly I wondered if they had any special ceremony for the occasion – perhaps a ritual stripping of the Panel Certificates or something of the sort.

I tried to put away the thought that more than the Ministry would be interested in my latest exploit. How about the Royal College? Did they strike you off for something like this? Well, it was possible, and in my serene state of mind I toyed with the possibilities of alternative avenues of employment. I had often thought it must be fun to run a secondhand book shop and now that I began to consider it seriously I felt sure there was an opening for one in Darrowby. I experienced a comfortable glow at the vision of myself sitting under the rows of dusty volumes, pulling one down from the shelf when I felt like it or maybe just looking out into the street through the window from my safe little world where there were no forms or telephones or messages saying, 'Ring Min.'

In Darrowby I drove round without haste to the knacker yard. I left my car outside the grim little building with the black smoke drifting from its chimney. I pulled back the sliding door and saw Jeff seated at his ease on a pile of cow hides, holding a slice of apple pie in blood-stained fingers. And, ah yes, there, just behind him hung the two great sides of beef and on the floor, the lungs, bowels and other viscera – the sad remnants of Mr Moverley's pedigree Aryshire.

'Hello, Jeff,' I said.

'Now then, Mr Herriot.' He gave me the beatific smile which mirrored his personality so well. 'Ah'm just havin' a little snack. I allus like a bite about this time.' He sank his teeth into the pie and chewed appreciatively.

'So I see.' I sorrowfully scanned the hanging carcase. Just dog meat and not even much of that. Ayrshires were never very fat. I was wondering how to break the news to him when he spoke again.

'Ah'm sorry you've caught me out this time, Mr Herriot,' he said, reaching for a greasy mug of tea.

'What do you mean?'

'Well, I allus reckon to have t'beast dressed and ready for you but

CLIPPING A FLEECE Some shearers used to sit at their work with the sheep on a cratch, or stool. Now shearers always stand and bend over the sheep. Above all, the fleece has to be kept clean and free of grass or soil. The shearers usually work in a barn or shed with the floor newly swept or spread with a sheet of canvas. They may wear soft slippers, or work without shoes. Hand-clippers were commonly used in the Dales until after 1945. The coming of mains electricity to farms from 1945 onward made it possible to use powered clippers.

you've come a bit early.'

I stared at him. 'But ... everything's here, surely.' I waved a hand around me.

'Nay, nay, that's not 'er.'

'You mean ... that isn't the cow from Moverley's.'

'That's right.' He took a long draught from the mug and wiped his mouth with the back of his hand. 'I 'ad to do this 'un first. Moverley's cow's still in t'wagon out at the back.'

'Alive?'

He looked mildly surprised. 'Aye, of course. She's never had a finger on 'er. Nice cow for a screw, too.'

I could have fainted with relief. 'She's no screw, Jeff. That's the wrong cow you've got there.'

'Wrong cow?' Nothing ever startled him but he obviously desired more information. I told him the whole story.

When I had finished, his shoulders began to shake gently and the beautiful clear eyes twinkled in the pink face.

'Well, that's a licker,' he murmured, and continued to laugh gently. There was nothing immoderate in his mirth and indeed nothing I had said disturbed him in the least. The fact that he had wasted his journey or that the farmer might be annoyed was of no moment to him.

Again, looking at Jeff Mallock, it struck me, as many times before, that there was nothing like a lifetime of dabbling among diseased carcases and lethal bacteria for breeding tranquillity of mind.

'You'll slip back and change the cow?' I said.

'Aye, in a minute or two. There's nowt spoilin'. Ah never likes to hurry me grub.' He belched contentedly. 'And how about you, Mr Herriot? You could do with summat to keep your strength up.' He produced another mug and broke off a generous wedge of pie which he offered to me.

'No ... no ... er ... no, thank you, Jeff. It's kind of you, but no ... no ... not just now.'

He shrugged his shoulders and smiled as he stretched an arm for his pipe which was balanced on a sheep's skull. Flicking away some shreds of stray tissue from the stem he applied a match and settled down blissfully on the hides.

'I'll see ye later, then,' he said. 'Come round tonight and everything'll be ready for you.' He closed his eyes and again his shoulders quivered. 'Ah'd better get the right 'un this time.'

It must be more than twenty years since I took a cow under the T.B. Order, because the clinical cases so rarely exist now. 'Ring Min' no longer has the power to chill my blood, and the dread forms which scarred my soul lie unused and yellowing in the bottom of a drawer.

All these things have gone from my life. Charles Harcourt has gone too, but I think of him every day when I look at the little barometer which still hangs on my wall.

LIFE ON THE ROAD Travelling the north Yorkshire roads, often following a regular yearly pattern, were several solitary 'Wold Rangers', or tramps. Some spent the winters breaking horses, and most spent the summers helping in hay and harvest fields. Among the tramps were men who had once been farmhands but had given up the relentless labour tied to one farm for a riskier but more independent life. They carried their few possessions with them, slept rough in the fields, caught – frequently poached – small creatures for food, and worked two or three days a week. They received payment when they completed the job – and quite often drank it away.

11

An emergency operation

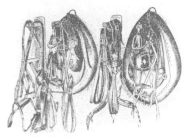

WORKING HARNESS The working horse was in its harness up to eight hours a day – more at harvest time – so it was vital for the harness to be comfortable as well as strong. Leather was the best material, with a frame of wood inside the collar. Chains or leather traces attached the haycart, plough or other load to the collar so that the horse took the strain on its chest and shoulders.

Occasionally my period in limbo was relieved when I was allowed out of camp into the city of Manchester. And I suppose it was the fact that I was a new-fangled parent that made me look at the various prams in the streets. Mostly the prams were pushed by women but now and then I saw a man doing the job.

I suppose it isn't unusual to see a man pushing a pram in a town, but on a lonely moorland road the sight merits a second glance. Especially when the pram contains a large dog.

That was what I saw in the hills above Darrowby one morning and I slowed down as I drove past. I had noticed the strange combination before – on several occasions over the last few weeks – and it was clear that man and dog had recently moved into the district.

As the car drew abreast of him the man turned, smiled and raised his hand. It was a smile of rare sweetness in a very brown face. A forty-year-old face, I thought, above a brown neck which bore neither collar nor tie, and a faded striped shirt lying open over a bare chest despite the coldness of the day.

I couldn't help wondering who or what he was. The outfit of scuffed suede golf jacket, corduroy trousers and sturdy boots didn't give much clue. Some people might have put him down as an ordinary tramp, but there was a businesslike energetic look about him which didn't fit the term.

I wound the window down and the thin wind of a Yorkshire March bit at my cheeks.

'Nippy this morning,' I said.

The man seemed surprised. 'Aye,' he replied after a moment. 'Aye, reckon it is.'

I looked at the pram, ancient and rusty, and at the big animal sitting upright inside it. He was a lurcher, a cross-bred greyhound, and he gazed back at me with unruffled dignity.

'Nice dog,' I said.

'Aye, that's Jake.' The man smiled again, showing good regular teeth. 'He's a grand 'un.'

I waved and drove on. In the mirror I could see the compact figure stepping out briskly, head up, shoulders squared, and, rising like a statue from the middle of the pram, the huge brindled form of Jake.

I didn't have to wait long to meet the unlikely pair again. I was examining a carthorse's teeth in a farmyard when on the hillside beyond the stable I saw a figure kneeling by a dry stone wall. And by his side, a

I had noticed the strange combination before ... it was clear that man and dog had recently moved into the district.

pram and a big dog sitting patiently on the grass.

'Hey, just a minute.' I pointed at the hill. 'Who is that?'

The farmer laughed. 'That's Roddy Travers. D'you ken 'im?'

'No, no I don't. I had a word with him on the road the other day, that's all.'

'Aye, on the road.' He nodded knowingly. 'That's where you'd see Roddy, right enough.'

'But what is he? Where does he come from?'

'He comes from somewhere in Yorkshire, but ah don't rightly know where and ah don't think anybody else does. But I'll tell you this – he can turn 'is hand to anything.'

'Yes,' I said, watching the man expertly laying the flat slabs of stone as he repaired a gap in the wall. 'There's not many can do what he's doing now.'

'That's true. Wallin' is a skilled job and it's dying out, but Roddy's a dab hand at it. But he can do owt – hedgin', ditchin', lookin' after stock, it's all the same to him.'

I lifted the tooth rasp and began to rub a few sharp corners off the horse's molars. 'And how long will he stay here?'

'Oh, when he's finished that wall he'll be off. Ah could do with 'im stoppin' around for a bit but he never stays in one place for long.'

'But hasn't he got a home anywhere?'

'Nay, nay.' The farmer laughed again. 'Roddy's got nowt. All 'e has in the world is in that there pram.'

Over the next weeks as the harsh spring began to soften and the sunshine brought a bright speckle of primroses on to the grassy banks I saw Roddy quite often, sometimes on the road, occasionally wielding a spade busily on the ditches around the fields. Jake was always there, either loping by his side or watching him at work. But we didn't actually meet again till I was inoculating Mr Pawson's sheep for pulpy kidney.

There were three hundred to do and they drove them in batches into a small pen where Roddy caught and held them for me. And I could see he was an expert at this, too. The wild hill sheep whipped past him like bullets but he seized their fleece effortlessly, sometimes in mid-air, and held the fore leg up to expose that bare clean area of skin behind the elbow that nature seemed to provide for the veterinary surgeon's needle.

Outside, on the windy slopes the big lurcher sat upright in typical pose, looking with mild interest at the farm dogs prowling intently around the pens, but not interfering in any way.

'You've got him well trained,' I said.

Roddy smiled. 'Yes, ye'll never find Jake dashin' about, annoyin' people. He knows 'e has to sit there till I'm finished and there he'll sit.'

'And quite happy to do so, by the look of him.' I glanced again at the dog, a picture of contentment. 'He must live a wonderful life, travelling everywhere with you.'

'You're right there,' Mr Pawson broke in as he ushered another bunch of sheep into the pen. 'He hasn't a care in t'world, just like his master.'

WENSLEYDALE SHEEP The Wensleydale, now very rare, belongs to the lower slopes of the Dales. It is a large sheep with a slate-blue face and pearled, or crimped, coat. Despite its prolific high-quality fleece, it has been out of fashion for some years. The growing demand for large but lean lamb joints may bring it back to breeders' attention.

Roddy didn't say anything, but as the sheep ran in he straightened up and took a long steady breath. He had been working hard and a little trickle of sweat ran down the side of his forehead but as he gazed over the wide sweep of moor and fell I could read utter serenity in his face. After a few moments he spoke.

'I reckon that's true. We haven't much to worry us, Jake and me.'

Mr Pawson grinned mischievously. 'By gaw, Roddy, you never spoke a truer word. No wife, no kids, no life insurance, no overdraft at t'bank – you must have a right peaceful existence.'

'Ah suppose so,' Roddy said. 'But then ah've no money either.'

The farmer gave him a quizzical look. 'Aye, how about that, then? Wouldn't you feel a bit more secure, like, if you had a bit o' brass put by?'

'Nay, nay. Ye can't take it with you and any road, as long as a man can pay 'is way, he's got enough.'

There was nothing original about the words, but they have stayed with me all my life because they came from his lips and were spoken with such profound assurance.

When I had finished the inoculations and the ewes were turned out to trot back happily over the open fields I turned to Roddy. 'Well, thanks very much. It makes my job a lot quicker when I have a good catcher like you.' I pulled out a packet of Gold Flake. 'Will you have a cigarette?'

'No, thank ye, Mr Herriot. I don't smoke.'

'You don't?'

'No – don't drink either.' He gave me his gentle smile and again I had the impression of physical and mental purity. No drinking, no smoking, a life of constant movement in the open air without material possessions or ambitions – it all showed in the unclouded eyes, the fresh skin and the hard muscular frame. He wasn't very big but he looked indestructible.

'C'mon, Jake, it's dinner time,' he said and the big lurcher bounded around him in delight. I went over and spoke to the dog and he responded with tremendous body-swaying wags, his handsome face looking up at me, full of friendliness.

I stroked the long pointed head and tickled the ears. 'He's a beauty, Roddy – a grand 'un, as you said.'

I walked to the house to wash my hands and before I went inside I glanced back at the two of them. They were sitting in the shelter of a wall and Roddy was laying out a thermos flask and a parcel of food while Jake watched eagerly. The hard bright sunshine beat on them as the wind whistled over the top of the wall. They looked supremely comfortable and at peace.

'He's independent, you see,' the farmer's wife said as I stood at the kitchen sink. 'He's welcome to come in for a bit o' dinner but he'd rather stay outside with his dog.'

I nodded. 'Where does he sleep when he's going round the farms like this?'

'Oh, anywhere,' she replied. 'In hay barns or granaries or sometimes out in the open, but when he's with us he sleeps upstairs in one of our rooms. Ah know for a fact any of the farmers would be willin' to have him in the house because he allus keeps himself spotless clean.'

'I see.' I pulled the towel from behind the door. 'He's quite a character, isn't he?'

She smiled ruminatively. 'Aye, he certainly is. Just him and his dog!' She lifted a fragrant dishful of hot roast ham from the oven and set it on the table. 'But I'll tell you this. The feller's all right. Everybody likes Roddy Travers – he's a very nice man.'

Roddy stayed around the Darrowby district throughout the summer and I grew used to the sight of him on the farms or pushing his pram along the roads. When it was raining he wore a tattered over-long gaberdine coat, but at other times it was always the golf jacket and corduroys. I don't know where he had accumulated his wardrobe. It was a safe bet he had never been on a golf course in his life and it was just another of the little mysteries about him.

I saw him early one morning on a hill path in early October. It had been a night of iron frost and the tussocky pastures beyond the walls were held in a pitiless white grip with every blade of grass stiffly ensheathed in rime.

I was muffled to the eyes and had been beating my gloved fingers against my knees to thaw them out, but when I pulled up and wound down the window the first thing I saw was the bare chest under the collarless unbuttoned shirt.

'Mornin', Mr Herriot,' he said. 'Ah'm glad I've seen ye.' He paused and gave me his tranquil smile. 'There's a job along t'road for a couple of weeks, then I'm movin' on.'

'I see.' I knew enough about him now not to ask where he was going. Instead I looked down at Jake who was sniffling the herbage. 'I see he's walking this morning.'

Roddy laughed. 'Yes, sometimes 'e likes to walk, sometimes 'e likes to ride. He pleases 'imself.'

'Right, Roddy,' I said. 'No doubt we'll meet again. All the best to you.'

He waved and set off jauntily over the icebound road and I felt that a little vein of richness had gone from my life.

But I was wrong. That same evening about eight o'clock the front door bell rang. I answered it and found Roddy on the front door steps. Behind him, just visible in the frosty darkness, stood the ubiquitous pram.

'I want you to look at me dog, Mr Herriot,' he said.

'Why, what's the trouble?'

'Ah don't rightly know. He's havin' sort of . . . faintin' fits.'

'Fainting fits? That doesn't sound like Jake. Where is he, anyway?'

He pointed behind him 'In t'pram, under t'cover.'

'All right.' I threw the door wide. 'Bring him in.'

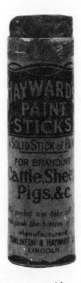

A MARKING STICK Almost solid paint encased in a metal tube made a marker for identifying animals temporarily. It was not an alternative to branding or dye-marking, because it wore off, but was used to show ownership or lot number at an auction, for example, or to indicate which animals had been treated when a whole herd was being inoculated or dosed. The paint stick was pushed up from the bottom of the tin as it was used up.

Roddy adroitly manhandled the rusty old vehicle up the steps and pushed it, squeaking and rattling, along the passage to the consulting room. There, under the bright lights he snapped back the fasteners and threw off the cover to reveal Jake stretched beneath.

He head was pillowed on the familiar gaberdine coat and around him lay his master's worldly goods; a string-tied bundle of spare shirt and socks, a packet of tea, a thermos, knife and spoon and an ex-army haversack.

The big dog looked up at me with terrified eyes and as I patted him I could feel his whole frame quivering.

'Let him lie there a minute, Roddy,' I said. 'And tell me exactly what you've seen.'

He rubbed his palms together and his fingers trembled. 'Well, it only started this afternoon. He was right as rain, larkin' about on the grass, then he went into a sort o' fit.'

'How do you mean?'

'Just kind of seized up and toppled over on 'is side. He lay there for a bit, gaspin' and slaverin'. Ah'll tell ye, I thought he was a goner.' His eyes widened and a corner of his mouth twitched at the memory.

'How long did that last?'

'Nobbut a few seconds. Then he got up and you'd say there was nowt wrong with 'im.'

'But he did it again?'

'Aye, time and time again. Drove me near daft. But in between 'e was normal. Normal, Mr Herriot!'

It sounded ominously like the onset of epilepsy. 'How old is he?' I asked.

'Five gone last February.'

Ah well, it was a bit old for that. I reached for a stethoscope and auscultated the heart. I listened intently but heard only the racing beat of a frightened animal. There was no abnormality. My thermometer showed no rise in temperature.

'Let's have him on the table, Roddy. You take the back end.'

The big animal was limp in our arms as we hoisted him on to the smooth surface, but after lying there for a moment he looked timidly around him then sat up with a slow and careful movement. As we watched he reached out and licked his master's face while his tail flickered between his legs.

'Look at that!' the man exclaimed. 'He's all right again. You'd think he didn't ail a thing.'

And indeed Jake was recovering his confidence rapidly. He peered tentatively at the floor a few times then suddenly jumped down, trotted to his master and put his paws against his chest.

I looked at the dog standing there, tail wagging furiously. 'Well, that's a relief, anyway. I didn't like the look of him just then, but whatever's been troubling him seems to have righted itself. I'll . . .'

My happy flow was cut off. I stared at the lurcher. His fore legs were

MAKING A HAY BURDEN To make up burdens, or bundles, of hay for supplementing hill-sheep's winter grazing, the farmer cut out three 'canches', or layers, from the stack in the barn. He put them one on top of another on a rope laid out ready on the ground and secured the rope at the top of the burden with one wisp of hay. Each burden weighed at least 4 stones, and often more than 8 stones.

on the floor again and his mouth was gaping as he fought for breath. Frantically he gasped and retched then he blundered across the floor, collided with the pram wheels and fell on his side.

'What the hell ...! Quick, get him up again!' I grabbed the animal round the middle and we lifted him back on to the table.

I watched in disbelief as the huge form lay there. There was no fight for breath now – he wasn't breathing at all, he was unconscious. I pushed my fingers inside his thigh and felt the pulse. It was still going, rapid and feeble, but yet he didn't breathe.

He could die any moment and I stood there helpless, all my scientific training useless. Finally my frustration burst from me and I struck the dog on the ribs with the flat of my hand.

'Jake!' I yelled. 'Jake, what's the matter with you?'

As though in reply, the lurcher immediately started to take great wheezing breaths, his eyelids twitched back to consciousness and he began to look about him. But he was still mortally afraid and he lay prone as I gently stroked his head.

There was a long silence while the animal's terror slowly subsided, then he sat up on the table and regarded us placidly.

'There you are,' Roddy said softly. 'Same thing again. Ah can't reckon it up and ah thought ah knew summat about dogs.'

I didn't say anything. I couldn't reckon it up either, and I was supposed to be a veterinary surgeon.

I spoke at last. 'Roddy, that wasn't a fit. He was choking. Something was interfering with his air flow.' I took my hand torch from my breast pocket. 'I'm going to have a look at his throat.'

I pushed Jake's jaws apart, depressed his tongue with a forefinger and shone the light into the depths. He was the kind of good-natured dog who offered no resistance as I prodded around, but despite my floodlit view of the pharynx I could find nothing wrong. I had been hoping desperately to come across a bit of bone stuck there somewhere but I ranged feverishly over pink tongue, healthy tonsils and gleaming molars without success. Everything looked perfect.

I was tilting his head a little further when I felt him stiffen and heard Roddy's cry.

'He's goin' again!'

And he was, too. I stared in horror as the brindled body slid away from me and lay prostrate once more on the table. And again the mouth strained wide and froth bubbled round the lips. As before, the breathing had stopped and the rib cage was motionless. As the seconds ticked away I beat on the chest with my hand but it didn't work this time. I pulled the lower eyelid down from the staring orb – the conjunctiva was blue, Jake hadn't long to live. The tragedy of the thing bore down on me. This wasn't just a dog, he was this man's family and I was watching him die.

It was at that moment that I heard the faint sound. It was a strangled cough which barely stirred the dog's lips.

CARRYING HAY BURDENS Two burdens of equal weight – or made equal by adding stones to one of them – were slung one each side of a Dales pony, which carried them up the hillsides to the sheep when winter grazing was sparse or snow lay on the ground. Once he reached the sheep, the farmer pulled out the wisp of hay that secured the rope round each burden, so that the hay immediately fell loose ready for the converging flock.

387

WRAPPING A FLEECE To make it into a neat bundle for transporting, a fleece is first laid cut side down on a creel, or stool, and the tail part is removed. Then the sides are folded in and the fleece is rolled tightly from the tail end. Wool drawn out from the neck end is twisted to serve as a rope, which is wrapped round the fleece and secured by having its end tucked in.

'Damn it!' I shouted. 'He *is* choking. There must be something down there.'

Again I seized the head and pushed my torch into the mouth and I shall always be thankful that at that very instant the dog coughed again, opening the cartilages of the larynx and giving me a glimpse of the cause of all the trouble. There, beyond the drooping epiglottis I saw for a fleeting moment a smooth round object no bigger than a pea.

'I think it's a pebble,' I gasped. 'Right inside his larynx.'

'You mean, in 'is Adam's apple?'

'That's right, and it's acting like a ball valve, blocking his windpipe every now and then.' I shook the dog's head. 'You see, look, I've dislodged it for the moment. He's coming round again.'

Once more Jake was reviving and breathing steadily.

Roddy ran his hand over the head, along the back and down the great muscles of the hind limbs. 'But ... but ... it'll happen again, won't it?'

I nodded. 'I'm afraid so.'

'And one of these times it isn't goin' to shift and that'll be the end of 'im?' He had gone very pale.

'That's about it, Roddy, I'll have to get that pebble out.'

'But how ...?'

'Cut into the larynx. And right now – it's the only way.'

'All right.' He swallowed. 'Let's get on. I don't think ah could stand it if he went down again.'

I knew what he meant. My knees had begun to shake, and I had a strong conviction that if Jake collapsed once more then so would I.

I seized a pair of scissors and clipped away the hair from the ventral surface of the larynx. I dared not use a general anaesthetic and infiltrated the area with local before swabbing with antiseptic. Mercifully there was a freshly boiled set of instruments lying in the steriliser and I lifted out the tray and set it on the trolley by the side of the table.

'Hold his head steady,' I said hoarsely, and gripped the scalpel.

I cut down through skin, fascia and the thin layers of the sterno-hyoid and omo-hyoid muscles till the ventral surface of the larynx was revealed. This was something I had never done to a live dog before, but desperation abolished any hesitancy and it took me only another few seconds to incise the thin membrane and peer into the interior.

And there it was. A pebble right enough – grey and glistening and tiny, but big enough to kill.

I had to fish it out quickly and cleanly without pushing it into the trachea. I leaned back and rummaged in the tray till I found some broad-bladed forceps then I poised them over the wound. Great surgeons' hands, I felt sure, didn't shake like this, nor did such men pant as I was doing. But I clenched my teeth, introduced the forceps and my hand magically steadied as I clamped them over the pebble.

I stopped panting, too. In fact I didn't breathe at all as I bore the shining little object slowly and tenderly through the opening and dropped it with a gentle rat-tat on the table.

'Is that it?' asked Roddy, almost in a whisper.

'That's it.' I reached for needle and suture silk. 'All is well now.'

The stitching took only a few minutes and by the end of it Jake was bright-eyed and alert, paws shifting impatiently, ready for anything. He seemed to know his troubles were over.

Roddy brought him back in ten days to have the stitches removed. It was, in fact, the very morning he was leaving the Darrowby district, and after I had picked the few loops of silk from the nicely healed wound I walked with him to the front door while Jake capered round our feet.

On the pavement outside Skeldale House the ancient pram stood in all its high, rusted dignity. Roddy pulled back the cover.

'Up, boy,' he murmured, and the big dog leaped effortlessly into his accustomed place.

Roddy took hold of the handle with both hands and as the autumn sunshine broke suddenly through the clouds it lit up a picture which had grown familiar and part of the daily scene. The golf jacket, the open shirt and brown chest, the handsome animal sitting up, looking around him with natural grace.

'Well, so long, Roddy,' I said. 'I suppose you'll be round these parts again.'

He turned and I saw that smile again. 'Aye, reckon ah'll be back.'

He gave a push and they were off, the strange vehicle creaking, Jake swaying gently as they went down the street. The memory came back to me of what I had seen under the cover that night in the surgery. The haversack, which would contain his razor, towel, soap and a few other things. The packet of tea and the thermos. And something else – a tiny dog collar. Could it have belonged to Jake as a pup or to another loved animal? It added a little more mystery to the man ... and explained other things, too. That farmer had been right – all Roddy possessed was in that pram.

And it seemed it was all he desired, too, because as he turned the corner and disappeared from my view I could hear him whistling.

HEDGE-LAYING The characteristic field dividers of the Dales are walls, but in some valley bottoms there are hedges of sycamore, ash or hazel, which need pruning about every five years to prevent them from growing into trees. During the dormant period, undergrowth and thick old branches are cleared out and newer shoots are cut with an axe or a billhook at the main stem – but not severed completely. Then they are carefully woven between stakes driven in about 2 ft apart. The hedger leads the growths to the left, and on sloping ground he prefers to work uphill.

12

The bright lights

They had sent me to Eastchurch on the Isle of Sheppey and I knew it was the last stop.

As I looked along the disorderly line of men I realised I wouldn't be taking part in many more parades. And it came to me with a pang that at the Scarborough Initial Training Wing this would not have been classed as a parade at all. I could remember the ranks of blue outside the Grand Hotel, straight as the Grenadier Guards and every man standing stiffly, looking neither to left nor right. Our boots gleaming, buttons shining like gold and not a movement anywhere as the flight sergeant led the officer round on morning inspection.

I had moaned as loudly as anybody at the rigid discipline, the 'bull', the scrubbing and polishing, marching and drilling, but now that it had all gone it seemed good and meaningful and I missed it.

Here the files of airmen lounged, chatted among themselves and occasionally took a surreptitious drag at a cigarette as a sergeant out in front called the names from a list and gave us our leisurely instructions for the day.

This particular morning he was taking a long time over it, consulting sheaves of papers and making laboured notes with a pencil. A big Irishman on my right was becoming increasingly restive and finally he shouted testily:

'For —— sake, sergeant, get us off this —— square. Me —— feet's killin' me!'

The sergeant didn't even look up. 'Shut your mouth, Brady,' he replied. 'You'll get off the square when I say so and not before.'

It was like that at Eastchurch, the great filter tank of the RAF, where what I had heard described as the 'odds and sods' were finally sorted out. It was a big sprawling camp filled with a widely varied mixture of airmen who had one thing in common; they were all waiting – some of them for remuster, but most for discharge from the service.

There was a resigned air about the whole place, an acceptance of the fact that we were all just putting in time. There was a token discipline but it was of the most benign kind. And as I said, every man there was just waiting . . . waiting . . .

Little Ned Finch in his remote corner of the high Yorkshire Dales always seemed to me to be waiting, too. I could remember his boss yelling at him.

'For God's sake, shape up to t'job! You're not farmin' at all!' Mr Daggett grabbed hold of a leaping calf and glared in exasperation.

Ned gazed back at him impassively. His face registered no particular emotion, but in the pale blue eyes I read the expression that was always there – as though he was waiting for something to happen, but without much hope. He made a tentative attempt to catch a calf but was brushed aside, then he put his arms round the neck of another one, a chunky little animal of three months, and was borne along a few yards before being deposited on his back in the straw.

'Oh, dang it, do this one, Mr Herriot!' Mr Daggett barked, turning the hairy neck towards me. 'It looks as though I'll have to catch 'em all myself.'

I injected the animal. I was inoculating a batch of twenty with preventive pneumonia vaccine and Ned was suffering. With his diminu-

SEED FIDDLE With this simple mechanism, a sower on foot distributed seed evenly across a 12 ft width and could sow 4 acres an hour. It was used mostly for sowing small fields with grass and clover. As the sower pulled the bow back and forth, a controlled amount of seed passed from the box on to a disc beneath it. The leather thong attached to the bow passed round the disc's spindle and made it whirl round with each bow movement, flinging out the seed in a wide arc.

tive stature and skinny, small-boned limbs he had always seemed to me to be in the wrong job; but he had been a farm worker all his life and he was over sixty now, grizzled, balding and slightly bent, but still battling on.

Mr Daggett reached out and as one of the shaggy creatures sped past he scooped the head into one of his great hands and seized the ear with the other. The little animal seemed to realise it was useless to struggle and stood unresisting as I inserted the needle. At the other end Ned put his knee against the calf's rear and listlessly pushed it against the wall. He wasn't doing much good and his boss gave him a withering glance.

We finished the bunch with hardly any help from the little man, and as we left the pen and came out into the yard Mr Daggett wiped his brow. It was a raw November day but he was sweating profusely and for a moment he leaned his gaunt six foot frame against the wall as the wind from the bare moorland blew over him.

'By gaw, he's a useless little beggar is that,' he grunted. 'Ah don't know how ah put up with 'im.' He muttered to himself for a few moments then gave tongue again. 'Hey, Ned!'

The little man who had been trailing aimlessly over the cobbles turned his pinched face and looked at him with his submissive but strangely expectant eyes.

'Get them bags o' corn up into the granary!' his boss ordered.

Wordlessly Ned went over to a cart and with an effort shouldered a sack of corn. As he painfully mounted the stone steps to the granary his frail little legs trembled and bent under the weight.

Mr Daggett shook his head and turned to me. His long cadaverous face was set in its usual cast of melancholy.

'You know what's wrong wi' Ned?' he murmured confidentially.

'What do you mean?'

'Well, you know why 'e can't catch them calves?'

My own view was that Ned wasn't big enough or strong enough and anyway he was naturally ineffectual, but I shook my head.

'No,' I said. 'Why is it?'

'Well I'll tell ye.' Mr Daggett glanced furtively across the yard then spoke from behind his hand. 'He's ower fond of t'bright lights.'

'Eh?'

'Ah'm tellin' ye, he's crazed over t'bright lights.'

'Bright . . . what . . . where . . .?'

Mr Daggett leaned closer. 'He gets over to Briston every night.'

'Briston . . .?' I looked across from the isolated farm to the village three miles away on the other side of the Dale. It was the only settlement in that bleak vista – a straggle of ancient houses dark and silent against the green fellside. I could recall that at night the oil lamps made yellow flickers of light in the windows but they weren't very bright. 'I don't understand.'

'Well . . . 'e gets into t'pub.'

'Ah, the pub.'

THE YORKSHIRE WAGON The three types of Yorkshire wagon differed in size rather than design – and the size suited the type of country where the wagon was used. The smallest was the Dales wagon at only 8 ft long. The Moors wagon was 10 ft and the Wolds wagon 12 ft. A distinctive feature of the Yorkshire wagon was that the long shafts, to hold two horses one behind the other, could be replaced by a pole to which the horses were harnessed side by side. The pole was used on hilly ground because it reduced the risk of the horses being pulled over if the cart overturned.

HARVESTING SWEDES Even a smallholding could afford to devote a few acres to growing swedes, for they were a multipurpose crop. Both green tops and roots were used as vegetables for the household, and the roots were valuable winter fodder for sheep and cows. Here, a farmer and his helper are chopping off the tops.

Mr Daggett nodded slowly and portentously but I was still puzzled. The Hulton Arms was a square kitchen where you could get a glass of beer and where a few old men played dominoes of an evening. It wasn't my idea of a den of vice.

'Does he get drunk there?' I asked.

'Nay, nay.' The farmer shook his head. 'It's not that. It's the hours 'e keeps.'

'Comes back late, eh?'

'Aye, that 'e does!' The eyes widened in their cavernous sockets. 'Sometimes 'e doesn't get back till 'alf past nine or ten o'clock!'

'Gosh, is that so?'

'Sure as ah'm standin' here. And there's another thing. He can't get out of 'is bed next day. Ah've done half a day's work before 'e starts.' He paused and glanced again across the yard. 'You can believe me or believe me not, but sometimes 'e isn't on the job till seven o'clock in t'morning!'

'Good heavens!'

He shrugged wearily. 'Aye well, you see how it is. Come into t'house, you'll want to wash your hands.'

In the huge flagged kitchen I bent low over the brown earthenware sink. Scar Farm was four hundred years old and the various tenants hadn't altered it much since the days of Henry the Eighth. Gnarled beams, rough whitewashed walls and hard wooden chairs. But comfort had never been important to Mr Daggett or his wife who was ladling hot water from the primitive boiler by the side of the fire and pouring it into her scrubbing bucket.

She clopped around over the flags in her clogs, hair pulled back tightly from her weathered face into a bun, a coarse sacking apron tied round her waist. She had no children but her life was one of constant activity; indoors or outside, she worked all the time.

At one end of the room wooden steps led up through a hole in the ceiling to a loft where Ned slept. That had been the little man's room for nearly fifty years ever since he had come to work for Mr Daggett's father as a boy from school. And in all that time he had never travelled further than Darrowby, never done anything outside his daily routine. Wifeless, friendless, he plodded through his life, endlessly milking, feeding and mucking out, and waiting, I suspected with diminishing hope for something to happen.

With my hand on the car door I looked back at Scar Farm, at the sagging roof tiles, the great stone lintel over the door. It typified the harshness of the lives of the people within. Little Ned was no bargain as a stocksman, and his boss's exasperation was understandable. Mr Daggett was not a cruel or an unjust man. He and his wife had been hardened and squeezed dry by the pitiless austerity of their existence in this lonely corner of the high Pennines.

There was no softness up here, no frills. The stone walls, sparse grass and stunted trees; the narrow road with its smears of cow muck.

Everything was down to fundamentals, and it was a miracle to me that most of the Dalesmen were not like the Daggetts but cheerful and humorous.

But as I drove away, the sombre beauty of the place overwhelmed me. The lowering hillsides burst magically into life as a shaft of sunshine stabbed through the clouds, flooding the bare flanks with warm gold. Suddenly I was aware of the delicate shadings of green, the rich glowing bronze of the dead bracken spilling from the high tops, the whole peaceful majesty of my work-a-day world.

I hadn't far to drive to my next call – just about a mile – and it was in a vastly different atmosphere. Miss Tremayne, a rich lady from the south, had bought a tumbledown manor house and spent many thousands of pounds in converting it into a luxury home. As my feet crunched on the gravel I looked up at the large windows with their leaded panes, at the smooth freshly-pointed stones.

Elsie opened the door to me. She was Miss Tremayne's cook-housekeeper, and one of my favourite people. Aged about fifty, no more than five feet high and as round as a ball with short bandy legs sticking out from beneath a tight black dress.

'Good morning, Elsie,' I said, and she burst into a peal of laughter. This, more than her remarkable physical appearance, was what delighted me. She laughed uproariously at every statement and occurrence; in fact she laughed at the things she said herself.

'Come in, Mr Herriot, ha-ha-ha,' she said. 'It's been a bit nippy today, he-he, but I think it'll get out this afternoon, ho-ho-ho.'

All the mirth may have seemed somewhat unnecessary, and indeed, it made her rather difficult to understand, but the general effect was cheering. She led me into the drawing room and her mistress rose with some difficulty from her chair.

Miss Tremayne was elderly and half crippled with arthritis but bore her affliction without fuss.

'Ah, Mr Herriot,' she said. 'How good of you to come.' She put her head on one side and beamed at me as though I was the most delightful thing she had seen for a long time.

She, too, had a bubbling, happy personality, and since she owned three dogs, two cats and an elderly donkey I had come to know her very well in her six months' residence in the Dale.

My visit was to dress the donkey's overgrown hooves, and a pair of clippers and a blacksmith's knife dangled from my right hand.

'Oh, put those grisly instruments down over there,' she said. 'Elsie's bringing some tea – I'm sure you've time for a cup.'

I sank willingly into one of the brightly covered armchairs and was looking round the comfortable room when Elsie reappeared, gliding over the carpet as though on wheels. She put the tray on the table by my side.

'There's yer tea,' she said, and went into a paroxysm so hearty that she had to lean on the back of my chair. She had no visible neck and the

continued on page 409

393

WOODCARVERS IN ROBERT THOMPSON'S WORKSHOP AT KILBURN, 1944.

HANDMADE
BY
COUNTRY
—CRAFTSMEN—

In workshops tucked away
in quiet places,
or out in the open air, craftsmen
preserve the traditional
skills of a past age

In the footsteps of the mouseman of Kilburn

The medieval craft of woodcarving, which produced the delicately carved choir stalls at Ripon Cathedral in the 1490s, has flourished again this century in the village of Kilburn.

Kilburn, in the Hambleton Hills, was the home of Robert Thompson, a village carpenter who, in 1919, was asked by the monks of nearby Ampleforth Abbey to make a large oak cross. Oak carvings from Thompson's workshop now appear in hundreds of churches and public buildings throughout Britain, each carrying his 'signature' of a carved mouse.

Thompson's finest work was the library of Ampleforth College. The first library table, made in the 1920s, weighed 1¼ tons, and the final work was completed in 1955, just before his death.

Inspired by Thompson, a 'school' of woodcarvers has grown up in north Yorkshire, and his own grandsons and great-grandsons continue the workshop at Kilburn.

A PAIR OF MICE A modern craftsman using traditional tools carves a pair of mice in a piece of English oak. The workshop was set up by Robert Thompson (above), photographed in 1944 aged 68.

The re-birth of the village blacksmith

Every village once had its blacksmith to make gates and pitchforks, fire grates and griddles. He usually shod the local horses, too, and he treated their various ailments before the arrival of vets in the 19th century.

The decline of the farm horse after the Second World War and competition from factory-made farm tools threatened the blacksmith with extinction. But a boom in horse riding and a fresh interest in hand-made ironwork have opened up a new future.

KITCHEN FITTING Basil Keep, a blacksmith at Grassington, makes a crane for a traditional kitchen range.

TWO GENERATIONS A blacksmith shoes a pony outside the Racehorses Hotel at Kettlewell, Wharfedale, in 1937 (right). Until his recent death, Phil Dowson of Kirkbymoorside was doing the same job at Rydale Forge (above).

Modern use of a skill from the Stone Age

Drystone walls, a characteristic feature of the Yorkshire Dales, are still built by a technique that Stone Age men knew nearly 5,000 years ago. The walls are built without mortar, and are held firm by the skill of the craftsman in fitting rough boulders and angular stones together. The free-standing stones can expand and contract in the changing temperatures of the hills without causing damage.

Some of the present-day field boundaries were originally laid in the Middle Ages by lay brothers of Fountains Abbey, which was one of the largest sheep and wool producers of the Middle Ages.

However, most drystone walls reflect the Enclosure Acts of the 18th century, when large areas of common land on the uplands were walled off into privately owned fields.

THROUGH-BANDS A pair of wallers, working on both sides, can build about 12 yds a day. Walls are built on a solid foundation and often have through-bands of flat stone to give stability and to serve as stiles (above).

The traditional rope-makers of Wensleydale

When the Royal Navy consisted of fleets of sailing ships, rope-making was a major craft in Britain. A ship the size of Nelson's *Victory* carried 15 miles of ropes in her rigging.

Rope was also widely used on farms, and many inland towns had their long rope-walks where hemp and other fibres were spun and twisted into standard lengths of 240 yds.

Nearly all rope is now made by machines, often in man-made fibres such as nylon and polypropylene. However one country rope-making business still thrives at Hawes, at the top of Wensleydale.

Traditional ropes are still made for cow halters and leading-reins for ponies, and the firm also produces ropes for church bells, rope quoits, skipping ropes – and hand-made nylon clothes lines.

WARPING UP Peter Annison, a former textiles lecturer, now runs the old rope firm of W. R. Outhwaite & Son at Hawes. 'Warping up' with yarn to make three strands is the first stage in rope-making. The strands are then twisted into rope.

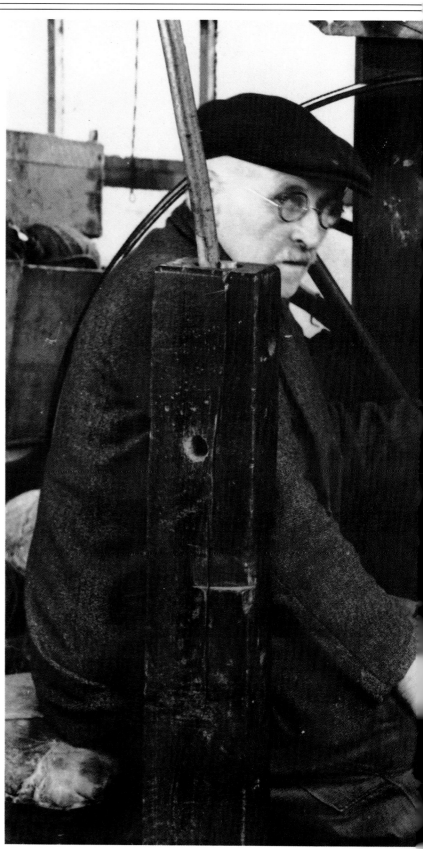

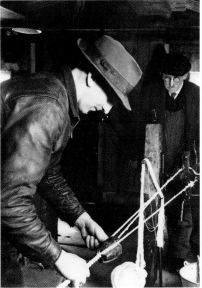

THE ROPE FORMS A strand-twister turns each of the three strands. The action causes the strands to twist themselves into a rope. Tom Outhwaite, who retired in 1975, controls the tension of the rope with a wooden 'top'.

SPINNING W. R. Outhwaite, who died in 1956 aged 81, spins the yarn for one of his ropes (left). Plough and wagon ropes for Dales farmers were made at the Hawes workshop by the simple and ancient technique which produced strong and durable ropes. Mr Outhwaite also made striped webbing for the halters and back-bands of Dales ponies. The webbing was woven on a wooden hand-loom (above).

403

The little miracle of the cooper's ancient craft

To take a bundle of wood strips and shape them into a watertight container involves a small miracle of woodworking skill.

For centuries barrels were used to transport all sorts of goods – wet and dry. They held beer, wine and spirits as well as flour and tobacco.

Every market town and many villages had their coopers, making barrels out of woods such as beech, elm and poplar. In exercising a craft that goes back to the ancient Egyptians, the cooper uses 20 different tools. And he makes barrels that hold as much as 100 gallons or more, or as little as a couple of pints.

But in recent years the craft of coopering has dwindled probably faster than any other, driven out by metal casks made without the need of the cooper's subtle skills.

MAKING A BARREL Clive Hollis, a cooper at Theakston's Brewery in Masham on the River Ure, shapes one of the oak staves for a beer barrel (above). As he fits the final stave in place (right), the barrel takes its shape. The brewery is one of the few places where wooden barrels are still made.

Red clay pottery for kitchens and gardens

Terracotta pottery for kitchens and gardens has been made for centuries by families of Yorkshire potters who dug the red clay – and sometimes the coal for firing the kilns – from their own land.

The main products of the red-ware-makers were mixing bowls, jugs, bread crocks and plant pots.

Littlethorpe Potteries, near Ripon, still makes the traditional ware that the pottery has produced for the past 150 years. Pots are now fired in electric kilns, but previously they went into a kiln that burned 7 tons of coal at one firing and required two and a half days to cool down.

MIXING BOWLS Roland Curtis, of Littlethorpe Potteries, near Ripon, makes traditional pancheons for mixing bread dough. At the turn of the century the pottery also made bricks.

'BIGWARE' A photograph taken in 1913 shows the Littlethorpe potters with the 'bigware' – crocks, bowls and drainpipes – for which they were renowned. Albert Kitson (with the dog) was famed as the finest of bigware throwers.

THATCHING Now rare in Yorkshire, thatching with wheat straw or heather was once a traditional form of roofing.

continued from page 393
laughter caused the fat little body to shake all over.

When she had recovered she rolled back into the kitchen and I heard her clattering about with pans. Despite her idiosyncrasies she was a wonderful cook and very efficient in all she did.

I spent a pleasant ten minutes with Miss Tremayne and the tea, then I went outside and attended to the donkey. When I had finished I made my way round the back of the house and as I was passing the kitchen I saw Elsie at the open window.

'Many thanks for the tea, Elsie,' I said.

The little woman gripped the sides of the sink to steady herself. 'Ha-ha-ha, that's all right. That's, he-he, quite all right, ha-ha-ho-ho-ho.'

Wonderingly I got into the car and as I drove away, the disturbing thought came to me that one day I might say something really witty to Elsie and cause her to do herself an injury.

I was called back to Mr Daggett's quite soon afterwards to see a cow which wouldn't get up. The farmer thought she was paralysed.

I drove there in a thin drizzle and the light was fading at about four o'clock in the afternoon when I arrived at Scar Farm.

When I examined the cow I was convinced she had just got herself into an awkward position in the stall with her legs jammed under the broken timbers of the partition.

'I think she's sulking, Mr Daggett,' I said. 'She's had a few goes at rising and now she's decided not to try any more. Some cows are like that.'

'Maybe you're right,' the farmer replied. 'She's allus been a stupid bitch.'

'And she's a big one, too. She'll take a bit of moving.' I lifted a rope from the byre wall and tied it round the hocks. 'I'll push the feet from the other side while you and Ned pull the legs round.'

'Pull?' Mr Daggett gave the little man a sour look. 'He couldn't pull the skin off a rice puddin'.'

Ned said nothing, just gazed dully to his front, arms hanging limp. He looked as though he didn't care, wasn't even there with us. His mind was certainly elsewhere if his thoughts were mirrored in his eyes – vacant, unheeding, but as always, expectant.

I went behind the partition and thrust steadily at the feet while the men pulled. At least Mr Daggett pulled, mouth open, gasping with effort, while Ned leaned languidly on the rope.

Inch by inch the big animal came round till she was lying almost in the middle of the stall, but as I was about to call a halt the rope broke and Mr Daggett flew backwards on to the hard cobbles. Ned of course did not fall down because he hadn't been trying, and his employer, stretched flat, glared up at him with frustrated rage.

'Ye little bugger, ye let me do that all by meself! Ah don't know why ah bother with you, you're bloody useless.'

At that moment the cow, as I had expected, rose to her feet, and the farmer gesticulated at the little man. 'Well, go on, dang ye, get some straw and rub her legs! They'll be numb.'

Meekly Ned twisted some straw into a wisp and began to do a bit of massage. Mr Daggett got up stiffly, felt gingerly along his back then walked up beside the cow to make sure the chain hadn't tightened round her neck. He was on his way back when the big animal swung round suddenly and brought her cloven hoof down solidly on the farmer's toe.

If he had been wearing heavy boots it wouldn't have been so bad, but his feet were encased in ancient cracked wellingtons which offered no protection.

'Ow! Ow! Ow!' yelled Mr Daggett, beating on the hairy back with his fists. 'Gerroff, ye awd bitch!' He heaved, pushed and writhed but the ten hundredweight of beef ground down inexorably.

The farmer was only released when the cow slid off his foot, and I know from experience that that sliding is the worst part.

Mr Daggett hopped round on one leg, nursing the bruised extremity in his hands. 'Bloody 'ell,' he moaned. 'Oh, bloody 'ell.'

Mr Daggett hopped round on one leg, nursing the bruised extremity.

Just then I happened to glance towards Ned and was amazed to see the apathetic little face crinkle suddenly into a wide grin of unholy glee. I couldn't recall him even smiling before, and my astonishment must have shown in my face because his boss whipped round suddenly and stared at him. As if by magic the sad mask slipped back into place and he went on with his rubbing.

Mr Daggett hobbled out to the car with me and as I was about to leave he nudged me.

'Look at 'im,' he whispered.

Ned, milk pail in hand, was bustling along the byre with unwonted energy.

His employer gave a bitter smile. 'It's t'only time 'e ever hurries. Can't wait to get out to t'pub.'

'Oh well, you say he doesn't get drunk. There can't be any harm in it.'

The deep sunk eyes held me. 'Don't you believe it. He'll come to a bad end gaddin' about the way 'e does.'

'But surely the odd glass of beer ...'

'Ah but there's more than that to it.' He glanced around him. 'There's women!'

I laughed incredulously. 'Oh come now, Mr Daggett, what women?'

'Over at t'pub,' he muttered. 'Them Bradley lasses.'

'The landlord's daughters? Oh really, I can't believe ...'

'All right, ye can say what ye like. He's got 'is eye on 'em. Ah knaw – ah've only been in that pub once but ah've seen for meself.'

I didn't know what to say, but in any case I had no opportunity because he turned and strode into the house.

Alone in the cold darkness I looked at the gaunt silhouette of the old farmhouse above me. In the dying light of the November day the rain streamed down the rough stones and the wind caught at the thin tendril of smoke from the chimney, hurling it in ragged streamers across the slate blue pallor of the western sky. The fell hung over everything, a black featureless bulk, oppressive and menacing.

Through the kitchen window I could see the oil lamp casting its dim light over the bare table, the cheerless hearth with its tiny flicker of fire. In the shadows at the far end the steps rose into Ned's loft and I could imagine the little figure clambering up to get changed and escape to Briston.

Across the valley the single street of the village was a broken grey thread in the gloom but in the cottage windows the lamps winked faintly. These were Ned Finch's bright lights and I could understand how he felt. After Scar Farm, Briston would be like Monte Carlo.

The image stayed in my mind so vividly that after two more calls that evening I decided to go a few miles out of my way as I returned homeward. I cut across the Dale and it was about half past eight when I drove into Briston. It was difficult to find the Hulton Arms because there was no lighted entrance, no attempt to advertise its presence, but I persevered because I had to find out what was behind Mr Daggett's tale

411

MAGNET MINDED MEN

For men like me

MAGNET
BRITAIN'S BEST BEER
JOHN SMITH'S TADCASTER BREWERY, LTD.

LOCAL BEER After a hot day's work in the fields, a 1930s farmhand could quench his thirst in the village pub with a pint of Magnet best bitter for seven old pence (3p.). It came from Tadcaster, which had been a brewing town from medieval times because of its numerous springs of hard water and the local crops of barley – two essentials for brewing. While it was a coaching stop on the route to the north, Tadcaster had plenty of customers for its beer, but the railways killed that trade. John Smith bought a run-down brewery in 1847 and developed a clear beer that pleased public taste at a time when pubs were beginning to serve beer in glasses, rather than in pottery mugs. By the 1930s, his successors were sending lorry loads of barrelled and bottled beers all over Yorkshire and into Lancashire and Cheshire.

of debauchery.

I located it at last. Just like the door of an ordinary house with a faded wooden sign hanging above it. Inside, the usual domino game was in progress, a few farmers sat chatting quietly. The Misses Bradley, plain but pleasant-faced women in their forties, sat on either side of the fire, and sure enough there was Ned with a half pint glass in front of him.

I sat down by his side. 'Hello, Ned.'

'Now then, Mr Herriot,' he murmured absently, glancing at me with his strange expectant eyes.

One of the Bradley ladies put down her knitting and came over.

'Pint of bitter please,' I said. 'What will you have, Ned?'

'Nay, thank ye, Mr Herriot. This'll do for me. It's me second and ah'm not a big drinker, tha knows.'

Miss Bradley laughed. 'Yes, he nobbut has 'is two glasses a night, but he enjoys them, don't you, Ned?'

'That's right, ah do.' He looked up at her and she smiled kindly down at him before going for my beer.

He took a sip at his glass. 'Ah really come for t'company, Mr Herriot.'

'Yes, of course,' I said. I knew what he meant. He probably sat on his own most of the time, but around him was warmth and comfort and friendliness. A great log sent flames crackling up to the wide chimney, there was electric light and shining mirrors with whisky slogans painted on their surface. It wasn't anything like Scar Farm.

The little man said very little. He spun out his drink for another hour, looking around him as the dominoes clicked and I lowered another contemplative pint. The Misses Bradley knitted and brewed tea in a big black kettle over the fire and when they had to get up to serve their customers they occasionally patted Ned playfully on the cheek as they passed.

By the time he tipped down the last drop and rose to go it was a quarter to ten and he still had to cycle across to the other side of the Dale. Another late night for Ned.

It was a Tuesday lunchtime in early spring. Helen always cooked steak and kidney pie on Tuesdays and I used to think about it all morning on my rounds. My thoughts that morning had been particularly evocative because lambing had started and I had spent most of the time in my shirt sleeves in the biting wind as my hunger grew and grew.

Helen cut into her blissful creation and began to scoop the fragrant contents on to my plate.

'I met Miss Tremayne in the market place this morning, Jim.'

'Oh yes?' I was almost drooling as my wife stopped shovelling out the pie, sliced open some jacket potatoes and dropped pats of farm butter on to the steaming surfaces.

'Yes, she wants you to go out there this afternoon and put some canker drops in Wilberforce's ears if you have time.'

'Oh I have time for that,' I said. Wilberforce was Miss Tremayne's ancient tabby cat and it was just the kind of job I wanted after my arm-aching morning.

I was raising a luscious forkful when Helen spoke again. 'Oh, and she had an interesting item of news.'

'Really?' But I had begun to chew and my thoughts were distant.

'It's about the little woman who works for her – Elsie. You know her?'

I nodded and took another mouthful. 'Of course, of course.'

'Well it's quite unexpected, I suppose, but Elsie's getting married.'

I choked on my pie. 'What!'

'It's true. And maybe you know the bridegroom.'

'Tell me.'

'He works on one of the neighbouring farms. His name is Ned Finch.'

This time my breath was cut off completely and Helen had to beat me on the back as I spluttered and retched. It wasn't until an occluding morsel of potato skin had shot down my nose that I was able to utter a weak croak. 'Ned Finch?'

'That's what she said.'

I finished my lunch in a dream, but by the end of it I had accepted the extraordinary fact. Helen and Miss Tremayne were two sensible people – there couldn't be any mistake. And yet ... even as I drew up outside the old Manor House a feeling of unreality persisted.

Elsie opened the door as usual. I looked at her for a moment.

'What's this I hear, Elsie?'

She started a giggle which rapidly spread over her spherical frame.

I put my hand on her shoulder. 'Is it true?'

The giggle developed into a mighty gale of laughter, and if she hadn't been holding the handle I am sure she would have fallen over.

'Aye, it's right enough,' she gasped. 'Ah've found a man at last and ah'm goin' to get wed!' She leaned helplessly on the door.

'Well, I'm pleased to hear it, Elsie. I hope you'll be very happy.'

She hadn't the strength to speak but merely nodded as she lay against the door. Then she led me to the drawing room.

'In ye go,' she chuckled. 'Ah'll bring ye some tea.'

Miss Tremayne rose to greet me with parted lips and shining eyes. 'Oh, Mr Herriot, have you heard?'

'Yes, but how ...?'

'It all started when I asked Mr Daggett for some fresh eggs. He sent Ned on his bicycle with the eggs and it was like fate.'

'Well, how wonderful.'

'Yes, and I actually saw it happen. Ned walked in that door with his basket, Elsie was clearing the table here, and, Mr Herriot.' She clasped her hands under her chin, smiled ecstatically and her eyes rolled upwards. 'Oh, Mr Herriot, it was love at first sight!'

'Yes ... yes, indeed. Marvellous!'

'And ever since that day Ned has been calling round and now he comes every evening and sits with Elsie in the kitchen. Isn't it romantic!'

'It certainly is. And when did they decide to get married?'

ROLLING-PINS Plain wooden pins (centre and bottom) about 16 in. long and made of sycamore or beech were used for rolling out pastry in the 1930s, as they still are. The usual pin was straight-sided and some had a knob at one end only. Less common was the convex-sided pin. This was sometimes used for rolling pastry, especially flaky pastry, very thin. Glass rolling-pins (top) were mainly ornamental, and frequently given by sailors to their girl-friends. This one of blown glass, clear with blue swirls, was filled with sugar, but others contained tea, or even liquor.

'Oh, he popped the question within a month, and I'm so happy for Elsie because Ned is such a dear little man, don't you think so?'

'Yes he is.' I said. 'He's a very nice chap.'

Elsie simpered and tittered her way in with the tea then put her hand over her face and fled in confusion, and as Miss Tremayne began to pour I sank into one of the armchairs and lifted Wilberforce on to my lap.

The big cat purred as I instilled a few drops of lotion into his ear. He had a chronic canker condition – not very bad but now and then it became painful and needed treatment. It was because Miss Tremayne didn't like putting the lotion in that I was pressed into service.

As I turned the ear over and gently massaged the oily liquid into the depths, Wilberforce groaned softly with pleasure and rubbed his cheek against my hand. He loved this anointing of the tender area beyond his reach and when I had finished he curled up on my knee.

I leaned back and sipped my tea. At that moment, with my back and shoulders weary and my hands red and chapped with countless washings on the open hillsides this seemed to be veterinary practice at its best.

Miss Tremayne continued. 'We shall have a little reception after the wedding and then the happy couple will take up residence here.'

'You mean, in this house?'

'Yes, of course. There's heaps of room in this big old place, and I have furnished two rooms for them on the east side. I'm sure they'll be very comfortable. Oh, I'm so excited about it all!'

She refilled my cup. 'Before you go you must let Elsie show you where they are going to live.'

On my way out the little woman took me through to the far end of the house.

'This, hee-hee-hee,' she said, 'is where we'll sit of a night, and this, ha-ha-ho-ho, oh dear me, is our bedroom.' She staggered around for a bit, wiped her eyes and turned to me for my opinion.

'It's really lovely, Elsie,' I said.

There were bright carpets, chairs with flowered covers and a fine mahogany-ended bed. It was nothing like the loft.

And as I looked at Elsie I realised the things Ned would see in his bride. Laughter, warmth, vivacity, and – I had no doubt at all – beauty and glamour.

I seemed to get round to most farms that lambing time and in due course I landed at Mr Daggett's. I delivered a fine pair of twins for him but it didn't seem to cheer him at all. Lifting the towel from the grass he handed it to me.

'Well, what did ah tell ye about Ned, eh? Got mixed up wi' a woman just like ah said.' He sniffed disapprovingly. 'All that rakin' and chasin' about – ah knew he'd get into mischief at t'finish.'

I walked back over the sunlit fields to the farm and as I passed the byre door Ned came out pushing a wheelbarrow.

LAMBING IN THE FIELDS Hill sheep are often brought into a field on lower ground when April and lambing time comes. Most sheep will not need help, but the shepherd keeps a close eye on the flock for difficult births and weak lambs. He makes sure that the lambs are being fed and finds a foster mother for the rare occasion when a ewe is not feeding her lambs adequately. The shepherd also puts the ewes that have lambed together, and to lead them to the right spot he carries the lambs while the ewe anxiously follows. Here the shepherd is carrying the lambs by their legs, a satisfactory method for a short distance, but for a longer distance he would carry them in his arms.

414

'Good morning, Ned,' I said.

He glanced up at me in his vague way. 'How do, Mr Herriot.'

There was something different about him and it took me a few moments to discern what it was; his eyes had lost the expectant look which had been there for so long, and, after all, that was perfectly natural.

Because it had happened at last for Ned.

FEEDING SHEEP Ewes will produce more milk, and thus rear strong lambs, if they are well fed themselves. They are often kept on a nursery field where the grazing is lush. It was once common to give them supplementary feeds of concentrates. These might be crushed oats, bran, flaked maize, or crushed cattle cake. The farmer here is scattering concentrate for the ewes, allowing about ½ lb as each animal's daily requirement. When it is time for the lambs to be weaned, the ewes' food is cut down so the milk supply dwindles.

13

Goodbye to the RAF

I knew it was the end of the chapter when I slammed the carriage door behind me and squeezed into a seat between a fat WAAF and a sleeping corporal.

I suppose I was an entirely typical discharged serviceman. They had taken away my blue uniform and fitted me with a 'demob suit', a ghastly garment of stiff brown serge with purple stripes which made me look like an old-time gangster, but they had allowed me to retain my RAF shirt and tie and the shiny boots which were like old friends.

My few belongings, including Black's *Veterinary Dictionary*, lay in the rack above in a small cardboard suitcase of a type very popular among the lower ranks of the services. They were all I possessed and I could have done with a coat because it was cold in the train and a long journey stretched between Eastchurch and Darrowby.

It took an age to chug and jolt as far as London then there was a lengthy wait before I boarded the train for the north. It was about midnight when we set off, and for seven hours I sat there in the freezing darkness, feet numb, teeth chattering.

The last lap was by bus and it was the same rattling little vehicle which had carried me to my first job those years ago. The driver was the same too, and the time between seemed to melt away as the fells began to rise again from the blue distance in the early light and I saw the familiar farmhouses, the walls creeping up the grassy slopes, the fringe of trees by the river's edge.

It was mid morning when we rumbled into the market place and I read 'Darrowby Co-operative Society' above the shop on the far side. The sun was high, warming the tiles of the fretted line of roofs with their swelling green background of hills. I got out and the bus went on its way, leaving me standing by my case.

And it was just the same as before. The sweet air, the silence and the cobbled square deserted except for the old men sitting around the clock tower. One of them looked up at me.

'Now then, Mr Herriot,' he said quietly as though he had seen me only yesterday.

Before me Trengate curved away till it disappeared round the grocer's shop on the corner. Most of the quiet street with the church at its foot was beyond my view and it was a long time since I had been down there, but with my eyes closed I could see Skeldale House with the ivy climbing over the old brick walls to the little rooms under the eaves.

That was where I would have to make another start; where I would find out how much I had forgotten, whether I was fit to be an animal doctor again. But I wouldn't go along there yet, not just yet ...

A lot had happened since that first day when I arrived in Darrowby in search of a job but it came to me suddenly that my circumstances hadn't changed much. All I had possessed then was an old case and the suit I stood in and it was about the same now. Except for one great and wonderful thing. I had Helen and Jimmy.

That made all the difference. I had no money, not even a house to call my own, but any roof which covered my wife and son was personal and special. Sam would be with them, too, waiting for me. They were outside the town and it was a fair walk from here, but I looked down at the blunt toes of my boots sticking from the purple striped trousers. The RAF hadn't only taught me to fly, they had taught me to march, and a few miles didn't bother me.

I took a fresh grip on my cardboard case, turned towards the exit from the square and set off, left-right, left-right, left-right on the road for home.

LEADING THE CORN When the corn was dry, it was ready for leading, or putting on carts to take back to the farmyard. It was forked up two sheaves at a time to a loader who stacked it on the wagon. The wagon often had a shelf jutting out from each side to allow it to carry a wider load. Horses drew the wagon from stook to stook – starting from the middle of the field – until it was carrying about 500 sheaves.

PART FOUR
Back to Darrowby

It seemed that all nature was rejoicing with me. It was
May 1947, the beginning of the most perfect summer
I can remember. The sun blazed, soft breezes swirled.
Everywhere new life was calling out its exultant message,
and my new little daughter was there in Darrowby.

1

Rickety gates and outsize calves

CHAROLAIS BULL The foremost beef animal of Europe is the pale cream Charolais from eastern central France. It was already established there in the 18th century, when it was used as a draught animal to pull ploughs and farm carts. This work no doubt intensified the animal's physical features – its heavy build and well-developed hindquarters. In 1962 the first 27 Charolais bulls were introduced into Britain, principally for crossing with dairy cattle. The bull calves that are born from such crosses make quick-maturing beef cattle.

When the gate fell on top of me I knew I was really back home.

My mind drifted effortlessly over my spell in the RAF to the last time I had visited the Ripleys. It was to 'nip some calves' as Mr Ripley said over the phone, or more correctly to emasculate them by means of the Burdizzo bloodless castrator, and when the message came in I realised that a large part of my morning had gone.

It was always something of a safari to visit Anson Hall, because the old house lay at the end of a ridged and rutted track which twisted across the fields through no fewer than seven gates.

Gates are one of the curses of a country vet's life and in the Yorkshire Dales, before the coming of cattle grids, we suffered more than most. We were resigned to opening two or three on many of the farms, but seven was a bit much. And at the Ripleys it wasn't just the number but the character.

The first one which led off the narrow road was reasonably normal – an ancient thing of rusty iron – and as I unlatched it it did at least swing round groaning on its hinges. It was the only one which swung; the others were of wood and of the type known in the Dales as 'shoulder gates'. I could see how they got their name as I hoisted each one up, balanced the top spar on my shoulder and dragged it round. These had no hinges but were tied at one end with binder twine top and bottom.

Even with an ordinary gate there is a fair amount of work involved. You have to stop the car, get out, open the gate, drive through, stop the car again, dismount and close the thing behind you. But the road to Anson Hall was hard labour. The gates deteriorated progressively as I approached the farm and I was puffing with my efforts as I bumped and rattled my way up to number seven.

This was the last and the most formidable – a malignant entity with a personality of its own. Over decades it had been patched and repaired with so many old timbers that probably none of the original structure remained. But it was dangerous.

I got out of the car and advanced a few steps. We were old foes, this gate and I, and we faced each other for some moments in silence. We had fought several brisk rounds in the past and there was no doubt the gate was ahead on points.

The difficulty was that, apart from its wobbly, loosely-nailed eccentricity, it had only one string hinge, halfway down. This enabled it to pivot on its frail axis with deadly effect.

With the utmost care I approached the right-hand side and began to unfasten the binder twine. The string, I noted bitterly, was, like all the others, neatly tied in a bow, and as it fell clear I grabbed hastily at the top spar. But I was too late. Like a live thing the bottom rail swung in and rapped me cruelly on the shins, and as I tried to correct the balance the top bashed my chest.

It was the same as all the other times. As I hauled it round an inch at a time, the gate buffeted me high and low. I was no match for it.

Another thing which didn't help was that I could see Mr Ripley watching me benevolently from the farmhouse doorway. While I wrestled the gate open, contented puffs rose from the farmer's pipe and he did not stir from his position until I had hobbled over the last stretch of grass and stood before him.

'Now then, Mr Herriot, you've come to nip me a few calves?' A smile of unaffected friendship creased the stubbled cheeks. Mr Ripley shaved once a week – on market day – considering, with some logic, that since only his wife and his cattle saw him on the other six days there was no point in scraping away at his face every morning with a razor.

I bent and massaged my bruised ankles. 'Mr Ripley, that gate! It's a menace! Do you remember that last time I was here you promised me faithfully you'd have it mended? In fact you said you'd get a new one – it's about time, isn't it?'

'Aye, you're right, young man,' Mr Ripley said, nodding his head in profound agreement. 'Ah did say that, but tha knaws, its one o' them little jobs which never seem to get done.' He chuckled ruefully, but his expression altered to concern when I wound up my trouser leg and revealed a long abrasion on my shin.

'Eee, that's a shame, that's settled it. There'll be a new gate on there by next week. Ah'll guarantee it.'

'But, Mr Ripley, that's exactly what you said last time when you saw the blood running down my knee. Those were your very words. You said you'd guarantee it ...'

'Aye, I knaw, I knaw.' The farmer tamped down the tobacco with his thumb and got his pipe going again to his satisfaction. 'Me missus is allus on to me about me bad memory, but don't worry, Mr Herriot, I've had me lesson today. I'm right sorry about your leg and that gate'll never bother ye again. Ah guarantee it.'

'Okay, okay,' I said and limped over to the car for the Burdizzo. 'Where are the calves, anyway?' Mr Ripley crossed the farmyard unhurriedly and opened the half door on a loose-box. 'They're in there.'

For a moment I stood transfixed as a row of huge shaggy heads regarded me impassively over the timbers, then I extended a trembling finger. 'Do you mean those?'

The farmer nodded happily. 'Aye, them's them.'

I went forward and looked into the box. There were eight strapping yearlings in there, some of them returning my stare with mild interest, others cavorting and kicking up their heels among the straw. I turned to the farmer. 'You've done it again, haven't you?'

'Eh?'

BULLDOGS This 8 in. long pair of bulldogs can be used whenever a bull or cow has to be grasped firmly at the head – for dosing with medicine, or for having a nose-ring inserted, for example. The jaws, with knobbed ends, swivel apart when the ring catch is slid down the stem. The ends are inserted in the animal's nostrils, and the ring is slipped into place to make the jaws grip the division between the nostrils.

I stood transfixed as a row of huge shaggy heads regarded me impassively.

'You asked me to come and nip some calves. Those aren't calves, they're bulls! And it was the same last time. Remember those monsters you had in the same box? I nearly ruptured myself closing the nippers and you said you'd get them done at three months old in future. In fact you said you'd guarantee it.'

The farmer nodded solemnly in agreement. He always agreed one hundred per cent with everything I said. 'That's correct, Mr Herriot. That's what ah said.'

'But these animals are at least a year old!'

Mr Ripley shrugged and gave me a world-weary smile. 'Aye, well, time gets on, doesn't it. Fairly races by.'

I returned to the car for the local anaesthetic. 'All right,' I grunted as I filled the syringe. 'If you can catch them I'll see what I can do.' The farmer lifted a rope halter from a hook on the wall and approached one of the big beasts, murmuring encouragingly. He snared the nose with surprising ease, dropping the loops over nose and horn with perfect timing as the animal tried to plunge past him. Then he passed the rope through a ring on the wall and pulled it tight.

'There y'are, Mr Herriot. That wasn't much trouble was it?'

I didn't say anything. I was the one who was going to have the trouble. I was working at the wrong end, nicely in range of the hooves which would surely start flying if my patients didn't appreciate having a needle stuck into their testicles.

Anyway, it had to be done. One by one I infiltrated the scrotal area with the local, taking the blows on my arms and legs as they came. Then I started the actual process of castration, the bloodless crushing of the spermatic cord without breaking the skin. There was no doubt this was a big advance on the old method of incising the scrotum with a knife, and in little calves it was a trifling business lasting only a few seconds.

But it was altogether different with these vast creatures. It was necessary to open the arms of the Burdizzo beyond right angles to grip the great fleshy scrotum and then they had to be closed again. That was when the fun started.

Thanks to my injection the beast could feel little or nothing but as I squeezed desperately it seemed that I was attempting the impossible. However it is amazing what the human frame can accomplish when pushed to the utmost and as the sweat trickled down my nose and as I gasped and strained, the metal arms inched closer until the jaws finally clicked together.

I always nipped each side twice and I took a rest before repeating the process lower down the cord. When I had done the same with the other testicle I flopped back against the wall, panting and trying not to think of the other seven beasts still to do.

It was a long, long time before I got to the last one and I was wrestling away, pop-eyed and open-mouthed when the idea came to me.

I straightened up and came along the side of the animal. 'Mr Ripley,' I said breathlessly, 'why don't you have a go?'

'Eh?' The farmer had been watching me with equanimity, blowing out slow clouds of blue smoke, but it was plain that I had jolted him out of his composure. 'What d'ye mean?'

'Well, this is the last one and I want you to understand what I've been talking about. I'd like to see you close those nippers.'

He thought the matter over for a moment or two. 'Aye, but who's goin' to hold t'beast?'

'That's all right,' I said. 'We'll tie him up short to the ring and I'll set everything up for you, then we'll see how you get on.'

He looked a little doubtful but I was determined to make my point and ushered him gently to the rear end of the animal. I enclosed the scrotum in the Burdizzo and placed Mr Ripley's fingers round the handles.

'Right,' I said. 'Off you go.'

The farmer took a long breath, braced himself and began to exert pressure on the metal arms. Nothing happened.

I stood there for several minutes as his face turned red then purple, his eyes protruded even further than mine and the veins on his forehead

421

FILLING THE FAMILY Those who ate most pudding could have most meat – or so a family would be told as they sat down at midday for their dinner. But the housewife well knew that those who had eaten most squares of the crisp, light pudding, with a generous pouring of savoury gravy, would have less appetite for the expensive roast beef.

stood out in livid ridges. Finally he gave a groan and dropped to his knees.

'Nay, lad, nay, it's no good, I can't do it.'

He got to his feet slowly and mopped his brow.

'But, Mr Ripley.' I put a hand on his shoulder and smiled kindly at him. 'You expect me to do it.'

He nodded dumbly.

'Ah well, never mind,' I said. 'You understand now what I've been talking about. This is an easy little job made difficult by leaving it until the beasts are as big as this. If you'd called me out when they were calves of three months I'd have been on and off your place in a few minutes, wouldn't I?'

'Aye, you would, Mr Herriot, you're right. I've been daft and I'll see it doesn't happen again.'

I felt really clever. I don't often have moments of inspiration but the conviction swelled in me that one of them had come to me today. I had finally got through to Mr Ripley.

The feeling of exhilaration gave me added strength and I finished the job effortlessly. As I walked to the car I positively glowed and my self-satisfaction deepened when the farmer bent to the window as I started the engine.

'Well, thank ye, Mr Herriot,' he said. 'You've taught me summat this mornin'. Next time ye come I'll have a nice new gate for ye and I'll never ask ye to nip big beasts like that again. Ah guarantee it.'

All that happened a long time ago, before the RAF, and I was now in the process of reinserting myself into civilian life, tasting the old things which I had almost forgotten. But at the moment when the phone rang I was tasting something very near to my heart – Helen's cooking.

It was Sunday lunchtime, when the traditional roast beef and Yorkshire pudding was served. My wife had just dropped a slab of the pudding on my plate and was pouring gravy over it, a rich brown flood with the soul of the meat in it and an aroma to dream of. I was starving after a typical country vet's Sunday morning of rushing round farms and I was thinking, as I often did, that if I had some foreign gourmet to impress with the choicest sample of our British food then this is what I would give him.

A great chunk of Yorkshire pud and gravy was the expedient of the thrifty farmers to fill their families' stomachs before the real meal started – 'Them as eats most puddin' gets most meat,' was the wily encouragement – but it was heaven. And as I chewed my first forkful I was happy in the knowledge that when I had cleared my plate Helen would fill it again with the beef itself and with potatoes, peas and runner beans gathered from our garden that morning.

The shrilling phone cut cruelly into my reverie but I told myself that nothing was going to spoil this meal. The most urgent job in veterinary practice could wait until I had finished.

But my hand shook as I lifted the receiver and a mixture of anxiety and disbelief flowed through me as I heard the voice at the other end. It was Mr Ripley. Oh please, no, not that long long trek to Anson Hall on a Sunday.

The farmer's voice thundered in my ear. He was one of the many who still thought you had to bawl lustily to cover the miles between.

'Is that vitnery?'

'Yes, Herriot speaking.'

'Oh, you're back from t'war, then?'

'Yes, that's right.'

'Well, ah want ye out here right away. One of me cows is right bad.'

'What's the trouble? Is it urgent?'

'Aye, it is! I think she's maybe broke 'er leg!'

I held the ear-piece away from me. Mr Ripley had increased his volume and my head was beginning to ring. 'What makes you think that?' I asked, suddenly dry-mouthed.

'Well, she's on three legs,' the farmer blasted back at me. 'And t'other's sort of hangin', like.'

Oh God, that sounded horribly significant. I looked sadly across the room at my loaded plate. 'All right, Mr Ripley, I'll be along.'

'You'll come straight away, won't ye? Right now?' the voice was an important roar.

'Yes, I'll come straight away.' I put down the receiver, rubbed my ear and turned to my wife.

Helen looked up from the table with the stricken face of a woman who can visualise her Yorkshire pudding sagging into lifeless ruin. 'Oh surely you don't have to go this minute?'

'I'm sorry, Helen, this is one of those things I can't leave.' I could picture only too easily the injured animal plunging around in her agony, perhaps compounding the fracture. 'And the man sounds desperate. I've just got to go.'

My wife's lips trembled. 'All right, I'll put it in the oven till you come back.'

As I left I saw her carrying the plate away. We both knew it was the end. No Yorkshire pud could survive a visit to Anson Hall.

I increased my speed as I drove through Darrowby. The cobbled market place, sleeping in the sunshine, breathed its Sunday peace and emptiness with all the inhabitants of the little town eating busily behind closed doors. Out in the country the dry-stone walls flashed by as I kept my foot on the boards, and when I finally arrived at the beginning of the farm track I had a sense of shock.

It was the first time I had been there since I left the service and I suppose I had been expecting to find something different. But the old iron gate was just the same, except that it was even more rusty than before. With a growing feeling of doom I fought my way through the other gates, untying the strings and shouldering the top spars round until finally I came to number seven.

YORKSHIRE PUDDING Some families liked their pudding cooked in individual small round tins but most had one large pudding cut into squares. Crisp corner pieces were the choice of some members of the family, while others preferred a softer square from the middle. To make Yorkshire pudding, add ½ teaspoon of salt to 4 oz of plain flour in a large mixing bowl and make a hollow in the centre. Drop 1 large egg into the hollow and gradually draw the flour into it, stirring vigorously and adding ½ pint of milk a little at a time until the batter is smooth. Leave the mixture to stand for an hour. Heat a little dripping in an 8 in. square baking tin, stir 2 tablespoons of cold water into the batter and pour it into the tin. Bake at 450°F (230°C), gas mark 8, for 25 minutes until puffy and golden-brown.

COOKING BY PARAFFIN In summer it was often too hot to keep the kitchen range lit. From the late 19th century, paraffin stoves were available and became widely used in north Yorkshire. The most common (top) was only 9 in. high and had several wicks giving flames beneath the flat stand where a kettle or stewpot could be boiled. The more elaborate Valor stove (bottom) was 2½ ft high and heated the space between the green-enamelled tinplate oven and the inner lining. The cabinet measured only about a cubic foot, but it had three shelves and a glass door to let the cook keep an eye on the baking.

This last and most terrible of the gates was still there, and unchanged. It couldn't be true, I told myself as I almost tiptoed towards it. All sorts of things had happened to me since I last saw it. I had been away in a different world of marching and drilling and learning navigation and finally flying an aeroplane, while this rickety structure stood there unheeding.

I eyed it closely. The loose-nailed wobbly timbers were as before, as was the single-string hinge – probably the same piece of string. It was unbelievable. And then I noticed something different. Mr Ripley, apparently worried lest his livestock might rub against and damage the ancient bastion had festooned the thing with barbed wire.

Maybe it had mellowed with time. It couldn't be as vicious as before. Gingerly I loosened the bottom string on the right-hand side, then with infinite care I untied the bow at the top. I was just thinking that it was going to be easy when the binder twine fell away and the gate swung with all its old venom on the left-hand string.

It got me on the chest first, then whacked against my legs, and this time the steel barbs bit through my trousers. Frantically I tried to throw the thing away from me, but it pounded me high and low and when I leaned back to protect my chest my legs slid from under me and I fell on my back. And as my shoulder hit the track, the gate, with a soft woody crunch, fell on top of me.

I had been nearly underneath this gate several times in the past and had got clear at the last moment, but this time it had really happened. I tried to wriggle out, but the barbed wire had my clothing in its iron grip. I was trapped.

I craned desperately over the timbers. The farm was only fifty yards away but there was not a soul in sight. And that was a funny thing – where was the anxious farmer? I had expected to find him pacing up and down the yard, wringing his hands, but the place seemed deserted.

I dallied with the idea of shouting for help, but that would have been just too absurd. There was nothing else for it. I seized the top rail in both hands and pushed upwards, trying to close my ears to the tearing sounds from my garments, then, very slowly, I eased my way to safety.

I left the gate lying where it was. Normally I meticulously close all gates behind me but there were no cattle in the fields and anyway I had had enough of this one.

I rapped sharply at the farmhouse door and Mrs Ripley answered. 'Now then, Mr Herriot, it's grand weather,' she said. Her carefree smile reminded me of her husband's as she wiped at a dinner plate and adjusted the apron around her ample midriff.

'Yes . . . yes . . . it is. I've called to see your cow. Is your husband in?'

She shook her head. 'Nay 'e hasn't got back from t'Fox and Hounds yet.'

'What!' I stared at her. 'That's the pub at Diverton, isn't it? I thought he had an urgent case for me to see.'

'Aye, well, he had to go across there to ring ye up. We haven't no

424

telephone here, ye know.' Her smile widened.

'But – but that was nearly an hour since. He should have been back here long ago.'

'That's right,' she said, nodding with perfect understanding. 'But he'll 'ave met some of his pals up there. They all get into t'Fox and Hounds on a Sunday mornin'.'

I churned my hair around. 'Mrs Ripley, I've left my meal lying on the table so that I could get here immediately!'

'Oh, we've 'ad ours,' she replied as though the words would be a comfort to me. And she didn't have to tell me. The rich scent drifting from the kitchen was unmistakably roast beef, and there was no doubt at all that it would have been preceded by Yorkshire pudding.

I didn't say anything for a few moments, then I took a deep breath. 'Well, maybe I can see the cow. Where is she, please?'

Mrs Ripley pointed to a box at the far end of the yard.

'She's in there.' As I set off across the cobbles she called after me. 'You can be lookin' at her till 'e gets back. He won't be many minutes.'

I flinched as though a lash had fallen across my shoulders. Those were dreadful words. 'Not many minutes' was a common phrase in Yorkshire and could mean anything up to two hours.

I opened the half door and looked into the box at the cow. She was very lame, but when I approached her she hopped around in the straw, dotting the injured limb on the ground.

Well, she hadn't a broken leg. She couldn't take her weight on it but there was none of the typical dangling of the limb. I felt a surge of relief. In a big animal, a fracture usually meant the humane killer because no number of plaster bandages could take the strain. The trouble seemed to be in her foot but I couldn't catch her to find out. I'd have to wait for Mr Ripley.

I went out into the afternoon sunshine and gazed over the gently rising fields to the church tower of Diverton pushing from the trees. There was no sign of the farmer and I walked wearily beyond the buildings on to the grass to await his coming.

I looked back at the house and even through my exasperation I felt a sense of peace. Like many of the older farms, Anson Hall had once been a noble manor. Hundreds of years ago some person of title had built his dwelling in a beautiful place. The roof looked ready to fall in and one of the tall chimney stacks leaned drunkenly to one side, but the mullioned windows, the graceful arched doorway and the stately proportions of the building were a delight, with the pastures beyond stretching towards the green fells.

And that garden wall. In its former glory the sun-warmed stones would have enclosed a cropped lawn with bright flowers but now there were only nettles. Those nettles fascinated me; a waist-high jungle filling every inch of space between wall and house. Farmers are notoriously bad gardeners but Mr Ripley was in a class by himself.

My reverie was interrupted by a cry from the lady of the house. 'He's

MILK DONKEY When milking out in the fields was going to yield more than one can of milk to take back to the farm, the milker might take a donkey or a pony with him. Wensleydale farmers used donkeys a great deal, but Swaledale farmers would use small ponies. A hebble, or two-platformed sling, was put across the animal's back to hold a can on each side.

LIMOUSIN BULL A major beef breed of Europe, second only to the Charolais, is the Limousin from west central France. It is a smaller animal than the Charolais, longer but finer-boned. It produces a high yield of lean beef. The Limousin matures quickly and is often reared for baby beef. At only ten months old the young bull will already weigh half a ton. A prize bull sold for breeding will bring a price of about £20,000.

comin', Mr Herriot. I've just spotted 'im through the window.' She came round to the front and pointed towards Diverton.

Her husband was indeed on his way, a black dot moving unhurriedly down through the fields, and we watched him together for about fifteen minutes until at last he squeezed himself through a gap in a wall and came up to us, the smoke from his pipe rising around his ears.

I went straight into the attack. 'Mr Ripley, I've been waiting a long time! You asked me to come straight away!'

'Aye, ah knaw, ah knaw, but I couldn't very well ask to use t'phone without havin' a pint, could I?' He put his head on one side and beamed at me, secure in his unanswerable logic.

I was about to speak when he went on. 'And then Dick Henderson bought me one, so I had to buy 'im one back, and then I was just leavin' when Bobby Talbot started on about them pigs he got from me last week.'

His wife chipped in with bright curiosity. 'Eee, that Bobby Talbot! Was he there this mornin', too? He's never away from t'pub, that feller. I don't know how his missus puts up with it.'

'Aye, Bobby was there all right. He allus is.' Mr Ripley smiled gently, knocked his pipe out against his heel and began to refill it. 'And ah'll tell you who else ah saw – Dan Thompson. Haven't seen 'im since his operation. By gaw it has fleeced him – he's lost a bit o'ground. Looks as though a few pints would do 'im good.'

'Dan, eh?' Mrs Ripley said eagerly. 'That's good news, any road. From what I heard they thought he'd never come out of t'hospital.'

'Excuse me,' I broke in.

'Nay, nay, that was just talk,' Mr Ripley continued. 'It was nobbut a stone in t'kidney. Dan'll be all right. He was tellin' me ...'

I held up my hand, 'Mr Ripley, can I please see this cow? I haven't had my lunch yet. My wife put it back in the oven when you phoned.'

'Oh, I 'ad mine afore I went up there.' He gave me a reassuring smile and his wife nodded and laughed to put my mind fully at rest.

'Well, that's splendid,' I said frigidly. 'I'm glad to hear that.' But I could see that they took me at my word. The sarcasm was lost on them.

In the loose-box Mr Ripley haltered the cow and I lifted the foot. Cradling it on my knee I scraped away the caked muck with a hoof knife and there, glinting dully as the sunshine slanted in at the door, was the cause of the trouble. I seized the metal stud with forceps, dragged it from the foot and held it up.

The farmer blinked at it for a few seconds, then his shoulders began to shake gently. 'One of me own hobnails. Heh, heh, heh. Well, that's a rum 'un. Ah must've knocked it out on t'cobbles, they're right slippery over there. Once or twice I've nearly gone arse-over-tip. I was sayin' to t'missus just t'other day ...'

'I really must get on, Mr Ripley,' I interposed. 'Remember I still haven't had my lunch. I'll just slip out to the car for an anti-tetanus injection for the cow.'

I gave her the shot, dropped the syringe into my pocket and was on my way across the yard when the farmer called after me.

'Have ye got your nippers with ye, Mr Herriot?'

'Nippers . . . ?' I halted and looked back at him. I couldn't believe this. 'Well, yes, I have, but surely you don't want to start castrating calves now?'

The farmer flicked an ancient brass lighter and applied a long sheet of flame to the bowl of his pipe. 'There's nobbut one, Mr Herriot. Won't take a minute.'

Ah well, I thought, as I opened the boot and fished out the Burdizzo from its resting place on my calving overall. It didn't really matter now. My Yorkshire pudding was a write-off, a dried-up husk by now, and the beef and those gorgeous fresh vegetables would be almost cremated. All was lost, and nipping a calf wasn't going to make any difference.

As I turned back, a pair of double doors at the end of the yard burst open and an enormous black animal galloped out and stood looking around him warily in the bright sunshine, pawing the ground and swishing his tail bad-temperedly. I stared at the spreading horns, the great hump of muscle on the shoulder and the coldly glittering eyes. It only needed a blast on a trumpet and sand instead of cobbles and I was in the Plaza de Toros in Madrid.

'Is that the calf?' I asked.

The farmer nodded cheerfully. 'Aye, that's 'im. I thowt ah'd better run 'im over to the cow house so we could tie 'im up by the neck.'

A wave of rage swept over me and for a moment I thought I was going to start shouting at the man, then, strangely, I felt only a great weariness.

I walked over to him, put my face close to his and spoke quietly. 'Mr Ripley, it's a long time since we met and you've had plenty of opportunities to keep the promise you made me then. Remember? About getting your calves nipped when they were little and about replacing that gate? Now look at that great bull and see what your gate has done to my clothes.'

The farmer gazed with genuine concern at the snags and tears in my trousers and reached out to touch a gaping rent in my sleeve.

'Eee, I'm right sorry about that.' He glanced at the bull. 'And I reckon 'e is a bit big.'

I didn't say anything and after a few moments the farmer threw up his head and looked me in the eye, a picture of resolution.

'Aye, it's not right,' he said. 'But ah'll tell ye summat. Just nip this 'un today, and I'll see nowt of this ever happens again.'

I wagged a finger at him. 'But you've said that before. Do you really mean it this time?'

He nodded vigorously. 'Ah'll guarantee it.'

LIMOUSIN HEIFERS The first rearing of Limousin cattle in Britain started in 1971, and there are already more than 16,000 pure-bred Limousins in the country. The cattle are able to tolerate widely differing extremes of temperature. These heifers have their thick winter coat, which is shed when the warm weather comes. The coat colour varies from deep yellow to reddish-brown, and round the eyes and mouth there are distinguishing pale rings. When they are two and a half years old, cows produce their first calves, and the breeders hope for a high proportion of bulls among them to rear for beef.

2

A pair of proper boots for Jimmy

'Hello! Hello!' I bellowed.

'Hello! Hello!' little Jimmy piped just behind me.

I turned and looked at my son. He was four years old now and had been coming on my rounds with me for over a year. It was clear that he considered himself a veteran of the farmyards, an old hand versed in all aspects of agricultural lore.

This shouting was a common habit of mine. When a vet arrived on a farm it was often surprisingly difficult to find the farmer. He might be a dot on a tractor half a mile across the fields, on rare occasions he might be in the house, but I always hoped to find him among the buildings and relied on a few brisk shouts to locate him.

Certain farms in our practice were for no apparent reason distinctive in that you could never find anybody around. The house door would be locked and we would scour the barns, cow-houses and fold yards while our cries echoed back at us from the unheeding walls. Siegfried and I used to call them the 'no-finding' places and they were responsible for a lot of wasted time.

Jimmy had caught on to the problem quite early and there was no doubt he enjoyed the opportunity to exercise his lungs a bit. I watched him now as he strutted importantly over the cobbles, giving tongue every few seconds. He was also making an unnecessary amount of noise by clattering on the rough stones with his new boots.

Those boots were his pride, the final recognition of his status as veterinary assistant. When I first began to take him round with me his first reaction was the simple joy of a child at being able to see animals of all kinds, particularly the young ones – the lambs, foals, piglets, calves – and the thrill of discovery when he came upon a huddle of kittens in the straw or found a bitch with pups in a loose box.

Before long, however, he began to enlarge his horizons. He wanted to get into the action. The contents of my car boot were soon as familiar to him as his toy box at home, and he delighted in handing out the tins of stomach powder, the electuaries and red blisters, the white lotion and the still-revered long cartons of Universal Cattle Medicine. Finally he began to forestall me by rushing back to the car for calcium and flutter valve as soon as he saw a recumbent cow. He had become a diagnostician as well.

I think the thing he enjoyed most was accompanying me on an evening call, if Helen would allow him to postpone his bedtime. He was in heaven driving into the country in the darkness, training my torch on a cow's teat while I stitched it.

A DRENCHING HORN FOR PIGS
Doses of liquid medicine – known as drenches – were given to cattle, sheep and pigs from a variety of vessels, including glass bottles and cows' horns. A flexible 'funnel' that many farmers found easy to use on pigs was an old boot, or a Wellington boot, with the toe cut off. Pigs would quickly crunch up a glass or horn drenching vessel.

The farmers were kind, as they always are with young people. Even the most uncommunicative would grunt, 'Ah see you've got t'apprentice with ye,' as we got out of the car.

But those farmers had something which Jimmy coveted; their big hob-nailed boots. He had a great admiration for farmers in general; strong hardy men who spent their lives in the open and who pushed fearlessly among plunging packs of cattle and slapped the rumps of massive cart-horses. I could see he was deeply impressed as he watched them – quite often small and stringy – mounting granary steps with twelve- or sixteen-stone sacks on their shoulders, or hanging on effortlessly to the noses of huge bullocks, their boots slithering on the floor, a laconic cigarette hanging from their lips.

It was those boots which got under Jimmy's skin most of all. Sturdy and unyielding, they seemed to symbolise for him the characters of the men who wore them.

Matters came to a head one day when we were conversing in the car. Or rather my son was doing the conversing in the form of a barrage of questions which I did my best to fend off while trying to think about my cases. These questions went on pretty well non-stop every day, and they followed a well-tried formula.

'What is the fastest train – the Blue Peter or the Flying Scotsman?'

'Well now ... I really don't know. I should say the Blue Peter.'

Then, getting into deeper water. 'Is a giant train faster than a phantom racing-car?'

'That's a difficult one. Let's see now ... maybe the phantom racer.'

Jimmy changed his tack suddenly. 'That was a big man at the last farm wasn't he?'

'He certainly was.'

'Was he bigger than Mr Robinson?'

We were launching into his favourite 'big man' game and I knew how it would end, but I played my part. 'Oh yes, he was.'

'Was he bigger than Mr Leeming?'

'Certainly.'

'Was he bigger than Mr Kirkley?'

'Without a doubt.'

Jimmy gave me a sidelong glance and I knew he was about to play his two trump cards. 'Was he bigger than the gas man?'

The towering gentleman who came to read the gas meters at Skeldale House had always fascinated my son and I had to think very carefully over my reply.

'Well, you know, I really think he was.'

'Ah, but ...' The corner of Jimmy's mouth twitched up craftily. 'Was he bigger than Mr Thackray?'

That was the killer punch. Nobody was bigger than Mr Thackray who looked down on the other inhabitants of Darrowby from six feet seven inches.

I shrugged my shoulders in defeat. 'No, I have to admit it. He wasn't

THRESHING THE CORN Ten or more farmhands were kept busy at threshing time. Men from neighbouring farms would join together in the work. Threshing needed an engine driver, a worker to feed sheaves into the machine, several forkers to move sheaves from the stack, and other workers to take away sacks of grain and bind and stack straw. The shortage of labour and high price of corn during the Second World War made the combine harvester an economic investment for more and more farmers.

SHEEP SHEARS Early July is the time for clipping. By then the rather matted fleece has been lifted a little from the sheep's skin by the growth of the new season's wool. The sheep-clipper's shears can cut into the new wool easily as long as they are kept sharp. Blacksmiths were busy in June supplying new shears or re-grinding the sharply pointed blades of old pairs on their rotary grindstones. On large farms where several extra hands were employed at clipping time, one man would have the task of sharpening blades with a hand stone during the day's work. The blades were not pivoted together as in scissors, but were fixed to an arched handle like a pair of tongs. Hand shears remained in use in the Dales until, and even after, the coming of mains electricity during the 1940s and 1950s had made it possible to use powered shears.

as big as Mr Thackray.'

Jimmy smiled and nodded, well satisfied, then he began to hum a little tune, drumming his fingers on the dashboard at the same time. Soon I could see he was having trouble. He couldn't remember how it went. Patience was not his strong point, and as he tried and stopped again and again it was plain that he was rapidly becoming exasperated.

Finally, as we drove down a steep hill into a village and another abortive session of tum-te-tum-te-tum came to an abrupt halt he rounded on me aggressively.

'You know,' he exploded, 'I'm getting just about fed up of this!'

'I'm sorry to hear that, old lad.' I thought for a moment. 'I think it's "Lilliburlero" you're trying to get.' I gave a swift rendering.

'Yes, that's it!' He slapped his knee and bawled out the melody at the top of his voice several times in triumph. This put him in such high good humour that he broached something which must have been on his mind for some time.

'Daddy,' he said. 'Can I have some boots?'

'Boots? But you've got some already, haven't you?' I pointed down at the little Wellingtons in which Helen always rigged him before he set out for the farms.

He gazed at his feet sadly before replying. 'Yes, I know, but I want proper boots like the farmers.'

This was a facer. I didn't know what to say. 'But, Jim, little boys like you don't have boots like that. Maybe when you're bigger ...'

'Oh, I want them now,' he moaned in anguished tones. 'I want proper boots.'

At first I thought it was a passing whim but he kept up his campaign for several days, reinforcing it with disgusted looks as Helen drew on the Wellingtons each morning and a listless slouching to convey the message that his footwear was entirely unsuitable for a man like him.

Finally Helen and I talked it over one night after he had gone to bed.

'They surely don't have farm boots his size, do they?' I asked.

Helen shook her head. 'I wouldn't have thought so, but I'll look around in any case.'

And it seemed that Jimmy wasn't the only little boy to have this idea because within a week my wife returned flushed with success and bearing the smallest pair of farm boots I had ever seen.

I couldn't help laughing. They were so tiny, yet so perfect. Thick, hob-nailed soles, chunky uppers and a long row of lace-holes with metal loops at the top.

Jimmy didn't laugh when he saw them. He handled them almost with awe and once he had got them on his demeanour changed. He was naturally square set and jaunty but to see him striding round a farmyard in corduroy leggings and those boots you would think he owned the place. He clumped and stamped, held himself very upright, and his cries of 'Hello! Hello!' took on a new authority.

He was never what I would call naughty – certainly never destructive

430

or cruel – but he had that bit of devil which I suppose all boys need to have. He liked to assert himself and perhaps, unconsciously, he liked to tease me. If I said, 'Don't touch that,' he would keep clear of the object in question but later would give it the merest brush with his finger which could not be construed as disobedience but nevertheless served to establish his influence in the household.

Also, he was not above taking advantage of me in awkward situations. There was one afternoon when Mr Garrett brought his sheepdog in. The animal was very lame and as I hoisted him on to the table in the consulting room a small head appeared for a moment at the window which overlooked the sunlit garden.

I didn't mind that. Jimmy often watched me dealing with our small animal patients and I half expected him to come into the room for a closer look.

It is often difficult to locate the source of a dog's lameness but in this case I found it immediately. When I gently squeezed the outside pad on his left foot he winced and a tiny bead of serum appeared on the black surface.

'He's got something in there, Mr Garrett,' I said. 'Probably a thorn. I'll have to give him a shot of local anaesthetic and open up his pad.'

It was when I was filling the syringe that a knee came into view at the corner of the window. I felt a pang of annoyance. Jimmy surely couldn't be climbing up the wistaria. It was dangerous and I had expressly forbidden it. The branches of the beautiful creeper curled all over the back of the house and though they were as thick as a man's leg near ground level they became quite slender as they made their way up past the bathroom window to the tiles of the roof.

No, I decided that I was mistaken and began to infiltrate the pad. These modern anaesthetics worked very quickly and within a minute or two I could squeeze the area quite hard without causing pain.

I reached for the scalpel. 'Hold his leg up and keep it as steady as you can,' I said.

Mr Garrett nodded and pursed his lips. He was a serious-faced man at any time and obviously deeply concerned about his dog. His eyes narrowed in apprehension as I poised my knife over the tell-tale drop of moisture.

For me it was an absorbing moment. If I could find and remove this foreign body the dog would be instantly rid of his pain. I had dealt with many of these cases in the past and they were so easy, so satisfying.

With the point of my blade I made a careful nick in the tough tissue of the pad and at that moment a shadow crossed the window. I glanced up. It was Jimmy, all right, this time at the other side, just his head grinning through the glass from half way up.

The little blighter *was* on the wistaria, but there was nothing I could do about it then, except to give him a quick glare. I cut a little deeper and squeezed, but still nothing showed in the wound. I didn't want to make a big hole but it was clear that I had to make a cruciate incision to

HORN-BURNS Flocks of moorland sheep know their own heugh, or pasturing area, and rarely wander off it. If a sheep does stray to another flock, or if it is stolen, the farmer cannot prove his ownership unless the animal bears his identifying mark. Brands were at one time made on the face, where they left the hair white, but horn-branding is more common. Each farm has its own mark, and it stays with the farm when the farm owner changes.

LEMON SQUEEZERS The juice from lemons was used in that favourite of the Yorkshire table, lemon curd, and for sprinkling on pancakes or making into lemonade and hot drinks for colds. An efficient lemon squeezer was essential and several types were popular, each one squeezing half a lemon at a time. The simplest was a fluted sycamore bulb pressed and twisted in the fruit. Hinged wooden and iron presses with inset perforated bowls were common, and, on a similar principle, a ridged pair of mahogany blades performed the task. One of the most elegant squeezers was a boxwood cup into which a plunger was forced by a screw.

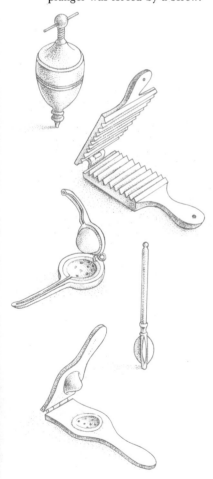

see further down. I was drawing the scalpel across at right angles to my first cut when from the corner of my eye I spotted two feet dangling just below the top of the window. I tried to concentrate on my job but the feet swung and kicked repeatedly, obviously for my benefit. At last they disappeared, which could only mean that their owner was ascending to the dangerous regions. I dug down a little deeper and swabbed with cotton wool.

Ah yes, I could see something now, but it was very deep, probably the tip of a thorn which had broken off well below the surface. I felt the thrill of the hunter as I reached for forceps and just then the head showed itself again, upside down this time.

My God, he was hanging by his feet from the branches and the face was positively leering. In deference to my client I had been trying to ignore the by-play from outside but this was too much. I leaped at the glass and shook my fist violently. My fury must have startled the performer because the face vanished instantly and I could hear faint sounds of feet scrambling upwards.

That was not much comfort either. Those top branches might not support a boy's weight. I forced myself back to my task.

'Sorry, Mr Garrett,' I said. 'Will you hold the leg up again, please.'

He replied with a thin smile and I pushed my forceps into the depths. They grated on something hard. I gripped, pulled gently, and, oh lovely, lovely, out came the pointed, glistening head of a thorn. I had done it.

It was one of the tiny triumphs which lighten vets' lives and I was beaming at my client and patting his dog's head when I heard the crack from above. It was followed by a long howl of terror then a small form hurtled past the window and thudded with horrid force into the garden.

I threw down the forceps and shot out of the room, along the passage and through the side door into the garden. Jimmy was already sitting up among the wallflowers and I was too relieved to be angry.

'Have you hurt yourself?' I gasped, and he shook his head.

I lifted him to his feet and he seemed to be able to stand all right. I felt him over carefully. There appeared to be no damage.

I led him back into the house. 'Go along and see Mummy,' I said, and returned to the consulting-room.

I must have been deathly pale when I entered because Mr Garrett looked startled. 'Is he all right?' he asked.

'Yes, yes, I think so. But I do apologise for rushing out like that. It was really too bad of me to . . .'

Mr Garrett laid his hand on my shoulder. 'Say no more, Mr Herriot, I have children of my own.' And then he spoke the words which have become engraven on my heart. 'You need nerves of steel to be a parent.'

Later at tea I watched my son demolishing a poached egg on toast, and then he started to slap plum jam on a slice of bread. Thank heaven he was no worse for his fall, but I still had to remonstrate with him.

'Look, young man,' I said. 'That was a very naughty thing you did out there. I've told you again and again not to climb the wistaria.'

Jimmy bit into his bread and jam and regarded me impassively. I have a big streak of old hen in my nature and down through the years even to this day he and later my daughter, Rosie, have recognised this and developed a disconcerting habit of making irreverent clucking noises at my over-fussiness. At this moment I could see that whatever I was going to say he wasn't going to take it too seriously.

'If you're going to behave like this,' I went on, 'I'm not going to take you round the farms with me. I'll just have to find another little boy to help me with my cases.'

His chewing slowed down and I looked for some reaction in this morsel of humanity who was later to become a far better veterinary surgeon than I could ever be – in fact to quote thirty years later a dry Scottish colleague who had been through college with me and didn't mince words, 'A helluva improvement on his old man.'

Jimmy dropped the bread on his plate. 'Another little boy?' he enquired.

'That's right. I can't have naughty boys with me. I'll have to find somebody else.'

Jimmy thought this over for a minute or so then he shrugged and appeared to accept the situation philosophically. He started again on the bread and jam.

Then in a flash his sangfroid evaporated. He stopped in mid-chew and looked up at me in wide-eyed alarm.

His voice came out in a high quaver. 'Would he have my boots?'

3

My first Caesarean

'It was Hemingway who said that, wasn't it?'

Norman Beaumont shook his head. 'No, Scott Fitzgerald.'

I didn't argue because Norman usually knew. In fact it was one of the attractive things about him.

I enjoyed having veterinary students seeing practice with us. They helped with fetching and carrying, they opened gates and they were company on our lonely rounds. In return they absorbed a lot of knowledge from us in our discussions in the car and it was priceless experience for them to be involved in the practical side of their education.

Since the war, however, my relationship with these young men had undergone a distinct change. I found I was learning from them just as much as they were learning from me.

The reason, of course, was that veterinary teaching had taken a leap

CUSTARD PIE This is a favourite week-end delicacy in many Yorkshire homes. It was a traditional dish on the Easter Sunday tea-table, especially round Whitby, but throughout the summer farmers' wives were glad to use the glut of milk and some of the daily eggs in this smooth, delicately flavoured dish.

To make custard pie, roll out 8 oz of shortcrust pastry to line an 8 in. pie dish. Prick the pastry base well to make sure there is no air trapped under it. Beat together 2 eggs, ½ pint of milk and 1 or 2 tablespoons of sugar. Strain into the pastry case and sprinkle lightly with grated nutmeg. Bake for 10 minutes at 425°F (220°C), gas mark 7, then at 350°F (180°C), gas mark 4, for a further 30 minutes or until the custard is just set.

CELL

forward. The authorities seemed to have suddenly discovered that we weren't just horse doctors and that the vast new field of small animal work was opening up dramatically. Advanced surgical procedures were being carried out on farm animals, too, and the students had the great advantage of being able to see such things done in the new veterinary schools with their modern clinics and operating theatres.

New specialist textbooks were being written which made my own thumbed volumes with everything related to the horse seem like museum pieces. I was still a young man, but all the bursting knowledge which I had nurtured so proudly was becoming irrelevant. Quittor, fistulous withers, poll evil, bog spavin, stringhalt – they didn't seem to matter much any more.

Norman Beaumont was in his final year and was a deep well of information at which I drank greedily. But apart from the veterinary side we had a common love of books and reading.

When we weren't talking shop the conversation was usually on literary lines and Norman's companionship lightened my days and made the journeys between farms seem short.

He was immensely likeable with a personality that was formal and dignified beyond his twenty-two years and which was only just saved from pomposity by a gentle humour. He was a solid citizen in the making if ever I saw one, and this impression was strengthened by his slightly pear-shaped physique and the fact that he was determinedly trying to cultivate a pipe.

He was having a little trouble with the pipe but I felt sure he would win through. I could see him plainly twenty years from now, definitely tubby, sitting around the fireside with his wife and children, puffing at that pipe which he had finally subjugated; an upright, dependable family man with a prosperous practice.

As the dry-stone walls rolled past the car windows I got back on to the topic of the new operations.

'And you say they are actually doing Caesareans on cows in the college clinics?'

'Good Lord, yes.' Norman made an expansive gesture and applied a match to his pipe. 'Doing them like hot cakes, it's a regular thing.' His words would have carried more weight if he had been able to blow a puff of smoke out after them, but he had filled the bowl too tightly and despite a fierce sucking which hollowed his cheeks and ballooned his eyeballs he couldn't manage a draw.

'Gosh, you don't know how lucky you are,' I said. 'The number of hours I've slaved on byre floors calving cows. Sawing up calves with embryotomy wire, knocking my guts out trying to bring heads round or reach feet. I think I must have shortened my life. And if only I'd known how, I could have saved myself the trouble with a nice straightforward operation. What sort of a job is it, anyway?'

The student gave me a superior smile. 'Nothing much to it, really.' He relit his pipe, tamped the tobacco down and winced as he burned his

LEE GAP HORSE FAIR For more than 800 years, since Henry I granted its first charter, the Lee Gap Horse Fair has been held at a site where ancient trackways met near Leeds. The fair is held now on St Bartholomew's Day (August 24) and on September 17, but until the 18th century it spanned the whole three weeks between these dates. It is still the most popular horse fair in Yorkshire. When horses were the main means of transport, dealers would be riding and driving their animals to the fair for days before it began. Many dealers were, and are now, gypsies, specialising in rearing and trading in horses.

finger. He shook his hand vigorously for a moment, then turned towards me. 'They never seem to have any trouble. Takes about an hour, and no hard labour.'

'Sounds marvellous.' I shook my head wistfully. 'I'm beginning to think I was born too soon. I suppose it's the same with ewes?'

'Oh yes, yes indeed,' Norman murmured airily. 'Ewes, cows, sows – they're in and out of the place every day. No problem at all. Nearly as easy as bitch spays.'

'Ah well, you young lads are lucky. It's so much easier to tackle these jobs when you've seen a lot of them done.'

'True, true.' The student spread his hands. 'But of course most bovine parturitions don't need a Caesarean and I'm always glad to have a calving for my case book.'

I nodded in agreement. Norman's case book was something to see; a heavily bound volume with every scrap of interesting material meticulously entered under headings in red ink. The examiners always wanted to see these books and this one would be worth a few extra marks to Norman in his finals.

It was August Bank Holiday Sunday, and Darrowby market place had been bustling all day with holidaymakers and coach parties. Each time we passed through I looked at the laughing throngs with a tiny twinge of envy. Not many people seemed to work on Sundays.

I dropped the student at his digs in late afternoon and went back to Skeldale House for tea. I had just finished when Helen got up to answer the phone.

'It's Mr Bushell of Sycamore House,' she said. 'He has a cow calving.'

'Oh damn. I thought we'd have Sunday evening to ourselves.' I put down my cup. 'Tell him I'll be right out, Helen, will you.' I smiled as she put down the receiver. 'One thing, Norman will be pleased. He was just saying he wanted something for his case book.'

I was right. The young man rubbed his hands in glee when I called for him and he was in excellent humour as we drove to the farm.

'I was reading some poetry when you rang the bell,' he said. 'I like poetry. You can always find something to apply to your life. How about now, when I'm expecting something interesting. "Hope springs eternal in the human breast".'

'Alexander Pope, *Essay on Man*,' I grunted. I wasn't feeling as enthusiastic as Norman. You never knew what was ahead on these occasions.

'Jolly good.' The young man laughed. 'You aren't easy to catch out.'

We drove through the farm gateway into the yard.

'You've made me think with your poetry,' I said. 'It keeps buzzing in my head. "Abandon hope all ye who enter here".'

'Dante, of course, *The Inferno*. But don't be so pessimistic.' He patted me on the shoulder as I put on my Wellingtons.

The farmer led us into the byre and in a stall opposite the window a small cow looked up at us anxiously from her straw bed. Above her

RESCUING A SNOWBOUND SHEEP
Moorland sheep are hardy enough to survive northern winters without being brought back to a fold near the farm. In snow their fleece insulates them, lack of food for some days is not fatal, and even under a snowdrift there is enough air to breathe. Danger comes as the snow melts. Then buried sheep drown, and wool on the belly and legs of long-wool breeds becomes caked with wet snow that turns to ice so thick and heavy that the animals cannot move. A farmer will carry an ailing sheep to shelter, or bring in a small flock to save the labour of taking hay to them.

435

SCRUFFLER This narrow, one-wheeled weed-clearer was drawn between the rows of a growing crop, potatoes or swedes perhaps, pulled by one horse and guided from behind by a man holding the two handles. Designs varied, but many scrufflers had a curved front blade to loosen the soil and two pointed blades to run flat just below the soil surface, slashing off thistles, docks and any other weeds.

head, her name, Bella, was chalked on a board.

'She isn't very big, Mr Bushell,' I said.

'Eh?' He looked at me enquiringly and I remembered that he was hard of hearing.

'She's a bit small,' I shouted.

The farmer shrugged. 'Aye, she allus was a poor doer. Had a rough time with her first calvin' but she milked well enough after it.'

I looked thoughtfully at the cow as I stripped off my shirt and soaped my arms. I didn't like the look of that narrow pelvis and I breathed the silent prayer of all vets that there might be a tiny calf inside.

The farmer poked at the light roan hairs of the rump with his foot and shouted at the animal to make her rise.

'She won't budge, Mr Herriot,' he said. 'She's been painin' all day. Ah doubt she's about buggered.'

I didn't like the sound of that either. There was always something far wrong when a cow strained for a long time without result. And the little animal did look utterly spent. Her head hung down and her eyelids drooped wearily.

Ah well, if she wouldn't get up I had to get down. With my bare chest in contact with the ground the thought occurred that cobbles didn't get any softer with the passage of the years. But when I slid my hand into the vagina I forgot about my discomfort. The pelvic opening was villainously narrow, and beyond was something which froze my blood. Two enormous hooves and resting on their cloven surfaces a huge expanse of muzzle with twitching nostrils. I didn't have to feel any more but with an extra effort I strained forward a few inches and my fingers explored a bulging brow squeezing into the small space like a cork in a bottle. As I withdrew my hand the rough surface of the calf's tongue flicked briefly against my palm.

I sat back on my heels and looked up at the farmer. 'There's an elephant in there, Mr Bushell.'

'Eh?'

I raised my voice. 'A tremendous calf, and no room for it to come out.'

'Can't ye cut it away?'

'Afraid not. The calf's alive and anyway there's nothing to get at. No room to work.'

'Well, that a beggar,' Mr Bushell said. 'She's a good little milker. Ah don't want to send 'er to the butcher.'

Neither did I. I hated the very thought of it, but a great light was breaking beyond a new horizon. It was a moment of decision, of history. I turned to the student.

'This is it, Norman! The ideal indication for a Caesar. What a good job I've got you with me. You can keep me right.'

I was slightly breathless with excitement and I hardly noticed the flicker of anxiety in the young man's eyes.

I got to my feet and seized the farmer's arm. 'Mr Bushell, I'd like to do a Caesarean operation on your cow.'

'A what?'

'A Caesarean. Open her up and remove the calf surgically.'

'Tek it out o' the side, d'ye mean? Like they do wi' women?'

'That's right.'

'Well that's a rum 'un.' The farmer's eyebrows went up. 'I never knew you could do that wi' cows.'

'Oh, we can now,' I said airily. 'Things have moved on a bit in the last few years.'

He rubbed his hand slowly across his mouth. 'Well, ah don't know. I reckon she'd die if you made a bloody great 'ole in her like that. Maybe she'd be better goin' for slaughter. I'd get a few quid for her and I allus think fust loss is best.'

I could see my big moment slipping away from me. 'But she's only a thin little thing. She wouldn't be worth much for meat and with a bit of luck we might get a live calf out of her.'

I was going against one of my steadfast rules – never to talk a farmer into doing something – but I was seized by a kind of madness. Mr Bushell looked at me for a long time, then without changing expression he nodded.

'Awright, what do you want?'

'Two buckets of warm water, soap, towels,' I replied. 'And I'll bring some instruments into the house to boil if I may.'

When the farmer had departed I thumped Norman on the shoulder. 'This is just right. Plenty of light, a live calf to aim for, and it's just as well poor Mr Bushell doesn't hear too well. If we keep our voices down I'll be able to ask you things as we go along.'

Norman didn't say anything. I told him to set up some straw bales for our equipment and had him scatter loose straw around the cow while I boiled the instruments in a pan in the farm kitchen.

Soon all was ready. Syringes, suture materials, scalpels, scissors, local anaesthetic and cotton wool laid in a row on a clean towel draped over one of the bales. I added some antiseptic to the water and addressed the farmer.

'We'll roll her over and you can hold the head down, Mr Bushell. I think she's too tired to move much.'

Norman and I pushed at the shoulder and Bella flopped on her side without resistance. The farmer put his knee against her neck and the long area of the left flank was exposed for our attention.

I nudged the student. 'Where do I make the incision?' I whispered.

Norman cleared his throat. 'Well, er, it's about ...' He pointed vaguely.

I nodded. 'Around the rumenotomy site, eh? But a bit lower I suppose.' I began to clip away in the hair from a foot-long strip. It would need a big opening for that calf to come through. Then I quickly infiltrated the area with local.

We do these jobs under a local anaesthetic nowadays, and in most cases the cow lies quietly on her side or even stands during the

THE WHEEL PLOUGH Greater ease in handling and less effort required for pulling it were the advantages of the wheel plough over the swing plough. The larger, furrow wheel ran on the turned earth and was adjustable to alter the width of the furrow. The smaller, land wheel ran on the unploughed surface and was adjustable up or down to alter the depth of the furrow. The two swingletrees at the front, to which the horses were harnessed, distributed the strain equally between them.

CATGUT A vet would usually stitch wounds and incisions within the body with catgut, which is prepared from the intestines of sheep or horses. External stitching of the skin would be done with silk or prepared horsehair. A screw-top glass bottle about 4 in. tall held three reels of catgut of different thicknesses. The bottle was filled with spirit to keep the gut sterile. Gut was drawn out through holes in the stopper. Man-made threads have now largely replaced other materials for stitching.

operation. The animal can't feel anything, of course, but I have a few extra grey hairs round my ears which owe their presence to the occasional wild cow suddenly rearing up halfway through and taking off with me in desperate pursuit to keep her internal organs from flopping on the ground.

But that was all in the future. On this first occasion I had no such fears. I cut through skin, muscle layers and peritoneum and was confronted by a protruding pink and white mass of tissue.

I poked at it with my finger. There was something hard inside. Could it be the calf?

'What's that?' I hissed.

'Eh?' Norman, kneeling by my side, jumped convulsively. 'What do you mean?'

'That thing. Is it the rumen or the uterus? It's pretty low down, it could be the uterus.'

The student swallowed a couple of times. 'Yes ... yes ... that's the uterus all right.'

'Good.' I smiled in relief and made a bold incision. A great gout of impacted grass welled out followed by a burst of gas and an outflow of dirty brown fluid.

'Oh Christ!' I gasped. 'It's the rumen. Look at all that bloody mess!' I groaned aloud as the filthy tide surged away down and out of sight into the abdominal cavity. 'What the hell are you playing at, Norman?'

I could feel the young man's body trembling against mine.

'Don't just sit there!' I shouted. 'Thread me one of those needles. Quick! Quick!'

Norman bounded to his feet, rushed over to the bale and returned with a trailing length of catgut extended in shaking fingers. Wordlessly, dry-mouthed, I stitched the gash I had made in the wrong organ. Then the two of us made frantic attempts to swab away the escaped rumenal contents with cotton wool and antiseptic but much of it had run away beyond our reach. The contamination must be massive.

When we had done what we could, I sat back and looked at the student. My voice was a hoarse growl. 'I thought you knew all about these operations.'

He looked at me with frightened eyes. 'They do quite a few of them at the clinic.'

I glared back at him. 'How many Caesareans have you seen?'

'Well ... er ... one, actually.'

'One! To hear you speak I thought you were an expert! And anyway, even if you'd seen only one you should know a little bit about it.'

'The thing is ...' Norman shuffled his knees around on the cobbles. 'You see ... I was right at the back of the class.'

I worked up a sarcastic snarl. 'Oh, I understand. So you couldn't see very well?'

'That's about it.' The young man hung his head.

'Well, you're a stupid young fool!' I said in a vicious whisper. 'Dishing out your confident instructions when you know damn-all. You realise you've killed this good cow? With all that contamination she'll certainly develop peritonitis and die. All we can hope for now is to get the calf out alive.' With an effort I turned my gaze from his stricken face. 'Anyway, let's get on with it.'

Apart from my first shouts of panic the entire interchange had been carried out *pianissimo* and Mr Bushell kept shooting enquiring glances at us.

I gave him what I hoped was a reassuring smile and returned to the attack. Getting the calf out alive was easy to say, but it soon dawned on me that getting the calf out in any way whatsoever was going to be a mammoth task. Plunging my arm deep below what I now knew was the rumen I encountered a smooth and mighty organ lying on the abdominal floor. It contained an enormous bulk with the hardness and immobility of a sack of coal.

I felt my way along the surface and came upon the unmistakable contours of a hock pushing against the slippery wall. That was the calf all right, but it was far, far away.

I withdrew my arm and started on Norman again. 'From your position at the back of the class,' I enquired bitingly, 'did you happen to notice what they did next?'

'Next? Ah yes.' He licked his lips and I could see beads of sweat on his brow. 'You are supposed to exteriorise the uterus.'

'Exteriorise it? Bring it up to the wound, you mean?'

'That's right.'

'Good God!' I said. 'King Kong couldn't lift up that bloody uterus. In fact I can't move it an inch. Have a feel.'

The student, who was stripped and soaped like myself, introduced his arm and for a few moments I watched his eyes pop and his face redden. Then he withdrew and nodded sheepishly. 'You're right. It won't move.'

'Only one thing to do.' I picked up a scalpel. 'I'll have to cut into the uterus and grab that hock. There's nothing else to get hold of.'

It was very nasty fiddling about away out of sight down in the dark unknown, my arm buried to the shoulder in the cow, my tongue hanging out with anxiety. I was terrified I might slash into something vital but in fact it was my own fingers that I cut, several times, before I was able to draw the scalpel edge across the bulge made by the hock. A second later I had my hand round the hairy leg. Now I was getting somewhere.

Gingerly I enlarged the incision, inch by inch. I hoped fervently I had made it big enough, but working blind is a terrible thing and it was difficult to be sure.

At any rate I couldn't wait to deliver that calf. I laid aside my knife, seized the leg and tried to lift it, and immediately I knew that another little nightmare lay ahead. The thing was a tremendous weight and it was going to take great strength to bring it up into the light of day. Nowadays when I do a Caesar I take care to have a big strong farm lad stripped off ready to help me with this lifting job, but today I had only

A BACK-CAN FOR MILK When milking was done in the open and by hand, there was no point in driving the cattle back to the farmhouse to be milked. The milker would go out to the pasture and kneel beside the cow to milk into the pail. He poured the milk into the tinplate back-can for carrying back to the farm. The can had a concave section to rest comfortably against his back. Cans were made in several sizes, and it was best to use a size that would be filled completely so that the milk did not swish about on the way back to the farm.

PLANT DUSTER This 1925 machine resembles a vacuum-cleaner but it was designed to puff dust out, not suck it in. As the horse pulled it along, an operator walked beside the machine turning a handle. This drove a chain-operated fan that blew through the hopper and along the hose and nozzle, sending out a powder for controlling insects, a fungus or weeds.

Norman.

'Come on,' I panted. 'Give me a hand.'

We reached down together and began to pull. I managed to repel the hock and bring the foot round and that gave us greater purchase but it was still agonisingly laborious to raise the mass to the level of the skin incision.

Teeth clenched, grunting with effort, we hauled upwards till at last I was able to grasp the other hind leg. Even then, with a foot apiece in our hands, nothing wanted to move. It was just like doing a tough calving except it was through the side. And as we lay back, panting and sweating, pulling with every vestige of our strength, I had a sudden wave of illumination which comes to all members of our profession at times. I wished with all my heart and soul that I had never started this ghastly job. If only I had followed Mr Bushell's suggestion to send the cow for slaughter I would now be driving peacefully on my rounds. Instead, here I was, killing myself. And even worse than my physical torment was the piercing knowledge that I hadn't the slightest idea what was going to happen next.

But the calf was gradually coming through. The tail appeared, then an unbelievably massive rib cage and finally with a rush, the shoulders and head.

Norman and I sat down with a bump, the calf rolling over our knees. And like a gleam of light in the darkness I saw that he was snorting and shaking his head.

'By gaw, he's a big 'un!' exclaimed the farmer. 'And wick, too.'

I nodded. 'Yes, he's huge. One of the biggest I've ever seen.' I felt between the hind legs. 'A bull, as I thought. He'd never have come out the proper way.'

My attention was whisked back to the cow. Where was the uterus? It had vanished. Again I started my frantic groping inside. My hand became entangled with yards of placenta. Oh hell, that wouldn't do any good floating around among the guts. I pulled it out and dropped it on the floor but I still couldn't find the uterus. For a palpitating moment I wondered what would happen if I never did locate it, then my fingers came upon the ragged edge of my incision.

I pulled as much as possible of the organ up to the light and I noticed with sinking disquiet that my original opening had been enlarged by the passage of that enormous calf and there was a long tear disappearing out of sight towards the cervix.

'Sutures.' I held my hand out and Norman gave me a fresh needle. 'Hold the lips of the wound,' I said and began to stitch.

I worked as quickly as I could and was doing fine until the tear ran out of sight. The rest was a kind of martyrdom. Norman hung on grimly while I stabbed around at the invisible tissue far below. At times I pricked the young man's fingers, at others my own. And to my dismay a further complication had arisen.

The calf was now on his feet, blundering unsteadily around. The speed with which newly born animals get on to their legs has always fascinated me but at this moment it was an unmitigated nuisance.

The calf, looking for the udder with that instinct which nobody can explain, kept pushing his nose at the cow's flank and at times toppling head first into the gaping hole in her side.

'Reckon 'e wants back in again,' Mr Bushell said with a grin. 'By 'eck, he is a wick 'un.'

'Wick' is Yorkshire for lively and the word was never more aptly applied. As I worked, eyes half closed, jaws rigid, I had to keep nudging the wet muzzle away with my elbow, but as fast as I pushed him back the calf charged in again and with sick resignation I saw that every time he nosed his way into the cavity he brought particles of straw and dirt from the floor and spread them over the abdominal contents.

'Look at that,' I moaned. 'As if there wasn't enough muck in there.'

Norman didn't reply. His mouth was hanging open and the sweat ran down his blood-streaked face as he grappled with that unseen wound. And in his fixed stare I seemed to read a growing doubt as to his wisdom in deciding to be a veterinary surgeon.

I would rather not go into any more details. The memory is too painful. Sufficient to say that after an eternity I got as far down the uterine tear as I could, then we cleared away a lot of rubbish from the cow's abdomen and covered everything with antiseptic dusting powder. I stitched up the muscle and skin layers with the calf trying all the time to get in on the act and at last the thing was finished.

Norman and I got to our feet very slowly, like two old, old men. It took me a long time to straighten my back and I saw the young man rubbing tenderly at his lumbar region. Then, since we were both plastered with caked blood and filth, we began the slow process of scrubbing and scraping ourselves clean.

Mr Bushell left his position by the head and looked at the row of skin stitches. 'Nice neat job,' he said. 'And a grand calf, too.'

Yes, that was something. The little creature had dried off now and he was a beauty, his body swaying on unsteady legs, his wide-set eyes filled with gentle curiosity. But that 'neat job' hid things I didn't dare think about.

Antibiotics were still not in general use but in any case I knew there was no hope for the cow. More as a gesture than anything else I left the farmer some sulpha powders to give her three times a day. Then I got off the farm as quickly as I could.

We drove away in silence. I rounded a couple of corners, then stopped the car under a tree and sank my head against the steering wheel.

'Oh hell,' I groaned. 'What a bloody balls-up.'

Norman replied only with a long sigh and I continued. 'Did you ever see such a performance? All that straw and dirt and rumenal muck in among that poor cow's bowels. Do you know what I was thinking about towards the end? I was remembering the story of that human surgeon of olden times who left his hat inside his patient. It was as bad as that.'

DRAINING OFF BUTTERMILK The time needed to churn butter varied according to the temperature. It could take hours for the butter to form in cool weather. When it had formed, the remaining liquid – the buttermilk – was drained off and the butter was scraped out to be worked between rollers which squeezed out the last of the buttermilk. The farmer's wife could make use of the buttermilk in the kitchen, in scones for example.

'I know.' The student spoke in a strangled undertone. 'And it was all my fault.'

'Oh, no it wasn't,' I replied. 'I made a right rollocks of the whole thing all by myself and I tried to blame you because I got in a panic. I shouted and nagged at you and I owe you an apology.'

'Oh no, no ...'

'Yes, I do. I am supposed to be a qualified veterinary surgeon and I did nearly everything wrong.' I groaned again. 'And on top of everything I behaved like an absolute shit towards you and I'm sorry.'

'You didn't, really you didn't ... I ...'

'Anyway, Norman,' I broke in, 'I'm going to thank you now. You were a tremendous help to me. You worked like a trojan and I'd have got nowhere at all without you. Let's go and have a pint.'

With the early evening sunshine filtering into the bar parlour of the village inn we dropped into a quiet corner and pulled deeply at our beer glasses. We were both hot and weary and there didn't seem to be anything more to say.

It was Norman who broke the silence. 'Do you think that cow has any chance?'

I examined the cuts and punctures on my fingers for a moment. 'No, Norman. Peritonitis is inevitable, and I'm pretty sure I've left a good-sized hole in her uterus.' I shuddered and slapped my brow at the memory.

I was sure I would never see Bella alive again, but first thing next morning a morbid curiosity made me lift the phone to find out if she had survived so far.

The 'buzz-buzz' at the other end seemed to last a long time before Mr Bushell answered.

'Oh, it's Mr Herriot. Cow's up and eatin'.' He didn't sound surprised.

It was several seconds before I was able to absorb his words.

'Doesn't she look a bit dull or uncomfortable?' I asked huskily.

'Nay, nay, she's bright as a cricket. Finished off a rackful of hay and I got a couple o' gallons of milk from 'er.'

As in a dream I heard his next question. 'When'll you take them stitches out?'

'Stitches ... ? Oh yes.' I gave myself a shake. 'In a fortnight, Mr Bushell, in a fortnight.'

After the horrors of the first visit I was glad Norman was with me when I removed the sutures. There was no swelling round the wound and Bella chewed her cud happily as I snipped away. In a pen nearby the calf gambolled and kicked his feet in the air.

I couldn't help asking. 'Has she shown any symptoms at all, Mr Bushell?'

'Nay.' The farmer shook his head slowly. 'She's been neither up nor down. You wouldn't know owt had happened to 'er.'

That was the way it was at my first Caesarean. Over the years Bella went on to have eight more calves normally and unaided, a miracle

MACHINE MILKING By the 1940s the milking parlour was rapidly becoming a workshop – no more a place for stools, pails and milkmaids, but one where vacuum pumps carried out hygienic 'in-can' milking. Each teat-cup assembly sent milk direct from the cow into a sealed container. Many Dales farms had no electricity supply until after 1945, but vacuum milk-pumps could also be powered by oil-fuelled engines.

which I can still hardly believe.

But Norman and I were not to know that. All we felt then was an elation which was all the sweeter for being unexpected.

As we drove away I looked at the young man's smiling face.

'Well, Norman,' I said. 'That's veterinary practice for you. You get a lot of nasty shocks but some lovely surprises too. I've often heard of the wonderful resistance of the bovine peritoneum and thank heavens it's true.'

'The whole thing's marvellous, isn't it,' he murmured dreamily. 'I can't describe the way I feel. My head seems to be full of quotations like "Where there is life there's hope".'

'Yes indeed,' I said. 'John Gay, isn't it – "The Sick Man and The Angel".'

Norman clapped his hands. 'Oh, well done.'

'Let's see.' I thought for a moment. 'How about "But t'was a famous victory".'

'Excellent,' replied the young man. 'Southey, "The Battle of Blenheim".'

I nodded. 'Quite correct.'

'Here's a good one,' the student said. ' "Out of this nettle, danger, we pluck this flower, safety".'

'Splendid, splendid,' I replied. 'Shakespeare, *Henry Fifth*.'

'No, *Henry Fourth*.'

I opened my mouth to argue but Norman held up a confident hand. 'It's no good, I'm right. And this time I *do* know what I'm talking about.'

4

Wetting my daughter's head

'Are you all right, Helen?'

I looked round anxiously as my wife fidgeted in her seat. We were in the one and ninepennies in the La Scala cinema in Brawton and I had a strong conviction that we had no right to be there.

I had voiced my doubts that morning. 'I know it's our half-day, Helen, but with the baby due any time don't you think it would be safer to stay around Darrowby?'

'No, of course not.' Helen laughed incredulously at the very idea of missing our outing. And I could see her point because it was an oasis of relaxation in our busy lives. For me it was an escape from the telephone and the mud and the Wellington boots and for my wife it meant a rest from her own hard slog plus the luxury of having meals cooked and

SHEDDING LAMBS When the shepherd wants to shed, or separate, the lambs from the ewes, the flock is herded along a narrowing passage – made by a wall and some hurdles perhaps – with a swing gate at the narrow end. As the animals approach the gate in single file, the shepherd swings it to one side or the other so that the lambs pass on one side of it into a pen and the ewes pass on the other side into another field. The separation may be carried out to give the lambs special feeding in the pen or to collect them for taking to market.

served by somebody else.

'But honestly,' I said. 'What if the thing comes on quickly? It's all right you laughing. We don't want our second child to be born in Smith's book-shop or the back of a car.'

The whole business had me worried. I wasn't as bad as when Jimmy was on his way. I was in the RAF then and I went into a sort of decline during which I lost two stones in weight, which wasn't all due to the hard training. People make jokes about this syndrome but I didn't find it funny. There was something about having babies which really got through to me, and lately I had spent a lot of time flapping around watching Helen's every move, much to her amusement. I just couldn't calm down about the thing. There isn't much of the Yogi in my make-up at any time and over the last two days the tension had built up.

But Helen had been adamant this morning. She wasn't going to be done out of her half-day by such a trifle and now here we were in the La Scala with Humphrey Bogart competing vainly for my attention and my blood pressure rising steadily as my wife squirmed around and occasionally ran a thoughtful hand over her swollen abdomen.

As I scrutinised her keenly from the corner of my eye she gave a convulsive jerk and her lips parted in a soft moan. An instant dew of perspiration had already sprung out all over me before she turned and whispered, 'I think we'd better go now, Jim.'

Stumbling over the outstretched legs in the darkness I guided her up the sloping aisle, and such was my panic that I felt sure the crisis would be upon us before we reached the usherette standing at the back with her torch.

I was thankful to reach the street and see our little car standing only a few yards away. As we set off I seemed to notice the rattles and bumping of the old springs for the first time. It was the only time in my life that I wished I had a Rolls-Royce.

The twenty-five miles to Darrowby seemed to take an eternity. Helen sat very quiet by my side, occasionally closing her eyes and catching her breath while my heart beat a tattoo against my ribs. When we reached our little town I turned the car to the right towards the market place.

Helen looked at me in surprise. 'Where are you going?'

'Well, to Nurse Brown's of course.'

'Oh, don't be so silly. It's not time for that yet.'

'But ... how do you know?'

'I just know.' Helen laughed. 'I've had a baby before, don't you remember? Come on, let's go home.'

Heavy with misgiving, I drove to Skeldale House and as we mounted the stairs I marvelled at Helen's composure.

It was the same when we got into bed. She lay there, obviously not very comfortable but quite patient and there was about her a calm acceptance of the inevitable which I could not share.

I suppose I kept dropping into what is termed a fitful slumber because it was 6 a.m. when she nudged my arm.

COOKING WITH OATMEAL Every north Yorkshire farm had its wooden ark, or box, full of oatmeal. It was dipped into frequently for making porridge and havercake, a local oat bread. Havercakes were made by many different recipes, but originally they were all cooked on a bakestone, a type of griddle made from a local mudstone, or iron hung over the fire. Later bakestones were often built in by the fireside. The cooked havercake might be placed on a wooden cake-stool or easel to dry out. Havercake was fried with bacon or crumbled into broth. It was also delicious eaten newly baked and spread with butter and treacle.

'Time to go, Jim.' Her tone was very matter-of-fact.

I shot from the bed like a jack-in-the-box, threw on my clothes and shouted across the landing to Auntie Lucy who was staying with us for the occasion. 'We're off!'

A faint reply came through the door. 'All right, I'll see to Jimmy.'

When I returned to our bedroom Helen was dressing methodically.

'Get that suitcase out of the cupboard, Jim,' she said.

I opened the cupboard door. 'Suitcase?'

'Yes, that one. It's got my nighties and toilet things and baby clothes and everything I'll need. Go on, bring it out.'

Suppressing a groan I carried the case out and stood waiting. I had missed all this last time because of the war and had often regretted it, but at that moment I wasn't at all sure whether I wouldn't rather be elsewhere.

Outside it was a glorious May morning, the air limpid with the new-day freshness which had soothed the irritation of many an early call, but it was all lost on me today as I drove across the empty market place.

We had only about half a mile to go and I was pulling up outside Greenside Nursing Home within minutes. There was a touch of grandeur about the name but in fact it was just the small dwelling-house of Nurse Brown. Upstairs there were a couple of bedrooms which for many years had seen the arrival of the local children.

I knocked at the door and pushed it open. Nurse Brown gave me a quick smile, put her arm round Helen's shoulders and led her upstairs. I was left in the kitchen feeling strangely alone and helpless but a voice cut in on my jumbled thoughts.

'Now then, Jim, it's a grand mornin'.'

It was Cliff, Nurse Brown's husband. He was sitting in the corner of the kitchen eating his breakfast and he spoke to me casually as though we had encountered each other in the street. He wore the broad grin which never seemed to leave his face, but I suppose I half expected that he would leap from the table, seize my hand and say, 'There, there,' or something of the sort.

However he continued to work his way phlegmatically through the stack of bacon, eggs, sausages and tomatoes on his plate, and I realised that over the years he must have seen hundreds of quivering husbands standing in that kitchen. It was old stuff to Cliff.

'Yes, Cliff ... yes ...' I replied. 'I think it will turn out hot later.'

He nodded absently and pushed his plate to one side to join an empty porridge bowl before turning his attention to bread and marmalade. Nurse Brown was a noted cook as well as a baby expert and it was evident that she believed in ensuring that her husband, a very big man and a lorry driver for one of the local contractors, would not grow faint from hunger during the morning.

Watching him slapping on the marmalade I cringed inwardly at the creaking sounds from the floorboards above. What was happening in that bedroom?

OATCAKES The havercake or oatcake recipes of the Dales varied from one locality to another. Some were leavened with yeast to make a rather rubbery bread, some were crumbly, biscuit-like mixtures of meal, water and a little fat. To make a simple, crisp type of oatcake, melt a walnut-sized piece of lard or dripping in 2 tablespoons of hot water and pour it on to 4 oz of medium oatmeal mixed with a pinch of salt. Knead the mixture into a ball, then flatten it with the hand into a disc about ⅛ in. thick – or make several small discs if the mixture is very crumbly. Slide the oatcake on to a hot griddle, or into a lightly-greased frying pan, and cook for a few minutes until crisp.

As he chewed, Cliff seem to notice that I was perhaps one of the more distraught type of husbands because he turned his big kind smile on me. He was and is one of the nicest men in our town and he spoke gently.

'Don't worry, lad,' he said. 'It'll be right.'

His words were mildly soothing and I fled. In those days it was unheard-of for the husband to be present at the birth and though it is now the in thing to observe it all I marvel at the fortitude of these young men. I know beyond all doubt that Herriot would be carried away unconscious at some time during the proceedings.

When Siegfried arrived at the surgery he was very thoughtful.

'You'd better stick around, James. I'll get through the morning round on my own. Take it quietly, my boy. All will be well.'

It was difficult to take it quietly. I found that expectant fathers really did pace the floor for long perods, and I varied this by trying to read the newspaper upside down.

It was around eleven o'clock when the long-awaited telephone call came. It was my doctor and good friend, Harry Allinson. Harry always spoke in a sort of cheerful shout and his very presence in a sick-room was a tonic. This morning the booming voice was like the sweetest music.

Over the years he must have seen hundreds of quivering husbands in that kitchen.

'A sister for Jimmy!' His words were followed by a burst of laughter.

'Oh great, Harry. Thank you, thank you. That's marvellous news.' I held the receiver against my chest for a few moments before putting it down. I walked with dragging steps to the sitting room and lay back in a chair until my nerves had stopped vibrating.

Then on an impulse, I leaped to my feet. I believe I have said before that I am a fairly sensible man with a propensity for doing daft things and I decided that I had to go round to the Nursing Home immediately.

At that time a husband was not welcome straight after the birth. I knew it because I had gone to see Jimmy too soon and had not been well received. But still I went.

When I burst into her establishment Nurse Brown's usual smile was absent. 'You've done it again, haven't you?' she said with some asperity. 'I told you with Jimmy that you should have given us time to get the baby washed, but it seems you took no notice.'

I hung my head sheepishly and she relented. 'Oh well, now you're here you might as well come upstairs.'

Helen had the same tired, flushed look that I remembered before. I kissed her thankfully. We didn't say anything, just smiled at each other. Then I had a look in the cot by the bed.

Nurse Brown regarded me with tight lips and narrowed eyes as I peered down. Last time I had been so aghast at Jimmy's appearance that I had mortally offended her by asking if there was anything wrong with him, and heaven help me I felt the same now. I won't go into details but the new little girl's face was all squashed and red and bloated and the sense of shock hit me as it had done before.

I looked up at the nurse and it was only too clear that she was waiting for me to say something derogatory. Her normally laughing face was set in a threatening scowl. One wrong word from me and she would have kicked me on the shins – I was sure of that.

'Gorgeous,' I said weakly. 'Really gorgeous.'

'All right.' She had seen enough of me. 'Out you go.'

She ushered me downstairs and as she opened the outside door she fixed me with a piercing eye. That bright little woman could read me without effort. She spoke slowly and deliberately as though addressing a person of limited intelligence.

'That . . . is . . . a . . . lovely . . . healthy . . . baby . . .' she said and closed the door in my face.

And, bless her heart, her words helped me because as I drove away I knew she must be right. And now, all these years later, when I look at my handsome son and my beautiful daughter I can hardly believe my own stupidity.

When I returned to the surgery there was one visit waiting for me, high in the hills, and the journey up there was like a happy dream. My worry was over and it seemed that all nature was rejoicing with me. It was the ninth of May, 1947, the beginning of the most perfect summer I can remember. The sun blazed, soft breezes swirled into the car,

447

carrying their fragrance from the fells around, an elusive breath of the bluebells, primroses and violets scattered everywhere on the grass and flowing among the shadows of the trees.

After I had seen my patient, I took a walk on the high tops along a favourite path of beaten earth on the hill's edge with Sam trotting at my heels. I looked away over the rolling patchwork of the plain sleeping in the sun's haze and at the young bracken on the hillside springing straight and green from last year's dead brown stalks. Everywhere new life was calling out its exultant message, and it was so apt with my new little daughter lying down there in Darrowby.

We had decided to call her Rosemary. It is such a pretty name and I still love it, but it didn't last long. It became Rosie at a very early stage and, though I did make one or two ineffectual stands, it has remained so to this day. She is now Doctor Rosie in our community.

On that May day I caught myself just in time. It has always been my practice to recline in the sunshine on the springy bed of heather which clusters on these hillsides and I was just settling down when I remembered I had other things to do today. I sped back to Skeldale House and began to telephone my glad news all over the country.

It was received rapturously by all, but it was Tristan who grasped the essentials of the situation.

'We've got to wet this baby's head, Jim,' he said seriously.

I was ready for anything. 'Of course, of course, when are you coming over?'

'I'll be there at seven,' he replied crisply, and I knew he would be.

Tristan was concerned about the venue of the celebration. There were four of us in the sitting-room at Skeldale House – Siegfried, Tristan, Alex Taylor and myself. Alex was my oldest friend – we started school together in Glasgow at the age of four – and when he came out of the Army after five years in the Western Desert and Italy he came to spend a few weeks with Helen and me in Darrowby. It wasn't long before he had fallen under the spell of the country life and now he was learning farming and estate agency with a view to starting a new career. It was good that he should be with me tonight.

Tristan's fingers drummed on the arm of his chair as he thought aloud. His expression was fixed and grave, his eyes vacant.

'We'd normally go to the Drovers but they've got that big party on tonight, so that's no good,' he muttered. 'We want a bit of peace and quiet. Let's see now, there's the George and Dragon – Tetley's beer, splendid stuff, but I've known them a bit careless with their pipes and I've had the odd sour mouthful. And of course we have the Cross Keys. They pull a lovely pint of Cameron's and the draught Guinness is excellent. And we mustn't forget the Hare and Pheasant – their bitter can rise to great heights although the mild is ordinary.' He paused for a moment. 'We might do worse than the Lord Nelson – very reliable ale – and of course there's always . . .'

continued on page 457

LIVING
TRADITIONS
OF WORK AND PLAY

People still gather to celebrate
customs that stem
partly from life on the farm,
partly from ancient
legends and rivalry in sport

Customs that echo an ancient way of life

People in north Yorkshire still maintain ancient customs with the enthusiasm of their ancestors.

Fertility rites such as plough blessing and the making of corn dollies have their origins in prehistoric prayers for the coming harvest. At Richmond the first farmer to bring a sheaf of the new season's wheat to the market cross is still given a gift of wine by the Mayor.

The curfew, which each evening for centuries warned people throughout the country to put out their fires, is still sounded in Ripon on a buffalo horn. A horn is sounded in the Wensleydale village of Bainbridge for a different purpose. At 10 o'clock each winter's night for 700 years it has been blown to guide foresters home from the long-since vanished forests.

PUNISHMENT PRESERVED The sticks set up on the shore at Whitby on the day before Ascension Day form a mock hedge which must survive three tides. This Penny Hedge commemorates the Penance Hedge which the Abbot of Whitby in 1160 ordered huntsmen to build each year for beating a hermit who shielded a hunted boar.

BARTLE HELD CAPTIVE At West Witton a straw figure is burned on a bonfire in August. It represents Bartle, a legendary ruffian of Wensleydale forest who was captured and killed by the dalesfolk.

DANCE AT GOATHLAND Sword-dancing and a play by ploughmen were part of a blessing of the plough in January. The ritual is still maintained in Goathland.

BETTY LUPTONS Morris dancing, a men's dance centuries old, grew out of ancient fertility rites. A women's group of dancers, called Betty Luptons after a Harrogate woman who sold spa water in the 19th century, now dance for charity.

ON WATCH The Ripon hornblower sounds the buffalo horn in the Market Place at 9 p.m. This once marked the start of the night watch for thieves and warned people to put out their fires.

SHROVETIDE RITE In Scarborough fishermen and townsfolk skip on the beach on Shrove Tuesday to ensure a good harvest from land and sea.

Festival of cricket, a county's passion

Every Yorkshire village has its own cricket team, not to engage in gentle sport but to compete fiercely in the local league. Families and friends watch the play, make tea in the pavilion, take a collection if a man scores 50 or performs the hat trick, and dream of a local hero having a trial for the county side.

Cricket is Yorkshire's game. Some exiles return for their children to be born – as only men born within the county can play for it. Yorkshiremen recall with pride their championship wins – four in the 1920s, seven in the 1930s, six in the 1960s. Talented past players are venerated, among them Hirst, Sutcliffe, Leyland, Rhodes, Bowes, Hutton and Trueman.

Partisanship is most fervent in the annual Whitsuntide match with Lancashire, but September's Scarborough Festival is for friendly celebration rather than cut-throat competition.

RECORD BATSMAN Len Hutton played for Yorkshire from 1934 to 1955 and was also the England opening batsman. At the Oval in a 1938 Test Match he scored 364 runs, a Test record that stood for 20 years until West Indian Garfield Sobers broke it with a score of 365 not out.

TEA INTERVAL Service was in the grand manner at Scarborough until about 1950 – formal waiters for the players and garden-party marquees for spectators.

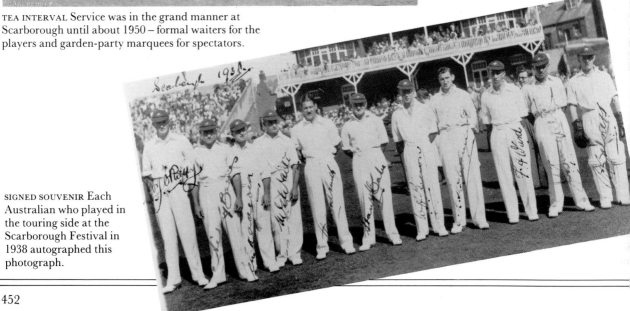

SIGNED SOUVENIR Each Australian who played in the touring side at the Scarborough Festival in 1938 autographed this photograph.

SCARBOROUGH FESTIVAL Since 1876 a cricket feast has been seen here each September except in wartime. The Test Match touring side always plays and many county stars take the field.

CAPTAINS' CALL Don Bradman of Australia and R.W.V. Robins of England go out for the toss at Scarborough in the late 1930s.

CATCHING THE SELECTORS' EYE Before play and during the intervals at any of the Scarborough matches, children or adults can play on the field – with a soft ball only, but even this is a rare concession for a county cricket ground.

The glittering show-place of Yorkshire farming

Throng and bustle fill Harrogate each July for the three-day Great Yorkshire Show. Horse-boxes and cattle-vans arrive along with dogs, hens, sheep, pigs, salesmen, coach parties and, the core of the whole event, the farmers and their families.

The show has been held on 128 occasions since 1838, at different towns until 1951, and since then at a permanent showground in Harrogate.

Parading and judging the stock plays a major part, but there is also an enormous range of exhibits related to farming and rural life – racing pigeons, forestry, bee-keeping, a flower show, angling, rural crafts.

In avenue upon avenue the latest machines and equipment are displayed. Sheep are sheared, horses shod and goats milked in demonstrations of farm work. In the main show-ring the heavy horses parade, glittering and jangling in their finery, four-in-hand drivers compete, packs of hounds are shown, and one of the biggest draws is the show-jumping competition.

WINNING PAIR Mare and foal receive their rosettes in a heavy horse class.

ALMOST A CHAMPION A handsome Jersey bull is first-prize winner of its class and runner-up champion of its breed.

JUDGMENT DAY A shepherdess in modern dress shows the judge a pair of entrants that patiently tolerate close scrutiny.

Marquees, machines and admirers fill the scene as farmers and friends enjoy a day at the show.

The grandstand fills for the parade of the cattle round the main show-ring.

TEST OF SKILL Perfect understanding between man and dog is seen at sheepdog trials. The dog gathers, drives, pens and separates sheep, as in its daily work. The contest is keen but shepherds enjoy the rare company of their own kind.

continued from page 448

'Just a minute, Triss,' I broke in. 'I went round to Nurse Brown's this evening to see Helen, and Cliff asked if he could come with us. Don't you think it would be rather nice to go to his pub since the baby was born in his house?'

Tristan narrowed his eyes. 'Which pub is that?'

'The Black Horse.'

'Ah yes, ye-es.' Tristan looked at me thoughtfully and put his finger tips together. 'Russell and Wrangham's. A good little brewery, that. I've had some first-rate pints in the Black Horse, though I've noticed a slight loss of nuttiness under very warm conditions.' He looked anxiously out of the window. 'It's been hot today. Perhaps we'd ...'

'Oh for heaven's sake!' Siegfried leaped to his feet. 'You sound like an analytical chemist. It's only beer you're talking about, after all.'

Tristan looked at him in shocked silence but Siegfried turned to me briskly. 'I think that's a pleasant idea of yours, James. Let's go with Cliff to the Black Horse. It's a quiet little place.'

And, indeed, as we dropped to the chairs in the bar parlour I felt we had chosen the ideal spot. The evening sunshine sent long golden shafts over the pitted oak tables and high-backed settles where a few farm men sat with their glasses. There was nothing smart about this little inn, but the furniture which hadn't been changed for a hundred years gave it an air of tranquillity. It was just right.

Reg Wilkey, the diminutive landlord, welcomed us and charged our glasses from his tall white jug.

Siegfried raised his pint. 'James, may I be the first to wish a long life, health and happiness to Rosemary.'

'Thank you, Siegfried,' I said, feeling suddenly very much among friends as the others said 'hear, hear' and began to drink.

Cliff, his face wreathed in his eternal smile, lowered the level in his glass by half then turned to the landlord. 'It gets better, Reg,' he said reverently. 'It gets better.'

As Reg bowed modestly Cliff said, 'Ye know, Jim, I've said for years that me two best friends are Mr Russell and Mr Wrangham. I think the world of 'em.'

Everybody laughed and the stage was set for a happy celebration. With my anxieties over I felt wonderful.

After a couple of pints Siegfried patted me on the shoulder. 'I'm off, James. Have a good time. Can't tell you how pleased I am.'

I watched him go and I didn't argue. He was right. There was a veterinary practice out there and somebody had to watch the shop. And this was my night.

It was one of those cosy evenings when everything seemed perfect. Alex and I recalled our childhood in Glasgow, Tristan came up with some splendid memories of Skeldale House in the bachelor days and over everything, like a beneficent moon, hung the huge smile of Cliff Brown.

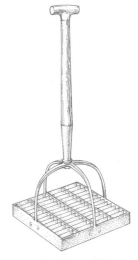

BARLEY HUMMELLER The awns, or long, bristly hairs that grow between the grains on an ear of barley, have to be removed before the grain is threshed. A hummeller, or humbler, is used to knock them off. This hand-hummeller, used before threshing machines incorporated a hummelling device, was stamped repeatedly on a heap of barley until the awns had been knocked off. Hummellers were made by the local blacksmith. They had wooden shafts and iron heads 12–18 in. square, consisting of parallel bars set 1–2 in. apart.

A great love of my fellow men mounted in me and I kept buying drinks for the local people around us. Finally I grew tired of fumbling for money and handed my wallet to the landlord. It was stuffed with notes because I had made a special visit to the bank that afternoon.

'Here, Reg,' I said. 'Just keep taking the drinks out of that.'

'Aye, right, Mr Herriot,' he replied without changing expression. 'It'll mek it easier.'

It did make it a lot easier. Men whom I hardly knew raised their glasses and toasted my new daughter repeatedly, and all I had to do was smile and raise mine in return.

When closing time was announced it didn't seem possible that it was all coming to an end.

As the little pub emptied I approached the landlord. 'We can't go home yet, Reg.'

He looked at me quizzically. 'Well, ye know the law, Mr Herriot.'

'Yes, but this is a special night, isn't it?'

'Aye, it is, I suppose.' He hesitated for a moment. 'Tell ye what. I'll lock up, then we could go down and 'ave one or two in the cellar, just to finish off.'

I put my arm round his shoulders. 'Reg what a delightful idea. Let's go down there.'

We descended a few steps into the pub cellar, switched on the light and pulled the trap door closed after us. As we disposed ourselves among the barrels and crates I looked around the company. Apart from the original four we were now augmented by two young farmers, one of the local grocers and an official from the Darrowby Water Board. We were a warmly knit little group.

It was much easier down there. No need to bother the landlord with his jug. We just went to a barrel and turned the tap.

'Still plenty in the wallet, Reg?' I shouted.

'Aye, there's plenty 'ere, don't worry. Help yourselves.'

We kept doing that and the party never flagged. It must have been past midnight when we heard the thumping on the outside door. Reg listened for a few moments then went upstairs. He returned soon but was preceded through the trap door by the long blue legs, tunic, cadaverous face and helmet of Police-Constable Hubert Goole.

A silence fell on the merry gathering as the constable's melancholy gaze passed slowly over us.

'Drinkin' a bit late, aren't ye?' he enquired tonelessly.

'Ah well.' Tristan gave a gay little laugh. 'It's a special occasion, you see, Mr Goole. Mr Herriot's wife gave birth to a daughter this morning.'

'Oh aye?' The Old Testament countenance looked down on my friend from its bony perch. 'I don't remember Mr Wilkey applyin' for an extended licence for tonight.'

It was the nearest he could get to making a joke, because PC Goole never made jokes. He was known in the town as a stern and unbending man, one who went by the book. It was no good riding a bike at night without lights when PC Goole was around. He was particularly merciless on this offence. He sang in the church choir, his morals were impeccable, he was active in community work, he did everything right. It was strange that in his mid-fifties he was still an ordinary constable.

Tristan bounced back. 'Ah yes, ha-ha, very good. But of course this was a totally impromptu thing. Spur of the moment, you know.'

'Ye can call it what ye like, but you're breakin' the law and you know it.' The big man unbuttoned his breast pocket and flipped open his notebook. 'I'll 'ave to 'ave your names.'

I was sitting on an upturned crate and I gripped my knees tightly. What an end to the happy evening. Nothing much happened in the town and this would make headlines in the Darrowby and Houlton Times. It would look great, with all my friends involved, too. And poor little Reg standing sheepishly in the background – he would really get it in the neck, and it was all my fault.

Tristan, however, was not beaten yet. 'Mr Goole,' he said coldly, 'I'm disappointed in you.'

'Eh?'

'I said I'm disappointed. I'd have expected you to show a different attitude on an occasion like this.'

The constable was unmoved. He poised his pencil. 'I'm a policeman, Mr Farnon, and I 'ave my duty to do. We might as well start with your name.' He wrote carefully then looked up. 'What's your address, now?'

'It seems to me,' said Tristan, ignoring the question, 'that you have forgotten all about little Julie.'

'What about Julie?' The long face showed a certain animation for the first time. Tristan's mention of PC Goole's beloved Yorkshire Terrier had found a tender spot.

'Well, as I recall,' Tristan went on, 'Mr Herriot sat up for several hours during the night with Julie when she was having pups. In fact if it hadn't been for him you might have lost the pups and Julie, too. I know it's a few years ago, but I remember it distinctly.'

'Now then, that has got nowt to do with tonight. I've told ye, I have my duty to do.' He turned to the official of the Water Board.

Tristan returned to the attack. 'Yes, but surely you could have a drink with us on a night like this when Mr Herriot has become a father for the second time. It's the same thing in a way.'

PC Goole paused and his face softened. 'Julie's still goin' strong.'

'Yes, I know,' I said. 'Wonderful little thing for her age.'

'And I still have one of them pups.'

'Of course. You've had him in to see me a few times.'

'Aye ... aye ...' PC Goole hitched up his tunic, delved in his trouser pocket and brought out a large watch. He studied it thoughtfully. 'Well, I'm off duty about now. Suppose I could have a drink with ye. I'll just phone in to the office first.'

'Oh, good!' Tristan moved quickly to the barrel and drew another pint.

REAPER-BINDER MACHINE
Horse-drawn reapers were first used in the Dales about 1890. Some had a slow gear for cutting cereal crops and a faster gear for mowing grass. Workers tying sheaves still had to follow the first machines, but within a decade or two a binding mechanism was combined with the reaper. A small farmer could hire a reaper for about £1 a day from a more well-to-do farmer who owned his own machine. Two or three smallholders sometimes put their funds together to buy a reaper between them. By the 1940s, farmers were using their tractors instead of horses to pull the reaper-binder.

LANDRACE GILTS The Danish breed of pig, the Landrace, was introduced into Britain from Sweden in the late 1940s. Because it is a good bacon producer it has become increasingly popular with pig breeders. Young females such as these four, which have not yet had litters of piglets, are called gilts. As soon as they farrow they are called sows.

When the constable returned from the phone he raised the glass solemnly. 'Here's wishin' t'little lass all the best,' he said, and took a long swallow.

'Thank you, Mr Goole,' I replied. 'You're very kind.'

He sat down on one of the lower steps, placed his helmet on a crate and had another deep drink. 'Both well, I 'ope?'

'Yes, just grand. Have another.'

It was surprising how soon he seemed to forget all about his notebook and the party picked up again rapidly. The relief of the escape added greatly to the festivities, and joy reigned unrestrained.

'It's bloody 'ot down 'ere,' PC Goole remarked after some time and removed his tunic. With this symbolic gesture the last barrier went down.

And yet, over the next two hours, nobody got really plastered. Nobody, that is, except PC Goole. With the rest of us it was a case of laughter, reminiscing and an undoubted heightening of the senses, but the policeman passed through various stages on the road to a fairly profound inebriation.

The first came when he insisted on a Christian-name relationship, then he became tearfully affectionate as he rhapsodised on the wonders of birth, human and canine. The latest phase was more sinister. He was turning aggressive.

'You're 'avin another, Jim.' It was a statement rather than an enquiry as the tall, shirt-sleeved figure bent, swaying slightly, over the tap of the barrel, glass at the ready.

'No thanks, Hubert,' I replied. 'I've had enough.'

He blinked at me owlishly. 'You're not 'avin' another?'

'No, honestly, Hubert, I've had it. I started long before you.'

He sent another pint frothing into his glass before continuing.

'Then you're a bloody piker, Jim,' he said. 'And if there's one thing I can't shtand, if there's one thing I can't bloody well shtand it's a bloody piker.'

I tried an ingratiating smile. 'I'm terribly sorry, Hubert, but I'm up to here, and anyway, it's half-past two. I really think we ought to be going.'

It seemed to be a general sentiment because the assembly all began to get to their feet.

'Goin'?' Hubert glared at me belligerently. 'Whassa matter with you? The night's young yet.' He slurped down another mouthful of beer indignantly. 'You ask a feller to 'ave a drink with you and next minute ye say we're goin'. Itsh not right.'

'Now, now, Hubert,' said little Reg Wilkey, sidling up to him, smiling and radiating the bonhomie which came from thirty years' practice at easing reluctant clients from his premises. 'Be a good lad, now. We've all 'ad a grand time and it's been lovely seein' you, but everybody's settin' off 'ome. Now where's your jacket?'

The constable muttered and grumbled as we helped him into his tunic and balanced his helmet on his head, but allowed us to lead him up the steps into the darkness of the pub. Outside, I installed him in the back of my car with Tristan and Alex on either side. Cliff sat with me in front.

Before we left, the landlord passed my wallet through the window. It had slimmed down to the point of emaciation and it occurred to me that my bank manager, who was always advising me in the kindest possible way to watch my overdraft, would be tossing uneasily in his bed if he knew.

I drove through the sleeping town and turned down the narrow street towards the market place. As we approached I could see that the cobbled square was deserted except for two figures standing at the edge of the roadway under a street light. With a twinge of alarm I recognised Inspector Bowles and Sergeant Rostron, our two head policemen. They were standing, very erect and trim-looking, hands behind their backs, glancing around them keenly. They looked as though they wouldn't miss any misdemeanours in their vicinity.

A sudden scream from the back seat almost sent me through a shop window. Hubert had seen them too.

'It's that bugger Rostron!' he yelled. 'I 'ate that bugger! He's 'ad it in for me for years and I'm goin' to tell 'im what I think about 'im!'

There was a thrashing of arms in the back as he wound down the window and started his tirade at the top of his voice. 'You bloody rotten . . .!'

For the second time that night an icy dread swept me that something awful was going to happen because of me.

'Quell him!' I shouted. 'For God's sake, quell him!'

However my friends in the rear had anticipated me. Hubert's cries were suddenly switched off as Tristan and Alex bundled him to the floor and fell on top of him. Tristan was actually sitting on his head when we came up to the two policemen and only muffled sounds drifted below.

As we passed, the inspector nodded and smiled and the sergeant gave me a friendly salute. It was not difficult to read their minds as they docketed away another item of information. Mr Herriot returning from yet another night call. A dedicated vet, that young man.

With their colleague writhing on the floor behind me I could not relax until we had turned off the square out of sight and sound. Hubert, when allowed to get up, seemed to have lost a lot of belligerence. In fact he was reaching the sleepy stage and when he reached his home he walked quietly and fairly steadily up his garden path.

Back in Skeldale House I went up to our bedroom. The big room with the double bed, wardrobe and dressing-table was eerily empty without Helen.

I opened the door to the long narrow apartment which had been the dressing-room in the great days of the old house. It was where Tristan slept when we were all bachelors together but now it was Jimmy's room and his bed stood in exactly the same place as my old friend's.

I looked down on my son as I had often looked down on Tristan in his slumbers. I used to marvel at Tristan's cherubic innocence but even he

461

BEET-LIFTER Sugar-beet, a widely grown root crop in Yorkshire, was sent to processing plants for the sugar to be extracted. This lifting machine was made in 1926 by Fowlers of Leeds, the world's leading manufacturer of steam-powered agricultural equipment. It was steered by one operator while it was winched back and forth across the field on cables driven by a steam engine at each end of the field. The machine lifted ten rows of beet at a time.

Treacle, dried fruits and ginger were the ingredients Yorkshire housewives used more than any other to flavour their baking. Gingerbreads have them all. To make gingerbreads, melt 8 oz of treacle or syrup in a pan with 2 oz of brown sugar and 2 oz of lard. Pour it on to 1 lb of flour mixed with 3 teaspoons of ground ginger and ½ teaspoon each of ground coriander, caraway seeds, powdered cinnamon and allspice. Knead to a dough. While it is soft, pull off pieces and press them into moulds of men or animals. Turn out on to greased baking sheets and decorate with currants for eyes or buttons. Bake for 20 minutes at 350°F (180°C), gas mark 4.

could not compete with a sleeping child.

I gazed at little Jimmy, then glanced at the other end of the room where a cot stood to receive Rosie.

Soon, I thought, I would have two in here. I was becoming rich.

5

A narrow escape for Rosie

'*I let my heart fall into careless hands.*' Little Rosie's voice piped in my ear as I guided my car over a stretch of rutted road. I had singing now to cheer the hours of driving.

I was on my way back to dress a wound on a cow's back and it was nice to hear the singing. But it was beginning to dawn on me that something better still was happening. I was starting all over again with another child. When Jimmy went to school I missed his company in the car but I did not realise that the whole thing was going to begin again with Rosie.

The intense pleasure of showing them the farm animals and seeing their growing wonder at the things of the countryside; the childish chatter which never palled, the fun and the laughter which lightened my days – it all happened twice to me.

The singing had originated in the purchase of a radiogram. Music has always meant a lot to me and I owned a record-player which gave me a lot of pleasure. Still, I felt I wanted something better, some means of reproducing more faithfully the sound of my favourite orchestras, singers, instrumentalists.

Hi-fi outfits hadn't been heard of at that time, nor stereo, nor wrap-around sound nor any of the other things which have revolutionised the world of listening. The best the music-lover could do was to get a good radiogram.

After much agonising and reading of pamphlets and listening to advice from many quarters I narrowed the list down to three models and made my choice by having them brought round to Skeldale House and playing the opening of the Beethoven Violin Concerto on one after the other, again and again. I must have driven the two men from the electric shop nearly mad but at the end there was no doubt left in my mind.

It had to be the Murphy, a handsome piece of furniture with a louvred front and graceful legs, and it bellowed out the full volume of the Philharmonia Orchestra without a trace of muzziness. I was enchanted with it, but there was one snag, it cost over ninety pounds and that was an awful lot of money in 1950.

'Helen,' I said when we had installed it in the sitting-room. 'We've got

462

to look after this thing. The kids can put records on my old player but we must keep them away from the Murphy.'

Foolish words. The very next day as I came in the front door the passage was echoing with '*Yippee ay ooooh, Yippee ay aaaay, Ghost riders in the skyyy!*' It was Bing Crosby's back-up choir belting out the other side of the 'Careless Hands' record and the Murphy was giving it full value.

I peeped round the sitting-room door. 'Ghost Riders' had come to an end and with her chubby little hands Rosie removed the record, placed it in its cover and marched, pig-tails swinging, to the record cabinet. She selected another disc and was halfway across the floor when I waylaid her.

'Which one is that?' I asked.

'The Little Gingerbread Man,' she replied.

I looked at the label. It was, too, and how did she know, because I had a whole array of these children's records and many of them looked exactly the same. The same colour, the same grouping of words, and Rosie at the age of three could not read.

She fitted the disc expertly on the turntable and set it going. I listened to 'The Little Gingerbread Man' right through and watched as she picked out another record.

I looked over her shoulder. 'What is it this time?'

'Tubby the Tuba.'

And indeed it was. I had an hour to spare and Rosie gave me a recital. We went through 'Uncle Mac's Nursery Rhymes', 'The Happy Prince', 'Peter and the Wolf', and many of the immortal Bing to whom I was and am devoted. I was intrigued to find that her favourite Crosby record was not 'Please', or 'How Deep is the Ocean' or his other classics but 'Careless Hands'. This one had something special for her.

At the end of the session I decided that it was fruitless to try to keep Rosie and the Murphy apart. Whenever she was not out with me she played with the radiogram. It was her toy.

It all turned out for the best, too, because she did my precious acquisition no harm and when she came with me on my rounds she sang the things she had played so often and which were word perfect in her mind. And I really loved that singing. 'Careless Hands' soon became my favourite, too.

There were three gates on the road to this farm and we came bumping up to the first one now. The singing stopped abruptly. This was one of my daughter's big moments. When I drew up she jumped from the car, strutted proudly to the gate and opened it. She took this duty very seriously and her small face was grave as I drove through. When she returned to take her place by my dog, Sam, on the passenger seat, I patted her knee.

'Thank you, sweetheart,' I said. 'You're such a big help to me all the time.'

She didn't say anything but blushed and seemed to swell with importance. She knew I meant what I said because opening gates is a

BEAGLE There were beagles hunting in Britain long before the Romans came, and until the 17th century royal gentlemen, lords of the realm and country squires used them in packs when they went out on foot to hunt hares. Elizabeth I had a pack of miniature beagles. When hunting on horseback for foxes became the prime sport in the 18th century, the beagle packs declined and were replaced by foxhounds.

The beagle is now back in favour, chiefly as a pet. It has a happy disposition and great stamina for covering miles of country and scrambling over obstacles.

chore.

We negotiated the other two gates in similar manner and drove into the farmyard. The farmer, Mr Binns, had shut the cow up in a ramshackle pen with a passage which stretched from a dead end to the outside.

Looking into the pen I saw with some apprehension that the animal was a Galloway – black and shaggy with a fringe of hair hanging over bad-tempered eyes. She lowered her head and switched her tail as she watched me.

'Couldn't you have got her tied up, Mr Binns?' I asked.

The farmer shook his head. 'Nay, I'm short o' room and this 'un spends most of 'er time on the moors.'

I could believe it. There was nothing domesticated about this animal. I looked down at my daughter. Usually I lifted her into hay racks or on to the tops of walls while I worked but I didn't want her anywhere near the Galloway.

'It's no place for you in there, Rosie,' I said. 'Go and stand at the end of the passage well out of the way.'

We went into the pen and the cow danced about and did her best to run up the wall. I was pleasantly surprised when the farmer managed to drop a halter over her head. He backed into a corner and held tightly to the shank.

I looked at him doubtfully. 'Can you hold her?'

'I think so,' Mr Binns replied, a little breathlessly. 'You'll find t'place at the end of her back, there.'

It was a most unusual thing. A big discharging abscess near the root of the tail. And that tail was whipping perpetually from side to side – a sure sign of ill-nature in a bovine.

Gently I passed my fingers over the swelling and like a natural reflex the hind foot lashed out, catching me a glancing blow on the thigh. I had expected this and I got on with my exploration.

'How long has she had this?'

The farmer dug his heels in and leaned back on the rope. 'Oh, 'bout two months. It keeps bustin' and fillin' up over and over again. Every time I thought it'd be the last but it looks like it's never goin' to get right. What's cause of it?'

'I don't know, Mr Binns. She must have had a wound there at some time and it's become infected. And of course, being on the back, drainage is poor. There's a lot of dead tissue which I'll have to clear away before the thing heals.'

I leaned from the pen. 'Rosie, will you bring me my scissors, the cotton wool and that bottle of peroxide.'

The farmer watched wonderingly as the tiny figure trotted to the car and came back with the three things. 'By gaw, t'little lass knows 'er way around.'

'Oh yes,' I said, smiling. 'I'm not saying she knows where everything is in the car, but she's an expert on the things I use regularly.'

GALLOWAY BULLOCK A hardy, sure-footed breed originating in the hills of south-west Scotland, the Galloway is suited to any cold, high region. Beneath its shaggy, black or dun, water-repelling coat there is a short, dense coat that retains body-heat. The Galloway matures slowly, but lives and breeds 15 or more years. It does best on natural hill grazing, not cereal fodder, and will fend for itself winter and summer. Many Dales farmers prized it for the qualities it gave to cross-breeds, especially when the sire was a Shorthorn bull.

464

Rosie handed me my requirements as I reached over the door. Then she retreated to her place at the end of the passage.

I began to work on the abscess. Since the tissue was necrotic the cow couldn't feel anything as I snipped and swabbed, but that didn't stop the hind leg from pistoning out every few seconds. Some animals cannot tolerate any kind of interference and this was one of them.

I finished at last with a nice wide clean area on to which I trickled the hydrogen peroxide. I had a lot of faith in this old remedy as a penetrative antiseptic when there was a lot of pus about, and I watched contentedly as it bubbled on the skin surface. The cow, however, did not seem to enjoy the sensation because she made a sudden leap into the air, tore the rope from the farmer's hands, brushed me to one side and made for the door.

The door was closed but it was a flimsy thing and she went straight through it with a splintering crash. As the hairy black monster shot into the passage I desperately willed her to turn left but to my horror she went right and after a wild scraping of her feet on the cobbles began to thunder down towards the dead end where my little daughter was standing.

It was one of the worst moments of my life. As I dashed towards the broken door I heard a small voice say 'Mama'. There was no scream of terror, just that one quiet word. When I left the pen Rosie was standing with her back against the end wall of the passage and the cow was stationary, looking at her from a distance of two feet.

The animal turned when she heard my footsteps then whipped round in a tight circle and galloped past me into the yard.

I was shaking when I lifted Rosie into my arms. She could easily have been killed and a jumble of thoughts whirled in my brain. Why had she said 'Mama'? I had never heard her use the word before – she always called Helen 'Mummy' or 'Mum'. Why had she been apparently unafraid? I didn't know the answers. All I felt was an overwhelming thankfulness. To this day I feel the same whenever I see that passage.

Driving away I remembered that something very like this had happened when Jimmy was out with me. It was not so horrific because he was playing in a passage with an open end leading into a field and he was not trapped when the cow I was working on broke loose and hurtled towards him. I could see nothing, but I heard a piercing yell of '*Aaaagh!*' before I rounded the corner. To my intense relief Jimmy was streaking across the field to where my car was standing and the cow was trotting away in another direction.

This reaction was typical because Jimmy was always the noisy one of the family. Under any form of stress he believed in making his feelings known in the form of loud cries. When Dr Allinson came to give him his routine inoculations he heralded the appearance of the syringe with yells of '*Ow! This is going to hurt! Ow! Ow!*'. He had a kindred spirit in our good doctor who bawled back at him, '*Aye. You're right, it is! Oooh! Aaah!*' But Jimmy really did scare our dentist because his propensity for noise

ROUGH FELL SHEEP The high, slaty fells of the Pennines are the home of the Rough Fell sheep, a breed that is placid but at the same time lively and nimble enough to find adequate grazing in such rough country. The sheep's black-and-white face has strong horns curling down beside it in both ram and ewe. The fleece is white, hangs right over the feet and is straight without a trace of a crimp. The fibres are about 8 in. long and the fleece weighs 5 lb, which is high for a hill sheep. The wool is not of fine quality, but is suitable for carpets and heavy fabrics.

LOOKING AFTER HORSES' FEET
When horses provided the power on farms, they were among the vet's most regular patients. Their feet especially needed prompt attention if they were damaged. Here the farmer shows the vet the trouble he has spotted, perhaps an infection, and has a shoeing hammer ready to remove the horseshoe – the first thing to be done before the vet makes his own thorough inspection and carries out treatment.

appeared to carry on even under general anaesthesia. The long quavering wail he emitted as he went under the gas brought the poor man out in a sweat of anxiety.

Rosie solemnly opened the three gates on the way back, then she looked up at me expectantly. I knew what it was – she wanted to play one of her games. She loved being quizzed just as Jimmy had loved to quiz me.

I took my cue and began. 'Give me the names of six blue flowers.'

She coloured quickly in satisfaction because of course she knew. 'Field Scabious, Harebell, Forget-me-not, Bluebell, Speedwell, Meadow Cranesbill.'

'Clever girl,' I said. 'Now let's see – how about the names of six birds?'

Again the blush and the quick reply. 'Magpie, Curlew, Thrush, Plover, Yellowhammer, Rook.'

'Very good indeed. Now name me six red flowers.' And so it went on, day after day, with infinite variations. I only half realised at the time how lucky I was. I had a demanding, round-the-clock job and yet I had the company of my children at the same time. So many men work so hard to keep the home going that they lose touch with the families who are at the heart of it, but it never happened to me.

Both Jimmy and Rosie, until they went to school, spent most of their time with me round the farms. With Rosie, as her schooldays approached, her attitude, always solicitous, became distinctly maternal. She really couldn't see how I was going to get by without her and by the time she was five she was definitely worried.

'Daddy,' she would say seriously. 'How are you going to manage when I'm at school? All those gates to open and having to get everything out of the boot by yourself. It's going to be awful for you.'

I used to try to reassure her, patting her head as she looked up at me in the car. 'I know, Rosie, I know. I'm going to miss you, but I'll get along somehow.'

Her response was always the same. A relieved smile and then the comforting words. 'But never mind, Daddy, I'll be with you every Saturday and Sunday. You'll be all right then.'

I suppose it was a natural result of my children seeing veterinary practice from early childhood and witnessing my own pleasure in my work that they never thought of being anything else but veterinary surgeons.

There was no problem with Jimmy. He was a tough little fellow and well able to stand the buffets of our job, but somehow I couldn't bear the idea of my daughter being kicked and trodden on and knocked down and covered with muck. Practice was so much rougher in those days. There were no metal crushes to hold the big struggling beasts, there were still quite a number of farm horses around and they were the ones which regularly put the vets in hospital with broken legs and ribs. Rosie made it very clear that she wanted country practice and to me this seemed very much a life for a man. In short, I talked her out of it.

This really wasn't like me because I have never been a heavy father and have always believed that children should follow their inclinations. But as Rosie entered her teens I dropped a long series of broad hints and perhaps played unfairly by showing her as many grisly, dirty jobs as possible. She finally decided to be a doctor of humans.

Now when I see the high percentage of girls in the veterinary schools and observe the excellent work done by the two girl assistants in our own practice I sometimes wonder if I did the right thing.

But Rosie is a happy and successful doctor and, anyway, parents are never sure that they have done the right thing. They can only do what they think is right.

However, all that was far in the future as I drove home from Mr Binns with my three-year-old daughter by my side. She had started to sing again and was just finishing the first verse of her great favourite: '*Careless hands don't care when dreams slip through.*'

6

A miner's remedy

'Was there no peace in a vet's life?' I wondered fretfully as I hurried my car along the road to Gilthorpe village. Eight o'clock on a Sunday evening and here I was trailing off to visit a dog ten miles away which, according to Helen who had taken the message, had been ailing for more than a week.

I had worked all morning, then spent an afternoon in the hills with the children and some of their friends, a long-standing weekly event during which we had managed to explore nearly every corner of the district over the years. Jimmy had set a brisk pace with his hardy young pals and I had had to carry Rosie on my shoulders up the steepest slopes. After tea there was the usual routine of baths, story-reading and bed for the two of them, then I was ready to settle down with the Sunday papers and listen to the radio.

Yet here I was back on the treadmill, staring through the windscreen at the roads and the walls which I saw day in, day out. When I left Darrowby the streets of the little town were empty in the gathering dusk and the houses had that tight-shut, comfortable look which raised images of armchairs and pipes and firesides, and now as I saw the lights of the farms winking on the fell-sides I could picture the stocksmen dozing contentedly with their feet up.

I had not passed a single car on the darkening road. There was nobody out but Herriot.

I was really sloshing around in my trough of self-pity when I drew up

AN ELEGANT STILE Part of the waller's craft was to build stiles, and in them he showed individual touches. A flagged path leading to Hawes received unusual treatment – curved flags set upright in the mortared wall ends.

DACHSHUND Familiarly known as the sausage dog, the dachshund was first bred in Germany for badger-hunting. With its short legs, strong, low-slung body and highly acute sense of smell, the dog was tenacious in following the scent and ideally built to pursue the quarry through thick undergrowth and even down its hole. It was introduced into England in the 19th century, and has long been a pet.

outside a row of greystone cottages at the far end of Gilthorpe. Mrs Cundall, Number 4, Chestnut Row, Helen had written on the slip of paper and as I opened the gate and stepped through the tiny strip of garden my mind was busy with half-formed ideas of what I was going to say.

My few years' experience in practice had taught me that it did no good at all to remonstrate with people for calling me out at unreasonable times. I knew perfectly well that my words never seemed to get through to them and that they would continue to do exactly as they had done before, but for all that I had to say something if only to make me feel better.

No need to be rude or ill-mannered, just a firm statement of the position; that vets liked to relax on Sunday evenings just like other people; that we did not mind at all coming out for emergencies but that we did object to having to visit animals which had been ill for a week.

I had my speech fairly well prepared when a little middle-aged woman opened the door.

'Good evening, Mrs Cundall,' I said, slightly tight-lipped.

'Oh, it's Mr Herriot.' She smiled shyly. 'We've never met but I've seen you walkin' round Darrowby on market days. Come inside.'

The door opened straight into the little low-beamed living-room and my first glance took in the shabby furniture and some pictures framed in tarnished gilt when I noticed that the end of the room was partly curtained off.

Mrs Cundall pulled the curtain aside. In a narrow bed a man was lying, a skeleton-thin man whose eyes looked up at me from hollows in a yellowed face.

'This is my husband, Ron,' she said cheerfully, and the man smiled and raised a bony arm from the quilt in greeting.

'And here is your patient, Hermann,' she went on, pointing to a little dachshund who sat by the side of the bed.

'Hermann?'

'Yes, we thought it was a good name for a German sausage dog.' They both laughed.

'Of course,' I said. 'Excellent name. He looks like a Hermann.'

The little animal gazed up at me, bright-eyed and welcoming. I bent down and stroked his head and the pink tongue flickered over my fingers.

I ran my hand over the glossy skin. 'He looks very healthy. What's the trouble?'

'Oh, he's fine in himself,' Mrs Cundall replied. 'Eats well and everything, but over the last week he's been goin' funny on 'is legs. We weren't all that worried but tonight he sort of flopped down and couldn't get up again.'

'I see. I noticed he didn't seem keen to rise when I patted his head.' I put my hand under the little dog's body and gently lifted him on to his feet. 'Come on, lad,' I said. 'Come on, Hermann, let's see you walk.'

As I encouraged him he took a few hesitant steps but his hind end

468

swayed progressively and he soon dropped into the sitting position again.

'It's his back, isn't it?' Mrs Cundall said. 'He's strong enough on 'is forelegs.'

'That's ma trouble, too,' Ron murmured in a soft husky voice, but he was smiling and his wife laughed and patted the arm on the quilt.

I lifted the dog on to my knee. 'Yes, the weakness is certainly in the back.' I began to palpate the lumbar vertebrae, feeling my way along, watching for any sign of pain.

'Has he hurt 'imself?' Mrs Cundall asked. 'Has somebody hit 'im? We don't usually let him out alone but sometimes he sneaks through the garden gate.'

'There's always the possibility of an injury,' I said. 'But there are other causes.' There were indeed – a host of unpleasant possibilities. I did not like the look of this little dog at all. This syndrome was one of the things I hated to encounter in canine practice.

'Can you tell me what you really think?' she said. 'I'd like to know.'

'Well, an injury could cause haemorrhage or concussion or oedema – that's fluid – all affecting his spinal cord. He could even have a fractured vertebra but I don't think so.'

'And how about the other causes.'

'There's quite a lot. Tumours, bony growths, abscesses or discs can press on the cord.'

'Discs?'

'Yes, little pads of cartilage and fibrous tissue between the vertebrae. In long-bodied dogs like Hermann they sometimes protrude into the spinal canal. In fact I think that is what is causing his symptoms.'

Ron's husky voice came again from the bed. 'And what's 'is prospects, Mr Herriot?'

Oh, that was the question. Complete recovery or incurable paralysis. It could be anything. 'Very difficult to say at this moment,' I replied. 'I'll given him an injection and some tablets and we'll see how he goes over the next few days.'

I injected an analgesic and some antibiotic and counted out some salicylate tablets into a box. We had no steroids at that time. It was the best I could do.

'Now then, Mr Herriot.' Mrs Cundall smiled at me eagerly. 'Ron has a bottle o' beer every night about this time. Would you like to join 'im?'

'Well ... it's very kind of you but I don't want to intrude ...'

'Oh, you're not doing that. We're glad to see you.'

She poured two glasses of brown ale, propped her husband up with pillows and sat down by the bed.

'We're from South Yorkshire, Mr Herriot,' she said.

I nodded. I had noticed the difference from the local accent.

'Aye, we came up here after Ron's accident, eight years ago.'

'What was that?'

'I were a miner,' Ron said. 'Roof fell in on me. I got a broken back,

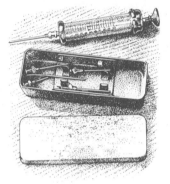

A VET'S SYRINGE SET The metal and glass syringe kept in a case with several sizes of needle was an indispensable instrument for a vet to carry on his rounds. It was made of glass and metal, materials that could be sterilised by boiling. The vet would carry with him one or two of each size of syringe, sterilised ready for use. He might have to use the needles more than once before he got back to his surgery to re-sterilise them. In the 1950s plastic syringes were introduced. These did not need such careful handling because they were not breakable. Now sterilising is not always necessary; a sterile plastic syringe can be taken from its sealed pack, used once and then thrown away.

469

crushed liver and a lot o' other internal injuries, but two of me mates were killed in the same fall so ah'm lucky to be 'ere.' He sipped his beer. 'I've survived, but doctor says I'll never walk no more.'

'I'm terribly sorry.'

'Nay, nay,' the husky voice went on. 'I count me blessings and I've got a lot to be thankful for. Ah suffer very little and I've got t'best wife in the world.'

Mrs Cundall laughed. 'Oh, listen to 'im. But I'm right glad we came to Gilthorpe. We used to spend all our holidays in the Dales. We were great walkers and it was lovely to get away from the smoke and the chimneys. The bedroom in our old house just looked out on a lot o' brick walls but Ron has this big window right by 'im and he can see for miles.'

The window commanded a wide view of the green slopes running down to the river.

'Yes, of course,' I said. 'This is a lovely situation.' The village was perched on a high ridge on the fell-side and that window would command a wide view of the green slopes running down to the river and climbing high to the wildness of the moor on the other side. This sight had beguiled me so often on my rounds and the grassy paths climbing among the airy tops seemed to beckon to me. But they would beckon in vain to Ron Cundall.

'Gettin' Hermann was a good idea, too,' he said. 'Ah used to feel a bit lonely when t'missus went into Darrowby for shoppin' but the little feller's made all the difference. You're never alone when you've got a dog.'

I smiled. 'How right you are. What is his age now, by the way?'

'He's six.' Ron replied. 'Right in the prime o' life, aren't you, old lad.' He let his arm fall by the bedside and his hand fondled the sleek ears.

'That seems to be his favourite place.'

'Aye, it's a funny thing, but 'e allus sits there. T'missus is the one who has to take 'im walks and feeds 'im but he's very faithful to me. He has a basket over there but this is 'is place. I only have to reach down and he's there.'

This was something that I had seen on many occasions with disabled people; that their pets stayed close by them as if conscious of their role of comforter and friend.

I finished my beer and got to my feet. Ron looked up at me. 'Reckon I'll spin mine out a bit longer.' He glanced at his half-full glass. 'Ah used to shift about six pints some nights when I went out wi' the lads, but you know I enjoy this one bottle just as much. Strange how things turn out.'

His wife bent over him, mock-scolding. 'Yes, you've had to right your ways. You're a reformed character, aren't you?'

They both laughed as though it were a stock joke between them.

'Well, thank you for the drink, Mrs Cundall. I'll look in to see Hermann on Tuesday.' I moved towards the door.

As I left I waved to the man in the bed and his wife put her hand on my arm. 'We're very grateful to you for comin' out at this time on a Sunday night, Mr Herriot. We felt awful about callin' you, but you understand it was only today that the little chap started going off his legs like that.'

'Oh, of course, of course, please don't worry. I didn't mind in the least.'

And as I drove through the darkness I knew that I didn't mind – now. My petty irritation had evaporated within two minutes of my entering that house and I was left only with a feeling of humility. If that man back there had a lot to be thankful for, how about me? I had everything. I only wished I could dispel the foreboding I felt about his dog. There was a hint of doom about those symptoms of Hermann's and yet I knew I just had to get him right . . .

On Tuesday he looked much the same, possibly a little worse.

'I think I'd better take him back to the surgery for X-ray,' I said to

Mrs Cundall. 'He doesn't seem to be improving with the treatment.'

In the car Hermann curled up happily on Rosie's knee, submitting with good grace to her petting.

I had no need to anaesthetise him or sedate him when I placed him on our newly acquired X-ray machine. Those hind quarters stayed still all by themselves. A lot too still for my liking.

I was no expert at interpreting X-ray pictures but at least I could be sure there was no fracture of the vertebrae. Also, there was no sign of bony extoses, but I thought I could detect a narrowing of the space between a couple of the vertebrae which would confirm my suspicions of a protrusion of a disc.

Laminectomy or fenestration had not even been heard of in those days so I could do nothing more than continue with my treatment and hope.

By the end of the week hope had grown very dim. I had supplemented the salycilates with long-standing remedies like tincture of nux vomica and other ancient stimulant drugs, but when I saw Hermann on the Saturday he was unable to rise. I tweaked the toes of his hind limbs and was rewarded by a faint reflex movement, but with a sick certainty I knew that complete posterior paralysis was not far away.

A week later I had the unhappy experience of seeing my prognosis confirmed in the most classical way. When I entered the door of the Cundall's cottage Hermann came to meet me, happy and welcoming in his front end but dragging his hind limbs helplessly behind him.

'Hello, Mr Herriot.' Mrs Cundall gave me a wan smile and looked down at the little creature stretched frog-like on the carpet. 'What d'you think of him now?'

I bent and tried the reflexes. Nothing. I shrugged my shoulders, unable to think of anything to say. I looked at the gaunt figure in the bed, the arm outstretched as always on the quilt.

'Good morning, Ron,' I said as cheerfully as I could, but there was no reply. The face was averted, looking out of the window. I walked over to the bed. Ron's eyes were staring fixedly at the glorious panorama of moor and fell, at the pebbles of the river, white in the early sunshine, at the criss-cross of the grey walls against the green. His face was expressionless. It was as though he did not know I was there.

I went back to his wife. I don't think I have ever felt more miserable. 'Is he annoyed with me?' I whispered.

'No, no, no, it's this.' She held out a newspaper. 'It's upset him something awful.'

I looked at the printed page. There was a large picture at the top, a picture of a dachshund exactly like Hermann. This dog, too, was paralysed but its hind end was supported by a little four-wheeled bogie. On the picture it appeared to be sporting with its mistress. In fact it looked quite happy and normal except for those wheels.

Ron seemed to hear the rustle of the paper because his head came round quickly. 'What d'ye think of that, Mr Herriot? D'ye agree with it?'

'Well ... I don't really know, Ron. I don't like the look of it, but I

472

suppose the lady in the picture thought it was the only thing to do.'

'Aye, maybe.' the husky voice trembled. 'But ah don't want Hermann to finish up like that.' The arm dropped by the side of the bed and his fingers felt around on the carpet, but the little dog was still splayed out near the door. 'It's 'opeless now, Mr Herriot, isn't it?'

'Well, it was a black look-out from the beginning.' I said. 'These cases are so difficult. I'm very sorry.'

'Nay, I'm not blamin' you,' he said. 'You've done what ye could, same as vet for that dog in the picture did what 'e could. But it was no good, was it? What do we do now – put 'im down?'

'No, Ron, forget about that just now. Sometimes paralysis cases just recover on their own after many weeks. We must carry on. At this moment I honestly cannot say there is no hope.'

I paused for a moment, then turned to Mrs Cundall. 'One of the problems is the dog's natural functions. You'll have to carry him out into the garden for that. If you gently squeeze each side of his abdomen you'll encourage him to pass water. I'm sure you'll soon learn how to do that.'

'Oh, of course, of course,' she replied. 'I'll do anything. As long as there's some hope.'

'There is, I assure you, there is.'

But on the way back to the surgery the thought hammered in my brain. That hope was very slight. Spontaneous recovery did sometimes occur but Hermann's condition was extreme. I repressed a groan as I thought of the nightmarish atmosphere which had begun to surround my dealings with the Cundalls. The paralysed man and the paralysed dog. And why did that picture have to appear in the paper just at this very time? Every veterinary surgeon knows the feeling that fate has loaded the scales against him and it weighed on me despite the bright sunshine spreading into the car.

However, I kept going back every few days. Sometimes I took a couple of bottles of brown ale along in the evening and drank them with Ron. He and his wife were always cheerful but the little dog never showed the slightest sign of improvement. He still had to pull his useless hind limbs after him when he came to greet me, and though he always returned to his station by his master's bed, nuzzling up into Ron's hand, I was beginning to resign myself to the certainty that one day that arm would come down from the quilt and Hermann would not be there.

It was on one of these visits that I noticed an unpleasant smell as I entered the house. There was something familiar about it.

I sniffed and the Cundalls looked at each other guiltily. There was a silence and then Ron spoke.

'It's some medicine ah've been givin' Hermann. Stinks like 'ell but it's supposed to be good for dogs.'

'Oh yes?'

'Aye, well ...' His fingers twitched uncomfortably on the bedclothes. 'It was Bill Noakes put me on to it. He's an old mate o' mine – we used to work down t'pit together – and he came to visit me last weekend.

MILK-BOTTLE TOPS Waxed discs of cardboard were used to seal milk bottles until the 1960s, when foil tops came into use. The cardboard disc fitted into the wide-necked bottle and had a perforated centre circle. This was pushed open to make a finger-hole for pulling out the bottle top. The top usually carried an advertisement for the farm, the retailer, or a wider interest.

473

Keeps a few whippets, does Bill. Knows a lot about dogs and 'e sent me this stuff along for Hermann.'

Mrs Cundall went to the cupboard and sheepishly presented me with a plain bottle. I removed the cork and as the horrid stench rose up to me my memory became suddenly clear. Asafoetida, a common constituent of quack medicines before the war and still lingering on the shelves of occasional chemist shops and in the medicine chests of people who liked to doctor their own animals.

I had never prescribed the stuff myself but it was supposed to be beneficial in horses with colic and dogs with digestive troubles. My own feeling had always been that its popularity had been due solely to the assumption that anything which stank as badly as that must have some magical properties, but one thing I knew for sure was that it could not possibly do anything for Hermann.

I replaced the cork. 'So you're giving him this, eh?'

Ron nodded. 'Aye, three times a day. He doesn't like it much, but Bill Noakes has great faith in it. Cured hundreds o' dogs with it, 'e says.' The deep-sunk eyes looked at me with a silent appeal.

'Well, fine, Ron,' I said. 'You carry on. Let's hope it does the trick.'

I knew the asafoetida couldn't do any harm and since my treatment had proved useless I was in no position to turn haughty. But my main concern was that these two nice people had been given a glimmer of hope, and I wasn't going to blot it out.

Mrs Cundall smiled and Ron's expression relaxed. 'That's grand, Mr Herriot,' he said. 'Ah'm glad ye don't mind. I can dose the little feller myself. It's summat for me to do.'

It was about a week after the commencement of the new treatment that I called in at the Cundalls as I was passing through Gilthorpe.

'How are you today, Ron?' I asked.

'Champion, Mr Herriot, champion.' He always said that, but today there was a new eagerness in his face. He reached down and lifted his dog on to the bed. 'Look 'ere.'

He pinched the little paw between his fingers and there was a faint but definite retraction of the leg. I almost fell over in my haste to grab at the other foot. The result was the same.

'My God, Ron,' I gasped. 'The reflexes are coming back.'

He laughed his soft husky laugh. 'Bill Noakes's stuff's working, isn't it?'

A gush of emotions, mainly professional shame and wounded pride, welled in me, but it was only for a moment. 'Yes, Ron,' I replied. 'It's working. No doubt about it.'

He stared up at me. 'Then Hermann's going to be all right?'

'Well, it's early days yet, but that's the way it looks to me.'

It was several weeks more before the little dachshund was back to normal and of course it was a fairly typical case of spontaneous recovery with nothing whatever to do with the asafoetida or indeed with my own efforts. Even now, thirty years later, when I treat these puzzling back

WHIPPET When rabbit and hare coursing began to be frowned on about the beginning of this century, owners of swift hounds turned to dog racing. The explosive starting speed of the whippet soon made it a popular racing dog; it can sprint 100 yds in six seconds. Miners in particular took to keeping whippets. The spare, tense-looking dog makes a warm and affectionate pet.

conditions with steroids, broad spectrum antibiotics and sometimes colloidal calcium I wonder how many of them would have recovered without my aid. Quite a number, I imagine.

Sadly, despite the modern drugs, we still have our failures and I always regard a successful termination with profound relief.

But that feeling of relief has never been stronger than it was with Hermann and I can recall vividly my final call at the cottage in Gilthorpe. As it happened it was around the same time as my first visit – eight o'clock in the evening, and when Mrs Cundall ushered me in, the little dog bounded joyously up to me before returning to his post by the bed.

'Well, that's a lovely sight,' I said. 'He can gallop like a racehorse now.'

Ron dropped his hand down and stroked the sleek head. 'Aye, isn't it grand. By heck, it's been a worryin' time.'

'Well, I'll be going.' I gave Hermann a farewell pat. 'I just looked in on my way home to make sure all was well. I don't need to come any more now.'

'Nay, nay,' Ron said. 'Don't rush off. You've time to have a bottle o' beer with me before ye go.'

I sat down on the bed and Mrs Cundall gave us our glasses before pulling up a chair for herself. It was exactly like that first night. I poured my beer and looked at the two of them. Their faces glowed with friendliness and I marvelled because my part in Hermann's salvation had been anything but heroic.

In their eyes everything I had done must have seemed bumbling and ineffectual and in fact they must be convinced that all would have been lost if Ron's old chum from the coal-face had not stepped in and effortlessly put things right.

At best they could only regard me as an amiable fathead and all the explanations and protestations in the world would not alter that. But though my ego had been bruised I did not really care. I was witnessing a happy ending instead of a tragedy and that was more important than petty self-justification. I made a mental resolve never to say anything which might spoil their picture of this triumph.

I was about to take my first sip when Mrs Cundall spoke up. 'This is your last visit, Mr Herriot, and all's ended well. I think we ought to drink some sort o' toast.'

'I agree,' I said. 'Let's see, what shall it be? Ah yes, I've got it.' I raised my glass. 'Here's to Bill Noakes.'

MODERN ROLE FOR THE SLED
Even in 1955 when farm machinery had become so commonplace that a small Wharfedale farmer had the use of a hay baler, there was still a use for the old equipment. Machine-made bales are pulled easily up a muddy track beside the Wharfe on the metal runners of a horse-drawn sled.

7

Fertility rites

AYLESBURY DUCKS Ducks lay more eggs over a longer period than hens, and are quicker to fatten for the table. They are also practically free of disease, and they do not attempt to fly away as hens do. A pond is not essential for them as long as they have a large trough of water. They like to be in an orchard, under the shade of trees. There they eat insects, slugs and snails and graze the grass as well as disposing of household food scraps.

However, ducks are very nervous, and farmers' wives have traditionally preferred keeping hens. Rough handling prevents ducks from laying or fattening. The Aylesbury duck, Britain's best table duck, reaches a table-weight of 5 lb in about ten weeks. It is broad and plump with pale, well-flavoured flesh. The pure-bred duck has white plumage, a pinkish bill and orange legs.

The bull with the bowler hat.

That was one of the irreverent terms for Artificial Insemination when it first arrived on the post-war scene. Of course AI was a wonderful advance. Up till the official licensing of bulls the farmers had used any available male bovine to get their cows in calf. A cow had to produce a calf before it would give milk and it was milk that was the goal of the dairy farmers, but unfortunately the progeny of these 'scrub' bulls were often low grade and weakly.

But AI was a great improvement on licensing. To use a high-class, pedigree, proven bull to inseminate large numbers of cows for farmers who could never afford to own such an animal was and is a splendid idea. Over the years I have seen countless thousands of superior young heifers, bullocks and bulls populate the farms of Britain and I have rejoiced.

I am speaking theoretically, however. My own practical experience of Artificial Insemination was brief and unhappy.

When the thing first began, most practitioners thought they would be rushing about, doing a lot of insemination on their own account, and Siegfried and I could hardly wait to get started. We purchased an artificial vagina, which was a tube of hard vulcanised rubber about eighteen inches long with a lining of latex. There was a little tap on the tube and warm water was run into this to simulate the temperature of a genuine bovine vagina. On one end of the AV was a latex cone secured by rubber bands and this cone terminated in a glass tube in which the semen was collected.

Apart from its use in insemination this instrument provided an excellent means of testing the farmers' own bulls for fertility. It was in this context that I had my first experience.

Wally Hartley had bought a young Ayrshire bull from one of the big dairy farmers and he wanted the animal's fertility tested by the new method. He rang me to ask if I would do the job and I was elated at the chance to try out our new acquisition.

At the farm I filled the liner with water just nicely at blood heat and fastened on the cone and glass tube. I was ready and eager for action.

The required cow in oestrus was in a large loose box off the yard and the farmer led the bull towards it.

'He's nobbut a little 'un,' Mr Hartley said, 'but I wouldn't trust 'im. He's a cheeky young bugger. Never served a cow yet, but keen as mustard.'

I eyed the bull. Certainly he wasn't large, but he had mean eyes and

476

the sharp curving horns of the typical Ayrshire. Anyway, this job shouldn't be much trouble. I had never seen it done but had flipped through a pamphlet on the subject and it seemed simple enough.

All you did was wait till the bull started to mount, then you directed the protruded penis into the AV. Apparently then, the bull, with surprising gullibility, thrust happily into the water-filled cylinder and ejaculated into the tube. I had been told repeatedly that there was nothing to it.

I went into the box. 'Let him in, Wally,' I said, and the farmer opened the half door.

The bull trotted inside, and the cow, fastened by a halter to a ring on the wall, submitted calmly as he sniffed around her. He seemed to like what he saw because he finally stationed himself behind her with eager anticipation.

This was the moment. Take up position on the right side of the bull, the pamphlet had said, and the rest would be easy.

With surprising speed the young animal threw his forelegs on the cow's rump and surged forward. I had to move quickly and as the penis emerged from the sheath I grabbed it and poised the AV for action.

But I didn't get the chance. The bull dismounted immediately and swung round on me with an affronted glare. He looked me carefully up and down as though he didn't quite believe what he saw and there was not an ounce of friendliness in his expression. Then he appeared to remember the rather pressing business on hand and turned his attention to the cow again.

He leaped up, I grabbed, and once more he suspended his activities abruptly and brought his forefeet thudding to the ground. This time there was more than outraged dignity in his eyes, there was anger. He snorted, shook the needle-sharp horns in my direction and dragged a little straw along the floor with a hoof before fixing me with a long appraising stare. He didn't have to speak, his message was unequivocal. Just try that once more, chum, and you've had it.

As his eyes lingered on me everything seemed to become silent and motionless as though I were part of a picture. The cow standing patiently, the churned straw beneath the animals, and beyond them the farmer out in the yard, leaning over the half door, waiting for the next move.

I wasn't particularly looking forward to that next move. I felt a little breathless and my tongue pressed against the roof of my mouth.

At length the bull, with a final warning glance at me, decided to resume his business and reared up on the cow once more. I gulped, bent quickly and as his slim red organ shot forth I grasped it and tried to bring the AV down on it.

This time the bull didn't mess about. He sprang away from the cow, put his head down and came at me like a bullet.

In that fleeting instant I realised what a fool I had been to stand with the animals between me and the door. Behind me was the dark corner of the box. I was trapped.

MOVING THE FLOCK When sheep are moved – to feed in a different field perhaps, or to be dipped, marked or treated by the vet – the shepherd finds his crook an invaluable aid. The hooked end will catch the leg of a breakaway sheep to bring it back into the flock. It also draws out from the flock an individual animal the shepherd wants to examine.

Fortunately the AV was dangling from my right hand and as the bull charged I was able to catch him an upward blow on the snout. If I had hit him on the top of the head he would never have felt it and one or both of those nasty horns would inevitably have started to explore my interior. But as it was, the hard rubber cylinder thumping against his nose brought him to a slithering halt, and while he was blinking and making up his mind about having a second go I rained blows on him with a frenzy born of terror.

I have often wondered since that day if I am the only veterinary surgeon to have used an artifical vagina as a defensive weapon. It certainly was not built for the purpose because it soon began to disintegrate under my onslaught. First the glass tube hurtled past the ear of the startled farmer who was watching, wide-eyed, from the doorway, then the cone spun away against the flank of the cow who had started to chew her cud placidly, oblivious of the drama being enacted by her side.

I alternated my swipes with thrusts and lunges worthy of a fencing master but I still couldn't jockey my way out of that corner. However, although my puny cylinder couldn't hurt the bull I obviously had him puzzled. Apart from a lot of weaving and prodding with his horns he made no sign of repeating his first headlong charge and seemed content to keep me penned in the few feet of space.

But I knew it was only a matter of time. He was out to get me and I was wondering how it felt to receive a cornada when he took a step back and came in again full tilt, head down.

I met him with a back-handed slash, and that was what saved me because the elastic holding the latex lining came off and the warm water from within fountained into the bull's eyes.

He stopped suddenly and it was then I think he just decided to give up. In his experience of humans I was something new to him. I had taken intimate liberties with him in the pursuit of his lawful duty, I had belaboured him with a rubber instrument and finally squirted water in his face. He had plainly had enough of me.

During his pause for thought I dodged past him, threw open the door and escaped into the yard.

The farmer looked at me as I fought for breath. 'By gaw, Mr Herriot, it's a 'ell of a job, this AI, isn't it?'

'Yes, Wally,' I replied shakily. 'It is, rather.'

'Is it allus like that?'

'No, Wally, no . . .' I looked sadly at my bedraggled AV. 'This is an exceptional case. I . . . I think we'd better get a specialist in to collect a sample from this bull.'

The farmer rubbed his ear where the tube had clipped it in passing. 'Awright, then, Mr Herriot. You'll let me know when you're comin', I suppose. It'll be another bit of excitement to look forward to.'

His words did nothing to ease the feeling of abject failure as I crept away from the farm. Vets were taking semen samples every day now

GATHERING OATS With a wooden-toothed rake the harvester drew up a bundle of mown oats against his knee to form into a sheaf for tying up. Oats was a fodder crop for both horses and cattle, and oatmeal was used extensively in the kitchen. A smallholder would mow his crop and afterwards make it into sheaves. Where more hands were available, a sheaf-maker followed on behind the mower.

with no trouble at all. What was the matter with me?

Back in the surgery I phoned the advisory service. Yes, they said, they would send out one of their sterility advisory officers. He would meet me on the farm at ten o'clock the next morning.

When I arrived there on the following day the officer was already in the yard and I thought there was something familiar about the back of the jaunty figure strolling over the cobbles and blowing out clouds of cigarette smoke. When he turned round I saw with a gush of relief that it was Tristan. I hadn't been looking forward to recounting my shameful performance to a stranger.

His broad grin was like a tonic. 'Hello, Jim, how are things?'

'Fine,' I replied. 'Except for this semen collection. I know you're doing it all the time but I had a shambolic experience yesterday.'

'Really?' He pulled deeply at his Woodbine. 'Tell me about it. Mr Hartley's just on his way in from the fields.'

We stepped inside the loose box, the scene of the previous day's debacle, and I began my tale.

I hadn't got far before Tristan's jaw dropped. 'You mean you just let the bull in here on his own, without any restraint?'

'That's right.'

'You daft bugger, Jim. You're lucky to be here. In the first place this job should always be done out in the open, and secondly the bull should always be held by a pole or a halter through the nose ring. I like to have two or three blokes helping me.' He shot me an incredulous glance as he lit another Woodbine. 'Anyway, go on.'

As I proceeded with my story his expression began to change. His mouth twitched, his chin trembled and little giggles burst from him. 'Are you trying to tell me that you grabbed him by his old man?'

'Well ... yes.'

'Oh dear, oh dear!' Tristan leaned back against the wall and laughed immoderately for a long time. When he had recovered he regarded me pityingly. 'Jim, old lad, you are supposed to put your hand only on the sheath to do the directing.'

I gave a wry smile. 'Oh, I know that now. I had another read at the pamphlet last night and realised I had made a lot of mistakes.'

'Well, never mind,' he said. 'Carry on with your story. You're beginning to interest me.'

The next few minutes had a devastating effect on my colleague. As I described the bull's attack on me he slumped, shouting, against the door and by the time I had finished he was hanging limply with his arms dangling over the woodwork. Tears coursed down his cheeks and feeble little moans issued from his mouth.

'You were ... you were in that corner, fighting the bull off with the AV. Clouting him over the nut with all that stuff ... flying around.' He reached for his handkerchief. 'For God's sake don't tell me any more, Jim. You'll do me an injury.' He wiped his eyes and straightened up but I could see that the whole thing had taken it out of him.

BULL LEADERS Most bulls have a ring fitted in the nose so they can be led. On a farm a length of rope would be slipped through the ring as leader, but bull breeders and farmers at shows will use a 3 ft wooden rod with a metal hook, clasp or spiral fitted at the end. Some use a shorter metal pincer without a handle, but the handle makes it easier to keep the bull's head at a distance.

MOULDING CHEESE CURD The curd formed by mixing rennet into heated milk was hung in a cotton cloth in the farm dairy to drain for three hours before being crumbled into a cotton-lined mould. The sinker, or loose cover, of the mould pressed the curd lightly. After about six hours, the curd was turned over on to a clean piece of cotton and put back into the mould under greater pressure for several hours or overnight.

He turned unsteadily as he heard the farmer's footsteps in the yard. 'Ah, good morning, Mr Hartley,' he said. 'We can get started now.'

Tristan was very businesslike as he directed operations. Yesterday's cow was still in oestrus and within minutes she was tied to a gatepost in the yard with a man on either side. 'That's to stop her swinging round when the bull mounts,' he explained to me.

He turned to the farmer and handed him the AV. 'Will you fill this with warm water, please, and screw the stopper on tightly.'

The farmer trotted into the house and as he returned another of his men led out the bull. This time my antagonist of yesterday was securely held by a halter through his ring.

Tristan had certainly got everything arranged in an orderly fashion.

The farmer had said that the bull was keen as mustard and his words were verified when the young animal took one look at the cow and started towards her, a picture of urgent lust. Tristan scarcely had time to get the AV into his hands before the bull was clambering eagerly aboard his quarry.

I had to admit that my young colleague was lightning fast as he stooped, seized the sheath, and sent the penis plunging into the AV. So that was how it was done, I thought wistfully. So very easy.

My feeling of shame was building up when the bull pushed out his tongue and emitted a long-drawn, deafening bellow of rage. And he had scarcely entered the AV when he withdrew with a backward leap and began to caper around on the end of his halter, filling the air with disapproving bawls.

'What the hell ...?' Tristan stared at the animal in bewilderment, then he poked his finger into the AV. 'Good God!' he cried 'The water in here is damned hot!'

Walley Hartley nodded. 'Aye well, the kettle had just come to the boil when I went into t'house, so ah just poured it straight in.'

Tristan clutched his brow and groaned. 'Oh, bugger it!' he muttered to me. 'I always check the temperature with a thermometer but what with talking to you and that young beggar going into action so fast, I clean forgot. Boiling water! No wonder the poor sod got out quick.'

Meanwhile the bull had stopped his noise and was circling the cow, sniffing her over and regarding her with a mixture of disbelief and respect. 'What a woman!' was clearly the dominant thought in his mind.

'Anyway, let's have another try.' Tristan made for the farmhouse. 'I'll fill the thing myself this time.'

Soon the stage was set once more. Tristan standing at the ready, and the bull, apparently undeterred by his recent experience, patently eager to join battle yet again.

It is difficult to know what an animal is thinking and at that moment I wondered whether the bull was in a torment of frustration, remembering the disasters of yesterday and the recent blow to his pride and comfort. By his attitude now he looked as though, come hell or high water, he was going to serve that cow.

My impression was confirmed when he made a sudden rush at her. Tristan, slightly pop-eyed, managed to jam the AV over the penis as it hurtled past him but as he did so the velocity of the charge caused the animal to lose his footing so that the bull slid on his back clean underneath the cow.

The AV was jerked from Tristan's grasp and soared high into the air. Mr Hartley followed it, open-mouthed, as it described a graceful parabola before landing on a pile of straw at the other end of the yard.

As the bull scrambled to his feet Tristan strolled unhurriedly towards the straw. The glass tube was still attached to the cylinder and my friend held it up at eye level.

'Ah yes,' he murmured. 'A nice 3 cc sample.'

The farmer came puffing up. 'You've got what you wanted, 'ave you?'

'Yes indeed,' Tristan replied airily. 'Exactly what I wanted.'

The farmer shook his head wonderingly. 'By 'ell, it's a complicated sort o' business, isn't it?'

'Ah well.' Tristan shrugged his shoulders. 'It can be just a little at times, it can be. Anyway, I'll get my microscope from the car and examine the sample.'

It didn't take long and soon afterwards we were all having a cup of tea in the kitchen.

My colleague put down his cup and reached for a scone. 'That's a fine fertile bull you have there, Mr Hartley.'

'Eee, that's champion.' The farmer rubbed his hands. 'I paid a fair bit o' brass for 'im and it's grand to know he's up to scratch.' He looked across at the young man with undisguised admiration. 'You've done a grand job and I'm right grateful to you.'

As I sipped my tea the thought occurred to me that despite the passage of years things hadn't changed. Just as that glass tube had landed on a soft bed of straw Tristan always landed on his feet.

NATURE IN HERRIOT COUNTRY

Moors, dales and farmlands support an abundance of plants and animals to delight the nature lover

Rich wildlife of the woodlands

Woods once covered north Yorkshire, but man and his animals have cleared most of them. Where any remain, ash dominates in limestone areas. Even in full leaf it lets through ample light, and shrubs – especially hazel – and many flowers grow under it.

On acid soil, sessile oak is the dominant tree among beech, elm and sycamore. Beneath them the shade is heavier and the wildlife less rich.

In the deep shade below the conifers planted on the moors, little grows.

Throughout the woods, millipedes, woodlice and insects live where there is plant life. Woodmice, bank voles and squirrels feed on the woodland fruits, and shrews and moles on grubs, insects and worms. The small mammals themselves are food for weasels, stoats, owls, sparrowhawks and foxes.

Woodpeckers and treecreepers probe the bark for insects. In ash woods, song thrushes feast on the abundant snails, and lizards and slow-worms bask on the rocks in sunny glades.

HERB PARIS All summer long, damp nooks in ash woodland hide herb paris, a rare, distinctive plant 6–16 in. tall with one green flower held above a single whorl of leaves.

ANGULAR SOLOMON'S-SEAL The rarer relative of Solomon's-seal is distinguished by its ridged stem. The powdered roots once made a poultice for sealing wounds – medical wisdom that King Solomon is said to have taught.

GIANT BELLFLOWER The toothed, heart-shaped leaves are similar to nettles, but the wide blue bells, borne on the 3–4 ft high plant in late summer, are more showy. They are wild campanulas, which thrive on a heavy woodland soil.

DOG'S MERCURY A plant to be wary of is the 12–16 in. dog's mercury, a poisonous plant that carpets shady dells. In early spring its foul-smelling female flowers attract midges which act as pollinators.

ASH The tall, domed tree is dominant in the natural woods left on the Dales' lime-rich soil. Its sooty buds open into leaves of nine or more leaflets, and its tiny purple flowers develop into single-winged seeds. The ash casts only a light shade.

HAZEL The commonest shrub in the profuse undergrowth of ash woods is hazel. It is tasselled with green-gold catkins in late winter, and in autumn bears nuts that feed mice, voles, squirrels and nuthatches.

BLUETIT Squabbling, acrobatic bluetits in the middle heights of the trees swing on thin twigs to reach juicy grubs.

WOOD WARBLER Lemon and green among the tree-tops, the wood warbler is hard to spot as it darts at insects, often while they are on the wing. This summer visitor makes a nest on the ground.

WHITETHROAT In summer this secretive visitor nests and feeds in the nettles and brambles that sprawl in the glades.

BLACKCAP The black-capped males and the brown-capped females build their nests in dense bushes on the woodland floor. They greet intruders with a loud sound like two stones struck together.

EUROPEAN LARCH In conifer woods, larches stand out against the general dark green. Their soft, emerald springtime needles darken and in autumn turn gold and drop. Grey squirrels eat the cones, and crossbills search out the seeds held among the scales.

COMMON SHREW Aggressive, squeaking and carnivorous, the long-nosed shrew rummages day or night on the woodland floor for millipedes, woodlice, worms and other small prey. Its orange-tipped, narrow teeth sink in, injecting a poisonous saliva that kills rapidly.

BANK VOLE A nest of grass in the roots of a shrub or tree is the home of the blunt-nosed, short-tailed bank vole. It eats berries and hazel nuts, sometimes climbing a trunk to reach them.

WOODMOUSE The varied food and ample cover in deciduous woods attract this russet-backed, shy mouse. It prefers rocky ground and feeds on nuts, berries and a few insects.

The moorland world of heather and grouse

Large areas of the Yorkshire Dales and the North York Moors consist of wide stretches of empty moorland. The land is covered by a thick blanket of peat with outcrops of a coarse sandstone called gritstone.

It is a treeless world in which the common heather – or ling – is the dominant plant, producing a rippling ocean of purple flowers in summer.

The most common bird is the red grouse, which rises from the feet of ramblers with an alarm cry that sounds like a terrier's bark. It feeds on the shoots and seeds of ling and on bilberries.

Moorland animals include field voles, stoats, weasels, foxes, badgers, rabbits and hares, and adders often sun themselves in sheltered places.

DUNLIN Trilling softly, the dunlin circles and hovers high above the wet parts of the moors where it comes in summer to breed.

MEADOW PIPIT A small brown-streaked bird, less than 6 in. long. At high altitudes it is one of the commonest song-birds.

REDSHANK If an intruder approaches, the redshank gives the alarm with a volley of harsh, piping notes.

SKYLARK A clear warbling song is sustained for minutes at a time as the skylark flies over the moors.

RED GROUSE The male has dark reddish-brown plumage and is 15 in. long. The female is smaller and paler. She lays her eggs in a hollow among the heather.

CURLEW The haunting cry – 'coor-li' – is heard over the moors for most of the year. It is the call of the curlew, a wader that breeds on wet moors. In winter, curlews move to the coast.

MERLIN One of the predators of the moors, together with its relative the kestrel. The merlin catches small birds, such as meadow pipits and skylarks, on the wing.

GOLDEN PLOVER A wader found in the wet parts of the moors. It feeds on insect larvae and worms around pools.

CHICKWEED
WINTERGREEN A small
plant found with
bilberries on the
eastern moors. It
grows a few inches
high and has white
flowers in early
summer.

BILBERRY In spring the knee-
high shrub bears drooping pink
flowers irresistible to bees.
Sharp-flavoured, juicy blue-
black berries follow in late
summer.

CROSS-LEAVED HEATH A member of
the heather family which grows in
wetter places than common
heather. Rose-pink flowers bloom
in late summer.

HEATHER Young shoots of
this knee-high, acid-loving
evergreen shrub are nibbled
by red grouse. When the
late summer flowers make
heather a purple sea, bees
are constantly busy on it,
taking the nectar.

ROUND-LEAVED
SUNDEW Found in the
wetter parts of the
moors, together with
bog moss, sundews
feed on insects
trapped by sticky
liquid on the leaves.

STOAT A lean-bodied carnivore that
preys on rabbits, voles and other
animals. In winter its coat often turns
white, and is called ermine.

WEASEL Similar in shape to the
stoat, but smaller. Weasels hunt
voles, frogs, rats and mice.

HARE Plant-eating
animal that lives above
ground. It is similar to a
rabbit, but larger.

The food chain of the upland ponds and streams

Ponds and streams in the dales and moors teem with food and support a great range of wildlife.

Nutrients in the water provide food for tiny plants which are eaten by small fish and by the insects which inhabit the water and swarm over its surface.

Larger fish, birds and small animals feed, in turn, on the insects and the smallest fish.

And at the top of the food chain come large predators such as the fierce pike and the heron which eat almost any creatures that come within their range – fish, water voles, frogs, and in the spring mallard and moorhen chicks as they paddle over the water.

KINGFISHER A swift, brilliant flash of orange and blue, the kingfisher dives from a branch above a river, and plunges into the water for small fish.

MOORHEN Often seen in ponds, streams and marshes where plants on the banks provide cover. The moorhen is about 13 in. long, and feeds mainly on seeds, fruit, leaves and moss.

GREY WAGTAIL Black, grey and yellow bird, 7 in. long. It feeds on insects picked from the mosses and plants growing beside an upland stream. In winter it moves south from the upland areas.

GREAT CRESTED GREBE The grebe, with its distinctive double crest, builds a floating nest in reeds on the edge of a lake. It is about 19 in. long.

TUFTED DUCK One of the 'diving ducks' found in freshwater lakes. It regularly dives in search of small fish, frogs and insects.

SAND MARTIN A small bird that flies over rivers catching insects. It nests in holes in sandy river banks.

HERON A large white-and-black bird, 3 ft long. It can be seen standing motionless in or beside ponds and streams, waiting for prey – fish, water voles or frogs.

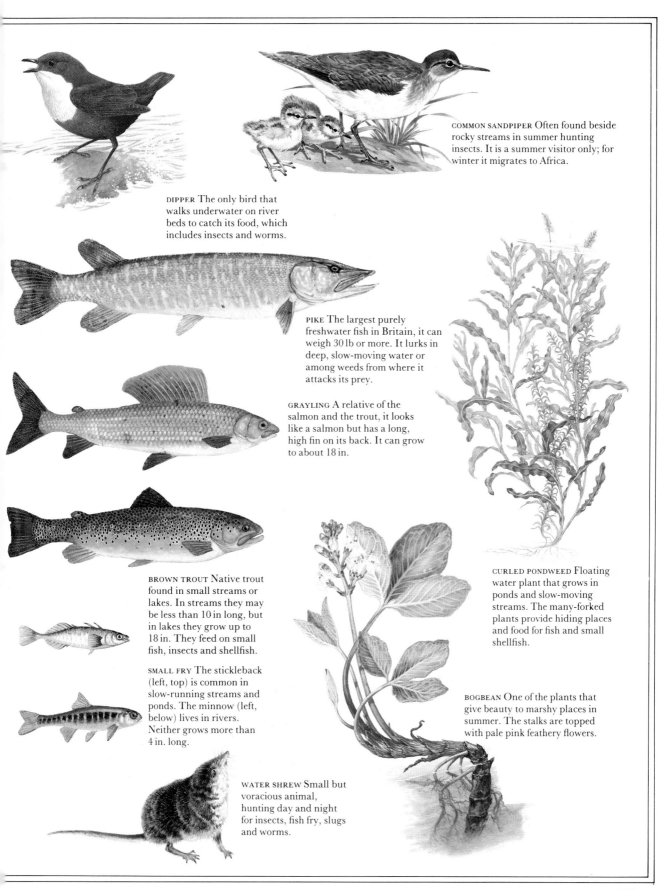

COMMON SANDPIPER Often found beside rocky streams in summer hunting insects. It is a summer visitor only; for winter it migrates to Africa.

DIPPER The only bird that walks underwater on river beds to catch its food, which includes insects and worms.

PIKE The largest purely freshwater fish in Britain, it can weigh 30 lb or more. It lurks in deep, slow-moving water or among weeds from where it attacks its prey.

GRAYLING A relative of the salmon and the trout, it looks like a salmon but has a long, high fin on its back. It can grow to about 18 in.

CURLED PONDWEED Floating water plant that grows in ponds and slow-moving streams. The many-forked plants provide hiding places and food for fish and small shellfish.

BROWN TROUT Native trout found in small streams or lakes. In streams they may be less than 10 in long, but in lakes they grow up to 18 in. They feed on small fish, insects and shellfish.

SMALL FRY The stickleback (left, top) is common in slow-running streams and ponds. The minnow (left, below) lives in rivers. Neither grows more than 4 in. long.

BOGBEAN One of the plants that give beauty to marshy places in summer. The stalks are topped with pale pink feathery flowers.

WATER SHREW Small but voracious animal, hunting day and night for insects, fish fry, slugs and worms.

Birds and flowers of farmland and high pastures

Intensive farming has removed almost all the original wildlife of the lowlands, except the hedgerows. Hawthorn is the hedge plant – early leafing, dense and thorny. Robins, dunnocks, song thrushes, yellow-hammers and partridges nest there. Redwings and fieldfares eat its berries in winter.

On upland farms wild flowers thrive because sheep keep the grass short. Thyme, eyebright, white clover and bird's-foot-trefoil attract insects and the caterpillars of butterflies. In the field barns, swallows, house martins and little owls nest. Among the rocky outcrops lizards bask.

Steep, rough pastures are loud in summer with the penetrating song of meadow pipits and skylarks, and the cries of peewits and curlews.

ROBIN Possessive and cocky, a robin jealously drives out other robins from the territory round its nest in a hedge bank.

REDWINGS Winter visitors from the north and Scandinavia, redwings find in the hedges of sheltered dales their favourite food – hawthorn berries.

GREY PARTRIDGE From its nest in the banking under a hedge, the partridge goes to open farmland to feed with pheasants and wood pigeons.

SONG THRUSH Hammering a snail shell on a stone or trilling loudly from a tall tree, the song thrush wins attention.

BIRD'S-FOOT-TREFOIL The sunny yellow flowers brighten summer pastures, and the leaves are the food for caterpillars of common blue butterflies.

EYEBRIGHT Among the turf of limestone grasslands wide-open white eyebright, marked with yellow and rose, nods on upright stems (left).

YELLOWHAMMER Low in the hedges on arable land, yellowhammers make their nests. They go to the fields in flocks to feed.

HAWTHORN The hedges bordering farmland are almost exclusively of hawthorn. They give dense cover and winter food to many birds and small mammals.

8

The piano-class concert

Mr Garrett's words about parents needing nerves of steel have come back to me many times over the years. One notable occasion was the annual recital given by Miss Livingstone's piano class.

Miss Livingstone was a soft-voiced, charming lady in her fifties who started many of the local children in piano lessons, and once a year she held a concert in the Methodist Hall for her pupils to show their paces. They ranged from six-year-olds to teenagers, and the room was packed with their proud parents. Jimmy was nine at the time and had been practising without much enthusiasm for the big day.

Everybody knows everybody else in a small town like Darrowby, and as the place filled up and the chairs scraped into position there was much nodding and smiling as people recognised each other. I found myself on the outside chair of the centre aisle with Helen on my right, and just across the few feet of space I saw Jeff Ward, old Willie Richardson's cowman, sitting very upright, hands on knees.

He was dressed in his Sunday best, and the dark serge was stretched tightly across his muscular frame. His red, strong-boned face shone with intensive scrubbing and his normally wayward thatch of hair was plastered down with brilliantine.

'Hello, Jeff,' I said. 'One of your youngsters performing today?'

He turned and grinned. 'Now then, Mr Herriot. Aye, it's our Margaret. She's been comin' on right well at t'piano and I just hope she does herself justice this afternoon.'

'Of course she will, Jeff. Miss Livingstone is an excellent teacher. She'll do fine.'

He nodded and turned to the front as the concert commenced. The first few performers who mounted the platform were very small boys in shorts and socks or tiny girls in frilly dresses, and their feet dangled far above the pedals as they sat at the keyboard.

Miss Livingstone hovered nearby to prompt them, but their little mistakes were greeted with indulgent smiles from the assembly and the conclusion of each piece was greeted with thunderous applause.

I noticed, however, that as the children grew bigger and the pieces became more difficult, a certain tension began to build up in the hall. The errors weren't so funny now and when little Jenny Newcombe, the fruiterer's daughter, halted a couple of times, then bowed her head as though she were about to cry, the silence in the room was absolute and charged with anxiety. I could feel it myself. My nails were digging into my palms and my teeth were tightly clenched. When Jenny successfully restarted and I relaxed with all the others, the realisation burst upon

This, he clearly thought, was going
to be a doddle.

me that we were not just a roomful of parents watching our children perform, we were a band of brothers and sisters suffering together.

When little Margaret Ward climbed the few steps to the platform her father stiffened perceptibly in his seat. From the corner of my eyes I could see Jeff's big work-roughened fingers clutching tightly at his knees.

Margaret went on very nicely till she came to a rather complicated chord which jarred on the company with harsh dissonance. She knew she had got the notes wrong and tried again . . . and again . . . and again, each time jerking her head with the effort.

'No, C and E, dear,' murmured Miss Livingstone and Margaret crashed her fingers down once more, violently and wrongly.

'My God, she's not going to make it,' I breathed to myself, aware suddenly that my pulse was racing and that every muscle in my body was rigid.

I glanced round at Jeff. It was impossible for anybody with his complexion to turn pale but his face had assumed a hideously mottled appearance and his legs were twitching convulsively. He seemed to sense that my gaze was on him because he turned tortured eyes towards me and gave me the ghastly semblance of a smile. Just beyond his wife was leaning forward. Her mouth hung slightly open and her lips trembled.

As Margaret fought for the right notes a total silence and immobility settled on the packed hall. It seemed an eternity before the little girl got it right and galloped away over the rest of the piece, and though everybody relaxed in their seats and applauded with relief as much as approval I had the feeling that the episode had taken its toll on all of us.

I certainly didn't feel so good, and watched in a half-trance as a succession of children went up and did their thing without incident. Then it was Jimmy's turn.

There was no doubt that most of the performers and parents were suffering from nerves, but this couldn't be applied to my son. He almost whistled as he trotted up the steps and there was a hint of a swagger in his walk up to the piano. This, he clearly thought, was going to be a doddle.

In marked contrast, I went into a sort of rigor as soon as he appeared.

491

PLUNGE BUTTER CHURNS The hardest physical labour in the numerous stages of making butter was the churning. The earliest type of churn (top) had a circular body about 2 ft high, made from oak strips held by iron hoops. The top of the churn was narrower than the base and on the lid, surrounding the central hole, was a splashguard to prevent drops of cream from jumping out as the perforated dasher was plunged up and down in the hole. Churns of the same design were sometimes made in red earthenware and glazed a rich brown (bottom).

My palms broke out in an instant sweat and I found I was breathing only with difficulty. I told myself that this was utterly ridiculous, but it was no good. It was how I felt.

Jimmy's piece was called 'The Miller's Dance', a title which is burned on my brain till the day I die. It was a rollicking little melody which of course I knew down to the last semi-quaver, and Jimmy started off in great style, throwing his hands about and tossing his head like Arthur Rubinstein in full flow.

Around the middle of 'The Miller's Dance' there is a pause in the quick tempo where the music goes from a brisk *ta-rum-tum-tiddle-iddle-om-pom-pom* to a lingering *taa-rum, taa-rum, taa-rum*, before starting off again at top speed. It was a clever little ploy of the composer and gave a touch of variety to the whole thing.

Jimmy dashed up to this point with flailing arms till he slowed down at the familiar *taa-rum, taa-rum, taa-rum*. I waited for him to take off again but nothing happened. He stopped and looked down fixedly at the keys for a few seconds then he played the slow bit again and halted once more.

My heart gave a great thud. Come on, lad, you know the next part – I've heard you play it a hundred times. My voiceless plea was born of desperation, but Jimmy didn't seem troubled at all. He looked down with mild puzzlement and rubbed his chin a few times.

Miss Livingstone's gentle voice came over the quivering silence. 'Perhaps you'd better start at the beginning again, Jimmy.'

'Okay.' My son's tone was perky as he plunged confidently into the melody again and I closed my eyes as he approached the fateful bars. *Ta-rum-tum-tiddle-iddle-om-pom-pom, taa-rum, taa-rum, taa-rum* – then nothing. This time he pursed his lips, put his hands on his knees and bent closely over the keyboard as though the strips of ivory were trying to hide something from him. He showed no sign of panic, only a faint curiosity.

In the almost palpable hush of that room I was sure that the hammering of my heart must be audible. I could feel Helen's leg trembling against mine. I knew we couldn't take much more of this.

Miss Livingstone's voice was soft as a zephyr or I think I would have screamed. 'Jimmy, dear, shall we try it once more from the beginning?'

'Yes, yes, right.' Away he went again like a hurricane, all fire and fury. It was unbelievable that there could ever be a flaw in such virtuosity.

The whole room was in agony. By now the other parents had come to know 'The Miller's Dance' almost as well as I did and we waited together for the dread passage. Jimmy came up to it at breakneck speed. *Ta-rum-tum-tiddle-iddle-om-pom-pom* then *taa-rum, taa-rum, taa-rum* . . . and silence.

Helen's knees were definitely knocking now and I stole an anxious glance at her face. She was pale, but she didn't look ready to faint just yet.

As Jimmy sat motionless except for a thoughtful drumming of his fingers against the woodwork of the piano, I felt I was going to choke. I glared around me desperately and I saw that Jeff Ward, across the aisle, was in a bad way. His face had gone all blotchy again, his jaw muscles stood out in taut ridges and a light sheen of perspiration covered his forehead.

Something had to break soon and once more it was Miss Livingstone's voice which cut into the terrible atmosphere.

'All right, Jimmy dear,' she said. 'Never mind. Perhaps you'd better go and sit down now.'

My son rose from the stool and marched across the platform. He descended the steps and rejoined his fellow pupils in the first few rows.

I slumped back in my seat. Ah well, that was it, the final indignity. The poor little lad had blown it. And though he didn't seem troubled, I was sure he must feel a sense of shame at being unable to get through his piece.

A wave of misery enveloped me, and though many of the other parents turned and directed sickly smiles of sympathy and friendship at Helen and me it didn't help. I hardly heard the rest of the concert, which was a pity because as the bigger boys and girls began to perform, the musical standard rose to remarkable heights. Chopin nocturnes were followed by Mozart sonatas and I had a dim impression of a tall lad rendering an impromptu by Schubert. It was a truly splendid show – by everybody but poor old Jimmy, the only one who hadn't managed to finish.

At the end, Miss Livingstone came to the front of the platform. 'Well, thank you, ladies and gentlemen, for the kind reception you have given my pupils. I do hope you have enjoyed it as much as we have.'

There was more clapping, and as the chairs started to push back I rose to my feet, feeling slightly sick.

'Shall we go then, Helen,' I said, and my wife nodded back at me, her face a doleful mask.

But Miss Livingstone wasn't finished yet. 'Just one thing more, ladies and gentlemen.' She raised a hand. 'There is a young man here who, I know, can do much better. I wouldn't be happy going home now without giving him another opportunity. Jimmy.' She beckoned towards the second row. 'Jimmy, I wonder . . . I wonder if you would like to have one more try.'

As Helen and I exchanged horrified glances there was an immediate response from the front. Our son's voice rang out, chirpy and confident. 'Aye, aye, I'll have a go!'

I couldn't believe it. The martyrdom was surely not about to start all over again. But it was true. Everybody was sitting down and a small familiar figure was mounting the steps and striding to the piano.

From a great distance I heard Miss Livingstone again. 'Jimmy will play "The Miller's Dance".' She didn't have to tell us – we all knew.

As though in the middle of a bad dream I resumed my seat. A few seconds earlier I had been conscious only of a great weariness, but now I was gripped by a fiercer tension than I had known all afternoon. As Jimmy poised his hands over the keys, a vibrant sense of strain lapped

BOX AND DISC BUTTER CHURNS
The box churn (top), a sycamore cube of about 15 in., remained still while inside it a cross-shaped dasher rotated as the handle was turned. A glass window in the lid allowed the farmer's wife or daughter to keep a check on how the butter was forming. The sycamore disc churn (bottom) was an improved box churn. Its container was raised on a four-legged stand, and its internal wooden dasher was in the shape of a convex disc. The side handle was turned by hand, but drove gears that made the disc rotate faster than the handle.

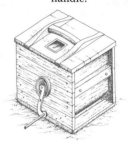

AN ANTI-BALANCE STEAM PLOUGH Invented in 1885 by Fowlers, a Leeds firm of agricultural engineers, the anti-balance plough was winched across the field by the cable of a winding drum set at one end of the field. Then it pivoted on the central wheels so that the side that had just ploughed tilted into the air while the other came down into the soil. The plough was then winched back by another winding drum at the other end of the field. The drums were powered by steam-engines. Such ploughs were still being used in the 1930s, but they were never as numerous as horse-drawn ploughs.

around the silent room.

The little lad started off as he always did, as though he hadn't a care in the world, and I began a series of long shuddering breaths designed to carry me past the moment which was fast approaching. Because I knew he would stop again. And I knew just as surely that when he did I would topple senseless to the floor.

I didn't dare look round at anybody. In fact when he reached the crucial bars I closed my eyes tightly. But I could still hear the music – so very clearly. *Ta-rum-tum-tiddle-iddle-om-pom-pom*, *taa-rum*, *taa-rum*, *taa-rum* ... There was a pause of unbearable length then, *tiddle-iddle-om-pom*, *tiddle-iddle-om-pom*, Jimmy was blissfully on his way again.

He raced through the second half of the piece, but I kept my eyes closed as the relief flooded through me. I opened them only when he came to the finale which I knew so well. Jimmy was making a real meal of it, head down, fingers thumping, and at the last crashing chord he held up one hand in a flourish a foot above the keyboard before letting it fall by his side in the true manner of the concert pianist.

I doubt if the Methodist Hall has ever heard a noise like the great cheer which followed. The place erupted in a storm of clapping and shouting and Jimmy was not the man to ignore such an accolade. All the other children had walked impassively from the stage at the end of their efforts, but not so my son.

To my astonishment he strode from the stool to the front of the platform, placed one arm across his abdomen and the other behind his back, extended one foot and bowed to one side of the audience with the grace of an eighteenth-century courtier. He then reversed arms and pushed out the other foot before repeating his bow to the other side of the hall.

The cheering changed to a great roar of laughter which continued as he descended the steps, smiling demurely. Everybody was still giggling as we made our way out. In the doorway we bumped into Miss Mullion, who ran the little school which our son attended. She was dabbing her eyes.

'Oh dear,' she said breathlessly. 'You can always depend on Jimmy to provide the light relief.'

I drove back to Skeldale House very slowly. I was still in a weak condition and I felt it dangerous to exceed twenty-five miles an hour. The colour had returned to Helen's face, but there were lines of exhaustion round her mouth and eyes as she stared ahead through the windscreen.

Jimmy, in the back, was lying full length along the seat, kicking his legs in the air and whistling some of the tunes which had been played that afternoon.

'Mum! Dad!' he exclaimed in the staccato manner which was so typical of him. 'I like music.'

I glanced at him in the driving-mirror. 'That's good, son, that's good. So do we.'

Suddenly he rolled off the back seat and thrust his head between us. 'Do you know why I like music so much?'

I shook my head.

'I've just found out,' he cried delightedly. 'It's because it's so soothing.'

9

Siegfried sees great days ahead

It was a Sunday morning in June and I was washing my hands in the sink in Matt Clarke's kitchen. The sun was bright with a brisk wind scouring the fell-sides, so that through the window I could see every cleft and gully lying sharp and clear on the green flanks as the cloud shadows drove across them.

I glanced back beyond the stone flags at the white head of Grandma Clarke bent over her knitting. The radio on the dresser was tuned to the morning service and, as I watched, the old lady looked up from her work and listend intently to some words of the sermon for a few moments before starting her needles clicking again.

In that brief time I had a profound impression of serenity and unquestioning faith which has remained with me to this day. It is a strange thing, but over the years whenever I have heard discussions and arguments on religion, on the varying beliefs and doctrines, on the sincerity or otherwise of some pious individuals, there still rises before me the seamed old face and calm eyes of Grandma Clarke. She knew and was secure. Goodness seemed to flow from her.

She was in her late eighties and always dressed in black with a little black neckband. She had come through the hard times of farming and could look back on a long life of toil, in the fields as well as in the home.

As I reached for the towel the farmer led Rosie into the kitchen.

'Mr Clarke's been showing me some baby chicks, Daddy,' she said.

Grandma looked up again. 'Is that your little lass, Mr Herriot?'

'Yes, Mrs Clarke,' I replied. 'This is Rosie.'

'Aye, of course. I've seen her before, many a time.' The old lady put down her knitting and rose stiffly from her chair. She shuffled over to a cupboard, brought out a gaily coloured tin and extracted a bar of chocolate.

'How old are ye now, Rosie?' she asked as she presented the chocolate.

'Thank you, I'm six,' my daughter replied.

Grandma looked down at the smiling face, at the sturdy tanned legs in their blue shorts and sandals. 'Well, you're a grand little lass.' For a moment she rested her work-roughened hand against the little girl's

STOPPING THE MILK SUPPLY
Lambs are sometimes reluctant to forage for themselves and be weaned from their mother's milk, but ewe and lamb have to be spained, or separated, for the breeding cycle to start again. One way of stopping the lamb sucking is to seal the ewe's teats with tar and pitch applied with a square of strong paper. A wet piece of turf was convenient for pressing the paper on firmly.

495

cheek, then she returned to her chair. They didn't make much of a fuss, those old Yorkshire folk, but to me the gesture was like a benediction.

The old lady picked up her knitting again. 'And how's that lad o' yours. How's Jimmy?'

'Oh, he's fine, thank you. Ten years old now. He's out with some of his pals this morning.'

'Ten, eh? Ten and six ... ten and six ...' For a few seconds her thoughts seemed far away as she plied her needles then she looked at me again. 'Maybe ye don't know it, Mr Herriot, but this is the best time of your life.'

'Do you think so?'

'Aye, there's no doubt about it. When your children are young and growin' up around ye – that's when it's best. It's the same for everybody, only a lot o' folk don't know it and a lot find out when it's too late. It doesn't last long, you know.'

'I believe I've always realised that, Mrs Clarke, without thinking about it very much.'

'Reckon you have, young man.' She gave me a sideways smile. 'You allus seem to have one or t'other of your bairns with you on your calls.'

As I drove away from the farm the old lady's words stayed in my mind. They are still in my mind, all these years later, when Helen and I are soon to celebrate our Ruby Wedding of forty years of marriage. Life has been good to us and is still good to us. We are lucky – we have had so many good times – but I think we both agree that Grandma Clarke was right about the very best time of all.

When I got back to Skeldale House that summer morning I found Siegfried replenishing the store of drugs in his car boot. His children, Alan and Janet, were helping him. Like me, he usually took his family around with him.

He banged down the lid of the boot. 'Right, that's that for another few days.' He glanced at me and smiled. 'There are no more calls at the moment, James, let's have a walk down the back.'

With the children running ahead of us we went through the passage and out into the long garden behind the house. Here the sunshine was imprisoned between the high old walls with the wind banished to the upper air and ruffling the top leaves of the apple trees.

When we reached the big lawn Siegfried flopped on the turf and rested on his elbow. I sat down by his side.

My partner pulled a piece of grass and chewed it contemplatively.

'Pity about the acacia,' he murmured.

I looked at him in surprise. It was many years since the beautiful tree which had once soared from the middle of the lawn had blown down in a gale.

'Yes, it is,' I said. 'It was magnificent.' I paused for a moment. 'Remember I fell asleep against it the first day I came here to apply for a job? We first met right on this spot.'

Siegfried laughed. 'I do remember.' He looked around him at the

GYPSIES' HOME The traditional round-topped, horse-drawn wooden caravans of gypsy families were a frequent sight in north Yorkshire in the 1930s.

They would cluster in woodland clearings or on roadside verges for a few days before moving off again. The journeys were usually made to reach the numerous horse fairs, such as Lee Gap Fair, near Leeds, because horse-dealing was the main source of income for the gypsies. The caravans were carefully maintained, and some were ornate. Billy Wright of Rothwell Haigh near Leeds made the finest ones.

496

mellow brick and stone copings of the walls, at the rockery and rose bed, the children playing in the old henhouse at the far end. 'My word, James, when you think about it, we've come through a few things together since then. A lot of water, as they say, has flowed under the bridge.'

We were both silent for a while and my thoughts went back over the struggles and the laughter of those years. Almost unconsciously I lay back on the grass and closed my eyes, feeling the sun warm on my face, hearing the hum of the bees among the flowers, the croaking of the rooks in the great elms which overhung the yard.

My colleague's voice seemed to come from afar. 'Hey, you're not going to do the same trick again, are you? Going to sleep in front of me?'

I sat up, blinking. 'Gosh, I'm sorry, Siegfried, I nearly did. I was out at a farrowing at five o'clock this morning and it's just catching up with me.'

'Ah, well,' he said, smiling. 'You won't need your book tonight.'

I laughed. 'No, I won't. Not tonight.'

Neither Siegfried nor I suffered from insomnia but on the rare occasions when sleep would not come we had recourse to our particular books. Mine was *The Brothers Karamazov*, a great novel, but to me, soporific in its names. Even at the beginning I felt those names lulling me. 'Alexey Fyodorovich Karamazov was the third son of Fyodor Pavlovich Karamazov.' Then by the time I had encountered Grigory Kutuzov, Yefim Petrovich Polenov, Stepanida Bedryagina and a few others I was floating away.

With Siegfried it was a book on the physiology of the eye which he kept by his bedside. There was one passage which never failed to start him nodding. He showed it to me once: 'The first ciliary muscle is inserted into the ciliary body and by its contraction pulls the ciliary body forward and so slackens the tension on the suspensory ligament, while the second ciliary muscle is a circular muscle embedded in the ciliary body and by its contraction drags the ciliary body towards the crystalline lens.' He had never managed to get much further than that.

'No,' I said, rubbing my eyes. 'I won't need any encouragement tonight.' I rolled on to my side. 'By the way, I was at Matt Clarke's this morning.' I told him what Grandma had said.

Siegfried selected a fresh piece of grass and resumed his chewing.

'Well, she's a wise old lady and she's seen it all. If she's right we'll have no regrets in the future, because we have both enjoyed our children and been with them from the beginning.'

I was beginning to feel sleepy again when my partner startled me by sitting up abruptly.

'Do you know, James,' he said. 'I'm convinced that the same thing applies to our job. We're going through the best time there, too.'

'Do you think so?'

'Sure of it. Look at all the new advances since the war. Drugs and procedures we never dreamed of. We can look after our animals in a way

THE GYPSY LIFE A gypsy family's life went on in the open near the caravan. The men made wooden clothes pegs and the women cooked the meals and made paper flowers.

The family moved on frequently to reach the next horse fair. While the men were making deals at the fair, the women would go from house to house hawking pegs and paper flowers, and offering to tell fortunes.

that would have been impossible a few years ago and the farmers realise this. You've seen them crowding into the surgery on market day to ask advice – they've gained a new respect for the profession and they know it pays to call in the vet now.'

'That's true,' I said. 'We're certainly busier than we've ever been, with the Ministry work going full blast, too.'

'Yes, everything is buzzing. In fact, James, I'd like to bet that these present years are the high noon of country practice.'

I thought for a moment. 'You could be right. But if we are on the top now does it mean that our lives will decline later?'

'No, no, of course not. They'll be different, that's all. I sometimes think we've only touched the fringe of so many other things, like small animal work.' Siegfried brandished his gnawed piece of grass at me and his eyes shone with the enthusiasm which always uplifted me.

'I tell you this, James. There are great days ahead!'

We were both silent for a while and my thoughts went back over the struggles and the laughter of those years.

Index

The page numbers refer to
illustrations and captions in
the margins of text pages
and to the colour features.

Acknowledgments

Some of the artwork in this book is based on photographs in Life and Tradition in the Yorkshire Dales, by Marie Hartley and Joan Ingilby, published by J. M. Dent and Sons Ltd.

Where no specific acknowledgment is given, artwork was supplied by:
David Baird, Leonora Box, Ray Burrows, Tony Graham, Robert Micklewright, Gilly Newman, Annette Robinson or Eric Robson.
All text illustrations by Victor Ambrus. Drawings on title page and pages 9, 165, 287 and 417 by Robert Micklewright.

Except where otherwise stated, acknowledgments for photographs and artwork read from left to right and top to bottom of the page. Work commissioned by the Reader's Digest is in *italics*.

7 Artist *Iain Stuart*. 10 The British Veterinary Association/*Eileen Tweedy*. 28 Syndication International/Daily Mirror. 34 *Eileen Tweedy*. 38 The Daily Telegraph/*Eileen Tweedy*. 42–45 Derek Widdicombe. 46–47 Derry Brabbs. 48–49 *Jon Wyand*.
50–51 *Jon Wyand*. 51 Derry Brabbs. 52 Derek Widdicombe. S. and O. Mathews. 52–53 Derek Widdicombe. 54–55 S. and O. Mathews. 56–59 Derry Brabbs. 60 Heather Angel. Derry Brabbs. 60–61 Derry Brabbs. 62–63 Colin Molyneux. 64 Derry Brabbs. 78 The Mansell Collection. 83 John Topham Pictury Library. 84 University of Reading, Institute of Agricultural History and Museum of English Rural Life. 89 Adam Woolfitt/British Tourist Authority. 90 Top right North Yorkshire County Library; overlap *Jon Wyand*. Bottom Marie Hartley; overlap *Jon Wyand*. 91 Top North Yorkshire County Library; overlap *Jon Wyand*. Bottom right Marie Hartley; overlap *Jon Wyand*. 92–93 Derry Brabbs. 94 Top right Harrogate Reference Library; overlap *Jon Wyand*. Malcolm Woods/England Scene. Colin Molyneux/England Scene/English Tourist Board. 95 Eric Rowell/British Tourist Authority. Colin Molyneux/England Scene/English

Tourist Board. Eric Rowell/British Tourist Authority. 96 Left K. M. Andrew. Sefton Photo Library. The Ephemera Society. 97 Colin Molyneux. Top right Malcolm Aird. Centre right Arnold Kidson/Bruce Coleman Ltd. Both Derry Brabbs. 98–99 *Patrick Thurston*.
100–1 Colin Molyneux. 101 Richard Jemmett. 102 Colin Molyneux. Marcus Brown/Photo Library International. 103 Marcus Brown/Photo Library International. 104 Derry Brabbs. 130 University of Reading, Institute of Agricultural History and Museum of English Rural Life. 133 By permission of IPC Business Press Ltd/*Eileen Tweedy*. By courtesy of Farmer's Weekly/*Eileen Tweedy*. 145 John Bethell Photography. 146–7 Colin Molyneux/British Tourist Authority. 147 Trevor Wood/England Scene/English Tourist Board. 148 John Bethell Photography. British Tourist Authority. John Bethell Photography. 149 Derry Brabbs.
150 Sefton Photo Library. *Jon Wyand*. 151–2 *Jon Wyand*. 159 Reproduced with the kind permission of The Yorkshire Evening Post/*Eileen Tweedy*. 162 Castle Museum, York.
202–3 England Scene. 204 John Bethell Photography. England Scene. John Bethell Photography. 205 *Patrick Thurston*. 206 *Patrick Thurston*. Derry Brabbs. 206–7 Sefton Photo Library. 208 S. and O. Mathews. 249 Raymond Hayes.
250 Top right North Yorkshire County Library; overlap *Jon Wyand*. Fox Photos Ltd. By permission of Keith Osborne/*Robert Osborne*. 251 Top right The Mansell Collection. Others *Jon Wyand*. 252–6 *Jon Wyand*. 297 J. and C. Bord. 298 J. and C. Bord. Anthony Howarth/Daily Telegraph Colour Library. Robert Estall. 299 Photoresources. *Jon Wyand*. Mike Freeman.
300 Artist Ivan Lapper. Photoresources. J. and C. Bord. Photoresources. 301 Derry Brabbs. 302–4 Richard Surman. 309 University of Reading, Institute of Agricultural History and Museum of English Rural Life. 330 Quadrille Antiques/reproduced by permission of EMI Music Publishing Ltd. Quadrille Antiques/reproduced by kind permission of Chappell Music Ltd (for Bradbury Wood Ltd). 332 The Ephem-

era Society. 333 University of Reading, Institute of Agricultural History and Museum of English Rural Life. 337 *Jon Wyand*. Vignette J. H. Cookson. 338–52 *Jon Wyand*.
355 University of Reading, Institute of Agricultural History and Museum of English Rural Life. 356 Robert Opie. 364 University of Reading, Institute of Agricultural History and Museum of English Rural Life. 385 University of Reading, Institute of Agricultural History and Museum of English Rural Life. 394–5 Keystone Press Agency. 396 Keystone Press Agency. 396–7 Roger Scruton/England Scene. 398 Richard Surman. Artist *Ivan Lapper*. 398–9 Marie Hartley.
400 *Jon Wyand*. 400–1 Richard Surman. 402–3 Bottom left, artist *Ivan Lapper*. Others North Yorkshire County Library. 404 artist Ivan Lapper. 404–5 David Morgan-Rees. 406 artist *Ivan Lapper*. 406–7 Mr Curtis. 408 John Edenbrow. 412 *Eileen Tweedy*. 449 Marie Hartley.
450–1 Homer Sykes. Harrogate Borough Council. Homer Sykes. Homer Sykes. Homer Sykes. Popperfoto. 452–3 Top right Patrick Eagar. Others Scarborough Cricket Club. 454–5 Yorkshire Agricultural Society. 456 *Derry Brabbs*. 482 Artists *Line Mailhe, Victoria Goman, Barbara Walker, Barbara Walker, Brian Delf, Brian Delf*. 483 Artists *Ken Wood, Norman Arlott, Norman Arlott, Norman Arlott, David Salariya, Norman Weaver, Norman Weaver, Norman Weaver*. 484 Artists *Trevor Boyer, D. W. Ovenden, Robert Morton, Norman Arlott*. Far left *Tim Hayward, Robert Morton, Trevor Boyer, Ken Wood*. 485 Artists *Marie-Claire Nivoix, Barbara Walker*, top right and centre *Marjory Saynor, Paul Wrigley, Ray Burrows, Ray Burrows, Pat Oxenham*. 486 Artists *Peter Barrett, Tim Hayward, D. W. Ovenden, John Francis, Robert Morton, Robert Morton, Robert Gillmor*. 487 Artists *Norman Arlott, John Francis, David Carl-Forbes*, centre right *Leonora Box, David Carl-Forbes, David Carl-Forbes*, bottom right *Guy Michel, David Carl-Forbes, David Carl-Forbes, Norman Weaver*. 488 Artists *Norman Arlott, Norman Arlott, Tim Hayward, Norman Arlott*, centre right *John Francis, Robert Morton, Ken Wood, Robert Morton*.

Printed and bound in 1989
by Everbest Printing Co. Ltd., Hong Kong
for Reader's Digest (Australia) Pty Limited (Inc. in NSW),
26-32 Waterloo Street, Surry Hills, NSW 2010
40/099/7